Direct Instruction Reading

Direct Instruction Reading

Fourth Edition

Douglas W. Carnine
University of Oregon

Jerry Silbert
University of Oregon

Edward J. Kame'enui
University of Oregon

Sara G. Tarver
University of Wisconsin, Madison

PEARSON

Merrill
Prentice Hall

Upper Saddle River, New Jersey
Columbus, Ohio

Library of Congress Cataloging-in-Publication Data
Direct instruction reading/Douglas W. Carnine . . . [et al.]— 4th ed.
    p. cm.
    Rev. ed. of: Direct instruction reading/Douglas W. Carnine, Jerry Silbert, Edward J.
Kame'enui. 3rd ed. c1997.
    Includes bibliographical references and indexes.
    ISBN 0-13-112308-4
    1. Reading—Direct instruction approach. 2. Reading—Code emphasis approaches. 3. Reading
comprehension. I. Carnine, Douglas. II. Carnine, Douglas. Direct instruction reading.

LB1050.365.D57 2004
372.41—dc21   2003050445

Vice President and Executive Publisher: Jeffery W. Johnston
Acquisitions Editor: Allyson P. Sharp
Editorial Assistant: Kathleen S. Burk
Production Editor: Linda Hillis Bayma
Production Coordination: Trish Finley, Carlisle Publishers Services
Design Coordinator: Diane C. Lorenzo
Cover Designer: Bryan Huber
Production Manager: Laura Messerly
Director of Marketing: Ann Castel Davis
Marketing Manager: Amy June
Marketing Coordinator: Tyra Poole

This book was set in Times Roman by Carlisle Communications, Ltd. It was printed and bound by R.R. Donnelley &
Sons Company. The cover was printed by The Lehigh Press, Inc.

Pearson Education Ltd.   Pearson Education Australia Pty. Limited
Pearson Education Singapore Pte. Ltd.   Pearson Education North Asia Ltd.
Pearson Education Canada, Ltd.   Pearson Educación de Mexico, S.A. de C.V.
Pearson Education—Japan   Pearson Education Malaysia Pte. Ltd.

10 9 8 7 6 5 4 3 2 1
ISBN: 0-13-112308-4

*To those teachers who are always looking for a better way to teach
and to improve student performance*

Educator Learning Center: An Invaluable Online Resource

Merrill Education and the Association for Supervision and Curriculum Development (ASCD) invite you to take advantage of a new online resource, one that provides access to the top research and proven strategies associated with ASCD and Merrill—the Educator Learning Center. At **www.EducatorLearningCenter.com** you will find resources that will enhance your students' understanding of course topics and of current educational issues, in addition to being invaluable for further research.

How the Educator Learning Center will help your students become better teachers

With the combined resources of Merrill Education and ASCD, you and your students will find a wealth of tools and materials to better prepare them for the classroom.

Research

- More than 600 articles from the ASCD journal *Educational Leadership* discuss everyday issues faced by practicing teachers.
- A direct link on the site to Research Navigator™ gives students access to many of the leading education journals, as well as extensive content detailing the research process.
- Excerpts from Merrill Education texts give your students insights on important topics of instructional methods, diverse populations, assessment, classroom management, technology, and refining classroom practice.

Classroom Practice

- Hundreds of lesson plans and teaching strategies are categorized by content area and age range.
- Case studies and classroom video footage provide virtual field experience for student reflection.
- Computer simulations and other electronic tools keep your students abreast of today's classrooms and current technologies.

Look into the value of Educator Learning Center yourself

Preview the value of this educational environment by visiting **www.EducatorLearningCenter.com** and clicking on "Demo." For a free 4-month subscription to the Educator Learning Center in conjunction with this text, simply contact your Merrill/Prentice Hall sales representative.

PREFACE

In April of 2000, the National Reading Panel, a panel of scientists charged by the U.S. Congress with the responsiblity of reviewing research in reading instruction and identifying methods that consistently relate to reading success, issued its long-awaited report.

The findings of the National Reading Panel confirmed the validity of the content and procedures that have been included in *Direct Instruction Reading* since the first edition. The panel pointed out the importance of teaching phonemic awareness (Chapter 6), letter-sound correspondences (Chapter 7), systematic and explicit phonics (Chapters 9, 10, 11, and 15), fluency (Chapter 18), vocabulary and language skills (Chapters 11 and 20), and strategies for comprehending narrative and content-area text (Chapters 21 to 24). Furthermore, the panel pointed out the importance of systematic and explicit teaching in all areas.

Direct Instruction Reading, unlike most textbooks, has not described multiple approaches to teaching beginning reading but instead has provided and continues to provide the reader with detailed information on how to systematically and explicitly teach essential reading skills. The direct instruction approach is highly congruent with the findings of the National Reading Panel. The approaches described in this text have been shown to benefit all students, but are especially powerful with the most vulnerable learners, children who are at risk because of poverty, disability, or limited knowledge of English.

This textbook is designed to provide teachers and soon-to-be teachers specific information that can help them to be effective with all their students. The text not only provides information on what to do but explains why particular procedures are recommended. Even though publishers have begun to incorporate more research findings into their reading programs, teachers will find great differences among programs regarding their effectiveness with at-risk students and must be prepared to make needed modifications and adjustments to ensure a successful learning experience for all students.

Direct Instruction Reading presents information on how to provide success to students through structuring initial teaching procedures so that the teacher presentation is clear; using language and demonstrations that can be understood by all children; sequencing the content to be sure that all essential skills and knowledge are taught in an aligned and coherent manner; using teacher presentation techniques that foster a high degree of interaction between teacher and student; and providing adequate practice and review to develop high levels of fluency and accuracy.

Direct Instruction Reading attempts to help teachers create a learning and instructional environment for teaching students in a humane and efficient manner. A learning environment is humane when the environment enhances the student's self-concept. Our experience, and our reading of the research, suggests that competence comes first, leading to increased self-concept. A learning environment is efficient when the maximum amount of learning occurs in the shortest possible time with the fewest resources.

The organization of *Direct Instruction Reading* has changed somewhat from the third edition. We have organized the chapters to be congruent with the five major areas of reading instruction identified by the National Reading Panel. We continue to devote a disproportionate amount of the book to beginning reading, because the first months of reading instruction are immensely important to later reading success.

The major change in this edition of *Direct Instruction Reading* is not in the instructional details for how to teach reading, but in the chapters that connect Direct Instruction with the findings of the National Reading Panel, the chapters on how to establish a classroom reading program, and the chapters that present the research base that supports the importance of direct, explicit instruction in reading. We have incorporated the research findings of the National Reading Panel in chapters throughout the text as well as in the research summaries. We have also updated the instructor's guide that accompanies this text.

As with previous editions, this edition is not intended to be a definitive handbook. As we work with students, we continue to learn, and this learning enables us to improve our procedures. Procedures can always be improved. The main purpose of the text is to empower teachers by providing them with specific suggestions for problems they will encounter in the classroom. It is our hope, however, that the systematic procedures recommended here will stimulate the development of even better procedures. Furthermore, we encourage teachers to view learning as an outcome of instruction, rather than a function of inalterable attributes of the learner. We also encourage commercial publishers to design better programs for students. Overall, we hope that this book contributes to better teaching methods for all students, particularly the hard-to-teach and at-risk students.

Acknowledgments

We are grateful to many people. Foremost we are grateful to Zig Engelmann, whose empirical approach to instructional design has resulted in the development of many highly effective instructional programs. Many of the procedures in this book were derived from *The Reading Mastery Series, Language for Learning,* and *The Corrective Reading Series,* authored by Engelmann and his colleagues. Englemann, more than 30 years ago, incorporated the systematic and explicit teaching of phonics, phonemic awareness, vocabulary, fluency, and comprehension into his programs. He recognized the importance of explicitly teaching foundational language and reasoning skills while students were learning how to read so that the door to higher-order comprehension could be opened to all children. His programs still remain in a class by themselves as models of how to create success for all children, particularly the most vulnerable learners.

In addition to ideas gained from these programs, many ideas were contributed by colleagues and students, including Kathy Jungjohann, Gary Davis, Vicky Vachon, Nancy Woolfson, Frank Falco, Mary Gleason, Ramon Alvarez, Linda Carnine, Billie Overholser, Conley Overholser, Abby Adams, Anita Archer, Scott Baker, Elain C. Bruner, Vonnie Dicecco, Robert Dixon, Phil Dommes, Jane Dougall, Ruth Falco, Mickey Garrison, Alex Granzin, Tracey Hall, Cheri Hansen, Lisa Howard, Sheri Irwin, Joleen Johnson, Jean Osborn, Mary Rosenbaum, Barak Rosenshine, Sandra Schofield, Marcy Stein, Marilyn Stepnoski, Candy Stevens, and Joan Thormann. Other colleagues provided important support and encouragement, namely, Barbara Bateman, Wes Becker, Mark Gall, Joe Jenkins, Marty Kaufman, Deb Simmons, and Ruth Waugh. Kathy Jungjohann, Gary Davis, and Nancy Wolfson were particularly helpful in providing feedback as we constructed drafts of several key chapters for this edition.

We sincerely appreciate the assistance of the following people who reviewed the manuscript and provided constructive feedback for changes: Carol Bunch, Hannibal LaGrange College; Mark Posluszny, Buffalo State College; Richard Robinson, University of Missouri; and Roberta Strosnider, Hood College.

The Prentice Hall Companion Website: A Virtual Learning Environment

Technology is a constantly growing and changing aspect of our field that is creating a need for content and resources. To address this emerging need, Prentice Hall has developed an online learning environment for students and professors alike—Companion Websites—to support our textbooks.

In creating a Companion Website, our goal is to build on and enhance what the textbook already offers. For this reason, the content for each user-friendly website is organized by topic and provides the professor and student with a variety of meaningful resources. Common features of a Companion Website include:

For the Professor—

Every Companion Website integrates **Syllabus Manager**™, an online syllabus creation and management utility.

- **Syllabus Manager**™ provides you, the instructor, with an easy, step-by-step process to create and revise syllabi, with direct links into the Companion Website and other online content without having to learn HTML.

- Students may log on to your syllabus during any study session. All they need to know is the web address for the Companion Website and the password you've assigned to your syllabus.

- After you have created a syllabus using **Syllabus Manager**™, students may enter the syllabus for their course section from any point in the Companion Website.

- Clicking on a date, the student is shown the list of activities for the assignment. The activities for each assignment are linked directly to actual content, saving time for students.

- Adding assignments consists of clicking on the desired due date, then filling in the details of the assignment—name of the assignment, instruction, and whether it is a one-time or repeating assignment.

- In addition, links to other activities can be created easily. If the activity is online, a URL can be entered in the space provided, and it will be linked automatically in the final syllabus.

- Your completed syllabus is hosted on our servers, allowing convenient updates from any computer on the Internet. Changes you make to your syllabus are immediately available to your students at their next logon.

For the Student—

- **Overview and General Information**— General information about the topic and how it will be covered in the website.

- **Web Links**—A variety of websites related to topic areas.

- **Content Methods and Strategies**— Resources that help to put theories into practice in the special education classroom.

- **Reflective Questions and Case-Based Activities**—Put concepts into action, participate in activities, examine strategies, and more.

- **National and State Laws**—An online guide to how federal and state laws affect your special education classroom.

- **Behavior Management**—An online guide to help you manage behaviors in the special education classroom.

- **Message Board**—Virtual bulletin board to post and respond to questions and comments from a national audience.

To take advantage of these and other resources, please visit the *Direct Instruction Reading,* Fourth Edition, Companion Website at

www.prenhall.com/carnine

CONTENTS

PART 3

Decoding

Note: Every effort has been made to provide accurate and current Internet information in this book. However, the Internet and information posted on it are constantly changing, and it is inevitable that some of the Internet addresses listed in this textbook will change.

Perspective

Perspectives on Reading Instruction

Reading is a complex process—complex to learn and complex to teach. Psycholinguists, information systems analysts, reading researchers, and cognitive psychologists each describe the reading process differently. While these descriptions are important to theoretical questions about the reading process, many of them do not address the needs of classroom teachers. Our purpose is not to survey the various theoretical positions, but to explain procedures that teachers can use to improve the reading performance of their students. Our position is that many students will not become successful readers unless teachers identify the essential reading skills, find out what skills students lack, and teach those skills directly.

Success in reading is very important to students, both for academic and vocational advancement and for the students' psychological well-being.

To teach reading effectively and efficiently, teachers must be knowledgeable in several areas. Teachers must know

1. The essential skills or objectives that make up the reading process and the procedures for teaching those skills.

2. The procedures for evaluating, selecting, and modifying reading programs to meet the needs of all students in their classrooms.

3. The techniques for effectively presenting lessons, including techniques for pacing tasks, motivating students, and diagnosing and correcting their errors.

4. How to utilize assessments to properly place students in a program and monitor their performance throughout the school year.

5. How to use the information from assessments to inform instruction.

6. How to organize classrooms to maximize the amount of time students spend engaged in reading instruction.

Perspectives on Improving Student Reading Performance

Effective and efficient instruction benefits all students but is essential for instructionally naive students who typically have trouble learning to read. *Instructionally naive students* are those students who do not readily retain newly presented information, are easily confused, and have difficulty attending to an instructional presentation.

There are four basic perspectives toward improving student reading performance. The first, the pessimist's viewpoint, states that the schools can do little unless the student's physical make-up or home and social environment are altered. The second, the generalist's viewpoint, states that the schools can improve reading performance by developing a wide range of abilities which supposedly underlie reading. The third, a constructivist or whole-language viewpoint, holds the individual reader's construction of meaning as central to reading, and views phonics and the "decoding" of words as strategies that trivialize the purpose of reading. The fourth, a direct-instruction viewpoint, involves an analysis of how to teach specific reading skills. Each orientation toward reading instruction is discussed below.

Pessimist's Viewpoint

The pessimist's viewpoint states that the schools can do little unless the student's physical make-up or home and social environment are altered, and that conditions outside the control of the schools are the predominant determiners of success. The pessimist orientation results in educators not examining what occurs in the school to explain why children have not been successful.

More than three decades ago, Becker (1973) pointed out the problem with the pessimist's orientation, an orientation tacitly minimizing the importance of teaching:

> As long as the educational climate was such that
> teaching failures could be blamed on the children,
> there was no pressure on the teacher to learn more
> effective means of dealing with children. Over the
> years, psychologists, mental health workers, and
> some educators have trained teachers to shift their
> failures to someone else or at least to blame the
> child's home background, his low IQ, his poor
> motivation, his emotional disturbance, his lack of
> readiness, or his physical disability for the teaching

failure. With the recent advent of the label learning disability (for children with normal IQ who fail to learn) there is no teaching failure which cannot be blamed on the child. (p. 78)

An orientation that blames students for their failure is unwarranted and harmful. *Teachers can bring about substantial improvements in students' reading performance.* Problems, such as poverty, a disruptive home life, and physiological impairments, often make teaching more difficult. However, we reject the assumption that improvement in reading achievement is not possible unless there are changes in the children's economic and social environments. Educators cannot use social and home environments as excuses for the poor performance of some students.

More than forty years of substantial and coercive research now supports the proposition that if students are taught fundamental reading skills directly, explicitly, strategically, and thoughtfully, they will learn to read (Adams, 1990; Becker & Carnine, 1980; Foorman, 1995; Kame'enui & Simmons, 1990; Lyon, 1995; National Reading Panel, 2000; Smith, Simmons, & Kame'enui, 1995).

Generalist's Viewpoint

Typical of the second orientation toward improving reading performance is the idea that reading performance can be improved by focusing on the *processes* or *abilities* that underlie learning. Focusing on reading skills is felt by this viewpoint's advocates to be an inappropriate emphasis. Once students "learn to learn," "become motivated," or "overcome auditory deficits," reading will be relatively easy for them. The attitudes reflected in this orientation are more constructive than those of the pessimists because the assumption is that students can succeed and what the teacher does will influence the learning of the students. However, the problems with the generalist's viewpoint are these:

1. It draws attention away from the quality of reading instruction. Instead of looking at the

way reading is taught, general skills such as visual perception are stressed.

2. Proposed solutions often inadvertently result in students receiving less actual reading instruction than in a normal situation.

3. Data from research reviews do not support a generalist viewpoint (Kavale & Forness, 1987; Lloyd, 1984).

Modality matching and learning styles approaches to reading instruction stem from the generalist viewpoint. In these approaches, learners are classified as either auditory or visual learners and assigned to either an auditory method of teaching reading or a visual method of teaching reading. The assumption is that auditory learners will benefit most from an auditory method and visual learners will benefit most from a visual method. However, reviews of the modality matching and learning styles research have revealed no evidence to support the approaches (Forness, Kavale, Blum, & Lloyd, 1997; Snider, 1992; Stahl & Kuhn, 1995; Tarver, 1996). These negative findings converge with findings that indicate that students, regardless of their modality preferences or their learning styles, benefit most from explicit and systematic instruction.

Constructivist or Whole-Language Viewpoint

Typical of the third orientation toward improving reading performance is the notion that children develop and progress at their own rate, and that learning to read is as natural a process as learning to speak and that both are comparable parts of overall language development (Foorman, 1995; Liberman & Liberman, 1990). Moreover, this orientation holds that children develop language naturally in environments that support meaningful and purposeful language usage. Thus, children will develop reading and writing skills within environments that promote meaningful and purposeful reading and writing experiences, but at their own individual pace. Differences in reading performance, therefore, are seen as reflective of developmental differences that will minimize over time.

The attitudes reflected in this "constructivist" orientation are certainly more productive than those of the pessimists because the constructivist's assumption is that students will succeed. However, "success" is often viewed as "getting the gist" of the story, for example, which is in contrast to correctly reading the words of a text. Additionally, the committed teacher's role is viewed much more as a facilitator or guide within the reading process and not as someone whose direct actions have a direct and instrumental influence on students' learning.

While some of the guidelines described in this orientation may be viewed as useful "truisms" for all classrooms (e.g., provide a supportive "literate" environment with functional print everywhere), the problems with the developmentalist or whole-language viewpoint are based on the assumption that learning to read is as natural as learning to speak. To assess this assumption, we must pose two questions: (a) Is reading, like speaking, natural? (b) What is required if the child is to read and write?

Liberman and Liberman (1990) answer the first question with an unqualified "no." Speech is primarily biological. Humans possess a predisposition for its development, whereas learning to read is gaining knowledge of and practice with an agreed-upon convention for the written representation of language. In response to the second question, much of the current research that focuses on beginning reading skills unwaveringly points to the child's need for well-developed phonological awareness skills and alphabetic understanding as prerequisite and corequisite requirements in learning to read and write. (See Part 2 for a more complete treatment of beginning reading skills.)

Although developmental differences are well-recognized, the viewpoint of reading as a constructivist activity that unfolds naturally within a supportive, enriched "literate" environment is one that might negatively affect "perhaps 20 to 25 percent (of the children) who will not discover the point of the alphabet except as it is made apparent to them by appropriate instruction" (Liberman & Liberman, 1990, p. 54).

Direct Instruction

The fourth orientation and, in our opinion, the best answer to the question of how educators can improve student reading performance is direct instruction. Direct instruction involves teaching essential reading skills in the most effective and efficient manner possible. Essential skills as well as effective and efficient teaching practices are identified by scientifically-based research about reading development, reading instruction, and reading disabilities. Scientifically-based research includes instructional research that compares the results of different practices and approaches (National Institute of Child Health and Human Development, 2000).

The research base for direct instruction is solid. It includes research which supports the approach as a whole, as well as research that supports the components that make up the whole. It includes large-scale experimental studies conducted in the real world of schools and classrooms, as well as small-scale experiments conducted in more highly controlled settings. It includes studies with students of all income levels, all grade levels, and a wide range of ability levels. It includes studies with both special-education and regular-education students. It includes studies using norm-referenced as well as criterion-referenced assessment instruments. It includes studies which investigated the characteristics of effective teachers.

Follow Through *Research With Disadvantaged Students*

The earliest and largest study of the effectiveness of Direct Instruction was a federally funded 16-year study called *Follow Through.* In *Follow Through,* several major approaches to educating low-income, primary-grade students were compared. Direct approaches were compared with approaches based on language-experience, Piaget's stages of learning, child-development theory, discovery learning, and open education. Only students in a direct-instruction approach consistently outperformed control students on basic, cognitive, and affective measures. Guthrie (1977) summarized the *Follow Through* results in this way:

> Final answers about teaching are not available from this study (*Follow Through*)—nor will they ever be—no more than final answers about medicine, engineering, or poetry. A fully complete explanation of education is not likely, since values of the public and research methods are constantly shifting. However, the results of the *Follow Through* experiment endow us with evidence about the effects of teaching programs at an unprecedented level of certainty. The edge that the more successful programs have over the less successful programs is wide enough to serve as a foothold in the climb to improved, intended education. (p. 244)

Research 25 Years Beyond Follow Through

The reading program used in the direct-instruction model in *Follow Through* was DISTAR (1974). Later, that program was revised and renamed Reading Mastery I and II. Still later, the Reading Mastery series was expanded through six levels. Several revisions of the series have occurred over the last 25 years. During these 25 years, a large number of experimental or quasi-experimental studies have been conducted to compare the effectiveness of direct instruction to other instructional approaches; most, but not all, of those studies were focused on direct instruction in reading. In *Research on Direct Instruction: 25 Years Beyond DISTAR,* Adams and Engelmann (1996) reported the results of their comprehensive review and meta-analysis of 34 studies. The 34 studies reported 173 comparisons, spanning the years from 1972 to 1996. Large gains were reported for both regular- and special-education students and for both elementary and secondary students. The average effect size calculated for the 34 studies was .87; for the 173 comparisons it was .97. This means that, on average, gain scores for students in Direct Instruction groups averaged nearly a full standard deviation above those of students in comparison groups. Effect sizes of this magnitude are rare in educational research.

Ellis and Fouts (1997) addressed the question of a possible conflict of interest in the Adams and Engelmann (1996) review because Engelmann is an author of commercial direct-instruction materials. Mindful of the fact that only 5 of the 71 researchers referenced in the Adams and Engelmann (1996) review were co-authors of commercial materials, Ellis and Fouts concluded:

> We do not believe this [a conflict of interest] to be an issue for several reasons. First, there are . . . other researchers who have studied D.I. who are not connected to its commercial aspects, and their findings are basically the same. Second, the research by prominent D.I. advocates is published in prestigious, peer-reviewed journals, an extremely important quality control point. Third, there has been no sustained or focused criticism that we could find that challenges the quality of the research. (pp. 223–224)

Teacher Effectiveness Research

Rosenshine's (1986) seminal review of research on teacher effectiveness provides support for many of the components of the direct instruction model. He described the variables that were associated with student academic success as "direct instruction" and included the following in his summary of direct instruction:

- High levels of student engagement
- Academic focus
- Teacher-directed
- Carefully sequenced and structured materials
- Clear goals
- Sufficient time allocated for instruction
- Extensive content coverage
- Monitoring of student performance
- Immediate, academically-oriented feedback to students
- Structured, but not authoritarian, teacher-student interactions

Although the research Rosenshine reviewed focused on the achievement of low-income, primary-grade

students, other researchers (Brophy & Good, 1986) report similar results with other types of students.

Research With Special-Education and Other Low-Achieving Students

Several independent reviews of special education research have added to the strong support for direct instruction. A 1988 meta-analysis of 25 studies that focused on special education populations showed large effect sizes for direct instruction, with no comparisons favoring the comparison group (White, 1988). A 1997 analysis of intervention programs for special-education students found direct instruction to be one of only seven interventions showing strong evidence of effectiveness (Forness, Kavale, Blum, & Lloyd, 1997). A 1997 *Current Practice Alert* sponsored by the Division for Learning Disabilities (DLD) and the Division for Research (DR) of the Council for Exceptional Children (CEC) states that a high level of effectiveness (for direct instruction) has been demonstrated by individual research studies, research reviews, and technical reports of informal studies (Tarver & DLD/DR, 1999). In addition, a 1990 review of intervention techniques and programs for students with academic performance problems (i.e., low achievers) revealed strong evidence of the effectiveness of direct instruction (Elliot & Sharpio, 1990).

Concern for At-Risk and Low-Achieving Students

As indicated by the kinds of research described above, the direct-instruction perspective reflects concern for the academic performance of all students. This includes large numbers of students who have been labeled variously as at-risk students, disadvantaged students, low-performing students, learning-disabled students, reading-disabled students, ESL students, and students with limited English proficiency (LEP). The umbrella term *diverse students* has been used to encompass the broad array of students with different backgrounds and different learning abilities and needs. From the direct instruction perspective, all of these students, like other students who experience no learning problems in school, benefit from effective instruction. However, students who are at risk for learning problems in school, regardless of the reason(s) for those problems or the labels used to describe the problems, are in greater need of research-based instruction; for them, success in school depends upon it. The general principles of effective instruction apply to the teaching of all students; however, the applications of those principles vary according to the needs of individuals. Throughout this textbook, we suggest ways of individualizing instruction to meet the needs of different students without violating the research-based principles of instruction that benefit all students.

Although the research described above was focused on direct instruction, it was not focused exclusively on direct-*reading* instruction. The direct-instruction model encompasses all basic academic subjects. However, reading is the most studied of the academic subjects and strong support for direct-reading instruction comes from the mainstream of reading research. In the largest, most comprehensive evidence-based review ever conducted of research on how children learn reading, the National Reading Panel (2000) concluded that effective reading instruction includes:

- teaching children to break apart and manipulate the sounds in words (phonemic awareness)

- teaching them that these sounds are represented by letters of the alphabet which then can be blended together to form words (phonics)

- having them practice what they've learned by reading aloud with guidance and feedback (guided oral reading)

- applying reading comprehension strategies to guide and improve reading comprehension

Direct instruction emphasizes all of these essential reading skills. Furthermore, direct-instruction procedures for teaching the skills effectively and efficiently are validated by scientific research and are consistent with the recommendations of the National Reading Panel. That is why we have adopted the report of the National Reading Panel as the research base for this textbook.

Illustrations of the Four Orientations

Four answers to the question of how to improve reading instruction have been discussed: Pessimists look outside the school, generalists look toward abilities that underlie reading, constructivists look toward enriching the environment and making it more meaningful and purposeful to the child, and direct instruction advocates look to improvements in teaching methodology that are based on research. The following description presents a series of well-defined student problems and solutions that are described through each of the four orientations.

The first student is Arthur who upon entering fourth grade is placed in a fourth-grade reading group. Each day an assignment is written on the chalkboard consisting of a story to read and several written exercises to complete. Unfortunately, Arthur can read only about 60% of the words that appear in the reader and, thus, cannot figure out many of the answers to the written exercises. At the end of the reading period, he hands in his papers. They are returned at the end of the day, full of Xs and sometimes a comment such as "Be more careful." After several days, Arthur begins spending more time roughhousing and talking with his neighbors. He seldom completes his assignments. The response from a pessimist's viewpoint might be that Arthur is suffering from attention deficit with hyperactivity disorder (ADHD), comes from a broken home, and is unmotivated.

Those who embrace a generalist's viewpoint might suggest moving Arthur to another class where the teacher empathizes with his situation and emphasizes "feeling good" and would work to develop Arthur's self-concept first, and his reading skills second. "After all," a generalist would argue, "You can't read when you don't feel good about who you are."

Constructivist or whole-language advocates might argue that the assignments are not meaningful and purposeful for Arthur. From a direct-instruction viewpoint, Arthur requires changes in the instructional program to enable him to succeed. First, the teacher must place Arthur at a more appropriate level in the reading program because he obviously cannot succeed in assignments that assume skills he does not have and has not been taught. Second, the teacher must examine the task to determine critical component skills and devise strategies to teach these skills. If Arthur is expected to know the meanings of various words and to draw inferences from a text, he must be taught vocabulary words and inference skills before he works the assignment. Finally, the teacher must institute a system to motivate Arthur because the high degree of failure he has encountered has made reading distasteful to him.

The next student is Janice, a first-grader. Janice makes numerous word reading errors during oral reading in small group instruction. In the most recent reading lesson, Janice said "at" for *it* and "hum" for *him.* The pessimist might assert that whatever Janice does in the classroom is irrelevant because her low IQ ostensibly prohibits her from becoming a fluent and successful reader. The generalist might argue that Janice will always have difficulty with reading, because she must first overcome her auditory processing deficits before she can begin to read visually. The constructivist or whole-language viewpoint might take two approaches: First, Janice is simply not ready to read and is too immature for reading. Second, the teacher's focus on word-reading errors is not a legitimate concern and trivializes the purpose of reading, which is to construct meaning from text. Moreover, a constructivist would argue that as long as what Janice is reading "makes sense" to her as an individual constructing meaning, decoding "words" is irrelevant. A direct instruction approach to Janice's reading performance would begin with assessment. First, one would test to see if Janice knows the sound of the letter *i* and has a strategy for reading words. For deficiencies in either skill, specific teaching procedures would be instituted immediately with specific goals set for improved reading accuracy.

The last student is Dale, a sixth-grader who forgets how to look up information on different topics in a textbook. The teacher explains that she taught Dale and the rest of the class several weeks ago how to use a subject index in a textbook. Yesterday, however, when Dale was given a worksheet assignment that required him to list the page numbers on the Egyptians in his history book, he did not remember the subject index or how to use it and began looking at every page in his book to find the pages that discussed the Egyptians. He ran out of time and was unable to finish his assignment. A pessimistic approach to Dale's problem might argue that Dale did not finish his assignment because he has too many worries about home and the care he must provide to his four brothers and sisters because his single mother works two jobs to support the family. A generalist might suggest memory training for Dale. The constructivist interpretation might argue that the assignment is simply meaningless to Dale and the time limit imposed by the teacher constrains Dale's ability to gain meaning from the text. A direct-instruction explanation would focus on providing Dale with more instruction and practice in using an index. If Dale had completed several exercises in using the subject index immediately following the teacher's initial explanation he would be more likely to remember when and how to use it. The recommendation from this approach would be to reteach the skill and provide more practice immediately after the reteaching. Once Dale has learned the *skills,* he would be taught to apply the skills to a wide range of questions involving multiple texts.

The Four Orientations and Reading Readiness

These four orientations also vary significantly in their approach to reading readiness, that is, how to prepare the students for beginning reading instruction. For example, some educators believe that teachers should delay reading instruction until the students have had enough experiences and demonstrate an interest in learning to read. While we would agree that a child who has participated in a broad range of experiences prior to beginning school may be well-prepared for instruction, delaying the instruction of students who do not arrive at the school door well-prepared denies

them the opportunity to catch up to their more prepared peers. Further, following this line of reasoning,
one must ask, "What is to be done if students do not
show an interest in reading?"

Those who subscribe to a constructivist orientation promote a child-centered approach to reading
readiness. To prepare children for reading, they suggest providing literate environments which include
reading aloud highly predictable stories that frequently repeat key words, modeling a strong interest
in reading by allowing children to observe adult
reading behavior, and having many books available.
Because of the assumption that learning to read is as
natural as learning to speak, and that children quickly
learn to speak in environments that provide meaningful and purposeful communicative events, then
children should naturally learn to read in these environments that present meaning and purposeful reading behavior that is developmentally appropriate.

The direct-instruction approach to reading
readiness recognizes the importance of preparing
children to succeed in reading instruction through
the systematic teaching of critical prerequisite skills
such as phonemic awareness and language concepts
that will be used by teachers later when teaching
reading. A direct-instruction approach recognizes
that teachers have limited instructional time to
teach an enormous amount of information to groups
of children who often present diverse learning pro-
files. Thus instruction must be designed and delivered carefully and efficiently.

It should be noted that in each situation, the
direct-instruction approach sought to improve the
instruction so that the students would be more likely
to succeed. As teachers, we need to seek out ways to
improve teaching *in the classroom.* Of course, some
students are more difficult to teach than others, but
highly skilled professionals who understand the skills
and teaching techniques involved can teach these students to read. Hopefully, this book will contribute to
improved reading instruction by providing detailed
explanations of effective teaching procedures.

CHAPTER 2

A Model of Reading Instruction

Direct instruction has been defined and described in various ways by different professionals across the years. Our current definition is reflected in the description that is presented in Figure 2.1, "What Is Direct Instruction?" (Schug, Tarver, & Western, 2001). As indicated by that description, our model is highly consistent with the findings of scientific research conducted over the last 50 years. A list of the major research studies and/or reviews conducted during that time appears below:

- Chall's (1967) review of studies comparing the relative effectiveness of whole-word ("look-say") versus phonics approaches to beginning reading instruction

- The USOE Cooperative Research Program's (1967) review of beginning reading programs (Bond & Dykstra, 1967; Dykstra, 1968)

- Syntheses of Project Follow Through findings regarding reading achievement of students in different educational models (Bereiter & Kurland, 1981–1982; Stebbins et al., 1977)

- A quantitative synthesis of 97 selected studies including 30 different methods (Pflaum, Walberg, Karegianes, & Rasher, 1980)

- *Becoming a Nation of Readers,* a report of the Commission on Reading, produced by the Center for the Study of Reading at the University of Illinois, Urbana–Champaign (1985), under the auspices of the National Academy of Education's Commission on Education and Public Policy, with the sponsorship of the National Institute of Education

- Rosenshine's reviews of teacher effectiveness variables (Rosenshine, 1979; Rosenshine & Stevens, 1986)

- Adams's (1990) review of research and theories of beginning reading, conducted in conjunction with the Reading Research and Education Center at the Center for the Study of Reading at the University of Illinois, Urbana–Champaign

- The National Reading Panel report (2000)

Because the most recent of the comprehensive reviews, the National Reading Panel review, encompasses the research included in the earlier reviews, we adopted it as the research base for this textbook. However, the other reviews and/or classic studies within reviews will be referenced as appropriate throughout the book.

Figure 2.1   What Is Direct Instruction?

Direct Instruction is an approach to teaching. It is skills-oriented, and the teaching practices it implies are teacher-directed. It emphasizes the use of small-group, face-to-face instruction by teachers and aides using carefully articulated lessons in which cognitive skills are broken down into small units, sequenced deliberately, and taught explicitly (see Carnine, 2000, pp. 5-6; Traub, 1999).

Direct instruction derives mainly from two lines of scholarship and curriculum development. One line of scholarship is based on a synthesis of findings from experimental studies (conducted by many different researchers, working independently, mostly in the 1980s) in which teachers were trained to use particular instructional practices. These practices then were assessed for their effects on student learning, and the effects were compared with effects for similar students who had not been taught according to the experimental method. The synthesis growing out of these studies identified common "teaching functions" abstracted from the experiments that had proved effective in improving student learning. These teaching functions included teaching in small steps with student practice after each step, guiding students during initial practice, and ensuring that all students experienced a high level of successful practice. Instruction of this sort was described variously by the people who used it and discussed it. It was sometimes called systematic teaching, or explicit teaching, or active teaching. In an influential essay, Barak Rosenshine and Robert Stevens (1986) called it direct instruction, and this is the name by which it is now most often known.

As Rosenshine and Stevens describe it, direct instruction is a teaching model, not a particular, fully elaborated program for teaching, say, reading or mathematics. It is abstracted from detailed procedures found, for example, in particular training manuals and materials, and it implies nothing definite about how teachers who make new uses of it might best fulfill the teaching functions it embodies (Rosenshine & Stevens, 1986, p. 389). It is a generic teaching model, in other words—one awaiting subsequent interpretation and development in particular applications.

Interpretation and development of this sort has been provided in a second line of scholarship associated primarily with the work of Siegfried Engelmann and his colleagues. Their work goes

beyond the generic direct instruction model, providing detailed teaching programs consistent with its main principles. Engelmann and his colleagues call their programs Direct Instruction or DI programs, using upper-case type to distinguish them from the earlier, generic formulations.

The texture of detail in Direct Instruction derives in part from its foundation in close analyses of the comprehension and reasoning skills needed for successful performance in, say, reading or mathematics. These skills provide the intellectual substance of Direct Instruction programs. In the case of reading, it is substance found in the sound system of spoken English and the ways in which English sounds are represented in writing. That is why Direct Instruction is associated with phonemic awareness, or phonics. But Direct Instruction is not the same thing as phonics, or "merely phonics." Direct Instruction can be used to teach things other than phonics—mathematics and logic, for example—and phonics can be taught (as it often has been) by means other than Direct Instruction.

The detailed character of Direct Instruction derives also from a learning theory (Engelmann & Carnine, 1991) and a set of teaching practices linked to that theory. The learning theory focuses on how children generalize from present understanding to understanding of new, untaught examples. This theory informs the sequencing of classroom tasks for children and the means by which teachers lead children through those tasks. The means include a complex system of scripted remarks, questions, and signals, to which children provide individual and choral responses in extended, interactive sessions. Children in Direct Instruction classrooms also do written work in workbook or activity sheets.

Many published instructional programs have made some use of insights from Direct Instruction (or direct instruction). Taken at a high level of generality, at least, those insights are not private property. But Direct Instruction to date is represented most clearly and extensively in instructional programs authored by Engelmann and published by SRA/McGraw-Hill. When educators talk about adopting Direct Instruction, the programs in question are most likely the Engelmann-authored SRA/McGraw-Hill programs. Other publishers, of course, could enter the market, if they chose to do so, by developing new applications of the underlying direct instruction principles.

The National Reading Panel (NRP) Report (2000)

The NRP was convened in 1997 in response to a congressional directive to review the scientific literature and determine the most effective ways to teach children to read. Leading scientists in reading research, representatives of colleges of education, reading teachers, educational administrators, and parents served on the NRP. The panel identified approximately 100,000 studies published since 1966 and 15,000 studies published before that time. From those studies, they selected for further review the experimental and quasi-experimental studies that met rigorous scientific standards. The panel's conclusions were based on the evidence from those scientific studies.

NRP identified five essential components of effective reading instruction:

- Phonemic awareness instruction
- Phonics instruction
- Fluency instruction
- Vocabulary instruction
- Text comprehension instruction

The NRP report (2000) contains comprehensive reviews of the scientific research within each of the five domains along with succinct summaries of the conclusions drawn from the research. To make this evidence-based reading research available to educators, parents, policy-makers, and others with an interest in helping all people learn to read well, a summarizing document titled *Put Reading First* (2001) was developed and disseminated. *Put Reading First* (2001) was published by the Partnership for Reading, a collaborative effort of the National Institute for Literacy, the National Institute of Child Health and Human Development, and the U.S. Department of Education. *Put Reading First* can be downloaded by going to the National Institute of Literacy website at *www.nifl.gov.* The complete NRP report can be downloaded or ordered from the NRP website at *www.nationalreadingpanel.org.* Drawing from the NRP report and *Put Reading First,* we constructed tables of major conclusions about each of the five essential components of effective instruction. Those tables are included in relevant chapters of this textbook.

The most promising overall conclusion from the NRP report was captured by Duane Alexander, Director of the National Institute of Child Health and Human Development:

> For the first time, we now have guidance—based on evidence from sound scientific research—on how best to teach children to read . . . the panel's rigorous scientific review identifies the most effective strategies for teaching reading.

Direct-Instruction Model

The direct-instruction model presented in this textbook is a comprehensive model that provides instruction in all five of the essential components identified by the NRP. Subcomponents within each of these major components are specified in the direct instruction model and are described in detail in later chapters.

Most importantly, the direct-instruction model goes further to:

- Sequence the components and subcomponents to produce a seamless progression from beginning to advanced reading skills
- Specify effective and efficient teaching techniques and procedures to ensure that students acquire components skills and strategies and progress from beginning to advanced reading

Teaching techniques and procedures employed in the model are described in detail in Chapters 3 and 4. Chapter 3 details the selection of instructional materials and organization of instruction. Chapter 4 details specific techniques and procedures for delivering instruction. The practices described in Chapters 3 and 4 are applied to particular reading components in later chapters. Research that supports the direct instruction techniques and procedures is summarized in Chapters 13 and 27.

Chall's Model of Reading Development

Chall's model of reading development grew out of her seminal research on the effectiveness of different beginning reading approaches (Chall, 1967). In her later book on the *Stages of Reading Development* (1983), Chall described six stages of development that are entirely consistent with the stages of instruction that constitute the direct-instruction model which we advocate. For that reason, we describe Chall's model briefly here and then discuss important commonalities among her model, the direct-instruction model, and the NRP report.

Stage 0 (up to Age 6)   Stage 0 (up to age 6) is a prereading stage that is characterized by children's growth in knowledge and use of spoken language. Increasing control of words (vocabulary) and syntax is apparent. In addition, children acquire some beginning understandings of the sound structures of words. For example, they learn that some words sound the same at the beginning (alliteration) and/or the end (rhyme), that spoken words can be broken into parts, and that the parts can be put together to form whole words. Most children also acquire some knowledge of print at this stage. They may, for example, learn the names of the letters of the alphabet and learn to print their names and some letters not in their names. Although much of their reading may best be described as "pretend reading," most children do learn to hold the book right-side up and turn the pages. Some may learn to point at a word on the page while saying the word. Reading to children provides them with opportunities to acquire this kind of prereading knowledge.

Stage 1 (Grades 1–2)   In Stage 1, children learn the letters of the alphabet and the correspondences between the letters and the sounds that they represent. By the end of this stage, they have acquired a general understanding of the spelling-sound system. Direct teaching of decoding accelerates development in Stage 1, particularly for those with limited readiness.

Stage 2 (Grades 2–3)   In Stage 2, confirmation of what was learned in Stage 1 takes place and children learn to apply the knowledge gained in Stage 1 to read words and stories. Children learn to recognize words composed of increasingly complex phonic elements and read stories composed of increasingly complex words. Through practice, oral reading of stories and passages becomes more fluent and sounds more like talking.

Stages 1 and 2 Together   Together, Stages 1 and 2 constitute a "learning to read stage," at the end of which children are no longer glued to the print on the page. They recognize most words automatically and read passages with ease and expression. Decoding the words on the page no longer consumes all of their cognitive attention; cognitive capacity is freed for processing meaning. At this point, children are ready to make the important transition from "learning to read" to "reading to learn."

Stage 3 (Phase A, Grades 4–6; Phase B, Grades 7–8 and/or 9)   In Stage 3, children begin to learn new knowledge, information, thoughts, and experiences by reading. Growth in word meanings (vocabulary) and background knowledge are primary goals. Children read selections from an increasingly broad range of materials (e.g., textbooks, magazines, encyclopedias) about an increasingly broad range of topics (e.g., history, geography, science). Most reading is for facts, concepts, or how to do things. In Phase A of Stage 3, when vocabulary and background knowledge are still rather limited, reading is best developed with materials and purposes that focus on one viewpoint. As students move through Phase B, they start to confront different viewpoints and begin to analyze and criticize what they read.

Stage 4 (High School)   In Stage 4, students must deal with more than one viewpoint. Topics in textbooks are treated in greater depth and from more than one viewpoint. Dealing with more than one set of facts, competing theories, and multiple interpretations provides not only multiple viewpoints, but knowledge of how to acquire new points of view and how to acquire increasingly complex concepts.

Study skills and practice in efficient reading are beneficial at this stage.

Stage 5 (Age 18 and Above)   At this highest stage of reading development, readers can read materials in the degree of detail and completeness that is needed to serve their purposes. Readers select materials to serve their purposes; they know what not to read as well as what to read. They analyze, synthesize, and make judgments about what they read. They balance their own comprehension of the words with their analysis of the content and their own ideas about the topic. At this stage, reading is constructive. The reader constructs knowledge and understanding from reading what others have written.

Chall (1983) attempted to prevent misunderstanding of her model by elaborating the following points:

1. The ages or grades at which the stages occur are approximate.

2. Whether reading develops as described at any given stage depends, to a considerable extent, upon the instruction that is provided in the classroom and/or at home.

3. Development at each stage is dependent upon adequate development at the prior stages. For example, Stage 1 reading is dependent upon the development of language in Stage 0; rhyming, alliteration, and vocabulary are particularly important prerequisites to beginning reading instruction. Reading development in Stage 4 (i.e., critical reading) is dependent upon the acquisition of a rich base of information and vocabulary in Stage 3.

4. The reading stages are not discrete; they are continuous and overlapping. For example, although most spelling-sound correspondences are learned in Stage 1, other more complex correspondences are learned throughout Stages 3 and 4 and perhaps even Stage 5. And, even though fluent passage reading does not become a clear focus of reading development until Stage 2, the rudiments of fluency are developing in Stage 1. Also, although comprehension is not emphasized in Stages 1 and 2, literal comprehension of simple passages is inherent in the development of word recognition skills (Stage 1) and fluency (Stage 2). Although not discrete, each of the stages is associated with particular aspects of development that are of primary importance.

A stage model has important implications for individualization of instruction. Because development at each stage is dependent upon adequate development at the prior stages, it is necessary that educators conduct assessments to determine students' levels of development. Assessments provide the information that will enable educators to provide children with instruction that starts where they are and then build on that base to help children advance to the higher levels. For example, the child who lacks knowledge of rhyming and alliteration (Stage 0) will need some instruction in those skills before moving on to the more formal phonics instruction that is associated with Stage 1. The child who lacks knowledge of most of the letter-sound correspondences will need some instruction in those basic phonics skills before fluency of passage reading is emphasized. The child who has not yet "learned to read" will need instruction in one or more aspects of decoding and fluency before moving on to the "reading to learn" stages. And, similarly, the child who has not acquired sufficient information and vocabulary in Stage 3 will likely have great difficulty when confronted with the need to deal with different viewpoints in Stage 5; explicit teaching of vocabulary and background knowledge will be necessary.

Stanovich (1988) coined the term "Matthew Effect" to describe the educational dilemma that students face throughout their schooling when they are expected to perform at particular levels even though they lack prerequisite knowledge and skills. Children who begin school with little or no phonemic awareness have difficulty learning letter-sound correspondences and therefore have trouble with word recognition. When word recognition places too many demands on cognitive capacity, less cognitive attention is available for allocation to higher-level comprehension processes. Trying to read for meaning without the necessary cognitive resources is not a rewarding experience. Unrewarding early experiences squelch motivation and lead to less involvement in reading-related activities. This lack of involvement, and therefore lack of practice, further delays the development of automatic word recognition. The negative spiral of cumulative disadvantage continues and troublesome emotional side effects begin to be associated with school experiences. The emotional problems, in turn, present yet another hindrance to school achievement.

In contrast, children who develop efficient decoding processes quickly and easily find reading enjoyable because they can concentrate on the meaning of the text. They read more; the additional exposure and practice further develops their reading abilities. The "Matthew Effect" analogy is used frequently to explain the rich-get-richer and poor-get-poorer effects that are embedded in the educational process. The term derives from the Gospel according to Matthew: "For unto every one that hath shall be given, and he shall have abundance; but from him that hath not shall be taken away even that which he hath."

Congruence of Our Direct-Instruction Model, Chall's Six-Stage Model, and the NRP Report

The direct-instruction model, on which this textbook is based, is highly congruent with both Chall's classic model of reading development and the research-based conclusions of the NRP. Although the terminology used in the three sources differs to some extent, the substance of the instructional implications and practices is essentially the same.

An explanation of some differences in terminology may prevent confusion about the substance of the messages in these three sources. Chall used the global term "development" to describe children's progression through the stages. To some ed-

ucators, the term "development" connotes an unfolding within the child that is independent of the environmental effects of schooling. It is clear, however, that Chall saw reading development as highly related to methods of teaching beginning reading in school. In both her classic 1967 book, *Learning to Read: The Great Debate,* and her 1983 book, *Stages of Reading Development,* she presented the evidence in favor of a code-emphasis approach in beginning reading instruction and continued throughout her career to expand upon that theme. Our direct-instruction model, like Chall's, is a code-emphasis model. (See Chapter 3 for a definition of what constitutes a code-emphasis approach.) In our direct-instruction model, however, we describe what children learn as they progress in reading as "skills," "knowledge," "concepts," and "strategies" and rarely use the term "development." Our focus is on "instruction" rather than "development."

Chall's 1967 analysis of the research evidence regarding beginning reading instruction is strikingly similar to that of the NRP (2000). Her stages mirror the five components identified by NRP: phonemic awareness (in Stage 0 and into Stage 1, if needed); phonics (emphasized in Stage 1, continued but with less emphasis in the higher stages); fluency (emphasized in Stage 2, continued but with less emphasis in Stage 3); vocabulary (emphasized in Stage 3 and continued throughout Stages 4 and 5); text comprehension (emphasized in Stages 3, 4, and 5, with increasing emphasis on higher-order comprehension at the more advanced stages). Furthermore, both Chall's analysis and the NRP analysis are highly consistent with the analyses of the other review teams listed at the beginning of this chapter. The findings of those review teams will be summarized in a later chapter on Research on Beginning Reading.

At this point in time, there is little room for doubt that the components of reading identified by NRP, Chall, and numerous other reviewers are non-negotiable components of reading instruction. Those who value scientifically-based research findings agree, for the most part, on *what* must be taught when we teach reading. There is less agreement about *how* to teach the identified components.

Our direct-instruction model encompasses all of the NRP components and emphasizes different components at different times as students progress from naive to mature readers. Furthermore, our model provides all of the advantages of a stage model even though we do not label the model as a stage model in the way that Chall did. In our model, components and subcomponents are sequenced and coordinated very carefully to ensure smooth transitions from phase to phase. Careful coordination of the various components and subcomponents also facilitates application and generalization to a broad range of reading assignments (Kame'enui & Carnine, 1998; Tarver, 2000). Because major changes in emphasis are less evident when instruction is designed to progress smoothly from task to task and from phase to phase, the progressive na-

ture of our model is not always apparent to the naive educator. Though not readily apparent, this careful sequencing and coordination is a critical feature of our model.

The major difference between our direct-instruction model, Chall's model, other scientifically-based models, and the NRP's instructional recommendations, is this: We specify in much greater detail both the *what* and the *how* of reading instruction. The sequencing and coordination of components (i.e., curriculum design) is the *what* of instruction. What teachers do to ensure that students really do learn the components as they proceed through the curriculum is the *how* of instruction. In the remaining chapters of this book, we describe in great detail the *what* and the *how* that we believe to be essential to effective reading instruction.

Classroom Reading Instruction

This book attempts to provide teachers with information that relates directly to what happens in the classroom. Our goal is to provide information that will empower teachers to provide instruction that maximizes student reading performance while improving the children's self-concept. This chapter will present an overview of three important components related to classroom instruction; instructional materials, assessments, and classroom organization.

Instructional Materials

What a teacher does in the classroom will be driven in good part by the instructional materials the teacher is using. The more carefully thought-out and constructed the materials the more energy the teacher can devote to his or her teaching interactions with students. A teacher with effective materials can concentrate on the students when teaching. A teacher with poorly constructed instructional materials will have a much more difficult job as constant modifications in materials will be needed.

Using a well-constructed reading program is critical for teachers working with at-risk students, because the quality of the materials can make the difference between success and failure. Teachers

working with more sophisticated students also need well-constructed programs, because poorly constructed programs can keep the students from learning at an optimal rate.

Specific criteria teachers can use when evaluating and selecting materials appear in later chapters.

Comprehensive Core Reading Programs

A comprehensive core reading program is a set of sequentially aligned teacher and student instructional materials that is designed to systematically teach reading and language arts content for students in kindergarten through sixth grade. The programs, which are produced by major publishing houses, are designed so that they will cover virtually all the content standards that are specified by a state. Some publishers produce specific programs for the larger states that have statewide adoptions, California, Florida, and Texas. There are at the time of this writing, five major publishers that account for the bulk of sales of these programs.

The advantage of these core programs is their inclusion of a wide range of content. This advantage can also be a disadvantage if the program contains so many topics that priority content does not receive deep coverage.

These comprehensive core programs used to be and still are referred to by many educators as basal reading programs. The more recently published core programs are somewhat different than previously published programs in that the newer comprehensive core programs include more language arts topics.

Beginning in the late 1990s, several large states, California, Texas, and Florida, required that basal programs to be adopted in their respective states be aligned with scientifically-based reading research. These requirements, along with the publication of the National Reading Panel Report, and the passage of the No Child Left Behind legislation, have had a major effect on the design of the programs. Since 2002, all the major publishers of comprehensive core reading programs have published new programs that are significantly more aligned with the research findings. Even though these programs are aligned with the research findings, there are still significant differences among the programs in their potential effectiveness as instructional tools, particularly for teachers responsible for the education of at-risk children. Throughout the remaining chapters of this book, information will be presented that teachers can use in selecting programs that can best meet the needs of their students.

Focused Core Reading Programs

These reading programs focus on what the authors consider to be the essential skills students need to be accomplished readers. These programs are not as inclusive as the comprehensive core reading programs. Some of these programs have been particularly effective with at-risk students because they do provide more in-depth treatment of the core content. Schools have adopted these programs and supplemented them with teacher-made materials to create a reading program that meets all content standards.

Supplementary Materials

Supplementary materials provide instruction or practice on just one or two areas of reading instruction. An increasing number of publishers are producing programs that focus on phonemic awareness and/or phonics, including exercises to teach letter-sound correspondences and word reading. Some publishers are producing programs focused on fluency development. Many publishers produce text materials designed for extra reading practice. There is a great difference in the quality with which these programs are constructed.

Teachers need to be careful to ensure that the supplementary materials that they are using are aligned with their core-reading program and are research-based.

Intervention Materials

Intervention programs and materials are designed for children who are performing below grade level. There are a few comprehensive intervention programs specifically designed for older children who have not mastered critical content from the early grades. We describe these programs in Chapter 26. These programs offer specific sequences of lessons for children at different stages. A program for a fifth-grader reading at second-grade level would need to be significantly different from a program for a child reading just 1 year below grade level. These programs need to be highly systematic and explicit.

Computer-Based Instruction

A variety of computer-based programs are available. Most are designed to supplement a core reading program.

A number of programs are aimed at teaching or providing practice to younger children on phonics and phonemic awareness. There are also programs designed to help teachers motivate children to read. These programs determine a child's reading level, indicate books at the child's reading level, provide comprehension questions for the books and include motivational-type record-keeping features. Some programs are more comprehensive providing aligned instruction in all critical areas of reading instruction.

A limitation of computers, particularly during the early stages of reading instruction, is that computers cannot yet reliably interpret children's oral responses and thus cannot give children reliable feedback on their verbal responses. Computer programs, though, can serve as useful supplementary tools that can provide practice for some skills and instruction in others. For example, a computer program might present comprehension strategies and then provide a series of application items to which the computer will provide immediate feedback to correct a wrong response. Some computer programs are becoming "intelligent," in that the amount of practice and what is practiced depends on student performance.

Constructing a School Reading Program

A teacher will not have the time to construct his or her own comprehensive reading program. A comprehensive reading program contains numerous activities from all the essential components of reading instruction (phonemic awareness, phonics, fluency, vocabulary, and comprehension). The introduction of all this content must be carefully sequenced within a grade level and across grade levels.

The reading program in a school should be designed to meet the needs of all the children in the school. The reading program should be carefully sequenced so that when a student moves from grade to grade each year the reading instruction presented is part of an aligned sequence. There should be materials available to meet the needs of children at, below, or above grade-level performance standards.

The core reading program in a school should be selected to meet the needs of the majority of children in the school. If the majority of children in a school are at-risk, the core reading program should be one that is highly systematic and explicit, containing adequate practice, carefully controlled rates of introducing new skills and clear teaching demonstrations. If the majority of the children in a school are more instructionally sophisticated, the reading program should still be grounded on scientifically-based reading research, but may be less explicit. In schools in which fewer children are at risk, a program that is more explicit and systematic may be

used with the few children who are identified as at risk. In all schools, it is important that children be assessed early in their school career so that children who are at risk can be identified and appropriate instruction initiated to avoid failure.

Intervention should be available for children below grade-level. These programs should include systematic and explicit teaching, and should include more comprehensive assessment procedures that help teachers determine students' instructional level.

Supplementary materials need to be available to meet particular student needs or areas of weakness in a particular program. For example, a school working with children who enter school as non-English speakers will need materials that provide systematic teaching on vocabulary and receptive and expressive language skills.

Focus on What Works

School personnel must act as very diligent consumers when selecting reading programs. The words "research-based" in a brochure cannot be relied on to indicate that a program is, in fact, research-based. Even among programs that are aligned with the findings of scientifically-based reading research, there are significant differences in regard to how well the programs can meet the needs of children who are at risk.

The most powerful evidence regarding the potential of a reading program to be an effective instructional tool is data on the student achievement that has been produced in schools that used a particular program with a similar student and teacher population. Teachers, particularly those serving populations with high numbers of at-risk children, should select programs that have produced high levels of student performance in comparable schools.

Effectiveness rather than inclusiveness should be the major factor in selecting a reading program. In the past, schools often used checklists with multiple factors to evaluate programs. The problem with these checklists was that the number of topics covered became the main factor in program selection. Thus, reading programs that provided only superficial coverage of critical content were given higher ratings than programs that had in-depth coverage of critical content because the former covered a wider range of content, though most of it was covered superficially.

Modifying Core Reading Programs for At-Risk Learners

Most core reading programs will require modifications in order to meet the needs of at-risk students. Below is a description of five common problems that will require modifications.

Many programs include a large number of activities that would take many hours each day to present; however, the program does not provide clear guidance regarding which tasks are the more essential. The teacher must be able to identify the most important tasks and schedule instruction so that priority topics are included in daily lessons.

Some programs do not provide clear directions to teachers on how to overtly teach specific skills. The teacher must be prepared to structure the teaching tasks. Teaching exercises must facilitate active involvement by all children. Teachers should be prepared to modify exercises so that teaching presentations are highly interactive with a great deal of student responding and immediate feedback by the teacher.

A third area of concern is the lack of assessments to help teachers in placing students in the program at the beginning of the school year and monitoring the extent to which the students are learning the content during the year. During the school year, frequent ongoing assessment is needed to ensure that children are learning the critical reading skills.

A fourth area of concern is the introduction of new information and skills at too fast a rate. Too much may be introduced at one time with too little practice provided in order to enable students to develop mastery before proceeding to more advanced topics. Teachers need to be prepared to analyze teaching exercises into their component tasks and create teaching demonstrations for each of these components and then provide adequate practice to facilitate student mastery.

A fifth area of concern is that some programs do not carefully control the vocabulary or syntax the teacher uses when presenting information to children. Word and sentence structures that are not commonly understood by the children will appear in teacher demonstrations. For example, some kindergarten programs will use the terms *same* and *different* in early lessons. Many at-risk kindergartners will not understand these terms; thus frustration is likely for student and teacher. Teachers will need to modify the wording in teacher presentations to ensure that all terms used are terms the children understand.

The above list is not a thorough listing of all potential problem areas. The remainder of this text will present examples of teaching that will show teachers how to deal with the problems described above and other problem areas. Our goal is to provide the reader with specific examples of how to make success possible for all children.

Assessment

Assessment is an essential part of any reading program. There are three types of assessments: screening assessments, diagnostic assessments, and progress-monitoring assessments. The on-going use of assessment is essential for maximizing student progress and for providing children with a successful learning experience.

Screening and Placement Assessments

Screening assessments are administered at the beginning of the year to inform the teacher if a child is able to participate productively in grade-level materials, or if the child is behind or at risk of not succeeding in reading instruction. Screening assessments generally are designed to take no longer than 5 to 15 minutes per child. There are two types of screening assessments: generic screening assessments and program-specific placement assessments. The generic assessment is not tied to a particular program; it will include short tests on several areas that have been identified as critical for that particular grade level. For example, a screening assessment for first grade might test the child on knowledge of letter-sound correspondences and the ability to blend isolated sounds to create a word. A test for third grade might include an oral reading test of a passage that is at beginning third-grade level. On the other hand, a program-specific screening assessment will be geared to a specific program.

Teachers must be careful in relying on screening assessment results. Some children, especially younger children, may be shy or reluctant to respond to an adult they do not know well. Other children may perform poorly on a test given the first days of school, but then after several days of instruction show they can perform at a much higher level than their performance on a screening indicated. Teachers must remember that screening assessments are just a tool to help the teacher get instruction started for children at what appears to be their instructional level. Teachers should expect to make adjustments for children during the first weeks of the school year as the teacher receives more information on how the child performs. Teachers should watch for children who can perform above their current level, as well as those who are struggling.

Diagnostic Assessments

Diagnostic assessments are in-depth assessments designed to provide the teacher with information on how a student performs on a wider range of critical component skills than is assessed by the screening assessment. Generally diagnostic assessments are administered to children who do poorly on a screening assessment or who are struggling during the school year. For example, a third-grade screening assessment might have a student orally read a passage at beginning third-grade level and answer several comprehension questions. The diagnostic assessment might include passages at a lower level and an assessment to test the child's knowledge of letter-sound correspondences for individual letters, and letter combinations (digraphs, blends, diphthongs), the child's knowledge of suffixes and prefixes, and the child's ability to use this information in reading words.

The teacher would use this information from the diagnostic assessment to provide focused instruction on particular skills or if a child's performance indicates severe deficits placement in an intervention program.

Progress-Monitoring Assessments

Progress-monitoring assessments are administered frequently and regularly during the school year to determine if children are mastering what is being taught. There are two types of progress-monitoring assessments: program-specific assessments and generic assessments. The program-specific progress-monitoring assessment is designed to provide an indication if children are in fact learning what is being taught in the specific reading program.

The generic progress-monitoring assessment is not related specifically to what is taught in any particular program, but is based on what a district expects students to be learning during the year. A district may require that oral reading fluency be tested every several months to determine if children are making adequate progress in this area. Written progress-monitoring assessments may also be administered periodically to determine how students are progressing in comprehension- and vocabulary-related standards.

Organization of Instruction

Classroom organization involves creating the structure within the classroom to facilitate the conditions for successful implementation of a reading program. Included in classroom organization are allocating time for instruction, arranging materials, and establishing classroom routines.

Allocating Time for Instruction

Reading-engaged time refers to the time students actually spend on reading exercises and activities. Researchers have found that time spent in reading yielded significantly higher correlation's with achievement than any other teacher or student behavior studied (Brophy & Good, 1986; Murphy,

Weil, & McGreal, 1986; Rosenshine & Stevens, 1986). Note that engaged time does not refer to scheduled time, but only to the time students actually spend engaged in reading activities.

Engaged time must be put to good use. First, if students are expected to learn to read, they must be engaged in reading-related activities. On the one hand, researchers found positive and usually significant correlations between achievement and engagement in reading activities. On the other hand, time spent on arts and crafts, active play, or child selection of activities *always* produced a negative correlation. Second, students should be placed in a reading series at a place appropriate to their skill level. They should not be placed in material that is too easy, where they just review previously learned material. Nor should their placement be at too advanced a lesson, where they lack essential preskills and make frequent mistakes.

Similarly, independent-reading exercises must be instructionally appropriate. Exercises should provide practice for new skills and for previously introduced skills that require continued practice. The exercises should neither be too easy nor too hard. The match between the content of reading exercises (both teacher-directed and independent exercises) and student skill is the essence of individualizing instruction. More than a decade ago, Brophy and Good (1986) pointed out the importance of appropriate independent work:

> Student success rates, and the effectiveness of seatwork assignments generally, are enhanced when teachers explain the work and go over practice examples with the students before releasing them to work independently. Furthermore, once the students are released to work independently, the work goes more smoothly if the teacher (or an aide) circulates to monitor progress and provide help when needed. If the work has been well chosen and well explored, most of these "helping" interactions will be brief, and at any given time, most students will be progressing smoothly through the assignment rather than waiting for help. (p. 364)

In allocating the number of minutes that is to be scheduled daily for reading instruction, a prime consideration should be how much content and information students need to learn in order to reach grade-level performance standards. If a child is performing significantly below the norm for his age, significantly more time should be scheduled for reading instruction. We recommend this extra time for reading because reading is a gateway for learning in all academic areas. A child who is not reading well is likely to struggle throughout the school day. By focusing on the essentials of reading until the child is at grade level, the teacher is preparing the child for later success.

Children who are at-risk of reading failure need to be identified when beginning kindergarten (or ideally preschool). An intensive program of instruction that begins in kindergarten can have a powerful effect on a student's academic career.

The authors of this text have worked extensively with high-poverty schools and have been privileged to have visited schools where bringing children to grade-level performance is the norm rather than the exception. In these schools, children who were behind would receive small group reading instruction in the morning and afternoon in reading, beginning in kindergarten. This amount of instruction combined with a strong reading program and well-trained teachers resulted in high degrees of success (Berkeley, 2000).

For children who are behind in the upper grades, there should not be a business-as-usual attitude. Children should receive reading instruction in the morning and afternoon and, if need be, after school and during the summer so that they can make more than 1 year's progress each year and catch up.

As Brophy and Good (1986) state:

> Achievement is maximized when teachers emphasize academic instruction as a major part of their own role, expect their students to master the curriculum, and allocate most of the available time to curriculum-related activities. (p. 360)

Teachers need to plan carefully in order to use time efficiently. They cannot spend 15 minutes getting the students settled in the morning, 5 minutes for transitions between activities, 5 minutes re-explaining assignments and rules that students should understand, and 5 minutes figuring out what to do next while students sit waiting. Teachers working with at-risk students must carefully schedule activities so that instructional time is well used and enough time is devoted to priority areas. In some classrooms, less important activities may need to be sacrificed temporarily so that enough time is available for reading instruction.

Arranging Materials

In addition to adequate instructional time, organized instruction involves arranging the physical setting and the instructional materials. A teacher might save several minutes daily by indicating the page different groups are on with clips in the teacher's guide (a different-colored clip for each group), so that the appropriate lesson can be easily and quickly located. Likewise, arranging student materials so the teacher can quickly hand them out when they are needed will save time.

Establishing Classroom Routines

Creating a classroom atmosphere that will be supportive of instruction is a major goal during the first weeks of school. Teachers must organize their classroom and create routines so that teachers can focus on instruction. Classroom routines refer to regularly occurring activities that can be completed by students with minimal assistance from teachers, such as turning in classwork and transitioning to and from reading groups. These routines must be carefully planned and taught. An in-depth discussion on teaching classroom routines can be found in *The Effective Classroom— Managing for Success* by Geoffrey Colvin and Mike Lazar (1997) and in *The Solution Book* by Randy Sprick (1991).

Delivery of Instruction

Adequate instructional time, well-designed materials, and effective presentation techniques are all essential ingredients of a successful reading program. An excellent reading series in the hands of a knowledgeable teacher will not produce significant gains if instructional time is too limited. Likewise, at-risk students will not do well in an excellent program with ample instructional time if the teacher cannot present and explain the content clearly. Finally, the potential advantages of adequate time and a teacher who presents well will not be realized if the reading program is too difficult or poorly designed.

No matter how well an instructional program is designed, teachers will have to make adjustments based on information provided through day-to-day student performance and through information provided through assessments.

This chapter presents an overview of two areas that a teacher can draw from when delivering instruction or modifying exercises in commercial materials: These areas are program design and teacher presentation techniques.

Program Design

Teachers must be able to evaluate reading programs so they can select programs to meet their students'

needs. In addition, they must be able to design lessons for teaching specific skills, which often requires modifying or supplementing certain aspects of a commercial program. Six aspects of direct instruction program design are relevant when selecting a reading program, writing lesson plans, and modifying reading programs:

1. Specifying objectives
2. Devising instructional strategies
3. Developing teaching procedures
4. Selecting examples
5. Sequencing skills
6. Providing practice and review

Specifying Objectives

Objectives must be stated as specific observable behaviors. Saying that students will be decoding at first grade level by the end of first grade is not specific. The types of words the students will be expected to read must be specified, along with accuracy and rate criteria. The way in which the words will be presented must also be described (e.g., in lists or in passages). For passage reading, the complexity of sentence structure should also be specified.

Objectives of a program should be carefully evaluated according to their usefulness. Since teaching time is limited, skills should be listed in order of importance, with essential skills being taught first. A skill is essential if it is a prerequisite for a more sophisticated skill or is important in its own right. An example of a nonessential skill is knowing where to place an accent mark in a word. Since students must be able to decode a word before they can place the accent mark, the skill is not a prerequisite for decoding. Knowledge of accent marks is necessary when students look up a word in a dictionary to figure out its pronunciation. However, that skill does not require the student to place the accent mark; its position is already indicated.

Devising Instructional Strategies

Whenever possible, programs should teach students to rely on strategies rather than require them to memorize information. Teaching strategies make instruction more efficient. For example, teaching the students the letter-sound correspondences and a sounding-out strategy enables children to read any word that contains these letter-sound relationships. Once children have mastered sounding out, each time a new letter-sound correspondence is taught the child will be empowered to read a number of new words. Let's say that the students already know the sounds for the letters *m, s, t, f, d, r, n, h, k, l, a, o,* and *c*. The introduction of the letter *i* results in the student being able to read these words: *sit, in, hid, lid, tin, Tim, hill, sin, miss, kiss,* and *fill*.

Lessons should be designed so that once children have learned a strategy, they receive practice in applying the strategy to a wide range of examples. For example, after the teacher presents the strategy for reading CVCe words (vowel says its name), the stories that students read would contain CVCe words so that the students can have practice applying that rule. More instructionally sophisticated students may learn strategies without being explicitly taught. For instructionally naive students, however, explicit instruction is necessary.

The importance of teaching strategies has been extensively analyzed and researched by Brown and her colleagues (Brown, 1987; Palincsar & Brown, 1984) and others (Billingsley & Wildman, 1990; Borkowski, 1992; Collins, Dickson, Simmons, & Kame'enui, 1996; Cornoldi, 1990; Meltzer, 1993; Wong, 1992). As Brown (1987) noted some time ago:

> Too often educators and psychologists draw conclusions about research on an educationally relevant problem without adequate analysis of the nature of the problem itself. We suspect that there are general teachable strategies that young children normally learn by trial and error which greatly facilitate his performance on these tasks. We therefore propose a study of these strategies with an eye toward making them an explicit part of reading education. The main problem is one of externalizing an internal mental event. (pp. 1, 5)

Some researchers now suggest that strategy deficits account for many, if not most, of the educational problems of students with disabilities (Armbuster, Echols, & Brown, 1983; Paris & Jacobs, 1984; Simmons, Kame'enui, & Darch, 1988). Research has shown that training students with disabilities to apply various strategies is definitely possible. In fact, the strategy used when reading a passage may be the primary determinant of what is remembered (Zimmer, 1978).

Throughout this text, a number of overt strategies will be presented. We want to provide teachers with tools that they can use to foster efficient learning for their students. Teachers must take the responsibility for fostering student use of these strategies by providing sufficient practice and prompting students to use the strategies; many students do not spontaneously apply a learned strategy in new situations. The practice and prompting are very important to foster generalization.

Developing Teaching Procedures

After a strategy has been devised, the strategy must be translated into a *format* that specifies exactly how the teacher is to present the strategy. Throughout this text, a number of formats will appear that specify exactly how the teacher can present specific strategies. The formats include directions on what the teacher and the students are to say and do. We have found that providing detailed formats is very helpful because teaching involves very specific behaviors. Teachers do not teach students to read words in some abstract fashion. They point to particular words, give information, ask questions, etc. Vague teaching procedures do not provide concrete suggestions for teaching a strategy in the clearest possible manner. The detailed formats in this book will hopefully be useful in teaching particular content and also serve as models for teachers in designing formats to teach content not covered in-depth in the text. Detailed formats planned in advance of teaching allow the teacher to focus their full attention on the students' performance.

Formats must be carefully constructed so that (1) the teacher's explanations can be easily understood by the students and (2) they contain only one new skill. For a format to be easily understood, the instructional language must be clear. Words and sentence structures that students do not understand should be avoided. This point is simple but often overlooked. Formats in the teachers' guides of commercial reading programs often contain words that average and above-average students may understand, but these same words often confuse at-risk students. Much student failure in day-to-day lessons is caused by teachers failing to preteach critical vocabulary.

Formats include only one new skill. Formats that attempt to teach more than one new skill cause two problems. First, when students have to learn two new skills at the same time, they are more likely to fail because the learning load is twice as great as when one new skill is introduced. Second, when students fail, the teacher cannot readily tell which skill caused the failure; this makes diagnosis and remediation difficult. For example, in teaching students to decode consonant-vowel-consonant-final *e* (CVCe) words, such as *like* or *fate,* a teacher presents this rule: When a word ends in *e,* say the name for the first vowel. Students who were not taught vowel names before encountering this rule would have to learn two new skills at once: vowel names and the rule. Students who say "lick" for *like*

may not know the vowel name for *i* or may not know how to apply the rule. Consequently, a teacher would not know whether to help the students with vowel names or with applying the rule.

Formats often contain two stages: introduction and guided practice. In the *introduction* stage of a format, the teacher demonstrates the steps in a strategy and then provides structured practice in using the strategy. In the *guided-practice* stage, the teacher gradually reduces help and prompting, and eventually the students apply the steps in the strategy independently. Including teacher guidance from prompted application to independent application of a strategy is referred to as scaffolded instruction. A final step in the guided practice stage, called discrimination, includes the teacher presenting a set of examples that provide practice on items applicable to the new strategy and items from similar previously taught strategies.

Selecting Examples

Selecting appropriate examples is a critical part of format construction. Examples at the introductory stage are appropriate only if the student can use the new strategy and information that was taught previously to come up with the correct answer. For example, when teaching students to decode regular words, the examples would be limited to words that contain only the letters for which students have been taught the letter-sound correspondences. If the students know the letter-sound correspondences for only the letters *m, s, a, d, f, r, t,* and *i,* the teacher should not present the word *met* since it contains an unknown letter (e).

Selecting appropriate examples for discrimination exercises involves creating a mix of examples. In addition to examples applicable to the new strategy, other examples must also be included. These other examples review previously taught strategies and are in some cases similar to the new examples. A range of examples is necessary so that students are required to differentiate when to use the new strategy and when to use previously taught strategies. If examples of the new CVCe word type are *cane* and *robe,* the teacher might include the words *can* and *rob* in the discrimination format. Including these similar words provides important discrimination practice.

Sequencing Skills

Sequencing involves determining an optimal order for introducing new information and strategies. Sequencing significantly affects the difficulty or ease students have when learning new skills. Five sequencing guidelines tend to reduce student error rates:

1. Preskills of a strategy are taught before the strategy itself is presented.

2. Instances that are consistent with strategy are introduced before exceptions.

3. High utility skills are introduced before less useful ones.

4. Easy skills are taught before more difficult ones.

5. Strategies and information likely to be confused are not introduced at the same time.

The most critical sequencing principle is *teaching components of a strategy before the entire strategy is introduced.* Since the components must be taught before the strategy itself, the components can be referred to as preskills. In the strategy for decoding CVCe words, knowing the names of the vowels is a preskill, which is introduced before the strategy is presented. Another illustration of preskills involves dictionary skills. To prepare older students to locate words in a dictionary, teachers should provide preskills instruction, including saying the alphabet; comparing target words to guide words by looking at the first, second, or third letter; and knowing whether to turn toward the front or back of a dictionary after opening it for a particular page. Another example is sounding out. The preskills of the strategy for sounding out words include: identifying the sound for each letter, knowing that words are read from left to right, blending the sounds, and then saying the blended sounds as a word. Teaching prerequisite skills and enabling

children to gain proficiency with these skills before a strategy is taught helps provide more success for students.

Introducing examples consistent with a strategy before introducing exceptions can be illustrated with the letter combination *ch* which usually represents the sounds as pronounced in the words *chart* and *much*. Students are taught a strategy to decode words with *ch* by saying the words with the above sound. A word like *chef* in which *ch* represents a different sound would not be introduced until the students had a good deal of experience with the regular sound for ch.

The procedure of sequencing *high-utility skills* before *less useful ones* can be illustrated with irregular words. Very common irregular words, which students encounter many times in primary readers (e.g., *was, said, have*), are introduced before less common and, therefore, less useful words (e.g., *tomb, heir, neon*). Another example involves letters: the letters *a, m, s,* and *i* are introduced earlier than the letters *v, x,* and *j* because they appear more often in words in primary readers. As students learn the more common letters, they will be able to decode more words.

The procedure of *introducing easy skills before more difficult skills* can be illustrated with letter-sound correspondences and word types. Easier to say sounds (e.g., *a* and *m*) should appear before more difficult to pronounce letters (e.g., *l* and *e*). Similarly, shorter regular words that are easier to sound out than longer regular words should be introduced first.

The procedure of *separating information and strategies likely to be confused* can be illustrated with the letters *b* and *d,* which are similar in shape and sound. If *b* and *d* are introduced within a close time span students are more likely to develop confusion between them than if they were separated by a longer time span. If *b* is introduced during the third week of a program, *d* might be introduced in the eighth week, after eight or nine other less similar letters have been introduced. Another illustration involves the similar irregular words *were* and *where.* Since they are similar in sound and appearance, they would be introduced several weeks apart.

It is important to note that the sequencing guidelines sometimes conflict with each other. For example, exceptions to a strategy often need to be introduced early because they are useful. For example, the letters *ai* represent the long-a sound in virtually all the words in which *ai* appears together. Students are taught a strategy of saying the long-a sound when they say ai. The word *said* is an exception to this strategy. It would be introduced early in a reading program as an irregular word because it is a very useful word. Similar conflicts arise when a skill is difficult, which suggests a late introduction, yet is very useful, which suggests an earlier introduction. Obviously, compromises are necessary to resolve these conflicts. The way a compromise is made usually depends on the relative importance of the guidelines in conflict.

Providing Practice and Review

Learning to read requires lots of practice to develop accuracy and fluency. Sufficient practice must be provided within each lesson and across lessons. When a new strategy is introduced, within-lesson practice includes a concentrated or massed presentation of examples. The practice is necessary if the student is to master the strategy. Review, which is sufficient practice across a number of lessons, is needed to ensure that students retain the strategies and information taught in a reading program. A pattern of massed practice in the first several lessons and systematic review later is critical for retention. Teachers must supplement reading programs that do not supply sufficient practice.

Presentation Techniques

Different presentation techniques are appropriate for different stages of reading instruction. For example, when children are first learning to read, instruction is in small groups and is highly interactive with children primarily making oral responses and the teacher responding immediately to confirm or correct their responses. Once children have learned to read accurately and with fluency, reading instruction will be more varied. The instruction in an upper-grade classroom in which all children are performing at grade level will include a variety of instructional activities. Sometimes the teacher may present lessons to the entire class. Other times, children may work collaboratively providing feedback to each other. If some children have difficulty with a particular concept or skill, the teacher may provide small-group instruction to the struggling students. An example of how a specific technique is used differently at different times involves monitoring of student performance by the teacher. During early reading instruction, the teacher listens to oral responses and watches children's mouths to see how they are pronouncing words. Monitoring in the later grades focuses more on the teacher reviewing student written work and providing a combination of oral and written feedback. In general, teachers teaching beginning reading skills must be proficient in presentation techniques needed to maintain student participation in highly-interactive oral exchanges between teacher and students. On the other hand, intermediate-grade teachers must be more skilled in managing students in a number of instructional settings.

The remainder of this section explains some of the direct-instruction teaching techniques designed for working with groups of students: unison oral responding, signaling, pacing, monitoring, correcting errors and teaching to mastery, diagnosing, and developing student motivation. Although most of the examples used involve situations in which younger students are being taught, teachers of older students, especially students who have not yet mastered primary-grade content, should find much of the discussion relevant.

Small-Group Instruction

The instructional techniques to be described here are designed for small groups composed of children who are at the same instructional level. Creating instructional groups in which children are at their instructional level requires a careful assessment of the students' skill level. Students should be assessed carefully to determine their knowledge of prerequisite skills, and groups should be formed with children at the same levels. Creating such groups is referred to as homogeneous grouping for instruction. The issue of homogeneous has been one of great controversy. If misused, homogenous grouping can lead to tracking where lower-performing students are placed and maintained in settings that do not bring out their full potential to learn. If used well, homogeneous grouping can lead to acceleration of student progress and higher success levels for students. Acceleration is possible because during the small group, the child can be more actively involved, and the teacher does not have to make significant compromises between meeting the needs of higher performers and lower performers. Higher success levels are possible because the teacher will more readily be able to spot and immediately correct any confusion or misinterpretation a student makes.

A critical condition that must be in place for homogenous grouping to be well implemented is that placement in groups must be *flexible.* That means that during the school year a child's placement in a group is not fixed, but can and will be changed based on the child's performance. If a child's performance indicates that the child is able to perform at a higher level, the child would be moved to a group that is further ahead in the program and visa-versa.

The number of children in an instructional group should depend on the instructional sophistication of the students. Children who are instructionally sophisticated, attentive to teacher's instruction and not likely to become confused easily, can be taught in instructional groups with more children. Children who are less attentive to teacher instruction, more likely to be easily distracted and likely to need more practice trials to master content, should be in instructional groups composed of fewer children. In earlier editions of this book, we used the term *instructionally naive* to describe these more vulnerable learners. Here is an illustration of those guidelines applied to a first-grade class of 22 children in a school with many at-risk children. The teacher might create 3 instructional groups; the group with higher performing students might contain 10 students, the middle group 7 students, and the group with lower performing students just 5 students.

During small-group beginning-reading instruction, students are more likely to be attentive if seated close to the teacher. For beginning reading

instruction, we recommend seating the students in chairs, without desks, in a semicircle or in two rows directly in front of the teacher. The teacher sits facing the group, looking out over the classroom so that the teacher can monitor the entire class. The students in the group should be facing towards the teacher and away from the other students so they will not be distracted. More distractable students should be seated closest to the teacher to make it easier for the teacher to monitor their performance and give encouraging pats or handshakes. It is interesting to note that just the opposite pattern often occurs with less proficient students seated farthest from the teacher. Teacher monitoring of distractible and instructionally naive students is easier when they are seated in the middle of the group rather than on the sides (see Figure 4.1). Lap boards may be given out to children for writing exercises.

Unison Oral Responding

When using small-group instruction, particularly during the beginning reading stage, the teacher maximizes students' active responding by structuring tasks to incorporate unison responses. Unison responding, in which all the students respond at the same time, facilitates a high degree of active student involvement. Much of the instruction in the learning-to-read stage is suitable for unison responding since the tasks are of a nature where there is just one correct answer (e.g., when shown the letter *m* and asked, "What sound?", the answer is /m/). The advantage of frequent unison responses is that all students actively practice each skill throughout an instructional period. Unison responses also provide the teacher with frequent information about each student's progress. Teachers should structure tasks to be highly interactive by keeping explanations short and immediately followed by student responses. That is, teachers should not talk for long without calling for a response to ensure students understand what has been said. Unison responding can significantly accelerate student progress, particularly for children who are more instructionally naive. If the teacher presented all tasks to each individual in a large group, some students may answer

Figure 4.1   Suggested Seating Arrangement. An open circle (O) indicates naive or distracted students. Note that these students are not placed next to each other.

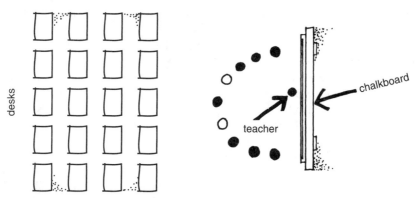

only once or twice during a period. Such infrequent responding often results in inattentiveness on some students' part and restricted information about student performance on the teacher's part.

Signaling

For the advantages of unison responding to be fully realized, teachers have to utilize a number of techniques. The first technique involves making it clear when students are to respond. Unison responding is more effective when all the children in a group create their own response rather than relying on mimicking other children's responses. Some children are initially less confident than others and will have a tendency to rely on others to come up with the answer. A technique referred to as *signaling* is used to facilitate active self-initiated responding.

A signal is a cue given by the teacher that tells students when to make a unison response. The effective use of signals allows participation by all students, not just the higher performers who, if allowed, tend to dominate the lower-performing students. For example, if a teacher neglects to use a signal when presenting a complex comprehension question, higher-performing students are likely to respond long before lower performers have had a chance to organize and produce their responses. As a result, the lower-performing students may learn to copy responses from the other students, or they may just give

up. Either result leads to a reduction in the amount of practice these lower-performing students receive. A signaling procedure can avoid this problem.

To signal a unison response, the teacher (1) gives directions, (2) provides a thinking pause, and (3) cues the response. In giving directions, the teacher tells the students the type of response they are to make and asks the question. For example, if presenting a word-list reading exercise on the board, the teacher might instruct the children: "Say the word when I touch it."

After the directions comes the thinking pause. The duration of the thinking pause is determined by the length of time the lowest-performing student needs to figure out the answer. (If one student takes significantly longer to answer than the other students in the group, the teacher should consider providing extra individual practice for that student or placing him or her in a lower-performing group.) For easier questions (simple tasks involving review of previously taught skills), the thinking pause may be just a split-second, while for more complex questions, the thinking pause may last several seconds. Carefully controlling the duration of the thinking pause is a very important factor in maintaining student attentiveness and providing students with a successful learning experience.

The final step in the signaling procedure is the actual cue to respond. A cue or signal to respond may be a clap, finger snap, hand drop, touching the board, or any similar type of action. In some tasks, the teacher would say, "Get ready" a second before signaling. The consistent use of "Get ready" a second before the actual signal to respond is given can help in ensuring a clear signal. The "Get ready" cue is particularly useful for teacher-directed worksheet tasks, since students are looking at their worksheets and cannot see a hand signal from the teacher.

The essential characteristic of any good signal is its clarity. The signal must be given so that students know exactly when they are expected to respond. If a signal is not clear, students will not be able to respond together. The teacher should use the students' behavior to evaluate the clarity of her signals. A repeated failure to respond together usually indicates that the signals are unclear or that the teacher has not provided adequate thinking time.

Pacing

Anyone who has observed young children watching TV shows such as *Sesame Street* can attest to the value of lively pacing in keeping students attentive. Teachers need not put on an elaborate show to foster attention but should be familiar enough with their material to present it in a lively, animated manner and without hesitation. Teachers who are well-versed with their materials will not only be able to teach at a more lively pace, but will also be able to focus their attention more fully on the students' performance.

However, providing a briskly paced presentation does not mean that a teacher rushes students, requiring them to answer before they have had time to figure out the answer. The key to providing an effectively paced presentation is to not have "downtime" after the students make a response. When the students respond, the teacher immediately either begins the directions for the next question (or the correction to the current task). A teacher working with younger students on oral tasks in which children identify the most common sound of letters would pace his or her presentation so that children are responding about 10 to 15 times a minute. The teacher works on a series of similar tasks for a period of time without interruption, then transitions to a new task with some kind of quick change-up between the

tasks. For example, during an early reading lesson, the teacher might work intensively for a period of 3 to 5 minutes on a letter-sound task and then spend 15 seconds during which time the teacher would acknowledge their efforts with verbal praise and physical contact in the form of handshakes, tickles, pats, etc., then proceed to a phonemic awareness task. As students become more mature, the time they work without a change-up increases.

Monitoring

When a group of students respond orally at the same time, it will generally be very difficult for the teacher to hear mistakes made by only one or two of the students, especially when an incorrect response sounds similar to the correct response. For example, if one student in a group of eight students says the word *sit* instead of *sick* or says the sound /m/ instead of /n/, the error will be difficult to detect. So besides listening to student responses, teachers monitor student performance by watching the children's eyes and mouths. By watching the mouth, the teacher can determine if children have positioned their lips and tongue in the position necessary to produce the correct response. For example, a teacher points to the letter *m,* and a child who is responding has her mouth open. Since producing the sound /m/ requires closed lips, the student's pronunciation is probably incorrect. The teacher also watches the eyes of the children to determine if they are attending. If a student is not looking at the board or presentation book displaying the stimulus, the child may be mimicking other students' responses rather than initiating his own answer.

A teacher cannot be looking at the faces of all children each time the group responds. Consequently, a teacher must systematically switch from student to student during the lesson, yet focus primarily on lower-performing students. For example, in a group of eight students, five children seldom have difficulty while the other three sometimes make errors. The teacher arranges the students' seats so that the three who are more likely to have difficulty are seated in or near the center of the group. The teacher watches them for two or three responses and then shifts his or her attention to the students on the left side of the group for a response or two. Then the teacher shifts his or her attention back to the students in the middle for several responses before watching the students on the right side. By always returning to the students in the middle and watching them respond, the teacher monitors their responses about twice as often as responses of the higher-performing students seated on either side.

Individual turns are a very important monitoring tool. Children may appear to be answering correctly and initiating their own responses during unison responding instruction, but they may in fact on some responses be mimicking other children. The teacher gives individual turns when the teacher feels the group has mastered all the steps in a format. By providing adequate group practice *before* calling on individuals, the teacher avoids needlessly embarrassing a student. Because individual tests are time-consuming, if a group is large, individual turns need not be given to every child. The teacher can test a sample of children on a sample of the tasks presented. The teacher presents individual turns to the more instructionally naive students and some of the higher-performers. The teacher presents tasks that were troublesome for children during the unison responding exercise or that were troublesome on past lessons. If a number of children make errors when individual turns are given, the teacher knows that he or she did not provide enough practice during the unison responding part. Likewise, if a particular student makes errors on individual turns, the teacher knows that more attention must be paid to monitoring that student's responses during unison responding in future lessons.

The importance of careful monitoring cannot be overemphasized. The sooner a teacher detects an error the easier it will be to remedy that error. Each day a student's confusion goes undetected the student is, in essence, receiving practice doing something the wrong way. For each day a student remains confused, a teacher may have to spend several days reteaching that skill to ameliorate the confusion. Thus, careful monitoring is a prerequisite for efficient instruction.

Correcting Errors and Teaching to Mastery

The correction procedure for incorrect responses during small-group instruction in the primary grades consists of as many as five steps: *model, lead, test, firm up, and delayed test.* For example, in presenting a letter-sound correspondence task, the teacher points to *o* and asks, "What sound?" A student responds, "/ŭ/." First, the teacher *models* the correct answer, saying, "ŏŏŏŏŏ." Second, the teacher may *lead* (respond with the children, "Say *o* with me. Get ready . . . ooo"). The teacher responding with the student (leading) provides a model as the students respond, ensuring they hear a correct response as they practice producing the response. Leading is needed only when students have difficulty making the response (saying the sound). Third, the teacher tests, asking the students to answer on their own.

The fourth step is the *firm up*. The teacher repeats the series of items that just preceded the missed item and the missed item itself. For example, during second grade, a word-reading exercise might include several lists of words, each list containing five words. If a student misses a word in a list, the teacher returns to the beginning of that list and repeats the list. The purpose of the firm-up step is to provide students with repeated practice on the missed item.

The last step is a *delayed test* in which the teacher tests the group on the missed item at a later time in the lesson. With instructionally naive students, several delayed tests may be given during a lesson so that they will receive repeated practice within a lesson if they need it. If the students make errors on the delayed test, the teacher corrects the mistake again. A teacher should keep track of student errors so that missed skills can be retaught and practiced on the next day's lesson.

Note that all these steps are directed to the entire group. When an individual makes an error, the teacher does not single out the child, but directs the correction to the group and has the entire group respond.

The goal of this correction procedure is to enable all children to master all the content as they progress from task to task and lesson to lesson. This process is referred to as *teaching to mastery*.

Teaching to mastery requires a great deal of teacher skill and awareness. Obviously, the teacher working with more instructionally naive learners will have to provide more practice and corrections than the teacher working with more sophisticated learners. Teachers have to be able to keep children motivated as they present this practice. Teachers should be positive and encouraging when correcting. Teachers should not be negative when children make errors. On the other hand, teachers should respond with a great deal of enthusiasm when children respond correctly to all items in a task without error.

Not teaching to mastery can lead to later problems for students. For example during beginning reading, if the students do not receive adequate practice to learn the letter-sound correspondences, they are likely to have difficulty later in the program when sounding out words is presented. Teaching to mastery can be a very efficient procedure in the long run. If teachers bring children to mastery on each task in each lesson, they will note that children need less repetitions each day to reach mastery.

The correction procedure for higher-order tasks is somewhat different in that rather than modeling the answer, the teacher would lead the students through a series of thinking steps to determine the answer. For example, let's say the students have read an expository passage containing the rule, "When objects are heated, they expand." The students read this item: "A metal ball was left outside. It was 40° in the morning. In the afternoon it was 95°. What do you know about the size of the metal ball in the afternoon?" and answered "It got smaller." The teacher corrects by asking a series of questions. What's the rule? What was the temperature of the ball in the morning? What was the temperature of the ball in the afternoon? Did the temperature get hotter or colder? So did the ball expand? What does expand mean? This procedure helps students apply the strategy for coming up with the answer and also provides the teacher with information about where specific problems may lie.

Diagnosing

As children progress in an instructional program, their errors on the current tasks will sometimes result from them not being firm on skills that were taught earlier that are prerequisite for the skill currently being taught. For example, when sounding out a word, the prerequisites are: knowing the letter-sound correspondence for each letter in the word, being able to blend the sounds to create a word, and then being able to translate the blended sounds into a word said at a normal rate. Diagnosis is sometimes very obvious. If, for example, a student says "sit" for the word *sat* and "mit" for *mat,* the teacher would diagnose the student's problem as a confusion of the letter-sound correspondence for *a* and *i,* since the student said the wrong sound for the letter *a* in both words. During a lesson, the teacher would immediately correct by telling the student the correct sound when the child makes an error. The teacher would also design future lessons to include more teaching and review of previously taught letter-sound correspondence that was missed.

Diagnosis becomes more challenging as the children do more complex activities. For example, a student may have missed a complex comprehension question because of not knowing a particular word (expand), not having enough background information about a particular topic, or not applying a series of steps to infer the answer. Teachers should work with students having trouble individually to determine the specific cause of the errors, and then structure lessons to provide more instruction on particular areas of weakness.

Motivation

Some students come to school eager to learn and eager to please the teacher. They respond well to simple praise. They work hard and have pride in their work. With such students, motivation is not a concern. Other students have less interest in learning, will give up easily and are not as eager to please the teacher. The teacher must accept these students regardless of their attitudes and use techniques to develop an interest in learning. A first step in motivating these students is demonstrating to them that they can succeed in reading. This is done by carefully designing and effectively presenting lessons. Second, the teacher shows students there is a reward in learning to read. At first, with younger students the teacher may use extrinsic rewards such as physical contact, tickles, pats, and handshakes. Eventually, the teacher works toward developing intrinsic motivation.

Accelerating Student Learning

The procedures in this text are intended to make learning to read easier by breaking complex tasks into their component skills, teaching these components, and demonstrating to students how these skills are applied. This simplification of complex tasks is particularly important for instructionally naive students, but can also accelerate the learning of instructionally sophisticated students if used appropriately.

The key to maximizing the progress of all students is to use information from assessments and from student performance during lessons to inform instruction. For example, at the beginning of first grade, the teacher would test all children on their knowledge of letter-sound relationships and blending and sounding-out skills. Obviously students who know many letter-sound correspondences and can already sound out words would progress much faster than children who began the year without this knowledge.

The importance of using information from assessments and student performance during lessons to guide instruction can not be overstated. Teachers must be aware of what prerequisite skills are needed to perform on reading tasks, and must know which of these skills the student knows already. Likewise, teachers must know when a student has demonstrated mastery on a skill during a lesson and can proceed to the next exercise. Just as not providing enough practice to enable students to reach mastery can be problematic, so can providing too much instruction on what children have

already mastered be problematic. Teaching is a constant challenge as teachers attempt to meet the needs of all students.

Some educators claim that explicit and systematic instruction may be appropriate for at-risk students but not for instructionally sophisticated students. The evidence in support of this position is sparse, particularly in the area of reading instruction (Carnine & Kame'enui, 1992; Cronbach & Snow, 1977). Engelmann and Carnine (1976) found that more sophisticated students perform very well as a result of direct instruction, scoring significantly above grade level on achievement tests and demonstrating an enthusiastic attitude toward learning. Similarly, Guthrie (1977) reported that direct instruction was the only approach in the *Follow Through* study that produced benefits with both low- and middle-income students.

Whole-Class Instruction

Large-group or whole-class teaching becomes more common as children progress from the "learning to read" stage to the "reading to learn" stage. Whole-class instruction utilizes some of the same techniques used in teaching a small group, particularly on tasks that call for responses in which there is only one correct answer, such as reading words in a list, and saying the most common sound of letter combinations. Whole-class and small-group instruction are the same in that the teacher has the students sit in an arrangement where the teacher can readily monitor the performance of the students most likely to have difficulty. If the classroom is arranged in rows, the teacher would have the more vulnerable learners sitting in the front rows in the middle so that the teacher can more readily monitor their performance. Signaling and pacing would be the same as in small groups. Corrections would as in small-group instruction, be directed to the group rather than individuals.

One difference between whole-class and small-group instruction is in regard to teaching to mastery. During whole-class instruction, if there are children who are performing significantly below the majority of the class participating in instruction, the teacher would not spend inordinate amounts of time during whole-class instruction repeating tasks until these children are firm. This repetition could result in other children becoming inattentive and embarrass the children having difficulty. Instead, the teacher would work with the struggling students during a small group session at another time. Ideally, the teacher's work with these children during the small group could avoid them having difficulty when participating in whole-class instruction.

Beginning Reading
The First Months of Instruction

CHAPTER 5

An Overview of Beginning Reading

The beginning reading stage refers to the period when students are learning to read the first several hundred words presented in the classroom reading program. Some students may come to school able to read many words. For these students, little instruction may be needed for them to complete the beginning stage. Other students will enter school with very little ability to read words. These students may require anywhere from 6 months to 1 year of instruction before completing the beginning stage.

From our perspective, the beginning stage is focused primarily on phonics instruction. For that reason we begin this chapter with a discussion of terms having to do with phonics instruction and a brief listing of different approaches to phonics instruction. Next, we discuss the controversies (or the *debates* or *wars*) that surround beginning reading instruction. We begin by contrasting code-emphasis and meaning-emphasis approaches to teaching beginning reading; that contrast was central to the debates of the 1970s and 1980s. Then we go on to relate that contrast to (a) direct instruction versus whole language and constructivist practices as they are employed today, and (b) the NRP's recommendations for explicit and systematic phonics instruction. Finally, we present practices for teach-

ing beginning reading skills from the perspective of our direct-instruction model. As the reader will see, our approach is a code-emphasis approach, and our methods of teaching phonics are highly explicit and systematic.

Although phonics is the primary focus in beginning reading instruction, beginning reading programs also include instruction in phonemic awareness, beginning vocabulary and language skills, and beginning comprehension skills. Phonemic awareness instruction is the topic of Chapter 6. Beginning vocabulary, language, and comprehension instruction are discussed in Chapter 11.

Phonics Instruction

Phonics instruction teaches the relationships between the letters of written language (graphemes) and the individual sounds of spoken language (phonemes). It also teaches how these relationships are used to read and write words. The following terms have been used to refer to these relationships:

- Letter-sound associations
- Letter-sound correspondences
- Sound-symbol correspondences

Figure 5.1   Six Approaches to Phonics Instruction

Synthetic phonics	Children learn how to convert letters or letter combinations into sounds, and then how to blend the sounds together to form recognizable words.
Analytic phonics	Children learn to analyze letter-sound relationships in previously learned words. They do not pronounce sounds in isolation.
Analogy-based phonics	Children learn to use parts of word families they know to identify words they don't know that have similar parts.
Phonics through spelling	Children learn to segment words into phonemes and to make words by writing letters for phonemes.
Embedded phonics	Children are taught letter-sound relationships during the reading of connected text. (Since children encounter different letter-sound relationships as they read, this approach is not systematic or explicit.)
Onset-rime phonics	Children learn to identify the sound of the letter or letters before the first vowel (the onset) in a one-syllable word and the sound of the remaining part of the word (the rime).

- Sound-spelling
- Grapheme-phoneme correspondences
- Graphophonemic relationships

The goal of phonics instruction is to help children learn and use the *alphabetic principle*—the understanding that written letters correspond to spoken sounds and that the correspondences are systematic and predictable. Knowledge of the alphabetic principle helps children to (a) recognize familiar words accurately and automatically, and (b) decode new words independently.

In Figure 5.1, we list and describe briefly six approaches to phonics instruction that were described in the NRP report and *Put Reading First*. As indicated by the descriptions, children pronounce sounds in isolation in some approaches (synthetic phonics, phonics through spelling); in others, they do not (analytic phonics, analogy-based phonics). Some approaches emphasize correspondences for units of sound larger than phonemes (analogy-based phonics, onset-rime phonics); others emphasize correspondences for individual phonemes (synthetic phonics, phonics through spelling). In embedded phonics, correspondences are not taught in isolation

but are taught only during the reading of connected text. Teaching phonics in context does not allow for explicit and systematic teaching of phonics; therefore, embedded phonics is neither explicit nor systematic.

As pointed out by the authors of *Put Reading First*, some programs of instruction combine elements from different approaches. Our direct-instruction model does just that. Although the beginning phonics instruction that we recommend is primarily synthetic phonics, elements of onset-rime phonics, analytic phonics, and analogy-based phonics are evident in some of the teaching formats that we present for teaching decoding skills after the beginning stage. Furthermore, writing letters for phonemes and phonemic spelling of regular words are inherent parts of the beginning reading instruction that we recommend.

The Great Debate: Code-Emphasis vs. Meaning-Emphasis Programs

Controversy surrounds the beginning reading stage. The intense "debates," even "wars," of the last 50 years are described, along with research relevant to those debates/wars, in a later chapter on research on beginning reading instruction. In this overview chapter, we focus on instructional practices.

Chall (1967) classified beginning reading approaches as either code-emphasis or meaning-emphasis approaches. Code-emphasis programs emphasize predictable letter-sound correspondences and the reading of words composed of those correspondences. Code-emphasis programs are usually referred to in lay terms as phonics programs. Programs that emphasize the reading of words that occur frequently in spoken language, regardless of the letter-sound irregularity of the words, are called meaning-emphasis programs.

Code-emphasis programs initially select words made up of letters and letter combinations representing the same sound in different words. This consistency between letters and their sound values enables students to read many different words by blending the sounds for each new word. For example, the word *sat* is sounded out as "sssaaat" and pronounced "sat." The word *land* is sounded out as "lllaaannnd" and pronounced "land." The letter *a* represents the same sound in *sat* and *land*, as well as in other words initially appearing in a code-emphasis program. In code-emphasis programs, a new word generally is not introduced until students have mastered the letter-sound correspondences that make up the word. For example, the word *mat* is not introduced until the students know the sounds for the letters *m, a,* and *t.*

In contrast, meaning-emphasis programs initially select words that appear frequently in print regardless of their letter-sound irregularity. The assumption is that frequently appearing words are familiar and, consequently, easier for students to learn. Students are encouraged to use a variety of sources—pictures, context of the story, word configuration, and initial letter—as cues to use in decoding words. Unlike the code-emphasis programs, the meaning-emphasis programs do not control words so that the same letter represents the same sound in most initially appearing words. For example, it would not be uncommon to see the words *done, to, not,* and *book* among the first 50 words introduced in a meaning-emphasis program. Note

that in each word, the letter *o* represents a different sound.

Some other differences between code-emphasis and meaning-emphasis approaches are:

1. Code-emphasis approaches emphasize oral reading; meaning-emphasis approaches emphasize silent reading.

2. Code-emphasis approaches emphasize sounding out of words, meaning-emphasis approaches emphasize whole word reading.

3. Code-emphasis approaches emphasize reading new words in isolation, meaning-emphasis approaches emphasize reading new words in context.

4. Code-emphasis approaches emphasize accuracy of reading words in sentences; meaning-emphasis approaches emphasize guessing at unfamiliar words or skipping unfamiliar words to maintain the flow of reading.

In a well-designed code-emphasis approach, the emphasis changes over time. For example, the initial emphasis on oral reading shifts to an emphasis on silent reading after students can read passages fluently. The initial emphasis on sounding out words shifts to an emphasis on automatic recognition of words; however, students are taught to sound out words that they do not recognize automatically throughout all stages of instruction.

Whole language is a meaning-emphasis approach which differs from most meaning-emphasis basals in this respect: words are not selected at all; instead, authentic literature is selected and students read whatever words are in the text. In whole-language teaching, meaning is not only the goal of reading instruction but also the means through which children learn to read. Goodman (1986) states that "The focus is on meaning and not on language itself, in authentic speech and literacy events" (p. 40). Children are thought to acquire literacy skills by reading. They do not first learn reading skills and then apply them to pronounce words and get meaning; instead, they first get the meaning and then use meaning cues to decode unfamiliar words. They move from understanding the whole text (i.e., the meaning) to recognizing the vehicles of that meaning (i.e., the paragraphs, sentences, phrases, and words).

Continuing Debate: Phonics vs. Whole Language

Whole language became increasingly popular in the 1970s and 1980s. Moats (2000) explained the growing popularity this way:

> Relying on theory derived largely from introspection into their own mental processes, Ken Goodman and Frank Smith in the late 1960s advanced the notion that meaning and purpose should be the salient goals in early reading instruction. Observing that adults appear to process the written word without recoding it letter by letter or sound by sound, and claiming that children should learn to read as naturally as they learn to speak, Smith asserted that the decomposition of words into sounds was pointless; that attention to letters was unnecessary and meaningless; that letter-sound correspondences were "jabberwocky" to be avoided; and that skill development was largely boring, repetitive, nonsensical, and unrelated to developing *real readers*. Smith, Goodman, and their disciples pushed ideas that were eagerly and readily embraced by progressive educators turned off by drab basal readers, mechanistic drills, and the knowledge that the basal readers in use had not solved all of their instructional challenges. Teachers were persuaded that the cause of most reading failure was insufficient emphasis on reading real books for real purposes. By the mid-1980s, schools were ready to throw out basal readers, phonics workbooks, spelling programs, and other "canned" material so that teachers could create individualized reading instruction with "authentic" children's literature. (p. 7)

Moats (2000) went on to delineate the major premises advanced by whole language advocates and to show how facts established by scientific investigations contradict those premises:

- *Premise:* Reading is acquired naturally.
  Fact: Learning to read is not a "natural" process. Most children must be taught to read

through a structured and protracted process in which they are made aware of sounds and the symbols that represent them, and then learn to apply these skills automatically and attend to meaning.

- *Premise:* Children will extract the structure and form of print if they are exposed to it sufficiently in the context of meaning-making activities.
  Fact: Our alphabetic writing system is not learned simply from exposure to print. Phonological awareness is primarily responsible for the ability to sound words out. The ability to use phonics and to sound words out, in turn, is primarily responsible for the development of context-free word recognition ability, which in turn is primarily responsible for the development of the ability to read and comprehend connected text.

- *Premise:* Learning to read and spell is just like learning to talk.
  Fact: Spoken language and written language are very different; mastery of each requires unique skills.

- *Premise:* Good readers can recognize words on the basis of a few sound-symbol correspondences, such as beginning and ending consonants, and don't really need to know the inner details, such as vowels; therefore, teaching all letter-sound correspondences and sounding out are unnecessary.
  Fact: The most important skill in early reading is the ability to read single words completely, accurately, and fluently; to read single words out of context, children use knowledge of phonic correspondences.

- *Premise:* When a child is reading and cannot recognize a word, the child should be asked to guess at the word from context and then sound the word out if guessing does not yield a word that would make sense in the sentence.
  Fact: Context is not the primary factor in word recognition; guessing from context leads to egregious errors.

Many of the unsupported ideas and practices associated with whole language live on under the guise of "balanced" reading instruction (Moats, 2000). The three-cueing system and Reading Recovery are examples of approaches touted as "balanced" though they clearly are outgrowths of Goodman's (1969) method of assessment that he called "miscue analysis" (Hempenstall, 1999, 2002; Moats, 2000; Wren, 2002). Goodman (1967) observed that young children made errors as they read that did not change the meaning of the text (e.g., "horse" for "pony"). Based on these observations, he concluded that good readers depend largely on context, and not on sounding out, to predict and read upcoming words in text. He defined reading as a "psycholinguistic guessing game" in which the reader need sample or look at only a few of the words on the page to confirm their predictions or guesses of upcoming words. Smith (1978, 1982) expanded on this theme, giving rise to the three-cueing system, which places greater emphasis on syntactic and semantic cues than grapho-phonemic cues. Similarly, the "running records" procedure employed in Reading Recovery emphasizes errors of meaning rather than phonic errors. Moreover, the Reading Recovery approach embraces a host of ideas and practices associated with whole language—teaching children to guess at words from context and initial letter, incidental phonics and decoding instruction as students compose their own sentences and stories, and predictable texts.

In summary, although the whole-language ideas and practices put forth by Goodman and Smith in the 1960s and 1970s have been thoroughly refuted by scientific research, they live on by masquerading as new approaches with new names. This lesson from our history suggests that knowing what scientific research really says about reading instruction is essential to avoiding sound-good fads that simply don't work. It is critically important that teachers know what the scientific research really says about reading instruction so that they can select practices and approaches that are research based and discard those that are not. It was toward that end that NRP was convened to analyze the massive body of research on beginning reading and render conclusions useful to classroom teachers.

NRP Recommendations

As indicated by the NRP conclusions shown in Figure 5.2, the NRP specifies that the phonics instruction that is most beneficial to children is both **explicit** and **systematic.** In the NRP report, system-

Figure 5.2 Scientifically-Based Conclusions About Beginning Phonics Instruction

Systematic and explicit phonics instruction is more effective than nonsystematic or no phonics instruction.

Systematic and explicit phonics instruction significantly improves kindergarten and first-grade children's word recognition, spelling, and reading comprehension.

Systematic and explicit phonics instruction is most effective when it begins in kindergarten or first grade; to be effective with young learners, it should begin with foundational knowledge involving letters and phonemic awareness.

Systematic phonics instruction includes teaching children to use their knowledge of phonics to read and write words.

Systematic and explicit phonics instruction is particularly beneficial for children who are having difficulty learning to read and who are at risk for developing future reading problems.

Systematic phonics instruction helped children at all socioeconomic levels make significantly greater gains in reading than did non-phonics instruction.

Systematic phonics instruction is effective when delivered through tutoring, through small groups, and through teaching classes of students.

Approximately 2 years of systematic and explicit phonics instruction is sufficient for most students.

Adapted from the NRP Report of the Subgroups, Chapter 2, Part 2, "Phonics Instruction," pp. 93–96.

atic phonics instruction was contrasted with instruction that is not systematic in this way:

> Systematic phonics instruction typically involves explicitly teaching students a prespecified set of letter-sound relations and having students read text that provides practice using these relations to decode words. Instruction lacking an emphasis on phonics instruction does not teach letter-sound relations systematically and selects text for children according to other principles. The latter form of instruction includes whole word programs, whole language programs, and some basal reader programs. (pp. 2–92)

The three types of programs that do not teach phonics explicitly and systematically were described this way in *Put Reading First* (p.17):

- Literature-based programs that emphasize reading and writing activities. Phonics instruction is embedded in these activities, but letter-sound relationships are taught incidentally, usually based on key letters that appear in student reading materials.

- Basal reading programs that focus on whole-word or meaning-based activities. These programs pay only limited attention to letter-sound relationships and provide little or no instruction in how to blend letters to pronounce words.

- Sight-word programs that begin by teaching children a sight-word reading vocabulary of from 50 to 100 words. Only after they learn to read these words do children receive instruction in the alphabetic principle.

Put Reading First (p. 16) stated that effective programs offer phonics instruction that:

- Helps teachers explicitly and systematically instruct students in how to relate letters and sounds, how to break spoken words into sounds, and how to blend sounds to form words;

- Helps students understand why they are learning the relationships between letters and sounds;

- Helps students apply their knowledge of phonics as they read words, sentences, and text;

- Helps students apply what they learn about sounds and letters to their own writing;

- Can be adapted to the needs of individual students based on assessment;

- Includes alphabetic knowledge, phonemic awareness, vocabulary development, and the reading of text, as well as systematic phonics instruction.

Direct Instruction, Constructivist Approaches, and Systematic/ Explicit Phonics Instruction

Today, the whole-language approach is included in the rubric of *constructivist* approaches to teaching. Constructivist philosophy, as applied to the teaching of reading, leads to the belief that readers *construct* meaning from text; they do not simply *get* the meaning conveyed by the text. From this philosophy stems practices that are very different from those employed in a direct instruction approach with a code-emphasis. Carnine (2000) contrasted a constructivist reading classroom with a direct instruction classroom in this way:

> First graders in a constructivist reading classroom might be found scattered around the room: some children are walking around, some are talking, some painting, others watching a video, some looking through a book, and one or two reading with the teacher. The teacher uses a book that is not specifically designed to be read using phonics skills, and when a child misses a word, the teacher will let the mistake go by so long as the meaning is preserved to some degree (for instance if a child reads "horse" instead of "pony"). If a child is stuck on a word, the teacher encourages her to guess, to read to the end of the sentence and then return to the word, to look at the picture on the page, and possibly, look at the first letter of the word.
>
> In a direct instruction classroom, some children are at their desks writing or reading phonics-based books. The rest of the youngsters are sitting with the teacher. The teacher asks them to sound out challenging words before reading the story. When

the children read the story, the teacher has them sound out the words if they make mistakes. (p. 5)

The practices employed in the direct instruction classroom are consistent with NRP's recommendation for systematic and explicit phonics instruction; the practices employed in the constructivist classroom are not.

In the remaining sections of this chapter, we provide the rationale for the practices which we recommend. In later chapters on beginning reading instruction, we provide detailed descriptions of the practices.

Rationale for a Direct Instruction Approach

We recommend using a code-emphasis program approach during the beginning stage over a meaning-emphasis approach because a code-emphasis approach more readily allows the teacher to present reading instruction in a more efficient and humane manner. Instruction is efficient when the teacher can present the maximum number of skills in the minimum amount of time. Instruction is humane when students encounter a high degree of success.

Instruction can be presented more efficiently in a code-emphasis approach than in a meaning-emphasis approach because a code-emphasis approach better facilitates generalization. The introduction of each new letter-sound correspondence results in the students reading many new words. For example, let's say that the students already know the sounds for the letters *m, s, t, f, d, r, n, h, k, l, a, o,* and *c.* The introduction of the letter *i* results in the students being able to read these words: *sit, in, hid, lid, tin, Tim, hill, sin, miss, kiss,* and *fill.* In a meaning-emphasis approach, each word is introduced as a separate unit.

Instruction can be presented in a more humane manner in a code-emphasis program than in a meaning-emphasis program. The former more readily allows the teacher to provide each student with a higher degree of success in the reading process. When word reading is introduced in a code-emphasis approach program, students are taught an overt strategy—saying the sounds for each letter in the word in a left-to-right progression, then saying the blended sounds at a normal rate. If a student misreads a word, the cause of the error and an effective correction procedure are clear. For example, if a student says "mud" when encountering the word *mad,* the teacher checks to see if the student knows the sound for the letter *u.* If the student does not know the correct sound, the teacher presents exercises to teach the missed sound. Words with the letter *u* would be avoided until the reteaching is accomplished. In summary, the code-emphasis approach facilitates the use of simple teaching procedures and allows for effective corrections. The students learn a strategy that is used again and again.

In contrast, meaning-emphasis programs do not teach the student to rely on a single strategy because there is little consistency between letter-sound relationships in the words students read, especially regarding vowel sounds. The students are encouraged to use a variety of strategies to decode words. Students are told to use the initial sound, the shape of the word, the context of the sentence in which the word appears, and the pictures on the page in which the word appears as cues to decoding the word. This reliance on a multifaceted approach results in relatively long, complex teacher explanations. For example, a typical meaning-emphasis program might introduce the word *cat* using the following steps:

1. The teacher writes a sentence on the board that has the word *cat,* and reads the sentence.

2. The teacher then displays flash cards containing the words *can* and *cat,* and asks the children how they are alike.

3. The teacher reminds the children that the middle letter represents the short vowel sound in each word.

4. Finally, the children are asked to read the word *cat* and identify the final sound.

This explanation contains words that more naive students may not understand (e.g., middle, final). Also, there is a relatively high degree of teacher talk. The higher the ratio of teacher talk to student response, the less attentive students are likely to be.

If a student misreads a word in a meaning-emphasis approach program, there is no simple correction available to the teacher that corrects the immediate mistake and prevents the error from reoccurring.

Let's say a student is reading the sentence: *The boy saw a little bird.* When coming to the word *saw,* the student says "said." A correction the teacher might use would involve explaining that the word *saw* could not be *said* because it does not end with *d* and does not make sense in the sentence. The correction tells the student why a word couldn't be *said,* but does not provide him with a strategy enabling him to figure out the word. The student might say "sees" the next time he or she encounters the word in a sentence.

The relatively complex teaching strategy and the relatively long teaching demonstrations inherent in a meaning-emphasis approach places the instructionally naive student at risk. Students who are inattentive to begin with are not likely to attend to teaching demonstrations that do not consistently demand active involvement.

We strongly recommend the use of a code-emphasis approach as the tool for teaching beginning reading. The importance of students receiving the highest quality of instruction available during the beginning reading stage cannot be overemphasized. For the child, initial reading instruction represents his or her first big challenge in the school setting. Every child should be guaranteed the right to successfully meet this challenge.

Our experience in the schools over the past 25 years has led us to a strong belief that virtually all the reading failure in the early grades could be avoided if teachers: (a) were given well-constructed code-emphasis instructional materials, and (b) received adequate on-the-job training in how to present beginning reading instruction. Our experience

in training teachers has shown that the average person will need 50 to 60 hours of preservice and in-the-classroom supervision to become skilled in presenting beginning reading instruction in a humane and efficient manner. This book cannot take the place of this type of training. What this book can do, however, is to help the teacher learn the specific details of what a code-emphasis approach reading program should include and to become aware of the specific teaching techniques that foster student attentiveness and success.

Key Terminology

Throughout these beginning chapters, we will use several key terms. The definition of these terms and an explanation of their importance follows.

Most Common Sounds

The most common sound of a letter is the sound that a letter most usually represents when it appears in a short, one-syllable word, such as *man* or *bled.* Table 5.1 lists the most common sound of each of the 26 letters. The word next to each letter illustrates the most common sound of that particular letter.

Table 5.1   Most Common Sounds of Single Letters

Continuous Sounds		Stop Sounds	
a	(fat)	b	(boy)
e	(bet)	c	(can)
f	(fill)	d	(did)
i	(sit)	g	(got)
l	(let)	h	(his)
m	(mad)	j	(jet)
n	(nut)	k	(kiss)
o	(not)	p	(pet)
r	(rat)	q	(quit)
s	(sell)	t	(top)
u	(cut)	x	(fox)
v	(vet)		
w	(wet)		
y	(yes)		
z	(zoo)		

Stop Sounds vs. Continuous Sounds

A continuous sound is a sound that can be said for several seconds without distorting the sound. A stop sound can be said for only an instant. Words beginning with a stop sound are more difficult for students to sound out than words beginning with a continuous sound. For example, the word *pad* is more difficult to sound out for beginning readers than the word *sad* because *pad* begins with a stop sound. Because of the difference, a slightly different procedure is used when the teacher presents stop sounds than is used to teach continuous sounds. The list in Table 5.1 designates which letters correspond to stop sounds and which letters correspond to continuous sounds.

Regular Words

A regular word is any word in which each letter represents its respective, most common sound. For ex-

ample, the words *am, cat, mud, best,* and *flag* are regular words because each letter represents its most common sound.

Irregular Words

During the beginning reading stage, any word in which one or more letters does not represent its most common sound will be considered an irregular word. The word *was* is irregular because the letters *a* and *s* do not represent their most common sounds.

Consonant Blends

A consonant blend occurs when two or three consonants appear consecutively in a word and each consonant represents its most common sound. Consonant blends may appear at the beginning or end of words. Table 5.2 illustrates common initial- and final-consonant blends. Words that begin with

Table 5.2 Consonant Blends

Initial-Consonant Blends								
Two-Letter Blends Continuous Sounds First				Two-Letter Blends Stop Sound First				Three Letters
fl	(flag)	sc	(scat)	bl	(black)	pl	(plug)	scr	(scrap)
fr	(frog)	sk	(skip)	br	(brat)	pr	(press)	spl	(split)
sl	(slip)	sp	(spin)	cl	(clip)	tr	(truck)	spr	(spring)
sm	(smack)	sq	(square)	cr	(crust)	tw	(twin)	str	(strap)
sn	(snip)	st	(stop)	dr	(drip)			
sw	(swell)			gl	(glass)			
				gr	(grass)			

Final-Consonant Blends						
Two-Letter Blends Continuous Sounds First				Two-Letter Blends Stop Sound First		Three Letters
ft	(left)	nd	(bend)	ct	(fact)	Words formed
ld	(held)	nk	(bank)	pt	(kept)	by adding an
lk	(milk)	nt	(bent)	xt	(text)	s to two-letter
lp	(help)	sk	(mask)	bs	(cabs)	blends (e.g.,
lt	(belt)	st	(west)	ds	(beds)	belts, facts)
mp	(lamp)	ls	(fills)	gs	(rags)	
ms	(hams)			ps	(hips)	
ns	(cans)			ts	(bets)	

consonant blends are more difficult to decode than words that begin with single consonants. An initial-consonant blend that contains a stop sound will make a word more difficult to decode than will a consonant blend with two continuous sounds.

Regular Word Types

Regular word types may be described by the patterns of vowels and consonants they contain. Table 5.3 lists word types in their relative order of difficulty. In the first column, the letters V and C are used to describe the various types. V stands for vowel and C stands for consonant. A CVC word begins with a consonant letter, followed by a vowel, and another consonant. The word *sat* is a CVC word since *s* is a consonant, *a* is a vowel, and *t* is a consonant. The second column indicates the reason for the word type's relative difficulty. The third column illustrates each word type. This table provides general guidelines,

not hard and fast rules for the teaching of each word type. Some students may find words of an earlier type more difficult than words of a latter type.

An Overview of Decoding Instruction—Beginning Stage

During the beginning stage, the major part of instruction revolves around teaching students how to decode regular words. We recommend teaching students an overt strategy of sounding out words. In sounding out, the students start at the beginning of the word and say the sound corresponding to the first letter. They then advance in a left-right progression, saying the sound for each successive letter and blending the sounds without pausing. The blending results in a word such as *Sam* being sounded as "Sssssaaaaaammmmmm." Finally the blended word is said at a normal rate "Sam."

Table 5.3 Simple Regular Words—Listed According to Difficulty

Word Type	Reason for Relative Difficulty/Ease	Examples	Notes
VC and CVC words that begin with continuous sound	Words begin with a continuous sound.	it, fan	VC and CVC are grouped together because there are few VC words.
VCC and CVCC words that begin with a continuous sound	Words are longer and end with a consonant blend.	lamp, ask	VCC and CVCC are grouped together because there are few VCC words.
CVC words that begin with stop sound	Words begin with a stop sound.	cup, tin	
CVCC words that begin with stop sound	Words begin with stop sound and end with a consonant blend.	dust, hand	
CCVC	Words begin with a consonant blend.	crib, blend, snap, flat	Words that begin with two continuous consonants are the easier of words that begin with blends. These words are grouped with the rest of blends since there are relatively few such words.
CCVCC, CCCVC, and CCCVCC	Words are longer.	clamp, spent, scrap, scrimp	

The following are preskills that help students to sound out words:

1. A knowledge of letter-sound correspondences in the word. (Note that word reading can begin as soon as the students know enough sounds of letters to form words. The students need not master all letter-sound correspondences before word reading begins.)

2. The ability to orally blend a series of sounds in which each sound is held several seconds with no pause (e.g., the teacher says "mmmaaannn" and the student says "mmmaaannn").

3. The ability to translate a series of connected sounds into a meaningful word (e.g., the teacher says "mmmaaan" and the student says "man").

The imitating and translating skills are auditory skills. They can be presented verbally without any reference to printed material. The first week of instruction will consist primarily of letter-sound correspondence and auditory-skill training.

Sounding-out instruction can begin when the students know four to six letter-sound correspondences. The first sounding-out exercises are word-list exercises in which the teacher points to the letters in a word while the students say and blend the sounds, then say the word at a normal rate.

When the students demonstrate mastery on teacher-prompted sounding out, the teacher introduces sounding-out exercises in which the students point to the letters as they blend sounds in a word that appears on a worksheet page.

Passage reading, in which the students read stories composed of words taught in word-list exercises, begins with passages that are just one or two sentences in length. The length of stories and the time devoted to passage reading grows gradually until, near the end of the beginning stage, almost two-thirds of decoding instruction focuses on passage reading.

A gradual transition is made over a period of weeks from sounding out to sight-word reading in which the students do not vocally sound out a word before saying it at a normal rate.

Initial word-reading exercises are done with regular VC and CVC words that begin with continuous sounds. More difficult regular word types are introduced only when students demonstrate mastery of easier types. Irregular words, words in which one or more letters do not represent their most common sound, are not introduced until students have developed ease in sounding out regular words.

In summary, decoding instruction begins with the teacher presenting component skills that students will need when reading words. The teacher presents letter-sound correspondences and auditory skills that students will employ when reading words. The initial word-reading instruction involves the teacher instructing the students how to sound out regular words. A gradual transition is made from exercises in which students vocally sound out words with a good deal of teacher prompting to later exercises in which students read words independently without vocally sounding them out. The key teacher behavior is to provide students with adequate practice to facilitate high accuracy before proceeding to new steps.

Comprehension

During the first year of reading instruction, the words students will be able to read will represent only a small fraction of the words in the students' expressive and receptive vocabulary. Text comprehension exercises are limited to relatively simple, literal, and inferential questions. Comprehension instruction on a wider range of topics can and should be presented verbally. All students can benefit from oral instruction in a wider range of comprehension and vocabulary skills than can be presented in written exercises.

The type and quantity of comprehension instruction during the beginning reading stage depends on the entering skills of the children. Since the words introduced in most commercial reading programs are selected to be within the vocabulary of the *average* child, relatively little work needs to be done on these words with most students. Comprehension teaching for instructionally sophisticated students can consist of oral training in reasoning skills and more sophisticated vocabulary.

At-risk students, however, may require a great deal of teaching of basic vocabulary and expressive language. They will not know the meaning of words encountered in primary reading books. Equally important, they may not understand many terms teachers commonly use during instruction. To prepare these students for the tasks they will encounter, a teacher should provide instruction in basic language and vocabulary. Early lessons should include instruction in various attributes of objects such as color, shape, texture, and size, labels for common classroom objects, use of comparatives and superlatives, pronoun usage, and prepositions.

In summary, oral-language training during the beginning reading stage will benefit all students, but it is especially critical for instructionally naive students. Without extensive oral training, these students are likely to have serious problems with later comprehension activities.

✳ Application Exercises

1. a. Write B if the word begins with a consonant blend.
   b. Write E if the word ends with a consonant blend.
   c. Circle the consonant blend in each word.

clip	step	desk	clamp
must	lamp	milk	splint

2. Classify each of the following words under the appropriate heading below.

strip	step	ant	crust
camp	fled	bets	bled
mud	must	snap	top
best	cop	brat	set
strap	ask	grab	bust

   a. VC and CVC words that begin with continuous sound:
   b. CVC words that begin with stop sound:
   c. CVCC and VCC words:
   d. CCVC words:
   e. CCVCC, CCCVC, and CCCVCC words:

3. Put *s* over each letter that represents a stop sound. Put *c* over each letter that represents a continuous sound.
   a b c d e f g h i j k l m n o p q r s t u v w x y z

4. Identifying words students will not be able to decode is an important teaching skill. Assume that students know the most common sound of all individual letters. Circle any single letter the student will not be able to decode, which means the word itself is probably not decodable. For example, the letter *g* in *gin* would be circled since *g* is not representing its most common sound.

cent	tab	put
must	cut	fat
cab	gin	send
pin	rust	son
was	ten	con
gas	some	hat
wish	fast	mind
tent	bent	dent
	walk	cub

Phonemic Awareness and Alphabetic Understanding

In the 1970s, the first edition of *Direct Instruction Reading* (Carnine & Silbert, 1979) described the importance of teaching "auditory" skills to beginning readers. The authors proposed ensuring that students were introduced to the sound structure of words and were able to manipulate sounds in words by teaching three auditory skills: telescoping, segmenting, and rhyming.

Much research in the l980s and 1990s led to refined understandings of the roles that these auditory skills play in reading. As that understanding grew, the term "auditory skills" was replaced by the terms "phonological awareness skills" and "phonemic awareness skills." With that research came increased understanding of the distinctions and the intricate relationships among phonological awareness, phonemic awareness, the alphabetic principle, and phonics.

Phonemic and Phonological Awareness

Both phonological awareness and phonemic awareness involve the identification and manipulation of parts of *spoken* language. *Phonological awareness,* the broader category, includes awareness of the larger parts of spoken language as well as awareness of the smaller parts. Included among the larger units of spoken language are words, syllables, onsets, and rimes; thus, phonological awareness refers to aspects of sound such as rhyming and alliteration. Phonemic awareness, on the other hand, refers only to awareness of phonemes, the smallest meaningful parts of spoken language.

Phonemic awareness is a subcategory of phonological awareness that is focused more narrowly on identifying and manipulating individual sounds within words. Phonemic awareness includes both an awareness that spoken words are composed of tiny, abstract sounds and the ability to manipulate those sounds in a variety of ways. Those tiny, abstract sounds are called *phonemes.* English consists of about 41 phonemes.

Alphabetic Awareness, Alphabetic Understanding, and the Alphabetic Principle

As stated above, phonemic awareness involves the ability to hear and manipulate sounds. *Alphabetic awareness* refers to a reader's knowledge of the letters of the alphabet coupled with the understanding that the alphabet represents the sounds of spoken language. *Alphabetic understanding* refers to understanding that letters represent sounds and that whole words embody a sound structure of individual sounds and patterns of groups of sounds. The *alphabetic principle* is the combination of alphabetic understanding and phonemic awareness. The alphabetic principle enables the reader to translate independently a visual symbol into a sound. Converging evidence provides strong support that a combination of *phonemic awareness* and *letter-sound correspondence* training is necessary to understand the alphabetic principle (Adams, 1990; Ball & Blachman, 1991; Byrne & Fielding-Barnsley, 1990; Mann, 1993; Rack et al., 1992; Snowling, 1991; Spector, 1995; Stanovich, 1986; Vellutino, 1991; Vellutino & Scanlon, 1987a).

Phonemic Awareness and Phonics

Phonemic awareness is not the same thing as phonics, though they have been frequently misunderstood as the same. Phonemic awareness is an understanding of how the sounds of *spoken* language work to form words, whereas phonics is the system by which symbols represent those sounds in an alphabetic writing system. Because the two are closely linked in beginning reading instruction, phonemic awareness activities are sometimes called beginning phonics activities, and beginning phonics activities are sometimes called phonemic awareness activities. As shown in Figure 6.1, the National Reading Panel concluded that phonemic awareness instruction is most effective when students use letters of the alphabet as they are taught to manipulate phonemes. When students use letters of the alphabet in phonemic awareness instruction, the instruction looks like what we usually consider to be beginning phonics instruction. To distinguish the two, the National Reading Panel explained that phonemic awareness instruction does not qualify as phonics instruction when it teaches children to manipulate phonemes in speech, but it does qualify when it teaches children to segment or blend phonemes with letters. In other words, when instruction teaches children to segment or blend phonemes with letters, the instruction can be termed either phonemic awareness instruction or phonics instruction. When letters are used in phonemic awareness instruction, the instruction

Figure 6.1   National Reading Panel Conclusions From Scientifically-Based Research on Phonemic Awareness Instruction

- Phonemic awareness can be taught explicitly.
- Phonemic awareness instruction helps children learn to read and spell.
- Phonemic awareness instruction is most effective when students use letters of the alphabet as they are taught to manipulate phonemes.
- Phonemic awareness instruction is most effective when it focuses on only one or two rather than several types of phoneme manipulation.
- Phonemic awareness instruction produces greater benefits in reading when it includes blending and segmenting of phonemes in words.
- Phonemic awareness instruction is most effective when it makes explicit how children are to apply phonemic awareness skills in reading and writing tasks.
- Phonemic awareness instruction helps all types of children improve their reading, including normally developing readers, children at risk for future reading problems, disabled readers, preschoolers, kindergarteners, first-graders, children in second through sixth grades with reading disabilities, and children across various socioeconomic levels.
- Phonemic awareness instruction should consume no more than 20 hours of instructional time over the school year.
- Phonemic awareness instruction is more effective when delivered to small groups of students than when delivered to individual students or to the whole class.

Adapted from the NRP Report of the Subgroups, Chapter 2, Part 1, "Phonemic Awareness Instruction," pp. 5–7.

overlaps phonics instruction. This overlap helps children understand how their phonemic awareness skills link up with their knowledge of letters of the alphabet. This understanding is critical. What we call the instruction is of less importance.

Research of the late 1980s and early 1990s showed clearly that students who enter first grade with a wealth of phonological and phonemic awareness are more successful readers than those who do not (Kame'enui, 1996; Smith, Simmons, & Kame'enui, 1995). Fortunately, phonemic awareness skills can be taught explicitly to students who lack these skills when they enter kindergarten or first grade. The National Reading Panel concluded that phonemic awareness instruction is most effective when it:

- uses letters of the alphabet as students are taught to manipulate phonemes

- focuses on only one or two rather than several types of phoneme manipulation

- includes blending and segmenting of phonemes in words

- makes explicit how phonemic awareness skills are applied in reading and writing tasks

The National Reading Panel report provides evidence that the three "auditory" skills described in the First Edition of Direct Instruction Reading (Carnine & Silbert, 1979) are critical prereading skills. Telescoping and segmenting correspond to the blending and segmenting skills to which the NRP conclusions listed above refer. The third "auditory" skill—rhyming—was identified as an important phonological skill that helps students focus on parts of spoken language that are smaller than syllables but larger than phonemes. A rime is the part of a syllable that contains the vowel and all that follows it (the rime of *man* is -an; of *shop,* -op).

Preskills for Sounding Out Words

In this section, we explain how telescoping, blending, and rhyming are preskills for sounding out

words and provide formats for teaching the three skills. It is important to note that these three skills are primarily spoken language skills, which means that the teacher does not present written letters or words to students. Instead, the exercises are conducted orally with the teacher saying sounds and requiring students either to repeat the sounds or say the sounds another way. The student is not required to look at a word and read it. The student merely listens to sounds and responds. Teaching these phonemic awareness skills early is necessary to lay the groundwork for later reading skills, such as sounding out words and blending.

Two skills directly related to sounding out words, which enhance phonemic awareness, are "telescoping" sounds to form a word and "segmenting" a word into sounds. Telescoping sounds to form a word begins with the teacher saying a series of blended sounds. The students then translate the series of sounds into a word said at a normal rate ("aaammm" becomes *am*). This procedure explicitly demonstrates that words are composed of strings of smaller units of speech or phonemes. In the telescoping task, the students are provided with extended opportunity to "hear" those smaller units of speech (i.e., phonemes) and then translate what they have heard into familiar spoken words.

The second skill is segmenting a word into sounds. (Note: The use of the word segmenting differs from common usage in the literature in that, as a preskill, for sounding out a word, segmenting is taught as "not stopping between the sounds." In the literature, phonemic segmentation generally refers to isolating the phonemes within a word. For example, *sad* becomes /s/ /a/ /d/, while for our purposes, *sad* is segmented as "sssaaad.") In the segmenting format, the teacher first models saying a word slowly, breaking it into component sounds. Then the students say the word slowly or segment the word.

The tasks of telescoping and segmenting words do the following:

1. Show the students that words are composed of discrete sounds (i.e., teaches phonemic awareness skills).

2. Provide practice in saying sounds before the letter-sound correspondences are introduced. This practice is particularly important for difficult-to-say sounds such as "th."

3. Prepare students for later sounding-out exercises that require blending (saying sounds without pausing between them).

Because auditory skills do not require knowledge of letter-sound correspondence and do not require students to look at written letters (graphemes) or words, instruction on these skills can begin on the first day of instruction, before any letter-sound correspondences have been introduced. Telescoping sounds to form a word is the easier skill and should be introduced first. Segmenting a word into sounds can be introduced when students are able to telescope a group of words with no errors. This is usually within several days. These auditory tasks should be continued for the first few months of instruction. Four to six words should be included in each exercise. As a general rule, auditory exercises should include words and sounds that students will be asked to decode in the near future.

Telescoping Sounds

Telescoping sounds requires the student to translate a series of blended sounds into words said at a normal rate. When sounding out a written word, students will hold each continuous sound for 1 to 2 seconds, thus producing a series of sounds, "mmmaaannn." Then they will have to telescope this series of sounds

into a word pronounced at a normal rate, "man." A format for teaching telescoping appears in Table 6.1. The teacher says a word slowly, pauses an instant, and then says, "What word?" The students reply by saying the word at a normal rate.

Correcting Mistakes

Students may make three types of mistakes when telescoping sounds to form a word: saying the word slowly (imitating the teacher), leaving out a sound (the teacher says "sssaaat," but the child leaves off the final consonant saying "saa"), and mispronouncing a sound (the teacher says "ssseeelll," but the student says "sil"). The correction procedure, which is the same for all types of mistakes, consists of the teacher's (a) modeling the correct response, (b) leading the students by responding with them, (c) testing the students on the missed word, and (d) returning to the first word in the format.

Here is a typical correction sequence: The teacher is presenting these words: *if, sat, Sid, am, fit.*

- Teacher says, "Ssssiiiiid." Student says "sad" instead of "Sid."
- Teacher says correct answer, "Sid."
- Teacher models entire task: My turn. (Pause.) "Ssssiiiid." What word? "Sid."
- Teacher leads—teacher and student respond together: "Ssssiiiid." What word? (Signal.) "Sid." (Teacher says, "Sid" with the students.)

Table 6.1 Format for Telescoping Sounds

Teacher	Students
1. (Teacher gives instructions.) Listen, we're going to play a say-the-word game. I'll say a word slowly, then you say the word fast.	
2. (Teacher says the word slowly, then students say it fast.) Listen. (Pause.) iiiiffffff. What word? (Signal.)	"If."
3. Teacher repeats step 2 with four more words: sat, Sid, am, fit.	
4. Teacher repeats the set of words until students can respond correctly to all the words, making no errors.	
5. Teacher gives individual turns to several students.	

- Teacher tests—only students respond. Your turn. (Pause.) "Ssssiiiid." What word? (Signal.) "Sid."

- Teacher returns to first word in format: Let's see if we can do all the words without making any errors.

Usually one or two students in a group will make an error while the rest of the students respond correctly. Teachers should occasionally begin the correction procedure by praising a student who responded correctly (e.g., "Good answer, Tommy"). This praise will demonstrate to students that the teacher places importance on correct responding. Teachers should not be negative with students who make errors. Praise a student who got the answer right. The praise keeps the lesson positive and motivates other students. The teacher does not generally single out the students who made the error, but presents correction to the entire group, having all the students respond. When presenting individual turns at the end of the format, the teacher should test a student on any word the student missed during the exercise.

Segmenting a Word

Segmenting a word format (see Table 6.2) teaches students to say a word slowly by holding each continuous sound for about 1½ seconds and by switching from sound to sound without pausing. The teacher models by saying a word slowly. Then the students imitate the teacher.

Correcting Errors

Students can make three types of mistakes in segmenting a word: not saying the correct sound, pausing between sounds, or not switching sounds when the teacher signals for the students to say the next sound. The correction procedure for not saying a correct sound includes these steps:

1. Stop the students as soon as you hear the wrong response and say the correct sound.

2. Model the correct response.

3. Lead the students in making the response.

4. Test the students.

Table 6.2 Format for Segmenting

Teacher	Students
1. We're going to say words slowly.	
2. First word: **sad.**	
I'll say it slowly. Listen. (Pause.) Ssssaaaddd.	
You say it slowly. Get ready. (Teacher signals each time students are to switch to the next sound.)	"Ssssaaaddd."
3. Teacher repeats procedure in step 2 with 3 more words.	
Next word: **me.**	
I'll say it slowly. Listen. (Pause.) Mmmmeee.	
You say it slowly. Get ready. (Signal.)	"Mmmmeee."
Next word: mom.	
I'll say it slowly. Listen. (Pause.) Mmmmooommm.	
You say it slowly. Get ready. (Signal.)	"Mmmmooommm."
Next word: **fit.**	
I'll say it slowly. Listen. (Pause.) Ffffiiittt.	
You say it slowly. Get ready. (Signal.)	"Ffffiiittt."
4. Teacher repeats the set of words until students can say every word slowly, making no errors.	
5. Teacher gives individual turns to several students.	

5. Return to the beginning of the exercise.

Here is a typical correction sequence:

- Examples being presented: am, not, rug, sad.

- Error when segmenting "nnnooot," a student says "nnnuuu."

- Teacher stops the student as soon as she hears "uuu."

- Teacher says correct sound, "Ooooo."

- Teacher models (emphasizing the sound the student said incorrectly): My turn. Nnn*ooo*t.

- Teacher leads: Listen. Nnnn*ooo*t. Say it with me. Get ready. (Signal.) "Nnnooot."

- Teacher tests: Listen. Nnnnooot. You say it slowly. Get ready. (Signal.) "Nnnooot."

- Teacher returns to first word in task.

The correction procedure for student pausing between sounds is basically the same as for mispronounced words except that the teacher does not have to say a missed sound. The teacher tells the students not to stop between sounds. Then the teacher models, leads, tests, and returns to the first word of the exercise.

The correction procedure for students failing to switch sounds when the teacher signals would begin with the teacher praising students who followed the signal, then modeling, leading, and testing as above.

Segmenting and Telescoping

The two auditory skills are combined in a single format in Table 6.3. This format can be introduced when students are able on the first trial to respond correctly to all the words in a segmenting format without making any errors.

Critical Behaviors—Saying the Word Slowly

Saying a word slowly allows students to hear each sound in the word for an extended period of time. When saying a word slowly in an auditory-skills format, the teacher: (a) says each continuous sound for about 1½ seconds, (b) does not pause between sounds, and (c) is careful not to distort any sound. When saying the final consonant of a word, the teacher must be careful not to add an "uh" sound, but to say the word *sad* as "sssaaad," not "sssaaduh." Similarly, teachers must be careful not to add an

Table 6.3 Segmenting and Telescoping—Combined Format

Teacher	Students
1. First you'll say a word slowly, then you'll say it fast.	
2. Listen. (Pause.) Rrrraaannn. Say it slowly. Get ready.	"Rrraannn."
(Teacher signals each time students are to switch to the next sound.)	
What word? (Signal.)	"Ran."
3. Listen. (Pause.) Sssiiiccck. Say it slowly. Get ready. (Signal.)	"Ssssiiiick."
What word? (Signal.)	"Sick."
4. Listen. (Pause.) Mmmmaaad. Say it slowly. Get ready.	
(Signal.)	"Mmmaaaad."
What word? (Signal.)	"Mad."
5. Listen. (Pause.) Iiiffff. Say it slowly. Get ready. (Signal.)	"Iiiifff."
What word? (Signal.)	"If."
6. Teacher repeats steps 2 through 5 until students are able to respond correctly to all words.	
7. Teacher gives individual turns to several students.	

"uh" sound to words that begin with stop sounds (*b, c, d, g, h, j, k, p, q, t*). The teacher pronounces a word such as *pin* by combining the /p/ and /ĭ/ sound and then elongating the /ĭ/ sound, pronouncing *pin* as "piiiiiiinnnnn" not as "puhiiiiinnnn."

Note that in all three formats the teacher is directed to pause before saying a word slowly (segmenting a word). The pause should be just for an instant. The purpose of the pause is to ensure that the students hear the word as a distinct unit.

Signaling

The telescoping and segmenting tasks are among the first tasks presented to students at the beginning of the year. When presenting the exercises to the students, the teacher not only teaches the telescoping and segmenting skills, but also teaches students how to respond as a member of a group. The teacher must present the signal to respond in a manner that makes it clear to the students exactly when they are to respond and when to listen. When speaking to the students the teacher can hold up his (or her) hand in front of him (as someone indicating another person to stop).

In the telescoping exercises, one way that the teacher can signal the students to respond is by moving his or her hand up and down in a quick drumbeat motion. The up-down motion should be done crisply and without hesitation. The students respond on the down motion, just as the teacher's hand hits an imaginary drum. The up-down motion should be done the same way every time. Any hesitation or inconsistency makes a unison responding difficult because the students don't know when to respond.

The signal for segmenting a word can begin the same way with the teacher holding his or her hand in the stop position. The teacher signals the students to begin responding by using the drum-beat motion. One-and-a-half seconds later the teacher repeats the up-down motion again, then 1½ seconds later the teacher repeats the motion. The students switch from sound to sound on each movement, not pausing between them. The signaling procedure is summarized in this way:

```
sssssssssssaaaaaaaaaaaaaammmmmm
|              |                    |
up-down    up-down          up-down
motion     motion           motion
```

A slightly different signaling procedure is necessary when words begin with stop sounds (*b, c, d, g, h, j, k, p, q, t*). When the teacher models these words, the teacher says the first two sounds of the word as one unit. For example, when segmenting the word *hat* the teacher says "haaat." The teacher says the initial-consonant sound for an instant and then begins the next sound without any pause or distortion.

To signal to the students that this type of word is different, the teacher makes two rapid drum-beat motions while saying the first two sounds of the word. The teacher holds the vowel slightly longer than usual (about 2 seconds), then makes another up-down movement, to signal students to say the third sound.

Monitoring Students

When students respond orally in unison, hearing an incorrect response can be difficult; therefore, the teacher should look at the students' mouths as they make the responses. The position of the students' lips and tongues helps to tell the sounds the students are making. For example, if a student's mouth is open when the student is supposed to be making the /m/ sound, the teacher knows the student is not making a correct response.

The teacher should also watch the students' eyes. The students' eyes should be directed toward the teacher's face. Young children unconsciously watch an adult's mouth movements to learn how to say sounds and words. Hence, students should watch the teacher's mouth as the teacher models. Watching the students' eyes also lets the teacher know if the students are attending to the teacher's signals.

Pacing

As a general rule, the teacher should keep the time between when the students respond and when the teacher begins the instructions for the next word to just an instant.

When presenting a format the teacher presents several words in a row, pausing no longer than several seconds to make a quick one- or two-word praise comment (e.g., good, great) between the student response and the instructions for the next word. After a set of several words, the teacher can spend 5 to 15 seconds praising students.

The concept of presenting a set of tasks with little extraneous language between each task is an important one. Presenting a set of tasks with no interruption is a very powerful method for keeping students attentive.

The number of words in a set and the relative intensity of teacher praise depends on the difficulty the students have with the formats. The less difficulty students have, the more words should be included in a set and the praise less effusive.

Individual Turns

As a general rule, when a format is presented, the teacher has the students respond in unison. The teacher has the students respond in unison until the teacher is fairly certain all students can respond correctly to all the words. Then individual turns are given. The main purpose of individual turns is to make a final check to see whether students are able to respond correctly. During the first week of instruction an individual turn on segmenting a word may be given to most students. Later, fewer individual turns are needed. The teacher may give an individual turn to each weaker student, but just to 1 or 2 stronger students. The purpose of giving individual turns to higher performers is not only to monitor their performance, but also to ensure that the teacher does not inadvertently stigmatize some students as lower performers by always calling on just them for individual turns.

Selecting Examples

Selecting words to use in telescoping and segmenting tasks is relatively simple. The basic rule is to use regular words that will appear in early word-reading tasks. On the first day of instruction, the teacher selects four words, including some from the first word-reading task in the program.

The initial auditory tasks are done with the easiest type of words, VC and CVC words beginning with continuous sounds. More difficult types of words are presented in auditory tasks a week or so before that type is introduced in word-reading exercises.

The teacher must make certain the list is not too predictable because a predictable list may cause the students to anticipate words and not attend carefully to what the teacher says. For example, if the same vowel appears in all words, the words form a predictable order; the students may then respond according to the pattern rather than to what the teacher says. If the teacher presented the following set: *Sam, lap, rat, man,* the students might start anticipating that all words have the /ă/ sound.

To avoid a predictable list, the teacher constructs a list in which the same letter does not appear in the same position in more than two consecutive words.

Rhyming

Rhyming is an important phonological awareness skill because it (1) prepares students to see the relationship between letter clusters that represent the same sounds in different words, such as *fan, pan, tan,* and *man,* and (2) prepares students for sounding out words that begin with stop sounds. Rhyming can be introduced when the students have mastered the segmenting and telescoping skills.

In the rhyming format (see Table 6.4), the teacher writes several letters on the board (e.g., *m, r, s*) and models by saying a series of rhyming words, beginning with those letters (e.g., *mat, rat, sat*), then tests the students. On the first lessons that rhyming is presented, the letters written on the board should have continuous sounds. After the students can correctly do the rhyming tasks with continuous sounds, words that begin with stop sounds can be included. For example, a set might include these words: *fill, hill, pill, mill.*

Table 6.4   Rhyming Format

Teacher	Students
(Teacher writes on board:)	

Teacher	Students
1. Listen. I'm going to rhyme with (Pause.) **at.** What am I going to rhyme with? (Signal.)	"At."
2. (Teacher models:) (Teacher puts finger on ball of first arrow and says:) My turn: Rhymes with **at.** (After a 1-second pause, teacher moves finger rapidly across arrow and says:) **Mat.**	
3. (Teacher repeats step 2 with remaining arrows.)	
4. (Teacher tests:) (Teacher puts finger on ball of first arrow and says:) You're going to rhyme with **at.** What are you going to rhyme with? (Signal.) Rhymes with **at.** (After a 1-second pause, teacher moves finger quickly across arrow.)	"At." "At." "Mat."
5. (Teacher repeats step 4 with remaining arrows.)	
6. (Teacher gives individual turns to several students.)	

The correction procedure follows these steps:

- Teacher says the correct answer.

- Teacher models: My turn. Rhymes with at. (Signal.) "Mat."

- Teacher leads: Let's do it together. Rhymes with at. (Signal.) "Mat." (Teacher responds with the students.)

- Teacher tests: Your turn. Rhymes with at. (Signal.) "Mat."

- Teacher returns to first word in format.

✦ Application Exercises

1. The teacher is presenting the format for telescoping a word. Specify all the steps in the correction procedure for the following error. Tell what the teacher says and does.

   Teacher says "mmmuud. What word?" Student says "mad."

2. The teacher is presenting the format for segmenting a word. Specify all the steps in the correction procedure for the following errors.

   Teacher says "fffiiit. Say it slowly." Student says "fff (pauses) iiiit."

3. Classify each of the following words under the appropriate heading below.

mud	hid	fled	ramp
stamp	ran	Sid	frog
cop	slid	hot	fit
best	stink	ten	strap
runt	lid	splint	

   a. VC and CVC words that begin with continuous sound:

   b. CVC words that begin with stop sound:

   c. CVCC and VCC words:

   d. CCVC words:

   e. CCVCC, CCCVC, and CCCVCC words:

4. Identifying words students will not be able to decode is an important teaching skill. Assume that students know the most common sound of all individual letters. Circle any single letter the student will not be able to decode, which means the word itself is probably not decodable. For example, the letter *g* in *gin* would be circled since *g* is not representing its most common sound.

chest	lamp	rub
bent	ten	find
cent	bath	fit
son	rust	slim
rob	camp	limp
was	mend	pen

5. The teacher is selecting words to use in teaching the segmenting format during the first week of instruction. Examine each list of words and indicate by specifying *acceptable* (A) or *unacceptable* (U) whether or not the teacher followed the example-selection guidelines for segmenting. If the teacher did not follow the guidelines specify the violations.

List A	List B	List C
brat	mud	mad
ham	sad	if
sit	lid	sit
fun	mad	Sam
last		

Letter-Sound Correspondence

Students should be taught letter-sound correspondence to prepare them for sounding out words. When students sound out words, they must produce the sound represented by each letter in the word, blend the sounds, and then identify the word. In this section, the details pertaining to teaching letter-sound correspondences are explained.

Sequence

Here are four guidelines for determining an order for introducing letters:

1. Introduce initially only the most common sound for a new letter.

2. Separate letters that are visually or auditorily similar.

3. Introduce more useful letters before less useful letters.

4. Introduce lower-case (small) letters before upper-case (capital) letters.

Introduce the Most Common Sound

The most common sound of a letter is the sound that is usually pronounced for the letter when it appears

in a short word, such as *man* or *sit*. The chart presented earlier in Table 5.1 illustrates the most common sound for each of the 26 letters.

The letters are grouped as continuous sounds or stop sounds. Remember, a continuous sound can be said for several seconds without distorting the sound. All vowels and some consonants are continuous sounds. A stop sound can be pronounced for only an instant. Next to each letter in Table 5.1 is a word in which the letter represents its most common sound. (Note: Phonemes and graphemes are the words used by linguists to describe sounds and the letters that represent them. Phoneme means sound. Grapheme is a letter or a series of letters that represents one sound.)

Separate Visually or Auditorily Similar Letters

The more similar two letters are, the more likely students will confuse them. Separating similar letters from each other in their order of introduction reduces the possibility of student confusion. The greater the similarity between two sounds or letters, the greater the number of letters that should separate them. Two factors determine the probability of confusion: auditory similarity (how alike the

60

most common sounds of two letters are) and visual similarity (how alike the appearance of two letters). The following sounds are auditorily similar: /f/ and /v/, /t/ and /d/, /b/ and /d/, /b/ and /p/, /k/ and /g/, /m/ and /n/, /ĭ/ and /ĕ/, and /ŏ/ and /ŭ/. The following letters are visually similar: *b* and *d, b* and *p, q* and *p, n* and *m, h* and *n, v* and *w,* and *n* and *r.*

Similar sounds should be separated by the introduction of at least three other dissimilar sounds. For example, if the sound /t/ is introduced on lesson 40, the sounds /r/, /l/, and /m/ might be introduced before /d/, which is auditorily similar. Students have the most difficulty with pairs of letters that are both visually and auditorily similar: (*b, d*), (*m, n*), (*b, p*). These letters (plus *e* and *i*) should be separated by at least 6 other letters. If possible, the members of these pairs should also be separated.

Introduce More Useful Letters First

More useful letters are those that appear most often in words. Learning such letters early enables students to decode more words than learning less useful letters. For example, knowing the sounds for the letters *s, a, t,* and *i* will allow students to decode more words than knowing the sounds for *j, q, z,* and *x.* Vowels are the most useful letters. More useful consonants are *b, c, d, f, g, h, k, l, m, n, p, r, s,* and *t.* Less useful consonant letters are *j, q, z, y, x, v,* and *w.*

Introduce Lower-Case Letters First

Lower-case letters should be taught before upper-case letters since the majority of words in reading material is composed of lower-case letters. A student knowing all lower-case letters would be able to decode all the words in the following sentence: "Sam had on his best hat." A student knowing only upper-case letters could read none of the words. An exception to this guideline can be made for lower-case and upper-case letters that look exactly the same, except of course for size (e.g., sS, cC). These lower- and upper-case letters may be introduced at the same time. Upper- and lower-case letters are classified according to their visual similarity in Table 7.1.

A Sample Sequence

Table 7.2 contains one possible order for introducing letters. We are not suggesting that this is the only or even the best sequence for introducing letters. It is just one sequence that derives from the guidelines specified here. Note the following about Table 7.2:

1. The letters visually and/or auditorily similar—*e, i; b, d; m, n;* and *b, p*—are separated by 13, 7, 13, and 6 letters, respectively. Other potentially confusing pairs (*d, t; f, v; h, n; k, g; v, w; n, r*) are also separated.

2. Upper-case letters not the same in appearance as their respective lower-case letters are

Table 7.1   Upper- and Lower-Case Letters Grouped According to Visual Similarity

Dissimilar				Same					Moderate Similarity			
aA	eE	qQ	bB	cC	kK	oO	pP	sS	fF	mM	jJ	nN
rR	dD	gG	hH	uU	vV	wW	xX	zZ	tT	yY	lL	iI

Table 7.2   An Acceptable Sequence for Introducing Letters

a m t s i f d r o g l h u c b n k v e w j p y T L M F D I N A R E H G B x q z J Q introduced after most lower-case letters have been introduced. Upper- and lower-case letters that are identical are introduced at the same time and, thus, these upper-case letters are not listed on the chart.

3. More useful letters are introduced before less useful letters. The lower-case letters *j, y, x, q,* and *z* are introduced toward the end of the sequence. The first two letters, *a* and *m,* were chosen not only because they are more useful letters, but also because they are easy to pronounce. Starting with easy-to-pronounce letters makes initial sounds tasks easier for instructionally naive students.

Rate and Practice

The rate at which new letters are introduced is always contingent on student performance. Teachers working with students who enter school with little knowledge of letter-sound correspondence will find an optimal rate (one which introduces new letters quickly while minimizing errors) for introducing new letters is about one each second or third day. This rate assumes that the teacher presents daily practice on isolated sounds. Without adequate daily practice, an optimal rate is not possible. However, the rate of introduction should always be dependent on the students' performance.

When the first five letters are being taught, a new letter should not be introduced if the students are unable correctly to produce the sound for each of the previously introduced letters. Rather than presenting a new letter, the teacher should review previously taught letters for several days, concentrating on the unknown letters. After the first five letters have been introduced, a new letter can be introduced if the students are having difficulty with just one letter-sound correspondence; however, that letter should not be similar to the letter being introduced. For example, a new vowel (e) can be introduced even though students are having difficulty with *b* and *d.* However, the vowel *e* should not be introduced if the students are having difficulty with any previously introduced vowel since all vowel sounds are similar.

Procedure for Teaching Letter-Sound Correspondences

The basic procedure for teaching letter-sound correspondences involves an introductory format and a discrimination format. In the introductory format, the teacher models and tests on the new letter-sound correspondence. In the discrimination format, the teacher tests the new letter-sound correspondence along with previously introduced letters. The introductory format is used in the first lesson or two when a new letter appears. The discrimination format starts after two letters have been introduced and appears in every subsequent lesson.

Introductory Format

In the introductory format, the teacher first models by saying the sound, then tests by having the group say the sound. The teacher first has the students respond in unison. Then when the teacher thinks that the group can respond correctly, the teacher tests students individually (see Table 7.3).

Discrimination Format

In the sounds-discrimination format, students receive the practice they need to quickly and accurately say the sound for different letters, a skill necessary for sounding out words. A new letter-sound correspondence is taught in the introductory format. If the students have no difficulty saying the sound, the letter can appear in the discrimination format.

The teacher writes the new letter several times on the board intermingled with previously introduced letters. The new letter is written several times to prevent the students from cueing on where the letter is written rather than on the shape of the letter. The teacher follows an alternating pattern in which he or she gradually increases the number of other letters pointed to between each occurrence of the new letter. The format shown in Table 7.4 illustrates the introduction of the letter *f.* During the first month of reading instruction, two isolated sound-discrimination exercises should be included in each

Table 7.3 Introductory Format for Letter-Sound Correspondences

Teacher	Students
1. (Teacher writes on the board: m.) When I touch under the letter, you say the sound. Keep saying the sound as long as I touch it.	
2. (Teacher *models* the sound. Teacher holds her finger under the letter and says:) My turn. (Teacher moves finger out and in, touching under the letter for 2 seconds if it is a continuous sound and for an instant if it is a stop sound. Teacher says the sound while touching under the letter, then quickly moves her finger away from the letter and immediately stops saying the sound.)	
3. (Teacher *tests* by having the group say the sound several times by themselves, and finally gives individual tests to all students. The purpose of the individual test is to enable the teacher to correct mispronunciations early.)	
a. (Teacher points under the letter and says:) What sound? (Signal.) (Teacher touches under letter for about 2 seconds.)	"mmmmmmm"
b. (Teacher repeats step *a* several times, touching under the sound from 1 to 3 seconds.)	
4. (Teacher tests the students individually.)	

Table 7.4 Discrimination Format for Letter-Sound Correspondences

Teacher	Students
(Teacher writes on board several letters that have been previously taught, along with the new letter. Note that the new letter appears several times in different positions:)	

```
                          i
   a          f                      m
        s          n            f
        r               f                   o
```

Teacher	Students
1. (Teacher gives instructions.) When I touch under a letter, you say the sound. Keep saying the sound as long as I touch under it.	
2. (Teacher tests new sound. He points to the first letter, pauses 2 seconds, moves his finger out and in, touching under the letter for about 2 seconds if it is a continuous sound, and for an instant if it is a stop sound.) (Teacher immediately either corrects or points to the next letter.)	Students say the sound.
3. (Teacher tests on all letters. He points to a letter, pauses 2 seconds, then moves his finger out and in, touching under the letter.) (The teacher follows an alternating pattern in which he gradually increases the retention interval for the newly introduced letter by pointing to more review letters before returning to the new letter. For example, if the new letter is *f,* the teacher points to the letters in this order:)	Students say the sound.

```
   f   a   f   r   m   f   s   i   o   f   n   i   r   o   f
```

Teacher	Students
4. (Teacher gives individual tests. Every day the teacher should test several students on all vowels introduced up to that time and test individual students on any sounds that have caused difficulty for them in the past week.)	

lesson: one early in the lesson and one later in the lesson. The reason is simply to provide extra practice. Later in the program when students begin reading words, the word reading itself will be a form of practice for letter-sound correspondences and only one discrimination letter-sound correspondence task needs to be presented in a lesson.

As with the introductory-sound format, the teacher has the group respond in unison until it appears all students are responding correctly to all sounds. Then the teacher gives individual turns.

Note that the discrimination format directs the teacher to pause 2 seconds after pointing to a letter before signaling the students to respond. This pause is to allow the students time to think of their response. After the students know about 12 letter-sound correspondences, the teacher can decrease the pause to about a second on letters introduced prior to the current week.

Critical Behaviors

Signaling

The teacher should concentrate on teaching students to respond to her signal during the first days of instruction. To follow the touching signal, students begin saying a sound as soon as the teacher touches under the letter and continue to respond as long as she touches it. Teaching students to say a sound continuously for several seconds is a very important preskill for sounding out words. When students initially sound out a word, they will say each sound for 1 to 2 seconds. During the time they are saying one sound, they simultaneously look ahead to the next one. For example, while the students say the /m/ sound in *mad,* they look ahead to figure out the sound for the letter *a.* Students who cannot hold a sound for several seconds are likely to have difficulty sounding out words.

When signaling, the teacher points under the letter (not touching the board), making certain that no students's vision is blocked by any part of the teacher's hand or body. The out-and-in motion is done crisply with the finger moving away from the board (about 3 inches) and then immediately back to the board (see Figure 7.1). When the finger touches the board below the letter, the students are to respond. The out-and-in motion is done the same way every time it is used. Any hesitation or inconsistency makes a unison response difficult because the students cannot tell when they are supposed to answer. The teacher signals the students to stop re-

Figure 7.1 Point, Out-In, and Touch Signal

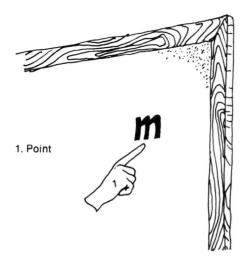

1. Point

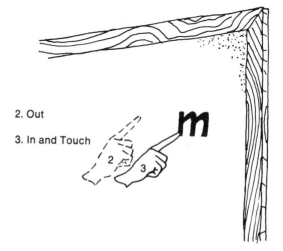

2. Out

3. In and Touch

sponding by moving his or her finger away from the board in a rapid, distinct movement.

A modified signaling procedure is used for the stop sounds (/b/, /c/, /d/, /g/, /h/, /j/, /k/, /p/, /q/, /t/, and /x/). Since these sounds can be pronounced for only an instant, the teacher signals by touching the board below the letter for only an instant.

Modeling

Continuous consonant sounds should be said without any distortion. The letter *m* is said "mmmm," not "uummm" or "mmmmmuuu." Saying a stop sound without adding a slight vowel sound is impossible. However, teachers should try to minimize the vowel sound. The letter *d* should not be pronounced "duh." Vowel sounds must also be pronounced accurately. Some teachers have a tendency to distort vowel sounds. They start out with a distorted sound and then change it into the correct sound (e.g., pronouncing *i* as "uuiii") or start with the correct sound and then distort it (e.g., pronouncing *i* as "iiieee"). Care should be taken to avoid distorting sounds.

Pacing

Pacing a task is not only an important method for maintaining student attention, but it also affects academic performance. Pacing should be fast enough to keep the students attending, but not so fast they begin to guess and make errors. A basic pacing rule in presenting the letter-sound correspondence discrimination format is for the teacher to provide a "thinking pause" before giving the signal for the students' response. Then after the students respond, quickly move to the next letter. The thinking pause gives all students enough time to come up with a response. A longer thinking pause may be given for sounds that have caused the students difficulty in previous lessons. However, the teacher should provide extra practice on the letter so that by the end of the discrimination format, the students can respond with only a 2-second pause.

The thinking pause concept is illustrated as follows. Let's say that the teacher is presenting a letter-sound correspondence task with the letters *m, s,* and *d.* The students had trouble with the letter *d* on the previous lesson. Note how the teacher gives more thinking time for the letter *d.*

- Teacher points to *m,* pauses 2 seconds, then signals.
- Immediately after students respond, teacher points to *s.*
- Teacher pauses 2 seconds, then signals.
- Immediately after students respond, teacher points to *d,* and says, "Remember this tough sound," then pauses 4 seconds before signaling.

Another critical aspect of pacing is immediately moving to the next letter after the students make a correct response. Note above that immediately after the students make the response for the letter *m,* the teacher moves to the next letter *s,* then gives the students time to think. The rapid movement after students respond is a big help in keeping students attentive.

Developing Automaticity

The goal of the letter-sound correspondence formats is not only to enable students to produce the sound associated with the letter, but also to allow them to make the response with relative ease.

In the discrimination format, we recommended that teachers use a 2-second thinking pause before signaling. As the school year progresses, the thinking pause should be gradually reduced; so, by the time 12 letter-sound correspondences have been introduced, the students can respond with no more than a 1-second thinking pause before each letter.

Teachers working with instructionally naive students may find the students need a great deal of practice to increase their rate. To keep the students' frustration level low, the teacher can start the discrimination format with a 2-second thinking pause before each signal. When the students can respond correctly to all the letters with no more than a 2-second pause, the teacher challenges the students by saying, "You did a great job. I'll go faster this time."

Monitoring

Monitoring student performance during group responding is done by listening to the students' responses and watching their mouths and eyes. Since the teacher cannot watch every student on every response, she watches only a few students at a time. She continually scans the group, focusing on one or two students for one response and then shifting attention to other students for the next response. The teacher looks at a student's eyes and mouth. If a student's eyes are not directed toward the letters, the student is probably not paying attention. Looking at the student's mouth indicates whether the student is responding correctly. To produce a sound, a student's lips and tongue must be in a certain position. For example, when a student makes the /l/ sound, his mouth should be open with the front edge of the tongue touching the upper palate. If the student's mouth or tongue is not in this position, he is probably not pronouncing the sound correctly. For some sounds—(c, g), (d, t), (f, v), (p, b), (s, z), and all short vowel sounds—the teacher cannot rely on looking at the student's mouth because the lips and tongue are placed in similar positions for more than one sound. Consequently, the teacher must listen very closely to these sounds.

Even when the teacher listens and watches carefully to unison student responses, she cannot be certain that all students are responding correctly. Individual turns at the end of a format are given to help the teacher find which letters the student does not know. In the introductory format, teachers give individual turns to every student. The purpose is to ensure that the students are saying the new sound correctly. The faster the teacher spots a mispronunciation error, the easier it will be for the teacher to correct the error. In the discrimination format, teachers test several students each day on the new letter, all the vowels introduced up to that time, plus any troublesome consonants.

Teachers should test all students weekly or bi-weekly on all letters introduced to date in order to determine if students can produce the sounds for all letters with no more than a 2-second pause. During this test, which is not to be presented during group instruction, the teacher should let students respond at their own rates. Teachers should record not only the sounds the students are unable to say correctly, but also the sounds the students *can* say correctly, yet take more than 2 seconds to produce.

Correcting Mistakes

Three types of errors are possible: a confusion error (saying the sound for a different letter), a pronunciation error (saying a sound in a distorted manner), and a signal error (not beginning the response when the signal is given). The basic correction for all the errors includes these four steps:

1. Modeling the correct answer.

2. Leading, if necessary.

3. Testing the group on the missed letter, then alternating between the missed letter and other letters in the format.

4. Retesting, later in the lesson, individual students who made an error.

Confusion Errors

In a confusion error, a student might say *m* for *n*. The teacher would do the following:

1. Model the missed letter. "Listen: mmm."

2. Test the students on the missed letter, then alternate between it and other previously identified letters that have been *correctly* identified. If the student said a sound represented by another letter, the teacher does not include this letter in the firm-up. If the student said *n* for the letter *m,* the letter *n* would not appear in the firm-up for *m*. The teacher gradually increases the number of review letters that are included. The teacher continues to alternate between the missed letter and familiar letters until the students

identify the missed letter correctly after at least three other letters are tested just prior to the missed letter. The examples might look like this: first a test on *m,* then an alternating pattern of *a, m, s, i, m, r, f, g, m.*

3. Retest students later in the lesson who have made errors on *m.* The teacher retests by pointing to *m* and asking, "What sound?" If the student misses the letter, the teacher should follow the procedure in steps 2 and 3.

Keep in mind that the sooner confusion errors are spotted, the easier it will be to correct them. Older students who have been confused on a pair of letters for years will take much more time to remedy than younger students.

If a student is having chronic problems with a pair of letters (e.g., *b* and *d*), the teacher might work on one letter of the pair and exclude the other letter from the practice sets. When the students are able to identify correctly the letter being presented for three consecutive days, the teacher can reintroduce the other letter of the pair.

Pronunciation Errors

Pronunciation errors can be as serious as confusion errors, especially if made on vowel sounds. The more distorted the pronunciation of a sound, the greater the students' difficulty will be in discriminating it from similar sounds appearing in later lessons. For example, if a student distorts the /ĭ/ sound so that it is very similar to the /ĕ/ sound, she will have difficulty when the /ĕ/ sound is introduced and may confuse /ĭ/ and /ĕ/ in word reading, saying "led" for *lid.*

The correction for a mispronunciation error is similar to that for a confusion error. When a student mispronounces a sound, the teacher does the following:

1. Models, saying the correct response. "Listen: Mmmmm."

2. Leads, checking to see whether the lips and tongue of the student who made the mistake are positioned properly. If the position is incorrect, the teacher models again saying,

"Watch my mouth when I say the sound." The teacher says the sound and watches the student's eyes to make certain the student is attending. Next, the teacher leads by having the students say the sound with him while watching the student's mouth. Leading is used most often when students mispronounce a sound. Listen: Mmmm. Say it. "Mmmm." (Teacher responds with students.) Listen again: Mmmm. Say it. "Mmmm." (Teacher responds with students.)

3. Tests, alternating between the missed letter and other letters, using the same pattern as for confusion errors. Teacher points to each letter and asks, "What sound?"

4. Retests later in the lesson.

The main difference in the correction procedure for pronunciation errors and the correction procedure for confusion errors is in the lead step. In the lead step, the teacher says the sound, then has the students say the sound with her. The teacher directs the students to watch her mouth as she says the sound. Watching the teacher's lips and tongue as she says the sound will help the students in placing their lips and tongues in the correct position to say the sound. The teacher may have to present 5 to 15 repetitions before the students make an acceptable response. Note above that before each student response, the teacher models saying the sound, then has the students say the sound with her.

The teacher should set a reasonable goal for the lead step. If the student does not have any speech problems, the goal is to have the student say the sound perfectly. If the student has a lisp or other speech problem, the teacher should set a reasonable approximation of the sound as a goal. The teacher should continue the lead step until the student can make two consecutive acceptable responses. Quite often a student who has an initial difficulty saying a sound will make an acceptable response, but on the next trial will make an unacceptable response. Providing extra practice for students to make two consecutive acceptable responses will result in steady improvement over a period of days. A student may need 15 repetitions before he's able to make an acceptable response the first day, then only 10 responses the next day, and fewer each following day. Providing practice to help students say sounds correctly is very challenging for the teacher. He or she must decide what response from the student will be the goal for each session. The teacher must be careful not to set up unreasonable goals. The outcome of instruction is not only for students to produce the desired response but also to see themselves as capable persons. During instruction the teacher should be very encouraging. After several student responses, the teacher should encourage the students and praise them for their effort: "You kids are working hard. This is a tough sound." When a student finally makes two consecutive acceptable responses, the teacher should act very excited and praise the student profusely: "That's great! You did it. I knew you would be able to do it. You didn't give up and you got it right. Great, great, great!"

Teachers working with students who have poor enunciation should provide extra practice in imitating sounds. The teacher should do a daily exercise in which students simply imitate sounds the teacher says. The teacher says a sound for several seconds, then has the student say it for several seconds. The teacher, therefore, can introduce a sound in imitating exercises a week or so before it appears in words presented during the auditory tasks.

Signal Errors

In a signal error, students do not begin and/or end their responses when the teacher signals. Teachers should expect some students to need many signal corrections the first several days of isolated sounds instruction. To make learning to follow signals easier during the first few days of instruction, the teacher can exaggerate each part of the signal. After pointing to the letter, the teacher exaggerates the "out" portion of the signal by moving his or her hand 6 inches from the board, rather than just 3 inches. The teacher can also emphasize when to begin responding by hitting the board to create a "thud," which tells the students to respond. To exaggerate the end of the signal, the teacher moves his or her hand 6 inches in a quick motion, away from the board.

A second prompt a teacher can use to train students to follow signals involves varying the interval for holding a sound. Each time the teacher signals the students to respond, the teacher touches under the letter for a different amount of time. For example, the teacher might touch under the letter for 3 seconds the first time, then 1 second, and finally 2 seconds. The purpose is to show the students that they should hold the sound as long as the teacher points to the letter and not for some fixed interval. If the teacher points to every letter for the same amount of time, the students will soon learn to ignore the signal.

During the first few days of sounds instruction, teachers should be effusive with their praise for students learning to follow the signals. Nearly all students can learn to follow sound signals in one or two days if they are motivated. The teacher can make the exercise into a game. The teacher can challenge the students with a statement such as, "I'm going to try to trick you. It's really hard to watch my finger and say the sound just when I'm touching the letter." This game format is usually very motivating for students.

After the first week of instruction, the teacher should correct a signal error by: (1) praising a student who responded correctly, (2) modeling, (3) testing the missed letter by alternating, and (4) retesting later in the lesson.

Selecting Examples

The introductory sounds format includes just the letter being introduced. A new letter appears for two or three consecutive lessons. The discrimination format includes 6 to 8 letters. For the first week or two, selecting examples is easy; all previously introduced sounds are included in the format. After the students know more than 8 letters, the teacher must select which letters to include. Including all the letters introduced so far makes the format too time consuming. The following guidelines can be used to select letters for the discrimination format:

1. **a.** As a general rule, include the new letter in the discrimination format on the 2nd day the letter appears in the introductory format.

b. If the new letter being introduced is visually and auditorily similar to a previously introduced letter, do not include the similar previously introduced letter in the discrimination format on the lessons in which the new letter appears in the introductory format. Thereafter include the similar letter every day for the next 2 weeks.

2. Once a new letter is introduced in the discrimination format, it should appear daily for about 2 weeks.

3. Put extra emphasis on vowels. Include all vowels introduced to date in almost every lesson.

The chart in Table 7.5 demonstrates the integration of example-selection criterion into daily lesson construction. The chart shows the examples that might be included in the introductory and discrimination formats during the time in which the letter *b* is introduced. Note that on days 1, 2, and 3, the letter *d* does not appear in the discrimination format since *b* is appearing in the introductory format. On day 4, the letter *d* appears along with the letter *b*. The teacher concentrates on providing discrimination practice on *b* and *d*, as well as reviewing other earlier introduced letters. Note also the extra review on vowel letters, as well as the consonant *c, l,* and *h* which were recently introduced.

Table 7.5   Sample 4-Day Example-Selection Sequence for Letter-Sound Correspondence Tasks

Day	1	2	3	4
Introductory Format	b	b	b	
Discrimination Format	cuh	hoi	bui	ucb
	log	bul	hat	odi
	ia	cr	cl	tf

❧ Application Exercises

1. Following are lists of letters in the order they are introduced in several hypothetical reading programs. Next to each letter is the sound value taught for the letter. Write *acceptable* (A) next to the *one* program in which the sequence is acceptable. Write *unacceptable* (U) next to the *one* program that has such severe violations it should not be used with low-performing students. Tell why the sequence is unacceptable. For the other programs, specify the sequencing guideline which is violated in each one and tell what step might be taken to modify it to increase the probability of student success.

Program A
1. a/ă/   2. i/ĭ/   3. e/ĕ/   4. u/ŭ/   5. o/ŏ/   6. b/b/   7. f/f/   8. d/d/

Program B
1. m/m/   2. a/ă/   3. f/f/   4. d/d/   5. s/s/   6. o/ŏ/   7. g/g/   8. h/h/

Program C
1. m/m/   2. M/m/   3. a/ă/   4. A/ă/   5. s/s/   6. S/s/   7. d/d/   8. D/d/

Program D
1. m/m/   2. a/ă/   3. d/d/   4. s/s/   5. i/ĭ/   6. b/b/   7. r/r/   8. n/n/

2. The sequences below indicate the letters (*s, a, m, r,* and *f*) a teacher presented in a sound-discrimination task. Next to each letter is a plus (+) if the student responded correctly or a minus (−) if the student responded incorrectly. For each series of responses, indicate by checking *acceptable* or *unacceptable,* whether the teacher followed the recommended correction procedure. If not, explain the violation.

    Sequence 1—acceptable/unacceptable why?

    s+   r+   m+   a−   (teacher corrects) a+   m+   a−   (teacher corrects) a−

    Sequence 2—acceptable/unacceptable why?

    s+   a+   m−   (teacher corrects) m+   s+   m+   a+   s+   m+   f+   r+   a+   m+

    Sequence 3—acceptable/unacceptable why?

    s+   a−   (teacher corrects) a+   m+   r+   f+   m+   s+   r+   m+

3. The teacher is presenting the sound-discrimination format. The task includes these letters: *m, a, s, d, i, f, c,* and *e.* The student has identified *m, a, s,* and *d* correctly, but then says /ĕ/ for the letter *i.* Specify the steps (including the examples) the teacher should take to correct the error.

4. **a.** Circle the lower-case letters not highly similar to the upper-case letters.

    b. Place an S over each letter that represents a stop sound.

    a   b   c   d   e   f   g   h   i   j   k   l   m   n   o   p   q   r   s   t   u   v   w   x   y   z

5. The letters:

    a   m   t   s   i   f   d   r   o   g   l   h   u   c   b   n   v

    have been presented to a reading group.

    a. A student does not know the letter *b.* The letter *e* is the next letter to be introduced. What should the teacher do?

    b. A student does not know the letter *i.* The letter *e* is the next letter to be introduced. What should the teacher do?

    c. A student does not know the letters *b* and *t.* The letter *e* is the next letter to be introduced. What should the teacher do?

CHAPTER 8

Sounding Out Regular Words

Regular words are words in which each letter represents its most common sound. For example, the word *sat* is regular because the letters, *s, a,* and *t,* each represents its most common sound.

Regular word-reading instruction can begin when students have mastered four to six letter-sound correspondences and the auditory skills of segmenting and telescoping the easiest word types to decode (i.e., CVC words beginning with continuous sounds).

Regular word-reading instruction begins with word-list exercises in which students are taught to sound out regular VC and CVC words that begin with continuous sounds. The teacher prompts the students by pointing to the letters in a word as the students blend the sounds together to form a meaningful word. Word-list sounding out is continued for several months. Passage-reading exercises, in which the students read a story, are introduced when they can sound out simple words in lists with relative ease. Passage reading is a more difficult task for students, since they can no longer rely on the teacher to prompt them by pointing to the letters.

Scope and Sequence

The chart in Figure 8.1 summarizes the decoding-related content of daily lessons during the early weeks of instruction. Sounding out, auditory preskills, and letter-sound correspondence exercises, as well as letter copying and writing, are included in lessons.

Keep in mind that this scope and sequence chart is based on the assumption that the students begin instruction with no knowledge of these reading-related skills. Students who enter school with some knowledge of these skills will be able to progress at a more accelerated rate.

Note on the chart that the first lessons include only letter-sound correspondences, auditory skills, and letter writing. During the first lessons, students learn not only these skills, but also how to respond to the teacher's signals. Sounding out is not introduced until the students know four to six letter-sound correspondences. All initial sounding out is done with VC- and CVC-regular words that begin with continuous sounds, the easiest type of word. Also note that only a couple of words are presented in the early word-list sounding-out exercises. Students can be

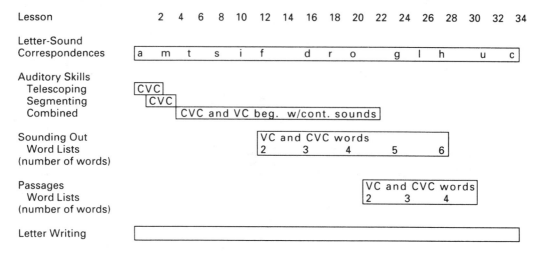

Figure 8.1   Scope and Sequence—Early Weeks of Beginning Instruction

expected to need quite a few practice trials before they are able to sound out a new word without distorting the sounds. Few words are included in the initial exercises so that a teacher can bring the students to a high level of performance on sounding out the words. A high level is reached when the students can correctly sound out each word in the task without error.

Passage reading is introduced after students have sufficient practice reading words in lists. Students will differ in the amount of practice they need on sounding out words in lists. Passage reading can be introduced when students can do a four-word, word-list exercise without making an error. On the chart we recommend that passage reading be introduced 10 days after sounding out is introduced. Remember, it is the students' performance that dictates when new skills are introduced. When a student can perform without error on a format, the teacher can introduce new skills. The chart in Figure 8.1 only shows "average" amounts of time a teacher can expect to present a skill.

Teaching Procedures

Sounding out is initially presented in *word-list* exercises in which the teacher writes the words in

lists, then prompts the students by pointing in a left-to-right progression to the letters in the words. The students say the sounds as the teacher points to the letters.

Passage reading, in which the students point to and concurrently say the sound in words, is introduced after students master the word-list exercises.

Word Lists

Word lists are the vehicles the teacher uses to introduce and provide initial practice for new word types. Word-list exercises are also used to introduce words that will appear in stories. Words can be written on a chalkboard, overhead, or on an 8½ × 11 sheet of paper. If the teacher writes the words on a sheet of paper, we recommend constructing a display made on one side with a piece of 10 × 12 cardboard and on the other with a piece of clear acetate. The acetate is fastened to the cardboard on one side and on the bottom. The teacher slips the paper on which the word list is written into the acetate container. The advantage of the container over the chalkboard is that teachers can hold the acetate container in front of them and point to the words without turning their back to the students.

Guidelines for Constructing Word Lists

- The initial word-list exercise should include only two to four words since in this initial exercise the students will be learning the mechanics of sounding out and are likely to need a good deal of repetition before they can sound out words correctly.

- The number of words in word lists should increase gradually. The number can be determined by the students' performance. A general rule is to include the number of words the student can be brought to mastery on within a 5- to 7-minute period. Mastery is reached when the students are able to respond consecutively to all the words in a list without making an error.

- Words should include only letters students have mastered in letter-sound correspondence tasks. Mastery is demonstrated when a student does not make an error on a particular sound for two consecutive lessons.

- When a new letter first appears in word-list exercises, that letter should appear in about a third to half of the words in the list.

- Word lists should be construed in an unpredictable manner. Generally the same letter should not appear in the same position for more than two words in a row. For example, a list such as *sat, mit, rut, fat* would be inappropriate since the same letter, *t*, appears in the same final position in all the words. The problem with lists such as this is that such predictability may inadvertently encourage student nonattentiveness as they anticipate rather than examine letters.

The chart in Figure 8.2 illustrates the integration of these example-selection guidelines into daily lessons. The chart shows instances presented in the letter-sound format and the word-list sounding-out format over a four-lesson period during the 6th week of instruction. The students already know about 15 letter-sound correspondences and have been sounding out words for about 3 weeks. The letter *u* is introduced in the introductory format for letter-sound correspondences in lesson 31. Previously introduced letters are reviewed in the letter-sound discrimination format. The words in the word-list exercise in lesson 31 include only letters previously mastered. Note that the letter *l* appears in three words. The letter *l* was recently introduced and receives more practice. Note also that the letter *u* does not appear in word-list exercises until lesson 34. There is a 3-day period for the students to practice the letter-sound correspondence for *u* before reading words with these letters. Remember that student performance dictates when new skills are introduced. If the students are having difficulty with *u* in the letter-sound correspondence format, words with *u* should not be presented. A final note concerns the word *fill*. Even though *fill* is technically a CVCC word, it is included as an easier word type since it includes only 3 sounds.

Figure 8.2 Integration of Example-Selection Guidelines Into Daily Lessons

Lesson	31	32	33	34
Letter-Sound Intro	u	u		c
Letter-Sound Disc	h l g a i r d f	u a i g h l t	u i r d h l a o	c r o u l h t d
Word-List Sounding Out	fill	ran	lot	rug
	if	fill	mad	in
	lot	it	lid	lad
	lad	lit	if	mud
	am	mom	Sam	mat

Teaching Procedure for Sounding Out Words in Lists

Introductory Format

The format for introducing sounding out appears in Table 8.1. The teacher introduces sounding out by demonstrating (modeling) how to sound out a word. The teacher points to each letter for about 1½ seconds and says the sounds for the respective letters, not pausing between the sounds. Note the similarity between this task and the auditory segmenting skills tasks. The students have learned in the auditory skills task to pronounce a series of sounds without pausing between each sound, and to follow a teacher's signal of when to switch from sound to sound. In the sounding-out task, the students say the sounds when teachers point to the letters. After the teacher models sounding out a word, the teacher has the students respond with him or her (lead). The purpose of responding with the students is to ensure that they hear the correct response. People who have not worked with young students usually do not realize how difficult sounding out is for them. To read a word, the student says the first sound, then, while saying the first sound, the student must examine the next letter to determine its sound. The student then says the next sound without distorting either sound. This is a diffi-cult coordination task for young students. The teacher responds with the students since it is predictable that they will make errors at first. The teacher repeats responding with the students until they appear able to respond correctly without prompting. Then the students respond without any leading (test).

The introductory format is presented daily until the students are able to sound out the words correctly in the format with no more than two practice trials for each word.

Critical Behaviors

Signaling

An illustrated explanation of the signaling procedure for sounding out appears in Figure 8.3.

Monitoring

The teacher monitors by watching the students' eyes and mouths and by listening to their responses. To coordinate pointing to the letters while watching students is difficult. The teacher should quickly glance at the letters to determine where to point next, and then look at the students before pointing to the next letter. All these movements are done in an instant. The key is to watch the students'

Table 8.1 Introductory Format for Sounding Out Words in Lists (Illustrated With the CVC Word Type)

Teacher	Students
(Teacher writes on board: am, fit.)	
1. Teacher states instructions. "Watch. When I touch a letter, I'll say its sound. I'll keep saying the sound until I touch the next letter. I won't stop between sounds."	
2. Teacher *models* sounding out the first word. "My turn to sound out this word." Teacher touches under each letter that represents a continuous sound 1 to 1½ seconds and under letters that represent stop sounds for only an instant. "Aaaammm."	
3. Teacher *leads* students in sounding out the word. Teacher points to left of word. "Sound out this word with me. Get ready." (Signal.)	"Aaaammm."
Teacher touches under letters. The teacher sounds out the word with students until they respond correctly.	
4. Teacher *tests* the students on the first word. Teacher points to left of word. "Your turn. Sound out this word by yourselves. Get ready." (Signal.)	"Aaaammm."
Teacher touches under letters.	
5. Teacher has several students sound out the word individually. "Billy, sound it out. Get ready." (Signal.)	"Aaaammm."
6. Teacher repeats steps 2 through 5 with the word *fit*.	

Figure 8.3   Signaling Procedure

1. Instructions: Teacher points to the page about an inch to the left of the first letter in the word. "Get ready."

2. The signal for the first sound: Teacher looks at the students to see if they are attending, then quickly touches under the *m*. Teacher holds finger under *m* for about 1 to 1½ seconds.

3. The signal for the second sound: Teacher *quickly* makes a loop, moving his finger from the first letter to the second letter, *a*, and holds his finger under *a* for about 1 to 1½ seconds.

4. The signal for the third sound: Teacher loops *quickly* from *a* to *d* and instantly removes his finger from the page. When signaling for the students to say a stop sound, the teacher touches under the letter for an instant and then moves his hand quickly away from the letter.

mouths when they say a new sound, since the position of their mouths provides feedback about the correctness of their responses and also informs the teacher whether students are responding.

Pacing

The teacher should point to each letter long enough for the students to say its sound and look ahead to the next letter. This will be between 1 and 1½ seconds for each continuous sound. Not pointing to a sound for a long enough time is probably the most common mistake teachers make. The importance of allowing adequate time cannot be overstated.

Students may have to sound out a word several times before they can blend the sounds without error. The pacing of these repetitions is important. For each repetition, the teacher says, "Again," points to the left of the word, and then pauses about 2 seconds before beginning the signal. Shorter pauses before beginning signaling may not give the students time to focus on the beginning of the word.

The teacher can expect more instructionally naive students to need 10 to 15 repetitions on the lead step during the first lessons when sounding out is taught. A great deal of skill is needed to give the children adequate practice and still to make the reading lesson enjoyable for the students. One way to keep lessons enjoyable is to provide a short 5 to 10-second change-up after each five or so practice trials. During the change-up, the teacher encourages the students: "You kids are working so hard.

Table 8.2   Discrimination Format—Sounding Out Words in Lists

Teacher	Students
1. Teacher states instructions. "You're going to sound out each word. After you sound out the word correctly, you'll say it fast."	
2. Teacher points to left of first word. "Sound it out. Get ready." Teacher touches under each letter (except stop sounds) for 1 to 1½ seconds. After the student sounds out the word correctly, the teacher immediately says, "What word?"	
3. Teacher repeats step 2 with remaining words written on the board.	
4. Teacher gives individual tests. Teacher calls on several students to sound out a word.	

These are really hard words and you've almost got them." When the students finally sound out all the words correctly, the teacher should act very excited and proud of the students. "You did it! I'm so proud of you. Let's clap our hands loud so everybody knows what hard workers we are."

Providing the practice students need to respond correctly to all words consecutively in the early days will result in steadily improving student performance. Not providing adequate practice will result only in minimal daily improvement.

Discrimination Format

In the discrimination format (see Table 8.2) for sounding out words in lists, the teacher tests the students on sounding out a set of words. The discrimination format replaces the introductory format when students' performance in the introductory format indicates they no longer require the teacher to lead. Specifically, after the teacher models sounding out a word in the introductory format, the students can (with generally only one or two practice trials) sound it out correctly.

Critical Behaviors

Pacing

The students should not be asked to say it "fast" (at the normal rate) until they have sounded out the word acceptably (i.e., saying each sound correctly and not pausing between sounds). The teacher should say, "Say it fast" immediately after the stu-

dents correctly sound out the word. Any pause makes translating the blended sounds into a word said at a normal rate more difficult. Likewise, in the discrimination format, the teacher should not praise after the students sounded out the word, but should hold the praise until after the students say the word at a normal rate.

Individual Turns

Remember, individual turns are given only when the students responding in unison appear to have mastered all the words. Keeping all the students in a group attentive while one student is given an individual turn is very important. The more students are attentive and actively practicing word reading, the faster they will progress.

During individual turns the teacher should tell the other students to read the words to themselves. The teacher can encourage students to read to themselves by initially using effusive praise: "Randy and Ginger are reading to themselves. They are going to be good readers because they are practicing. Let's clap for them."

Correcting Mistakes

Two common errors made during sounding out are pausing between sounds and saying a sound incorrectly. Pausing errors involve the student's stopping between sounds, which can result in the student leaving out a sound when saying the word the fast way. For example, in sounding out the CVC word *sat,* a student pauses between the first and second sounds, "sss (pause) aaat." When translating these blended sounds into a word, the student may leave off the sound preceding the pause, translating "sss (pause) aaat" into "at."

Below is the correction procedure for pausing errors. The teacher:

1. **Models.** As soon as the teacher hears the error, she says: "Don't stop between sounds. Listen to me sound out the word without stopping." (Teacher points to letters and sounds out the word.)

2. **Leads** by responding with the students. "Sound it out. Get ready." (Teacher responds with students.)

3. **Tests** by having the students sound out the word themselves. "Sound it out. Get ready."

4. **Returns** to the first word in the list and repeats all the words in the list until the students can sound out all the words consecutively without an error. (Note: If there are more than four words in a list, the teacher simply returns to a word four words earlier in the list rather than to the beginning of the list.)

5. **Individual turns.** At the completion of the list, individual turns are given to students who missed the word.

The teacher should sometimes begin the correction procedure by praising one of the students who responded correctly. "Nice job, Randy. You didn't stop between the sounds."

Teachers sometimes cause pausing errors and sound errors by not pointing long enough to each letter. If the teacher moves too quickly from one letter to the next, some students will not have time to look ahead to the next letter and, consequently, will guess or pause. If students make many of these errors, the teacher should consider whether he or she is causing the error and try pointing longer. Teachers also sometimes cause student errors by not signaling clearly. Teachers should make certain their signals are not causing student errors.

Sound errors involve the student's saying a sound that is not the most common sound of a letter. In sounding out the word *fat,* a student says the sound /ĭ/ when the teacher points to the letter *a.*

The correction for sound errors is somewhat different. In correcting a sound error, the teacher uses a limited model, which involves first modeling and testing only the sound missed rather than the entire word. For example, if the teacher points to the letters in *sip* and the student responds "sssaaa," the teacher immediately says "iiii." Next, the teacher points to *i* and asks, "What sound?" The teacher then tests students on the entire word. Below is a sample sounds correction for a student who said /ă/ for *i* in sounding out the word *sit.*

1. *Limited model.* As soon as the teacher hears the sound error, the teacher says the correct sound, "/iiiii/."

2. *Tests.* The teacher tests the whole group on the missed sound, carefully monitoring individuals who originally made the error. Teacher points to *i.* "What sound?" Teacher signals by touching *i.*

3. *Tests.* The teacher tests the whole group on sounding out the word. "Sound it out. Get ready." (Signal.)

4. The teacher returns to the first word in the list and repeats all the words until the students can correctly sound out each word in the task. (Note: If there are more than four words in the list, the teacher just goes back four words.)

5. *Individual turns.* At the completion of the list, individual turns are given to students who made errors.

A third type of error that occurs when the teacher is presenting the discrimination format involves the student saying the word incorrectly after sounding it out, usually leaving out the initial sound. For example, the student sounds out "sssaat" and when the teacher asks "What word?" the student says "at."

This type of error is usually a result of the student pausing between the first two sounds when sounding out the word (e.g., *sat* is sounded out "ssss [pause] aaaat"). The steps in the correction procedure for this type of error are:

1. The teacher says the word. "That word is *sat.*"

2. The teacher models sounding out and saying the word. "My turn. Sssăăăt. What word?" "Sat."

3. The teacher tests and leads if necessary. "Sound it out. Get ready. (Signal.) What word?" (Signal.)

4. The teacher returns to earlier word in list.

5. Individual turns.

Teachers should record the errors students made. Table 8.3 shows a simple recording form that can be used over a week's time. The names of the students in a group are written in the spaces in the left column. Across from each student's name are boxes for each day of the week. The teacher records errors the student made in the appropriate box. If a student makes an error in a letter-sound-correspondence task, the teacher writes the letter and over the letter writes the sound that the student said. In a sounding-out task, the teacher can write the word the student was reading, then write the response the student said over it.

Precorrecting

Precorrecting is a valuable technique for minimizing errors students make in a lesson. In a sounding-out precorrection, the teacher prompts the students on a letter that has caused them difficulty in earlier lessons before having them sound out a word with that letter. For example, if the students were having difficulty with *e*, the teacher would point to *e* in the word *met* before having the students sound out the word and ask, "What sound?" The teacher would then have the students sound out the word.

A possible danger with using precorrections is in using them too much, making some students dependent on them. If precorrections are overused, the students will not try to remember difficult sounds because they expect the teacher to identify them. Teachers can avoid developing dependency by precorrecting a sound only for a few lessons. Precorrections are particularly appropriate when new,

Table 8.3 Weekly Recordkeeping Form

Student	Monday	Tuesday	Wednesday	Thursday	Friday
		Weekly Recordkeeping Form			
Bill	(n) m				
Francine	(sad) sid	(t) (mit) d mid			
José					
Elwin	(i) e	(i) (lid) e led			
Marcy					

difficult letters appear in words or when a letter that has caused students difficulty appears in a word.

Introducing New Word Types

Regular words can be classified by type according to their relative difficulty to decode. The types are listed below, according to their relative difficulty—easy to difficult:

- VC and CVC that begin with continuous sounds (e.g., *at, Sam*)
- CVCC that begin with continuous sounds (e.g., *runs, lamp, fist*)
- CVC that begin with stop sounds (e.g., *hot, cap*)
- CVCC that begin with stop sounds (e.g., *cast, hand*)
- CCVC in which both of the initial consonants are continuous sounds (e.g., *slap, frog*)
- CCVC in which one of the initial sounds is a stop sound (e.g., *crib, stop*)
- CCVCC words (e.g., *brand, clump*)
- CCCVC and CCCVCC words (e.g., *split, sprint*)

Sounding-out instruction begins with VC and CVC words that start with continuous sounds. Instructionally naive students may require 20 to 30 lessons of practice with this type of word before they are able to sound out a set of these words with relative ease. Teachers often underestimate the amount of practice needed by lower performing students to become proficient in sounding out words. During these first months of instruction the students will be learning many new letter-sound correspondences. Integrating all the new correspondences when sounding out words requires a great deal of practice. The amount of practice needed will vary from student to student.

The students' performance tells the teacher when the student is ready to learn a new skill. When a student can sound out a set of four CVC words beginning with continuous sounds without error on the first trial for two consecutive days, CVCC words beginning with continuous sounds can be introduced. No special teaching procedure is required for introducing CVCC words. The teacher writes three CVCC words on the board and uses the introductory sounding-out format. This format is repeated daily until the students can sound out the three words with no more than one error during the format. Then the introductory format is dropped and CVCC words are included in the discrimination format. Half the words in the discrimination format should be CVC words while the other half should be CVCC words.

Words Beginning With Stop Sounds

CVC words beginning with stop sounds can be introduced when students master CVCC words. Remember, student performance is always the key factor that determines when something new can be introduced.

Several modifications in the teaching procedure are necessary for words that begin with a stop sound. First, the sounding-out signaling procedure has to be modified slightly. The letter for the stop sound is touched for just an instant, followed by a quick movement to the next letter, which is pointed to for slightly longer than usual, about 1½ to 2 seconds. When modeling how to sound out the word, the teacher does not pause at all between the initial stop sound and vowel. The word *can* would be modeled "caaaannnn" with no pauses. (Note: Words beginning with the stop sound /h/ often cause students particular difficulty. When words beginning with *h* are introduced, include at least three such words in a format, such as *hit, hug,* and *him,* to provide massed practice.)

During the first week when words that begin with stop sounds first appear, the teacher can use a precorrection in which she has the students say the sound of the letter following the stop sound before they sound out the word. For example, before the students sound out the word *cut,* the teacher points to *u* and asks, "What sound?" If this precorrection is used, the teacher should have the students sound out the entire word list again later without using the precorrection so that the student does not become overly dependent on the precorrection. Furthermore, the precorrection should not be used for more than one week.

CVCC words beginning with stop sounds (e.g., camp, hunt, test) can be introduced when students are able to sound out CVCC words beginning with continuous sounds and CVC words beginning with stop sounds.

Words Beginning With Blends

Words that begin with initial blends (two consecutive consonants) are introduced next. This type can be divided into words that begin with two continuous sounds (e.g., *snap, frog, sled*), and words in which one of the initial consonants is a stop sound (e.g., *stop, club, grab, spin*). There are not many regular words that begin with two continuous consonants; moreover, these words will usually not present difficulty for students. Words where one of the two initial consonants is a stop sound, such as *step* and *skin,* will require careful teaching and a great deal of practice.

In addition to providing sounding-out practice, the teacher can also present several supplementary exercises. First is the auditory-skills task in which students telescope a series of blended sounds into a word said at a normal rate. (See page 53.) This auditory exercise can be started a week or so before students begin reading words containing initial blends, then can be continued daily for about two weeks. When presenting the auditory format, the teacher includes words the students will be asked to decode within the next few days.

Precorrections can also be used when words containing blends are first introduced. The precorrection involves the teacher pointing to the letter with which students are likely to have problems. If the word contains a stop sound, the teacher points to the letter following that stop-sound letter (e.g., in *step,* the teacher would point to *e,* and in *cram, r*). If the word does not contain a stop sound, the teacher would point to the second consonant in the blend (e.g., the teacher would point to *l* in *flap* and *r* in *frog*).

Example Selection

Example selection criteria are very important. Word lists, in the discrimination format, should contain a mix of words from the various types introduced to the current day. About half the words should be of the most recently introduced type and half a mix of words from earlier types. The purpose of the mix is to buttress against students not attending carefully to the letters in a word. For example, if students read lists of words all having the letter *l* as the second letter, some students might become careless and often include the /l/ sound when sounding out a word.

Passage Reading

Passage reading refers to an activity where each student is given a story and expected to read the words orally. Sounding-out passage reading is significantly more difficult than word-list sounding out. In word-list exercises, the teacher points to the letters and the students say the sounds. In passage-reading exercises, the student must learn to coordinate independently moving from letter-to-letter and concurrently saying the sounds.

When to Introduce

Sounding-out passage reading can be introduced when students are able to sound out the words in a word-list task with relative ease. This level of mastery would be indicated by the students not making more than one error on a five-word sounding-out word-list task for two consecutive days.

As students progress through the beginning stage, the proportion of the lesson devoted to passage reading gradually increases until late in the beginning stage nearly two-thirds of decoding instruction revolves around passage reading.

Constructing Passages

During the first weeks of passage reading, the passages students read should contain only words that have previously appeared in word-list exercises. Including previously taught words will help make the transition from word-list reading to sounding-out passage reading easier.

Initially the passages should be very short, containing only two to four words. The teacher should expect to correct some students many times when passage reading is introduced. If the initial passages are too long, students may find passage reading too frustrating. The passage length should increase gradually. Passage-reading exercises, during the beginning stage, should be structured so that students are likely to attend to the letters in the words and nothing else. Consequently, picture cues should be avoided because some students will try to use them as an aid in decoding words. A student might look at the first letter in a word, then look at the picture to find an object whose name starts with that letter. For example, when reading the sentence "Tom had a rock," a student might look at a picture, then begin reading "Tim had a . . . ," and then, not knowing the /o/ sound in the next word, *rock,* refer to the picture for help in figuring out the word. If the picture shows a child holding a rock, the student is likely to use the picture as a cue for decoding the word. An effective way to avoid problems with pictures is to construct pages so that pictures appear only at the end of the passage. The students see the picture only after they read the passage.

Teaching Procedures

We recommend that students respond in unison, saying each sound as they move their fingers from letter to letter. Words to be read in early passage-reading exercises should be written large enough to allow the student to place his finger under each letter. Passages to be read during the first 5 weeks should be written with an arrow under each word. The arrows would resemble these:

(A big ball appears at the beginning of each arrow; small dots appear under each letter.) Requiring students to respond in unison and to touch each letter encourages students to apply the sounding-out strategy, fosters attentiveness and maximizes the amount of active practice students receive. Such a procedure is especially important with instructionally naive students, who tend to be very distractible. The touching procedure and unison responding also make monitoring easier, since they enable the teacher more easily to see and hear students respond. The format for sounding-out passage reading appears in Table 8.4. Note that the signaling procedure for unison responding needs to be done precisely. In a teacher-training program at the University of Oregon, numerous hours are spent in preservice, training prospective teachers to use the signaling procedure for conducting unison-response passage reading. If these procedures are not implemented correctly, they will not be productive. It would be more productive simply to call on students to read individually while other students follow along.

Critical Behaviors

Signaling

Because the students are looking at their stories and not at the teacher, the signal for unison responding must be audible. Students cannot look at the passage while simultaneously watching for the teacher's signal. The audible signal we recommend has two parts—a "get ready" and series of claps (or finger snaps). The "get ready" tells the students to prepare; the clap indicates that they are to begin the response. The critical teacher behavior in making the signal effective is a consistent 1-second pause between the "get ready" and the first clap. Consistency is necessary so that students will be able to use the "get ready" as an effective cue by expecting the clap 1 second after they hear "get ready."

During the first days of passage reading, the students may need to sound out each word several times. To ensure that repetitions are done quickly and with little confusion, the teacher must use a clear signal for instructing the students to return to the first letter of a word. The teacher can do this by saying, "Again, back to the big ball of the arrow." After giving this instruction several times, it can be abbreviated to "Again." The teacher should make certain all the students are touching the ball of the arrow before signaling the group to sound out the word another time.

Table 8.4   Format for Sounding-Out Passage Reading

Teacher	Students
1. "Everybody, touch the big ball for the first word."	Students touch ball of first arrow.
2. "We are going to sound out the words. When I clap, touch the first little dot and say the sound above it. Keep on saying it until I clap again, then move your finger and say the next sound. Don't stop between sounds."	
3. "Get ready." Teacher pauses 1 second then claps. After 1 to 1½ seconds, teacher claps for next sound. Then 1 to 1½ seconds later she claps for last sound.	Students say sounds, pointing to the dots under the letters as they say sounds.
Step 3 is repeated until the students sound out the word without an error. Then the teacher asks, "What word?"	Students say the word at a normal rate.
4. a. "Touch the big ball of the next arrow."	Students put finger on ball of next arrow.
b. "Get ready." Teacher pauses 1 second then claps. After 1 to 1½ seconds teacher claps for next sound. Then 1 to 1½ seconds later, she claps for last sound.	Students say sounds, pointing to dots under the letters as they say sounds.
c. After students sound out the word without any errors, the teacher asks, "What word?"	Students say the word at a normal rate.
5. Teacher repeats step 4 with the remaining words in the sentence.	
6. Teacher repeats steps 4 and 5 with the next sentence.	
7. Teacher gives individual turns. Several students sound out a word or two.	

Monitoring

The monitoring techniques used in sounding out passages in unison are similar to those a teacher uses in word-list exercises. As in word-list reading, the teacher watches the student's mouth and notes if the student's lip movement is appropriate for each sound. For example, if a student's lips do not come together at the end of the word *ham,* the teacher knows that the student made an error. To say the word *ham,* the lips must be pressed together for the final "mmmmm" sound. The teacher also watches the student's fingers, noting if the student is pointing to the appropriate letter.

Individual turns are also used to monitor students' performance. As a general rule, individual turns should not be given until the group has read the passage in unison with no errors. Individual turns serve as a check to see if students are actual participants in the group reading (students often become quite good at mimicking other students rather than actually reading), and to see if the teacher has provided enough practice. During individual turns, the students who are not reading should follow along, touching the letters as the reader says the sounds. Since the teacher can hear the responses of the student who is reading, he or she watches the eyes and fingers of the other students who are following along. The students who are not reading are more likely to be inattentive. To increase the probability of students being attentive, the teacher should instruct the nonreaders to whisper the sounds as they point to them.

Correcting Mistakes

Initially some students will have difficulty following the signal for shifting from letter to letter. The teacher corrects by modeling and, if necessary, by leading (physically moving the student's finger from one letter to the next). Some students may initially require 10 to 20 repetitions before they respond to the signal by touching and saying the next letter. The teacher should use the same techniques discussed in the pacing section (see page 76) to motivate students and to keep them from getting discouraged.

Students may misidentify a sound. The correction is similar to that specified in the word-list reading section. The instant the teacher hears an error, she models the correct sound, and tests by having the students sound out the word again. As the final part of the correction, the teacher has the students return to the beginning of the sentence and reread the sentence. When the students reach the missed word again (after having returned to the beginning of the sentence), they are receiving a delayed test on that word. The purpose of rereading the sentence is to demonstrate to the students that the teacher places a great importance on reading a passage accurately.

If the students miss a sound in a word near the end of a sentence, the teacher can let the students continue reading the sentence, then say, "Let's go back to the beginning of the sentence and read it again with no mistakes." Again, a good deal of teacher skill is required to help students reach a high level of performance and, at the same time, keep the lesson positive and motivating for the students. A series of videos illustrating the sounding-out procedures is available from the Association for Direct Instruction (*www.ADIhome.org*).

✤ Application Exercises

1. (For an aid in doing this exercise, see the word lists in Appendix A.)
   a. Students have been taught to read CVC words that begin with continuous sounds and know the most common sounds for these letters: *f, t, l, m, d, s, r, a, i, o.* List four words that could be included in a word-reading task.
   b. Students have been taught to read CVC words that begin with continuous and stop sounds and know the most common sounds for these letters: *f, l, m, d, t, s, r, h, i, o, a.* Assume the letter *h* has been introduced 3 days earlier. Make a list of 10 words for a word-reading task. Four of the words should include the letter *h.* Four of the words should begin with continuous sounds.

2. The teacher is presenting a word-list sounding-out format. In the following situations, specify what the teacher would do and the wording the teacher would use to correct the student's error when it occurs.
   a. When sounding out the word *mud,* student pauses after saying *m.*
   b. When sounding out the word *mud* a student says /i/ when the teacher points to *u.*

3. Assume that you have taught a group of students the following skills:
   The most common sound of these individual letters

   a i o u b c d f g h k l m n p r s t v w

   How to decode these word types: VC and CVC that begin with continuous sounds; CVC that begin with stop sounds; CVCC that end with consonant blends.

   Circle each of the following words students will not be able to decode. Next to each circled word write the abbreviation for the explanation below that tells why students cannot decode the word. These are the possible explanations:

Letter (L)—The word is regular, but a letter, the students do not know appears in the word.

Word Type (WT)—The word is a type that has not been taught.

Not Regular (NR)—The word is not regular. Some letter(s) do not represent its most common sound.

jet	_____	rag	_____	said	_____
slim	_____	hot	_____	stand	_____
big	_____	clap	_____	tag	_____
red	_____	put	_____	of	_____
last	_____	best	_____	ramp	_____
trap	_____	list	_____	stop	_____
was	_____	talk	_____	sink	_____
if	_____	Sam	_____	fit	_____

4. The words in a word-reading task are *Sam, rid, mad, it, at.* Below are four sequences of examples a teacher presented to different groups. A plus (+) indicates a correct response; a minus (−) indicates an error. (1) Tell whether each sequence represents an acceptable firm up, and (2) explain what is wrong with the unacceptable sequences. Assume all errors were word-identification errors.

    a. Sam (−) (teacher corrects) rid (−) (teacher corrects) mad (−) (teacher corrects) if (+) at (+)

    b. Sam + rid + mad + if + at +

    c. Sam + rid + mad − (teacher corrects) Sam + mad − (teacher corrects) Sam + rid + mad + it +

    d. Sam + rid − (teacher corrects) Sam + rid − (teacher corrects) mad + if + at + Sam + if + at +

5. Assume the students know the common sound of the following letters: *a, m, t, s, i, f, d, r, o, g, l, h, u, c, b, n.* The teacher has created two word lists that are unacceptable. Examine the word lists below. For each word list, indicate whether the list is *acceptable* or *unacceptable* and explain your answer.

List A	*List B*	*List C*
dug	dad	rug
run	rim	bat
hut	den	fin
fun	got	hot
hug	hug	dig

6. List these words according to their relative difficulty to sound out. Provide a brief explanation for your sequence.

    lamp, stop, bet, clamp, slam, run, best

7. The students are sounding out the sentence: "Sam sat in mud." When sounding out mud, a student says "a" for *u.* Tell all the steps in the correction procedure. Tell what the teacher says and does.

Sight-Word Reading

In sight-reading exercises, the students do not sound out words vocally, but say them at a normal rate. Sight-word reading[1] is introduced in the word-list exercises. Students initially sight-read several words they sounded out earlier in the lesson. The number of words in sight-reading exercises increases gradually until the students sight-read all of the words in a list.

Sight-reading words in passages follows the same pattern as sight-reading words in lists. Initially, students might sound out a 10-sentence story, then sight-read one of the sentences. The number of sentences a student sight-reads increases gradually until he or she can read the entire story by sight-reading.

Sight-Reading in Word Lists

Sight-reading in word lists may be introduced when students can consistently sound out a set of four

---

1. We use the term *sight-word reading* to refer to the reading of *regular* words (as well as some irregular words) without sounding out the words orally. In contrast, some beginning reading approaches use the term to refer exclusively to the reading of *irregular* words.

CVC words that begin with continuous sounds without an error.

Introducing Sight-Reading in Lists

Two formats—an introductory format and a practice format—can be used to teach sight-reading. The introductory format (see Table 9.1) is designed to teach students to sound out a word to themselves (subvocally), then say it out loud at a normal rate. This format begins with the teacher modeling how to sound out words subvocally, then say the words out loud at a normal rate. The model is followed by a step in which the teacher instructs the students to sound out words to themselves (as the teacher points to the sounds), then say the words out loud at a normal rate. This step is very important, especially for instructionally naive students. It overtly shows them what to do in sight-reading exercises. Without this step, some more passive students might not sound out words but rely on guessing. The format is presented daily until the students are able to respond correctly to all words on the first trial for two consecutive days. Then a sight-reading practice exercise where the students practice sight-reading without any teacher prompting replaces the introductory format.

Table 9.1   Format for Introducing Sight-Reading Words

Teacher	Students
Teacher writes on board: sat, mud, fit, sad.	
1. Teacher models.	
a. "You are going to read these words without saying the sounds out loud."	
b. "My turn. Watch my mouth. I'll say the sounds to myself, then I'll say the word." Teacher points to the first word, moving lips and whispering each sound as she points to each letter. After saying the sounds subvocally, she says "What word?", signals, and says the word "sat."	
c. Teacher models with one more word.	
2. Teacher tests group on all the words.	Students sound out words, whispering sounds. "Sssaaat."
a. "Your turn." Teacher points to left of first letter. "As I point to the letters, sound out this word to yourselves." Teacher loops from letter to letter touching under each continuous sound letter for about one second. "What word?" (Signal.)	Students say word at normal rate. "Sat."
b. Teacher repeats step 2(a) with remaining words in list. Teacher presents the list until students correctly identify all words.	

Practicing Sight-Reading in Lists

Table 9.2 contains the format for practicing sight-reading in word lists. In this format, the teacher tells the students to sound out the words to themselves, then say the word the fast way out loud when the signal is given. The students read the list of words at least two times. The goal of the first reading is to have students identify each word within 3 seconds. The goal of the second reading is to have students identify each word with only a 2-second pause.

Critical Behaviors

A critical teaching behavior is deciding how long a pause should be given to enable the students to figure out a word. The goal of the first reading of a list is to enable the students to respond to each word with no more than a 3-second pause before the signal. Some students may need longer than 3 seconds to sound out a word. During the first several weeks, up to 5 seconds can be allowed to let the students figure out a word. After 5 seconds, the teacher should give the signal for the students to respond, even if it appears that not all students have figured out the word. Allowing the students too much time may inadvertently reinforce student indecisiveness.

Some students take a long time to figure out a word because they start to sound it out, say 1 or 2 sounds to themselves, then stop and start over again. Allowing too long a period may inadvertently show students that this behavior is acceptable. Remember, the teacher can usually determine what a student is doing by watching the student's mouth.

If any student in the group needs more than 3 seconds to figure out a word in a list, the teacher should provide extra practice. This is done by either returning to the beginning of the list or returning four words earlier in the list, whichever is less, and representing the words. When the words are represented, the students receive extra practice. The extra practice is critical to enabling the students to develop adequate fluency.

A problem with repeating a set of words several times is that the students may memorize the words on the page according to their position. If the teacher covered all the words with his or her hand, the students could say the words. To minimize the possibility of students memorizing the position of words, the teacher can present the words in a different order each time the list is repeated.

The teacher should be certain to keep the student's motivational level high by using praise. Remember, praising students when they respond

---

Table 9.2 Practice Format for Sight-Reading Words in Lists

Teacher	Students
Teacher writes on board: sad, not, fit, am, sun, fin.	
1. "You're going to read these words the fast way. When I point to a word, sound it out to yourself. When I signal, say the word the fast way."	
2. Students read words with a 3-second pause.	
a. Teacher points to left of the first word, pauses 3 seconds, then says, "What word?", and signals.	"Sad."
b. The teacher continues the same procedure, as in step 2(a), with the remaining words.	
3. Students read entire word list again with a 2-second pause.	
a. Teacher has the students read words again with only a 2-second pause.	
4. Teacher gives individual turns.	
a. Teacher points to word, pauses 2 seconds, then calls on a student.	
b. Teacher repeats step 4(a) with remaining words.	

---

correctly is a very powerful motivator for young students. When returning to an earlier word in a list, the teacher can make a comment such as, "You certainly are working hard. Let's go back and see if we can read a little faster." Be certain to praise effusively when a student who has had difficulty finally succeeds.

Signals

The teacher points just to the left of a word, pauses to let the students figure out the word, then says, "What word?", and moves her finger using the same out-in motion described earlier for the isolated letter-sound correspondence format (see Figure 7.1).

The teacher should be watching the students when she gives the signal for the students to respond. Watching the students is critical. It enables the teacher to see if the students are attentive and helps to determine if the students made a correct response.

Individual Turns

Keeping students attentive during individual turns is a challenge for the teacher. The teacher should not call on students in a predictable order. Pacing is very important. The teacher points to a word, pauses long enough for all the students to figure out

the word, then calls on an individual student to respond. The critical behavior involves allowing enough time for *all* the students to figure out the response, *before* calling on an individual student.

The teacher can make up an activity game such as "I'm going to see if I can trick you. I'll point to a word and give you time to figure it out, then I'll call on someone. You won't know who until I call on you. Don't get tricked." The teacher should strongly praise students who answer correctly immediately when their name is called. "That was great. You are a hard-working reader."

Sometimes teachers call a student's name before pointing to a word. The problem with doing this is that once a student knows that he won't be called on, the student is much less likely to be attentive.

Correcting Mistakes

The correction procedure for misidentification errors involves: giving a limited model identifying the missed sound (e.g., if student says "fat" for *fit*, teacher points to *i* and says, "This says *i*"), having the students sound out the word vocally and say it fast, then returning to an earlier word in the list. The teacher goes back three or four words and re-presents the words. At the end of the lesson, the teacher retests students individually on any words they have missed.

Below is an example of a limited model-correction procedure. A student said "fat" for *fit*.

1. Teacher gives limited model: (Teacher points to *i*.) "This says *i*. What sound?" (Signal.) "i."

2. Teacher has students sound out word: "Let's sound out the word. Get ready." (Teacher points to left of first letter, pauses, then loops under each letter.) "What word?" (Signal.) "Fit."

3. Teacher goes back several words in the list and repeats the list. "Let's read these words perfectly."

Example Selection

The criteria for constructing word lists to be sight-read is basically the same as for selecting words for sounding-out exercises.

• Words should include only letters that students have demonstrated mastery on in letter-sound correspondence tasks.

• Words should be listed in an unpredictable order. The same letter should not appear in the same position in more than two consecutive words.

• Words of a new type should make up one-third to one-half of the list.

The word-list exercises during the beginning stage will include both sounding-out and sight-reading activities. When sight-word reading is first introduced, the introductory sight-reading format should be presented with just 3 or 4 words the students sounded out earlier in the lesson. The number of words to be sounded out increases gradually over a period of weeks until the students sight-read all the words sounded out earlier in the lesson. In future lessons, the teacher can change the pattern by gradually reducing the number of words that are sounded out. Word-list reading exercises, near the end of the beginning stage, might include 15 words. The students sound out 5 words of the newest type introduced, then sight-read all the words. Keeping sounding out alive throughout the beginning stage is important to buttress against the possibility of students adopting guessing strategies.

Table 9.3 includes a summary of the number of words that might be included in word-list exercises throughout the beginning stage. Note that the word-list exercises do *not* grow above 15 words. The reason is that during the beginning stage, most of the practice will be in the form of passage reading.

Passage Reading

Passage reading refers to activities in which students read stories. Sight-word passage reading involves the students reading a story, and saying the words at a normal rate rather than sounding them out vocally.

Introducing Sight-Word Reading

Sight-word passage reading can be introduced when students have had adequate practice with the sight-word list reading to enable them to read the words with no more than a 3-second thinking pause for each word on the first reading.

In sight-reading stories, students simply say the word after the teacher signals. They do not

Table 9.3 Relationship of Sounding Out and Sight-Reading During Beginning Reading Stage

Lesson	30	50	70	90	110
Words to be sounded out only	6	8			
Words to be sounded out, then sight-read		4	10	6	5
Words to be sight-read only				8	10

Table 9.4 Introductory Format for Passage Sight-Reading

Teacher	Students
1. Teacher says, "You're going to read the words in this story the fast way. When I signal, you'll say a word the fast way."	
2. Students read the first sentence, teacher says:	
a. "Touch the first word."	Students touch under first letter of first word.
b. "Figure out the word. Move your finger under the sounds and say the sounds to yourself." (Pause up to 3 seconds.) "Get ready." (Signal.)	Students touch letters and sound out word subvocally.
c. "Next word. Say the sounds to yourself." (Pause up to 3 seconds.) "Get ready." (Signal.)	Students say the first word. Students sound out word subvocally.
d. Teacher repeats step 2(c) with remaining words in the sentence.	Students say the next word.
e. Students are to reread the sentence if they needed more than 3 seconds to figure out any word in the sentence.	
3. Teacher repeats step 2 with remaining sentences.	
4. Teacher has individual students read a sentence.	

sound out the word vocally. To facilitate the transition from sounding-out to sight-reading passages, the teacher has the students first sound out a passage, then sight-read one or two sentences in the same passage.

A format for introducing sight-reading passages appears in Table 9.4. This format is presented for one week. In this introductory format, the teacher prompts the students to sound out each word to themselves before saying the word. We recommend unison responding to increase student attentiveness. A sentence is reread until the students are able to identify each word in the sentence with no longer than a 3-second pause.

Critical Behaviors

Signaling

When reading a passage, the students are looking at their stories, not at the teacher. The signal for students to respond in sight-word passage reading must be an auditory signal. We recommend the signal begin with the teacher saying, "Get ready," pausing for a second, then making a noise such as a clap or finger snap. The length of time between the "Get ready" and the clap should be consistent. Think of it as hitting a drum. The drummer says,

"Get ready," then lifts his or her drumstick and hits the drum.

Monitoring

The procedures for monitoring unison responding during sight-reading are the same as those used during sounding out: Listen carefully to the students' response, check whether the students are pointing to each word, and watch their lips and eyes.

The teacher should tell students always to keep their eyes on their story. Sometimes students may look up after each word. This looking up slows down the task. The teacher should praise students for keeping their eyes on the book during the entire story.

Pacing

Immediately after the students say a word correctly, the teacher should say, "Next word." The students are immediately to begin sounding out the next word to themselves. The teacher allows them time to figure out the word, then says, "Get ready," and signals. If the students respond correctly, the teacher immediately says, "Next word," then pauses several seconds to let the students figure out the word. (Teachers should allow for longer pauses for words that occur at the beginning of a new line of print, since students must move their fingers down to the next line and back to the left side of the page to locate the next word.)

Practicing Sight-Word Passage Reading

We recommend that students continue sounding out the words in stories for several weeks after sight-word passage reading is introduced. The purpose is to buttress against the possibility of students adopting a guessing strategy. Students can read half of the story sounding out words, then read the entire story by sight-reading. Table 9.5 contains a format for presenting sight-word passage reading after the first week.

The format has three parts. In part 1, the students sight-read the story a sentence at a time in unison. (The teacher no longer prompts the students to sound out the words themselves.) In part 2, the teacher writes on the board any words the students missed during the passage reading and conducts a sight-word-list reading exercise. In part 3, the teacher calls on individual students to read a sentence at a time.

Critical Behaviors
Comprehension

The teacher asks comprehension questions periodically. The comprehension questions should include literal questions such as who, where, what, and when questions, and some simple inferential questions such as, "Why were they sad?"

Adequate Practice

The teacher should provide students with adequate practice to gradually increase their reading rate. The teacher works toward increasing fluency by gradually decreasing the number of seconds allowed to figure out words when conducting sight-word-unison passage reading. During the first weeks of passage sight-reading, students repeat sentences until they are able to read all the words with no longer

---

Table 9.5   Format for Practicing Sight-Reading a Passage

Teacher	Students
Part 1: Students sight-read story in unison.	
1. Teacher says,"We're going to read the words in the story the fast way. Each time I signal, say a word the fast way."	
2. "Touch the beginning of the story." (Pause.)	Students touch.
3. "Figure out the first word." (Pause.) "Get ready." (Signal.)	Students say first word.
4. a. "Next word." (Teacher pauses while students figure out the next word.) "Get ready." (Signal.)	
b. Teacher repeats step 4(a) with remaining words in sentence.	
c. (If students need more than specified pause time for any word or make an error, the teacher has students reread the sentence.)	
5. "Touch the first word in the next sentence." (The teacher has the students read the sentences using the same procedure as in steps 3 and 4.)	
Part 2: Teacher firms up missed words.	
1. Teacher writes missed words on the board. The students sound out, then identify each word.	
2. Students sight-read the list.	
Part 3: Individual turns.	
1. Teacher calls on individual students to read a sentence at a time, asking comprehension questions.	

than a 3-second pause. This translates to an appropriate rate of 20 words per minute. Higher-performing students may require few, if any, rereadings to read at this rate. Lower-performing students, however, may require numerous repetitions. When the students are able to read at the rate of 20 words per minute without the need of rereading, the teacher can decrease the pause time to about 2 to 2½ seconds (a rate of about 25–30 words per minute). This rate in turn can be increased later by decreasing the pause time to 1½ seconds between words. Teachers working with lower-performing students may note that students need repetitions on virtually every sentence before they are able to read at the specified rate. We strongly recommend scheduling another 15 to 20-minute reading period later in the day for such students. This practice is necessary to enable the students to develop adequate fluency. Without the extra practice, the students will fall behind their peers. The importance of providing extra practice for students during 1st grade cannot be emphasized too much. Beginning in 2nd grade, an increasing proportion of school activities (e.g., social studies, science, etc.) are conducted with the whole class. Students who read too slowly may not be able to keep up. Not only may they be subjected to frustration, but they will not be able to benefit from the practice other students receive during these activities.

Motivation

The teaching procedures call for students to reread a sentence if a word is missed or if the students have taken too long to figure out a word. Providing such practice is necessary for students to read a passage fluently and accurately. However, teachers must be prepared to use a combination of techniques to keep students from viewing reading as a dull, repetitive task.

One important technique teachers can use is making the rereading a challenge. If students need to reread a sentence, the teacher challenges them to read better. For example, the teacher might say, "Let's read this sentence again. You did pretty well.

I bet you'll do it perfectly this time." The teacher rewards the students when they meet the challenge. Phrasing the challenge positively is important, since it contributes to a positive attitude toward reading. For students who require several rereadings before reading a sentence acceptably, physical rewards, such as handshakes, should be given as well as verbal praise. When rewarding students, the teacher comments on their persistence, saying, for example, "Good reading. You worked hard and didn't give up. You worked till you got it right. I'm proud of you." In addition to using challenges and rewards, teachers can keep rereading from being boring by inserting short breaks after each 5 to 10 minutes of reading. During the break, the teacher can conduct an enjoyable game such as "Simon Says" for about 30 seconds. Remember, that the teacher's most powerful motivation tool is praising students who perform in a desired manner. Praise should always be stated specifically so it's clear to the other students what behaviors the teacher considers important.

Signaling and Pacing in Individual Reading

No signals are necessary during individual reading since the students are not responding in unison. However, to encourage attentiveness, students who are not reading aloud should point to each word as it is read.

The teacher calls on students in an unpredictable order. If students can predict when they will be called on to read, some are likely not to attend until it is almost their turn. Others may look ahead to find "their" sentence and practice it. Sometimes inattentive students should be called on to read again after only one other student has read. This indicates to students that, even though they may have just finished a sentence, they cannot become inattentive because they might be called upon again soon. Students should read only one or two sentences in a row, since the longer one student reads, the greater the probability some other students will become inattentive. The more inattentive the students in a group, the fewer the number of consecutive sentences any one student should read.

Students should be instructed to stop at periods in order to read in more meaningful units. The pause also enables the teacher to call on a new student to read. The teacher calls on the new student immediately after one student says the last word of a sentence. This quick pace enhances student attentiveness and maintains story continuity.

During individual turns, some students will read in a very quiet voice, making it difficult for other students to follow along. Imploring or nagging a student to read louder will not usually change the student's behavior. Providing strong reinforcement for students who do speak in an acceptably loud voice will often be effective in eliciting louder responses from a student who is reading too quietly. The reinforcement can be in the form of praise after a student reads, such as "Great job, Erika. You read with a big voice," or the teacher can reward the student with a tangible reinforcer (e.g., stickers) at the end of the group session for reading in a "big" voice.

Correcting Errors

During unison reading the teacher should make a correction if any student says the wrong word. The correction procedure for misread words during sight–passage reading in the beginning stage is to (1) stop the students; (2) instruct the group or individual to sound out the word, then say it at a normal rate; and (3) direct the students to return to the beginning of the sentence and reread the sentence. For example, if during unison reading the students are reading "A cat went in it," and the teacher hears a student say "was" for *went,* the teacher should say "Everybody, let's sound out the word. Put your finger on the first sound. Get ready." (Signal.) After the students sound out the word correctly, the teacher tells the students to return to the beginning of the sentence and has the student reread the sentence.

The words missed during passage reading should be included in the part 2 firm-up and in the next lesson's word-list exercise.

A second type of error that might occur during unison sight-passage reading is the signal error. A student does not respond when the signal is given, either responding an instant after the rest of the group or not at all. The correction procedure for this type of error is the same as for the wrong-word error. The teacher has the students sound out the word, then return to the beginning of the sentence. A teacher must be very careful in handling signal errors. If several students in a group make signal errors, a high probability exists that the teacher is not allowing students adequate time to figure out the word. In such cases, the teacher should increase the amount of time she gives students to figure out words before signaling.

During the first week of unison sight–passage reading, the teacher should make it clear through praise that she wants the students to respond on her signal. She can do this by having the students read the first sentence of a story, continuing to the end of the sentence even if some students make signal errors then effusively praising the students who read on signal: "Mary read great. She said every word when I signaled. Let's clap for Mary." The teacher then challenges the students and repeats the sentence. "I wonder if you can all answer as well as Mary did. This is difficult stuff." The teacher repeats the sentence until all students are responding on signal. Thereafter, the teacher challenges the students: "Let's see if I can trick you on the rest of the story. Let's see if you can answer correctly on signal every time." As a general rule, any signal errors thereafter should be handled by having the group sound out the word, then returning to the beginning of the sentence. To keep the instructional setting positive, the teacher should be very encouraging: "That was a tough word. Let's sound it out . . . Now let's go back to the beginning of the sentence. I bet that word won't trick us again."

Finding the Beginning of a Sentence

A critical part of the story-reading correction procedure is to have the students immediately reread a sentence in which they made an error. After telling the students to sound out the missed word, the teacher instructs the students to go back to the first word in the sentence.

A great deal of time can be saved if the students are able to find the first word of the sentence quickly. A format for teaching this skill appears in Table 9.6. This format should be presented early in the school year. The format has four parts. In part 1,

the teacher holds up a story and models how to find the end of a sentence. In part 2, the teacher has the students go through the story, finding the end of each sentence. During this part, the teacher must monitor the students carefully to make certain they move their fingers word-by-word until they get to the period. Part 2 is presented daily until the students are able to find the end of sentences in a story without making any errors.

Table 9.6 Format for Finding First Word of Sentence

Teacher	Students
Part 1: Teacher models finding end of sentences.	
1. Teacher holds up a story that is at least 4 sentences long.	
2. "You can tell where a sentence ends by looking for a little dot, called a period."	
3. (Teacher points to first word in the story.) "This is where the first sentence begins. I'll move my finger and stop at the period."	
4. (Teacher moves finger from word to word and stops at the period.) "This period tells us that this is the end of the first sentence."	
5. "I'll move my finger from word to word; say 'period' when I get to the next period." (Teacher moves finger from word to word, pointing at the space between each word for an instant.)	
6. Teacher repeats step 5 with remaining sentences.	
Part 2: Teacher tests finding end of sentences.	
1. "Put your finger on the first word of the story."	
2. "Move your finger from word to word. Stop when you get to the period at the end of the sentence."	
3. Teacher repeats step 2 with remaining sentences.	
4. Teacher repeats steps 1 through 3 if students had any difficulty.	
Part 3: Teacher models finding beginning of sentences.	
1. "I'll show you how to find the beginning of a sentence."	
2. (Teacher holds up a story and points to the period at the end of the last sentence in the story.) "Here's the end of the last sentence in the story."	
3. "Watch me find the beginning of that sentence." (Teacher moves finger from word to word until she reaches the preceding period.) "Here's the period." (Teacher points to word after period.) "This is the first word of that sentence."	
4. "Now I'll find the first word of this sentence." (Teacher points to preceding sentence, moves from word to word, and stops just before period.)	
Part 4: Students practice finding the beginning of sentences.	
1. "Look at your stories."	
2. "Touch the period at the end of the story."	
3. "Move your finger back until you come to the first word of that sentence."	
4. (Teacher points to last word of preceding sentence.) "Move your finger back until you come to the first word of this sentence."	
5. Repeat step 4 with remaining sentences.	

Parts 3 and 4 teach the students how to go back and find the first word in a sentence. In part 3, the teacher models. The teacher holds up a copy of the story and models how to return to the beginning of sentences. In part 4, the students practice finding the beginning of sentences.

Individual Checkouts for Rate and Accuracy

We recommend that students be tested weekly on reading an entire passage. The individual checkouts begin when the students are sight-reading passages about 40 words in length. The teacher would put in some type of motivator to ensure that students really try (e.g., "If you can read this whole passage in less than 2 minutes with three or fewer errors, you'll get two stars on the chart next to your name. If you have trouble, I'll let you practice by yourself and you can try again, for one star."). The individual checkouts will provide valuable information to the teacher. The checkouts will show if the student is receiving adequate practice in developing rate and accuracy. The students should read a story that is of equal length to the stories currently being read. The teacher times the student and records any errors the student made.

Table 9.7 shows a chart that can be used to record student performance over a period of several weeks. The teacher records the time it took each student to read the passage and the words the student missed. This data, along with the data on student performance during daily lessons, will help teachers diagnose and remediate errors.

Diagnosis and Remediation

A student's performance on individual checkouts will often indicate the need for remediation procedures, either in regard to specific skills or fluency. Teachers should record daily errors on a form like that shown earlier in Table 8.3. Teachers should also use the student's performance on individual checkouts, story reading, and word-list exercises to look for error patterns. Error patterns may indicate

that a student needs extra practice on a previously taught component skill or that a teacher is making an error in the way he or she is presenting a format. A teacher error is indicated if several students in a group are making the same type of mistakes. For example, if several students are responding late during unison reading, the teacher may not be providing adequate time to figure out a word before signaling; thus, the teacher should alter his or her presentation to provide students with a longer thinking pause.

The type of error patterns teachers should look for in word-reading tasks are specific letter-sound correspondence errors, word-type errors, fluency errors, and random-guessing errors.

Letter-Sound Correspondence Errors

A specific letter-sound correspondence error is indicated when students mispronounce the same letter in several words. For example, a student says "mat" for *mit*, "hum" for *him*, and "ten" for *tin*. The student's performance seems to indicate that the student does not know the most common sound for the letter *i*. The teacher should test the student individually by asking the student to say the sound for *i*. If the student does not know the sound, the letter-sound correspondence should be reintroduced in the next lesson. The teacher presents the letter in an introductory format, then stresses it in a letter-sound-discrimination format for several days. During the days the letter is being reintroduced, the teacher precorrects words containing that letter. In the precorrection, the teacher tells the students the letter's sound before asking them to read words that contain the letter.

After several days, the teacher presents an introductory word list of 3 to 5 words, all containing that particular letter. This list is followed by a discrimination list of 8 to 10 words in which about half of them include the letter students had missed.

Word-Type Errors

A word-type error is indicated when a student misses several words of a particular type. For ex-

Table 9.7   Record Form—Individual Checkouts

Student	Lesson		Lesson		Lesson	
Name	Time	Errors	Time	Errors	Time	Errors

ample, a student says "lam" for *lamp* and "ben" for *bent.* On both words, the student left off the second consonant of a final consonant blend in a CVCC word. To remediate a word-type error, a teacher presents daily word-list reading exercises focusing on that particular word type. The teacher first presents an introductory list of four words, all of which are of that particular type. (For example, if students had difficulty with CVCC words, the teacher might include the words *lamp, sink, bust,* and *bent,* all of which are CVCC words.) Next the teacher presents a discrimination list of about eight words. Half the words should be of that particular type. The other half should be from easier types and provide dis-

crimination practice. A list focusing on CVCC words might include these words: *sand, tan, bust, bus, bent, can, lamp,* and *men.*

Fluency Errors

If a student reads much more slowly than the rest of the group, he or she should either be provided with extra practice or be placed in a lower group. The extra practice can be done on isolated letter-sound correspondences, word-list reading, and passage reading. Sometimes late responding is caused by a student's lack of ability to say the sounds for letters at a rapid enough rate to sound out words quickly.

As a check, the teacher can ask the student to produce the sounds of all letters introduced to date. The teacher then notes the letters the student was unable to recognize instantly and provides practice on them. In addition to extra practice, the teacher can also use a slightly longer thinking pause on word-reading tasks so that the student does not develop a habit of copying the responses of higher-performing students.

Random-Guessing Errors

A random-error pattern is indicated when a student is making errors on more than 10% of the words in exercises, and the errors do not involve a specific letter or word-type pattern. Random-error patterns often simply result from the student's not examining a word carefully. The student might just look at several letters and say any word that contains those letters. Sometimes this guessing is caused by a student not being able to respond at the rate the teacher is signaling. If so, practice should be provided and a longer thinking pause used during group reading. If the student is able to read at the rate the group is reading, the remedy lies in increasing the student's motivation to read accurately. (See Chapter 18 for a discussion on motivational techniques.)

❧ Application Exercises

1. A teacher is having a group of students sight-read the following sentence in unison: "Sam had a big cast." Several students say "cat" when the teacher signals for "cast." Specify all the steps the teacher takes to correct this error. Tell what the teacher says and does.

2. Assume that you have taught a group of students the following skills: Letter-sound relationships:

   a, i, o, u, b, c, d, f, g, h, l, n, m, p, r, s, t, w

   How to decode these word types: VC, CVC, and CVCC words that begin with either continuous or stop sounds:

   a. Circle each of the following words the students will not be able to decode. Next to each of those words write the letters for the explanation below that tells why the student can not decode the word:

   Letter (L)— A letter the students do not know appears in the word.

   Word Type (WT)—The word type has not been taught.

   Not regular (NR)—The word is not regular; a letter(s) does not represent its most common sound.

cop	_____	tin	_____	spot	_____	drug	_____
said	_____	test	_____	mad	_____	kept	_____
last	_____	bust	_____	sip	_____	sand	_____
gram	_____	was	_____	can't	_____	Stan	_____
must	_____	gin	_____	don't	_____	big	_____
had	_____						

   b. The errors for each of the two students below are listed. For each student (1) diagnose the problem, (2) specify whether an isolated letter-sounds task is called for, and (3) construct an introductory word list and a discrimination word list to remediate the problem. Be certain to include only letters the students have been taught.

   Student A
   Errors: The word was *tin,* student said "tun."

   The word was *sit,* student said "sat."

Diagnosis: _____

Sound tasks: yes _____ no _____

Examples for introductory list _____

Examples for discrimination list _____

Student B

Errors: The word was *land,* student said "lad."

       The word was *first,* student said "fit."

Diagnosis: _____

Sound tasks: yes _____ no _____

Examples for introductory list _____

Examples for discrimination list _____

c. Below are three word lists a teacher constructed for a practice exercise. Two are unacceptable. Tell why.

List A	List B	List C
bunt	hunt	bent
mint	win	win
hunt	sand	rust
pant	past	sand
lint	wig	will
	till	top

3. A teacher is presenting a practice sight-reading word-list exercise with these words: rag, must, sink, fun, fin. The goal of the exercise is for students to identify each word with no longer than a 2-second think pause. When the students come to the word "sink," several students need 4 seconds to figure out the word. Tell what the teacher is to do.

4. In a practice sight-word-list reading exercise, a student says "ham" when the teacher signals for the students to respond to "him." Tell what the teacher says and does to correct this error.

Irregular Words

Irregular words are words that a student cannot read by applying the letter-sound correspondence knowledge that the student has learned in the reading program. For example, the word "was" is irregular because the letters *a* and *s* both do not represent the sound typically associated with the particular letters.

In designing a reading program, the teacher needs to be aware that words that are irregular at one point in a reading program may not be irregular at a later point in the reading program. For example, the word *park* would be irregular early in a reading program when the students have only been taught to associate the letter *a* with the short-a sound. In the word *park,* the letter *a* does not represent the short-a sound. Later in the program, students will be taught the letter correspondence for the letter combination *ar.* The letter combination *ar* is highly consistent in representing the *r* controlled vowel sound heard in words like *park, hard,* and *start.* Once students learn the *ar* sound, the word *park* would no longer be considered an irregular word.

Some words will always be considered irregular because they contain letter-sound correspondences unique to that word or a few words. Examples of this

type of irregular word include *was, they, said,* and *break.* In these words, one or more letters represent a sound that is not common for that particular letter. The term *sight words* is sometimes used to refer to irregular words.

The manner in which irregular words are introduced in a reading program can be an important factor in determining if students develop confusions regarding how to apply word attack strategies. This chapter will present suggestions for introducing irregular words when using a program that uses a systematic and explicit phonics approach.

When to Introduce

Learning to decode irregular words is an important step for beginning readers because a new strategy is involved. The reader cannot simply sound out a word, then translate the blended sounds into a word. For example, *was* is sounded out as "wwwăăăsss" but is pronounced "wuz."

For teachers working with instructionally naive children, we recommend delaying the introduction of irregular words until students can read regular CVC words in a list at a rate of about a word every 3 seconds. This rate, though quite slow in terms of the advanced reader, is adequate at the beginning stage to indicate student mastery of the sounding-out skill. The reason for delaying the introduction of irregular words is to make initial reading instruction easier for the students by simply letting them concentrate on the mechanics of sounding out regular words.

Because of the complexity of decoding irregular words, students need a great deal of practice to master each individual word. Therefore, the introduction of the first several irregular words should be carefully spaced out—1 every 4 to 6 lessons. The next 10 or so irregular words can be introduced at a somewhat faster rate of about 1 new word every 3 lessons. The students' performance, of course, is the key determinant of how quickly new irregular words can be introduced. During the introduction of the first 10 irregular words, a new irregular word should not be presented if students miss any previously introduced irregular words in word-list reading or in passage reading.

After several weeks, a teacher can introduce a new irregular word even if a student is having difficulty with a previously introduced irregular word. However, the new word should not be similar to the word the student is having difficulty with. For example, a teacher would not introduce the word *where* if students are having difficulty with *were,* but could introduce *where* if students are having difficulty with *said.* If students are having difficulty with more than one previously introduced word, no new words should be introduced.

Sequence

If a teacher is using a commercial program, the words in upcoming passages will dictate the order that irregular words are introduced. The teacher will introduce irregular words according to the order they appear in the program.

If a teacher is constructing a program, the following factors should be considered when making a sequence: frequency, similarity, type of irregularity, and presence of related words.

Frequency

As a general rule, words that appear more often in children's literature should be introduced before words that appear less often. The sequence of words is not particularly critical as long as the general rule is followed. Appendix B contains a list of 400 high-frequency words.

Similarity

Some irregular words are very similar to other irregular words (e.g., saw–was, of–off, were–where). The introduction of these pairs should be planned so that one of the two words is introduced at least 15 lessons before the other. The separation allows students to master the first word before encountering the second and, thus, decreases the probability of the students confusing them.

Type of Irregularity

As the students progress through a reading program, they will begin to learn the letter-sound correspondences for letter combinations (e.g., *ar* in shark, *ea* in seat; a list of common letter combinations appears in Table 15.1) and patterns of letters such as the VCe pattern which produces a long vowel sound, as in *hate, like,* and *note.*

As a general rule, words that contain a VCe pattern in which the vowel is long and words containing a letter combination representing its common sound should not be presented as irregular words during the beginning stage, with the exception of very common words such as *name* and *told.* The reason is that later in the program students will learn generalizable strategies that allow them to decode these words. Spending time in the beginning stage teaching a word as an individual word is not efficient if soon thereafter the students learn a strategy which allows them to decode a wide range of words, one of which is that word.

Related Words

Some irregular words will be related because they have the same letter-sound correspondences. Examples of some common related irregular words appear below:

walk	none	some	other
talk	done	come	mother
chalk			brother
give	to	any	most
live	do	many	post
			ghost

As a general rule, related words should be taught one after another or introduced together.

Teaching Procedure

The teaching procedure to use when introducing irregular words should (1) require the student to examine all the letters in a word and (2) point out to students the irregularity in one or more of the letter-sound correspondences.

The strategy we recommend for introducing the first 10 to 20 irregular words involves the teacher alerting the children that the word is a "funny" word, then having the student sound out the word as it is written, saying the sound they have been taught for each letter, then translating that series of sounds into the correct pronunciation. *Was* is sounded out as "wăăăsss," but is pronounced "wuz." The word *walk* is sounded out as "wwwăăălllk," but is said "wauk." Even though this procedure is somewhat cumbersome, it has several advantages. First, it increases the probability that students will carefully continue to attend to all the letters in the word in a left to right progression. It shows students that the same basic strategy (i.e., to start with the first letter, say the sound, then blend the sounds for the remaining letters in left to right sequence, one sound for one letter) can be used to decode all words, even though some are pronounced differently from what the blended sounds indicate. Without this demonstration, some students may develop the misrule that since sounding out does not work on some words, it will no longer work on many words. Second, it prepares students for later spelling exercises by demonstrating that students cannot rely solely on how a word sounds to spell words.

Table 10.1 contains the format for introducing irregular words with this sounding out strategy. The format starts with a model: The teacher says the irregular word, then sounds it out saying the most common sound for each letter, then says it again as a meaningful word. The teacher then tests the students, asking them to say the word, sound it out, then say the word again as it is pronounced.

Table 10.1   Introductory Format for Irregular Words

Teacher	Students
1. Teacher tells students a new word, then sounds it out. Teacher points to *was.*	
"Everybody, this is a funny word. The word is 'was.' What word?" (Signal.)	"Was."
"Listen to me sound out the word." Teacher touches each letter. "Wwwwăăăsss. That's how we sound out the word. But here's how we say it: *was.* How do we say it?" (Teacher touches word.)	"Was."
"Yes, *was.*"	
2. Teacher has students sound out the word and then say it. Teacher points to the left of *was.* "Now you are going to sound out *was.* Get ready." Teacher touches under each letter for about a second.	"Wwwwăăăsss."
"But how do we say the word?" (Signal.)	"Was."
"Remember, how do we say the word?" (Signal.)	"Was."
3. Teacher gives individual turns on step 2.	

Critical Behaviors

Demonstrating

The teacher must clearly demonstrate that the irregular word is pronounced differently than it is sounded out. When sounding out the word, the teacher must say the most common sounds. To keep students from making errors when sounding out a word, the teacher can point to a letter in the word that is pronounced differently from its most common sound, and ask the students "What sound?" before having the students sound out the word.

Correcting Mistakes in Introductory Format

Students make two types of errors in step 2 of the introductory format: (1) when sounding out the word, they may say the sounds for how the word is pronounced, rather than the most common sound for each letter (e.g., when sounding out the word *was,* the students say /ŭ/ instead of /ǎ/ for *a*); and (2) after sounding out the word, they may say the word as it is sounded out, rather than as it is said (e.g., after sounding out the letters in *was* as "wwwǎǎǎsss," the student says "wǎs" instead of "wuz").

The correction procedure for both errors is (1) to model by repeating the task and saying the correct answer; (2) to test by returning to the beginning of step 2; and (3) to retest by repeating the format later in the lesson. For example:

- Error. Student says /ŭ/ when sounding out the word *was.*
  Teacher models.
  My turn to sound out *was.* Listen:
  Wwwǎǎǎsss.
  Teacher tests.
  Sound out *was.* Get ready. (Signal.)
  "Wwwǎǎǎss."
  How do we say the word? (Signal.) "Was."
  Later in the lesson the teacher repeats the format.

- Error. After sounding out *of,* student responds "off" when the teacher asks, What word?

Teacher models.
We say *of.*
What word? (Signal.) "Of."
Teacher tests sounding out and saying word.
Sound out *of.* Get ready. (Signal.) "ŏŏŏfff."
How do we say the word? (Signal.) "Of."
Later in the lesson, the teacher repeats the format.

Modified Introductory Format

A procedure for introducing irregular words after the first 10 to 20 words have been presented involves the teacher telling the students the word, then having the students repeat the word, spell it by letter names, and say the word again:

1. This word is *giant.* What word? (Signal.)"Giant."

2. Spell *giant.* (Signal.)"G-i-a-n-t."

3. What word did you spell? (Signal.)"Giant."

4. Yes, *giant.*

The purpose of having students spell words is to ensure they attend to the letters in the word. Spelling replaces sounding out because spelling the word allows for a faster-paced presentation. Obviously, this format would not be introduced until the students know the names of all letters.

Facilitating Retention

Students will require considerable exposure to a word before they can be expected to recognize it on sight. New words should be systematically introduced and practiced.

A new irregular word should be presented daily for 3 to 4 days using one of the introductory formats. On the 3rd day, the new irregular word is incorporated into a practice sight word-list exercise along with regular words and previously introduced irregular words. The new irregular word appears daily in the word-list exercise until the students are able to identify it correctly for two consecutive days. Then the new irregular word is incorporated into stories to be read in passage-reading exercises; the new word appears at least every 2nd day for several more weeks in either a word-list or passage-reading exercise.

Correcting Mistakes in Word-Reading Exercises

When the teacher asks students to identify an irregular word in a word reading exercise, students may make two types of misidentification mistakes: (1) saying the word as it is sounded out (saying "wăs" instead of "wuz"), or (2) saying a different word (saying "saw" instead of "wuz"). The correction procedure for either errors is the same:

1. The teacher tells students the word and asks them to repeat it. "This word is *was*. What word?"

2. The teacher has students sound out the word or say its letter names, depending on what procedure was used to introduce the word.

3. The teacher asks how the word is pronounced. "How do we say that word?" or "What word?"

4. The teacher backs up four words in the list and has the students reread that part of the list.

5. Later in the lesson, the teacher retests by calling on the student who missed the word to identify it.

If a previously introduced irregular word is missed more than once, it should be reintroduced in the next lesson and stressed in the word-list exercise for several days. For example, if students had trouble with the word *put* in Monday's lesson, the teacher should reintroduce *put* in an introductory format on Tuesday and include it in sight-word-list exercises daily until the students correctly identify the word for 2 consecutive days on the first trial.

The teacher can incorporate a more powerful correction technique into a word-list exercise by using an alternating pattern: The teacher presents the missed irregular word, one of the other words, and then returns to the missed word. She returns to the missed word several times during the task, but each time only after having presented more review words. For example, if the irregular word *said* is in a word list with *was, the, walk,* and *lamp,* and the student misread *said,* the teacher could present the words in this order: *said, was, said, walk, the, said, walk, the, lamp, said.* Note that more words appear between each successive presentation of *said.* The teacher keeps alternating between the missed word and review words until the student is able to identify the new irregular word correctly three times.

✎ Application Exercises

1. Assume that you have taught a group of students the following skills: The most common sound for all single letters except *e, b, q, w, x, y,* and *z.* How to decode these word types: VC, CVC, CVCC, and CCVC words that begin with continuous or stop sounds.

   a. Circle each of the following words the students will not be able to decode. Next to each of those words, write the abbreviation for the explanation below that tells why the student cannot decode the word.

   Letter (L)—The word is regular, but contains a letter that the students do not know.

   Word Type (WT)—The word is a type that has not been taught.

Irregular (I)—The word is irregular.

fled ____	list ____	you ____	nest ____	hot ____
clap ____	stamp ____	slam ____	rump ____	slug ____
push ____	bet ____	was ____	son ____	stink ____
led ____	stop ____	tint ____	spot ____	bent ____
cut ____	said ____	snag ____	free ____	home ____

b. A teacher circled the errors students made when reading stories. The word above the circled word is what the student said. Your assignment is to first diagnose what skill the student needs help with, then to specify what the teacher would include in the remediation exercise. Remember if a student has difficulty with a particular letter, include isolated-sounds practice and a group of introductory and discrimination words. If the problem is with a word type, only introductory and discrimination words are called for. Be specific. List the examples you would include in the tasks. Be certain to include only letters students have been taught.

Student 1   fat   sap
Dan had a (flat) hat with a (snap).

Student 2   cot   dad
Tim's hand had a (cut) on it. His mom did act fast. His mom is not a (dud).

Student 3 fat   lip
Tam has a (fast) cat. It has a (limp).

Student 4

This student missed no words; however, he read quite slowly when given an individual turn. What should the teacher do?

2. This exercise introduces letter combinations (two or more letters which usually represent the same sound(s) in a significant number of words). Although letter combinations will not be discussed until later in the book (Chapter 15), we include them now so the reader may receive adequate practice to develop fluency in recognizing and pronouncing them. Assume the students know the most common sound of all single letters and these letter combinations: *th, sh, ch, ck, ar, ee, ea,* and *or.* Circle any letter or letter combination the students will not be able to decode, which means the word itself is probably not decodable. For example, the *ar* in warm would be circled because it does not represent its most common sound (see list of letter combinations in Table 15.1).

charm	east
par	sea
warm	head
shark	porch
need	worm
been	corn
peek	world
dead	short
weak	chef

3. A teacher is presenting the introductory format for irregular words. In step 2, the teacher has the student sound out "w˘as," then asks how the word is pronounced. Some students say "wăs," pronouncing the word phonetically. Specify what the teacher says and does in correcting.

4. Put a check next to each of the six irregular words below that would not warrant frequent review during the first year of decoding instruction.

knob	was	scent
your	scenic	see
said	good	route
any	of	talk
pry	scarce	they

5. The teacher is presenting a discrimination sight-reading format which includes the words *flag, must, said, him, slip,* and *was.* A student says "sad" for *said.* Specify what the teacher would do and the wording the teacher would use to correct the student's error when it occurs, then tell what the teacher would do after making the correction.

Vocabulary and Language Skills
Beginning Stage

During the beginning stage, vocabulary, language, and comprehension tasks can be presented orally. During this stage, students will be able to read only a small fraction of the words in their receptive and expressive vocabularies. Oral instruction makes it possible to teach a much wider range of concepts than if the teacher limits the instruction to the words students are taught to decode.

The scope of skills presented depends on the student's language skills. Many at-risk students do not enter school with adequate vocabulary and sufficient language skills. They do not understand the meaning of many words commonly used in directions given by teachers (for example, find the letter *under* the *last* car, touch the *narrow stripe* in the first column, find the letter in the *lower right-hand corner*). For these students, instruction in basic vocabulary and oral language is needed to succeed in reading instruction. For students who enter school with basic language skills, instruction can begin with more advanced concepts such as inferences and reasoning skills.

A screening assessment should be administered to all at-risk children upon entering kindergarten. A sample screening assessment appears in Chapter 12. Children who have poor language skills should re-ceive at least 30 minutes daily small-group direct instruction in vocabulary, language, and comprehension skills. This is additional time beyond the 30- to 35-minute block devoted for decoding.

Vocabulary Teaching

The procedures for teaching vocabulary are critical for teachers working with instructionally naive students. Teaching vocabulary to average and above-average students is relatively easy because these students have a good understanding of language and a sizeable vocabulary. Instructionally naive kindergartners, on the other hand, do not know many common words, have difficulty repeating statements of more than four or five words, and are confused by unclear demonstrations.

Vocabulary can be taught orally by the use of modeling, synonyms, and definitions. Modeling is used when verbal explanations of a new word include words students do not understand. For example, when teaching the preposition *over,* the teacher cannot explain why something is *over* without using the term *over* or a synonym for *over* such as above. Modeling is used primarily to teach the word labels for common objects, actions, and attributes.

Synonyms are used when a student knows a word(s) that can explain the meaning of a new, unknown word. For example, a student knows the word *over* but does not know *above*. Instead of introducing *above* through modeling examples, the teacher tells the students that *above* means *over* and then tests the students to make sure that they understand the synonym. Similarly, if a student knows the meaning of *wet,* the teacher can use a *little wet* to explain the meaning of *damp.* (Note: Initial synonyms do not have to be precise. They must, however, be designed to give students an approximate meaning that can be refined as they encounter the word in later reading.)

Definitions are used when students have adequate language to understand a longer explanation and when the concept is too complicated to be explained through a synonym. The teacher constructs a definition by specifying a small class to which a new word belongs and then by telling how the word differs from other members of the class. For example, a simple definition of *service station* might be "a place where gasoline is sold and cars are repaired." Service station is in the class of *places*. It differs from other places because gas is sold and cars are repaired there. After a definition is given, examples are presented to test the students' understanding of the definition.

Example Selection

The most important aspect of teaching vocabulary, regardless of the procedure used, is selecting a set of appropriate examples. A set of examples is appropriate only if it demonstrates the teacher's intended meaning. A set of examples may be inappropriate if the student can learn an interpretation other than the intended one. For example, a thick pen and a thick pencil are presented as examples of *thick*. Since both of these objects are writing tools, some students might interpret *thick* as having something to do with writing rather than with size.

Learning a vocabulary word implies applying the word correctly to a set of examples. When a baby first learns the word *dog,* the baby may think that the word *dog* refers solely to the dog in his

house. Through further experience, the child learns to expand his definition of *dog* to a whole set of dogs, many with different appearances. For learning to take place in the classroom, a teacher must provide enough positive examples of a new word so the student can respond to a full range of possibilities.

Selecting examples that show the range of *positive examples* is the first step in constructing a set of examples. To teach the class the word *container,* the positive examples might be a garbage can, a cardboard box, a drawer, and a glass vase. Having this wide variety of positive examples rules out the possibility of the student misconstruing the concept of container as being something square or something made of metal. The examples also set a base for fostering generalization to things not presented in the lesson (e.g., a plastic can or metal box). When teaching the preposition *over* (as in "the pencil is over the table"), the pencil should not just be presented above the center of the table, since young children might think that *over* has something to do with "in the middle" or a height of about 1 foot. To illustrate the full range of possibilities, the teacher presents the pencil in many different positions by holding it an inch or two above the table, then several feet above it, and then over the table's left and right side.

In addition to positive examples, an appropriate set of examples should also include *negative examples.* Negative examples rule out incorrect generalizations. For example, in teaching the concept *pet,* if only positive examples of *pet* were presented (dog, cat, goldfish, canary), some students might generalize that all animals are pets. In presenting the term *vehicle,* some positive examples might include an airplane, truck, boat, train; negative examples might include a kite and a buoy. When possible, negative and positive examples, which are exactly alike except for the presence or absence of the new concept, should be presented. The positive and negative examples form a pair. Each pair of examples can be referred to as a *minimally different pair.* Minimally different pairs focus student attention on the characteristics that determine whether an example is positive. The advantage of using minimally different pairs is illustrated in the following examples for teaching the color *orange.* A teacher might use these minimally different pairs of objects for teaching *orange:*

1. Two identical shirts, except that one is orange and one is red.
2. Two identical pieces of paper, except that one is orange and one is blue.
3. Two identical plastic disks, except that one is orange and one is brown.
4. Two identical crayons, except that one is orange and one is green.

By varying just the color in each pair of objects, the teacher demonstrates the critical characteristics. Misinterpretations that orange has something to do with shape, texture, or size are ruled out. Likewise, any confusion between *orange* and *red* is ruled out by including *red* as a negative example.

Teaching Procedure for Modeling

Modeling is used when it is impossible to use language to explain the meaning of a word. Modeling is used primarily to teach concepts like color, size, and shape covered in preschool and kindergarten. Modeling's basic procedure involves three steps: (1) modeling positive and negative examples of the new concept, (2) testing the students on their mastery of the examples for the new word, and (3) presenting different examples of the new word, along with examples of other previously taught words. As in decoding, review should be cumulative. Newly introduced words should be reviewed heavily at first by appearing daily for at least two or three lessons, then less frequently by appearing every other day for a week or two, and then intermittently thereafter. Also, as in the case of introducing new decoding skills, the introduction rate of vocabulary words is dependent on the students' mastery of previously introduced words.

Table 11.1 includes object, color, adverb, and adjective formats for teaching basic vocabulary. Each format has three basic steps: model, test, and integrated test. Each format contains positive and negative examples and instructional wording. The examples in each presentation were selected to show the range of positive examples and eliminate possible incorrect generalizations. For example, in teaching *mitten* the positive examples vary in color and material, showing that color and material are irrelevant to whether an object is a mitten. Also, minimally different positive and negative pairs are included (e.g., a mitten and a glove of the same size, material, and shape). Similarly, the positive examples of the color *orange* in Table 11.1 include a range of objects and minimally different positive and negative examples. Also, note the minimum use of language. Teacher talk is minimized to facilitate pacing and student attentiveness.

The students are tested by asking them to respond to the object as an example or not an example of the new concept (e.g., *heavy* vs. *not heavy*). Requiring students to say "heavy" or "not heavy" provides better practice than a "yes/no" response when the question "Is this heavy?" is presented.

Critical Behaviors

Modeling. When modeling, examples must be presented rapidly in order to keep a student's attention. The teacher should present the examples in a lively fashion, stressing the key words: "This is a *mitten.*" "This is *not* a *mitten.*"

Testing the New Word. The teacher presents the task until students can respond correctly in consecutive order to a group of at least three positive and three negative examples (six in all). A teacher can conclude only *after* students make correct responses to all the positive and negative examples that the students understand the new word. Examples should not be presented in a predictable order. Never use a yes-no-yes, no-yes-no pattern. Vary the number of consecutive positive and negative instances.

Teaching Procedure for Synonyms

Teaching new vocabulary through synonyms is similar to the procedure of teaching modeling examples, except that the teacher first equates a new word (*huge*) with a known word(s) (*very big*) rather

Table 11.1   Format for Teaching Vocabulary: Modeling Examples

	Object	Adjective (Color)	Adverb	Adjective (Texture)
Step 1: *Teacher models positive and negative examples.*	"This is a mitten" or "This is not a mitten." *Examples:* brown wool mitten brown wool glove red nylon glove red nylon mitten blue sock blue mitten	"This is orange" or "This is not orange." *Examples:* 2″ red disk 2″ orange disk 4 × 4″ orange paper 4 × 4″ brown paper	"This is writing carefully" or "This is not writing carefully." *Examples:* write on board, first neatly, then sloppily hang up coat, first carefully, then carelessly arrange books, first carelessly, then carefully	"This is rough" or "This is not rough." *Examples:* red flannel shirt red silk shirt piece of sandpaper piece of paper smooth book cover rough book cover
Step 2: *Teacher tests.* Present positive and negative examples until the students make six consecutive correct responses.	"Is this a mitten or not a mitten?"	"Is this orange or not orange?"	"Is this _____ carefully or not carefully?"	"Is this rough or not rough?"
Step 3: *Teacher tests by asking for names.* Present examples until students make six consecutive correct responses.	"What is this?" glove mitten sock mitten mitten glove	"What color is this?" orange brown orange red	"Show me how you _____ carefully" or "Tell me about how I'm writing" (quickly, slowly, carefully, etc.).	"Find the _____ that is rough" or "Tell me about this shirt" (rough, red, pretty, etc.).

than modeling examples. The teacher gives the synonym: "Here's a new word, *huge*. Huge means very big." Next, the teacher tests a set of positive and negative examples for the new word saying, "Tell me if it is huge or not huge." Then, the teacher provides practice in applying several recently taught synonyms: "Is this huge? How do you know? Find the one that is huge." The purpose of this review is to build retention.

The selection of synonyms must be made very carefully. Students *must* understand the meaning of the familiar word because it is intended to "explain" the new word. It is inappropriate to use the term *textile* to explain *fabric* because most students do not understand the synonym *textile*. On the other hand, using the synonym *strong* to explain *sturdy* is reasonable because most students know the meaning of *strong*.

Teachers can find potential words to use for synonyms by referring to a children's dictionary or thesaurus. One or more of the words will probably be familiar to students and appropriate to use.

Table 11.2 illustrates a synonym teaching format with the word *sturdy*. The major steps include the teacher presenting the synonym, testing positive and negative examples, and then reviewing the new word and previously introduced words.

Teaching Procedure for Definitions

The third procedure for teaching vocabulary is through definitions. Although definitions can be constructed in several ways, we will focus on a procedure that is applicable to most words and suited to most young students. The procedure includes two steps:

Table 11.2   Format for Teaching Vocabulary Through Synonyms

Teacher	Students
1. Teacher states the new word and the equivalent, familiar word and then tests.	
a. "Here is a new word. *Sturdy. Sturdy* means strong."	
b. "What does *sturdy* mean?" (Signal.)	"Strong."
2. Teacher presents positive and negative examples until the students make 6 consecutive correct responses. Examples are not repeated in the same order.	
a. "Tom leaned against a pole. The pole fell over. Was the pole sturdy or not sturdy?" (Signal.)	"Not sturdy."
b. "Tom leaned against another pole. The pole didn't move. Was the pole sturdy or not sturdy?" (Signal.)	"Sturdy."
c. "A house didn't shake at all in a high windstorm. Was the house sturdy or not sturdy?" (Signal.)	"Sturdy."
d. "A different house fell down when the wind started blowing. Was the house sturdy or not sturdy?" (Signal.)	"Not sturdy."
Note: The teacher can also provide practice by asking the students to generate examples. "Tell me about something that is sturdy."	
3. Teacher reviews new word and other previously introduced words.	
a. "Is it mild out today? How do you know?"	
b. "Is that bench sturdy? How do you know?"	
c. "Is my desk tidy? How do you know?"	

1. Identifying a small class to which a word belongs.

2. Stating how the word differs from other members of that class.

In constructing definitions, teachers must make them understandable to students, rather than make them technically correct. For example, a *liquid* might be defined as something poured. Although scientists might disapprove of this definition, it is adequate to teach the meaning of *liquid* to young children. Definitions are also kept understandable by using words that students understand.

Following are some sample definitions. Note the effort to keep them as simple as possible.

Class	Differs From Other Things in the Class
1. Container:	an object you can put things in
2. Vehicle:	an object that can take you places
3. Seam:	a place where two pieces of material are sewn together
4. Glare:	to look at someone as if you are angry

The format for teaching vocabulary through definitions appears in Table 11.3. First, the teacher tells the students the definition and has them repeat it. Sec-

ond, the teacher tests the students on positive and negative examples to ensure that students understand the definition and that they are not just memorizing a series of words that has no meaning. Third, review of previously introduced words is presented.

Written Vocabulary Exercises

During the beginning reading stage, written vocabulary exercises usually involve students selecting a word or phrase related to a picture. A student may either: (1) look at a picture and select a word, (2) read a word and select a picture, or (3) answer a question based on an attribute of the object illustrated in the picture. Each type of exercise is illustrated in Figure 11.1.

The simplest type of picture-related vocabulary item is multiple choice with one obviously correct alternative. Items increase in difficulty as more alternatives seem reasonable, even though only one answer is correct. For example, a picture shows a young boy. The answers are: *boy, kitten,* and *man.* A student may think that *man* is correct. However, the correct answer is *boy* because the person in the illustration is young. Vocabulary items are also more difficult when they ask about object attributes rather than object names. In Figure 11.2 item a,

Table 11.3 Format for Teaching Vocabulary With Definitions

Teacher	Students

1. Teacher states the new word and its definition and has students say definition.
  a. "An exit is a door that leads out of a building."
  b. "What is an exit?" (Signal.)
	"A door that leads out of a building."

2. Teacher presents positive and negative examples.
  a. Teacher holds up a picture or points to an open closet door. "Is this an exit or not an exit?" (Signal.)
    "How do you know?"
	"Not an exit."
	"It doesn't lead out of the building."

b. Teacher holds up a picture of a movie theater, points to an open exit door and asks, "Is this an exit or not an exit?" (Signal.)
    "How do you know?"
  c. Teacher continues presenting examples until the students answer six consecutive questions correctly.
	"An exit."
	"It leads out of the building."

3. Teacher reviews words recently introduced.
  a. Teacher holds up picture of barracks. "What is this?" (Signal.)
    "How do you know?"
  b. Teacher holds up a picture of an exit. "What is this? How do you know?" etc.
	"A barracks."
	"It's a building where soldiers live."

Figure 11.1

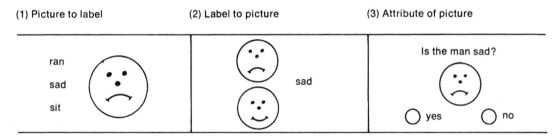

(1) Picture to label   (2) Label to picture   (3) Attribute of picture

which involves naming an object, is easier than item b, in which the students must identify an attribute of an object. In item b, the student must make the association between pillow and soft.

Many students can work this simple type of picture-related item without any teacher guidance. Obviously, these students do not need the teaching procedure. However, instructionally naive students may need directed teaching. Students should be led through several structured examples daily for 2 or 3 days. The items should include only words that are labels for objects. The teacher (1) asks the students what they see in the picture, (2) tells them to touch and read each word, and (3) asks if the picture shows that word.

Students should be taught to examine all the choices in a multiple-choice exercise before selecting the correct answer, preparing them for more difficult items that contain more than one plausible answer.

A significant proportion of students will need directed teaching on items that involve object characteristics. For example, an item shows a picture of a pillow and has the words *set, soft,* and *still* under the picture. The teacher first has the students say the name of the object in the picture and decode each word, asking if that word names the object. Next, the teacher tells the students that since no word names the object, one of the words must tell about the object. The teacher has the students decode each

Figure 11.2

(a)   (b)

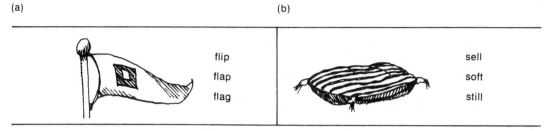

flip	sell
flap	soft
flag	still

word and asks, "Is a pillow _____?" The students must know the vocabulary words used in the task (e.g., the students must know the meaning of *soft*).

Language Skills

Beginning language teaching should include not only vocabulary but also a multitude of other skills such as plurals, pronouns, classification, polar concepts, information, and reasoning.

In this section, we'll discuss just three language skills to exemplify the activities that should be included in the curriculum for instructionally naive students. The skills are statement repetition, sentence comprehension, and similarity comparisons. We'll conclude with a discussion of how language and vocabulary skills are presented in commercial programs.

Statement Repetition

Statement repetition refers to a student's ability to say verbatim a statement said by the teacher. Instructionally naive students typically have difficulty repeating statements verbatim. In kindergarten it would not be unusual to find a significant number of students who could not repeat the sentence "The big tree does not have round leaves."

The inability to repeat statements often handicaps students in the later grades when they attempt comprehension activities. The students have difficulty studying because they cannot say sentences to themselves accurately.

Teachers should test statement repetition ability during the first school week by asking students to repeat several 6- to 10-word sentences (e.g., A little boy walked to the store yesterday; My friend has a big dog and a little cat). If a student does not repeat the sentence correctly, the teacher repeats it again and asks the student to say it again. Students who are not able to repeat the sentence correctly within two trials will need practice on statement repetition. Such practice should consist of short drills (3 to 5 minutes) in which students practice saying statements. Practice should start on sentences of a length a word or two longer than those a student can say without error.

Teaching Procedure

Providing sufficient practice is the key to improving statement repetition performance. Table 11.4 presents a format. The teacher first models by saying the statement and then tests by asking the students to repeat it. If the students are unable to say the statement, the teacher says it again, stressing deleted or mispronounced words. After two such corrections, the teacher can lead the students by responding with them. The teacher might say the statement several more times. Then the teacher judges how close the students are to repeating the statement correctly. If they need only a few more trials, the teacher continues modeling and leading. On the other hand, if the students appear to need many more trials, the teacher uses a part firming technique in which the teacher first models, leads, and tests on just the first part of the statement and then the entire statement. The final step in the format is modeling the statement in a normal speaking manner and testing the students on saying the

Table 11.4 Format for Statement Repetition

Teacher	Students
1. a. Teacher models and tests entire statement. "Listen. The little cat is under the old table. Say that." (Signal.)	
b. If students cannot say the statement, the teacher repeats step 1(a), stressing words the students left out. "The *little* cat is under *the old* table. Say it."	
c. If students cannot say the statement after several attempts, the teacher goes on to step 2.	
2. a. Teacher models, leads, and tests, saying the entire statement. "Listen. The *little* cat is under *the old* table. Say it with me." (Signal.) "The *little* cat is under *the old* table."	"The little cat is under the old table."
b. If the students cannot say the statement after several leads, the teacher goes on to step 3.	
3. a. Teacher models, leads, and tests on the first part of the statement and has students repeat it. "Listen. The *little* cat is under." (Signal.) "Say it with me." (Signal.) "The little cat is under." "Say it by yourselves." (Signal.)	"The little cat is under." "The little cat is under." "The little cat is under."
4. Teacher models, leads, and tests, saying the entire statement. "Listen. The little cat is under *the old* table. Say it with me." (Signal.) "The *little* cat is under *the old* table."	"The little cat is under the old table."
5. Teacher models and tests, saying the statement at a normal pace. "Listen, the little cat is under the old table. Say it by yourselves." (Signal.)	"The little cat is under the old table."

statement in a normal fashion. Without this final step, students may develop a stilted, singsong way of saying statements.

Critical Behaviors

Modeling and Pacing.   Each word in the sentence should be said at a normal pace. Teachers have a tendency to speak slowly in statement repetition tasks. A slow model makes repeating the statement more difficult for the students.

Correcting Mistakes.   When the teacher models the entire statement, some students may leave out a word. For example, the teacher says, "This ball is not big," but the student says, "This ball not big." The correction procedure is to model the statement again, stressing the word left out, "This ball *is* not big."

A second type of error involves mispronunciation. If the word is one or two syllables, the teacher corrects by stressing the missed sound. If

the student says "ba" instead of "bat," the teacher says "bat," stressing the final /t/ sound. If the student says "mid" instead of "mud," the teacher says "mud," stressing the /u/ sound. If the word is more than two syllables, the teacher can use a part firming procedure: model, lead, and test on the first part of the word, and then the entire word. For example, if a student has difficulty saying the word *experiment,* the teacher could model, lead, and test on "experi," then *experiment.*

Sentence Comprehension
Introducing Question Words

Sentence comprehension begins with exercises to teach students how to identify *what* happened in a sentence, *who* was involved, *when* the event happened, *where* the event occurred, and *why* the event occurred. Who, what, when, where, and why are referred to as question words.

Students should be able to repeat five- to seven-word statements (e.g., The boy ran in the park; The girl hit the ball) before questions about sentences are introduced. If students cannot retain the information in a sentence long enough in order to repeat that sentence, they are unlikely to remember the information from the sentence needed to answer simple *who* or *what* questions.

The rate for introducing new question words is determined by student performance. A new question word is not introduced until the students have mastered questions involving previously introduced question words.

Sequence

Who and *what* questions (see Table 11.5) should be presented first because they are easiest: "John went to the store. Who went to the store?" "John." "What did John do?" "Went to the store?" *Where* and *when* can be introduced next. And *how* and *why* are introduced later because they are more difficult.

When students answer *who* and *what* questions without difficulty, *where* questions can be intro-

duced. A phrase telling *where* would be inserted in each sentence and a *where* question asked in addition to the *who* and *what* questions.

For example:

Sentence: A girl played soccer in the park.
Questions: Who played soccer?
   What did a girl do?
   Where did the girl play soccer?

When students are able to answer the who, what, and where questions without difficulty, *when* phrases can be introduced. Table 11.6 includes a format for presenting *when* and *where* phrases.

After students can discriminate between *when* and *where* phrases, they can be introduced to *when* and *where* questions. The teacher uses all four question words to do this (see Table 11.7).

The next step is to introduce *how*. The procedure for doing this is to model the answer for one or two *how* questions and then test the students on a series of sentences (see Table 11.8).

The last step is to introduce *why* (see Table 11.9). The procedure for teaching why is similar to the procedure for teaching earlier question words because the teacher gives examples with *why* and

---

Table 11.5 Format for Introducing Question Words *Who* and *What*

Teacher	Students
1. Teacher models. "John ran in the park. Who ran in the park? John. What did John do? Ran in the park."	
2. Teacher provides practice and tests.	
a. "Listen. Tom fell off his bed. Say that." (Signal.)	"Tom fell off his bed."
b. "Who fell off the bed?" (Signal.)	"Tom."
c. "What did Tom do?" (Signal.)	"Fell off the bed."
3. Teacher repeats steps 2(a–c) with these sentences and questions:	
a. "Ann hit the ball. Say that." (Signal.)	"Ann hit the ball."
"Who hit the ball?" (Signal.)	"Ann."
"What did Ann do?" (Signal.)	"Hit the ball."
b. "The cat ate the food. Say that." (Signal.)	"The cat ate the food."
"Who ate the food?" (Signal.)	"The cat."
"What did the cat do?" (Signal.)	"Ate the food."
c. "The dog jumped up and down. Say that." (Signal.)	"The dog jumped up and down."
"Who jumped up and down?" (Signal.)	"The dog."
"What did the dog do?" (Signal.)	"Jumped up and down."

Table 11.6 Format for Introducing Question Words *When* and *Where*

Teacher	Students
1. Teacher models.	
a. "I'll say phrases that tell *when*. Yesterday morning tells when. Last night tells when. Before it got dark tells when. After dinner tells when."	
b. "Now I'll say phrases that tell *where*. In the park tells where. At the beach tells where. On my chair tells where. Under the couch tells where."	
2. Teacher tests. "I'll say a phrase. You say if it tells when or where."	
a. "In the park." (Signal.)	"Where."
b. "After dinner." (Signal.)	"When."
c. "Yesterday morning." (Signal.)	"When."
d. "On my chair." (Signal.)	"Where."
e. "At the beach." (Signal.)	"Where."
f. "Last night." (Signal.)	"When."

Table 11.7 Format for Using Four Question Words

Teacher	Students
1. Teacher says, "John played in the park yesterday morning. Say the sentence." (Signal.)	"John played in the park yesterday morning."
a. "Who played in the park?" (Signal.)	"John."
b. "What did John do in the park?" (Signal.)	"Played."
c. "Where did John play?" (Signal.)	"In the park."
d. "When did John play?" (Signal.)	"Yesterday morning."

Table 11.8 Format for Introducing *How*

Teacher	Students
1. Teacher models.	
"She ran like a deer. How did she run?	
Like a deer."	
2. Teacher tests.	
a. "He worked quickly. How did he work?" (Signal.)	"Quickly."
b. "He wrote carefully. How did he write?" (Signal.)	"Carefully."
c. "They worked like dogs. How did they work?" (Signal.)	"Like dogs."

then provides discrimination practice. A teacher should not always include the word *because* in sentences that call for a response to *why* questions, since students may acquire a misrule that *because* is the only word that tells why. To prevent students from learning this misrule, teachers include examples containing *to* (He went home to get his coat), *since* (He ran home since it was late), and finally *and* (He fell down and cried).

After several days of practice on *why* questions, they can be introduced into exercises that include other question word items.

Table 11.9 Format for Introducing *Why*

Teacher	Students
1. Teacher models. "He cried because he was hungry. Why did he cry? He was hungry."	
2. Teacher provides practice and tests.	
a. "Since she was late to school, she ran. Why did she run?" (Signal.)	"She was late."
b. "He went home to get his coat. Why did he go home?" (Signal.)	"To get his coat."
c. "She tried her best and won the race. Why did she win the race?" (Signal.)	"She tried her best."
d. "They lost because they made mistakes. Why did they lose?" (Signal.)	"They made mistakes."

Similarity Comparisons

Similarity comparisons involve examining several objects or actions and determining ways they may or may not be similar. Student success on similarity comparison items particularly depends on the student's knowledge of the common dimensions between objects and events. Some major dimensions are listed:

1. *Classification* (A knife and a saw are the same because they are both tools.)

2. *Use* (A knife and a saw are the same because they both cut.)

3. *Materials* (A knife and a saw are the same because their blades are both made of metal.)

4. *Parts* (A knife and a saw are the same because they both have handles.)

5. *Location* (A toothbrush and a hairbrush are the same because they are both found in a bathroom.)

6. *Attributes* (Many objects are the same because of their shape, color, and texture.)

If students are not knowledgeable about the dimensions relevant to the comparison of items, they will have difficulty with similarity items. For example, if students do not know the class of tools or that a knife and a saw both have blades, they may fail an item that asks how a knife and a saw are the same.

The first step in teaching similarity comparisons involves expanding the students' understanding of *same* by showing them that things are the same when they possess similar attributes.

Many students understand the concept *same* in a limited sense (i.e., whether two objects look alike). Table 11.10 includes a format designed to expand the students' understanding of *same*.

Students have more trouble with items when asked how two objects differ than they do with items that ask how objects are the same. This difficulty is sometimes caused by the students not knowing what *different* means and sometimes by a lack of vocabulary. The format in Table 11.11 presents the concept of *different*. Note how similar it is to the format for teaching how objects are the same.

Commercial Programs

Although all basal reading programs include exercises designed to teach vocabulary and language skills, none of these programs provides for the comprehensive and systematic teaching of language skills that at-risk children will need to learn at an optimal rate. Most programs use inappropriate teaching demonstrations and provide insufficient practice (Jitendra & Kame'enui, 1988, 1994).

Major modifications are necessary to make basal reading programs suitable tools for teaching vocabulary and oral language skills to at-risk students. However, modifying the vocabulary and oral language component of a program is much more difficult than modifying the decoding component of a program, since constructing demonstrations to teach the meaning of a new word can require many illustrations or objects. Our suggestion is not to modify the vocabulary and language teaching component of reading programs, but to

Table 11.10 Format for Teaching the Concept of *Same*

Teacher	Students
1. Teacher says, "Let's see some ways a chair and a table are the same."	
a. "Does a chair have legs?" (Signal.)	"Yes."
"Does a table have legs?" (Signal.)	"Yes."
"So a chair and a table are the same because they both have legs. A chair and a table are the same because they both . . ." (Signal.)	"Have legs."
b. "Can a chair be made of wood?" (Signal.)	"Yes."
"Can a table be made of wood?" (Signal.)	"Yes."
"So a table and a chair are the same because they both . . ." (Signal.)	"Can be made of wood."
c. "Is a chair in the class of furniture?" (Signal.)	"Yes."
"Is a table in the class of furniture?" (Signal.)	"Yes."
"So a table and a chair are the same because they are both . . ." (Signal.)	"In the class of furniture."
d. "Name three ways a chair and a table are the same." Teacher calls on individuals and accepts appropriate answers.	

Table 11.11 Format for Teaching the Concept of *Different*

Teacher	Students
1. Teacher says, "Let's see how a chair and a table are different."	
a. "Does a chair have a back?" (Signal.)	"Yes."
"Does a table have a back?" (Signal.)	"No."
"So a table and a chair are different because a chair has a back but a table doesn't."	
b. "Do you usually sit on a chair?" (Signal.)	"Yes."
"Do you usually sit on a table?" (Signal.)	"No."
"So a table and a chair are different because . . ." (Signal.)	"You sit on a chair but you don't sit on a table."
c. "Does a table have a top?" (Signal.)	"Yes."
"Does a chair have a top?" (Signal.)	"No."
"So a chair and a table are different because . . ." (Signal.)	"A table has a top but a chair doesn't."
d. "Tell me three ways a chair and a table are different." Teacher calls on individuals.	
e. "Now tell me some ways a chair and a table are the same." Teacher calls on individuals and accepts appropriate answers.	

obtain a program specifically designed to teach vocabulary and language skills to instructionally naive students. When selecting a program, teachers should spend most of their time examining *how* the programs teach skills, rather than determining what skills are taught, since most programs cover basically the same content. Teachers should look at individual lessons, noting the formats and examples used. The wording in the formats should be simple and direct. The examples, as mentioned

earlier, are critical. Example selection is the key to effectively teaching vocabulary. Note if positive and negative examples are provided. If the program does not provide adequate examples, it will not be effective with instructionally naive students.

After looking at the way several tasks are constructed, teachers should look at 5 to 10 consecutive lessons to see how many times each new skill or word is reviewed. The purpose is to determine the adequacy of initial practice and review. If a new skill or word is not reviewed, many students will not learn it. Programs with inadequate review are difficult to modify.

In summary, examine a beginning language program by looking at *how* it teaches language skills and vocabulary rather than by looking at what it claims to teach. Look at (1) the language used in the formats, (2) the adequacy of example selection, and (3) the provision for review.

An example of an effectively constructed program designed to teach basic vocabulary and language skills is *SRA'S Language For Learning* program written by Siegfried Engelmann (1999). The program uses an explicit and systematic instructional approach, including clear teaching demonstrations, highly interactive formats, immediate error correction, cumulative review, and frequent progress-monitoring assessments. *Language for Learning* is comprised of six learning strands: actions, descriptions of objects, information and background knowledge, instructional words and problem-solving concepts, classification, and problem-solving strategies. A typical 30-minute class lesson might include a number of exercises drawn from any or all of the strands. It was written to teach oral language skills to 4-year-old preschoolers, 5- and 6-year-old children whose language is inadequately developed, to primary students for whom English is their second language, to Title 1 and special-education students, and to children in speech/language classes.

Language for Learning is unique in that it provides for cumulative introduction and practice of skills (as new skills are introduced, previously introduced skills are reviewed) and introduces new material at a realistic rate. For example, prepositions are introduced at the rate of about one each 5 to 10 lessons; *on* appears in lesson 28, *over* in lesson 31, *in front of* in lesson 36, *in* in lesson 47, *in back of* in lesson 57, *under* in lesson 67, *next to* in lesson 76, and *between* in lesson 86. When a new preposition is introduced, previously taught ones are reviewed.

Language for Learning also uniquely emphasizes expressive language. Tasks range from simple identity statements (e.g., "This is a dog," or "This is not a dog") to more complex statements (e.g., "If the teacher touches her arm or her nose, all the girls will stand up"). A companion program *Language for Thinking* can be used when children finish *Language for Learning. Language for Thinking* (2002) reviews the vocabulary from *Language for Learning* and presents more complex reasoning tasks like absurdities, descriptions, definitions, multiple classifications, and analogies.

✎ Application Exercises

1. For each of the following sets of examples, specify at least one misinterpretation a student might learn.
   a. rough
      positive examples: wool shirt and burlap bag
      negative examples: desk top and mirror
   b. narrow
      positive examples: a picture of a narrow European street and a narrow alley next to the school, with buildings on each side.
      negative examples: none
   c. vehicle
      positive examples: 4-door sedan, 2-door sedan hatchback
      negative examples: none
2. Assume you are working with young children (5-6 years old). Tell which method—examples only, synonyms, or definitions—you would use to teach the following words. (A synonym can be a word or a phrase.)

  a. huge

  b. damp

  c. striped

  d. in

  e. between

  f. delivery truck

  g. cashier

3. On the following picture-comprehension item, the student makes this wrong response: How would you determine what caused the error?

4. Specify the correction procedure for the following error:

The teacher asks students to repeat this statement: The old man is walking the little dog. A student says, "The man walking dog."

5. Assume that a group of students knows the most common sound for all individual letters and the most common sound for the following letter combinations: *ai, ar, ay, ch, ea, ee, ing, oa, or, ou, sh,* and *th.* Underline every letter that the students will not be able to decode:

spout	some	peach	round	chef
boat	broad	gain	pour	mind
walk	tough	chord	starch	hound
again	round	steak	put	been
much	stain	gray	park	road
bread	street	beach	groan	storm
four	strap	steel	torn	none

6. Construct a set of 8 examples to teach the concept "tall." Half the examples should be positive examples and half negative examples. Specify the teacher wording in presenting and testing the examples you constructed to teach "tall."

Using Commercial and Teacher-Constructed Materials
Beginning Reading Stage

The learning-to-read stage is the time during which students learn about the alphabetic system—letter-sound correspondences, word blending, word reading, sight-word reading, text reading, and how to become fluent when reading. Approximately 2 years of phonics instruction is sufficient for most students. If phonics instruction begins early in kindergarten, it should be completed by the end of first grade. If phonics instruction begins early in first grade, it should be completed by the end of second grade (Ambruster & Osborn, 2001). This chapter deals with the first part of these 2 years of instruction.

Classroom activities discussed in this chapter include: selecting instructional materials, scheduling instructional time, and using assessments. The discussion of these activities is followed by specific classroom implementation suggestions for both kindergarten and first grade.

Selecting Instructional Materials

In selecting materials for a reading program, teachers must be careful and informed consumers. First, they cannot rely on a publisher's claims that a pro-

gram is based on sound scientific research. Instead, they must examine the materials to see if the teaching is in fact consistent with the scientific evidence. Second, as mentioned earlier, there are significant differences between materials that are research-based in the degree of explicitness, appropriate content, and skill emphasis. Some materials are much more explicit, with the right balance of skill emphasis and therefore more potent, instructional tools than other programs.

Determining If a Program Is Research-Based

The National Reading Panel report (NRP, 2000) provided an analysis and discussion of five components of reading instruction: phonemic awareness, phonics, fluency, vocabulary, and text comprehension. A comprehensive reading program that spans the elementary grades should include instruction in all of these components; however, different components are emphasized at different stages of instruction. Phonics and phonemic-awareness instruction are emphasized in the beginning reading stage.

The major differences between beginning reading programs that are aligned with sound scientific reading research findings and those not aligned with those findings are related to how phonemic awareness and phonics instruction are presented.

In a research-based program, phonemic awareness and phonics are taught explicitly and systematically. The program specifies a set of letter-sound correspondences and an appropriate sequence for introducing the correspondences. The set includes the major sound-spelling relationships for both consonants and vowels. Materials provide for substantial practice in applying knowledge of these relationships to read words, both in isolation and in text. Phonemic awareness instruction is aligned with phonics instruction.

A teacher can determine if a program is research based by examining and evaluating the first 15 to 30 lessons of the program which deal with teaching reading. If the program is research based, all of the following questions will be answered affirmatively:

1. Are the letter-sound correspondences taught explicitly? Is sufficient practice provided to ensure mastery? Are both vowel and consonants introduced, and do vowels receive equal emphasis? Vowels are often neglected in literature-based programs and other whole-word programs with a meaning emphasis.

2. Are students taught to use a word reading strategy in which sounds for all the letters in a word are combined (e.g., a blending strategy) as their primary strategy to read words? Does the program avoid reliance on context or picture cues as a strategy to read unknown words?

3. Is ample practice in applying the word reading strategy to read word lists and stories provided?

4. Are the stories that students read written so that a high percentage of words are decodable, the words contain only letters for which students have been taught the letter-sound correspondences? In a meaning-emphasis approach, words in stories are not selected on the basis of regularity of letter-sound correspondences. Instead, words are selected be-

cause they appear frequently in print. Many frequently-occurring words are irregular. Therefore, it is common, for example, to see the words *done, to, not,* and *book* among the first 50 words introduced in a meaning-emphasis program. Note that in each word, the letter *o* represents a different sound.

Determining Potential Effectiveness With At-Risk Students

Some research-based programs are better instructional tools for at-risk students than other research based programs. The more explicit, systematic, and prescriptive the program, the more effective it is likely to be with at-risk children. The following criteria can be used to evaluate a program in order to determine its potential effectiveness as an instructional tool for at-risk students.

Phonemic Awareness Instruction

Phonemic awareness instruction includes:

• Clear demonstrations of how to model segmenting and blending of spoken words and sounds

• Highly interactive teaching in which the teacher models segmenting and blending of sounds in spoken words, leads the students through segmenting and blending exercises, and tests the students by asking individual students to perform the tasks independently

• Sufficient practice in blending and segmenting of spoken words

• Phonemic awareness exercises that are aligned with phonics instruction such that blending and segmenting of sounds in spoken words precedes sounding out of written words composed of those same sounds

• Lesson construction that avoids too many different types of phonemic awareness skills being taught simultaneously

Letter-Sound Correspondences

Letter-sound correspondence instruction includes:

- Specific explanations to teachers on how to clearly model letter-sound correspondences

- Highly interactive teaching in which the teacher models sounds, monitors students as they pronounce the sounds, and asks students to pronounce the sounds to evaluate their performance

- Sequence of letter-sound correspondences that avoids confusion of similar letters and sounds

- Realistic rate of introducing new letter-sound correspondences: The introduction of a new sound is separated by 3 to 4 days before another new sound is taught assuming students do not know letter names. The introduction of a new sound is separated by 2 to 3 days before another new sound is taught assuming students do know letter names.

- Daily practice with cumulative review of previously introduced letter-sound correspondences

Use of Letter-Sound Correspondence Knowledge to Read Words

Word-reading instruction includes:

- Specific explanations to teachers on how to clearly model blending sounds to read words

- Highly interactive teaching in which students blend sounds for all letters, and teacher provides immediate feedback

- Sufficient practice in applying sounding-out strategy to read words in isolation and in connected text

- Logical sequence from easier to more difficult words

- Careful introduction and control of irregular words

Application to Spelling

Application to spelling includes:

- Ample opportunities for students to apply phonics to spell words

- Careful coordination of phonics and spelling instruction to ensure that students have learned the letter-sound correspondences needed to spell the words that appear in spelling exercises

Assessment

Assessment includes:

- Frequent assessments that teachers can use to monitor progress as students learn phonemic awareness skills, letter-sound correspondences, blending and sounding-out skills

- Assessment procedures that identify students who need additional practice

- Clear directions on how to provide extra assistance to students having difficulty; extra assistance is consistent with initial instruction

A Note on Letter Names and Letter Sounds

Most basal programs begin actual word-reading instruction with the assumption that children already know the names of letters. In these programs, letter names are taught early in kindergarten before reading instruction begins.

Logically, we can see why children who know letter names before starting reading instruction may be less likely to fail. First, children who have learned to discriminate letter figures as they learn the letter names have already had practice with working with letters. Second, letter names provide cues to the letter sounds. The letter *m,* for example, is pronounced by combining the short *e* sound with the letter sound: /*eemm*/. Similarly, the letter names for *f, l, n,* and *x* are pronounced by saying the short *e* sound and blending it with the sound of the letter. The letter names for *b, d, p, t, v,* and *z* are pronounced by saying the sound of the letter and blending it into the long *e* sound. For example, the letter name of *t,* for example, is pronounced by saying the sound of the letter and then the long *e* sound.

Although a child who is able to name letters of the alphabet upon beginning actual reading exercises will probably be able to learn letter-sound correspondences more rapidly than a child who does not know letter names, knowledge of letter names is *not* an essential prerequisite for learning to read. There is substantial evidence that one program that teaches letter sounds first, *Reading Mastery,* has been highly effective with a wide range of students and particularly effective with students at risk of reading failure when they enter school. The *Reading Mastery* program was designed to facilitate maximum acceleration for children who entered school with very few literacy-related skills. By teaching letter-sound correspondences first children would be more quickly prepared to read words, and the overall progress of children in learning to read could be accelerated. The authors recognized that children who did not know letter names would be more instructionally naive and so developed a specialized orthography to make learning the letter-sound correspondences simpler.

In *Reading Mastery,* some letters are connected (e.g., sh, wh, qu, th) to help children distinguish between the sound of the letter combination and the sound of the individual component letter; macrons (long letters over vowels) differentiate long vowels from short vowels; some letters are altered to reduce the confusion children typically have between pairs of letters that appear very much alike in traditional orthography; letters in words that do not directly correspond to a sound are printed in a smaller font (e.g., the *e* on *like* would be printed in a smaller font). This modified orthography is gradually faded as the students progress through the second level of the program. Letter names are also taught in the second level.

When examining a beginning-reading program, the focus is not on whether the program teaches letter names or letter sounds first. Both approaches have proven effective in well constructed research-based programs. The main focus should be on how well the program is designed. In either letter-sound first or letter-name first approaches, problems arise if too much information is introduced at once. For example a program that introduced upper-case letters, lower-case letters, letter names, and letter sounds concurrently would be likely to cause serious confusion for at-risk children. Likewise a program that introduced all the sounds of a letter or letter combination at once or had a sequence with similar letters in near proximity could cause confusion for the at-risk child.

Oral Language Component

In Chapter 11, we pointed out the importance of teaching foundational language skills and concepts to children at-risk because they enter school with poorly developed language skills. Unfortunately, none of the commercial basal reading programs we examined include what we consider to be sufficient systematic and explicit teaching of critical language skills in their kindergarten level. A language concept would be taught for a couple of lessons and not reviewed in later lessons.

It is essential for the at-risk child that foundational language skills and concepts be taught prior to and concurrent with beginning reading instruction. SRA's *Language for Learning* and *Language for Thinking* are two excellent research-based programs that systematically and explicitly develop receptive and expressive language skills. These programs incorporate all the features we mentioned in Chapter 11 and can serve as a model for how a language program for the at-risk child should be constructed.

Recent Changes in Commercial Programs

Beginning in the early years of the new millennium, significant changes in published beginning reading programs became evident. The publication of the National Reading Panel report in 2000, the incorporation of these findings in the No Child Left Behind legislation, the pressure of the accountability movement, and new adoption requirements by California, Texas, and Florida seem to have led many publishers to produce materials more congruent with the research findings.

Since the year 2002, all the major publishers of comprehensive reading programs have published new basal programs that are significantly more aligned with the research findings. However, there are still significant differences in levels of explicitness, emphasis and extent to which skills are taught systematically. Educators must be aware of these differences so that they can select programs that will be of most benefit to their students.

Selecting a Program

There is no particular formula that has yet been developed to evaluate beginning reading programs. For a school staff, the most reliable evidence regarding the potential of a reading program to serve as an effective instructional tool is evidence that documents success of the program in schools with similar students and teachers. Programs that have consistently produced high levels of achievement in similar schools are programs that should be carefully considered for adoption. Schools serving lower-income student populations, in particular, should select a program that has been demonstrated to be highly effective in schools serving comparable students.

Sometimes schools may locate a reading program that has produced high levels of student performance in schools serving similar student populations, but the program may not include coverage of every topic included in state standards. We suggest that in such instances that the school seriously consider adopting the program that has produced good results, and then obtaining or constructing supplementary materials to teach the content for the other standards.

In selecting materials for the first years of instruction, it is essential to determine that all of the critical components of reading instruction are aligned or integrated to produce a coherent program. Phonemic awareness activities, for example, should be coordinated with phonics activities which, in turn, should be coordinated with passages in texts. The stories that students read should be carefully controlled and coordinated with phonics and fluency instruction. Comprehension is taught initially through teacher read stories and oral language activities. Text-related comprehension activities should be a part of story-reading activities as soon as children start to read stories.

Examining comprehensive reading programs is a very time consuming task. Assistance is available. As of the writing of this text, the federal and state governments are funding organizations to examine programs. One such resource is the What Works Clearinghouse (*http://w-w-c.org/*). This clearinghouse is a project of the U.S. Department of Education's Institute of Education Sciences established to provide educators, policy makers, and the public with a central, independent, and trusted source of scientific evidence of what works in education.

Scheduling Instructional Time

Sufficient time must be allocated for reading instruction if all children are to meet grade-level performance standards by the end of first grade. To ensure that children who enter kindergarten with limited literacy and language skills accomplish that goal, substantial time for reading instruction must be provided. For children who enter school with a great deal of knowledge, less teacher-directed instructional time will be needed.

We recommend that kindergarten and first-grade classrooms in which there are many children who are at-risk because of limited literacy and language knowledge schedule at least two and a half hours a day of literacy instruction each day during the school year. During this time, every child should receive at least 30 minutes of small-group instruction in reading and 30 minutes of small-group instruction in language. Children who are not progressing at a rate to reach grade level performance should have additional 15 to 30 minute blocks of small-group instruction daily in both reading instruction and language instruction. In addition, more time after school and during the summer should be scheduled for children who do not make the necessary progress during the regular school day and/or year.

We realize that scheduling this amount of instruction for literacy teaching will not be easy. However, scheduling this time is of utmost importance for at-risk children from low-socioeconomic environments. These children must learn to read as quickly as possible so that they can use reading as a tool for learning new information independently, and have a vehicle for competing with their more advantaged peers. The positive effects on the childrens' self image as they see themselves as highly competent readers will be a reward for school staffs that go the extra mile to provide these children with an instructional program that truly prepares them for success.

Using Assessments

Screening, diagnostic, and progress-monitoring assessments are utilized during the beginning reading stage. Screening assessments help teachers identify children who are behind, and help to determine a starting place for children in instruction. Diagnostic assessments provide additional information about specific reading skill strengths and weaknesses of individuals. Diagnostic information is particularly important for children who are struggling. Progress-monitoring assessments serve to provide information to determine if children are learning the skills that the teacher has presented.

Some reading programs provide comprehensive assessment packages. Unfortunately, many do not. In our analysis of commercial programs, we noted particular shortcomings in progress monitoring assessments. Teachers need to be prepared to construct their own informal, curriculum-based progress monitoring assessments. Brief progress-monitoring assessments should be administered each week or two to monitor performance in critical skills such as letter-sound correspondences and word reading. More extensive assessments should be given every 6 to 9 weeks to provide a more complete view of student progress.

Constructing informal progress-monitoring assessments during the beginning reading stage is relatively simple because a small sample of what is being taught is assessed. For example, early during the first year of instruction when students are first learning to sound out words, a progress-monitoring assessment might include five recently introduced letters and five words. The teacher instructs the students to say the sounds for the letters and read the words. Later in the year, when students are reading passages, the teacher may monitor progress by administering oral reading fluency measures in which students read for one minute and rate (i.e., words per minute) and accuracy (i.e., number of errors) are recorded. Oral reading tests that yield measures of both rate and accuracy are excellent tools for monitoring progress.

Using Assessment Data to Inform Instruction

Information from progress-monitoring assessments can be used in three ways. First, it can be used to monitor performance of a group as a whole. If several students perform poorly, their poor performance tells the teacher that he or she must improve daily monitoring and correcting procedures to ensure that students are receiving enough practice to master important skills.

Second, the results of informal progress-monitoring assessments can be used to identify students in need of extra instruction. Children who perform poorly on an assessment are given a more thorough assessment to determine more specific problem areas. For example, a student who makes errors on two of five sounds and two of five words would be tested on all letter-sound correspondences and all word types that had been introduced previously. Then the teacher reteaches all previously introduced material that the student did not know. If this reteaching does not prove successful, the teacher might place the student in a lower-performing group. Conversely, a student who is noticeably more fluent than other students in the group might be considered for placement in a higher-performing group.

Third, the results of informal progress-monitoring assessments can be used to plan lessons to remedy specific skill deficits that are common to several children in a group. If more than one-third of the children in a group make errors on a particular skill(s), the teacher should repeat several lessons and concentrate on those particular skill(s). If the students read words accurately, but slowly, the teacher should concentrate on providing the practice needed to increase fluency.

Classroom Instruction in Kindergarten

The questions of how much and what kind of reading instruction to provide in kindergarten are important, particularly in schools with high percentages of children who lack prerequisite literacy and language skills.

Most state standards require that in kindergarten, children learn letter names, letter-sound correspondences, and phonemic awareness skills. Few states require children to do extensive reading of words and sentences in kindergarten. However, we have witnessed the effectiveness, particularly in low-income schools, of starting structured reading instruction, coupled with structured language instruction, in kindergarten. In the low-income schools in which we have worked, teachers have found that intensive academic instruction in kindergarten is essential if the gap between the knowledge of their students and the knowledge of more advantaged students is to be closed. These educators feel that their students must learn to read early so that they can use reading as a means of learning new information and vocabulary at a rate that will enable them to catch up and compete with their more privileged peers. The success that these educators have had in bringing at-risk populations to grade level and above is strong evidence of the potential benefits of teaching reading in kindergarten (Berkeley, 2002; Carlson & Francis, 2002). The kindergarten reading programs used in these successful schools are highly explicit and systematic, constructed to cover essential component skills, sequenced so that new information and skills are introduced at a realistic rate, scripted to ensure carefully controlled wording of explanations and corrections, and designed to ensure systematic practice and cumulative

review. In these schools, children who were way behind when entering kindergarten score at- or above-grade level on standardized tests by the end of first grade. (Carlson & Francis, 2002).

Though few in number, there are some commercial programs that are designed to provide explicit and systematic instruction to kindergarten children. We strongly recommend that teachers who work with children who enter school with limited literacy related skills obtain such a program. One such program is *Reading Mastery*. The authors have witnessed *Reading Mastery* produce success in kindergarten in schools located in high poverty urban and rural schools. In order to produce success, the program must be implemented with great care, utilizing all the mastery-teaching techniques discussed throughout the first part of this book. A series of 12 video tapes, titled "Reading Mastery Training Series," presents the rationale of the *Reading Mastery* program and demonstrates teaching techniques. This series is available from the publisher, Science Research Associates (ISBN: 0-07-584122-3).

Kindergarten teachers must teach receptive and expressive language concepts and skills as well as reading skills. Selecting a well-designed language program is as critical as selecting a well-designed reading program, particularly if many students in the class have limited knowledge of foundational language skills and are at risk of academic failure in school. Major modifications are necessary to make most commercial kindergarten materials suitable for teaching students with significant language needs. Modifying the vocabulary and language component of a program is much more difficult than modifying the decoding component of a reading program because illustrations and/or objects may be required to teach the meaning of a new word or concept. Our suggestion is not to attempt to modify the language and vocabulary components of inadequate programs, but rather to obtain a more adequate, instructionally sound program with research to document its effectiveness such as *Language for Learning* and *Language for Thinking.*

Problems With Kindergarten Level of Basal Reading Programs

The kindergarten level of most recently produced basal reading programs includes instruction in phonemic awareness and other skills related to the alphabetic principle and some word-attack instruction. However, many of these programs have serious program-design deficits. Among the problems commonly detected in the kindergarten level are:

- *Too much information is presented at once.* Letter names and letter-sound correspondences, as well as upper- and lower-case letters are often introduced simultaneously.

- *Too little practice and review.* Neither letter-sound correspondences nor critical language concepts are reviewed systematically. A particular concept or correspondence might be taught for a couple of lessons and then not appear again for weeks.

- *Confusing language in teaching demonstrations.* Many of the teacher explanations are too wordy and potentially confusing for students with limited knowledge of language. For example, words like *same* and *different* might appear early in the program. In one program that we reviewed, this was a typical task: "Listen as I say two words. If both words end with the same sound as *pig,* raise your hand. Bug, dog." In high poverty schools, many entering kindergartners do not know the terms *end* and *same.*

Using the Kindergarten Level of a Basal Program

Kindergarten teachers may find themselves in a situation where they have been given an instructional program that is not instructionally sound. In such instances, we recommend that the program be modified by incorporating direct instruction principles. In the following paragraphs, we offer suggestions for making modifications.

Letter-sound correspondences can be taught, using the principles specified in Chapter 7. Preparing letter-sound correspondence exercises is not very time-consuming. The teacher can follow the sequence for introducing letter-sound correspondences in the basal program, unless there are serious violations of sequencing principles (e.g., *b* and *d* or the vowels letters are too close together in the sequence). Serious sequencing violations should be remedied by altering the sequence. If upper- and lower-case letters are introduced simultaneously, the teacher can delay the introduction of the upper-case letters if it appears that students are having difficulty.

Phonemic awareness instruction can be modified to make it more explicit and systematic by incorporating the principles and procedures presented in Chapter 8. Modifications should be designed to ensure that not too many different types of tasks are presented simultaneously and that blending and segmenting are taught to mastery.

Teachers should be prepared to modify complex tasks by teaching component skills. For example, a worksheet task might have pictures of a frog, a hat, and a rug and instructions that say "Circle the words that end with the same sound as the word *dog.*" Teachers should not assume that students understand what is meant by the term *last* (or *first* or *middle*). Nor should they assume that students can extract a sound from a word. Instead, the teacher should be prepared to present exercises designed to teach the prerequisite skills and knowledge. Below is a an example of such teaching.

Teacher	*Students*
• My turn. I'll say the sounds in mud.	
• Listen: mmmuuud.	
• The first sound in mud is /m/.	
• The middle sound is /ŭ/.	
• The last sound is /d/.	
• Your turn. Say mmmuuud.	
• Get ready. (Signal.)	"Mmmmuuud."
• What's the first sound? (Signal.)	"Mmmm."
• What's the middle sound? (Signal.)	"Uuuu."
• What's the last sound? (Signal.)	"D."

The teacher models and assesses student performance on several words, then presents several words without modeling the answers first. The exercise is continued daily until the students can respond correctly to four words presented without a teacher model. These preskill exercises give the teacher an effective correction procedure to use if a student makes an error on a workbook exercise in which they are to circle words that end with the same sound.

Advances in Kindergarten Programs

Recently, some newer programs have been developed for kindergarten that provide more systematic and explicit instruction. One such program, the *Early Reading Intervention Program,* was developed at the University of Oregon's Institute for the Development of Educational Achievement (IDEA) in the College of Education (*http://idea. uoregon.edu/*). The *Early Reading Intervention Program* is now published by Scott Foresman.

The *Early Reading Intervention Program* is designed for children who need early, intensive intervention in phonological awareness, letter names, letter sounds, word reading, spelling, and simple-sentence reading. The target grade is kindergarten. The activities are designed to increase children's skills and knowledge in phonological awareness and alphabetic understanding. The intervention consists of 126 lessons that emphasize the strategic and systematic instruction of phonemic awareness and alphabetic understanding. Each lesson consists of two 15-minute components delivered consecutively in daily, 30-minute lessons. In the first 15 minutes, instruction establishes and reinforces the phonologic skills of (a) first and last sound isolation, (b) sound blending, and (c) sound segmentation. In addition, the intervention emphasizes the acquisition and application of fundamental alphabetic skills and strategies of (a) letter-name identification, (b) letter-sound identification, (c) letter-sound blending to read consonant-vowel-consonant (CVC) words, (d) selected irregular

word reading, and (e) sentence reading of controlled text. The second 15 minutes reinforce previously taught phonological awareness and alphabetic skills and extend these skills through instruction in handwriting (e.g., letter dictation and formation), integrated phonologic and alphabetic tasks, and spelling. The spelling component begins with tracing and writing previously taught letters and progresses to writing initial and final sounds in words, and then to the systematic sequential analysis and synthesis of all sounds and letters in CVC and CVCC (consonant-vowel-consonant-consonant) words. This program was experimentally tested with kindergartners and the evidence for its effectiveness is significant (Simmons & Kame'enui, 2003).

Screening Assessment in Kindergarten

There are a number of excellent commercial screening instruments that can be used in kindergarten. A review of a number of commonly used assessments that have been found to be reliable and valid appears on the web site for the Institute for the Development of Educational Achievement (IDEA) in the College of Education (*http://idea.uoregon.edu/*).

We have also included in this text an informal screening assessment for identifying kindergarten children with limited oral language–related knowledge. In addition to this assessment, a teacher could also quickly assess students for alphabetic knowledge by asking the child to say the name and the sound of ten common consonants (m, s, r, d, t, f, k, p, g, n) and the five vowels.

Oral-Language Screening Test

A screening assessment for language concepts appears in Table 12.1. It should be administered during the first few days of school. This oral language screening test is designed primarily to alert teachers to students who have vocabulary and/or language deficits. Children who miss four or more items will likely need intensive language instruction.

Table 12.1   Record Form for Oral Language Screening Test

Student's Name	1 yellow	2 brown	3 statement (1)	4 statement (2)	5 where	6 when	7 different	8 days	9 dentist	10 wood

Materials

The teacher needs a test form (Figure 12.1) and a class-record form (Table 12.1).

Teacher Directions

Start at item 1 and test all items.

Recording

The teacher uses the class-record form (Table 12.1). For a correct answer, the teacher writes a plus (+) under the appropriate heading. For an incorrect answer, the teacher writes a zero (0).

Grouping and Scheduling in Kindergarten

For at-risk children in kindergarten, we recommend small group instruction for reading and language. In a class with a high percentage of at-risk children, the teacher should try to form three groups—a high-performing group, a middle-performing group, and a lower-performing group. In a class of 20 students, for example, the groupings might be something like this: high-performing group of 8 to 10 students, middle-performing group of 6 to 8 students, and lower-performing group of 4 to 6 students. Screening test results can be used to initially group students.

We recommend that all groups receive at least 30 minutes a day of small group instruction in reading-related skills and 30 minutes a day in language-related skills. In addition, afternoon sessions of 15 to 30 minutes should be provided daily to children who need more practice to reach the desired levels of performance.

Classroom Instruction in First Grade

It is very important that children become established readers by the end of first grade. A successful experience in learning to read contributes to a

Figure 12.1   Oral Language Screening Test

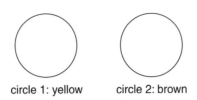

circle 1: yellow   circle 2: brown

Directions—Color circle 1 yellow. Color circle 2 brown.

1. (Point to circle one and ask) "What color is this?"
2. (Point to circle two and ask) "What color is this?"
3. "I'll say sentences. Say them just the way I say them. Listen." (pause) "A big boy sat on a dirty bench." (Repeat the sentence once if the student did not say it verbatim. If the student says it correctly verbatim on the first or second trial, score the item correct.)
4. "Listen." (pause) "Mary was baby-sitting for her little sister last night. Say that." (Repeat the sentence once if the student did not say it verbatim. If the student says it correctly verbatim on the first or second trial, score the item correct.)
5. "I'm going to say a sentence, then ask you some questions. Listen carefully. A little cat slept in the park yesterday. Listen again. A little cat slept in the park yesterday." "Where did the cat sleep?" (In the park.)
6. "When did the cat sleep in the park?" (Yesterday)
7. "How are a mouse and a cow different?" (Accept reasonable answers.)
8. "Listen. Monday, Tuesday, Wednesday, Thursday, Friday. Say that." (Repeat the days once if the student did not say them correctly. If the student says them correctly on the first or second trial, score the item correct.)
9. "What is a person who fixes your teeth called?"
10. "What is a pencil usually made of?"

child's self esteem and is a predictor of later reading success. For children from disadvantaged backgrounds, the successful early experience is a critical first step toward enabling them to compete with their more privileged peers.

The goal of having nearly all children read at grade level by the end of first grade is reachable, even in schools serving children from the highest poverty areas if (a) the teacher uses a well-designed, research-based program, (b) the teacher has received adequate training and professional development, and (c) instructional time is adequate.

By the end of first grade, children should be able to read late-first-grade materials with accuracy, fluency, and comprehension. They should read at a rate of at least 60 words per minute with expression. Children should know all letter-sound correspon-

dences for single letters and for more common letter combinations. They should know common prefixes and suffixes, and be readily able to apply this knowledge to read words. In the remaining sections of this chapter, we describe assessment and teaching practices that will enable students to reach the goal of grade-level reading by the end of first grade.

Using Assessments in First Grade

A screening assessment should be administered at the beginning of the school year to determine if children have the skills needed to be successful in the first-grade program. Most programs do not include well constructed screening tests, so the teacher will need to either construct her own or select one that has been constructed by others. We prepared the following screening assessment that tests students' knowledge of letter-sound correspondences and ability to sound out regular words.

Screening Test of Word-Attack Skills— Beginning Level

The Beginning Level Screening Test of Word-Attack Skills (Table 12.2) tests students' knowledge of letter-sound correspondences and ability to read simple regular words. The test is to be administered individually. It should take no longer than 5 minutes per child. Forms to use when administering this assessment can be found on the web site for the Association for Direct Instruction (*www.adihome.org*).

Materials

The teacher needs a copy of the test form (Table 12.2), a class-record form (Table 12.3), and a

Table 12.2 Screening Test of Word-Attack Skills—Beginning Readers' Section

a	m	t	s	i	f	d	r	o	g	l	h	
u	c	b	n	k	e	v	p	y	j	x	w	q

D   A   R   H   G   B   E   Q

1	2	3	4	5
it	cat	must	flag	stamp
am	him	hats	step	strap
if	hot	hand	drop	split
Sam	tag	last	skin	skunk
mad				

Table 12.3 Record Form for Screening Test of Word-Attack Skills—Beginning Level

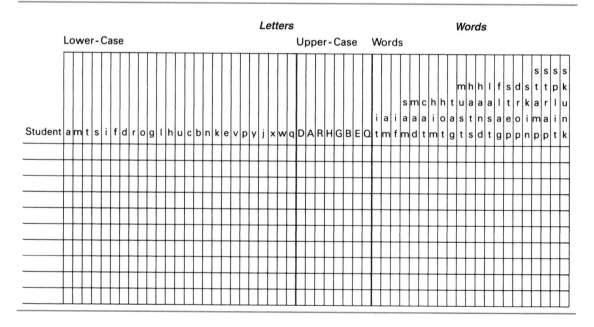

group-answer form (Table 12.4). When preparing the test form for reproduction, the teacher should use print with large letters.

Seating Arrangement

The student should be seated at a desk facing away from the rest of the class. The teacher should be seated to the side of the student so that the student cannot see the teacher recording errors.

Administering and Scoring

Step 1—Test Letter-Sound Correspondences (Lower-Case Letters).   Point to each letter and ask the student "What sound does this make?" On the class-record form (Table 12.3), write a plus (+) for each sound correctly produced. If a student tells you the letter name, say to the student, "Yes, that's the letter name, but can you also tell me the *sound* it makes?" If the student cannot tell you the sound but

Table 12.4 Group-Answer Form

Letters, Sounds, and Words		*Students*	
	1/25/03	*1/25/03*	*1/25/03*
Letters/Sounds	*Jim*	*Sarah*	*Tammy*
m	+	+	+
a	+	+	+
s	+	+	+ L
d	+	+	+ L
f	+	+	+
l	+	+	+ L
r	+	+	+
t	+	+	+
c	−NR	+	+ L
o	+	+	+
n	+	+	+
g	+	+	+
b	+	+	+
u	+	+	− ŏ
k	+	+	+
Irregulars			
was	+	+	+ L
put	+ L	+	+ L
pull	+	+	+ L
walk	+	+	+ L
said	+ L	+	− sad
Regulars			
last	+	+	+ L
cent	+	+	+ L
ask	+	+	+ L
lift	+	+	+ L
sand	+	+	+ L

does know the letter, write LN (Letter Name) next to the letter. If a student does not respond in 5 seconds and seems unable to answer, tell the student the sound, mark the letter with a zero, and move to the next letter. Continue testing letters until the student makes three incorrect responses in a row.

Step 2—Test Letter-Sound Correspondences (Upper-Case Letters).   The procedure is the same as for step 1 above.

Step 3—Test Regular Words.   Point to each word and ask "What word is this?" Repeat this question with each word in column 1, then columns 2, 3, 4, and 5. On the class-record form, write a plus (+) next to words correctly read. Write a zero (0) next to each word not read correctly. If the student misidentifies a word then immediately corrects himself, count it as

correct. If a student does not respond in 5 seconds, give the answer, then move to the next word. Continue testing until the student misses 3 words in a row.

Summarizing Assessment Results

The results of the tests can be recorded on a class summary form (Table 12.5). The students should be listed according to the total number of letter-sound correspondences correctly identified on the diagnostic test of word-attack skills. Students who made the fewest correct responses should be listed first. Across from the student's name, the number of correctly identified sounds (total of lower- and upper-case) and words should be written along with the number of items the students answered correctly on the language test. The class summary form is the basis for grouping students.

Table 12.5   Class Summary Form for Beginning-of-the-Year Testing

	Phonics Test		*Language Test*
	Letters Correct	*Words Correct*	*Items Correct*
Song Yan	0	0	6
Samuel	0	0	8
Jason	2	0	4
Cheryl	2	0	5
Elvin	2	0	9
Eric	3	0	6
James	4	0	8
Mary	5	1	8
Roberto	5	0	5
David R.	5	1	8
Lois	9	2	6
Alex	9	0	9
Phillipe	9	2	7
Gerald	10	2	8
Dianne	10	1	8
David P.	10	3	9
Sean	11	2	9
Toni	12	4	10
Dina	14	3	8
Jerome	14	2	10
Sandy	20	12	10
Alfred	21	14	10

Grouping and Scheduling in First Grade

Sufficient time must be allocated for reading instruction if all children are to read at grade level by the end of first grade. For teachers working with children who enter first grade behind the norms in literacy and language skills for children their age, this will mean significant time allocations.

We recommend at least 150 to 180 minutes a day for reading and language instruction for at-risk children. Some schools will have a 150-minute block devoted to reading and language in the morning. Some schools will have 90 minutes in the morning and 60 minutes in the afternoon. This time should be devoted to teacher-directed instruction. In addition, more time after school and during the summer should be scheduled for children who do not make the necessary progress during the regular school day or year.

Children should be placed in groups with other children who are at the same skill level for reading instruction. Grouping should be very flexible, so that children can be moved to a higher- or lower-performing group when the child's performance indicates the current placement is not appropriate.

The question of whether reading instruction should be provided in small group or in larger group settings is an important one. The number of students in a group should depend on the skill and attention levels of the students. In the earliest stage of reading instruction, small group instruction is preferred because teacher monitoring of oral responses and immediate corrective feedback are such important parts of instruction. Once children have mastered most letter-sound relationships and are able to accurately and fluently apply this knowledge to read passages orally, group size can be increased. For a first-grade classroom in which the children had reading instruction in kindergarten, we recommend groups of 8 to 12 children. Children who enter first grade with few skills would be placed in groups with fewer children.

When forming groups, the number of letter-sound correspondences and words the student knows is a good factor to consider. The teacher should try to form groups in which the number of letter-sound correspondences the students know are within four or five letters of each other.

Let's examine the class summary of a typical first-grade classroom in a low- to mid-socioeconomic area (see Table 12.5). We start with the students who know the most sounds—Alfred and Sandy. Alfred and Sandy both know 20 or more letter-sound correspondences and have identified 12 or more words. These students are performing at a much higher level than the students just below them. However, forming a group of just two higher-performing students would not be efficient use of teacher time. The optimal solution would be to collaborate with other first-grade teachers to see if they have children performing at a similar level and to create a group with 10 or 12 students. If the alternative of grouping students from several first-grade classrooms is not available, however, the teacher might consider grouping the higher-performing first-graders with a second-grade group.

Now let's look at the remaining 20 students in Table 12.5. Let's say the teacher wants to form three reading groups. The 10 students who know 9 to 14 letter-sound correspondences could form one group. The 8 students who know 3, 4, or 5 letter-sound correspondences could form a second group. And the two students who know zero letter-sound correspondences could form a third group.

Teachers must keep in mind that the initial groupings are tentative. No matter how much time is devoted to pretesting, some regrouping will always be necessary. Regrouping should be done after the first week or two of instruction. The student's performance should serve as a basis for changing group assignments. A student who is more accurate and faster in reading words during instruction might be moved to a higher group, while a student who makes more errors than other members of the group might be moved to a lower group.

Indications that a student might be ready to be moved to a higher group include mastering new skills with much less practice than required by the other students in the group and being ready to answer before the other students. A student might be moved to a lower group if he needs more practice than other members of the group and/or he is not able to answer as quickly as other members of the group.

Early regrouping is very important. If regrouping is delayed too long, students who could progress at a faster rate will lose valuable time and, furthermore, the transition to the higher group will be more difficult because the higher group will have learned a good deal more than the child who has been in the lower-performing group.

Some reading programs require whole-class instruction with follow-up instruction to small groups of students struggling with particular skills. In such cases, we highly recommend school-wide grouping with one class having the high-performers, another the middle-performers, and another the lower-performers. The class with the lower-performers should have the fewest students.

Using a Research-Based Program in First Grade

As stated repeatedly in this book, we strongly recommend that teachers use a program grounded in scientifically based reading research and that teachers working with children who are at risk of failure use a program that is highly explicit and systematic.

Unfortunately, many programs that claim to be research-based are limited in some respects. We have identified two characteristics of basal programs that can be particularly troublesome in first grade. First, the first-grade materials of most basal programs generally have a sequence that moves very rapidly, with letter-sound relationships and word-reading skills introduced at a rate that could be frustrating for a child who entered school with little knowledge of letter-sound relationships, phonemic awareness, or word reading ability.

Second, some programs contain more activities than it is possible to present in a single day. In many cases, in fact, what is to be presented on any day is unclear.

Because of these and other shortcomings of published programs, teachers should be prepared to modify a program in response to the performance of their students. Modifications to the program are needed when children have difficulty with tasks presented in a program, or when the children's performance indicates that they are not being sufficiently challenged. Following are some important points to remember:

- If the first-grade screening assessment indicates children have little knowledge of letter-sound correspondence and the program begins word reading very early, the teacher will have to create extra lessons to slow down the rate of introduction and provide children with adequate practice. For students who do not have any word attack skills, the teacher may want to use a teacher-made program focusing on phonemic awareness and phonics to prepare the students. Appendix C outlines a 20-lesson sequence for introducing letter-sound correspondences and sounding out regular words. Another possibility is to use a supplementary program. One such program was constructed by three teachers who read the first edition of this text. They spent several years developing a set of teacher and student materials for teaching beginning reading skills. The program is entitled the *BEST Phonics Program.* Information on this program and other supplementary programs can be obtained by writing to: Jerry Silbert, P.O. Box 10459, Eugene, Oregon 97440.

- If the program contains too many activities, the teacher will have to modify the program to ensure that priority activities are presented in every lesson and that children master the priority skills. Priority skills at the beginning stage are oral blending and segmenting, letter-sound correspondences, word attack skills (sounding out), and passage reading.

- If teaching procedures are not clear and interactive, teachers will need to modify formats to make them clear and interactive.

Here are some suggestions for presenting lessons from code-emphasis programs that need modification. The first step is to examine the words in the upcoming five lessons. The teacher notes (1) any regular-word types more difficult than the types previously intro-duced; (2) irregular words; and (3) new letter-sound correspondences to be introduced.

The teacher then constructs tasks for the daily lessons. Each lesson should have the following parts:

1. **Letter-Sound Correspondence Task.** Introduce and review letter-sound correspondences us-ing the procedures in Chapter 7.

2. **Phonemic Awareness Skills.** Present a telescoping and segmenting exercise in which difficult type words to be introduced in the near future in word-list exercises are practiced. Use procedures in Chapter 6.

3. **Word-List Exercises.** Construct word lists that contain regular words to be introduced in upcoming stories. Focus on words with newly introduced letters and words of the more-difficult type. Sound out some words and sight-read some words. Use procedures in Chapters 8 and 9.

4. **Irregular Words.** Introduce irregular words several lessons before they appear in passages. After the first 10 to 15 words have been introduced, the teacher no longer needs to sound out irregular words, but can say the word and have the students spell the words (assuming the students know letter names). See Chapter 10.

5. **Passage Reading.** Incorporate the procedures in Chapters 8 and 9. The students should read the story twice. In the first reading, the teacher concentrates on decoding. In the sec-ond reading, the teacher concentrates on de-coding and comprehension.

Using Programs That Are Not Research-Based in First Grade

In meaning-emphasis or literature-based programs, words are not controlled according to the relation between letters and sounds. This means that be-tween one-half and three-fourths of the words will be irregular when the student encounters them ini-

tially. This high level of irregularity makes it ex-ceedingly difficult, even impossible for many stu-dents, to learn the correspondences and/or apply that knowledge when reading words in a story.

Children who enter school with a good deal of knowledge about literacy and a great deal of continu-ing support from the home environment may survive what is potentially very confusing initial instruction in meaning-emphasis and/or literature-based pro-grams. However, it is not unusual to see a significant percent of students from middle- and high-income homes struggle in these kinds of programs that are not supported by research. A disproportionately larger percentage of students from low-income homes struggle and fail in such programs. Any student who enters first-grade without knowledge of many indi-vidual letter-sound relationships, without highly de-veloped oral language and without the ability to readily blend sounds represented by letters in phonet-ically regular words is at significant risk of failure if placed in a meaning emphasis program.

Our first recommendation is that teachers ap-peal to the principal and request that research based programs be obtained for the children who are struggling. Teachers should show the principal data from screening and progress-monitoring assess-ments. Teachers can also refer the principal to the National Institute for Literacy web site for informa-tion on the importance of research-based programs.

A second possibility is to obtain and use with struggling readers a supplementary program that teaches children letter-sound correspondence and how to blend sounds and includes decodable stories coordinating with the sequence of letter introduction. The same criteria that were listed earlier for evaluat-ing comprehensive core reading programs should be used to evaluate these supplementary reading pro-grams. The teacher can use this program for the first several months of school before beginning instruc-tion in the meaning-based program. While this sec-ond option is not ideal, obtaining these supplementary materials will at least provide the teacher with an im-portant instructional tool. One such program entitled PALS (Mathes, 2001) is available from Sopris West Educational Services. Another source of information is a web site maintained by the Florida Center for Reading Research (*www.fcrr.org*).

Teaching Bilingual Students to Read at Wilson Elementary School

In 1994, at Wilson Elementary School, just east of downtown Houston, approximately two-thirds of the children came from low-income homes in which Spanish was the first language. A high proportion of these children entered school speaking limited or no English. The principal, Ramon Alvarez, Jr., a native of southwest Texas, felt a certain urgency about educating these children. Even though the test scores at the school were in the acceptable range, Alvarez saw evidence that most of the children who entered Wilson with little English left it grossly unprepared for the demands of middle-school. The problem was not simple; the teachers were dedicated, yet the children did not learn enough.

With a commitment to teachers that the school would provide staff development, Alvarez engaged his staff in the search for effective tools. The first tool the Wilson School staff selected was a teacher-made beginning Spanish reading program that used systematic and explicit teaching of phonemic awareness and phonics. Because Spanish has great consistency in its letter-sound correspondences, Spanish reading is easier to master than English reading. With this new program, the children breezed through the process of learning to decode in Spanish. By December, over half of the first-graders could comfortably read first-grade books in Spanish. In addition to teaching the children to read Spanish, the teachers devoted several periods a day to teaching English vocabulary and sentence structure through the use of *Language for Learning*. A component of this program, entitled *Espanol to English*, provided a transition for non-English speakers.

The Wilson School staff's second goal was to find an effective tool for teaching reading in English. The consonant sounds in English are basically the same as they are in Spanish, except for a few letters (e.g., *ñ*, *rr*). The challenge is the vowels, which are quite different. The staff selected an English

reading program, *Reading Mastery* that taught sounds, blending, and phonemic awareness skills explicitly and systematically. Teachers began instruction in English reading only when a child had learned enough English vocabulary and sentence structure to understand the stories to be read.

A pleasant surprise for all came as the children readily transferred the blending skills they had learned while reading Spanish to their reading of English. Compared to previous years, the end-of-year results were impressive. Virtually all children were fluent readers in Spanish and two-thirds were reading at or above first-grade level in English. The lower-third of the children were near completion of the first-grade level reading in English. The next year results were even more impressive as kindergarten children who had learned English in pre-kindergarten entered the kindergarten. Teachers decided to begin reading instruction in English since the children had already developed a good deal of competence with English. Many children were fluent readers in first-grade materials at the end of kindergarten and were using reading to expand their knowledge of English. Likewise in first-grade, virtually all the children who had been at the school in kindergarten ended the year reading on grade level in English.

Technology

An increasing number of computer programs are being produced and marketed to serve as tools in teaching reading. Some of these programs have proved effective in teaching phonemic awareness skills and as practice vehicles for phonics, fluency, and comprehension. Teachers must be very careful in selecting these programs. Just as with print materials, teachers must be cautious in accepting claims that these programs are research based. Below are some specific points to consider when evaluating computer programs:

- Computers cannot provide adequate feedback on beginning reading tasks that require children to make oral responses. They cannot replace direct instruction with immediate feedback on tasks that require children to say sounds, blend sounds, and pronounce blended sounds as words.

- Teachers working with young children should be sure that the computer program teaches skills in an order aligned with the core program that is being used in the classroom.

- Computer programs that take advantage of the computer's capability to individualize instruction can be more powerful instructional tools. The individualization would come through the computer providing re-teaching and more practice on any particular skill that causes difficulty for the student.

- Programs that provide teachers with clear, comprehensive, and easily accessible reports are most useful.

When using a computer program, the teacher must take an active role. The teacher first must teach the children how to use the program. Then the teacher should watch the children as they use the program to see if students are using the program as intended. Some earlier computer programs were designed so that children did not have to attend very carefully to what was happening on the screen. The teacher should monitor the students' performance on the program regularly to ensure that students are benefiting from the computer instruction or practice.

✂ Application Exercises

1. Below are the first 20 words in two hypothetical reading programs.

Program A

sat	ram	fat	mam	am	it	cat	ram	was	sit	fit
ham	go	tan	Sid	mad	dad	had	sad	dim		

Program B

Robin	Larry	house	go	into	the	was	happy	new
soon	at	if	when	there	what	did	them	you	find

Which program is probably a code-emphasis program? Which program is probably a meaning-emphasis program? Explain your answers.

2. Below are the words introduced in the first 20 lessons of three hypothetical code-emphasis programs.

Lesson	Program A	Program B	Program C	
1	Sam, am	at, tam	a	During the
2	at, sat	Tim, mit	m	first 15
3	mad, tam	rat, rim		lessons, the
4	Tad, mat	sit, sat, Sam	s	program
5	it, sit	mad, rid, did		teaches
6	Tim, mit, miss	if, fat	t	auditory
7	rim, ram, rat	gas, dig, tag		skills but
8	rid, mam	ham, him, his		not word
9	fit, fat	hot, hit, rot	r	reading.
10	if, dim	lit, hill, till		

11	rag, tag	tan, man, Don	
12	gas, go	pan, pot, Pam	i
13	fill, till	hut, mud, hum	
14	lad, lid, to	tub, but, sub	f
15	had, ham, has	kiss, kit, kid	
16	hug, him	cat, sick, lock	if, sat
17	cat, sick	net, ten, bet	am, Sam
18	tack, sack	wet, wing, was	rat, at
19	hot, sock, lock	tax, Tex, box	sad, sit
20	mom, lot, Tom	yes, yet	Sid, ram

a. For each program, fill in the chart below with the letters introduced in each lesson.

	1	2	3	4	5	6	7	8	9	10	11	12	13	14	15	16	17	18	19	20
A																				
B																				
C																				

b. Tell which program would be the easiest to use with low-performing students. Explain why.

c. Tell which program would be the next easiest to use with low-performing children. Explain why.

d. Tell which program would be the most difficult to use with low-performing students. Explain why.

3. Below is a summary table which shows the performance of Mr. Andrews' first graders on the diagnostic phonics test. Make two groups. Tell which students would be in each group

	m	a	s	d	f	i	c	n	t	o	r	l	h	g	u	b	T	L	M	F	k	th	e	v	p
John	o	o	o																						
Ann	+	+	+	+	+	+	o	+	+	o	+	+	+	+	o	+	+	+	+	+	+	o	o	o	
Sue	+	+	+	+	+	+	+	+	+	o	+	+	+	o	o	o									
Ramon	+	+	+	+	+	+	+	+	+	+	+	+	o	+	+	+	+	o	+	+	+	o	+	+	
Dina	+	+	+	o	+	o	+	+	+	+	o	o	o												
Rachel	+	+	+	o	+	o	+	+	+	+	o	+	+	o	o	o									
Sandy	o	o	o																						
Thomas	+	+	+	+	+	o	+	+	o	o	o														
Jill	o	+	o	o	o																				
Jason	o	o	o																						

4. Below is a scope-and-sequence chart of the skills taught in a hypothetical reading program.

Lesson	Letter-Sound Correspondences	When the Word Types First Appear	Irregular Words
1	m		
4	s		
6	a		
9	t		
11	r		
14	g		
16	i		
19	f	CVC (continuous)	
22	n		
25	d		
28	o		
31	h		
34	l	CVC (stop sounds)	was
37	b		said
40	u		have
46	c	CVCC	give
50	k		no, go
55	p		the
60	v	CCVC	were
63	e		of
68	j		most

a. Specify the tasks you would include in Lesson 31 of this program. For each task, write the page in this book on which the format appears. Also write the examples you would use in each task. Use the lessons in Appendix C as a guide.

b. Specify the tasks you would include in Lesson 68 of this program. For each task, write the page in this book on which the format appears. Also write the examples you would use in each task. See page 135 for an outline of tasks to include.

C H A P T E R

Research on Beginning Reading Instruction

This chapter includes an overview and description of some important research findings relevant to reading instruction during the beginning stage.[1] Our review is not meant to be exhaustive. Such a review would necessitate more space than is available. The creation of the internet and the realization of the importance of relying on research to guide education reform has resulted in access to quality research being much more available now than it was when the first edition of the text was written. The No Child Left Behind Act of 2001 (P.L. 107–110) authorized The Partnership for Reading, a national reading research dissemination project. The Partnership for Reading's mission is to make scientifically-based reading research more accessible to educators, parents, policy makers, and other interested individuals. As of the writing of this edition, The Partnership for Reading web site offers a database containing abstracts of approximately 460 research studies related to the teaching of reading in grades K to 3. These studies have met high standards of research, *http://www.nifl.gov/ partnershipforreading/.*

---

1. This chapter utilizes sections of the third edition of *Direct Instruction Reading* which were authored by Vicky Vachon, Deborah C. Simmons, Geneva Blake, David Evans, and Cynthia C. Griffin.

Phonics Instruction

Few areas of education and pedagogy have been debated as exhaustively, continuously, and perhaps as rancorously as those on how to teach beginning reading. This debate is age old—perhaps more than 100 years old—and according to Stanovich reaches back to the "beginning of pedagogy" (Bower, 1992, p. 138).

The report of The National Reading Panel (NRP) finally has changed the nature of this debate. The NRP concluded that their examination of numerous studies provided solid support for the conclusion that systematic phonics instruction makes a bigger contribution to children's growth in reading than alternative programs providing unsystematic or no phonics instruction, and that the evidence indicated that systematic phonics instruction was successful with children from all SES backgrounds (2000). This definitive conclusion is aligned with similar findings by Snow, Burns, & Griffin (1998), who concluded that reading instruction that builds phonemic awareness and phonemic decoding skills, fluency in word recognition and text processing, construction of meaning, vocabulary, spelling and writing skills is generally more effective than instruction that does not include these components.

While phonics is the term directly associated with code-emphasis programs, it is often utilized as an inclusive term to describe a wide range of greatly differing reading activities and programs. As explained in Chapter 5, analytic phonics describes an approach wherein children derive letter-sound correspondences from words. In contrast, synthetic-phonics approaches teach letter-sound correspondences directly in isolation and require students to blend the individual sounds to form whole words.

The National Reading Panel (2000) concluded that synthetic phonics programs were especially effective for younger, at-risk readers and for disabled readers. The panel's conclusions regarding the synthetic-analytic contrast were:

> For children with learning disabilities and children who are low achievers, systematic phonics instruction, combined with **synthetic phonics instruction** produced the greatest gains. **Synthetic phonics instruction** consists of teaching students to explicitly convert letters into phonemes and then blend the phonemes to form words.
>
> Moreover, systematic synthetic phonics instruction was significantly more effective in improving the reading skills of children from low socioeconomic levels. Across all grade levels, systematic synthetic phonics instruction improved the ability of good readers to spell. (p. 5)

Phonemic Awareness

As we noted previously, phonemic awareness refers to the conscious awareness and knowledge that words are composed of separate sounds or phonemes and the ability to manipulate sounds in words (Smith, Simmons, & Kame'enui, 1995). Research of more than two decades has affirmed the importance of phonemic awareness and its relation to reading acquisition. Thus, reviews of the literature (Hurford, Darrow, Edwards, Howerton, Mote, Schauf, & Coffey, 1993; Mann, 1993; National Reading Panel, 2000) indicated that the presence of phonemic awareness is a hallmark characteristic of good readers while its absence is a consistent characteristic of poor readers.

Findings from a large body of research converge to suggest that students who enter first grade with little phonemic awareness experience less success in reading than peers who enter school with a conscious awareness of the sound structure of words and the ability to manipulate sounds in words (Adams, 1990; Liberman & Shankweiler, 1985; Mann & Brady, 1988; Spector, 1995; Stanovich, 1985, 1986, 1988; Wagner, 1988; National Reading Panel, 2000). The most encouraging lines of research give strong evidence that significant gains in phonemic awareness can be achieved with teaching and that the gains in phonemic awareness directly affect the ease of reading acquisition. In addition, a review of the research indicates that phonemic awareness is relatively independent of overall intelligence, a finding of particular importance for diverse learners (Torgesen, 1985; Vellutino & Scanlon, 1987; Wagner & Torgesen, 1987; National Reading Panel, 2000).

Phonemic awareness has been heavily researched because of its direct relation with the ability to read unfamiliar words independently and with ease (Cornwall, 1992; Lenchner, Gerber, & Routh, 1990; Mann & Brady, 1988; Rack et al., 1992; Snowling, 1991; Stanovich, 1985, 1986; Torgesen, 1985; Vellutino & Scanlon, 1987, 1987a; Wagner, 1988; Wagner & Torgesen, 1987; National Reading Panel, 2000). In addition, the ability to hear and consciously use sounds in language can be manifested in many processes fundamental to reading.

There has been growing support for a causal relation between phonemic awareness and reading acquisition. A number of reviews specifically concluded that converging evidence is sufficiently strong to establish a causal relationship (Mann & Brady, 1988; Wagner, 1988; Wagner & Torgesen, 1987; National Reading Panel, 2000). Phonemic awareness reliably predicted reading achievement across the age levels of participants from preschool through sixth grade (Cornwall, 1992; Hurford et al., 1993; Mann, 1993). Alone, the predictive evidence does not establish causal relations, however, powerful evidence for a causal relation results when predictive findings with high validity are combined with highly significant effects of beginning reading measures in intervention studies prior to formal reading instruction (Wagner, 1988; National Reading Panel, 2000).

The practical importance of this reciprocal relation between reading and phonemic awareness development has been argued extensively and passionately by several authors (e.g., Adams, 1990; Stanovich, 1985; Vellutino & Scanlon, 1987a; Wagner & Torgesen, 1987). The literature includes consistent recommendations for early identification of students at-risk for reading failure (e.g., low ability in phonemic awareness) and early explicit instruction in phonemic awareness prior to and in tandem with beginning reading instruction (e.g., Ball & Blachman, 1991; Cunningham, 1990; O'Connor et al., 1993).

Phonemic Awareness and Instruction

Synthesis of studies of the effects of phonemic awareness interventions on phonemic awareness development, reading, and spelling acquisition of normally achieving students and diverse students indicate that phonemic awareness is teachable (National Reading Panel, 2000).

The effects of teaching phonemic awareness were among the most instructionally salient findings in a review of seven intervention studies (Ball & Blachman, 1991; Byrne & Fielding-Barnsley, 1990; Cunningham, 1990; Lie, 1991; Lundberg et al., 1988; O'Connor et al., 1993; Vellutino & Scanlon, 1987). All seven studies reported positive effects on reading, spelling, or phonological awareness development. Six of the seven studies pointed to significant effects on various measures of phonological awareness, reading, or spelling. All studies looked at effects on reading; roughly 80% looked at effects of phonological awareness instruction on subsequent phonological awareness development, whereas roughly 60% looked at effects on spelling.

In addition to those short-term effects, two studies reported positive long-term transfer effects on reading and spelling and long-term maintenance

effects spanning 1 to 2 years on phonological tasks (Lie, 1991; Lundberg et al., 1988). Long-term maintenance means that the effects were evident when measured again long after the intervention stopped. Three studies reported differential effects of phonological awareness training (Lie, 1991; Lundberg et al., 1988; O'Connor et al., 1993). For example, Lundberg et al. (1988) noted larger effects of phonological awareness training on segmentation than on tasks requiring rhyming. Particularly pertinent were the greater effects for diverse learners (Lie, 1991) and the significant facilitation of reading acquisition for diverse learners and normally achieving children in studies that compared both types of learners (O'Connor et al., 1993; Vellutino and Scanlon, 1987).

The National Reading Panel (2000) concluded that teaching letter as well as phonemic awareness to beginning readers is essential. The Panel also indicated that teaching students to segment and blend benefit reading more than a multiskilled approach and that teaching students to manipulate phonemes with letters yields larger effects than teaching children without letters. Finally, the panel concluded that phonemic awareness helps many different children learn to read, including, preschoolers, kindergartners, first-graders who are just starting to learn to read, and older disabled readers. The findings are consistent among various SES groups.

Phonemic Awareness and Alphabetic Understanding

Phonemic awareness involves the ability to hear and manipulate sounds. *Alphabetic awareness* refers to a reader's knowledge of the letters of the alphabet coupled with the understanding that the alphabet represents the sounds of spoken language. *Alphabetic understanding* refers to understanding that letters represent sounds and that whole words embody a sound structure of individual sounds and patterns of groups of sounds. The alphabetic principle is the combination of alphabetic understanding and phonological awareness. The alphabetic principle enables the reader to translate independently a visual symbol into a sound.

Again, the National Reading Panel (2000) cites converging evidence that provides strong support that a combination of *phonemic awareness and letter-sound correspondence* training is necessary to understand the alphabetic principle (Adams, 1990; Ball & Blachman, 1991; Byrne & Fielding-Barnsley, 1990; Mann, 1993; Rack et al., 1992; Snowling, 1991; Spector, 1995; Stanovich, 1986; Vellutino, 1991; Vellutino & Scanlon, 1987a; National Reading Panel, 2000).

The results of an intervention study with kindergartners clearly indicated that phonemic awareness and letter-sound correspondence significantly enhanced later reading and spelling performance more so than training in letter-sound correspondence alone (Ball & Blachman, 1991). Similarly, in teaching young preliterate children to acquire the alphabetic principle, Byrne and Fielding-Barnsley (1989) found that only those who learned phonemic segmentation and phoneme identification skills and graphic symbols for initial sounds were able to correctly choose between *mow* and *sow* after they had been taught *mat* and *sat.*

A third study examined the effects of a metacognitive component on phonemic awareness and letter-sound correspondence instruction with kindergarten and first grade children (Cunningham, 1990). The study compared two instructional approaches across kindergarten and first grade: (1) letter-sound correspondence and skill training in phonemic awareness, and (2) letter-sound correspondence, skill training, and instruction in strategic use of phonemic awareness skills in context of reading. Adding explicit instruction in strategic application of the skills to instruction in letter-sound correspondence and skill training in phonological awareness resulted in significant improvement in reading. Specifically, improvement was noted in letter-sound correspondence knowledge, word recognition, and reading comprehension. Cunningham (1990) concluded that the difference was explained by contextualized instruction that included (1) in-

struction in and demonstration of conspicuous strategies, (2) guided practice, and (3) strategic and purposeful review of previous lessons in addition to the combination of phonemic awareness and letter-sound correspondence instruction.

Key Phonics and Phonemic Awareness Studies in the NRP Report

As stated explicitly in the NRP report, phonological and phonemic awareness can be taught and coordinated with systematic phonics instruction that is explicit and synthetic.

Several comprehensive studies were highlighted in the NRP report as examples of what can be accomplished when early phonemic awareness instruction is coordinated with continuing phonics instruction that is systematic, explicit, and synthetic.

Blachman, Tangel, Ball, Black, and McGraw (1999) conducted a study with low SES, inner-city children in which instruction began in kindergarten and continued through second grade. Kindergarten teachers delivered eleven weeks of instruction that was focused on phonemic awareness training. This was followed by explicit, systematic instruction in the alphabetic code in first grade. This phonics instruction continued in second grade for children who did not complete the program in first grade. The explicit systematic phonics instruction included: teaching sound-symbol relationships explicitly, teaching phoneme analysis and blending, reading words on flashcards to promote automatic word recognition, reading text containing phonetically controlled words, and writing words and sentences from dictation. Children in a control group received instruction in the school's regular basal reading program that included a phonics workbook that children used independently. Although children in the control group engaged in letter-learning and phonemic awareness activities, they were not explicitly taught to use these skills to read and write. The findings showed that the children who received explicit systematic instruction in phonics (preceded by eleven weeks of instruction in phonemic awareness) made greater progress in reading than the children who received the less explicit and systematic basal instruction.

In another comprehensive study, Torgesen, Wagner, Rashotte, Rose, Lindamood, Conway, and Garvan (1999) compared two forms of phonics instruction throughout the primary grades. One form provided very explicit and intensive instruction in phonological awareness plus synthetic phonics; the other provided less explicit instruction in phonemic decoding and more instruction in text comprehension. The latter form of instruction was called embedded phonics; instruction began by teaching children to recognize whole words. Both forms of instruction were provided by tutors rather than classroom teachers. Comparisons of the two groups revealed superior performance by the explicit and intensive phonics group on measures of phonological awareness, phonemic decoding accuracy and efficiency, and word reading accuracy. Thus, intensive training in synthetic phonics produced word reading performance that was superior to that produced by embedded phonics training.

Another important study (O'Connor, Jenkins, & Slocum, 1995) examined the effectiveness of focused rather than broad phonological awareness training. In the broad treatment, children performed a variety of sound manipulation activities that included isolating, segmenting, blending, and deleting phonemes; segmenting and blending syllables and onset-rime units; and working with rhyming words. The focused treatment was focused on the segmenting and blending of onsets, rimes, and phonemes. A control group received only letter-sound instruction. Comparisons showed that the focused and broad training were equally effective in teaching phonemic awareness; however, the focused training contributed more to the reading of words. The findings of this study are consistent with the NRP's conclusion that segmenting and blending have a greater impact on reading outcomes than does multiskill phonemic awareness instruction.

Castle, Riach, and Nicholson (1994) examined the effects of adding phonemic awareness training to whole language instruction for kindergartners with low phonemic awareness. Phonemic awareness training consisted of segmentation, blending, substitution, deletion, and letters during the latter part of the training. The results showed that adding phonemic awareness instruction to the whole language program enhanced students' decoding of pseudowords and spelling skills but not their other reading skills. These findings, when considered in concert with the highly positive findings of the two comprehensive studies by Blachman et al. (1999) and Torgesen et al. (1999) that were described above, suggest that add-on phonemic awareness instruction is of limited benefit unless it is added to systematic and explicit phonics instruction.

Foorman, Francis, Fletcher, Scharschneider and Mehta (1998) reported a dramatic reduction in overall failure rate of children based on the percentage of children remaining below the 30th percentile for children taught direct instruction in phonemic awareness and letter-sound correspondences practiced in controlled vocabulary text.

Specific Instructional Strategies

Although it is clear that beginning reading instruction that provides explicit and systematic instruction in phonemic awareness and phonics can have a significant effect on children's reading performance, teachers must pay careful attention to a variety of instructional variables to maximize the potential benefits. In the following section, we describe two instructional variables that we believe to be especially important—separating the introduction of similar letters and sounding out. As explained in the section on sounding out, blending is a necessary prerequisite to sounding out. Our emphasis on blending is consistent with the NRP's conclusion that blending and segmenting are particularly important phonemic awareness skills.

Separating the Introduction of Similar Letters

Carnine (1976d, 1980b, 1981a) demonstrated the superiority of teaching sequences that separate the introduction of visually and/or auditorily similar stimuli over methods that simultaneously introduce similar stimuli. In all three studies, preschoolers who participated in treatments wherein similar stimuli (either auditorily or visually or both) were separated in the order of introduction required significantly fewer trials to correctly complete associated tasks than did those for whom the presentation placed similar stimuli together for initial teaching.

Sounding Out Words

Teaching students to sound out words provides a conspicuous strategy (i.e., the steps necessary to achieve an instructional outcome) for the application of phonological awareness and alphabetic awareness to promote alphabetic understanding (i.e., the understanding that, in principle, the left-to-right spelling of printed words represent their phonemes from first to last).

The effects of pausing vs. not-pausing between sounds when blending was investigated by Weisberg and Savard (1993). In work with nine preschool children, they found that segmenting by pausing led to poor blending. They also found that (a) not-pausing-based blending errors were different and easier to correct than pausing-based blending errors, and (b) sound identification was necessary but not sufficient for decoding. In an earlier study, Weisberg, Andrachhio, and Savard (1989) studied the differential effects of no-pauses, 1-second pauses, and 3-second pauses between sounds. They found that kindergartners' and first graders' oral blending of dictated sounds was significantly better when no pauses intervened between sounds. These studies indicate that the specific practices employed in a synthetic phonics approach can make a difference; not all so-called "synthetic" approaches are equally effective.

Vocabulary and Language Skills

The National Reading Panel (2000) identified vocabulary instruction as one of the five areas of reading instruction. Beginning readers bring a variety of vocabulary and language skills to instructional settings (Baker, Simmons, & Kame'enui, 1995; Stanovich, 1986). The importance of these skills in relationship to beginning reading instruction is well established and studies indicate that students who do well on oral language tasks tend to do well on written comprehension tasks (Anderson & Freebody, 1983; Baker, Simmons, & Kame'enui, 1995).

Explicit vocabulary instruction may be most appropriate for beginning readers who by virtue of their limited decoding skills, are unable to utilize context in written material to derive word meanings. However, even after students become proficient decoders, explicit vocabulary instruction may be used to augment more contextual and natural learning strategies (National Reading Panel, 2000; Stahl & Fairbanks, 1986).

One of the points made in Chapter 11 is that *a presentation should be consistent with only one interpretation.* If a presentation is consistent with several interpretations, students may learn an interpretation other than that intended by the teacher. An application of this principle is illustrated in Figure 13.1, which contains positive and negative examples of the discrimination *on.* The pair of examples from teaching set *a* illustrates the minimum difference between positive and negative examples of *on.* In set *a* the number of possible interpretations for *on* is minimized because of the small differences between the positive and negative examples. In contrast, the subsequent sets of examples (sets *b* through *e*) differ in terms of several features, which suggest additional interpretations. A student with set *e* examples might learn that *on* means a block, something not held in a hand, horizontally positioned objects, etc. None of these interpretations is possible from set *a*. When Williams and Carnine (1981) presented examples similar to those in Figure 13.1 to different groups of preschoolers, they found a significant linear trend between the

Figure 13.1

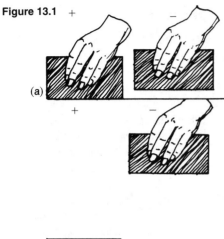

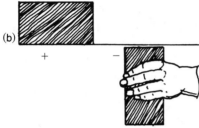

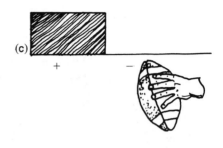

number of possible interpretations and errors on a transfer test. Preschoolers presented with set *a* examples responded correctly to 10.2 transfer items, whereas, preschoolers presented with set *e* responded correctly to 5.0 transfer items. In other words, the greater the number of possible interpretations consistent with a teaching demonstration, the greater the likelihood some students will learn an interpretation other than the one intended by the teacher. Designing a presentation as in set *a* that is consistent with only *one* interpretation increases the likelihood of students not becoming confused with what is relevant.

Summary

Direct instruction reading provides explicit instruction in those areas that are now recognized as integral to beginning reading skills:

1. Phonemic awareness skills through auditory skill training in conjunction with,

2. Letter-sound correspondences explicitly taught with attention to the order of introduction, and

3. Explicit teaching of a sounding-out (phonetic coding) strategy to make clear the utility of the alphabetic principle in the context of reading first words followed by phrases and then stories.

4. Ongoing instructional development of vocabulary and language skills, which serves as a critical basis for skillful reading and writing.

PART 3

Decoding

CHAPTER 14

Overview of Decoding

The remainder of this book will deal with skills taught after the beginning stage. The relationship between decoding and comprehension instruction changes as students progress through the grades. At the beginning of the primary grades, a good deal of time is devoted to teaching decoding skills because students need to learn generalizable skills that will enable them to decode many words. By the end of the primary grades, most specific word-attack skills have been taught. The proportion of the lesson devoted to teaching comprehension skills grows as the time spent on decoding decreases.

Decoding Instruction

A phonetic language is a language in which each letter always represents only one sound, regardless where the letter appears in a word. For the aspiring reader, English is not, unfortunately, a highly phonetic language. Although about half the letters in the English language are highly regular in that they nearly always represent the same sound, the other half of the letters are quite irregular. The sound these letters make varies considerably, depending on the context in which they appear. To determine

what sound a particular letter represents, the reader must take into account the letters that follow it in a word. For example, if the letter *o* is followed by another *o*, the letter *o* may make the /oo/ sound as in *moon,* or the /oo/ sound as in *blood.* Similarly, when *o* is followed by the letter *u,* the /ou/ sound as in the word *sound,* or the /oo/ sound as in the word *would* is produced. The letter *o* can also represent or combine with other letters to make the /ŏ/ sound as in the word *mom,* the /ō/ sound as in the word *hope,* and the /ŭ/ sound as in the word *done.* Obviously, the sound the letter *o* makes is determined by the letters that follow it.

The consonant *t* is also not consistent. If *t* is followed by the letter *h,* the *t* and *h* join to represent either the voiced /th/ sound as in *that,* or the unvoiced /th/ sound as in *thought.* But if *t* is followed by *ion,* the *t* represents the /sh/ sound as in *action.* Again, the sound the *t* represents is determined by the letters that follow it.

If English were a highly phonetic language, the job of teaching students to decode would be practically finished by the end of the beginning stage. The students would learn the letter-sound correspondences and how to blend in a left-right progression. The only major teaching steps remaining would be to provide practice and introduce longer words.

However, since English is not a highly phonetic language, much teaching needs to be done after the beginning stage to produce literate readers. One should look at the beginning reading stage as the time when the foundation for future learning is being established.

During the beginning reading stage, students learn the foundational skills that will enable them to succeed in later instruction. As students practice the skill of sounding out words letter by letter, they develop the ability to see units of letters rather than merely individual letters. As the students progress through the beginning reading stage, they should receive adequate practice to enable them to read one-syllable words relatively quickly, without subvocally sounding out the word first. The nearly instantaneous decoding of words indicates that the students are processing letters as a unit rather than as a series of individual letters.

Teaching students to decode in the primary and intermediate grades is discussed in three chapters: *Phonic-analysis* which deals with teaching students how combinations of letters represent sounds; *structural-analysis,* which deals with teaching children to read multisyllabic words, and *irregular words,* which deals with teaching students strategies to figure out irregular words.

Phonic Analysis

Phonic analysis refers to teaching students the relationship between units of letters and sounds. During the beginning stage, we recommend teaching the most common sound for individual letters. In the next stage, students learn sound correspondences for groups of letters we refer to as letter combinations. An example of a letter combination is *ar,* which usually represents the /ar/ sound as in the word *far.* Learning the sound for this letter combination enables students to decode a set of previously "irregular" words (e.g., *bark, barn, farm, cart, hard, start, card, star, dark, harm*).

We also recommend teaching students a rule for decoding words with a VCe pattern such as *like, made,* and *hope.* In VCe words, a single vowel is followed by a consonant and a final *e.*

Structural Analysis

Structural analysis involves teaching students to decode words formed by adding prefixes, suffixes, or another word to a base word. The word *repainting* is formed by adding the prefix *re* and the ending *ing* to the base word *paint* (*re + paint + ing = repainting*). Spelling changes are often needed when word parts are combined. For example, note what happens when the ending *ed* is added to *hope* and *hop* (*hope + ed = hoped, hop + ed = hopped*). *Hoped* is formed by dropping the *e* in *hope. Hopped* is formed by doubling the final *p* in *hop.* These spelling changes require the students to learn skills to discriminate similar words such as *hoped* and *hopped.* Another example of a spelling change occurs with words that end with the letter *y.* The *y* is often changed to an *i* (e.g., *try + ed = tried, happy + est = happiest, marry + ed = married*). Exercises that show students how word parts are combined will help students decode words with spelling changes.

Irregular Words

Teaching students phonic- and structural-analysis skills will allow them to decode a great number of words. However, there will still be words the students are not able to decode because the words contain letter-sound correspondences that are unusual. We call these words "irregulars." Teachers need to determine which words students will not be able to decode and introduce those words overtly so that students will be prepared to read these words in upcoming text. Teachers also need to teach students strategies for figuring out these difficult words. These strategies include teaching students to use the context in which a word appears as well as phonic and structural cues.

There has been a great deal of confusion regarding the use and misuse of context as a strategy for reading unknown words. Introducing the use of context when students are in the beginning stage of reading instruction can be very problematic as it is likely to result in student confusion. However, once students have mastered all basic phonic and structural analysis skills, the use of context can be a useful tool to help students in decoding irregular words.

Teaching students to use context involves teaching students to rely on the syntax (word order) and semantics (word meaning) of the sentence in which a word appears, as well as letter-sound-correspondence knowledge as an aid to decoding the word. The first type of context cue, syntax (word order), limits the number of possible words that can come next in a sentence. Thus, syntax cues allow students to make inferences regarding the possible pronunciation of a word. For example, the next word in the sentence "John ran to the _____" might be any of several nouns (e.g., *store, shore, station*), but could not be a verb (e.g., *stay, shave*), adverb (e.g., *slowly*), or pronoun (e.g., *she*). The second type of context cue, semantics (word meaning), further limits the number of possible words that can come next in a sentence. For example, although the next word in the sentence "Alice threw away the _____" must be a noun, only certain nouns

make sense (e.g., *cup, old clothes, broken TV*). Other nouns would not make sense and would not come next in the sentence (e.g., *Jerry, woman, railroad*). Since context cues (semantic and syntactic) restrict the words that can come next in a sentence, students are more likely to be able to figure out the pronunciation of an unknown word in context than when it appears in a list of words.

Students also use context cues to check their decoding of words in passages. If a student reads the sentence "The rabbit went *hopping* down the street" as "The rabbit went *hoping* down the street," he can infer he made a decoding error since the sentence does not make sense. The student needs to reanalyze *hoping* to correct the sentence.

Comprehension

The emphasis of reading instruction gradually shifts as students move through the grades from learning to read (decoding) to reading to learn (comprehension). By the intermediate grades, passage-reading instruction focuses primarily on comprehension. Most of the reading lesson at this point deals with teaching specific comprehension strategies and applying these strategies to comprehend passages.

Phonic Analysis

Systematic and explicit phonics instruction during the primary grades, after the beginning phonics instruction described in earlier chapters, includes instruction in a wide array of letter-sound correspondences. The National Reading Panel (NRP) stressed the importance of this more advanced phonics instruction in this way:

> A key feature that distinguishes systematic phonics instruction from nonsystematic phonics is in the identification of a full array of letter-sound correspondences to be taught. The array includes not only the major correspondences between consonant letters and sounds but also short and long vowel letters and sounds, and vowel and consonant digraphs (e.g., oi, ea, ou, sh, ch, th). Also it may include blends of letter-sounds that recur as subunits in many words, such as initial blends (e.g., st, sm, bl, pr), and final stems (e.g., -ack, -end, -ill, -op). Learning vowel and digraph spelling patterns is harder for children; therefore, special attention is devoted to learning these relations. (2000, p. 12)

During the primary grades, phonics instruction includes teaching students: (1) the most common sound(s) represented by several consecutive letters (referred to as letter combinations), and (2) strategy for decoding words which contain a VCe pattern in which the initial vowel represents its long sound and the final *e* is silent as in *make, hope,* and *use.*

NRP conclusions regarding the importance of phonic analysis beyond the beginning stage are summarized in Figure 15.1.

Words With Letter Combinations

A letter combination is a group of consecutive letters that represents a particular sound(s) in the majority of words in which it appears. Knowing the most common sounds of letter combinations greatly expands students' abilities to decode new words. For example, a student who can decode all types of regular words and has just learned the *ee* letter combination will be able to decode these new words: *bee, bleed, beet, breed, peel, see, teen, wee, creek, deer, flee, fleet, green, greet, jeep, keep, weep, canteen, indeed, upkeep,* and *fifteen.*

Table 15.1 lists the letter combinations that we suggest presenting. We recommend presenting the letter-sound relationship for a letter combination if the letter combination represents one sound in over half the words in which it appears and if it appears in five or more common words. The letter combinations are listed alphabetically in the left column of the table. The second column contains words that illustrate the most-common sound of each letter combination. The third and fourth columns give

Figure 15.1   Scientifically-Based Conclusions About Phonics Instruction After the Beginning Reading Stage

- Systematic and explicit phonics instruction improves word reading and oral text reading skills for students in second through sixth grades.
- Systematic phonics instruction is significantly more effective than non-phonics instruction in helping to remediate reading difficulties in disabled readers.
- Systematic phonics instruction improves word-reading skills for older struggling readers.
- Systematic and explicit phonics instruction is most effective for children with learning disabilities, children who are low achievers, and children from low socioeconomic levels when it is combined with **synthetic** phonics instruction.
- Systematic **synthetic** phonics instruction improves the ability of good readers to spell across all grade levels.
- Systematic phonics instruction is beneficial to students regardless of their socioeconomic levels.
- Systematic phonics instruction is effective when delivered through tutoring, through small groups, and through teaching classes of students.
- For readers beyond first grade, it is important to emphasize reading fluency, reading comprehension, and spelling instruction as well as phonics.

Adapted from the NRP Report of the Subgroups 12, Chapter 2, "Phonics Instruction," pp. 92–96.

data from a computer analysis of the most common 17,300 English words (Hanna et al., 1966). The third column lists the percentage of total words in which the letter combination represents its most common sound. (Note that these percentages vary from study to study, depending on the sample of words used.) The fourth column gives the number of words in which the particular letter combination represented its most common sound. In the fifth column, the letter combinations are classified as vowel digraph, consonant digraph, *r*-controlled vowel, or diphthong. A digraph consists of two consecutive letters that represent one sound. An *r*-controlled vowel is a vowel followed by the letter *r*. A diphthong consists of two consecutive vowels, each which contributes to the sound heard.[1]

Preskills

The first letter combinations can be introduced after students know the most common sounds of about 20 single letters and can decode passages made up of regular words at a speed of about 20 words per minute. This speed indicates that students are no

longer laboriously sounding out but beginning to perceive words as units, which makes decoding words that contain letter combinations much easier.

Sequence

Two factors determine the order in which letter combinations are introduced in a reading program. The first is the number of words in which the letter combination appears. When planning a sequence for introducing letter combinations, the number of words containing the letter combination should not only be considered in terms of total occurrence, but also in terms of how many words are common in primary grade literature. For example, although the digraph *ph* appears in a large number of words, many of these words are fairly uncommon words (words which would not appear in primary grade books). Consequently, *ph* would not be introduced as early as indicated by its frequency of occurrence. However, the letter combination *ol* appears in relatively few words, yet the words are very common (*hold, told, cold*). Thus, *ol* would be introduced relatively early.

The second sequencing consideration is the similarity of letter combinations. If letter combinations make similar (but not identical) sounds, they should be separated by at least three other combinations. Letter combinations to be separated include:

1. The distinction between which letter combinations and digraphs, dipthongs, or r-controlled vowels is more important to speech teachers than to reading teachers. Nonetheless, reading teachers should be aware of the terms since they often appear in teachers' guides and professional literature.

Table 15.1 Letter Combinations

Letter Combination	Sample Word	Percentage	Frequency	Type
ai[a]	maid	90%	254	vowel digraph
al[b]	halt	NA	NA	l-controlled
ar	car	75%	518	r-controlled
au	haul	94%	146	vowel digraph
aw	lawn	100%	75	vowel digraph
ay	stay	97%	131	vowel digraph
ch	chip	63%	313	consonant digraph
ea[a]	beat	60%	294	vowel digraph
ee[a]	need	98%	285	vowel digraph
er	fern	97%	313	r-controlled
igh	high	100%	88	vowel digraph
ir	first	100%	104	r-controlled
kn	know	100%	41	consonant digraph
oa	load	94%	126	vowel digraph
ol[b]	hold	NA	NA	l-controlled
oo	boot	59%	173	vowel digraph
or	short	55%	312	r-controlled
ou	cloud	84%	285	vowel diphthong
ow	own	50%	124	vowel digraph
oy	toy	98%	48	vowel diphthong
ph	phone	100%	242	consonant digraph
qu	quick	100%	191	none
sh	shop	100%	398	consonant digraph
th[c]	thank	74%	411	consonant digraph
ur	burn	100%	203	r-controlled
wh	whale	85%	89	consonant digraph
wr	wrap	100%	48	consonant digraph

[a]When computing percentages from the Hanna et al. study (1966), we combined some combinations that were followed by *r* (air, eer) with the respective combination without *r* (ee, ai). We found that even though there is a sound difference when *r* follows the combinations, students can decode words by pronouncing the most common sound of the letter combination and then saying the /r/ sound.

[b]The percentage and frequency of the l-controlled letter combination was not available.

[c]Although /th/ represents the unvoiced sound in most words (e.g., think), in many high-frequency words (this, that, them, than, then, the, those, these) the *th* is voiced. We recommend introducing this less-common, or minor sound of *th* first, because students use it in sounding out many high-frequency words.

1. *sh* and *ch:* These consonant digraphs are made by forming the lips in a very similar manner. This factor, along with their similar sound and appearance (both contain the letter *h*), can cause confusion.

2. *oa, oi, oo,* and *ou:* In addition to the fact that these letter combinations sound somewhat similar, they are part of a bigger group of letter combinations that begin with *o* (*oa, oi, ol, oo, ou, ow,* and *oy*). The large number of combinations beginning with the same letter and similar sound can confuse students.

3. *r*-controlled vowels: The three sounds produced by *r*-controlled vowels (/ar/ as in arm, /ur/ as in fur, bird, her, and /or/ as in sport) all sound similar. Thus, the letter combinations which represent these sounds should be separated.

Letter combinations representing the same sound (*ee* and *ea, ai* and *ay, ir* and *ur, oi* and *oy, au* and

Table 15.2 Sample Order for Introducing Letter
Combinations

1. th	10. ea	19. ir
2. er	11. oo	20. ur
3. ing	12. ee	21. kn
4. sh	13. ai	22. oi
5. wh	14. ch	23. oy
6. qu	15. or	24. ph
7. ol	16. ay	25. wr
8. oa	17. igh	26. au
9. ar	18. ou	27. aw

aw) need not be separated. Only letter combinations which represent *similar* sounds should be separated.

In Table 15.2 we have constructed a sample order for introducing letter combinations. Keep in mind that the order suggested is *not* meant to represent the only order for introducing letter combinations. It is only an example of how the sequencing guidelines can be applied.

Here is the rationale for determining the placement of specific letters in Table 15.2.

1. *Th, wh,* and *ol* are introduced early because they appear in very common, high-frequency words (e.g., this, that, when, where, and sold).

2. *Er* and *ing* are introduced early because, in addition to serving as letter combinations, they also function as affixes (e.g., cutter, cutting).

3. *Sh* and *ch* are separated by nine other combinations because, if introduced too near each other, they might be confused by some students.

Rate of Introduction

Learning to decode words containing a new letter combination is more difficult than simply learning the sound of a letter combination in isolation. When reading a word that contains a letter combination, the student can no longer decode by looking at the word letter by letter, but must see the word as being composed of one or more combinations of letters. For example, to decode the word *sheet,* the student must see that *sh* and *eet* are units within the word.

This transition, from decoding letter by letter to decoding words as units, requires extensive practice. The students' performance in decoding words containing previously taught letter combinations determines when to introduce a new letter combination, rather than their ability to identify a letter combination in isolated sound tasks.

As a general rule, students should be able to read a list of words containing letter combinations introduced to that date with no errors on the first trial at a rate no slower than every 2 seconds with 95% accuracy before a new letter combination is introduced. There are exceptions to this rule. If a student has developed a confusion between two letter combinations, the teacher (while working on alleviating the confusion) might introduce another letter combination. The new letter combination should not be similar to the ones with which the student is having difficulty. For example, if a student is having difficulty with the combinations *oo* and *ou* the teacher might introduce combination *ir* which is not similar to either of the pair the student has confused. If, however, a student is having difficulty with more than one pair of previously introduced combinations, the teacher should work generally on firming up the student's knowledge of these combinations before introducing a new one. In a developmental program being taught to average-ability students, nearly all letter combinations can be introduced by the end of the second year of reading instruction. This translates into a new letter combination being introduced about each 5 to 10 days.

Teaching Procedure

Two basic formats can be used in teaching students to decode words that contain letter combinations: an isolated-sounds format in which students learn to identify letter combinations in isolation and a sight-word-list format in which the students identify words that contain a letter combination.

Isolated-Sounds Format

The isolated-sounds format (see Table 15.3) is similar to the formats used to teach the most common sounds of individual letters. The teacher writes the

---

Table 15.3 Isolated Sounds for Letter Combinations (This Format Introduces the Letter Combination *ea*)

Teacher	Students
Teacher writes on the board: *ea, or, ee, ea, th, sh, ea,* and *ing*.	
1. Teacher models by saying the sound of the new letter combination and tests by having the students pronounce it. Teacher points to *ea*. "These letters usually say /ē/. What sound?" (Signal.)	"ē"
2. Teacher alternates between the new combination and other combinations. Teacher points to a letter combination, pauses 2 seconds, says "What sound?" and signals with an out-in motion.	Says the most common sound.
3. Teacher presents the remaining letter combinations using an alternating pattern similar to this: *ea, or, ea, ee, th, ea, sh, ing, or, ea*.	
4. Teacher calls on several individual students to identify one or more letter combinations.	

---

new letter combination, along with several previously introduced letter combinations, on the board. The teacher models the sound of the new letter combination and tests the students on saying the sound. Then the teacher alternates between the new letter combination and previously introduced letter combinations. The teacher uses the same signaling procedures and alternating procedure discussed in Chapter 7.

Critical Behaviors for Teaching Isolated Sounds

Signals, Pacing, and Individual Turns. The signaling procedure would be the same as described on pages 64–65 for isolated letter-sound correspondences. The teacher points to a letter combination, pauses to let the student recall the sound, then signals with an out-in motion.

The pacing should be rapid from letter to letter. When the students respond correctly to a signal, the teacher quickly moves to another sound, allows the students time to recall the sound, and then signals.

Correcting Mistakes. If a student misidentifies a letter combination or responds late, the teacher tells the student the correct sound, has the student say the sound, and then alternates between the missed letter combination and other letter combinations the student knows. If a student continues to make errors on a previously introduced letter combination, extra

practice should be provided on that combination in the next lessons.

Example Selection. The format should include 6 to 8 letter combinations. The following are guidelines for selecting examples:

1. Review the most recently introduced letter combinations daily until students correctly produce the correct sound for the letter combination on the first trial for three consecutive lessons.

2. Exclude previously taught, similar letter combinations the first day a new letter combination appears. On the second day after the new combination appears, include any previously introduced letter combinations similar to the newly introduced combination. For example, on the second day *ch* is introduced, the combination *sh* should be included because it sounds similar. Similarly, on the second day after the letter combination *or* is introduced, the letter combination *ar* should be included. Do not, however, include a similar letter combination unless it has been taught earlier.

Word-List Format

The word-list format (see Table 15.4) gives students practice reading words with letter combinations. Words containing a new letter combination can be introduced when the students correctly produce the

Table 15.4 Format for Words With Letter Combinations

Teacher	Students
Teacher writes on the board: b<u>ou</u>t, r<u>ou</u>nd, l<u>ou</u>d, b<u>oo</u>t, b<u>ea</u>m, tr<u>ou</u>t, stain, proud, moon, pound.	
1. **a.** Students identify the sound of the letter combination, then read the word. Teacher points under the underlined letters and asks, "What sound?" (Signal.)	"Ou."
b. Teacher points to left of word. "What word?" (Signal.)	"Bout."
c. Teacher repeats step 1(a–b) with remaining words.	
2. **a.** Students reread the list without first identifying the sound of the letter combination. Teacher points to *bout,* pauses 2 seconds, and asks, "What word?" (Signal.)	"Bout."
b. Teacher repeats step 2(a) with remaining words.	
3. Teacher calls on individual students to read one or more words.	

sound of the combination for two consecutive days in the isolated-sounds format. The word-list format should include 10 to 15 words. In the first half of the words, the letter combinations are underlined. The students first read the words with the underlined combination. For each word, the students first say the sound for the letter combination, then they say the entire word. The students then reread those words and the remaining words without first identifying the sound of the letter combination.

Critical Teaching Behavior When presenting word-list exercises, the teacher uses the same procedures discussed for practicing sight-word reading in the beginning stage (see pages 86–88). The teacher points to the left of a word, pauses to let students figure out the word, then signals by using an out-in motion. The teacher monitors the students by watching their eyes and mouths. When giving individual turns, the teacher points to a word, pauses to let students figure out the word, then calls a student's name. This procedure increases the probability of high student attentiveness.

Correction Procedure for Word Reading. If a student misidentifies a word or does not respond, the teacher points to the letter or letter combination pronounced incorrectly, then asks the student to say its sound. For example, if a student says "boot" for *bout,* the teacher points under *ou* and says "What

sound do these letters make?" If the student does not respond or responds incorrectly, the teacher tells the sound and has the student repeat it. After the student produces the correct sound for the letter (or letter combination), the teacher asks, "What word?" Then she returns to the beginning of the list or four words earlier in the list, whichever is fewer and represents the words.

Example Selection

- The first three words in the list should contain the newly introduced letter combination.

- Of the remaining words in the list, a third to a half should include the newly introduced letter combination.

- Include words that will appear in passages students will read within the next few lessons.

(Appendix A includes words the teacher can use in constructing word-list exercises.)

Multisyllabic Words Containing Letter Combinations

Two-syllable words containing a letter combination (e.g., *loudest, leader, beetle*) should be introduced several weeks after the first one-syllable words with that letter combination are introduced. A format for introducing multisyllabic words is discussed in Chapter 16.

Words With a VCe Pattern

In a VCe pattern word, a single vowel is followed by a consonant, which, in turn, is followed by a final *e*. Note the VCe patterns in the following words:

lake

stripe

smile

In approximately two-thirds of the one-syllable words containing VCe patterns, the initial vowel represents the long sound (the letter name.) In the other one-third of the words in which there is a VCe pattern, the vowel sound is sometimes the most common sound of the initial vowel (give) and sometimes a sound that is neither the most common sound nor the long sound (done).

Since the initial vowel represents its long sound in many one-syllable VCe pattern words, we recommend teaching the rule that when a word ends in *e,* the initial vowel says its name. The one-syllable, VCe pattern words in which the initial vowel makes a sound other than its long sound should be treated as irregular words.

Preskills

The strategy to decode VCe pattern words should be introduced after students have been taught to identify six to eight letter combinations and can decode words containing those combinations. Reading words with letter combinations gives students practice in looking at units of letters. This skill will prepare students for VCe words in which the initial vowel sound is determined by a letter at the end of a word (the final *e*).

Students should also be able to discriminate vowel letter names from vowel letter sounds before VCe pattern words are introduced. Many students will already know letter names.

For those students who do not know the name of the vowel letters, the teacher will need to make a mini-program to teach vowel names. On the first day, the teacher writes two vowels on the board, then tells the students the names of each vowel. "You know the sound these letters make. Today you're going to learn their names." (Points to *a*.) "This letter's name is *a*." (Points to *o*.) "This letter's name is *o*." The teacher then tests the students asking, "What's the name of this letter?" for each letter. The next day, the teacher begins by testing the students: (Points to *a*.) "What's the name of this letter?" (Points to *o*.) "What's the name of this letter?" If the students know both letter names, the teacher can introduce another letter name, then test on all three letter names. The procedure is repeated daily until the students can say the letter names for all vowels.

When the students know all vowel letter names, a discrimination format should be introduced. The teacher writes two letters on the board: *o* and *a*. The teacher models, pointing to the *o* and says, "This letter's name is ō. It's sound is /ŏ/." The teacher then tests the students by asking, "What's its name? What's its sound?" The same procedure is followed with the letter *a*.

The next day the teacher begins by testing. She writes *a* and *o* on the board and for each letter asks, "What's its name? What's its sound?" If the students are able to produce the name and the sound correctly for each letter, the teacher introduces the third letter: *i*. The teacher models saying the name and sound for *i*, then tests for that letter. Afterwards, the teacher tests all three letters (*a, o, i*) by asking students to say the name and sound for each letter. The teacher provides daily practice on saying the name and sound of the vowels, *a, i,* and *o*. When the students can respond without making any errors for two consecutive days, the teacher can introduce VCe pattern words. Note that we did not include the letters *e* and *u* in the discrimination format. There are relatively few VCe pattern words in which these letters are the initial vowel. We recommend delaying the introduction of VCe pattern words with either *e* or *u* as the initial vowel. This delay reduces the initial demands on the students. The letters *e* and *u* can be introduced when students can decode VCe words that have *a, i,* or *o* as initial vowels.

Table 15.5 Introductory Format for VCe Words

Teacher	Students
Teacher writes on the board: game, rope, mine, tape, note.	
1. Teacher states the rule: "An *e* at the end tells us to say the name of this (pointing to *a*) letter."	
2. Teacher guides students in applying the rule.	
a. Teacher points to game. "Is there an *e* at the end of this word?" (Signal.)	"Yes."
b. Teacher points to *a*. "So we say the name of this letter."	
c. "What's the name of this letter?" (Signal.)	"A."
d. "Get ready to tell me the word." Teacher pauses 2 seconds, then says, "What word?" (Signal.)	"Game."
e. Teacher repeats step 2(a–d) with the remaining 4 words.	
3. Students read all the words without guidance from the teacher.	
a. "You're going to read these words."	
b. Teacher points to *game,* pauses 2 seconds, then signals.	"Game."
c. Teacher repeats step 2(b) with remaining words.	
4. Teacher calls on individual students to read one or more words.	

Table 15.6 Discrimination Format for VCe Words

Teacher	Students
Teacher writes on board: make, sit, hope, like, ram, hop.	
1. Teacher reminds students of the rule: Remember, an *e* at the end of a word tells us to say the *name* (points to initial vowel) of this letter.	
2. Teacher guides students.	
a. Teacher points to *make.* "Is there an *e* at the end of this word?" (Signal.)	"Yes."
b. Teacher points to *a* in make. "Do we say /ā/ or /ă/ for this letter?" (Signal.)	"/ā/."
c. Teacher points to left of *make,* pauses, then says, "What word?" (Signal.)	"Make."
d. Teacher repeats step 2(a–c) with remaining words.	
3. Students read words without teacher guidance.	
a. "When I signal, tell me the word."	
b. Teacher points to *make,* pauses 2 seconds, then asks, "What word?" (Signal.)	"Make."
c. Teacher repeats step 3(b) with remaining words.	
4. Teacher calls on several individual students to read one or more words.	

Teaching Procedure

Two formats are used to teach VCe pattern words. First, there is an introductory format in which the teacher presents the rule and leads the students through decoding VCe pattern words.

In the introductory format (see Table 15.5), the teacher tells students about the VCe rule and prompts its usage. The students tell the teacher first the name of the initial vowel, then say the word. Note that the teacher does not use the term "initial vowel," but instead, points to the initial vowel and says, "An *e* at the end tells us to say the name of this letter." This wording is used because at this stage, students have not learned the terms *vowel* or *initial*.

The VCe concept can be taught without first teaching the meaning of these words.

A discrimination format (see Table 15.6) is used when students can answer the questions in the introductory format without error for two consecutive lessons. Included in the discrimination format is a six-word list with three CVCe words: one with *i* as the initial vowel, one with *a* for the initial vowel, and one with *o* for the initial vowel. The remaining three words should consist of regular CVC words: one with *i* as the initial vowel, one with *a* as the initial vowel, and one with *o* as the initial vowel. One or two minimally different pairs should be included (e.g., *hope–hop, dime–dim*). The list would be constructed in an unpredictable order (a CVCe word is not always followed by a CVC word). A list might include these words: *make, sit, hope, like, ram, hop.* Few words beginning with consonant blends (e.g., *globe, crime*) should appear in the introductory or discrimination format for the first two weeks of practice with VCe pattern words.

The students read the list twice. During the first reading, the teacher guides the students, asking about the presence of an *e* at the end of the word, then asking if the initial vowel says its name. In the second reading, the students simply say the word without teacher prompting. The sight-word list is presented daily (not using the identical words from day to day) until the students are able on the first trial to respond correctly to all the words for at least two consecutive days. Thereafter, VCe pattern words are incorporated into passage-reading stories and mixed into sight-word-list exercises that contain words with letter combinations, as well as irregular words. VCe pattern words with *e* and *u* can be introduced at this time.

Correcting Mistakes

The most common error is the students saying a CVCe word with the short sound of the initial vowel (e.g., saying "pan" for *pane*.) The correction procedure is illustrated below:

1. Teacher asks "Is there an *e* at the end of this word?" and prompts rule "Remember, if there is an *e* at the end, we say its (pointing to vowel) name."

2. Teacher asks "What's the name (pointing to initial vowel) of this letter?"

3. Teacher has students say the word. "What word?"

4. Teacher returns to the beginning of the list and re-presents the words.

The same correction procedure is used for any type of mistake involving the vowel sound (e.g., student says "some" for *same* or "dime" for *dome*).

✂ Application Exercises

---

1. Assume you have taught students the following skills:
   - Most common sound of all individual letters;
   - How to decode all regular word types;
   - Strategy to decode VCe words with long vowel sounds;
   - The most common sound of the following letter combinations: *ar, ea, ee, oa, th, sh, wh, ck.*

   Circle each of the following words the student would not be able to decode. Next to each of the circled words, write the abbreviated explanation below that tells why the student could not decode the word.

   - Letter (L)—The word contains a letter combination that the student does not know.
   - Irregular (I)—Some letter or letter combination is not representing its most common sound.

_____ ground	_____ those	_____ warn
_____ boat	_____ which	_____ farm

_____ speak		_____ spoil		_____ break
_____ wish		_____ cheer		_____ sack
_____ stew		_____ stick		_____ done
_____ went		_____ groan		_____ build
_____ broad		_____ spout		

2. Circle the three pairs of letter combinations below that students are most likely to confuse:

   ch–sh   ph–wr   ai–ea

   ea–ou   ou–oo   ar–ir

3. Below are sequences in which teachers introduced letter combinations. State the problems with each sequence.

   Sequence 1: *au, ea, ph, oy, th, ar*

   Sequence 2: *ar, er, th, sh, ch, ou, oi*

4. Describe the differences in teachers' presentation of words such as *like, made,* and *hope,* and words such as *have, none,* and *live.*

5. Below are the words three teachers included in VCe discrimination format. One teacher's examples are acceptable. Identify that teacher's examples. Tell why the other examples are unacceptable.

   Teacher A: *lake, hope, time, bake, rode, made*

   Teacher B: *tape, tap, side, Sid, hope, hop*

   Teacher C: *rope, time, sad, Tim, made, lot*

6. The following letter combinations have been taught so far in a program: *th, sh, wh, er, ai, oo, ar,* and *ea*. On an individual test, a student identifies all the letter combinations correctly except *oo*. Assume the program introduces the letter combination *ch* on the next lesson.

   Should the teacher delay *ch*? If so, why?

   What if the program introduced the letter combination *ou* on the next lesson?

   Should the teacher delay *ou*? If so, why?

7. In the following situations, specify what the teacher should do and the wording the teacher would use to correct the error. Then describe what the teacher should do next after the students have responded correctly to the missed item.

   a. During an isolated-sounds format, the student says "o" for *ou*.

   b. During the word-list format, for one-syllable words containing a letter combination, a student says "bat" for *bait*.

   c. During the VCe format, a student says "hop" for *hope*.

8. (Review item)

   Describe 6 examples (3 positive and 3 negative) that could be used to teach the concept, *plastic*. Specify what the teacher says and does with each example.

Structural Analysis

Structural analysis refers to an analysis of words formed by adding prefixes, suffixes, or other meaningful word units to a base word. Structural analysis is sometimes referred to as morphemic analysis, morphemes being the smallest meaningful units of language. In this section, we will present strategies for teaching students to decode words formed by adding morphemes (prefixes, suffixes, or inflected endings) to a base word.[1]

The chart in Table 16.1 lists major word types formed by adding morphemes to base words. The word types appear in their approximate order of introduction into a reading program. Each word type is described in the first column, illustrated in the second column, and special difficulties that arise are commented on in the third column.

Words Formed by Adding Common Endings to Base Words That End With a Consonant

Two factors should be taken into consideration when designing a sequence for introducing prefixes

and suffixes: (1) the number of primary level words in which each prefix or suffix appears, and (2) the relative similarity of the prefixes or suffixes. As always, any similar word parts should not be introduced too close to each other. For example, the suffix *le* would not be introduced soon after the suffix *ly* because they both contain the letter *l*, but represent significantly different sounds.

Table 16.2 lists prefixes and suffixes in one possible order of introduction. Although it is not the only acceptable sequence, it does serve as a concrete example of how our recommendations are applied. In column 1 is a word that represents the most-common pronunciation of the particular suffix or prefix. Column 2 tells whether the word part is a prefix, suffix, or inflected ending.

Words formed by adding a suffix or prefix to a base word can be introduced when students are able to sight-read one-syllable words at a rate of about 20 words per minute. The basic procedure for teaching students to read words formed by adding a common prefix or suffix to a base word ending in a consonant is to (1) introduce a prefix or suffix in the letter-sound correspondence format; (2) practice the prefix or suffix in isolation for several days; (3) introduce words containing that prefix or suffix in a word-list exercise; and (4) then include

---

1. Dr. Vicky Vachon, National Institute for Direct Instruction, contributed to the development of this chapter.

Table 16.1 Word Types Formed by Adding Morphemes to Base Words

Word Type	Illustration	Comment
Common ending or prefix added to a known base word ending with a consonant	bat + er = batter farm + ing = farming sun + y = sunny re + pack = repack	When suffixes that begin with a vowel are added to words ending with a consonant-vowel-consonant pattern (CVC), the final consonant is doubled.
ed added to words ending with a consonant	stop + ed = stopped hum + ed = hummed hand + ed = handed	When *ed* is added to a base word, the final consonant sound may be /d/ (hummed) or /t/ (stopped). Sometimes adding *ed* adds an extra syllable (handed).
Compound words	in + to = into some + times = sometimes	
An ending added to a word that ends with the letter *e*	hope + ing = hoping like + able = likable care + less = careless	When an ending that begins with a vowel is added to a word that ends with *e*, the *e* is dropped. Students must deal with discriminating word pairs such as *hopped* and *hoped*.
An ending added to base word ending with the letter *y*	cry + ed = cried happy + ness = happiness stay + ed = stayed	When the based word has a consonant before the *y*, the *y* is changed to an *i*. The *i* may represent the /ē/ or /ī/ sound, depending on the sound of the *y* represented in the base word.
Suffixes or prefixes added to a multisyllabic word	in + action = inaction	

Table 16.2 Sample Sequence for Introducing Common Prefixes and Suffixes

	Column 1	Column 2
er	batter	inflected ending
ing	jumping	inflected ending
ed	jumped	inflected ending
y	funny	suffix
un	unlock	prefix
est	biggest	inflected ending
le	handle	suffix
a	alive	prefix
be	belong	prefix
re	refill	prefix
de	demand	prefix
ic	heroic	suffix
ful	careful	suffix
ly	sadly	suffix

words of that type in passage-reading stories.

The presentation procedure begins with the teacher introducing a new ending or prefix in isolation. The teacher writes the new word part on the board along with several other prefixes or endings that have already been introduced. The teacher:

- Models the sounds made by the suffix: (Teacher points to *er.*) "At the end of a word, these letters usually say 'er.'"

- Tests the students: (Teacher points to *er.*) "What do these letters say?" "Er."

- Provides practice: Teacher alternates between the new ending and other letter combinations and endings. "What do these letters say?"

(Note that the teaching procedure is similar to that described in Chapter 7 for teaching isolated letter-sound correspondences.)

The new word ending is practiced for several days in the letter-sounds format, then words containing that ending are introduced in the following manner: Four or five words in which the new ending is added to a known base word are written on the board. The base word is underlined. (Note: In many words there will be a double consonant. The base word is underlined through the double consonant.)

jump<u>ing</u>   trick<u>ing</u>

bett<u>ing</u>   hopp<u>ing</u>

swimm<u>ing</u>

The teacher has the students read the list twice. On the first reading, the teacher prompts the students. For each word, the teacher first has the students say the underlined part ["Say the underlined part." (Signal.)], then pronounce the entire word ["Say the whole word." (Signal.)]. After completing the list, the students reread the list without reading the underlined part.

After several days, a discrimination exercise with 8 to 12 words is presented. In each word, the base word is underlined. The students read the discrimination list twice. The first time they say the underlined part, then the whole word. The second time they only say the whole word.

The newly introduced word ending should appear in about half the words. The other words should have previously introduced endings. Below is a sample list that might be used to present the ending *est* in a discrimination list. Assume that the endings *er, ing,* and *y* have previously been introduced.

bigg<u>est</u>   small<u>est</u>

funn<u>y</u>   small<u>er</u>

smart<u>est</u>   sunn<u>y</u>

hopp<u>ing</u>   tall<u>est</u>

bett<u>er</u>   runn<u>ing</u>

The most important criteria in selecting words for word-list exercises is that base words to which the prefix or suffix is added must be words the student is able to read (i.e., either an irregular word that has been previously taught or a word that contains letter-sound correspondences the student has been taught). (A list of words containing common prefixes can be found in Appendix A.)

A new prefix or suffix can be introduced when students are able to read the discrimination list without error on the first trial for two consecutive days.

Introducing Words Formed by Adding "ed"

The *ed* ending may represent one of three pronunciations. When *ed* is added to a word that ends in *d* or *t*, the *ed* is pronounced as a separate syllable (e.g., *handed, batted*). When *ed* is added to other words, the *ed* sometimes represents the /t/ sound (e.g., *jumped, tricked*), and sometimes, the /d/ sound (e.g., *hummed, begged*). The suffix *ed* can be introduced when students are able to read words with the endings *ing* or *er*.

The teaching procedure for words that contain the *ed* suffix consists of two steps. The first step involves a verbal format (see Table 16.3) in which the teacher writes *ed* on the board, says a word, then says the word with the *ed* ending (e.g., "I'll say hop with this ending. Hopped."). The teacher repeats this procedure with two more words, each ending with a different sound. Then the teacher tests the students on a set of six words. In two words, the *ed* represents the /d/ sound (e.g., *filled, hummed*), in two other words the /t/ sound (e.g., *jumped, hopped*), and in the remaining two words the /ed/ sound (e.g., *handed, landed*). The base words should be words the students have learned to decode. A sample list might include: *handed, jumped, filled, landed, hopped,* and *hummed.*

The advantage of using this verbal format is that it clearly demonstrates how the base word determines the sound the *ed* ending will make. Because the students do not have to read the base word, they can concentrate on saying the ending appropriately. The *ed* ending is *not* presented in an isolated-sounds task. Presenting *ed* in an isolated-sounds task would be inappropriate since *ed* can represent one of three sounds.

In the second format (see Table 16.4), written words are presented. This format can be introduced when the students can do the verbal *ed* format without errors for two consecutive days.

The first 3 days the format is presented, the teacher writes on the board a set of 6 regular words

Table 16.3 Format for Verbally Presented "ed" Words

Teacher	Students
1. Teacher writes *ed* on the board. Teacher then models and tests, saying different words with the *ed* suffix.	
a. "Say hop." (Signal.)	"Hop."
"I'll say hop with this ending."	
Teacher points to *ed*. "Hopped."	
b. Teacher points to *ed*. "Say hop with this ending." (Signal.)	"Hopped."
Teacher repeats step 1(a–b) with *hum* and *lift*.	
2. Teacher tests students.	
a. Teacher points to *ed*. "Say hop with this ending." (Signal.)	"Hopped."
b. Teacher repeats step 2(a) with *hum, jump, lift, hand,* and *rub*.	
3. Teacher calls on individual students.	

Table 16.4 Format for Presenting Written "ed" Words

Teacher	Students
Teacher writes on the board:	

hummed	begged
jumped	tripped
lifted	handed

Part I—Introducing "ed" Words (presented for 3 days only)

Teacher	Students
1. Students read each word by first identifying the root word and then saying the whole word.	
a. Teacher points to *humm*ed. "Say the underlined part." (Signal.)	"Hum."
b. "Say the whole word." (Signal.)	"Hummed."
c. Teacher repeats step 1(a–b) with remaining words.	
2. Teacher tests students on reading words.	
a. Teacher points to *hummed*. "What word?" (Pauses 2 seconds, then signals.)	"Hummed."
b. Teacher repeats step 2(a) with remaining words.	
3. Teacher gives individual turns.	

Part II—Discrimination Practice (begins on 3rd day)

Teacher writes on the board:

lifted	stopped	handed
handing	skipper	running
hummed	picked	lifting
biggest	picking	tagged

Teacher	Students
1. **a.** Teacher points to *lifted,* pauses 2 seconds, says "What word?" (Signal.)	"Lifted."
b. Teacher repeats step 1(a) with remaining words.	
2. Teacher gives individual turns.	

to which *ed* had been added. (The same example selection procedure as described above for the verbal format is used.) The teacher underlines the base word (e.g., <u>hand</u>ed, <u>fill</u>ed, <u>humm</u>ed, <u>batt</u>ed, hopped, jumped). The students read the list twice. On the first reading, the students say the base word, then the whole word. On the second reading, the students only say the entire word. On the third day, a practice list that contains 8 to 12 words is presented. The list should include a mix of word endings. Half with the various *ed* sounds and half with previously introduced endings. The practice list is presented daily. Words with new parts are incorporated into the list.

VCe Derivatives

A VCe derivative is created by adding a word ending to a VCe pattern word (e.g., care + less = careless, hope + ing = hoping).

The easiest VCe derivative is that formed by adding the letter *s* to a VCe word (hope + s = hopes). This word type can be introduced when students have demonstrated mastery of the discrimination between VCe words and CVC words (*hate–hat*). The teacher presents an introductory list of four words. Each word is a VCe word to which *s* has been added (e.g., *hates, likes, names*). The VCe base word is underlined (e.g., <u>hate</u>s). For each word, the teacher has the students say the underlined part, then the whole word.

A discrimination exercise can be presented when the students can do the introductory exercise without error for two consecutive days. The discrimination word list should include a mix of CVC and VCe words to which the letter *s* has been added (e.g., <u>hate</u>s, <u>cop</u>s, <u>name</u>s, <u>hope</u>s, <u>tap</u>s, <u>tape</u>s). The teacher has the students read the list twice. The first time, students say the underlined part, then the entire word. The second time, students only say the whole word. This format would be presented for several days with different words each day. When the students can do the exercise with no errors for two consecutive days, the teacher can write the list without the underlining and have them read the words in a regular, unprompted sight-word-list exercise. Keep in mind that the list should be written in a nonpredictable order; a VCe word should not always follow a CVC word. When the students can read this type of list without error for two consecutive days, VCe words with *s* endings can be integrated into word-list exercises containing a mixture of regular and irregular words to which various endings have been added (e.g., *handed, lifting, hopes, bigger, likes, hats, jumped, sitter, ropes, funny*).

VCe derivatives formed by adding endings other than *s* are introduced when students can read lists formed by adding *s* to CVCe and CVC words without error.

The teaching procedure for these words must take into account the effect of a spelling rule: *When an ending that begins with a vowel is added to a VCe word, the e is dropped* (e.g., hope + ing = hoping, love + able = lovable, use + ed = used). The difficulty caused by this spelling rule arises because of the likelihood that students may see a CVCe-derivative word as a CVC word plus an ending (e.g., hoping is seen as hop + ing rather than hope + ing). This word structure can lead to confusion between words such as hoping and hopping which are minimally different.

A three-step teaching sequence is used to teach CVCe derivatives:

1. Introduce VCe derivatives formed by adding a suffix beginning with a consonant to a VCe word (e.g., hopeful, careless).

2. Introduce VCe derivatives formed by adding a vowel to CVCe base (e.g. hoping, hoped).

3. Teach a strategy for discriminating CVCe derivatives formed by adding a vowel from CVC derivatives (e.g., hoping vs. hopping and hoped vs. hopped).

The introduction of words formed by adding suffixes that begin with consonants to CVCe words can be similar to the procedure for introducing words formed by adding *s* to CVCe derivatives.

The teacher constructs a list of about six words, a third with *a* as the initial vowel, a third with *o* as the initial vowel, and a third with *i* as the initial vowel. A mix of common endings is incorporated. The CVCe base word is underlined. Here is a sample list:

<u>care</u>ful	<u>use</u>ful
<u>hope</u>less	<u>care</u>less
<u>like</u>ly	<u>nice</u>ly

The students read the list twice: the first time identifying the underlined part, then saying the whole word; the second time only saying the whole word. This format is presented daily until students make no errors for two consecutive days.

Table 16.5 Format for Introducing CVCe Derivatives Formed by Adding "ing"

Teacher	Students
Teacher writes on the board:	

hope + ing = hoping
care + ing = caring
ride + ing = riding

	Students
1. Teacher tells students about spelling rule: "Here's a rule about spelling words that end with an *e*. When you add the ending *ing,* you drop the final *e.*" (Points to *hoping, caring,* and *riding*.). "These are words formed by using this rule."	
2. (Points to *hope.*) "What word?" (Signal.)	"Hope."
(Points to *hope.*) "Spell *hope.*" (Signal.)	"H-o-p-e."
(Points to *ing.*) "What ending?" (Signal.)	"ing."
(Points to *ing.*) "Spell *ing.*" (Signal.)	"i-n-g."
(Points to *hoping.*) "What word?" (Signal.)	"Hoping."
(Point to *hoping.*) "Spell *hoping.*" (Signal.)	"H-o-p-i-n-g."
3. Teacher repeats step 2 with remaining sets.	
4. Teacher has students read 2-syllable words.	
a. (Points to hoping.) "What word?" (Signal.)	"Hoping."
b. Repeats step 4(a) with remaining words.	

A miniformat for introducing words formed by adding suffixes beginning with a vowel can be introduced when students are firm discriminating CVCe + s words from CVC + s words and are practicing discriminating words formed by adding a suffix that begins with a consonant. This format (see Table 16.5) demonstrates how the CVCe spelling rule works. The teacher writes several sets which include the base word, the ending, and the word formed by combining the base and ending (e.g., hope + ing = hoping). The teacher explains why the *e* is dropped when combining the base word and the ending. The teacher then has the students identify and spell each part of each word set. The same format can be used with the endings *ed, er,* and *est.* The rule could be changed to say, when you add an ending that begins with a vowel, you drop the *e* from the end of the word (e.g., tape + ed = taped).

Two discrimination formats can be used to teach students to discriminate CVCe derivatives from CVC derivatives. In the first discrimination format, which is highly prompted, the teacher constructs a list of eight words—half CVC derivatives, half CVCe derivatives. Following is a sample list:

ho<u>pp</u>ed	lik<u>e</u>d
hop<u>e</u>d	bak<u>e</u>r
tim<u>e</u>r	hi<u>tt</u>er
ma<u>dd</u>er	cli<u>pp</u>er

The base part is underlined. Note that the underlining extends through the double consonant in CVC derivatives and through the *e* in CVCe derivatives. The students read the list twice: the first time saying the underlined part, then the entire word; the second time they only say the entire word.

Note that CVCe derivatives that end in *ing* cannot be used in the above format. If the base were underlined (i.e., <u>hop</u>ing) the format would induce the students to say the wrong word.

A special format for discriminating CVCe and CVC derivatives ending with *ing* appears in Table 16.6. Remember to not introduce this format until students can identify words formed by adding a suffix beginning with a vowel to both CVC and CVCe base words. In this format, the teacher shows the students how to use the number of consonants in the middle of the word as a cue to the

---

Table 16.6 Discrimination Format—CVCe Derivatives vs. Regular Word Derivatives

Teacher	*Students*

Teacher writes on the board:

h<u>o</u>ping	t<u>a</u>ping
t<u>a</u>pping	b<u>a</u>tting
f<u>i</u>lling	r<u>o</u>bbing
p<u>i</u>ling	r<u>o</u>ping

1. Teacher models presence of double consonants.
   "Some of these words have double letters after the underlined letter. Some of these words have single letters after the underlined letter."
   Teacher points to h<u>o</u>ping.
   "There's one *p* after the underlined letter. That's a single letter."
   Teacher points to t<u>a</u>pping.
   "There's two *p*'s after the underlined letter. Those are double letters."
2. Teacher tests on presence of double letters.
   a. Teacher points to h<u>o</u>ping. "What comes after the underlined letter. A single letter or double letters?" (Signal.)   —   "A single letter."
   b. Repeat step 2(a) with remaining words.
   c. Teacher gives individual turns.
      (Note: Steps 3 through 5 are not introduced until students are firm on step 2.)
3. Teacher presents rules about what to say.
   a. "Here are the rules about what to say for the underlined letter.
   b. If double letters come next, say the sound. If a single letter comes next, say the name.
   c. What do you say if a single letter comes next? (Signal.)   —   "The name."
   d. What do you say if double letters come next?" (Signal.)   —   "The sound."
4. Teacher leads through steps in applying rule.
   a. (Points to h<u>o</u>ping.) "Does a single letter or double letters come next? (Signal.)   —   "Single letter."
   b. (Points to o.) Do we say the name or the sound for this letter? (Signal.)   —   "The name."
      What word?" (Signal.)   —   "Hoping."
   c. Teacher repeats steps 4(a) and 4(b) with remaining words.
5. Teacher tests.
   a. "This time you'll just say the whole word when I signal.
   b. (Points to hoping.)
      What word?" (Signal.)   —   "Hoping."
   c. Teacher repeats step 5(b) with remaining words.

---

pronunciation of the initial vowel. To discriminate between words such as *tapping* and *taping,* students must cue on the number of consonants in the middle of the word. One consonant in the middle of a word indicates that the word was derived from a VCe pattern and that the initial vowel *will probably* represent its long sound. Two consonants in the middle of a word indicates that the word was *not* derived from a VCe-pattern word and that the initial vowel will *not* represent its long sound.

The format is designed to keep language usage simple. The terms *consonant* and *vowel* are not used. The initial vowel is underlined in each word. The rule students learn is: Double letters after the underlined letter tell you to say its sound. A single letter after the underlined letter tells you to say its name.

Steps 1 and 2 teach students to determine if a word contains a single letter or double letters after the underlined letter. Step 3 presents the rules, while in Step 4 the teacher leads students through applying the rules. Appendix A lists words that can be used in this format.

Y Derivatives

Y derivatives are formed by adding an ending to a word that ends in *y* (e.g., marry + ed = married, dry + ed = dried, happy + est = happiest). Y derivatives can cause difficulty because of the variety of sounds that may occur. When an ending is added to a base word that ends in *y*, there is usually a spelling change. The *y* is changed to an *i*. Note that in the following examples, the letters *ie* represent a variety of sounds. In the word *married*, the *ie* represents the /ē/ sound. In *dried*, the *ie* represents the /ī/ sound. And in *happiest*, the *ie* represents two sounds—the long *e* sound followed by the short *e* sound. A procedure for teaching students to decode *y* derivatives must deal with this variability.

Y derivatives can be introduced when the students know at least five words in which the *y* represents the /ē/ sound (e.g., *happy, funny, silly, carry, sunny*) and five words in which the *y* represents the /ī/ sound (e.g., *cry, fly, try, sky, dry*).

We recommend a two-step procedure. The first step involves using spelling word sets to illustrate how *y* derivatives are formed. Each set contains a base word, an ending, and the word formed by adding the ending to the base (e.g., funny + er = funnier). The examples should be carefully controlled. All the variations of sounds that *ie* represents should be included. Note that the list below contains an equal number of words in which the *ie* represents different sounds.

bunny + es = bunnies

funny + er = funnier

try + es = tries

carry + ed = carried

happy + er = happier

cry + ed = cried

The students read the list twice: the first time for each set they say the base word, then the *y* derivative (e.g., bunny, bunnies). In the second reading the teacher erases the base word plus the ending, then the students read only the derivatives. This exercise is continued until the students can do it without error for two consecutive days.

In the second step, which can be added after several days practice with the first step, a discrimination list focusing on *y* derivatives is presented. Half the words are *y* derivatives, including words in which the *ie* represents different sounds. The other half of the words are CVC and VCe derivatives. Below is a sample list:

sillier	drier
hoped	names
tried	funniest
runner	dropped
bunnies	candies

The students read a different list each day. When students can read the lists without error for two consecutive days, stories containing *y* derivatives can be presented.

Multisyllabic Words Formed With Prefixes and Suffixes

As students enter the late primary and early intermediate grades, they encounter increasing numbers of multisyllabic words, especially in content area texts. Estimates from Nagy and Anderson (1984) suggest that from fifth grade on, students encounter thousands of new words per year in print. Many of these new words are longer words composed of two or more word parts. Furthermore, these multisyllabic words may carry most of the meaning in passages, particularly in content passages.

A systematic introduction of prefixes and suffixes, and their incorporation into multisyllabic words should occur throughout the late-primary and intermediate grades.

The average number of syllables in the words students read increases steadily throughout these grades. At the end of first year of instruction in beginning reading programs, students are reading primarily one- and two-syllable words. A year later, students will be reading more two- and three-syllable words with occasional four- and five-syllable words appearing.

By third grade, many multisyllabic words appear. The following word list might be presented to students reading at a third-grade level:

belonging	unfairly	complaining
surrounded	respected	enjoyable
returning	carefully	prevented

The length of words grows as students progress through the grades. The word list below might be presented to students reading at a fifth-grade level:

occasional	professional	investigation
incredible	poisonous	entertainment
advantage	discovered	assortment

Common prefixes and suffixes should be systematically introduced throughout the primary and intermediate grades. Table 16.7 presents a possible sequence for introducing prefixes and suffixes. Not all the endings listed in Table 16.7 are suffixes. For example, *tion* and *sion* are not actual suffixes. They are formed by adding the suffix *ion* to a word ending in *t* or *s* (inspect + ion = inspection, profess + ion = profession). Similarly, *ation* is formed by combining *ate* + *ion* (e.g., invite + ate + ion = invitation). From a decoding viewpoint, it makes sense to present *tion* as an ending because it occurs in many words. Similarly, giving special treatment to *ation* is warranted since it appears in quite a few high-frequency words (e.g., *invitation, congratulations*).

Table 16.7 Sample Sequence for Introducing Common Prefixes and Suffixes

	Sample Word	Type
con	confuse	prefix
ment	payment	suffix
teen	sixteen	suffix
ful	handful	suffix
dis	distant	prefix
able	enjoyable	suffix
less	useless	suffix
ness	darkness	suffix
pro	protect	prefix
tion	invention[a]	suffix
ist	artist	suffix
ad	address	prefix
ible	sensible	suffix
age	package	suffix
sion	mission[a]	suffix
ence	sentence	suffix
ish	selfish	suffix
ation	vacation	suffix
pre	preschool	prefix
ex	expect	prefix
over	overtime	prefix
ion	million	suffix
ship	friendship	suffix
com	compare	prefix
ure	adventure	suffix
ive	detective	suffix
ac	accuse	prefix
ous	joyous	suffix
inter	interfere	prefix
ward	forward	suffix
ize	realize	suffix

[a]The suffix *tion* is often formed by adding *ion* to a word ending in *t* (interruption). We list *tion* as a high-frequency suffix for convenience. In addition, *sion* is formed by adding *ion* to a word ending with *s* (miss + ion = mission).

When introducing, prefixes and suffixes teachers need to keep in mind that their pronunciation often differs from their phonetic representation. For example, the suffix "able" is pronounced differently than the word "able."

The teacher introduces the suffix or prefix in isolation, telling the students how it is pronounced.

After introducing the new prefix or suffix in isolation, a group of words containing the new prefix or suffix is presented. The newly introduced affix is underlined (e.g., inven<u>tion</u>, frac<u>tion</u>, inspec<u>tion</u>) The teacher has the students read the list twice. On the initial reading, the students first say the underlined part, then read the entire word. On the second reading, they just read the entire word without first saying the underlined part.

After several days, words containing that new affix are mixed in with words containing previously introduced affixes. One or more word parts in each word are underlined. The students again read the list twice: The first time, they identify the underlined word parts ("What does this part say?"), then they say the word ("What's the word?"); the second reading of the list, students only say the word. Following is a sample list:

profe<u>ssion</u>al	<u>tre</u>mend<u>ous</u>	instinct<u>ive</u>ly
<u>temperature</u>	<u>tri</u>angle	unus<u>able</u>
occa<u>sion</u>ally	expo<u>sure</u>	incred<u>ible</u>

Review should be cumulative with previously introduced affixes being systematically reviewed.

Several resources are available to assist teachers in teaching multi-syllabic words. Appendix A includes lists of words for each suffix and prefix shown in Tables 16.2 and 16.7. Anita Archer, and her colleagues, Mary Gleason and Vicky Vachon, have developed a program that is highly explicit and systematic for teaching multi-syllabic words. Their program REWARDS, published by Sopris West, provides an example of explicit and systematic teaching of multisyllabic words that is integrated with passage reading and fluency development.

❧ Application Exercises

1. Each word in the list below contains a phonic or structural element. Circle the phonic (letter combination or VCe word) or structural element(s) unique to each word (see Table 16.1). Identify the type of phonic or structural element represented in each word.

batter	celebration	doting
helped	fried	humming
sail	saves	hardest

2. Assume students know the letter combinations *sh, th, ol,* and *wh,* all single letters, and the suffixes *ing* and *er.* Below are discrimination word lists various teachers prepared several days after the suffix *est* was introduced. Tell which teacher constructed an acceptable list. Specify the problem with the other two lists.

   Teacher 1

biggest	hottest	hotter	fattest	coldest	colder	hitting

   Teacher 2

hottest	biggest	fattest	coldest	maddest	wettest

   Teacher 3

cheapest	cheaper	shortest	trainer	smallest	falling

3. Assume the students know the most common sounds of all single letters and can decode all types of regular words. Circle the prefixes and suffixes below which the students would not be able to decode.

ment	ist	un	pro	re	ion

4. Specify what the teacher would say and do to correct the following error made when reading a list of words:

   a. A student says "*hop-ped*" for the word *hopped.*

   b. A student says "*hopping*" for the word *hoping.*

5. Below are word lists a teacher used in the format for presenting written *ed* words. Two lists are unacceptable. Identify those lists and tell why they are not acceptable.

   List A: handed, lifted, rented, sanded, melted

   List B: fainted, hopped, pounced, jumped, steered, called

   List C: hopped, hummed, handed, jumped, lifted, filled

6. Why are students likely to make more decoding errors on the words *taping* and *hoping* than the words *taped* and *hopes?*

7. Construct a 10-word discrimination list. Assume the students know all single letters, and the letter combinations and suffixes *ar, ee, ea,* and the endings *er, ing, ed, y,* and *est.* The teacher is introducing words that end in *le.*

   Construct a 6-word introductory list for presenting *y* derivatives. Assume the students know all single letters and the letter combinations *ar, ee, ou, er,* and *ai.*

Irregular Words
Primary and Intermediate Grades

As students learn more phonic- and structural-analysis skills, the number of words to be treated as irregulars significantly decreases. However, there are two types of words that will always be considered irregular; namely:

- words containing a letter combination which will not be taught to the students either because of its low frequency of appearance or lack of consistency in representing any particular sound (e.g., *duel, build, ceiling*). (See Table 17.1 for a list of these combinations.)

- words containing common letters or letter combinations not representing their respective, most common sounds. (For example, in the word *break*, the *ea* is not representing its most common sound.)

We present two procedures that can be used after the beginning stage for teaching irregular words. First, we discuss the introduction and review of irregular words in word-list to prepare students for up coming passage-reading exercises. Second, we discuss teaching students to use the context of a sentence and the known letter-sound relationships in the word to figure out unknown irregular words.

Systematic Introduction of Irregular Words

The sequencing guidelines for introducing irregular words remain the same as during the beginning reading stage. More common words should be introduced before lower-frequency words. Also, words very similar to each other should not be introduced too near each other. Teachers using basal reader textbooks use the words that will appear in upcoming passages. The teacher examines the words from upcoming passages to identify irregular words to be taught.

Rate

During the beginning reading stage, we recommend introducing irregular words at a relatively slow rate. Initially, one word is introduced every several lessons, then one word each second or third lesson. The rate gradually increases until several new words are introduced each day. The students' performance is the factor that determines the rate at which new words can be introduced. If students are able to identify previously introduced words with no difficulty, the teacher can introduce more new words. If students misidentify previously intro-

Table 17.1   List of Letter Combinations NOT to Be Taught

Letter Combination	Sample Word	Percentage of Words with Sound
ae	algae	83
	aesthetic	17
ei	reign	40
	deceit	26
	foreign	13
	seismic	11
eo	pigeon	67
	leopard	20
	people	13
ie	chief	64
	tie	36
gh	rough	45
	ghost	48
oe	foe	59
	shoe	22
ue	clue	75
ui	build	47
	fruit	29
uy	buy	100

Note: The words in this table either appeared in less than 10 words and/or did not represent the same sound(s) in more than half the words in which they appeared. The source for these figures is Burmeister (1968), who also utilized Hanna and Hanna's (1966) computer analysis of letter-sound correspondences.

duced words, the teacher concentrates on reteaching these words, rather than introducing new words.

Review

Irregular words require systematic review. New words should appear in word-list exercises for several days, then appear in either or both passages and word-list exercises. The more difficult the irregular word, the more review is required. Two factors determine the difficulty of an irregular word. First is the difference between how the word is sounded out and how the word is pronounced. The greater the discrepancy between the sounds and the actual pronunciation, the more difficult the word is. The word *though,* for example, is more difficult to decode than the word *put* because several letters in *though* do not represent their most common sound (*ough*); whereas, in *put* only one letter does not represent its most common sound (*u*). The second factor that de-

termines the relative difficulty of an irregular word is familiarity. The more familiar a word is to students, the easier it will be for them to decode. A word such as *tough* will be easier for students to remember than a word such as *agile,* because *tough* is more likely to be in the students' speaking vocabulary. Therefore, *agile* needs more review.

Teaching Procedure

The format for introducing and reviewing irregular words appears in Table 17.2. The format has two parts. In part 1, the teacher presents the new irregular words being introduced in the current lesson, as well as those introduced in the previous lesson. These words appear in a column. To introduce each new word, the teacher:

- tells the students the word. "This word is *fuel.*"

- has the students say the word. "What word?"

Table 17.2 Format for Introducing and Reviewing Irregular Words

Teacher	*Students*
Part 1: (Teacher introduces new words.)	
Teacher writes on board:	

New Words	Review Words	
ghost	agile	
pour	fuel	
zero	anchor	
weight	chew	
earth	zero	
wrong		

1. Teacher models and has students spell words in new word column.	
a. Teacher points to *ghost.* "This word is *ghost.* What word?" (Signal.)	"Ghost."
b. "Spell *ghost.*" (Signal.)	"G-h-o-s-t."
c. "What word?" (Signal.)	"Ghost."
d. Teacher repeats step 1(a–c) with remaining words in the new word column.	
Part 2: (Students sight-read words in new word column and review word column.)	
1. a. "When I signal, tell me the word."	
b. Teacher points to *ghost,* pauses 2 seconds. "What word?" (Signal.)	"Ghost."
c. Teacher repeats step 1(b) with all remaining words.	
2. Teacher calls on individual students to read several words.	

- has the students spell the word. "Spell *fuel.*"
- has the students say the word again. "What word?"

The teacher repeats the above procedure with each word, then has the students read the column again, just saying each word.

In part 2, irregular words introduced over the three prior days, as well as any previously introduced words students may have misidentified, are reviewed. The students read each word without any prompting from the teacher. Any error is corrected by telling the students the word, having them spell it, then say it again, then returning to an earlier word in the list and re-presenting the list.

Table 17.2 shows words that might be presented in a series of mid-third grade lessons. Three new words are introduced each day. The first three words in the new word column (*ghost, pour,* and *zero*) are being introduced for the first time. The next three words (*weight, earth,* and *wrong*) are being reintroduced. They were presented in the previous lesson. The words in the review column were introduced two and three lessons prior to the current lesson.

Minor Sounds

Some consonants and most letter combinations have minor sounds; the minor sound of a letter or letter combination is a sound represented in a minority of the words in which it appears.

The consonants *c* and *g* and the letter *y*, as well as a number of letter combinations, have minor sounds, sounds that appear in less than half of the words in which the particular letter appears.

When the letter *c* is followed by the vowels *e* or *i*, the *c* represents an /s/ sound. When the letter *g* is followed by *e* or *i*, the *g* represents the /j/ sound. Note also that whenever *c* is followed by *y*, the *y* acts as a vowel and the *c* represents its minor sound, (e.g., fancy).

The letter *y* can represent a consonant sound and one of two vowel sounds, a long *i*, as in *fly,* and a long *e*, as in *happy.*

Many letter combinations have minor sounds that occur with some frequency. Note *ea* often represents the short *e* sound as in *head*, and *oo* often represents the sound made in the word *book.*

Minor Sound for C and G   The consonants *c* and *g* both say their minor sounds when followed by the vowels *e*, *i*, and *y* (when *y* functions as a vowel). For example, giant, gem, age, ledge, cell, cinder, ace, ice. Since there are a number of words that have these minor sounds, a generalizable strategy can be taught. The strategy would teach application of a simple rule, "When *i* or *e* follow *c*, we say the sound /s/ for *c*."

A format for teaching the rule for the minor sound for *c* would have the teacher present a word list containing five words in which the rule applies (mice, cent, rice, cell, lace). The teacher leads the students in applying the rule ("What letter comes after the *c*?" "So what sound do we say for the *c*?" "What word?"). After several days, a discrimination format would be presented with half the words having *c* represent its major sound, and half its minor sound (nice, tack, cent, can't, cell, call, mice, mick). A similar procedure can be utilized with the letter *g* and with words in which *c* is followed by *y*.

In addition to the above discrimination format, the teacher could also present word families containing these minor sounds of *c* and *g*.

ace	ice	age	dge
face	mice	page	badge
grace	spice	cage	bridge
lace	dice	wage	ledge
place	nice	rage	wedge
mace	rice		fudge
pace	slice		budge
race	spice		
space			

The teacher writes on the board a word family, for example a group of words ending with the letters *ace* (lace, face, race, place, space). The teacher says, "The letters a-c-e say *ace*. All these words rhyme with *ace*." Then the teacher has the students read the set of words. This exercise is repeated for several days. After 2 days of practice, these words are randomly integrated into a practice sightreading word list. Several days later, words with this word family would be placed into stories.

Y as a Minor Sound   The letter *y* functions as both a consonant (yes) and a vowel (my, happy). At the end of one-syllable words, the *y* represents the long *i* sound (my, shy, fly, cry). At the end of multisyllabic words, it represents the long *e* sound (baby, happy, lily). A teaching procedure for introducing one-syllable words would present a list of words ending in *y* (fly, shy, cry, pry). The teacher would tell the students the sound the *y* makes and have the students read the list. This format would be presented for about a week, then words ending with *y* would be integrated into the word-list exercises with other type words.

Letter Combinations   Words that contain minor sounds of letter combinations would be introduced as irregular words. The teacher uses a format like the one in Table 17.2. The teacher tells the student the word, has the student spell the word, then say it. Word families containing the same sound can be introduced together (e.g., caught and taught).

Providing Extra Practice

Some students may need more practice to develop automaticity in reading irregular words. A peer-practice/testing procedure can be used to provide more practice and to ensure that students are, in fact, mastering irregular words. In this procedure, the teacher makes a list of 30 to 50 recently introduced irregular words on a sheet of paper and distributes copies of the list to the students. Students practice reading the list in pairs. To ensure students are attentive, the teacher directs the student who is not reading to point to the words being read. If the reader misses a word, the checker says "Stop," and tells the student the word. The reader says the word, moves back four words in the list, then continues to read. The teacher should put in a group reward to encourage cooperation and discourage arguing.

After several days of practice periods, the teacher has a testing period. Higher-performing students or adults (volunteers or aides) can be the testers. The instructions to the tester are kept simple. If a student misidentifies a word, the tester says the correct word and makes a mark next to the missed word. If a student takes longer than 3 seconds to say a word, the tester tells the student the word, then makes a mark next to the word. The students' goal is to read the list without error at a rate of one word per second.

A new set of words can be introduced after 30 to 50 new words have been presented. The teacher keeps old word lists and has students review them periodically. For example, after the students have been given three worksheets, they might be directed to review worksheets one and two. A danger with this procedure is that the students will memorize the order of words in a list. This danger can be minimized by sometimes having the student begin at the end of the list and read the list from end to front.

Context as a Cue

A teacher cannot systematically introduce all the irregular words students will encounter. As students progress through the grades, they increasingly read more outside the structured reading lesson. In this reading, they will encounter irregular words (i.e., words that contain letter-sound correspondences the students do not know). The context of the sentence can offer an important cue that can be used, with phonic- and structural-analysis cues, to decode these unknown irregular words.

A great deal of confusion has surrounded the use and misuse of context as a strategy for reading unknown words. Introducing the use of context when students are in the beginning stage of reading instruction can be very problematic, as it is likely to result in student confusion. Once students have learned the most common sound of all individual letters, most common letter combinations, common prefixes and suffixes, and can apply this knowledge accurately to reading words, teaching students to use the context of a sentence to help figure out a new unknown word is appropriate.

The vowel sounds are generally the most problematic part of reading unknown irregular words. In one-syllable words the difficulty often arises because a low-frequency letter combination (e.g., the *ue* in *fuel,* the *ei* in *neither*) is present or a letter or letter combination representing a vowel sound that it represents infrequently (e.g., *ea* in *steak, ee* in *been, ai* in *said, u* in *put*) is present.

In two-syllable words, the difficulty with the vowel sound often arises when there is a single consonant between two vowels in the mid-part of the word and the word is not a derivative of a CVCe word (e.g., *camel, hotel, topic, bacon, cupid, study, petal, meter*). Note that in some of these words the initial vowel sound is the long sound of the first vowel and, in some words, the short sound of the initial vowel.

Teaching Procedure

The teaching procedure we present provides students with a strategy to use when they come to a word in which there is no phonic or structural cue for the vowel sound. When the students come to such a word, they are first to pronounce the word with the initial vowel representing its long sound.

The students then determine if the word pronounced with the long-vowel sound makes sense within the sentence context. If the word pronounced with its long-vowel sound does not make sense, the students pronounce the word with the short-vowel sound to see if it is a word that does make sense in the context. This strategy should not be presented until students have mastered the discrimination between CVCe derivatives and CVC derivatives (*hopped* vs. *hoped*). Introducing the strategy too early can cause confusion.

Two formats are presented to teach the above strategy. The first (see Table 17.3) is a preskill format in which the teacher presents a list of six to eight words. Half the words should have a long-vowel sound and half should have a short-vowel sound. (See Appendix A for a list of words.) The initial vowel is underlined. For each word, the teacher tells the student whether the initial vowel says its name or sound, then has the student say the word. The purpose of this format is simply to give the students practice in saying words in which they have

been told the vowel sound. This preskill format is presented daily until the students can answer with no errors on the first trial for two consecutive days.

The second format (see Table 17.4) introduces students to the actual strategy of what to do when they encounter a new word with a difficult-to-determine vowel sound. The teacher first explains that to figure out a new word the students may have to try several sounds for the underlined letter (the initial vowel). Furthermore, the teacher tells the students that the first time they sound out the word they can say the name of the underlined letter. The teacher then leads the students through decoding a set of four to six words, half with a long initial vowel sound and half with a short initial vowel sound. For each word, the teacher prompts the students to pronounce the word, saying the long sound for the initial vowel. Then the teacher says a sentence and asks if what the student said makes sense within the sentence's context. If not, the teacher asks the students to say the word with a different sound. The word should make sense within the context of that sentence. All words should either be in

---

Table 17.3 Preskill Format

Teacher	Students
Teacher writes on board:	

bugle   fuel
rapid   topic
neither   silent

Teacher	Students
1. "These are funny words. In some words, the underlined letter says its name. In some words, the underlined letter says its sound."	
2. "For each word, I'll tell you if the underlined letter says its name or sound. You'll tell me what the letter says. Then you'll say the word."	
3. a. Teacher points to the *u* in *bugle*. "This letter says its name."	
b. "What's the name of this letter." (Signal.)	"Ū."
c. "Say the word." (Signal.)	"Bugle."
4. a. Teacher points to the *a* in *rapid*. "This letter says its sound."	
b. "What's the sound?" (Signal.)	"Ă."
c. "What word?" (Signal.)	"Rapid."
5. Teacher repeats steps 3 or 4 with the remaining words.	
6. Teacher gives several students individual turns on step 3 (a–c) or step 4 (a–c) with one or more words.	

Table 17.4 Strategy for Words That Have Difficult-to-Determine Vowel Sounds

Teacher	*Students*
Teacher writes on board:	

c<u>a</u>mel   n<u>ei</u>ther   t<u>o</u>pic   b<u>a</u>gel

1. "These are new words. When you try to figure out a new word, you may have to sound out the word with several different sounds for the underlined letter before you can figure out the word."	
2. "Here's a rule: the first time you figure out the word, say the name of the letter."	
3. a. Teacher points to c<u>a</u>mel. "What's the name of the underlined letter?" (Signal.)	"a."
b. Teacher points to <u>a.</u> "Figure out the word to yourself, saying /ā/ for this letter." (Pause.)	
c. "Say the word." (Signal.)	"Cāmel."
d. "I'll say a sentence with that word: A cāmel is an animal that has humps on its back. Does cāmel make sense in that sentence?" (Signal.) NOTE: If the answer to step 3(d) is "yes," do not do step 3(e–g).	"No."
e. Teacher points to *a*. "So let's try the sound. What's the sound?" (Signal.)	"ă"
f. "Get ready to pronounce the word saying the sound." (Pause and signal.)	"Camel."
g. "I'll say the sentence with that word. A camel is an animal that has humps on its back. Does camel make sense in that sentence?" (Signal.)	"Yes."
4. Repeat step 3 with remaining words.	

---

the students' vocabulary or have been presented earlier in a vocabulary exercise.

This format is presented daily until students make no errors on the first trial for two consecutive days. Then a new set of words can be introduced. A worksheet exercise similar to that in Figure 17.1 can be presented after several sets of words have been taught. In the worksheet exercise, four to eight irregular words that have not been previously introduced are written. Sentences with a missing word are written below the words. The students are to fill in the blanks in the sentences with one of the listed words.

Figure 17.1 Sample Worksheet for Context Usage

> Instructions: Fill in the blanks below with one of these words:
>
> salad   camel   bacon   hotel   copy
>
> **1.** They stayed in a nice _____ .
>
> **2.** I love _____ and eggs.
>
> **3.** The teacher said, "Do not _____ ."
>
> **4.** They rode on top of a _____ .
>
> **5.** We put tomatoes in the _____ .

The range of examples in the context exercise can be expanded to include words which are irregular either because they (1) contain letter combinations not taught because they appear infrequently, or (2) contain letter combinations representing a sound other than its most common sound. For example, the word *steak* contains the letter combination *ea* which usually makes the /ē/ sound as in the word *neat*. The teacher presents *steak* to the students by saying, "In this word, *e–a* does not say /ē/. I'll say the sentence. You figure out what the word must be. He cooked a big blank. What word?" (Signal.) "Yes, *steak*."

Multisyllabic Words

Students should also be taught how to use context as a cue to decode multisyllabic irregular words. Table 17.5 includes a format for teaching students

---

Table 17.5   Format for Introducing Multisyllabic Irregular Words

Teacher	Students
A. Teacher writes on board: isolation recognize demonstrate relationship graduation	
B. Teacher introduces word.	
1. Teacher has students say familiar parts of the word.	
a. Teacher points to *isolation*. "Let's say the parts in this word."	
b. Teacher points to *ol*. "What do these letters usually say?" (Signal.)	"Ol."
c. Teacher points to *ation*. "What do these letters usually say?" (Signal.)	"Ation."
2. Teacher gives context hint. "Listen, I'll say a sentence: The doctors put him in an (points to *isolation*) ward because they didn't want anyone to catch his disease. Raise your hand when you know the word." Teacher calls on an individual. After the student says the word, teacher asks the group to say it. "What's the word?" (Signal.)	"Isolation."
3. Teacher repeats steps 1 and 2 with all remaining words.	
4. Teacher has students reread words giving only context cues.	
a. "I'll say a sentence that has a missing word. You'll say the missing word."	
b. Teacher points to *isolation*. "The doctors put him in a blank ward. What word?" (Signal.)	"Isolation."
c. Teacher points to *recognize*. "I could not blank him. What word?" (Signal.)	"Recognize."
d. Teacher points to *demonstrate*. "We asked the salesman to blank how the machine worked. What word?" (Signal.)	"Demonstrate."
e. Teacher points to *graduation*. "When he finishes school, he will have a blank party. What word?" (Signal.)	"Graduation."

to use context to figure out multisyllabic irregular words. The teacher has the students identify known word parts, then says the sentence in which the word appears as a cue to help the students figure out the word. The instances presented in Table 17.5 are appropriate for the late-intermediate grades.

The unknown word must be a word that is in the students' receptive vocabulary. If the student has never heard the word before, or does not know what it means, context will not be a useful cue. After several days, worksheet exercises such as those described above can be presented.

❧ Application Exercises

1. Assume the teacher has taught the following skills:
   - Decoding all types of 1- and 2-syllable regular words and words containing letter combinations;
   - The most common sounds of all single letters;
   - The most common sound of these letter combinations and affixes: *ai, ar, ea, ee, ck, ou, th, sh, wh, ch, er, ing, ed, y, igh, al,* and *oa;*
   - VCe words with long sounds for initial vowel.

   Circle each of the following words the student would not be able to decode. Next to each of the *circled* words, write the abbreviation for the explanation below that tells why the student could not decode the word.
   - Letter (L)—The word contains a letter combination the students do not know.
   - Irregular (I)—Some letter or letter combination is not representing its most common sound.

_____ spoil	_____ float	_____ cough
_____ ground	_____ blame	_____ smell
_____ blew	_____ steak	_____ warn
_____ trait	_____ cheer	_____ done
_____ groan	_____ bleach	_____ roam
_____ soup	_____ sigh	_____ shame
_____ broad	_____ rough	_____ build

2. When teaching the strategy for words that have difficult-to-determine vowel sounds, the teacher states the following sentence and question to which the student answers, "No." Tell the likely reason for this error.

   Teacher: "I'll say a sentence with the new word. Listen: He ate a bagel.

   Does *bagel* make sense in that sentence?"

3. Below are the irregular words a teacher presented in word lists on each day. Tell why the lists are not adequate. Tell what the teacher should do to teach the words.

   Monday: fuel, reign, chauffeur

   Tuesday: bias, puny, tour

   Wednesday: sewn, plaque, chef

4. Put a check in front of the irregular words which can be part of a related set.

_____ said	_____ grace	_____ suit
_____ throw	_____ stood	_____ me
_____ fly	_____ cage	_____ soup

5. It is possible for a teacher to predict the relative difficulty students will have decoding new words. Put a check in front of the six words below students are most likely to have difficulty decoding. Assume students have mastered all phonic- and structural-analysis skills taught during the primary stage.

_____ predictable	_____ inactive	_____ peril
_____ hilarious	_____ ratio	_____ invention
_____ detective	_____ souvenir	_____ basketball
_____ hopelessly	_____ returning	_____ buttercup
_____ sodium	_____ inspection	_____ malaria

6. Construct a worksheet exercise that provides practice for using context to decode two-syllable words with a single consonant in the middle. (See word list in Appendix A.)

Fluency Instruction and Passage Reading

Fluency

Fluency is the ability to read a text quickly and accurately with ease and expression. When fluent readers read aloud, it sounds like they are speaking. In contrast, the oral reading of readers who have not yet developed fluency is slow, word by word, choppy, and plodding.

Although the terms automaticity and fluency frequently have been used interchangeably, they are not the same. Automaticity refers to fast, effortless recognition of words in isolation or in lists. Fluency refers to fast, effortless reading of words in sentences and passages. Automatic word recognition is a necessary, but not sufficient, condition of fluency. Some students may recognize words in isolation or in lists automatically and still lack fluency when reading those same words in sentences. They need instruction in fluency.

Fluency is important because it is a bridge between word recognition and comprehension. Fluent readers can focus their attention on the meaning of text because they do not need to concentrate on decoding the words. Because less fluent readers must focus their attention on figuring out the words, they have less attention left to devote to understanding the text. Fluency is essential to comprehension and

automatic word recognition is essential to fluency. Thus, fluency is a bridge that the reader must traverse to get from word recognition to comprehension. Automatic word recognition, fluency, and comprehension are inextricably intertwined reading skills. The main findings of the National Reading Panel (2000) on fluency appear in Figure 18.1. As stated in Figure 18.1, instructional procedures that improve fluency also have a positive impact on word recognition and comprehension.

Two major instructional approaches to fluency have been investigated by researchers:

1. Repeated reading approaches in which students read passages aloud several times and receive guidance and feedback from the teacher as they read aloud.

2. Independent silent reading approaches in which students are encouraged to read extensively on their own.

The National Reading Panel pointed out that research has not yet confirmed independent silent reading as a means of improving fluency and overall reading achievement. Research has, however, confirmed that repeated oral reading with feedback and guidance improves fluency and has a positive

Figure 18.1   National Reading Panel Conclusions From Scientifically-Based Research on Fluency Instruction

- Classroom practices that include repeated oral reading with feedback and guidance lead to improvements in reading for good readers, as well as those who are experiencing difficulties.
- Guided, repeated oral-reading procedures that improve reading fluency also have a positive impact on word recognition and comprehension.
- Repeated reading procedures have a clear impact on the reading ability of non-impaired readers through at least grade 4, as well as on students with various kinds of reading problems throughout high school.
- Fluency can be improved by having students read and reread text a certain number of times or until certain levels of speed and accuracy are reached.
- No research evidence is available currently to confirm that instructional time spent on silent, independent reading improves reading fluency and overall reading achievement.
- The lack of demonstrated effectiveness of strategies encouraging independent silent reading suggests that explicit are more important than implicit instructional approaches for improving reading fluency.

Adapted from the NRP Report of the Subgroups, Chapter 3, "Fluency," p. 29.

impact on comprehension. In repeated oral reading, students read and reread a text a specified number of times or until specified levels of speed and accuracy are reached. Listening to good models of fluent reading also promotes fluency; however, students must reread the text themselves after listening to the model.

In the remainder of this chapter, we provide examples of teaching procedures that incorporate modeling of fluent reading and repeated oral readings to specified levels of speed and accuracy. These procedures are carried out in the context of passage-reading activities.

Passage Reading

Passage reading refers to a structured activity in which students read stories designed to provide practice and application of decoding and comprehension skills. Passage reading provides students with the practice to become accurate and fluent readers. Fluency refers to the ease with which a student reads. Accuracy refers to the student's ability to read without making errors.

An emphasis on accuracy in early reading instruction will enable students to develop habitual accuracy. They will develop the concentration to read accurately without great effort. The need for accurate reading becomes increasingly observable when students encounter complex scientific materials where misreading one word can change the meaning of a sentence.

The teacher must take the responsibility to develop both accuracy and fluency. Students who do not receive the practice to develop adequate fluency may be handicapped in later grades. Students who read significantly slower than their peers can develop a negative attitude toward themselves as they note that they are not performing at a level equal to their peers. Such students may also encounter frustration as the workload grows in the upper grades and their slower reading rate results in those students needing more time than their peers to do assignments.

Story Selection

A successful passage-reading component is possible only if the stories presented in the passage-reading exercises are carefully controlled to ensure the student has a strategy to decode every word in the passage. Stories during the first and second years of instruction that are carefully controlled to include only words with taught phonic and structural elements and previously taught irregular words are referred to as decodable stories.

Not every word appearing in the story must have appeared in an earlier word-list exercise. If a word contains a phonic element the student has already mastered in earlier word-list exercises, the word need not be presented in a word-list exercise prior to its appearance in a story. For example, after the students have read about 15 to 20 words containing the letter combination *ar* in word-list exercises, a word containing *ar* that has not appeared in a word list exercise could appear in a story. Any word containing a phonic or structural element the student does not know should be presented as an irregular word in word-list exercises prior to its appearance in the passage.

The terms *independent level, instructional level* and *frustration level* are used to indicate the appropriateness of text for various purposes. Independent level is text that includes only words that the students have the knowledge to decode and is appropriate for exercises in which teachers will not preteach words specific to that text. Instructional level is text that is challenging, but manageable. Text at the instructional level should be at a level that with adequate word-list exercises just before reading the story, the children can read it with few errors. Frustration level is text that is so difficult that even with pre-teaching, students will find many words not readable.

Teaching Procedure

This section first will present procedures for presenting passage reading during the second year of instruction. Modifications in the passage-reading procedures to be made in later grades will be discussed next. Most passage-reading during the second year of reading instruction should be devoted to the students orally reading stories under the teacher's direct supervision. If possible, passage reading should be conducted in small groups. Higher-performing students can be placed in groups of up to 10 to 12 students. Groups composed of lower-performing students should be smaller.

The challenge for the teacher is to (1) motivate the students to be attentive while other students read, (2) provide motivation to foster careful and accurate reading by the students when it is their own turn to read, (3) provide adequate practice for all students to develop fluency, and (4) provide instruction in specific skills, such as reading with expression.

The following teaching and motivation procedures are based on the assumption that the students in the group have received sufficient teaching to decode all the words appearing in the stories. The stories are at the students' instructional level. If one or more students in the group are not able to decode the words in the story or read at a significantly slower rate than the other students in the group, the teacher should do something to increase the student's likelihood of having a successful experience during passage-reading exercises. The most practical procedure involves the student reading stories individually to a volunteer or peer before reading it as part of a group.

The basic procedure for conducting story reading during the second year of instruction involves the students reading a story several times. In the first reading, the teacher concentrates on decoding. If the students perform at an acceptable mastery level on the first reading, the teacher then focuses in the second reading on comprehension and decoding skills. A third reading would focus on fluency with students rereading the story chorally or in pairs.

The teacher conducts the first and second reading by calling on individual students to read as the others follow along. The student whose turn it is reads one to four sentences. The teacher calls on different students to read several sentences until the passage is completed. The teacher records any errors the students make. If the group reads the passage with an acceptable number of errors (a 97% criterion—no more than 3 errors per 100 words), the teacher has the students reread the story and asks comprehension questions as the students read. If the students make too many errors on the first reading (more than 3 per 100 words), they reread the story with the teacher solely concentrating on decoding skills, not asking comprehension questions.

Individual checkouts, in which the teacher has each student read a 100-word passage, should be done at least every second week. The checkouts serve to test whether students are developing sufficient accuracy and fluency. The teacher designates a 100-word excerpt from a recently read passage. The teacher records the time the student took to read, as well as the number of errors made.

Table 18.1   Format for Introducing Passage-Reading Decoding

---

1. Introducing story-reading procedure
   a. "You're going to read this story out loud. I'll call on different students to read. When you're reading, talk in a big voice so everyone can hear you. Pause when you come to a period. If I don't call on another student, read the next sentence. If it's not your turn to read, point to the words that are being read."
   b. "I'll show you how I want you to read. You point to the words as I say them." (Teacher reads several sentences. Students touch words as teacher reads.)
   c. Teacher repeats step 1(b) until all students follow along as she reads.
2. Students read story—decoding
   a. "Your turn to read. When I call on you, read in a mature voice. Pause when you come to a period. If I don't call on another student, read the next sentence. If it's not your turn to read, point to the words that are being read."
   b. "Our error limit for today's story is 8. If you read the story with only 8 errors or fewer, we'll read the story again, and I'll ask comprehension questions."
   c. Teacher calls on students to read individually. Teacher calls on a new student each one to three sentences.
3. Students read story—comprehension
   a. Teacher calls on student to read individually. Teacher asks comprehension questions.

A format for introducing passage reading appears in Table 18.1. The format begins with the teacher telling the students they will be reading individually when called upon. The teacher instructs the students to talk in a "big" voice and to pause at each period when they read. When other students are reading, the students are to point to the words being read. At this early stage, we recommend requiring students to point to words as other students read as a means to increase the probability they will stay actively involved throughout the entire lesson, not only when they are called upon to read. When students read for several weeks without losing their places, the teacher can give them the privilege of not pointing.

After explaining the procedure, the teacher reads several sentences, modeling how to read with expression and how to pause at the end of sentences. The teacher reads at a rate quickly enough to model good expression, but slowly enough to allow students to follow along.

Next, the teacher explains to the students the error limit for reading the story. (A description of procedures for setting error limits appears later in this section, along with a discussion of techniques to motivate students to read accurately.)

The students read the story without the teacher asking comprehension questions. If the students read the story making fewer errors than

specified, they read the story again. During this second reading, the teacher asks comprehension questions. If the students make more errors than allowed on the first reading, they read the story for a second time with the teacher concentrating again on accuracy.

Critical Behaviors

- Call on students to read in an unpredictable order. Students will be more attentive when they do not know when it will be their turn. Sometimes have a student read one sentence, sometimes several sentences.

- Watch the students carefully to make certain they are following along when another student is reading.

- Good timing will facilitate the transition from student to student. When the teacher wants a new student to read, the teacher says the name of the next student as the student who is reading finishes the last word in the sentence. The teacher should keep her talk to a minimum.

Corrections

The correction procedure a teacher uses depends on the group size the teacher is working with.

When a teacher is working with more than three students, the teacher must consider how his or her actions affect the attentiveness of the group. If the teacher spends too much time with an individual student, this extended time increases the probability of the other students becoming inattentive. The following correction procedure is designed for use with a group of more than three students and is used when a child misidentifies a word.

1. When a student makes an error, the teacher tells the student the missed word. "That word is *astounded*." The teacher should not use an abrupt or loud voice.

2. The teacher has the student say the correct word. "What word?"

3. The teacher tells the student to read the sentence from the beginning. ("Go back to the beginning of the sentence and read the sentence again.") The purpose of rereading the sentence is to make certain the student gains the proper meaning.

4. The teacher records the missed word and provides review on that word before students reread the story and in the next day's word list exercises.

If the student error was not a misidentification error, the teacher tells the student the error that was made and has the student read the sentence again. "You left out a word. Please read the sentence again."

In a one-to-one situation or with a small group, the teacher can use a more sophisticated correction procedure when the student makes an error. The teacher points to the missed word and attempts to prompt the student to determine the correct word. The prompt depends on the type of error. If a student misidentifies a word with a letter combination, the teacher points out the letter or letter combination missed, asks the student the sound of the letter(s), then if the student identifies the sound(s) correctly, asks the student, "What word?" For example, if a student says "beat" for beach, the teacher would point to ch and ask, "What do these letters say? What's the word." If the student cannot

identify the letter combination, the teacher tells the student the sound, has the student say the sound, then asks, "What word?" If the student misidentifies an irregular word, the teacher simply tells the student the word, because a phonic or structural cue will not help to figure out an irregular word. For all errors, the student should go back to the beginning of the sentence and reread the sentence.

As a general rule, the less said by the teacher when making corrections during passage reading, the smoother the lesson probably will progress.

The teacher then works on fluency. Procedures for this will be discussed in a later section in this chapter.

Modifications for Higher Grades

The procedure for presenting passage reading changes as the students progress through the grades. When students have successfully completed the second year of reading instruction, the teacher can introduce structured silent reading. The student reads most of the passage orally, then a small part silently. The teacher asks comprehension questions immediately after the students read silently on the content of the part read silently. The proportion of the story read silently gradually grows until one-third is read orally and two-thirds silently. This silent reading is only done if the students have developed sufficient accuracy and fluency.

Fluency—Reading With Expression

Training in reading with expression is necessary to demonstrate to students that written passages express meaning in the same way spoken language does. Oral-reading behaviors that characterize reading with expression include pausing at periods and punctuation marks, dividing text into meaningful chunks, emphasizing the appropriate words, and when reading quotations, using inflections that reflect the mood of the character speaking. Expression training can begin when students are able to read at a rate of about 50 to 60 words per minute. A 10- to 15-minute training session can be incorporated into the lesson following the reading of the passage.

We recommend a modeling procedure for teaching students to read with expression. The teacher says, "We're going to practice reading this story as if we were telling a story. I'll read a sentence. Then you read it the same way as I read it." The teacher then reads the first sentence or two, using slightly exaggerated expression. Students should be instructed to keep their fingers on the first word in the sentence and simply follow along with their eyes as the teacher reads. (Pointing to the first word enables the students to quickly find the beginning of the sentence when it is their turn to read.) After the teacher reads, he or she calls on the group to read the sentence in unison several times. Then the teacher calls on several individuals to read the sentence with expression. If a student does not read with expression, the teacher repeats the model and has the group read the sentence. The teacher then reads the first sentence(s) and the next sentence together modeling expression, then calls on the group and individuals to read with expression from the beginning. This procedure is repeated for each new sentence, so that the children are able to practice reading a cluster of sentences with fluency

Exercises for teaching reading with expression should be done daily until students read new material with expression without first receiving a teacher model. This can take months and months of practice.

Teachers can also have children practice reading with expression together in pairs as well as read chorally.

Recordkeeping

During oral passage-reading instruction, the teacher should maintain a recordkeeping system to keep track of student performance during oral passage reading. Two student behaviors are recorded: decoding errors and lost places.

A recording system should provide maximum information with minimum disruption of the group, enabling the teacher to record student performance without becoming distracted from teaching the group.

We recommend that the teacher record student performance on a photocopy of the passage the students are reading.

Recording Errors

The system described below is one possible system for recording errors. For an error, the teacher needs to indicate who made the error and the kind of error made. To record who made the error, the teacher can write the student's initials in capital letters over the missed word. Lower-case letters can be used to describe the decoding error.

The teacher needs a consistent system for describing student errors. Below is one possible system for recording various types of decoding errors:

- Student says word incorrectly: The teacher writes the reader's initials in capital letters over the word. The teacher then writes what the student said over the word, using lower-case letters. The teacher need not write the entire student response. If the student left off an ending (e.g., saying "mark" for marked), the teacher might make a slash through the ending (e.g., marked). The teacher's slash indicates that the ed ending was not said. If the student says one sound incorrectly, the teacher can write the lower-case letter representing that sound (e.g., pörk). The a indicates that the student said park instead of pork. Remember, the teacher uses lower-case letters when writing what the student said and upper-case letters to designate who made the error (e.g., we ate ^{EM}pörk). The teacher wrote EM for a student named Ellen Manco, and the a because the student said park instead of pork.

- Student is unable to identify a word within a reasonable amount of time: The teacher writes the initials for the student's name in capital letters over the word and circles the word (e.g., ^{EM}(mystery)). As a general rule, the teacher should allow the student no more than 5 seconds to figure out a word. Allowing the student too much time can be punishing for the student unable to figure out the word and can disrupt the flow of the lesson. However, not allowing sufficient time for a student to attempt a word can also be frustrating to the student. The teacher must use his or her judgment. If the student seems on the verge of figuring out the word, the teacher can allow the student several more seconds.

- Student omits a word: The teacher writes the initials for the student's name in capital letters over the omitted word and writes an "o" with a slash through it above the word (e.g., The man went to the ᴱᴹ ǿld house).

- Student inserts a word: The teacher writes ʌ to indicate that the student said a word not appearing in the text and writes student's initials in capital letters next to the inserted word. The teacher writes the word the student inserted (e.g., The student read the sentence, "He went to the game" as "He went to the big game." The teacher writes "He went to the bigᴮᴶ game").
  ʌ

- Students sometimes will pronounce a word incorrectly, but immediately correct themselves. This is referred to as a self-correction. The teacher writes the student's initials in capital letters and records the error by writing the letters "sc" over the word.

- When a student is called on to read, the student should say the first word of the sentence to be read within a second or two after being called on. If the student does not start reading within this time, it is probably because the student has not been attending. The teacher writes the student's initials over the period and a circled Ⓛ for lost place (e.g., went home. They play). Some students may not start reading when called on because their reading rate is slow. If it is obvious a student has been following along, the teacher need not record a circled L. Similarly, if the first word is a difficult word, the teacher should allow more time. The teacher must, however, make it clear to the students that she expects

them actively to follow along when other students read.

Group and individual performance during passage reading should be kept on summary sheets. This data serves as information for motivation systems and as indicators of student performance. As a general rule, any error is counted as a mistake. Omissions and insertions, as well as misread words, count as errors. Group performance can be recorded on graph paper. Lesson numbers are written across the horizontal axis, while the number of errors is recorded up and down the vertical axis. Table 18.2 displays a sample chart. Numbers 1 through 9 on the vertical axis refer to the number of errors. Note that only one space is provided for more than 9 errors. Numbers 30 through 40 across the horizontal axis refer to lesson numbers.

Individual student performance could be recorded on a simple table as shown in Table 18.3. The students' names are listed vertically. Lesson numbers are written horizontally. Daily performance is recorded on the table.

Motivation System

A motivation system during oral reading instruction of text selections should focus on two behaviors: accurate reading and student attentiveness.

Accurate Reading

A motivation system to foster careful reading begins with the teacher setting up pay-offs based on the number of errors a group makes when reading stories. The fewer the number of mistakes, the greater the pay-off.

The criteria for accurate reading should be set at a high level. We recommend a 97% accuracy goal (no more than 3 errors per 100 words). This criterion is based on the assumptions that students have received adequate practice to master word-list exercises and that the word-list exercises have been adequately designed and implemented to prepare students to read all the words in the assigned stories. One purpose of oral story reading is to provide students with practice employing decoding skills they have already mastered. If the students have not had

Table 18.2   Group Performance Chart

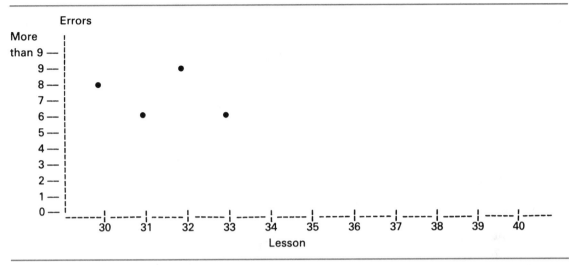

Table 18.3   Individual Student Performance Table

Name	43	44	45	46	47	48	49	50
Billy								
John								
Sally								
Tim								

adequate preparation in word-list exercises, the high criterion will be unreasonable and cause frustration. If students have had adequate preparation, the 97% criterion will be a realistic goal.

A variety of pay-offs may be used. The pay-offs employed should be based on the type of students involved. Teachers working with higher-performing, more intrinsically motivated students can rely primarily on verbal and written acknowledgements of performance. Teachers working with less intrinsically motivated students may need initially to utilize more powerful pay-offs, such as extra recesses, and tangibles, as well as acknowledgements of good performance. In all cases, the teacher should respond

with enthusiasm when students read with high levels of accuracy.

Following is a sample system used by a teacher. The students were reading stories of approximately 300 words. The students would be reading at a 97% accuracy rate if 9 errors were made in reading the story. The teacher set up an economy in which the students' performance earned an extra recess once a week. (Note: The recess was not awarded during reading time, but at another time during the day. Missing 15 minutes of reading a week would deprive students of nearly 10% of their instructional time.) The students earned minutes of recess each day if they read at a 97% accuracy level. They

Table 18.4   Reward Schedule for Passage Reading

Student Errors	Minutes of Extra Recess
0–1 errors	4
2–4 errors	3
5–7 errors	2
8–9 errors	1

earned more minutes if they read at a higher accuracy level. Table 18.4 shows the schedule the teacher used for a 300-word story.

Attentiveness

A motivation system also should be designed to keep students attentive throughout the oral-reading exercise and particularly when it is not their turn to read individually. A good indicator of attentiveness is the student knowing his or her place when called on to read.

A minimal consequence can be used to discourage inattentiveness. A second lost place in a week might result in a 5-minute practice session during recess time in which the teacher reads while the student follows along. For most students, this minimal consequence will be effective. If, however, a student continues to have problems with lost places, the teacher must take further actions to alleviate the problem.

First, the teacher should test the student's reading rate to determine if the problem results from the student's reading rate being significantly slower than other members of the group. If the student's rate is not adequate, the teacher should provide extra practice. Ideally, the student should have a chance to read the story to a volunteer the day before the group reads the story. If the student's reading rate is adequate, the teacher then can set up a more powerful motivation system. We recommend setting up a system whereby gradual improvement by the student enables the whole group to earn a reward. For example, if a student loses his place an average of three times a lesson, the teacher might set up a system wherein the student's improvement

to only two lost places per lesson earns a small reward for the group. Once the student improves to only two lost places per lesson, the teacher would up the criterion to one lost place per lesson, then two or three per week. It is important to maintain the reward system after the student improves. Paying attention to students when they are performing well and constantly acknowledging their good performance is very important.

Other Behaviors

Two student behaviors very important to a smoothly run passage-reading exercise are: (1) students pausing when they reach a period, and (2) students talking in a loud enough voice when called on for an individual turn.

During the story-reading exercise, the teacher should use specific praise frequently (e.g., "Good stopping at the period," "You talked in a big voice," "Good reading"). This praise will usually be effective with most students in the group. If some students have difficulty, the teacher should make individual systems with those students (e.g., "Billy, each time you read loud, I'll give you a point. When you get 10 points, you'll earn a bonus point for everyone in the group.").

A motivation system is not a fixed thing. A teacher must continually monitor the motivation system to ensure that each student is feeling successful and competent. The teacher must always resist the temptation to nag students having difficulty or implore them to work harder. Both of these teacher behaviors rarely result in student improvement. Instead, the teacher should always test individually to determine if a skill deficit is involved or if motivation procedures need to be strengthened.

Diagnosis and Remediation

Any student whose accuracy rate is below 97% in passage reading should receive extra instruction. The type of instruction to be provided depends on the basic cause of the errors. Errors can be divided into two broad categories: context-related errors and skill-deficit errors. Context-related errors are usually indicated by inconsistent student performance. The student reads a word correctly in one sentence and, later in the passage, reads it incorrectly. Specific-skill deficits are indicated by a consistent error pattern (e.g., the student misses all words with the letter combination *ou*).

The first step in any diagnosis procedure is to present an exercise similar to the one on which the student has been performing poorly and to make available a powerful reinforcer for improved performance. The teacher might give a student who has been reading inaccurately a passage to read and say, "If you read this passage with two or fewer errors, you'll earn a sticker for you and two of your friends." The purpose of the motivator is to determine if there is a significant improvement in the student's performance with only the introduction of an increased motivator.

If the student reads significantly more accurately with the increased motivator in force, the teacher should provide a more powerful motivator to the student for reading performance during group reading. As a general rule, we recommend letting a student earn something extra for the entire group. This procedure prevents students from figuring out that poor performance can eventually lead to greater rewards for themselves.

If the increased-motivation procedures do not result in significant improvement, the teacher administers an in-depth test to find specific phonic and structural weaknesses. A diagnostic test that focuses on phonic and structural analysis appears in Chapter 25 on page 311. A test of irregular words can also be created by going through the text being used and making a list of the irregular words introduced to that point.

Students with deficits in previously taught phonic, structural, or irregular word skills should receive daily instruction on the specific deficits. This instruction would include the systematic reintroduction and practicing of the skills the student has not mastered. For example, if the student did not know one or more letter combinations, the teacher would reintroduce the letter combination(s) one at a time using the procedures specified in Chapter 15. While the word-list remediation is being provided, the teacher would prompt the students in passage reading on words containing the unknown elements (e.g., "That word has the letters o–u. Remember, those letters say /ou/.").

Ideally, this extra instruction should be provided by the teacher in a 5- to 10-minute daily one-on-one or small-group setting. The realities of the classroom however, often, make it impossible for the teacher to provide ongoing individualized remediation. Several options are available: The teacher can integrate the remediation into the word-list presentations being made to the group or set up peer tutoring. In peer tutoring, the teacher prepares word-list exercises and trains a higher performing student to work with the student having difficulty.

Context errors may involve either an over- or under-reliance on context cues. An over-reliance on context cues is indicated by the student misidentifying many words (more than 3 per hundred) which the student is able to identify correctly in isolation. A context error is indicated when the student says a word that is syntactically correct but not similar to what is written (e.g., reading "The boy was not healthy" as "The boy was not happy").

The remediation procedure for a pattern that indicates an over-reliance on context involves instituting a motivation system to encourage accurate reading. The criteria depends on the student's current performance. The teacher should set up a system to improve performance in graduated steps. If a student is currently reading at a 90% accuracy level, the system could be set up so that a student is awarded for reading at a 92% or higher criterion. The criterion would gradually be increased as the student's performance improved.

Inaccurate readers often make many self-corrections (misidentifying a word, then immediately saying it correctly). Whereas, an occasional self-correct is not important, frequent self-corrects hamper the story flow. A student who makes too many self-corrects should be put on a motivation system like the one described in the previous paragraph.

Some students who overrely on context will also have a reading-rate deficit. The teacher should not work on remediating both types of deficits at first, but should work first on developing accuracy. Only after the student has begun reading accurately on a consistent basis should the teacher work on increasing rate. Remember, the key to a successful remediation is ensuring that the passage contains no words that have phonic or structural elements or irregular words the students do not know.

An underreliance on context would be indicated by a student saying words that do not make sense in the context of a passage. For example, when reading, The man went to the shop, a student reads, "The man went to the she." If students make many errors that indicate the student is not attentive to the context of the sentence, the teacher should institute oral-language training exercises to teach students to identify context errors. In one type of exercise, the teacher says sentences, and students indicate what word in the sentence does not make sense. Once students learn to identify errors in spoken sentences, they are more likely to identify context errors when they read. In presenting this exercise, a teacher might say, "I'll say some sentences. You tell me whether they make sense."

1. "The boy played on the pouch. Does that make sense?"

2. "The girls ran to the sore. Does that make sense?"

In addition to exercises such as this one, the teacher should establish a motivation system to encourage more careful reading.

Protecting a Student's Self-Image

In addition to providing remediation exercises, the teacher should take other actions to ensure that the self-image of lower-performing students is not being hurt. If one student makes a disproportionate number of errors during group passage reading, the other students may react negatively toward that stu-

dent. One way of dealing with this situation is to not count the student's errors when determining how many errors the group makes when reading a story. The teacher might tell the group, "Jerry is working hard now to catch up on some skills. While he is catching up, I won't count any errors he makes when you read the story."

Another action that can protect a lower-performing student's self-image is to arrange for the student to receive a tutoring session on the story *before* it is presented to the group. The prereading increases the probability of the student performing well when the story is presented to the group.

If a student's performance is significantly below other members of the group, and extra instruction is not making it possible for the student to fully benefit from instruction in that group, the teacher should try to place that student in a lower-performing group.

Fluency—Reading Rate

Reading rate refers to the speed at which a student reads a passage. A student's reading rate is usually expressed in words per minute. The question of how quickly children should be reading at various levels is one that is not clearly answered by research. In order to recommend desired reading rates, we examined studies that showed correlations between reading rates and students' performance on reading comprehension assessments (Hasbrouck & Tindal, 1992). Table 18.5 shows what we consider to be desired reading rates at various levels. These rates are based on examination of reading rates of students who were performing very well on standardized tests. We created desired reading rates that are challenging. We recommend setting these challenging rates because in our work with children in high-poverty schools, we have found that helping the children achieve high rates of fluency in early grades leads to more reading by the student and overall makes school a more enjoyable experience since children with high fluency rates can genrerally finish assignments more easily.

Exercises to develop reading rate should be part of daily lessons until students are able to read at least 135 words a minute. During passage reading, after students read a passage individually, they

Table 18.5   Desired Reading Rates for Various Instructional Levels

Instructional Level	Words per Minute on First Reading
Second third of grade 1 materials	45
Last third of grade 1 materials	60
First third of grade 2 materials	75
Second third of grade 2 materials	90
Last third of grade 2 materials	110
First half of grade 3 materials	120
Second half of grade 3 materials	135
Fourth grade and higher	150

can reread it chorally as a whole group and then individually in pairs.

We recommend extra rate-building exercises for students whose reading rate is 10% or more below the desired level for their instructional level. Note that a student's instructional level may be different than the student's grade level. If a student is reading in a book designated for late-second grade, the student's instructional level is at late-second grade, regardless of whether the child is a first-, second-, or third-grader.

The rate-building exercises involve students doing repeated readings of 100 to 200 word excerpts from previously read passages until they can read them at a desired targeted higher rate. Following is one possible system for doing rate building. It involves repeated reading exercises.

To prepare for the rate building exercises, the teacher first sets a target-rereading rate. The target-rereading rate should be 40% higher than the student's current reading rate. The purpose of setting the rereading criterion significantly higher than the student's current rate is to ensure that students receive massed practice on familiar material needed to improve his rate on new material. We found that having lower performers reread a story one time results in minimal improvements in rate. Yet, if students reread a passage until they read it at a rate significantly higher than their rate on the first reading, their rate on new material gradually improves.

If a student currently reads at a rate of 50 words a minute, the teacher would set the target rate at 70 words per minute (50 + [40% of 50 = 20] = 70).

If a student were reading at a rate of 90 words a minute, the target rate would be 126 words a minute (90 + [40% of 90 = 36] = 126).

The teacher prepares the reading material by marking off several 100-word excerpts in a previously read story. A teacher might put a star at the beginning and a bracket at the end of each 100-word excerpt.

The teacher can use Table 18.6 to translate the target-rereading rate into seconds needed to read a 100-word passage. In order to read a 100-word passage at a target rate of 70 words a minute, the student would have to read a passage in about 1:26 seconds.

The teacher begins the rereading exercises by pointing out the excerpt a student is to read and telling the student how long he has to complete it. The teacher would let the student time himself while reading the story. The student practices reading the excerpt to himself or to a partner until he is able to read it within the specified time. When the student feels he is able to read at the specified time, he raises his hand for the teacher to check him out. The teacher times the student as the student reads the excerpt orally. The student's reading of the excerpt would be deemed acceptable if the student read the passage in the specified time with two or fewer errors. If the student read acceptably, he would begin practicing another excerpt. During one 15-minute session, the student might work on three to five 100-word excerpts. If a teacher is working with a group of students, the teacher should structure the session so that while one student is being tested, the other students are practicing reading to themselves.

Table 18.6   Translation of Seconds Required to Read 100 Words Into Reading Rate

Seconds	Words per Minute	Seconds	Words per Minute
:30	200	1:46	57
:32	187	1:48	56
:34	176	1:50	55
:36	167	1:52	54
:38	158	1:54	53
:40	150	1:56	52
:42	143	1:58	51
:44	136	2:00	50
:46	130	2:02	49
:48	125	2:04	48
:50	120	2:06	48
:52	115	2:08	47
:54	111	2:10	46
:56	107	2:12	45
:58	103	2:14	45
1:00	100	2:16	44
1:02	97	2:18	43
1:04	94	2:20	43
1:06	91	2:22	42
1:08	88	2:24	41
1:10	86	2:26	41
1:12	83	2:28	40
1:14	81	2:30	40
1:16	79	2:32	39
1:18	77	2:34	39
1:20	75	2:36	38
1:22	73	2:38	38
1:24	71	2:40	37
1:26	70	2:42	37
1:28	69	2:44	37
1:30	67	2:46	36
1:32	65	2:48	36
1:34	64	2:50	36
1:36	62	2:52	35
1:38	61	2:54	34
1:40	60	2:56	34
1:42	59	2:58	34
1:44	58	3:00	33

A motivational system should be incorporated into rate-building exercises. For example, each excerpt read at a faster rate might earn a point with a 2-point bonus for reaching the target rate. Each 20 points can lead to some type of reward.

Every 2 weeks, the teacher has a student read a passage the student has never read before. The passage should be one that is at the student's independent level (a level at which the student has the skills to read all words correctly). The passage should be of a similar difficulty level to the passages being read in the rate-building exercises. The student's performance tells the teacher if the rate-training exercises are, in fact, working. If the student's rate has improved, the teacher increases the target rate on rereading exercises to the student's new rate plus 40%. For example, if a student had been reading at a rate of 60 words a minute at the beginning of the year and is now reading at 75 words a minute, the target rate for rereading exercises would increase from 84 words a minute (60 + 24) to 105 words a minute (75 + 30).

The exercise just described may be conducted in a small-group setting with one adult and three or four students. Parent volunteers or paraprofessionals could be used to conduct the training sessions. The length and number of training exercises each day would depend on a student's relative deficit. Students reading at a very slow rate might participate in two 15- to 20-minute sessions daily.

In addition to the rereading exercises, teachers can establish extra rereading times, using peers and parents.

Reading Outside School

We strongly recommend establishing a program that facilitates a great deal of student reading of books and other forms of written materials outside of the school environment. In order to do this, the teacher will need to have books that are at the student's independent reading level readily available. A book is at a student's independent level when the student can read the book with relative ease, having the word-attack skills to figure out virtually all the words in the book. In addition, the vocabulary and sentence structure used in the book should be readily understandable by the child. If possible, some of this reading should be done orally with an adult and some silently.

Here is a series of steps the teacher can follow to encourage home reading:

- The teacher contacts the parent and explains the importance of extra reading. The teacher asks the parent to arrange, at a minimum, a 5-minute daily period during which the student reads a hundred-word excerpt three times to the parent. The teacher needs to send home materials that are appropriate for the student to read.

- In addition to the oral repeated readings, the teacher can also send home books that a child can read silently or to the parent. These books must be at the child's independent level.

- The student brings home a weekly calendar (see Table 18.7). Each day the parent writes how many minutes the child read. The student brings the calendar to school once a week on a specified day.

Table 18.7   Student's Home Reading

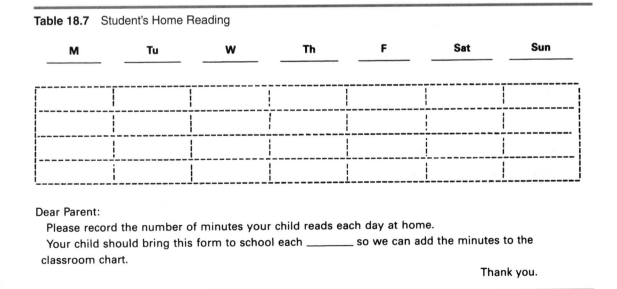

M	Tu	W	Th	F	Sat	Sun

Dear Parent:

Please record the number of minutes your child reads each day at home.

Your child should bring this form to school each _____ so we can add the minutes to the classroom chart.

Thank you.

- As a motivator, the teacher can put the minutes read by each student on a chart.

- A goal with a special event can be planned. "When our class reads 10,000 minutes at home, the principal will come down and give our class a special award."

- Individual motivation systems might be necessary for some children (e.g., "When you read 100 minutes at home you can be in charge of cleaning the erasers for a week").

✸ Application Exercises

1. The errors in each item below reflect a deficit in a particular passage-reading skill. State the skill and describe the procedure for remedying the deficit.
   a. When reading the sentence, *The girl tripped when running down the stairs,* a third grade student says "stars."
   b. When reading the sentence, *Ann built a large house,* student says "bought" for *built.* The student has missed *built* several times.
   c. When reading two sentences, the student ignores the period. The student has done this several times.
   d. A student reading late-second grade material reads at a rate of one word each 2 seconds.
   e. A student reads "bet" for *beat* and "set" for *seat.*

2. Specify the desired reading rates for the following students (see Table 18.5).
   a. A third grade student reading at a mid-second-grade level.
   b. A second grade student reading at a late-first-grade level.
   c. A fifth grade student reading at a late-first-grade level.
   d. A second grade student reading at a beginning-third-grade level.

3. For each student described below, tell if they should receive training to improve their reading rate. If they need such training, specify what the acceptable criterion would be on rereading exercises.
   a. William—A third-grader whose instructional level is at early-second grade. He is reading at a rate of 75 words per minute.
   b. Jackie—A third-grader whose instructional level is at mid-third grade. She is reading at a rate of 75 words per minute.
   c. Andra—A second-grader whose instructional level is at early-second-grade level. He is reading at a rate of 40 words a minute.

4. Listed below are the errors made by two students when reading the following passage. The word the student said is in quotes next to the missed word from the passage.

   The farmer had a gleam in his eye. He was hoping that all his wheat would be cut by that night. Later he would load it on his truck and take it to the coast.

   For each student, tell if the student's errors indicate a specific skill deficit. If so, state the deficit. Remember skill deficits are indicated by patterns of errors rather than a single incorrect response.
   a. Bill—gleam, "glow," load, "lay"
   b. Wilma—load, "land," coast, "cost"

5. Explain the differences between the correction procedure a teacher would use during the large group passage reading and the correction procedure for a one-to-one reading situation.

6. During passage reading, a student is constantly losing his place. To remedy this problem, the teacher has decided to call on students in a predictable order as a way of cueing students to their reading turn. Tell the potential problems the proposed remediation may cause. Describe an alternative remediation to correct the student's losing his place.

7. Below is a passage students will be reading. Pick 3 words from the passage that fourth grade students are likely to have difficulty decoding. Specify what the teacher would do and say in presenting each word. Assume students have mastered all phonic and structural skills.

   Alice had an older friend. It was Ann Lewis, a sophomore, who was the school's star soccer player. Ann gave Alice a great deal of encouragement. Some day Alice would be the team's leader. One day the two young women were talking. Alice said, "I want to be a star. I want to tour the country."

PART 4

Comprehension

Overview of Comprehension Instruction

Reading comprehension can be defined narrowly as instruction that promotes the ability to learn from text or more broadly as instruction that gives students access to important domains of knowledge and provides a means of pursuing affective and intellectual goals (RAND Reading Study Group, 2002). From either perspective, reading-comprehension instruction necessarily entails multiple teaching procedures designed to promote students' acquisition of numerous comprehension skills and strategies.

The critical state of reading comprehension among our nation's middle- and high-school students was captured in this description by the RAND Reading Study Group (RRSG):

> One of the most vexing problems facing middle and secondary school teachers today is that many students come into their classrooms without the requisite knowledge, skills, and dispositions to read the materials placed before them. These students are, for one reason or another, poor comprehenders. Poor comprehenders are students who can neither read nor demonstrate satisfactory understanding of texts appropriate for their grade level. Many teachers are frustrated by what they see as an ever-increasing number of students who are poor comprehenders. (2002, p. 34)

In response to a charge from the Office of Educational Research and Improvement of the U.S. Department of Education to study pressing literacy issues, RRSG chose to focus on comprehension. That focus was motivated by a number of factors, including the following:

- High school graduates are facing an increased need for a high degree of literacy, but comprehension outcomes are not improving.

- Students in the United States are performing poorly in comparison with students in other countries as they enter the later years of schooling when they encounter discipline-specific content and subject-matter learning.

- Unacceptable gaps in reading performance persist between children in different demographic groups despite extensive efforts to close those gaps.

- Not enough attention has been paid to helping teachers develop skills they need to promote reading comprehension, ensure content learning through reading, and deal with the differences in comprehension skills that their students display.

Studies conducted across the last 30 years suggest that inadequate time and attention to comprehension instruction is a factor that contributes to the state of poor comprehension among our students. In the late 1970s, Delores Durkin (1978–79) found that only 2% of the time designated for reading instruction was used to actually teach students how to comprehend what they read. Recent studies by Pressley (2000) and Taylor, Pearson, Clark, and Walpole (1999a) indicate that this situation has not changed much in the last 20 years despite a growing base of knowledge supporting the value of comprehension instruction. We now know that effective comprehension instruction is complex; adequate time and attention to the details of that instruction will be required to reverse the trend of increasing numbers of poor comprehenders. It goes without saying, however, that additional time and attention to comprehension instruction is likely to accomplish little unless the instruction is in accord with what research tells us about *effective* comprehension instruction.

Good instruction is the most powerful means of promoting proficient comprehension and preventing comprehension problems (RRSG, 2002). What we already know about comprehension instruction was summarized by RRSG. That summary converges with NRP's research-based conclusions about comprehension instruction to produce a solid base of information on which educators can rely. The two reports summarize the information in slightly different ways, for that reason, we include summaries from both reports in Figure 19.1 (NRP conclusions) and Figure 19.2 (RRSG conclusions).

As indicated by information provided in those figures, both reports emphasize that effective comprehension instruction includes the teaching of *specific* comprehension strategies. Four important components of effective strategy instruction are:

1. Explicit teaching in which the teacher explains the comprehension strategy clearly, models the strategy, guides the students as

Figure 19.1   Scientifically-Based Conclusions About Comprehension Instruction

- Text comprehension can be improved by instruction that helps readers use specific comprehension strategies.
- Six strategies that appear to have a firm scientific basis for improving text comprehension are: monitoring comprehension, using graphic and semantic organizers, answering questions, generating questions, recognizing story structure, and summarizing.
- Two additional strategies that have received some support from research are (1) making use of prior knowledge, and (2) using mental imagery.
- Individual strategies that can be used in content area instruction appear to have strong scientific support for their effectiveness and for their inclusion in classroom programs on comprehension instruction; however, teachers and students must keep in mind that not all comprehension strategies work for all types of text.
- Effective comprehension strategy instruction is explicit; explicit instruction typically includes

(1) direct explanation of why the strategy helps comprehension and when to apply the strategy, (2) teacher modeling of how to apply the strategy, usually by "thinking aloud" while reading the text, (3) guided practice in which the teacher guides and assists as students learn how and when to apply the strategy, and (4) application in which the teacher helps students practice the strategy until they can apply it independently.
- Effective comprehension strategy instruction promotes flexible use of multiple comprehension strategies in combination.
- Effective strategy instruction can be accomplished through cooperative learning activities in which students work together as partners or in small groups on clearly defined tasks.
- Comprehension instruction appears to be most effective in grades three through six; however, teachers in the primary grades can begin to build the foundation for reading comprehension.

Adapted from the NRP Report of the Subgroups, Chapter 4, Part 2, "Text Comprehension," pp. 5–10.

Figure 19.2 Scientifically-Based Conclusions About Comprehension Instruction

- Fluency instruction leads to gains in comprehension.
- Repeated reading of the same texts is an effective means of increasing fluency for normal readers through grade four and for students with reading problems throughout high school.
- Engaging students in identifying the big ideas in a text and in graphically depicting the relationships among these ideas improves their recall and comprehension of text.
- Engaging students in elaborative questioning improves their comprehension of text read during instruction and their comprehension of new text read independently.
- Teaching students to self-question while reading text enhances their understanding of the text used in the instruction and improves their comprehension of new text.

- Learning to paraphrase a text, identify the gist of a text, and identify and integrate the big ideas in a text enhance recall and the understanding of new text.
- The explicitness with which teachers teach comprehension strategies makes a difference in learner outcomes, especially for low-achieving students.
- Integrating strategy instruction into content domains requires a balance between the priority of instructing for reading comprehension and the priority of teaching the content area itself.
- A knowledge of text structure fosters comprehension.

Adapted from Catherine E. Snow, *Reading for understanding: Toward a research and development program in reading comprehension.* Rand Reading Study Group Report, 2002, pp. 30–43.

they learn and apply the strategy, and provides practice with the strategy until students can apply it independently.

2. Explicit teaching of how to use multiple strategies in combination.

3. Explicit teaching of how to apply strategies flexibly to different types of text.

4. Integration of strategies into content area instruction.

Each of these components is addressed in the following chapters on comprehension instruction. In Chapters 21 and 22, we present specific comprehension skills and strategies for the primary and intermediate levels. Chapter 21 is focused primarily on literal comprehension skills while Chapter 22 has more to do with inferential comprehension skills and strategies. Formats for teaching the skills and strategies explicitly are provided.

Vocabulary plays a critical role in reading comprehension. We use the term *vocabulary* to refer to knowledge of the meanings of individual words. In

the NRP report, the relationships among oral vocabulary, knowledge of letter-sound correspondences, and comprehension of printed text were described this way:

> As a learner begins to read, reading vocabulary encountered in texts is mapped onto the oral vocabulary the learner brings to the task. The reader learns to translate the (relatively) unfamiliar words in print into speech, with the expectation that the speech forms will be easier to comprehend. Benefits in understanding text by applying letter-sound correspondences to printed material come about only if the target word is in the learner's oral vocabulary. When the word is not in the learner's oral vocabulary, it will not be understood when it occurs in print. (4-3)

Although children learn the meanings of many words indirectly through everyday experiences with oral and written language, there is a need for direct instruction of vocabulary items required for comprehension of a specific text (NRP, 4-4). Our recognition of the need for direct vocabulary instruction is indicated by our inclusion of vocabulary instruction in Chapters 11, 20, and 24 of this text-book. In Chapter 11, we addressed vocabulary instruction as a part of early language instruction. In Chapter 20, we explain that although many students learn vocabulary indirectly through independent reading, low readers do not engage in enough independent reading to acquire the vocabulary needed to comprehend the increasingly complex materials that they encounter as they progress through school. Direct teaching of vocabulary is essential for poor comprehenders. Methods of teaching vocabulary directly are described in both Chapter 20 and Chapter 24 of this textbook.

Knowledge of text structure also fosters comprehension. The NRP reported that instruction of story structure improves students' ability to answer questions and recall what was read. This improvement was more pronounced for less able readers; good readers may not need this kind of instruction. In Chapter 23, narrative comprehension strategies designed to promote understanding of the text structure of stories (i.e., story grammar) are presented. In Chapter 24, Archer and Gleason explain how narrative text differs from expository text and why students need to use different strategies with different types of text.

Content-area instruction is particularly important for several reasons. First, some evidence suggests that strategy instruction is most effective when it is embedded in in-depth learning of content. Second, the evidence suggests that students are more likely to learn the strategies fully and apply them in new learning situations when the strategies are closely linked with content knowledge. However, in attempting to integrate strategy instruction into content instruction, it is important that teachers keep this caveat in mind (RRSG, 2002):

> Integrating strategy instruction into content domains requires a balance. The priority of instructing for reading comprehension must be balanced with the priority of teaching the content area itself. . . If comprehension strategies are taught with an array of content and a range of texts that are too wide, then students will not fully learn them. If strategies are taught with too narrow a base of content or text, then students do not have a chance to learn how to transfer them to new reading situations. (pp. 39–40)

In Chapter 24, Archer and Gleason describe ways of integrating strategy instruction into content instruction without sacrificing content. In so doing, they provide specific examples of how to:

1. Use graphs and concept maps to organize content such that big ideas, relationships, and critical distinctions are communicated clearly.

2. Teach specific strategies individually and then apply them in combination (see discussion of Reciprocal Teaching).

3. Conduct guided reading activities in which the teacher models the types of self-questioning that promotes prediction, identification of important information, and summarization.

The myriad of comprehension skills and strategies contained in the Archer and Gleason chapter is organized as prereading, reading, and postreading activities. This makes the teacher's task of organizing comprehension instruction more manageable.

Prereading activities include the preteaching of difficult-to-decode words, difficult vocabulary, and how to read and interpret graphic material. It also includes constructing concept diagrams and concept maps and previewing the selection.

Reading activities begin with guided reading in which the teacher asks questions that prepare students for the reciprocal teaching, partner reading, and learning strategies instruction that follow the guided reading.

In postreading activities, students write summaries and complete written exercises. Feedback on written assignments and review of major concepts are also important postreading activities.

Vocabulary Instruction

Vocabulary used in primary-grade reading books is usually controlled in that nearly all words appearing in stories are in the average student's speaking vocabulary. From about fourth grade on, students encounter a large number of words not known to them in any way. Many passages are written at almost adult reading levels, particularly texts in the content areas of social studies, science and math. They contain difficult to read words that are not already in the students' oral vocabularies. Teachers must be prepared to spend time teaching vocabulary, especially to children who have limited language backgrounds. They must work on increasing students' general vocabulary, as well as knowledge of specific words that will appear in upcoming passages that students will read during reading instruction or in other content-area classrooms.

In this chapter, we discuss strategies for teaching vocabulary during the intermediate grades.[1] We present strategies for teaching specific word meanings as well as strategies that students can use to help determine meanings of new words they encounter during independent reading. In addition, we highlight components of vocabulary instruction that promote comprehension of text containing taught words.

Prior to presenting strategies for teaching vocabulary, it's important to provide some background on the nature of vocabulary acquisition. One overarching research finding is that while most vocabulary is learned indirectly, some vocabulary must be taught directly (The Partnership for Reading, 2001). Indirect and direct vocabulary learning are discussed in the sections that follow.

Indirect Vocabulary Learning

Children's vocabularies increase at a rate of approximately 3,000 new words each year, or about 8 words per day (Nagy & Anderson, 1984). A child's vocabulary size approximately doubles between grades three and seven (Jenkins & Dixon, 1983). Most researchers agree that the magnitude of this vocabulary growth cannot be ascribed to classroom instruction. Rather, they suggest children learn the meanings of most words indirectly, through everyday experiences with oral and written language. Children learn meanings of words indirectly by engaging in conversations, listening to adults read to them, and by reading on their own. In fact, it's thought that by the third grade the major determinant of a student's vocabulary growth is amount of

---

1. This chapter was written by Carrie Thomas-Beck, Coordinator, Oregon Reading First Center.

time spent free reading (Nagy, Anderson, & Herman, 1987).

Relying on learning word meanings from independent reading is not an adequate way to deal with students' vocabulary development. Researchers who have studied indirect word learning through reading have found that word learning from context actually occurs only in small increments. Studies estimate that of 100 unfamiliar words met in reading, only between 5 and 15 of them will be learned (Nagy, Herman, & Anderson, 1985; Swanborn & de Glopper, 1999). Factors such as students' grade level, level of reading ability, and amount of text surrounding target words affect the probability of learning unknown words. Moreover, natural contexts frequently are not informative for deriving word meanings. Students must read widely to learn a substantial number of unfamiliar words. One reason we place such a strong emphasis on making children fluent, accurate readers by the end of first grade is to increase the likelihood that children will read extensively and thereby increase vocabulary growth. Nonfluent readers simply do not engage in the amount of free reading necessary to promote large gains in vocabulary knowledge.

Direct Vocabulary Learning

Researchers agree that direct vocabulary instruction is a useful adjunct to natural word learning from context. About 300 more words can be learned each year as a result of direct vocabulary instruction. This would account for between 6 and 30% of a student's vocabulary growth (Stahl & Fairbanks, 1986). Direct instruction is highly effective for vocabulary learning (The National Reading Panel, 2000). Direct instruction of vocabulary includes both directly teaching specific word meanings and teaching word-learning strategies.

Teaching Specific Word Meanings

It is reasonable to teach thoroughly about 8 to 10 words per week (The Partnership for Reading,

2001). The words that are taught and the sequence in which they are introduced will be dictated primarily by the text that the students will be expected to read. A teacher must review upcoming lessons and select words that are important, useful, and difficult.

Important words are words that are critical to understanding the passage. Useful words are those that students will find useful in many contexts. Priority is given to words that students are likely to see and use again and again. For example, it is probably more useful for students to learn a word like *substantial* or *critical* than the word *exigent*. The more likely students are to encounter a word in the future, the more critical it is to teach it. If the word is both important and useful, then a teacher must check that the word is, indeed, difficult for the students.

When selecting words to teach directly, it's important to keep in mind that students do not either know or not know words, rather they know words to varying degrees or levels (Beck, McKeown, & Kucan, 2002). Beck and colleagues have identified three levels of word knowledge: *unknown, acquainted,* and *established* (Beck, McKeown, & Omanson, 1987). At the *unknown* level, the meaning of the word is completely unfamiliar. If a word is at the *acquainted* level, the basic meaning is recognized after some thought. If a word is at the *established* level, meaning is easily, rapidly, and automatically recognized. Although it is enough for students to have a superficial acquaintance with some words in a selection, for most words—and all important words—students must have an established level of knowledge if they are to comprehend what they read (Nagy, Herman, & Anderson, 1985).

Teachers need to be careful in relying on the guidance in basal reading programs for identifying target vocabulary words. Most programs include lists of vocabulary words to teach, however sometimes these words are not appropriate. Researchers have found that children are likely to know a substantial proportion of those words—more than 75%—before encountering them in basal selections (Stallman et al., 1990). On the other hand, important words which the students do not know the meaning of may not be included in the list of words designated for vocabulary instruction. If a program does not provide reliable guidance on vocabulary, teachers, especially those working with at-risk students, will need to preview selections and locate important, useful words that students are not likely to know at the established level.

Another aspect of word knowledge relates to expressive versus receptive usage. Expressive vocabulary refers to how a student uses words to communicate with other people, whether in speaking or in writing. Receptive vocabulary refers to a student's understanding of the words another person has said. Receptive vocabulary also includes recognizing words in print. Teachers should keep in mind that *expressive usage* (using a word properly) is much more difficult than *receptive usage* (understanding the word).

The current depth of knowledge a student has about the meaning of a particular word will determine how the word should be taught. Researchers have identified four different kinds of word learning: (1) learning a new meaning for a known word; (2) learning the meaning for a new word representing a known concept; (3) learning the meaning of a new word representing an unknown concept; and (4) clarifying and enriching the meaning of a known word (Graves, Juel, & Graves, 1998). These types of word learning vary in difficulty. Each different kind of word learning requires different instructional procedures. In the sections that follow, we discuss each type of word learning and describe the instructional procedures appropriate for that level of word knowledge.

Learning a New Meaning for a Known Word

In some instances, students have a word in their oral vocabulary but are learning a new meaning for it. For example, the student knows what a tree *branch* is, but is learning about *branches* of government in social studies. It's estimated that 80% of our words have multiple meanings. Words with multiple meanings are also known as polysemous words.

Words such as *bank, run, bay, shot,* and *coach* are all examples of polysemous words. Consider the meaning of the following sentence: *Football coaches not admitted unless booked in advance* (Irvin, 2001). This sentence contains five polysemous words: *football, coaches, admit, book,* and *advance.* A reader's first interpretation may be that the individuals who train and direct athletes will not be admitted unless they make a reservation. The sentence is actually referring not to individuals, but to motor buses.

Teachers should directly teach students the new meaning of a word before the children read a selection in which understanding the new meaning for the word is needed. One way of teaching a new meaning is to utilize a dictionary. To teach the new meaning, the teacher presents the sentence in which the word appears and has the children find the word in their dictionary. The teacher points out that there are several definitions for the word. The teacher reads the definitions aloud one at a time. The class discusses which of the definitions would best fit the context of the sentence. Students eliminate the inappropriate definitions. The teacher then has students substitute the most likely definition for the word in the original sentence to verify that it makes sense. As a follow-up activity, teachers can have students create their own sentences using a variety of definitions for the polysemous word. For example, The criminal was *booked* downtown at the police department. He *booked* a ticket from San Francisco to Washington, D.C. As students become more sophisticated, teachers can provide less guidance and eventually have students use this process for finding a new meaning independently.

Many words have different meanings in different content areas. The word *division,* for example, has a very different meaning in math than it does in science or social studies. Students might be learning long *division* in math, studying cell *division* in science, and discussing *divisions* of the army in social studies. Teams of teachers can reinforce different meanings across disciplines by explicitly teaching that they are using "one" meaning of this word, reminding students that there are other meanings.

Table 20.1 Figurative Speech Example Worksheet

Draw a line from each numeral to the correct letter.

Phrases	*Meanings*
1. down and out	**a.** in trouble
2. in hot water	**b.** very happy
3. high as a kite	**c.** without hope
4. heavy heart	**d.** sad

Fill in the blanks with the phrases.

1. That kid was _____ after she spilled the ink on her dad's shirt.

2. With a _____ the coach told the team that he was leaving.

3. We were _____ after winning the game.

4. The old tramp was _____.

Figurative Expressions

Intermediate-grade textbooks contain hundreds of figurative or idiomatic expressions such as *down and out, bottom of the heap, in hot water,* and to be *out of line.* These expressions require students to learn new meanings for familiar words and should be taught directly. Teachers should preview upcoming passages students will read and select figurative or idiomatic expressions students may not understand and are not explained by the passage's context. These expressions should be taught before the passage is presented. As extra practice, the teacher can prepare worksheets in which the students must match figurative expressions with their meanings, then have them fill in the blanks in sentences with the appropriate expressions (see Table 20.1).

Learning a Meaning for a New Word Representing a Known Concept

In other situations, the student is familiar with the concept, but does not know the particular word for the concept. For example, the student knows about *leaves,* but does not know that the *leaf* of a palm tree is a called a *frond.* In Chapter 11 on oral-language training, we discussed teaching through synonyms when students know a word with a meaning similar to a new word. Synonym teaching can be continued throughout all grade levels. Some examples of less common words that can be taught through synonyms are:

- merge-join
- exterior-outside
- amity-friendship
- assault-attack
- secure-safe
- brief-short
- vary-change
- mentor-teacher

Definitions are used more often than synonyms as students progress through the grades and the meanings of words become increasingly more complex. The major way to define a word involves putting the new word in a class, then specifying the unique characteristics of that word distinguishing it from other words in that same class:

- decathlon—an athletic contest that includes 10 track-and-field events;
- pediatrician—a doctor who works with children;
- slander—a false report that says bad things about someone;

Table 20.2 Format for New Vocabulary (Respite)

Teacher	Students
1. Teacher models the pronunciation and definition of *respite*.	
a. "Listen, *respite*.	
Say that." (Signal.)	"Respite."
b. "A respite is a short rest.	
What is respite?" (Signal.)	"A short rest."
2. Teacher tests definition.	
a. "John worked hard all day. Then he went home and worked all night.	
Did he take a respite?" (Signal.)	"No."
"How do you know?"	"He didn't take a rest."
b. "Ann worked hard all morning. At twelve, she stopped and relaxed for awhile then she went back to work.	
Did she take a respite?" (Signal.)	"Yes."
"How do you know?"	"She took a short break."
c. "Sue did fifty push-ups. Then she splashed cold water on her face and lay down for five minutes. Then she did twenty-five more push-ups.	
Did she take a respite?" (Signal.)	"Yes."
"How do you know?" (Signal.)	"She rested for five minutes."
d. "Bill did fifty push-ups this morning, then he slept on the bed all night.	
Did he take a respite?" (Signal.)	"No."
"How do you know?" (Signal.)	"He slept too long."
3. Teacher reviews recently introduced words.	

- cutlery—tools used for eating;
- nonentity—a thing that is of no importance.

There are two steps to teach the meaning of a new word representing a known concept. First, the teacher communicates the meaning of the word, by presenting a synonym or definition. Second, the teacher presents a series of examples, some positive and some negative and asks the students to tell if the instance is an example of the new word. This step ensures that students really understand the meaning of the word and are not simply memorizing a rote definition. The teaching procedure is illustrated in Table 20.2. In the format, the teacher presents the word *respite* using a synonym (a short rest), then tests the students on a series of positive and negative examples. Note that for testing new vocabulary, the teacher asks, "How do you know?" after each question (e.g., "The bear slept all winter. Is that a

respite? How do you know?"). Words would be reviewed daily for several days than intermittently.

Learning a Meaning of New Word Representing an Unknown Concept

Much of learning in content areas requires that students learn a meaning of a new word representing an unknown concept. The student is not familiar with either the concept or the word for the concept, and so must learn both. For example, as students learn about *evaporation* and *photosynthesis* they may be learning both new concepts and new words. Similarly, literature selections in intermediate grades often contain difficult new concepts such as *altruism, pragmatism,* and *homage.* Learning the meaning of a new word that represents an unknown concept is the most difficult of the four types of word learning and requires the most elaborate instruction. The teacher can directly present the meaning of the new word by using a definition. However, for more complex concepts simply presenting a definition is not sufficient. Students will need a deeper understanding. Semantic mapping and concept definition maps are two techniques that can be used to more thoroughly teach the meaning of new concepts. Both utilize graphic organizers. The use of semantic mapping is explained below. Chapter 24 on content area instruction includes an in-depth discussion of concept definition maps.

Semantic Mapping

Semantic mapping encourages concept development by graphically displaying words in categories and showing how they are related to each other. The teacher prepares a graphic, writing the new word in the middle of the graphic and providing categories under which to list information about that word. For example, if the teacher presented the word *osprey,* the teacher might make these categories: what it looks like, how it hunts, where you find it, what kind of shelter it builds. Figure 20.1 illustrates a graphic that could be used for a presentation on the word *osprey.*

Figure 20.1   Semantic Map for the Word *Osprey*

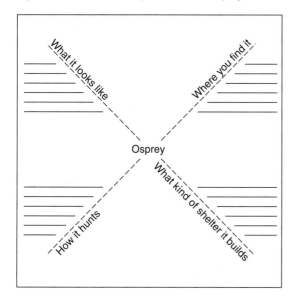

The teacher presents a source of information about the new concept, either having students read a passage about the new concept, present a lecture on the new concept or if the concept is one that she thinks some children may already be familiar with conducting a group discussion. The teacher and students would fill out the graphic using the information provided from the text or discussion.

Semantic mapping can also be used to show how related words are the same and different. For example, for a presentation on whales, the teacher could make a graphic with categories that describe all whales and then spaces to tell characteristics of specific whales. Building the map can generate much thought and discussion among students.

Classroom discussion is an especially effective medium for vocabulary learning because it allows for preconceptions and misconceptions to be discussed openly and be clarified (Stahl & Shiel, 1999). Students can think together about their experiences and how to make sense of them. Semantic mapping is especially useful for children with low vocabularies because these children not only learn the target word, but also many related words in the same semantic field. By using whole-class discussion, the teacher can take advantage of knowledge of higher performing students.

Clarifying/Enriching the Meaning of a Known Word

The fourth type of word learning occurs when students learn more precise definitions for a known word. In many cases the student has some idea of the basic meaning of a word, but needs to learn finer, more subtle distinctions in the meaning and usage. For example, the student knows that the words *jogging, trotting, dashing,* and *sprinting* have something to do with the word *running,* but does not know the specific meaning of each word.

Clarifying meanings of words can be done by explaining the difference between words in a similar category. Instruction would involve presenting more precise definitions and explanations of the words. For example, a teacher can explain, "*Sprinting* is a word we use when a person is running as fast as they can. *Jogging* is a word we use when a person is not running anywhere near as fast as the person can run."

Simply telling the students the definition is not adequate. Teachers should also provide practice in applying the definitions. One way to structure this application is by providing sentences and having the child fill in the appropriate word. For example, the teacher would present the sentence *Jason _____ down the street when he saw the school bus door closing* and ask, "What word fits best in the blank, *sprinted* or *jogged?*"

Enriching students' understanding of a word involves providing examples of the word's use in multiple contexts, particularly those that go beyond its use in the story in which it was first introduced. If a student's understanding of a word is limited to one narrow definition or a single context (e.g., *stern* is always used in association with a teenager's father), then students may not be able to comprehend many applications of the word and have limited use of the word in speech and writing (Beck, McKeown, & Kucan, 2002). Teachers can show the range of meaning of a word by presenting the word in a variety of contexts. For example, in enriching the meaning of *stern* as a serious and demanding person, the teacher can present several descriptions of a person as examples of *stern*.

> We had a stern teacher. He was very strict. He never smiled. He demanded that all our work be perfect. If we made any errors at all on our work, he would make us do the whole assignment over again.
>
> Our basketball coach was very stern. She made us practice our plays over and over again until we did them perfectly. She never seemed to be satisfied.

Providing Practice to Reach Established Level

A major goal of vocabulary instruction is to increase the number of words the student knows at the established level, the level at which the student readily and easily understands the meaning of a word. Providing a variety of applications that require students to use words and apply definitions will help students reach the established level of word knowledge. Beck, McKeown, and colleagues have developed numerous activities to enrich students' vocabulary knowledge (Beck et al., 2002). These researchers recommend that teachers have students talk about situations a word would describe. In one activity, "Have You Ever . . . ?", students associate newly learned words with contexts from their own experience. For example, after learning the meanings of the words *covertly* and *impressed,* the teacher can present an activity in which students are asked to describe a time when they might have acted *covertly* or tell about when they *impressed* their teacher. Another activity to promote word usage is to provide students with sentence stems that require them to integrate a word's meaning into a context in order to explain a situation. For example, "The man *covertly* hopped onto the bus because . . ." or "Nancy's teacher was very *impressed* because . . ." Teachers can have students respond to and explain examples as well as creating their own by asking questions such as, "If you had a friend who watched TV all the time, how might you *coax* him into getting some exercise?"

To provide additional practice on word usage, teachers can ask students to determine instances when the word would be an appropriate choice. For example:

> Which of these things might be *extraordinary*? Why or why not?
>   A shirt that was comfortable or a shirt that washed itself? (Beck et al., 2002, p. 56)

> I'll say some things, if they sound *leisurely,* say "Leisurely." If you'd need to be in a hurry, say "Hurry."
>   Taking a walk in the park.
>   Firefighters getting to a fire.
>   Runners in a race.
>   Sitting and talking to friends.
>   A dog lying in the sun. (Beck et al., 2002, p. 57)

Teachers can also ask students to differentiate between two descriptions by labeling them as an example or nonexample of the target word.

> banter
>   A husband and wife argue about what to have for dinner.

A husband and wife kid each other about who ate more at dinner.

(Beck et al., 2002, p. 74)

Beck and colleagues recommend presenting words in semantic groups of 8 to 10 words. For example, one semantic group could include words that describe people such as *covert, peculiar, raucous, stern, glum,* and *impatient.* These researchers stress that students' word knowledge is stored in networks of connected ideas. By making the connections between words explicit, teachers provide more opportunities for student to access that knowledge. One way to build connections between new and known words is to ask students to associate one of their new words (e.g., *peculiar, raucous, covert, stern*) with a presented word or phrase, such as "Which word goes with spy?"(*covert*). Another activity is to present questions that juxtapose two target words, such as "Could a *raucous* presenter *covertly* leave the room?" The purpose is to make students think about whether a relationship between the words exists. Students are always required to justify their answers.

As a culminating activity, the teacher can ask students to place a series of related words on a word line that represents a continuum. The teacher gives students a list of 4 to 8 related words. Students are to rank the words on a continuum based on intensity of meaning. There may not be one correct ordering of the words. The purpose of the activity is to elicit students explanations that involve target word meanings. See Figure 20.2.

Figure 20.2 Word Continuum: Shades of Meaning
Developed by MaryBeth Munroe, Southern Oregon ESD.

Rank the words on the continuum based on intensity of meaning:

scuffle	fight		altercation	riot
argument	disagreement		brawl	conflict

Teaching Word-Learning Strategies

Skilled reading depends not only on knowing a large number of words, but also on being able to deal effectively with unknown words that are encountered as one reads text. Skilled readers are not readers who never encounter words they do not know, but rather are readers who cope effectively with words that are new to them (Irvin, 1998). It is critical that teachers present students with strategies to facilitate independent word learning. Such strategies include: (1) teaching students within-word parts, (2) teaching students to be more proficient at figuring out a word's meaning from context, and (3) teaching students how to use a dictionary as an aid to determining meanings of unknown words. Each strategy will be discussed in the sections that follow.

Word Parts

Teaching of within-word parts is a productive type of vocabulary instruction. All words are composed of *morphemes,* the smallest linguistic units that have meaning. Morphemes may be free (whole words) or bound (found only as parts of words such as prefixes, suffixes, and non-word bases). Morphemic analysis as a vocabulary aid involves dividing a word into its component morphemes, then using the meanings of the individual morphemes to figure out the meaning of the entire word. Morphemic analysis can be illustrated with the word *unworkable,* which includes three morphemes: *un* meaning *not, work,* and *able* meaning *able to.* Through morphemic analysis, *unworkable* can be translated as *not able to work.* Teaching students the meanings of morphemes will give them a strategy for analyzing some unknown vocabulary words. This strategy may be especially important for content-area reading, where many of the words contain identifiable word parts which have the same meaning in many different words.

Teachers must realize that this strategy does have limitations. Three factors limit the usefulness of morphemic analysis. The first factor is the difficulty of translating individual morphemes into a functional definition. For example, the word *accurate* is composed of three morphemes: *ac,* which means *toward; cure* which means *care;* and *ate* which means *that which is.* The literal morphemic definition of *accurate* is *that which is toward care.* For a sophisticated reader, this definition might be helpful; however, for the less sophisticated students, such a definition would be difficult to use.

A second reason why morphemes are of limited value in figuring out word meanings is that many morphemes have dual meanings. For example, the morpheme *dia* sometimes means *through* as in *diameter* and sometimes means *day* as in *diary.*

A third reason for the limitations of morphemic analysis is that students often cannot determine the morphemes that have been combined to make up the word. For example, the word *recognition* is composed of the morphemes *re + cogno + ite + ion.*

Teachers must decide which morphemes are worth teaching. Table 20.3 includes some morphemes that lend themselves to relatively easy translation. Next to each morpheme is a word that

Table 20.3   Morpheme Meanings*

Morpheme	Sample Word	Approximate Meaning
able	portable	able to be
bi	bicycle	two
dis	dishonest	not
	disappear	opposite of
est	biggest	the most
ful	hopeful	full of
il	illegal	not
inter	interstate	between
intra	intrastate	inside
less	fearless	without
pre	preschool	before
re	repay	again
sub	submarine	below
tri	tricycle	three
un	unable	not
	untie	opposite of

*For a more thorough listing of morpheme meanings see *Dictionary of English Word-Roots* (R. Smith, 1966).

illustrates use of that morpheme and the morpheme's common meaning. Note that the meaning we use is designed to be functional rather than technically correct. We tried to construct definitions to make morphemic analysis easier for students.

Two rules for sequencing the introduction of morphemes are: (1) to introduce the most functional ones first, and (2) to separate morphemes likely to be confused. Morphemes are functional when they enable students to understand words they could not understand without knowledge of the morpheme. The morpheme *re,* which means *again,* is an example of a morpheme that is quite functional. Morphemes *inter* and *intra* can serve as examples of morphemes likely to be confused. The introduction of these morphemes should be separated by at least five other morphemes.

Directly teaching the most commonly used morphemes along with a strategy for decomposing words is recommended. Table 20.4 presents a format for teaching the meaning of new morphemes and reviewing previously taught morphemes. Table 20.5 includes written work that could also be used as a review. The rate of introducing new morphemes depends on the students' performance. A new morpheme can be introduced when the students can do the verbal and written exercises that review previously introduced morphemes without error.

The format in Table 20.4 includes several steps. In the first step, the teacher tells the students the meaning of a new morpheme, then tests students on the meaning of several words that contain that morpheme (e.g., the morpheme *less* added to the word *win* creates the word *winless* which means *without a win*). In the second step, the teacher provides practice for the meaning of the new morpheme and previously taught morphemes. In the third step, students use their knowledge of those morphemes to determine word meanings.

Practice on morphemic analysis in Table 20.5 includes two parts. In Part 1 of the worksheet, students write the correct meaning for each morpheme. In Part 2, students select words for sentence completion items. The students are given a written exercise with 5 to 10 sentences. A list of words appears above the sentences. From the list, the stu-

Table 20.4 Format for Introducing Morphemes

Teacher	Students
1. Teacher introduces a new morpheme.	
a. "Listen. *Less* usually means *without*."	
b. "What does *less* usually mean?" (Signal.)	"Without."
"So *careless* means without a care."	
"What does *careless* mean?" (Signal.)	"Without a care."
c. "What does less usually mean?" (Signal.)	"Without."
"So what does the word *winless* mean?" (Signal.)	"Without a win."
d. "What does *less* usually mean?" (Signal.)	"Without."
"So what does *homeless* mean?" (Signal.)	"Without a home."
2. Teacher reviews morphemes.	
a. "What does *pre* mean?" (Signal.)	"Before."
b. "What does *un* mean?" (Signal.)	"Not."
c. "What does *tri* mean?" (Signal.)	"Three."
d. "What does *less* mean?" (Signal.)	"Without."
e. "What does *able* mean?" (Signal.)	"Able to be."
3. Teacher applies morphemes to figuring out meaning.	
a. "Listen. *Careful*. Tell me the first morpheme in *careful*." (Signal.)	"Care."
"What's the next morpheme in *careful*?" (Signal.)	"Ful."
b. "What does *ful* mean?" (Signal.)	"Full of."
c. "What does *careful* mean?" (Signal.)	"Full of care."
d. Teacher repeats step 3(a–c) with these words: *preschooler* (one who is before school), *triangle* (three angles), *winless* (without a win).	

Table 20.5 Worksheet for Morphemic Analysis

Part 1: Write the correct meaning next to each morpheme.

un _____   less _____   re _____   mis _____
ful _____   able _____   est _____   er _____

Part 2: Fill in the blanks using these words:

hopeful   hopeless   misspell   winless   preschool

a. Tom did not want to _____ any words on the test.
b. My brother is too young for this school; he goes to a _____.
c. We are _____ our team will win.
d. After trying for two months to get his dog to sit, Tom thought it was _____ to continue.
e. The team was sad because it was _____.

dents are to select the words that should be in each sentence and fill in the blanks.

Lessons may be extended by asking students to create word journals. Students create one page per morpheme and whenever they encounter a word with that part, they place it on the page and note where they encountered the word. Likewise, teachers can create word walls to reinforce each morpheme. Teachers let students add to the walls as they find words using the morphemes they are studying.

Context Clues

In contextual analysis, a reader uses the words in a sentence surrounding an unknown word to figure out the unknown word's meaning. Contextual analysis is an essential skill for students in the intermediate grades because it allows them to determine the meaning of many unknown words they will encounter. Writers often define words they feel the reader is unlikely to know. Many times the definition is given through the use of an appositive construction containing a synonym or definition which immediately follows the unknown words in the passage:

1. The *drouge,* a small parachute for slowing down an object, shot out of the rear of the space capsule at 10,000 feet.

2. The *surplus,* that is, the amount left over, was so great that the storage bins were full and grain was lying on the ground.

A definition or synonym can also be stated as a negation, a form more difficult for students to understand:

1. The older brother was quite *affable,* not argumentative, as his younger sibling.

2. Jamie was a *versatile* athlete, while Ann, who was not so versatile, was able to play only one sport.

Contextual analysis is made more difficult not only when negative examples are used, but also when a synonym or definition is separated from the unknown word in a passage. In example 1 below, the definition immediately follows the new word. In example 2, the definition is separated from the new word, which makes example 2 more difficult:

1. The food is *preserved,* or kept from spoiling, by special refrigeration cars.

2. The food is *preserved* by special refrigeration cars. These specially made cars keep the food from spoiling.

Contextual analysis is also more difficult when the meaning of a word is implied by description rather than by direct use of a synonym. Often a paragraph or series of sentences provides example(s), either positive or negative, that students must use as the basis for inferring the meaning of a new word:

1. Byron's muscles strained as he pulled at the door. He leaned back and pushed as hard as he could. He *exerted* all the force he could.

2. In the sea, bones and shells are not eaten away and harmed by the air. Objects are covered with protective layers of sand so that years from now they will be undamaged. Life from the sea is being *preserved* for the future.

One way to teach students how to use contextual analysis to determine the meaning of an unknown word involves leading students through a series of short passages. For each passage, the teacher (1) points out the unknown word, (2) has the students find the words that tell what the unknown word means, and (3) has the students restate the sentence substituting a synonym or description for the unknown word. The definition or synonym would be derived through contextual analysis. Table 20.6 shows a format that can be used in the intermediate grades for teaching students to infer meaning from a passage.

A more general way of teaching students to derive meanings of words from context is to use a talk-through technique (Stahl & Shiel, 1999). In this technique, the teacher first provides a model by talking through the processes he or she is using to figure out a word's meaning from context. Next, the teacher leads the students through using context to derive the meaning of several words by using prompts such as, "What words around you tell you something about the word (_____) ?"; "What do you think the word (_____) means?"; "Does that meaning make sense when we substitute it for the word (_____) in the sentence?"

What's important to remember is that effective instruction in contextual analysis incorporates direct instruction procedures, including direct explanation of the purpose of the instruction, modeling, careful transition from guided to independent practice, and extensive practice in deriving word mean-

---

Table 20.6   Format for Teaching Vocabulary Through Context

Teacher	*Students*
An advanced exercise might include four to six passages such as this one: When the first people came to our country, they saw a dark, living cloud of birds. The cloud was so huge that it almost <u>eclipsed</u> the sun. When this happened, the people could hardly see what was happening.	
1. Teacher calls on a student to read the passage and identify the unknown word.	
a. "Read the passage."	
b. "A new word is underlined, what word is that?" (Signal.)	"Eclipsed."
2. Teacher calls on a student to find the synonym or definition.	
a. "What happened when the birds eclipsed the sun?"	"The people could hardly see."
b. "Because of the eclipse of the sun, the men could hardly see. What do you think an eclipse does to the sun?" (Signal.)	"Covers it up."
c. "Yes, it covers it up."	
3. Students say the sentence substituting the meaning of the new word.	
a. "Read the sentence with *eclipse* in it." (Signal.)	"The cloud was so huge that it almost eclipsed the sun."
b. Teacher calls on a student. "Say the sentence using a different word for *eclipse*." (Signal.)	"The cloud was so huge that it almost covered up the sun."
4. Teacher repeats steps 1 through 3 with several more passages.	

---

ings from context with specific feedback (Stahl & Shiel, 1999). Other critical aspects of teaching contextual analysis involve the sequencing of examples from easy to difficult and providing adequate independent practice. Students will learn the skill if they are given enough practice and review on the various types of context construction: synonym or definition (which can be close to or separated from the new word), negation, and inference. Providing sufficient and appropriate examples is as important as the teaching procedure itself.

Dictionary Use

Using the dictionary to determine a word's meaning is more difficult for the young student than an adult may suppose. First, a dictionary definition may include words a student does not understand. For example, a dictionary may define *habituate* as to *accustom;* unfortunately, many students will not know what *accustom* means. Teachers should try to select dictionaries written at an appropriate level for the students. The dictionary itself should use clear definitions composed of words with which students are familiar.

Second, many words have more than one meaning listed for them (e.g., the word *bark* can mean (1) covering of a tree; (2) a noise a dog makes; or (3) a small sailing ship). Teachers cannot take for granted that students will know how to find the appropriate meaning. Exercises to teach students how to determine which of several meanings listed for a word is appropriate for a given sentence were presented earlier in the chapter. Initial exercises should be limited to words in which the differences between the meanings are fairly obvious. For example, two possible meanings for the word *cold* are chilly and unfriendly. In the sentence, "I was surprised at how cold my friend acted towards me when we met yesterday", the meaning of *cold* is somewhat obvious.

Teachers should encourage students to look up new words encountered during independent reading, however, they should not require students to look up so many words that reading becomes tedious. Looking up every unknown word makes reading too laborious, while never looking up words can result in students' reading without understanding what they read. The decision of whether a word is important depends on the students' purpose for reading the passage. When reading to learn new information, students should look up most unknown words. Yet, students do not need to look up all adjectives or adverbs during pleasure reading. Knowing when to figure out the meaning of a new word is an important skill usually not taught.

The basic strategy students need to learn when encountering an unknown word, is that they should continue reading the paragraph in which the word appears to see if the context gives the word meaning. If the context does not give the meaning, the students decide if knowing the word's meaning is important to understanding the paragraph. If so, the students look up the word. To demonstrate when looking up a word is necessary, a teacher should conduct exercises where he leads students through several passages, helping them to see if the context gives the unknown word's meaning. If the context does not provide the meaning, the teacher asks if knowing the meaning of that particular word is essential to understanding the passage. The teacher then needs to model how to look up the meaning of an unknown word, choosing the appropriate definition from an entry to make sure it fits a particular context.

Relation of Vocabulary Instruction to Improving Comprehension

In the preceding sections, we presented a number of strategies for teaching vocabulary words to intermediate-grade students. Strategies for learning a new meaning for a known word, learning the meaning for a new word representing a known concept, learning a new concept, and enriching the meaning of a known word were described. Tech-

niques for teaching independent word-learning strategies such as using word parts, contextual analysis, and teaching independent use of the dictionary were also discussed. To date, no single best method of vocabulary instruction has been identified. Rather as Graves (1986) points out, it seems that "different methods will be more or less appropriate and effective depending on the particular word-learning task students face" (p. 65).

Research suggests that a high level of word knowledge is needed to effect comprehension (Beck, McKeown, & Omanson, 1987). Not all methods of vocabulary instruction result in comprehension gains. Three characteristics of vocabulary instruction appear important to effecting comprehension. These characteristics are: (1) including both definitional and contextual information, (2) encouraging deep processing of words, and (3) providing multiple exposures to words. In the sections that follow, we describe each critical feature.

Definitional and Contextual Information

In order to know a word, students must have definitional information and contextual information (Stahl, 1986). Definitional knowledge is knowledge of logical relations between a word and other known words. Contextual knowledge refers to knowledge of the core concept the word represents and how that core concept is changed in different contexts. For example, the word *run* means something slightly different when one *runs* a race than when one *runs* for office or one *runs* into trouble.

Examples of words in context can often demonstrate a meaning more powerfully than a definition alone and are essential in teaching how a word is used (Nagy, 1988). For example, the meaning of the word *cater,* "to act with special consideration," does not adequately convey the connotations of the word. Without additional contextual instruction, a student might produce a sentence such as "The mayor *catered* when the corporate executives visited the city" (Nagy, 1988, p. 9). Clearly, teaching only the definition of a word will not allow a student to use it in a variety of contexts. If the objective is to improve comprehension, research supports including a mix of definitional and contextual information (Stahl & Fairbanks, 1986; The National Reading Panel, 2000).

Deep Processing

Deep processing can be defined as (1) making more connections between new and known information, and (2) spending more of one's mental effort on learning (Stahl, 1986; Stahl & Fairbanks, 1986). Deep processing is facilitated by drawing on students' background knowledge or existing schema of word knowledge (Mezynski, 1983). Making semantic interrelationships explicit helps students create bridges between new and known words, and acquire an in-depth understanding of each word's meaning. The notion of connecting target words played a significant role in the rich instruction of Beck et al. (2002). By organizing words into semantic categories, Beck and colleagues made the relationships the words shared with each other explicit for the students. In addition, the category labels (e.g., *covert* and *impatient* were "people" words) provided an anchor for the students, allowing them to draw upon whatever prior knowledge of the category they possessed.

In addition to making connections between words, methods that require students to actively process information about each word's meaning promote comprehension. Rather than simply having students associate a word and a definition or a word and a single context, teachers should have students demonstrate understanding of the word by classifying the word with other words or completing fill-in-the-blank sentences. For greater depth of processing, teachers can ask students to generate a novel product such as relating the word to personal experiences or creating contexts for the word. Requiring students to justify why a particular word would be appropriate to use in a given situation also promotes greater depth of processing. Research indicates that increasingly deep levels of processing have differential effects on comprehension (Stahl, 1985, 1986; Stahl & Fairbanks, 1986).

Multiple Exposures

Researchers hypothesize that comprehension is best facilitated when virtually all the words in a given text are highly accessible (Beck, Perfetti, & McKeown, 1982). If a student can quickly and effortlessly access word meanings, attention can then be directed toward the overall meaning of a sentence or passage. Methods that build accuracy and fluency of word knowledge through multiple exposures to words are likely to have a greater effect on comprehension than methods that give students limited exposures to words. However, instruction must consist of more than drill and practice. Words must be presented in a variety of contexts to develop a breadth of knowledge about each word. Demonstrating how a word can be used in a variety of contexts seems to have large effects (The National Reading Panel, 2000).

Summary

The National Reading Panel reviewed the research in the area of vocabulary instruction. Fifty studies dating from 1979 to 2000 were reviewed in detail. There were 21 different methods of vocabulary instruction represented in the studies reviewed. In April of 2000, the National Reading Panel issued a report that summarized the scientific evidence on effective vocabulary instruction. Figure 20.3 presents a summary of their conclusions.

The conclusions from the National Reading Panel mirror the information presented in this chapter and should be treated as organizing principals of vocabulary instruction. As we stated earlier, no single best method of vocabulary instruction has been identified. The members of the panel stressed that "the collective body or research clearly indicates that vocabulary increases with instruction of many different sorts" (The National Reading Panel, 2000, pp. 4–24). Teachers must remember that effective vocabulary instruction requires a careful consideration of the specific learning goal, the words to be instructed, and the word knowledge students bring to the classroom.

Figure 20.3 National Reading Panel Conclusions From
Scientifically-Based Research on Vocabulary Instruction

- Vocabulary should be taught both directly and indirectly.
- Encountering vocabulary words often and in various ways can have a significant effect on vocabulary learning.
- Vocabulary words that students will find useful in many contexts should be selected.
- Restructuring tasks to be certain students fully understand the task and the components of vocabulary learning can lead to increased vocabulary learning, particularly for low-achieving and at-risk students.
- Actively engaging students results in larger vocabulary gains.
- Emerging support for the use of computer technology to increase vocabulary.
- Vocabulary words can be learned through incidental and indirect ways. Repetition, richness of context, and student motivation may add to the efficacy of incidental learning.

✎ Application Exercises

1. Circle the five words in which the use of morphemes will enable intermediate-grade students to figure out the meaning of a word. Assume the students know the meaning of the root word.

unusable	emphasis
decisive	discord
misspell	dejected
careless	rewashable
absent	useful

2. Rank the following three passages according to the difficulty students would have determining the meaning of each underlined word through contextual analysis. Write 1 for the easiest, 2 for moderate, and 3 for most difficult. Explain why 2 is more difficult than 1 and why 3 is more difficult than 2.
   - Our center fielder, Bill, is <u>ambidextrous</u>. He bats third in the lineup. He can use his right hand and his left hand.
   - I wish I were <u>ambidextrous</u>. Then I would be able to use my left hand as well as my right.
   - Our center fielder, Bill, is not <u>ambidextrous</u>. He bats third in the lineup. He can use his right but not his left hand.

3. Which three of the following dictionary definitions would be most difficult for fifth graders to understand? Why?

   malpractice—dereliction of professional duty

   mammoth—a very great size

   burnish—to polish using something hard

fossil—trace or impression of the remains of a plant or animal preserved in the earth's crust from past ages

infirm—deficient in vitality

fortunate—coming by good luck

Rewrite the more difficult definitions to make them more understandable.

4. Tell which method (synonym, definition) you would use to teach the meaning of the following words. Specify the wording you would use.

a. residence   d. invalid

b. retrospect   e. sanctuary

c. diabolic

5. Specify a set of examples (two positive and two negative) you would use in the teaching of *residence.*

6. Which five of the following vocabulary words should a fourth grade teacher review in later lessons when working with more naive students?

congress   region

impend   myriad

defend   professional

ensconced   suspend

wrest   trough

7. The following words are to appear in passages the students will be reading several days from now. Write V in front of each word that should be included in a vocabulary exercise. Write D in front of each word that should be included in a decoding exercise. (Some words need not be included in either type of exercise.)

_____ pauper	_____ exported	_____ extinction	_____ cleft
_____ surround	_____ finch	_____ gymnasium	_____ footstep
_____ essay	_____ architect	_____ void	_____ dynamite
_____ noun	_____ swear	_____ neutral	_____ brittle

Specific Comprehension Skills for the Early Primary Level

In this chapter, we illustrate the aspects of program design with three early primary-grade comprehension skills: literal comprehension, sequencing, and summarization. Literal comprehension involves teaching students to retrieve information stated in a passage. The discussion of literal comprehension is presented to demonstrate how attention to specific details can help instructionally naïve children succeed in the early stages of learning.

Sequencing requires students to order several events from a passage according to when they happened in a passage. The discussion on sequencing also is meant to illustrate how a step-by-step procedure can help the instructionally naïve student succeed.

Both the discussions of literal comprehension and sequencing present rather mechanical-type skills that show students how to extract information from a passage. Teachers working with average and higher-performing students will likely not have to utilize the strategies presented in this section because their students will be able to do the tasks without teacher guidance.

Summarization involves teaching students to generate or select a sentence that expresses the main idea. The discussion is designed to show how a teacher can introduce a higher-level thinking skill in a manner that can foster success for all students.

These three skills would be taught as text comprehension skills beginning during the later part of the first year of reading instruction or the early part of the second year when students are able to adequately decode enough words to construct written exercises.

These simple text comprehension items are introduced during the beginning reading stage. The complexity of early text comprehension items in a reading program is limited because the students' decoding skills enable them to read only a limited number of words. During the time when children are at the early part of the learning-to-read stage, the teacher can introduce more complex comprehension skills through verbal exercises in which the teacher reads stories to children and asks a variety of questions. An example of a commercial program that includes comprehension teaching based on orally read stories is *Reasoning and Writing Level A,* authored by Engelmann and Davis (2001).

Literal Comprehension

Literal comprehension, which is the simplest written comprehension exercise, is the first type of

---

Table 21.1 Literal and Nonliteral Comprehension Items

Passage:

A cat was sleeping in the sun. Then a dog walked by. The cat jumped up and hid in a can.

Items: Write the right word in the blank.

    literal   **1.** The cat hid in a _____. can   house   box

    nonliteral **2.** The cat was _____. happy   afraid   big

---

written exercise introduced in reading programs. In a literal comprehension exercise, the answer is directly stated in the passage. The difference between literal and nonliteral comprehension is illustrated in the passage and items in Table 21.1. Item 1 is literal because the answer is directly stated in the passage. In contrast, Item 2 is not literal since the answer (afraid) does not appear in the passage. In Item 2, students must infer that, since the cat ran from the dog and hid, the cat was afraid.

Teaching Procedure for Literal, Passage-Related Items

The following procedure is designed to introduce literal comprehension items. The procedure would be used only if students were unable to work literal items on their own. Even with students who initially require the structured teaching procedure, the procedure should be faded as soon as students can accurately work literal items independently.

In presenting passage-related items (see Table 21.2), the teacher (1) has the students decode the passage until they can do so fluently, (2) explains and tests the students' understanding of the instructions, and (3) has the students read the first question, asks for the answer, and if students cannot come up with the answer, directs them to reread the passage until they come to the sentence that contains the answer.

Developing Student Retention

After a few days of teacher-directed instruction, the students should do several passage-related items independently. The teacher watches students carefully while they read the passage and answer the items. She notes the strategy students use: Do students refer to the passage for every item or just for unknown items?

If students refer to the passage to answer most of the items, they should be encouraged to remember what they have read. One way of doing this is to present a passage and items on separate pages or require the students to cover the passage before they begin answering the items. The teacher says, "Today you're going to have to remember what you read. When you remember what you read, you can write your answers without looking back at the story. Let's try it. Read the story over until you remember what happens. Then cover the story like this (demonstrates) and write the answers." The teacher monitors the students to make certain they cover the passage before they begin to work the items. When students make an error or cannot remember an answer, they are allowed to refer to the passage. The teacher calls attention to students who correctly answer all the items without looking at the passage; for example, "Students who didn't have to look at the story are in the good remembering club." The teacher reads the names of students who are members of the club for that day. This procedure for building retention can be used on almost all comprehension exercises. In order to ensure a successful experience for instructionally naive students, initial exercises should include relatively short passages. Passage length should be increased gradually.

Difficulty of Literal Comprehension Items

Several variables affect the difficulty of passage-related items: (1) the degree to which the items are

---

Table 21.2 Format for Literal Comprehension

Passage:

A little cat lived in a mud house. It rained. A bug ran in the house. The mud house got wet and fell apart.
The cat and the bug sat in the rain and got wet.

Items: Fill in the blanks.

1. What got wet and fell apart? _____
2. A cat lived in a mud _____. house bug hut
3. The _____ and the bug sat in the rain. bug dog cat

Teacher	*Students*
1. The teacher focuses on decoding fluency. **"Touch the first word."** Teacher checks pointing. The teacher alternates between unison and individual responses until the students read the passage fluently. Students may need to reread the story several times.	Students read the passage.
2. Teacher tests students' understanding of the instructions. Often the instructions for early comprehension activities are not written because the students do not have the decoding skills necessary to read the words that appear in instructions. Whether the teacher gives the instructions or the students read them, the teacher then asks, **"How are you going to answer the question? Tell me what you're going to do. Show me where you put the answer."**	
3. Students read the first item and then mark the answer. If necessary, they find the appropriate sentence in the story that answers the item.	
a. **"Touch the first question."** Teacher calls on a student to read.	Student reads the question.
b. **"Raise your hand if you know the answer to that question."** If the question has only one possible correct answer, the teacher calls on the group to respond. If the question has several possible correct answers, she calls on individuals to respond. **"What's the answer?"**	Students answer.
c. If any students do not remember the answer, the teacher says, **"Let's find the answer in the story. Find the words get wet and fell apart."** If students cannot find the words, have them read each sentence. After students find the sentence, the teacher repeats the item. **"What got wet and fell apart?"** "Right, *the mud house.* **Write the answer."**	Students write the answer.
d. The procedure in step 3 is repeated until the students have completed all the items.	

---

literal, (2) the length of the passage, (3) the order in which questions are asked, (4) the complexity of the instructions, and (5) the use of pronouns.

Literal Items

The easiest type of passage-related item is one that can be answered by matching words in the item with those in the sentence. The following item, written in a nonsense language, illustrates a strictly literal item.

    Sentence: yjr, sm gr;; gpp jod jptdr

    Item: yjr, sm gr;; gpp jod_____

Adults cannot decode the nonsense item; yet, they can answer it correctly by matching the words in the item with those in the sentence and writing *jptdr* in the blank. Similarly, a child can answer a completion item by using a matching strategy rather than decoding each word.

    Items become less literal when they are not identical to a corresponding sentence in a passage.

    Question word items are also less literal (e.g., *Where did the cat live?*) because the word order is altered and the student must understand particular question words (e.g., *where* calls for a location answer).

Passage Length

Finding the sentence that contains the answer to a completion item is more difficult in longer passages. For example, extracting the answer to the question, "Who sat on a mat?" is easier in the sentence "A mad cat sat on a mat" than in this passage: "A rat sat on a mitt. A mad cat sat on a mat. A sad man sat on a bed."

Question Order

Items ordered so that they parallel the sequence of events in a passage are easier than items that do not. When items follow the sequence of a passage, students can start at the beginning of the passage and work through the items in order. Otherwise, they must skip around in the passage to locate the answers. Below are two sets of items, one that follows the sequence of events in the passage (set a) and one that does not (set b).

Passage:
Sam ran in a hut. He sat in a cup. He said, "I am hot." He fell off the cup. He got wet. "I am not hot," he said.

Items: Fill in the correct answer.

  a. Items follow the order of events in the passage:
  Did Sam run in a hut? _____
  Where did Sam sit? _____
  He said, "I am not _____."

  b. Items do not follow the order of events in the passage:
  He said, "I am not _____."
  Did Sam run in a hut? _____
  Where did Sam sit? _____

Instruction Complexity

Instructions indicating how students are to respond range from simple ones in which students circle the word that goes in a blank or fill in a missing word

to more complex ones in which students make several different responses, e.g., "Circle the word that tells what the boy did. Underline the word that tells what the girl did."

Pronouns

Pronouns increase the difficulty of items because students must identify a pronoun antecedent before they can answer the item. Note the differences between passage a and passage b.

Passage a: Tom got a car. It was dirty.

Passage b: Tom got a car. The car was dirty.

Item: Was Tom dirty?
A naïve student would be more likely to answer incorrectly yes after reading passage a because of the pronoun *it*. Passage b is easier because it directly states that the car was dirty. If students do not understand pronouns, they will have some difficulties with comprehension. To prevent these difficulties, teachers should present oral-language exercises to teach pronouns. Students can then apply their understanding of pronouns when reading. Although most students will *not* require instruction in pronouns, teachers should be prepared to work with students who need the instruction.

Teaching Procedure for Pronouns

The first step in teaching proper pronoun usage involves oral exercises to ensure that students know the meaning of key pronouns: *he, she, we, they, it, you, them, her, him.* Pronouns that cause particular difficulty are *it, they,* and *them* because they can refer to inanimate objects. The format in Table 21.3 which assumes students know *he, she,* and *it,* demonstrates how the pronoun *they* might be taught. Note that students are taught that the pronoun *they* refers to objects as well as people. This is an example of including a full range of positive examples.

The second step in teaching pronoun usage involves leading the students through a series of passages containing pronouns. A sample passage appears on the following page.

Table 21.3 Format for Teaching Pronouns

Teacher	Students
1. Teacher demonstrates. "Here's a new pronoun. *They. They* tells about more than one."	
2. Teacher provides practice on saying the definition. "What does the pronoun *they* tell about?"	"More than one."
3. Teacher provides practice on applying the definition. "Listen: John and Mary. Do we say *they* when we talk about John and Mary?" "How do you know?"	"Yes." "John and Mary are more than one."
4. "Listen: John. Do we say *they* when we talk about John?" "How do you know?" "What pronoun could tell about John?"	"No." "John is only one." "He."
5. "Listen: fork. Do we say *they* when we talk about a fork?" "Why not?" "What pronoun could tell about a fork?"	"No." "Fork is only one." "It."
6. "Listen: fork and spoon. Do we say *they* when we talk about a fork and spoon?" "How do you know?"	"Yes." "Fork and spoon are more than one."
7. "Listen: boys. Do we say *they* when we talk about boys?" "How do you know?"	"Yes." "Boys are more than one."
8. "Listen: Mary. Do we say *they* when we talk about Mary?" "Why not?" "What pronoun could tell about Mary?"	"No." "Mary is only one." "She."

Passage:

Tom and Lisa got in trouble with their parents. They had to stay in all weekend. He cried. She got mad.

Item:

a. Did Lisa stay in all weekend?

b. Did Tom get mad?

c. Who cried?

The teacher or students read the passage. The teacher asks questions after each sentence:

1. "Tom and Lisa got in trouble. Who got in trouble?" "Tom and Lisa."

2. "They had to stay in all weekend. Did Tom have to stay in?" "Yes." "Did Lisa have to stay in?" "Yes."

3. "He cried. Did Tom cry?" "Yes." "Did Lisa cry?" "No."

4. "She got mad. Did Tom get mad?" "No." "Did Lisa get mad?" "Yes."

If students make errors, the teacher refers to the pronoun (e.g., "She got mad. She tells about a girl. Is Tom a girl?").

Sequencing

Sequencing requires ordering several events according to when they occur in a passage. For example, a student reads a passage and then writes numbers in front of several phrases that describe events, writing 1 in front of the event that occurred first, 2 in front of the event that occurred next, etc. The difficulty of sequencing items depends on the length of the passage and the number of items to be sequenced. Obviously, the longer a passage and the more items to be sequenced, the more difficult the exercise will be.

Teaching Procedure

The strategy we recommend works only for very simple passages in which the first action appears in

Table 21.4 Format for Sequencing

Passage:

Alice went home after school. Later she went to the park. At the park she saw her friend, Bob. Alice and Bob played catch all day. Then they got an ice cream cone.

Directions:

Write 1 in front of what happened first, a 2 in front of what happened next, and a 3 in front of what happened third.
Items:

_____ Alice went home.

_____ Alice got an ice cream cone.

_____ Alice and Bob played catch.

Teacher	*Students*
1. Teacher has students read the story and directions.	
a. Read the story.	Students read the story.
b. Read the directions.	Students read directions.
2. Touch the item that says *Alice went home.*	Students find event below directions.
3. Now find in the story where it says *Alice went home* and underline those words.	Students locate and underline the sentence.
4. Teacher repeats steps 2 and 3 for the remaining two events.	
5. Look at the passage, find the first event in the story that is underlined and place a 1 over it. Then place a 2 over the second underlined event, and a 3 over the third underlined event.	Students locate the first event and write a 1 over it. Students locate the next item and write a 2 over it, etc.
6. **a.** Look at the items. Touch *Alice went home.*	Students locate item and touch it.
b. Now touch where it says *Alice went home* in the passage.	Students touch sentence in the passage.
c. What number is written over the words *Alice went home?*	"One."
d. Write that number in front of *Alice went home.*	Students write 1.
e. Teacher repeats steps a–d with remaining items.	

the story first; the second action appears second, and so forth. The strategy involves these steps (see Table 21.4): (1) the students read the passage and items; (2) for each item, the students underline the words in the passage that coincide with the event; (3) the students number the events underlined in the passage, beginning with 1; and (4) the students then write the numbers in front of the appropriate items in the question.

The teacher can fade the structure of the format over a period of days. When the students do the items without teacher help, the teacher need not insist on students using the underlining strategy if they are able to answer the items correctly without underlining.

The length of the passage, and the number of items to be sequenced, should increase gradually.

The increases in difficulty can occur when the students are able to do the current type without error for 2 consecutive days.

Summarization

Summarization not only allows the students to identify the key ideas from a passage, but it also reduces the information in a passage to key ideas that students can remember. Since students cannot remember everything they hear or read, acquiring summarization skills ensures they will remember major events rather than random details. A summary condenses a passage into a few sentences. A one-sentence summary can be considered a main idea.

Teaching Procedure

The teaching procedure we recommend begins with exercises in which the students create main idea sentences for short passages in which the subjects are persons or things, and the predicates include actions that can be easily classified.

The first type of item involves one person doing a series of actions that can be easily classified. Table 21.5 includes a sample set of items. Note that in each item the main idea can be written by naming the person, then telling the main thing the person did in all the sentences. The teaching procedure includes these steps: (1) the teacher tells the students a rule for writing a main idea sentence (e.g., "Name the person and tell the main thing the person did in all the sentences"); (2) the students read the passage; (3) the teacher asks the students to figure out a main idea sentence by naming the person and telling what the person did in all the sentences; (4) the teacher calls on a student to say the sentence, and the teacher corrects the student by telling the correct answer; (5) the teacher repeats the same procedure with the remaining passages; (6) the teacher has the students write the main idea sentence for each paragraph (difficult-to-spell words would be written on the board).

A slightly more complex–type item is introduced when the students master writing main idea sentences for the item type described above. This type includes sentences that name different persons or things and tell the actions they did. The students must give the people or things a group name, then say a verb that classifies the action. Following is a typical item:

Mr. Smith dug holes for the rose bushes. Mr. Jones put rose bushes in the holes. Mr. Adams put dirt back in the holes around the rose bushes.

An acceptable main idea sentence for the item above would be "The men planted rose bushes."

The teaching procedure for this type of item is basically the same as described above, except that the teacher directs the students to construct the sentence by naming the group (the men) and telling the main thing the group did (planted rose bushes).

The value of these exercises is that they demonstrate that main idea sentences tell what an entire passage is about.

Multiple-choice items, in which students are asked to select the sentence that is the main idea sentence for a passage, could be introduced next. Below is a sample item.

Passage:

A dog walked on its back legs. A bear rode a bicycle. A seal balanced a ball on its nose.

Which sentence is the best main idea sentence?

1. An animal walked on its back legs.

2. The animals wanted food.

3. The animals did tricks.

4. A dog did a trick.

Note the variety of possible main idea sentences used in the item. The correct answer is "The animals did tricks." Two sentences do not express the main idea because they merely describe one of the animals. One incorrect answer names the group (the

---

Table 21.5 Items for Main Idea Single-Person Class Action

Tom cooked two eggs. He poured orange juice into a glass. He put cereal in a bowl. He poured milk into the bowl.	Ann went to the park. She swung on the swings. She slid down a slide. She climbed on the bars.
Sally took the flat tire off her bike. She put a patch on the hole in the tire. She put the tire back on her bike. She filled the tire with air.	Robert gave a carrot to the horse. He poured milk in a bowl for a cat. He put hay in the barn for the cows.

animals) but makes an inference (the animals *wanted* food).

The teaching format includes these steps: (1) the students read the passage; (2) the teacher tells the students that one of the sentences is a good main idea sentence for the passage; and (3) the teacher has the students read each sentence and asks if it is a good main idea sentence for the passage, asking why or why not after each response.

The next step in the sequence is to introduce passages in which one or more sentences are not related to the main idea. We can call these sentences *distractors*. When distractors appear, the rule for creating a main idea changes from telling what a person or group did in all the sentences to telling the main thing the person or group did in most of the sentences. Look at the following passage.

Passage:

Tom got home and took out his school books. He did three pages of math. He liked math. He studied twenty spelling words. He wrote a report about birds. Tom was very interested in birds.

Note that two sentences in the above passage do not tell what Tom did. The main idea is still clearly "Tom did his homework."

The teacher introduces the passage by saying, "Most of the sentences in this passage tell about the main thing a person did. The main idea sentence for the passage tells what the passage is mainly about."

Multiple-choice items in which the possible answers the students must select from are written as questions can be introduced next.

A preskill for these types of items is sentence analysis, which teaches students to determine if a sentence tells where, why, when, etc. (see Chapter 12). Below are examples of paragraphs that tell why something occurred and paragraphs that tell where

something occurs. This paragraph tells *why* a boy was sad:

Bill got an F on his test. Bill lost his favorite toy. Bill's team lost the big game. Bill's best friend moved to another school.

Circle the best main idea:

1. Why Bill failed his test.
2. Why Bill was sad.
3. What happened to Bill's friend?
4. What Bill is going to do.

This paragraph tells *where* you can do something:

Football is lots of fun. You can play football in the street. You can play football in the park if there aren't too many trees. You can play football on a soccer field.

Circle the best main idea:

1. What you can do in a street.
2. Why football is fun.
3. Where you can play football.
4. When you can play football.

Where and *why* items can be introduced concurrently because they are relatively easy to distinguish from each other.

The teaching procedure presents the strategy of having the students examine each possible main idea, noting how many sentences tell about that particular main idea. The teacher leads the students through several examples, then has them do several independently.

Passages that tell when something occurs, how something is done, or how something looks may be introduced later.

✂ Application Exercises

1. Specify whether each question below is a literal question or a nonliteral question: The rocket landed on the soft sand. Minutes later Zorn walked out of the rocket. He had never seen such a place. The sky was black. He could see nothing but sand.

   a. Did Zorn land at noon time?

   b. What landed on the soft sand?

   c. What color was the sky?

   d. Did Zorn land in New York City?

2. Assume some teachers are presenting sets of examples to teach the range of the word *it*. Tell which of the three teachers below has constructed the best set of examples. Explain why.

   Teacher A—a pen, a fork, a pencil, a knife

   Teacher B—a bed, a chair, a table, a dresser, a stool

   Teacher C—a lion, a dresser, the moon, a pen, a spider

3. Specify the teacher wording to correct the following errors made by a student on a worksheet assignment. (Assume the student can decode all the words.)

   a. Passage: The beach was crowded. It was Sunday, and it was hot. Babies played in the sand. Children jumped in the waves. Parents sat and talked.

   Item: Circle the best title.

   1. Babies make sand piles.

   2. People had a good time at the beach.

   3. Children play in the waves.

   b. Passage: Bill and Sally walked to the park this morning. Sally played baseball and Bill ran around the track. They got a drink of water. Then they went home.

   Item: Write 1, 2, 3 in front of the events in the order they happened.

   3 They got a drink of water.

   1 They went home.

   2 Bill and Sally went to the park.

4. A teacher tested a group of students and found the students did not know the meaning of the following words that will appear in a written comprehension task within the next few days: daring, contented, rudder, and parallelograms. For each word,

   a. describe the procedure you would use to teach the word (examples, synonyms, or definitions) and, if applicable, write the synonym or definition.

   b. Write a set of four examples that could be used in teaching *daring* (specify two positive and two negative examples).

Specific Comprehension Skills for the Late Primary and Intermediate Levels

As stated earlier, reading comprehension is a complex cognitive activity which entails a myriad of skills and strategies. In the early primary grades, the skills and strategies are focused on literal comprehension exercises in which the answers to questions are stated explicitly in the text. In the late primary grades, the focus shifts to inferential comprehension exercises in which the answers are not stated explicitly in the text. To answer inferential comprehension questions, students must know and use a variety of complex thinking skills and strategies. Space does not allow for coverage of the full range of skills and strategies involved in inferential comprehension; in this chapter, we discuss five that we consider to be important and provide suggestions for teaching those directly.

First, we provide an example of how to teach students to discriminate literal and inferential questions. This is an important skill that students must acquire as they make the transition from exercises that focus primarily on literal comprehension to exercises that focus primarily on inferential comprehension. Second, we provide formats for teaching inferencing when critical relationships are stated and when critical relationships are not stated.

Next we discuss the need to identify and preteach background information that enhances understanding of upcoming stories or passages. Cognitive psychologists refer to this kind of background information as "prior knowledge." Many inferential questions assume background knowledge that many students may not have. We believe that critical background knowledge can and should be identified and taught directly.

Knowledge of the syntactic structures of sentences is also essential to good inferential comprehension. Syntactic structure of sentences becomes increasingly varied and complex as students progress through the intermediate grades. We describe sentence structures that are encountered frequently and provide explicit examples for teaching one such construction—passive voice.

We conclude with a section on critical reading that includes several formats for teaching students to identify the author's conclusion, discriminate evidence from opinion, and identify invalid conclusions and faulty arguments. Each of these component skills of critical reading requires reasoning and higher order thinking. Many reading comprehension programs assume that students have these reasoning skills when, in fact, many do not. These important skills and strategies can and should be taught directly.

Discriminating Literal and Inferential Questions

The introduction of inferential items can begin with simple questions asking students to predict based on what has already happened in the story. For example, a teacher may be reading a story to children about a boy who is very considerate. When a new situation requires a choice of actions by the boy, the children can be asked to predict how the boy may behave given what they already have learned about the boy.

Teaching students how to make inferential judgements can also be taught more formally. Below is a sample early exercise that can teach the children to discriminate between questions that you must think about (infer) to determine the answer versus questions that you can answer by finding the words in the text (literal).

Passage:

There was a big race. A girl in our class came in first. Her sister came in second. Jill's brother came in third.

After the students read the passage, the teacher poses questions to lead the students through a series of steps to determine if the question can be answered by finding words in the passage or by "thinking" to figure out the answer.

Here's a question based on the text:

Who came in third in the race?

The teacher asks:

Can you find the exact words that tell who came in third? (yes)

What is the answer? (Jill's brother)

Here's another question:

Did James come in second in the race?

The teacher asks:

The sentences don't tell about James. But you can use the information in the sentence and think to find the answer.

What do you know about who came in second? (A girl came in second.)

So could James have come in second? (no)

You used thinking to figure out the answer.

A more complex item is illustrated below. This item is an excerpt from a program entitled "Comprehension" which is part of the *Corrective Reading Series* authored by Sigfried Engelmann et al. (1999).

Passage:

If you don't get all the vitamins you need, you can get bad diseases. Children who don't get any vitamin D may get soft bones. This disease is called rickets (p. 102).

Questions for this text excerpt include:

What can happen if you don't get all the vitamins you need? (literal)

If Jim gets lots of vitamin D and Bill doesn't get any, which person is likely to have stronger bones? (inferential)

The teacher would lead the students through the items asking the students to tell the answer and indicate how they got the answer. A great deal of practice on this type exercise is likely to be needed for more instructionally naive students. Carefully written passages in which some questions can readily be answered by referring directly to words in the passage and other questions that can be answered by making inferences based on the information in a passage would need to be utilized.

Inference

Inferential questions require knowledge of relationships between two objects or events. The statement "When people run faster, their hearts beat faster" implies a relationship between changes in running rate and changes in heartbeat. Sometimes the relationship is directly stated in a passage (see example A in

Table 22.1   Inferential Questions

Relationship Stated	Relationship Not Stated	
	Knowledge of Relationship Is Assumed	Examples for Figuring Out the Relationship Are Provided
A. When people run faster, their hearts beat faster. On Monday, Rachel ran a mile in 5 minutes. On Tuesday, she took 7 minutes. On Wednesday, she took 4 minutes.	B. On Monday, Rachel ran a mile in 5 minutes. On Tuesday, she took 7 minutes. On Wednesday, she took 4 minutes.	C. On Friday, Rachel ran a mile in 8 minutes. Her heart was beating 78 times a minute. On Saturday, Rachel ran a mile in 6 minutes. Her heart was beating 93 times a minute. On Sunday, she ran a mile in 9 minutes. Her heart was beating 68 times a minute. On Monday, Rachel ran a mile in 5 minutes. On Tuesday, she took 6 minutes. On Wednesday, she took 4 minutes.
On which day did Rachel's heart beat fastest? Monday Tuesday Wednesday	On which day did Rachel's heart beat fastest? Monday Tuesday Wednesday	On which day did Rachel's heart beat fastest? Monday Tuesday Wednesday

Table 22.1). More often, the relationship is not specified; students are expected to know a particular relationship (see example B in Table 22.1) or are expected to infer the relationship using the information stated in a passage (see example C in Table 22.1). In passage A the relationship "When people run faster, their hearts beat faster" is directly stated. Since the relationship is stated, students are more likely to answer the item about Rachel correctly. In passage B, the relationship is not stated, and examples are not provided that allow the reader to figure out or induce the relationship. Obviously, students who do not know the relationship between exertion and heart rate have no basis for answering the item. Although the relationship is not directly stated in passage C either, several examples illustrate the relationship between running rate and heartbeat. When Rachel ran a mile in 8 minutes, her rate was 78 beats per minute. When she ran faster (a mile in 6 minutes), her rate was faster (93 beats per minute). Students are given information that enables them to induce the relationship and then figure out the answer. (Using specific information to derive a general relationship, as in example C, is called

induction. Applying a stated relationship to come up with a specific answer is called deduction.)

First, we discuss procedures for teaching students to make inferences based on stated relationships. Second, we discuss procedures for teaching students to answer inferential questions when a relationship is not stated. This type of item accounts for the majority of inference items in commercial programs. Third, we discuss procedures for teaching students to induce relationships when examples are provided to illustrate the relationship.

When introducing inference items, the teacher can refer to them as "detective" problems. The students must use the information in the passage to figure out the answer to the question.

Relationship Stated

Much of the material students read in the intermediate grades is expository. It is designed to convey information. A common characteristic of expository material is the inclusion of key sentences which specify a relationship. Table 22.2 includes examples

Table 22.2 Simple Relationships and Items for Teaching Inference

Relationship	*Items*
1. Students who study *hardest* make the best grades.	1. Jim got a lower mark on the test than Bill. Who studied *harder*?
2. The steeper a stream, the faster the water flows.	2. Bill is fishing in a stream on some flat land. Sarah is fishing in a stream on a hill. Which stream is moving faster?
3. The higher you go up, the less oxygen in the air.	3. There is less oxygen where Ann is walking than where Margie is walking. Who is walking at a higher place?
4. The greater the rainfall, the greener the grass.	4. There were 5 inches of rain in Oregon last month, 2 inches in New York, and 1 inch of rain in Arizona. Where is the grass greener?
5. When you buy a lot of the same thing, the price is cheaper.	5. Ann, Tom, and Jill bought some cans of chicken soup. Ann paid 14 cents for each can. Tom paid 13 cents for each can. Jill paid 11 cents for each can. Who bought more cans of soup?
6. The more weight you lift, the bigger your muscles get.	6. Bob's and Susan's muscles were the same size in November. Now Bob's muscles are smaller than Susan's muscles. Who lifted more weight?
7. The faster you run, the more energy you use.	7. On Monday Agnes ran 3 miles in 15 minutes. On Tuesday she ran 3 miles in 13 minutes. On which day did she use more energy?
8. The less a car weighs, the farther it goes on a gallon of gas.	8. Tim's car went 23 miles on a gallon of gas. Bill's car went 17 miles on a gallon of gas. Who's car is heavier?
9. The less you eat, the thinner you get.	9. Bill lost 4 pounds in January, 3 pounds in February, and 5 pounds in March. In which month did he eat the least?

of sentences which specify relationships with items that can be used to test students' ability to draw inferences from a stated relationship.

Table 22.3 includes a sample worksheet exercise that can be used to teach students to work from stated rules. The rule is presented; then a series of questions that contain information relating to the rule are given. Note that after each question, the students are expected to explain why they gave a particular answer.

Teaching Procedure

The teaching procedure always begins with the students reading the rule, then saying it. Some students may have a lot of trouble saying the rule. See the statement repetition procedures on pages 111 through 112 for suggestions.

Table 22.3 Sample Worksheet—Rule-Related Inference

Rule: The faster you run, the more oxygen you use.

Item I:

a. John and Bill had a race. John lost the race.
   Who used more oxygen? _____
b. How do you know? _____

Item 2:

a. Ann and Sally ran a race. Ann breathed more oxygen than Sally.
   Who ran faster? _____
b. How do you know? _____

Item 3:

a. Jerry ran 3 miles in 15 minutes. Al ran 3 miles in 12 minutes.
   Who used more oxygen? _____
b. How do you know? _____

The first several days these worksheets are presented, the teacher models by relating the answer to the rule (e.g., "My turn. Item 1: Who used more oxygen?" Bill. "How do you know?" Bill ran faster than John. "The rule says: The faster you run, the more oxygen you use."). After modeling several items, the teacher repeats the items, calling on different students to respond, then presents new items.

When students can do rule worksheets without error for two consecutive days, simple passages containing "rules" can be introduced. A sample passage appears below. Note that the rule sentence is underlined.

John runs around the track every day. When he finishes, he counts his breath to see how hard he ran. <u>When he breathes harder, it means that he ran faster.</u> On Monday he took 100 breaths in 1 minute. On Tuesday, he took 90 breaths in 1 minute. On Wednesday, he took 110 breaths in 1 minute. When do you think John ran the hardest? Why?

The teacher tells the students that the underlined sentence gives the rule they should use to find the answer. The teacher (1) has the students read the entire passage; (2) find the rule and say it; (3) points out what the information given tells ("We know how many breaths he took on each day"); (4) reminds students of the rule; and (5) asks students why they gave that answer.

Relationship Not Stated

In many inference items, the student is assumed to have the prerequisite information and knowledge of a less common relationship needed to answer the question. For example, a social studies book might ask, "Is the border between the United States and Mexico or the border between Oregon and Washington more heavily watched by police?" To answer the question, the students must know that since the United States and Mexico are separate nations, that border is more closely watched than the border between Oregon and Washington, which are states. Knowledge of the relationship between the type of boundary and how heavily it is guarded is assumed.

Teachers, especially those working with lower-performing students, should preview inference items in all types of material—content area, literature, and workbooks. When previewing the materials, the teacher notes what information the student needs to comprehend the material and answer questions. The information may be a simple fact (e.g., Oregon is a state) or an unstated relationship (e.g., international boundaries are watched more closely than state boundaries). Teachers should preteach prerequisite information or relationships students are not likely to know and not stated in the passage.

The distinction between items which do and do not require preteaching can be seen in the following sets of passages and items. Note that the first set will not require preteaching because it assumes knowledge of a relationship most students will, in fact, know ("When you play in the rain you may get a cold."). The second set assumes knowledge of a less well-known relationship ("If a cactus is watered every day it will die."). This relationship should be taught before students are assigned the item.

Exercise 1—obvious relationship, no preteaching needed

Passage:
Thomas was big for his age and tired quickly; but, today he kept on playing handball even after the rain started. He was so concerned about improving his serve, he didn't care about being tired or notice the cold rain beating down on his head and arms.

Item: Circle the best answer.
Thomas _____

  1. is probably a ninth-grader.

  2. plays soccer every day.

  3. may get a cold.

Exercise 2—less common relationship, preteaching required

Passage:
Tom bought his mother two plants, a cactus and a fern, for her birthday. He watered the plants every

day for three weeks. He wanted the plants to look nice when he gave them to his mother.

Item: Circle the best answer.
Tom _____

1. probably will be very happy when he gives his mother the plants.
2. will be disappointed because one of the plants will be dead.
3. probably took a course in how to care for plants.

Induced Relationships

Relationship-based inference items, in which students must induce a relationship (i.e., the relationship is unstated), are much more difficult than items in which a relationship is directly stated in a passage. Items of this type can be introduced after students have learned to answer questions based on stated and assumed relationships.

Teaching Procedure

A format for teaching students to induce a relationship based on information in a passage appears in Table 22.4. First the students read a passage about what happens when several beggars make different types of requests of a girl named Alice. If the request will cost Alice money, she says "no." If the request will not cost Alice money, she says "yes."

Difficulty Variables

Three factors contribute to the difficulty of inference items:

1. the degree to which the stated relationship is separated from the relevant information;
2. the ease with which relevant information can be used in drawing an inference;

3. the number of distractors that appear in the passage. (A distractor is irrelevant information that calls attention to a plausible but incorrect answer.)

These three difficulty variables are illustrated in the two passages that appear in Table 22.5. Most students find passage A easier because relevant information is directly stated, the sentences containing the stated relationship and the relevant information appear together, and passage A contains no distractors.

1. In passage A, the information about the speed of the planes immediately follows John's statement about wanting to fly on fast planes. In passage B, John's statement about wanting to fly on fast planes is separated from the relevant information about the speed of planes. Students reading passage B must remember the stated relationship that John's major concern is flying on a fast plane.
2. In passage A, relevant information can be easily processed since the flying time for each plane is stated: 1 hour and 1½ hours. On the other hand, students reading passage B must know to translate departure and arrival times into a total flying time: "The Air Worst plane is a small jet which leaves at 10:30 and arrives at 11:30."
3. Finally, passage A contains few distractors. In passage B, many advantages of one plane are listed: it is big, serves a good meal, and shows movies. Students who read passage B must be careful to apply John's criterion for selecting a plane and not be misled by all the benefits listed for the plane.

While no single format can prepare students to handle all inference items, a general teaching procedure can be helpful. The first step is to teach students to find the stated relationship and the information needed to draw an inference based on the stated relationship. Instructionally naive students must be shown that they sometimes have to skim a passage to find both the stated relationship and the information

Table 22.4 Format for Inducing Relationships

Passage:

A beggar asked Alice Jones for some food. Alice said, "No." Another beggar came by and asked to sit on the porch and rest. Alice said, "Yes." The next day a different beggar came to the house. He asked to stand by the fire and warm up. Alice said, "Yes." A week later, a beggar asked for some gas for his car. Alice said, "No."

Items:

1. A beggar asked to lay in Alice's yard and sleep. What do you think Alice said?
2. Another beggar asked for some clothes. What do you think Alice said?

Teacher	Students
1. "You're going to read about Alice and some beggars. We're going to figure out why Alice treats them the way she does. Start reading the story."	Students begin reading the passage. "A beggar asked Alice Jones for some food. Alice said, 'No.' Another beggar came by and asked to sit on the porch and rest. Alice said, 'Yes.'"
2. "One time Alice said yes; one time she said no. What happened before she said yes?" "What happened before she said no?" "Why do you think Alice said no to food and yes to sitting and resting? How is letting someone have food different from letting someone sit down and rest?" If students do not indicate that food costs money but letting someone sit and rest doesn't, the teacher should point out this relationship. "Let's read on and see if Alice says no when beggars ask for things that cost money."	"The beggar asked to sit and rest." "The beggar asked for food." "The next day a different beggar came to the house. He asked to stand by the fire and warm up."
3. "Would it cost money to let the beggar stand by the fire?" "So what do you think Alice will do?" "Read on and see if she does."	"No." "Let him stand by the fire." "Alice said, 'Yes.' A week later, a beggar asked for some gas for his car."
4. "Would it cost money to let the beggar have some gas?" "So what do you think Alice will do?" "Read on and see what happens."	"Yes." "Not give him any gas." "Alice said, 'No.'"
5. "You were right. Giving the man gas would cost money, so Alice said no. Read and work the items on your own."	

they need to draw an inference based on the stated relationship. For example, if students had just read the item asking about which plane John will take, the teacher would say, "In what kind of plane does John like to fly?" "Fast planes." "Find the part of the story that tells about how long it takes the planes to get to San Francisco." Note that this passage assumes student knowledge of the unstated relationship: Vehicles that get to a place the quickest travel the fastest. This relationship may have to be taught to some naive students before presenting the passage.

Next, students must learn to translate any relevant information into a form that directly fits the stated relationship. In the example about John, who likes to fly on fast planes, the student must be able to subtract time notations and determine that 10:30 until 11:30 is 1 hour while 9:30 to 11:00 is 1½ hours. When students do not have the skills needed to translate information into a direct form, they will have trouble with comprehension items. Consequently, teachers must preview comprehension exercises and identify assumed preskills. The teacher

Table 22.5 An Illustration of Passage-Related Difficulty Variables

---

Passage A

John was planning a short vacation. He walked into a travel agency and said, "I like to visit big cities. The city I enjoy visiting the most is San Francisco."

"Are you sure you want to go to San Francisco?" asked the agent. "It's raining there and you won't be able to enjoy the parks and beaches."

"Yes, I'm sure," John replied. "It's a beautiful city with many interesting people and lots of fun things to do. I can see friends, go to museums, see new plays, and enjoy good food. The last time I was in San Francisco the weather was stormy. It was a holiday and there was a special show at a theater. I went and saw folk dancers, listened to music, and watched a magic show. There is always something new and exciting to do there."

"Let me tell you about the flights to San Francisco then," said the agent. "There are two planes that travel non-stop to San Francisco."

"Well," said John, "when I travel, all I care about is flying on fast planes."

The agent said, "The Air Worst plane takes one hour. The USA plane takes one-and-a-half hours."

Which plane do you think John will take?

Passage B

John was planning a short vacation. He walked into a travel agency and said, "I want to fly to San Francisco. When I travel, all I care about is flying on fast planes."

The agent said, "Are you sure you want to go to San Francisco? It's raining there and you won't be able to enjoy the parks and beaches."

"That's all right," said John, "I don't mind rain. I'm sure I want to go to San Francisco. It's my favorite city. There is always something new and exciting going on there. I can visit friends, go to concerts, see new plays, and enjoy good food. I always have a good time in San Francisco. The rain won't matter."

"Let me tell you about the flights to San Francisco," said the agent. "There are two planes that fly non-stop. The Air Worst plane is a small jet which leaves at 10:30 and arrives at 11:30. The USA plane is a huge jet. It has one of the fastest engines built. It carries 300 passengers, serves a great meal, and shows a movie. If you don't want to see the movie you can listen to music with headphones. Or, you can just rest comfortably. The USA plane leaves at 9:30 and arrives at 11:00. I think you would enjoy flying on the USA plane, but it's up to you."

Which plane do you think John will take?

---

must then either teach preskills that students do not have or delete items requiring those preskills.

Finally, students must learn to deal with distractors in a passage. The distractors in the item about John consist of the positive aspects of the USA plane, which is the slower plane. The USA plane is bigger, serves a meal, and has music and a movie. Students who do not carefully attend to the statement that John wants to fly in the fastest plane might think that John would take the USA plane. When introducing items with distractors, teachers must emphasize the statement that determines the answer to the item. For example, after students read, "Which plane do you think John will take?" the teacher says, "In what kind of plane does John

want to fly?" "The fastest plane." "Did John say he wanted a plane with a meal or with a movie?" "No." "So what kind of plane are you going to look for when you answer the item?" "The fastest plane." "Figure out what plane John picked." Whenever students make a mistake because of a distractor, the teacher should require the students to locate the part of the passage that specifies the stated relationship. The teacher then points out that the distractor has nothing to do with the stated relationship and does not lead to the correct answer.

Although teachers can and should use formats for teaching students to handle the various difficulty variables, the most critical aspect of teaching involves providing a carefully designed sequence of items in which difficulty variables are introduced one at a time.[1] They should sequence items from simple to complex and provide sufficient practice on easier types before introducing more difficult types. When sequencing items, teachers should begin with relatively simple items which call for commonly known relationships; complexity of passages should be gradually increased, and new difficulty variables should be introduced one at a time. More specifically, teachers should pretest and, if necessary, teach students to make inferences based on stated relationships. Next, items based on assumed relationships can be introduced. Less common relationships should be pretaught. Items for both stated and unstated relationships should be drawn from the students' reading assignments. Next, the difficulty variables can be introduced, one at a time: separation, ease of using relevant information, and distractors. Finally, induction items should be presented. Again, the items should be taken from literature and content area assignments.

Prior Knowledge

Learning information about a topic before reading stories or content passages in which that topic plays an important role enhances comprehension. We dis-

cuss two examples from *Reading Mastery V and VI* (Engelmann et al., 1988) to illustrate the kinds of general knowledge that can be identified and pretaught directly to enhance comprehension. The general knowledge that students learn as a result of such preteaching activities can be viewed as "prior knowledge" that prepares the students to better understand and appreciate the upcoming stories or passages.

In *Reading Mastery V,* prior to reading the first part of a six-part story about Jackie Robinson, students read passages that explain the rules of baseball. In one passage, students view a picture of a baseball field with nine players in blue caps stationed at their positions (positions are labeled) and an umpire behind the catcher. Then they participate in teacher-guided reading and discussion of the following passage:

> The picture shows a game between two baseball teams. There are nine players on each team. The blue team is in the field. One player from the other team is at bat. The pitcher on the blue team throws the ball toward the catcher, who plays behind home plate. There are players at first base, second base, and third base. Between second and third base is another player called the shortstop. In the outfield, there are three more players: the left fielder, the center fielder, and the right fielder. The player from the other team is standing at home plate, holding a bat. When the pitcher throws the ball, the batter tries to hit it to a spot where nobody on the blue team can catch it. Then the batter runs as far as possible around the bases, starting with first base. If the batter can come all the way back to home plate, the batter scores a run. The picture also shows an umpire right behind the catcher. The umpire calls out "Strike" for good pitches and "Ball" for bad pitches. (p. 252)

Over the next several lessons, several more passages explaining baseball are presented. By the time the students read the series of passages about Jackie Robinson, they are knowledgeable about baseball.

Students who are familiar with the game of baseball probably already know the basic information presented in these exercises. For those

---

1. Education has long been enamored with higher order or inference questions. While educators are correct in calling for numerous inferential items, they must realize that large doses of inferential items will not necessarily improve students' inference skills, especially for instructionally naive students. The problem occurs when the inference items assume knowledge and skills the students do not have; and yet, teacher guidance is not provided. For example, consider this inference item: "As the location of a subatomic particle becomes more precise, what would you infer about its momentum?" Or consider this example: "When John walked out onto the street, he nictitated rapidly. Where do you think John had been?" These are inference items, but working many items similar to these would not improve an average adult's skill in drawing inferences. Similarly, exposing students, especially low-performing ones, to inference items is not sufficient. The examples must be carefully selected and sequenced, and careful instruction must be provided. Students must know relevant vocabulary, assumed relationships, and how to draw inferences if practice exercises are to be helpful.

students, a quick reading of the short passages will be sufficient to "prime" their preexisting knowledge of baseball; for some, this kind of "preteaching" and/or "priming" is unnecessary. For students who are unfamiliar with the game of baseball, however, this preteaching of basic information is critical to their understanding and appreciation of the remaining five parts of the Jackie Robinson story.

In *Reading Mastery VI,* before reading a 30-chapter version of Tom Sawyer, students participate in four lessons in which critical background information about the United States in the 1840s is presented. Information is presented about:

- the location of Hannibal, Missouri, on the Mississippi River.

- the importance of the Mississippi River to Hannibal.

- steamboats (how they work, what types of goods they transported, what types of passengers used them).

- what schools and newspapers were like in the 1840s.

- how houses got water in the 1840s and why they didn't have electricity in the 1840s.

- what breakfasts were like in the 1840s.

- what diseases were common in the 1840s and how people tried to protect themselves from the diseases.

This background information prepares students for deeper understanding and appreciation of Tom Sawyer.

Sentence Structure

During the intermediate grades, sentence syntax becomes increasingly complicated. A great variety of sentence constructions are introduced including these:

1. Participles (underlined words):

    The man <u>taking the money</u> looked to his side.

    The mountain <u>towering above the plain</u> was 12,000 feet high.

    <u>Thinking about the upcoming test,</u> Jack decided not to go out last night.

    <u>Wearing her new sneakers to the meet,</u> Ann was confident she would be the next state champion.

2. Clauses:

    Trig, who comes from the planet Floss, was over 80 feet tall.

    Eugene, which is in west-central Oregon, has a population of 100,000.

3. Sentences containing these connectives: consequently, although, therefore, provided that, unless, so that, as, whether, yet, whether or not, while, during, some, all, none, either, or, neither, nor.

    Note the difference in the meanings in these sentence pairs:

    a. Neither Jim nor John will win.
       Either Jim or John will win.

    b. They played while it rained.
       They played until it rained.

    c. He gave pencils to some of the students.
       He gave pencils to all of the students.

4. Passive constructions:

    John was carried down the mountain by Liz.

    The man was led into the arena by a black stallion.

5. Numerical and class-inclusive notations:

    The lion and the gladiator walked into the arena, the former snarling and vicious, the latter tense and alert. (*Former* and *latter* are numerical terms.)

    His dog barked a lot during the night. The animal seemed to be on edge. (Dog is included in the class of animals.)

6. Pronouns referring to an action or series of actions:

    The baseball game went into extra innings. This caused Tom to worry if he would be late getting home.

The rocket took off. Faster and faster it went until it had climbed 386 feet. It was the beginning of the space age.

The teaching procedure for each type of construction is somewhat different. Since we cannot discuss the procedures for each type of syntactic construction, we will illustrate direct instruction procedures that can be used to show students how passive voice construction functions. Similar procedures can be used for other constructions. (Note: Directly teaching all types of syntactic structures is not necessary since many may not cause difficulty for students. However, syntactic structures that cause students difficulty in comprehension could be taught using the steps similar to those outlined for passive constructions.)

Passive Voice

In the procedure for teaching students to understand passive voice, the teacher asks questions about a pair of minimally different active- and passive-voice sentences. The format involves the teacher's presenting an active-voice sentence and asking (1) who was acted upon; and (2) who did the acting. After each active-voice sentence, the teacher presents a passive-voice sentence and asks the same questions. By answering these questions, students will learn to comprehend both active and passive constructions. For example:

1. "I'll say sentences and then ask a question."

   "John hit Mary." (Active)

   "Who was hit?" ("Mary")

   "Who did the hitting?" ("John")

2. "Listen to a different sentence."

   "John was hit by Mary." (Passive)

   "Who was hit?" ("John")

   "Who did the hitting?" ("Mary")

In the active construction ("John hit Mary"), Mary was hit. In the passive construction ("John was hit by Mary"), John was hit. Since the question, "Who was hit?" is identical for both the active and passive constructions, the students must attend carefully to the words *was* and *by*. These words signal a passive construction, in which the subject is the recipient of the action ("John *was* hit *by* Mary. Who was hit? John"). Only by carefully watching for the words that signal a passive construction will students learn to distinguish passive from active constructions and, thereby, be able to answer questions such as, "Who was hit?"

The situation is almost identical for the "Who did the hitting?" question. This question is asked about both the active and passive constructions. Again, only by watching for the words that signal a passive construction (*was* and *by* in this example) will the students learn to distinguish active from passive voice and, thereby, be able to answer the question. More specifically, "John hit Mary" is active so the subject (John) did the hitting. "John was hit by Mary" is passive so the subject (John) didn't do the hitting; Mary did. The verbal exercises should include three to five pairs of sentences. Corrections should involve modeling and testing.

After several days, a worksheet exercise can be presented in which pairs of similar sentences, one in the active voice and one in the passive voice, are followed by literal-comprehension questions (see Table 22.6). Note that in both sentences in each item the names appear in the same order; e.g., in item 1 the order is rabbit-chicken. Maintaining a consistent order prevents students from learning a misinterpretation that the actor in a sentence always comes first.

The items included in these tasks should be low-probability items. That means the answer should not be one that would be expected based on common knowledge. An example of a poor item is "The child was bitten by the dog." Since the answer is highly predictable from common knowledge (dogs bite children), the item is of high probability. It can be answered through common sense without the students carefully attending to the words that signal a passive-voice construction.

In contrast, the items on our sample worksheet are low-probability items. Common sense does not indicate whether a rabbit or a chicken is more likely to be helpful, whether a dog would sell a cat, or whether John would find Mary rather than Mary

---

Table 22.6 Worksheet Practice on Passive-Voice Constructions

Item 1: **a.** The rabbit helped the chicken.
Who got helped? _____
Who did the helping? _____
b. The rabbit was helped by the chicken.
Who got helped? _____
Who did the helping? _____

Item 2: **a.** John was found by Mary.
Who was found? _____
Who did the finding? _____
b. John found Mary.
Who was found? _____
Who did the finding? _____

Item 3: **a.** The dog sold the cat.
Who was sold? _____
Who did the selling? _____
b. The dog was sold by the cat.
Who was sold? _____
Who did the selling? _____

---

find John. Since the answers for items 1, 2, and 3 are not based on common knowledge, students must learn sentence structure to determine who is the actor and who is the recipient of the action.

Critical Reading

Critically evaluating assertions, arguments, and proposals, whether presented orally or in print, is possibly the most important comprehension skill related to preparing students for their various roles in life. Many personal, professional, and social decisions are based on what we are told by other people. Because faulty arguments and propaganda are so common, critical thinking has a role in almost every important decision we make. To simplify instruction in critical reading, we will outline a standard procedure students can apply to increasingly sophisticated arguments. As in all comprehension instruction, sequencing exercises from simple to complex and providing sufficient practice for students to master one level of complexity before introducing the next are indispensable if students are to learn a strategy for critical reading. The steps in

teaching critical reading involve teaching students to do the following:

1. Identify the author's conclusion; that is, what does the author want the reader to believe?

2. Determine what evidence is presented; that is, what does the author present to convince the reader? Evidence or opinion?

3. Determine the trustworthiness of the author; that is, can the reader trust what the author says?

   a. Does the evidence come from a qualified person?

   b. Does the person have biases?

4. Determine if the conclusion derives from the evidence. Identify any faulty arguments:

   a. Tradition, either old or new (sometimes called a bandwagon effect)

   b. Improper generalization

   c. Confusing correlation with causation (or coincidence)

A rather advanced example of the propaganda devices students will encounter and how students should analyze them is illustrated in the following passage and discussion:

> Thomas Edison, the inventor of the lightbulb, was seriously concerned about the increasing use of alternating current as a form of electricity. Edison believed that because alternating current involved so much more current than direct current, alternating current was a threat to the nation. Many fires were caused by alternating currents. In fact, alternating current was used in Sing Sing to electrocute criminals. Direct current was used with lightbulbs for many years. Edison felt direct current was still the best form of electricity.

First, the students must use details from a passage (seriously concerned, a threat to the nation, direct current is still the best) to form a main idea (or an author's conclusion). Identifying an author's conclusion is a continuation of summarization skills (main idea, best title) discussed earlier.

The second step is for the student to decide whether the author's conclusion is based on opinion or evidence. If a conclusion is based on opinion, students should know that the author's conclusion is really nothing more than a suggestion by the author about what people should think. A conclusion based on opinion does not imply the student should believe or act on it. In the alternating current example, both opinion and evidence are used to support the author's conclusion. The statement that alternating current is a threat to the nation is an opinion. The other details are evidence used to justify the author's interpretation (i.e., the occurrence of fires, electrocution of criminals, and the initial use of direct current as an energy source).

The third step consists of several questions, all relating to the reliability or trustworthiness of the person presenting the argument. Question a is whether the evidence comes from a qualified person. Since Edison was definitely an expert on electricity in the late 1800s, he was qualified. Question b concerns biases the expert might have. In Edison's case, two major biases existed. One was his deep personal and financial involvement in a company that provided direct current. He stood to lose money if alternating current replaced direct current. Also, his reputation was at stake. He became famous, in part, because of his discovery of the lightbulb and a distribution system for electricity based on the use of direct current. If alternating current replaced direct current, his reputation might be diminished. Since Edison's biases contribute to the passage's conclusion, the evidence he cites may not be trustworthy.

Since there is doubt about the trustworthiness of the author, students must seek information from different experts. The statement that direct current is the best form of electricity is disputed by many experts. Alternating current can be transmitted great distances, but direct current cannot. If remote areas are to receive electricity at a reasonable rate, alternating current is a necessity. Since the expert is biased and alternative interpretations of the evidence are compelling, the evidence is probably not trustworthy.

The final step in the critical-reading process is deciding whether a conclusion legitimately derives from the evidence. In many arguments, valid evidence will be presented, but then a conclusion will be drawn that does not derive from the evidence. In the alternating-current example, one possible interpretation is that since direct current has been used with lightbulbs for many years, it should continue to be the best form of electricity. This faulty argument illustrates the use of tradition; what has been the best must continue to be the best. Conclusions based on tradition are not necessarily true. What has worked well may continue to be the best procedure, or a better procedure may be developed. Students can disregard conclusions based on tradition. (Note that the same attitude can be taken toward newly developing traditions; i.e., "Everybody is starting to use alternating current; therefore, you should, too." A conclusion that a product or procedure is better because it is popular is faulty.)

Since the passage about alternating current does not illustrate the other two types of improper arguments (improper generalization and confusing correlation with causation), the following additional passages provide illustrations of these invalid forms of conclusions. The first additional passage illustrates improper generalization. One valid example is presented, but then a conclusion is drawn that applies to all examples:

> Another example of the dangers of alternating current has just occurred. A house wired with alternating current caught fire and burned to the ground. The fire started when an electrical wire became so hot that a wall caught fire. Alternating current will eventually cause a fire whenever it is used. Direct current rather than alternating current should be used for lighting.

One fire caused by alternating current does not mean that alternating current will cause a fire every place it is used. Improper generalization occurs often: "I saw a rich person who was rude. What makes rich people so rude?" "We sat next to a long-haired man in the movies. He smelled. I'll bet he hadn't bathed in weeks. Long-hairs should take better care of their bodies."

The next passage involves a confusion of causation and correlation. An event that is associated with success or some other positive outcome through coincidence is erroneously concluded to be the cause of the positive outcome:

> *The Daily Post* used direct current to light its press room for over a year. Reporters are much happier now. They write more interesting stories. Sales of the newspaper have increased dramatically. *The Daily Post* is now the most popular newspaper.

Direct-current lighting is associated with happier reporters, more interesting stories, and greater sales; however, direct current did not necessarily cause reporters to be happier. The electric lighting that produced the positive outcomes could have been achieved with direct or alternating current. Conclusions suggesting causation that are, in fact, based on correlation can be disregarded. Confusion of correlation and causation is often made: "Joe Blow uses Squirt-Squirt deodorant, and girls always chase him." "Sally took You-Bet-Your-Life vitamins every day. She lived to be 106!"

Sequence

Before the complete critical-reading strategy can be introduced, the component skills must be taught separately, then combined to form the strategy. The four steps in the critical-reading process can be treated as the major component skills: (1) identifying the author's conclusion; (2) distinguishing opinion from evidence; (3) determining the trustworthiness of evidence (qualifications of evidence source, biases, alternative interpretations of evidence); and (4) identifying faulty arguments (tradition, improper generalization, and a confusion of correlation and causation).

Students can be taught relatively early to identify an author's conclusion and details that support the conclusion. Next, procedures for discriminating evidence from opinion can be introduced. After that, instruction in determining the reliability of evidence and then the validity of arguments can occur. Finally, the component skills can be combined to form the complete strategy.

Teaching Procedure

We will discuss separately teaching procedures for the four component skills of the critical reading strategy.

Identifying an Author's Conclusion

This skill is closely related to selecting a main idea. The major difference is that students must generate a conclusion rather than select the best alternative in a multiple-choice format. Since every passage is unique, specifying a detailed format to teach students to generate an author's conclusion is difficult. This skill, however, can be taught through modeling and extensive practice. A teacher models by presenting a passage, identifying the author's conclusion, and listing supporting details from the passage that led to the conclusion. Then the teacher tests by presenting a series of passages, asking students to identify the author's conclusion, and then justify their conclusion by citing supporting details. The teacher and the students should discuss unacceptable answers by pointing out why they are unacceptable. At first, items should be quite simple. Following are examples of items that might be presented initially:

1. I hope Tom comes back to our team. Since he left, we have lost every game. (Conclusion: We are losing because Tom isn't on the team.)

2. Those ABC tires are great. I've been getting super gas mileage on my new car with ABC tires. (Conclusion: I'm getting better gas mileage because I'm using ABC tires.)

3. Mary has looked so sad since our team lost the game. She doesn't go out at night. I never see her in the store after school. (Conclusion: Mary doesn't go out any more because she's sad about our team losing the game.)

Verbal exercises are conducted for several days and then replaced with written exercises. The length of the passages should be increased gradually.

Discriminating Evidence From Opinion

Teaching students to discriminate fact from opinion is done in two stages. In the first stage, all opinion statements include phrases that indicate that an opinion is being given (I think, I believe, I feel, in my opinion, in my judgment). The examples include about 10 statements, half of which are opinions and half of which are facts. Below is a set of statements that might be included in such a format.

1. I believe Tom won the race.

2. Tom won the race yesterday.

3. I believe he is faster than his brother.

4. He beat his brother in a race.

5. I think it will rain.

6. It is raining.

7. I think chocolate is the best flavor.

8. More people eat chocolate than any other flavored ice cream.

9. In my opinion she is the best player on the team.

10. She is the oldest girl on our team.

The teacher might introduce the items by explaining the difference between fact and opinion saying, "When somebody tells you something that actually happened they are telling you a *fact*. When somebody tells you how they feel about something they are telling you an *opinion*. Sometimes the way a person tells you something lets you know if it's an opinion. If a person says 'I think,' 'I believe,' or 'I feel,' they are giving an opinion." The teacher would then present the statements asking the students to tell if the statement is one of fact or opinion.

The second stage of the procedure introduces more sophisticated items which do not include phrases such as "I think" or "I believe." Teaching students to distinguish fact from opinion with this type of statement involves consensus. If, on the one hand, a person says something with which almost everybody who is knowledgeable agrees, the statement is one of fact. If, on the other hand, it is a statement with which knowledgeable people disagree, the statement is one of opinion. Consider the following statements:

1. *Traveling by train is not as exciting as traveling by car.* This is a statement of opinion. No special knowledge base is needed. In the general population, there are many people who would not agree with this statement.

2. *Traveling across the country by plane is faster than by car.* This is a statement of fact. Most people knowledgeable about travel agree.

3. *It rains too much in Oregon.* This is a statement of opinion. It reflects how some people feel, but not how all people feel.

4. *Oregon has more rain than New Jersey.* This is a fact.

Distinguishing opinion from fact is not easy. It will require lots of practice with a great variety of statements. For example, when an author uses opinion rather than evidence to sway the reader, he may use emotional words as a tactic. (See Table 22.7 for teaching students how to identify emotionally charged words when evaluating conclusions. Since this format is independent of the other formats, it can be introduced at a teacher's discretion.)

Determining the Trustworthiness of an Author

An important aspect of determining author trustworthiness is examining the qualifications of the person stating the argument. Much advertising is based on nonexpert endorsements. Sometimes a popular figure will endorse products about which he or she has no knowledge.

The first step in determining the trustworthiness of the author is determining his expertise regarding what he is talking about. A second step involves examining the motives of an author to determine if he or she has anything to gain by convincing the reader of his position. For example, if a student knows that a person invented an object and stands to make a

---

Table 22.7 Format for Identifying Emotional Words

Teacher	Students
1. Teacher explains emotionally charged words. **a.** "Most people like some words and don't like other words. Here are some words that most people like: love, freedom, beauty, democracy, kindness, confidence, creativity. Here are some words that most people do not like: murder, hate, ugliness, loneliness, cruelty, selfishness. Sometimes words people like are used to convince people to accept a conclusion."	

2. Teacher models.
    a. "Listen to this conclusion. The F.U.N. Reading Program is colorful, fun packed, and enlightening. All teachers should use the F.U.N. Reading Program."
    b. "When you read or hear an argument, ignore words that people like or dislike. When we get rid of the words people like or dislike, we see that there is no evidence for using the F.U.N. Reading Program. It's just someone's opinion."	

3. Teacher tests.
    a. "I'll make a claim. You tell me the words people like or dislike. Then you tell me if any evidence is left to support the conclusion."
    b. "Everybody should use Smiley Toothpaste. It makes them pleasant all day and free to do all the things they really want to do."
    c. "What are the words people like or dislike?" Teacher calls on individuals.
    d. "Is there any evidence left to support the conclusion?"
	
	 "Pleasant, free."
	
	 "No."

4. The teacher presents several more items. After students can correctly respond to verbally presented items, they should be assigned written items. The students cross out emotionally charged words and then indicate what evidence remains to support the conclusion.	

---

good deal of money if the object is sold, there is good reason to be suspicious of the person's claims. Passages such as the one below could be presented to develop the concept of author motive:

> Edwin Water, an inventor of the Sunglass Water Camera and owner of Water Camera Company of America, made the following remarks at a photographer's convention: "I was a professional photographer for several years. During that time I felt that a PHXTVW-23 Sunglass Water Camera gave me the greatest resolution, both with close work and when using a telephoto lens. Its lightweight and small size make it very convenient.

I don't need to tell you the importance of quality and convenience when it comes to cameras."

After students have been taught to evaluate an author's trustworthiness, they should work exercises that incorporate the critical-reading skills discussed thus far. A sample exercise appears as follows. (Assume that the students have previously learned to identify an author's conclusion and to distinguish evidence from opinion.)

> Thomas Edison invented the electric lightbulb and a system for distributing direct current to people to light their homes and businesses. He owned part of

a company that made lightbulbs and one that sold direct current. After direct current had been in use for a few years, alternating current was invented. Many people bought alternating current because it was cheaper and could be distributed long distances. Edison opposed the use of alternating current, though. He felt it was a threat to the nation. Edison argued that people should continue to use direct current.

1. What was the author's conclusion?

2. Was evidence or opinion used to support the conclusion?

3. Was Edison a qualified expert on electricity? Explain your answer.

4. Was Edison biased? Did Edison have any personal reason for opposing alternating current? Explain your answer.

5. Would you be suspicious of Edison's conclusion? Why?

Items 1 and 2 assume that students have been taught to identify an author's conclusion and to distinguish evidence from opinion. To answer items 3 and 4, students use information in the passage about Edison. If students have doubts about the trustworthiness of an author, they must seek additional information about the subject. Item 5 requires the student to synthesize the information from items 1 to 4.

Identifying Faulty Arguments

Earlier we mentioned three types of fallacious arguments: those based on tradition ("It's been done this way in the past, so it should be done this way in the future."), improper generalization ("X is no good, X is a Y, so Y is no good."), and coincidence or a confusion of causation and correlation ("S and Y happened at the same time, so S must cause Y."). We picked these three fallacies since they occur relatively often.

The formats are similar for each of the three types of invalid arguments (tradition, improper generalization, and a confusion of causation and correlation). The teacher states a rule about an invalid form and presents a series of examples, asking whether the argument in each example is valid. After students have learned the first two forms of invalid conclusions, they receive discrimination practice in determining which form accounts for an invalid conclusion. In this discrimination exercise, the teacher presents a series of examples and asks, "Is the argument faulty?" If students answer yes, the teacher asks, "Why?" The students then have to indicate what invalid argument was used to draw the conclusion. This discrimination exercise also appears again after the third form of invalid argument is introduced; students identify which of three forms accounts for an invalid conclusion. Table 22.8 contains a format for identifying invalid conclusions based on *tradition*. Table 22.9 contains a format for identifying invalid conclusions based on *improper generalization*. Note that the format for improper generalization is identical to the format for tradition. Only the rule for explaining why the argument is invalid is different.

After arguments based on improper generalizations are introduced, a discrimination exercise in which students must discriminate between tradition and improper generalization should be given (see Table 22.10). The teacher reviews the definitions of tradition and improper generalization and then presents a series of items.

The final type of faulty argument is a confusion of correlation with causation. When two things happen at the same time, one does not necessarily cause the other.

Table 22.11 presents a format for introducing this type of faulty argument. A discrimination exercise with all three types will be presented later.

Illustrations of procedures to teach other fallacies can be found in an instructional program entitled *Reasoning and Writing—Level D* published by SRA.

An Overall Critical-Reading Strategy

Exercises in which students must apply several of the critical-reading-component skills in analyzing the validity of an author's conclusion should be presented after students have been

Table 22.8 Format for Identifying Invalid Conclusions Based on Tradition

Teacher	Students
1. "Sometimes an author makes a conclusion that is based on faulty argument."	
2. "One type of faulty argument is called tradition. A conclusion based on tradition says that something should be a certain way because it has always been that way. What does a conclusion based on tradition say?" (signal)	"That something should be a certain way because it has always been that way."
3. "Here is an example. Mr. Rotter said our family has always bought Brand-X shoes and should keep on buying Brand-X shoes. The conclusion that we should continue doing something just because we have done it in the past is based on the faulty argument of tradition."	
4. "Listen to this argument: Mr. Jones said the Yankees are a sure bet to win this year since they won last year. Do you agree with Mr. Jones's conclusion?" (signal)	"No."
"Why not?" Teacher calls on individual students and accepts reasonable answers. "Correct, his conclusion was based on tradition. Just because something has been done a certain way in the past doesn't mean that is the way it should be done."	
5. "Listen to this argument. Mrs. Spencer told her daughter, 'When I was a young girl, my mother had me come home at 9 P.M. from a date. So when you go out, you should be home at 9 P.M.' Do you agree with Mrs. Spencer's conclusion?" (signal)	"No."
"Why not?" Teacher calls on individual students and accepts reasonable answers. "Correct, the conclusion was based on tradition."	

Table 22.9 Format for Identifying Invalid Conclusions Based on Improper Generalization

Teacher	Students
1. "Sometimes authors make a conclusion that is based on improper generalization. An improper generalization says that because a part has a certain characteristic, the whole thing must have that characteristic. What does an improper generalization say?" (signal)	"That because a part has a certain characteristic, the whole thing must have that characteristic."
2. "Here are some examples. When a store sells a gallon of spoiled milk, that doesn't mean that all the milk they sell is spoiled. The conclusion that the store always sells spoiled milk because it once sold some spoiled milk is based on the faulty argument of improper generalization. When a student does well in sports, that doesn't mean that all the student's brothers and sisters are athletic. The conclusion that everyone in the family is athletic because one person is athletic is based on improper generalization."	
3. "Listen to this argument. The cobra car has super tires. You should buy the cobra car. Do you agree with the conclusion?" (signal)	"No."
"Why not?" Teacher calls on individual students and accepts reasonable answers. "Correct, that argument is faulty because it is based on improper generalization. Just because one part of something is good doesn't mean the whole thing is good."	

Table 22.10 Discrimination Format

Teacher	Students
1. "An argument may be faulty because it is based on tradition or because it is based on an improper generalization."	
2. "What does an argument based on tradition say?" (signal)	"Something should be a certain way because it has always been that way."
3. "What does an argument based on improper generalization say?" (signal)	"That because a part has a certain characteristic, the whole thing must have that characteristic."
4. "I'll say some arguments that are faulty. You tell me why the argument is faulty, because of tradition or because of improper generalization."	
a. "Thomas can spell very well. I bet he is the smartest student in the class. Why is that argument faulty?"	"It is based on improper generalization."
b. "New York had the first good subway system. Its subway system must be the best. Why is that argument faulty?"	"It is based on tradition."
c. "Mr. Ricardo has lived on this street since 1970. He'll never move. Why is that argument faulty?"	"It is based on tradition."
d. "That restaurant serves delicious pies. It is the best restaurant in town. Why is that argument faulty?"	"It is based on improper generalization."

Table 22.11 Format for Identifying Faulty Arguments Based on Coincidence

Teacher	Students
1. "An argument is faulty if it is based on coincidence. An argument is based on coincidence when we say that one event caused another event just because they both happened at the same time. When is an argument based on coincidence?" (signal)	"When we say that one event caused another event just because they both happened at the same time."
2. "Here are some examples. Joe is shown eating muscle-man hotdogs. Joe is handsome and strong. Eating muscle-man hot dogs and looking handsome and strong happen at the same time. A conclusion that muscle-man hot dogs caused Joe to be handsome would be faulty. Just because two things happen at the same time, you cannot make a conclusion that one caused the other to happen. That argument is based on the faulty argument of coincidence."	
3. "Listen to this argument. Sam fights a lot, and he has lots of friends. Sam has lots of friends because he fights a lot. Do you agree with the conclusion?" (signal)	"No."
"Why not?" Teacher calls on individual students and accepts reasonable answers. "Correct, a conclusion that fighting causes people to have friends would not be reasonable; it is based on coincidence. Just because two things happen to the same person, you cannot make a conclusion that one caused the other."	

taught the component skills (identifying conclusion, distinguishing evidence from opinion, determining reliability of evidence, and spotting faulty arguments). Exercises should include a mixture of supportable and unsupportable conclusions so that students do not develop a habit of automatically disagreeing with an author's conclusion. There should be variety among the passages that have unsupportable conclusions. In some passages, the cause of the invalid conclusion should be lack of evidence; in others, faulty arguments; and in others, lack of reliable evidence. Following is a sample worksheet exercise:

Mrs. Asper was talking to her neighbor, Mr. Trump. Mrs. Asper told him she thought it would be terrible if he sold his house to the Parkinson family. Mrs. Asper said that the Parkinsons were from that terrible country, Lispania. Her husband had been in the war against Lispania. She had worked with a person from Lispania who always came late to work and did not dress neatly. She said that if the Parkinsons moved into the neighborhood, it would never be the same.

1. What is Mrs. Asper's conclusion?

2. Did Mrs. Asper use evidence? If so, list the evidence used.

3. Would you be suspicious of Mrs. Asper's evidence? If so, explain why.

4. Are faulty arguments used? If so, tell which type.

5. Do you agree with Mrs. Asper's conclusion? Explain your answer.

When initially presenting exercises of this type, the teacher instructs the students to answer the questions one at a time, occasionally inserting additional instructions. More specifically, before students identify the author's argument, the teacher instructs the students to cross out all emotionally charged words. In the preceding example, the students cross out the phrase *terrible country*. The teacher also makes certain the students explain why Mrs. Asper's opinions are unreliable. The teacher checks the students' answers to each item before instructing them to answer the next time.

After carefully monitoring student performance on several exercises, teachers should allow students to work independently. After students can successfully work items independently, the teacher can omit the first four items, and only present the question, "Do you agree with the author's conclusion? Explain your answer." In explaining their answers, students should discuss the reliability of the author's opinions, the evidence, and any faulty arguments. Working exercises of this final form is difficult and requires extensive practice.

✆ Application Exercises

1. Label each passage with an *RS* (relationship stated), *PKA* (prior knowledge assumed), and *IIP* (information for induction provided).

_____ Fresher vegetables contain more vitamins. The two pounds of carrots in the blue bag were picked today. The two pounds of carrots in the red bag were picked three days ago. Which carrots have more vitamin A?

_____ The two pounds of carrots on the ground have four hundred units of vitamin A. They were picked today. The two pounds of carrots on the table have two hundred units of vitamin A. They were picked a week ago. The two pounds of carrots in the can were picked yesterday. Which carrots have the most vitamin A?

_____ These carrots are all from the same garden. The two pounds in the sack were picked today. The two pounds in the box were picked a week ago. Which carrots have more vitamins?

2. Specify what the teacher should say to correct a student who answered the question below incorrectly. "Fresher vegetables contain more vitamins," Mrs. Ampston told her boy, Robbie. "When you go to the store,

always try to buy the freshest vegetables." Saturday morning Robbie went shopping for his mother. When he got to the vegetable counter he asked the man about carrots. The man told him they had two types of carrots. Mighty-Fine carrots and Blue Label carrots. Mighty-Fine carrots were delivered to the store Tuesday. They were from the biggest farm in the state. They were also on sale today, one pound for 36¢. Blue Label carrots had been delivered just after the store opened this morning. They were packed in plain wrappers and cost 38¢ a pound. They had been grown on a small farm outside the city. Which carrots should Robbie buy? (The student answers, "Mighty-Fine carrots.")

3. For each of the following selections:
   a. Identify the author's conclusion;
   b. List the evidence;
   c. Determine the author's trustworthiness by indicating whether she is qualified or has biases;
   d. Identify any faulty arguments.
   - Mr. Ragster had been a top race car driver and mechanic when he was young. Now he was a salesman for the Snazy Truck Company. Mr. Ragster had heard that Kevin McNeer wanted to buy a new truck. Wednesday morning Mr. Ragster called Kevin. He said "Kevin, you should by a Snazy truck. Your Dad always drove a Snazy truck. I bet I sold him 10 different Snazy trucks. *Automotive News,* a magazine that has reports on trucks, says that the new Snazy truck gets better mileage than any truck that is comparably priced. You'd be making a mistake if you didn't buy a Snazy truck."
   - Tom Jackson was a star baseball player. He worked for the Ace Toothpaste Company during the winter. He said, "I think Ace toothpaste is the best toothpaste there is. I have white shiny teeth and I use Ace toothpaste. If you want bright shiny teeth, you, too, should use Ace toothpaste."

4. For each of the following inference items, state any information students must know to answer the item correctly:
   a. Tim lived in San Francisco. Bill lived in New York. When waking up each morning, one of the boys would look out his window and watch the sun rise over the ocean. Tell which boy. Tell why you chose that boy.
   b. Janice was a star athlete. She hoped to make the Olympic team; however, first she wanted to complete medical school. It was now 1996. Janice had 3 years of medical school left. Do you think Janice will try out for the next Olympics? Why?
   c. Bill and Susan were carpenters who were building a house. They had completed everything, except putting in the floor. Jack, their good friend, told them that he had lots of cedar wood left over and would sell it to them for a cheap price. Do you think they will buy the cedar? Why?

5. Which two of the following four sentences would not be good items for a passive-voice exercise?
   a. The dog was put in the house by Tom. Who was put in the house?
   b. Bill was put in the house by Bob. Who was put in the house?
   c. Ann is getting a scolding from Jill. Who is scolding?
   d. Ann is getting a scolding from her mother? Who is scolding?

6. (Review)
   The following words will appear in passages the students will read several days from now. Write *V* in front of each word that should be included in a vocabulary exercise. Write *D* in front of each word that should be included in a decoding exercise:

	anvil		bragging		reins
	enjoyment		uranium		alley
	breech		efficient		coil
	harmlessly		plague		deerskin
	suffix		pollster		choir

Narrative-Comprehension Strategies

Overview

During the early primary grades, commercial basal-reading programs mainly include narrative reading passages. In the late primary grades, expository or textbook reading is introduced; however, a significant part of these programs still includes narrative stories.

This section deals with teaching students to comprehend narrative stories. Stories have their own text structure called *story grammar*. This structure often revolves around the conflicts or problems faced by the characters in the story and the characters' attempts to resolve the problem. The story-grammar components of (1) conflict, (2) goal, (3) resolution of the conflict, (4) plot, and (5) the characters' thoughts and feelings are common to many stories. By keying on the presence of these components in a story, the reader is better able to comprehend the story. The structure of a story can be simple (e.g., the components are few and written in a predictable sequence) or complex (e.g., the components are numerous and their sequence unpredictable).

Students who do not have problems with literal comprehension may still have problems answering questions about the structure of a story. For example, a student may be able to identify the characters in a story, but not the characters' goals and motives and actions for achieving those goals. For these students, the teacher needs to demonstrate a strategy for identifying, understanding, and relating these different components of story grammar to each other in comprehending the story's general message.

This section presents procedures for presenting the components of story grammar during story-reading activities. These procedures are designed for students who decode passages accurately, do not have significant fluency problems, and can accurately answer literal-comprehension questions.

Story Selection

The primary rule for developing a sequence for introducing stories in story-grammar exercises is to progress from simple stories to more complex stories. Factors to consider are (1) the number of characters, plots, goals, and subgoals, (2) the number of attempts by characters to achieve the goals, (3) the explicitness of the story-grammar components (the main characters, goals, conflict), (4) the length of the story, (5) the readability of the story (structure of sentences, multisyllabic words), and (6) the amount of background knowledge required of students.

Stories can differ in the amount of background knowledge required for students to comprehend the story. Some stories may rely heavily on a reader's background knowledge about a topic, while others may provide the reader with the information necessary to comprehend the story. For example, in some stories the information the reader needs to comprehend the characters' goals, conflicts, motives, and actions is given in the story. This type of story is called *textually explicit* because the text gives the reader all the information needed to comprehend fully what's going on in the story. Stories somewhat dependent on the reader's background knowledge

are called *textually implicit*. Stories heavily dependent on the reader's background knowledge are called *scripturally implicit*.

Figure 23.1 includes an example of a textually explicit text, the fable of "The Mouse and the Hawk." In this fable, the actions of the mouse in wanting to help the people of the town get rid of the hawk are explicit. The relationship between the mouse's motivation for ridding the town of the hawk and the goal are stated in the text.

Figure 23.2 contains an example of a textually implicit text, the fable of "Clover and the King." In the fable, Clover wants the lettuce, knows the King dis-

Figure 23.1   Example of Textually Explicit Text

The Mouse and the Hawk

Long ago in a small western town lived a hawk that attacked almost all the chickens in the whole town. He ate them one by one until finally there were only two chickens left.

Nobody in the town could kill the hawk. They talked about it in the big tent where a little mouse was listening when she heard the bad news. The little mouse was very brave and she also liked to help people. The mouse wanted to help the people in the town, so she worked out a plan.

First, she cut a small hole in the top of the tent. Then she made a very sharp point on one end of a stick. She put that stick through the hole. Next she went outside and sat on top of the tent very close to the sharp stick.

She knew the hawk would see a tiny mouse and come diving down from the sky to get her. Even though she was afraid that the hawk would kill her, she sat there waiting.

Finally, the hawk saw the brave mouse and came flying toward her ready to attack. The mouse waited until the hawk was almost on her. Then she jumped aside and the hawk flew onto the sharp stick and was killed instantly.

The mouse was a hero and everyone in the village came to the big tent to praise and thank her.

Figure 23.2   Example of Textually Implicit Text

Clover and the King

Clover was a very clever rabbit who, along with the other rabbits, loved lettuce. They lived outside the King's castle, and soon they had all the lettuce from nearby gardens except for the King's own garden.

The King loved his garden and grew the best lettuce in all the land. He did not want the rabbits to get any of his lettuce so his garden was well guarded. The rabbits didn't like the King either and just wanted his lettuce.

One day Clover got an idea. A rabbit could not sneak into the King's garden, but a rabbit could sneak into the King's kitchen. Clover sneaked into the King's kitchen every morning for several days. Each day the King's men brought in some lettuce for dinner, and each day Clover poisoned the lettuce. Soon, everyone in the King's palace was sick.

The King was very sad when he learned that his lettuce was making everyone sick. He ordered his soldiers to dig up the lettuce from his garden. Then he ordered the lettuce dumped outside the castle, near where the rabbits lived.

The King was very pleased with himself. He would solve two problems at once.

Figure 23.3 Example of Scripturally Implicit Text

The Fox and the Grapes

One day a sly fox was running along a dry, dusty road and he was very hot and thirsty. After a long period, he saw a large bunch of purple grapes hanging from a tree on a vine in a garden by the side of the road. These grapes were large, ripe, and very juicy looking. They looked especially good to the fox. "How I wish I could eat some of those beautiful grapes," said the fox as he licked his lips. The fox jumped high into the air to get the grapes, but he did not get them the first time he tried. He jumped again and again, but he still could not reach the grapes. He was still very thirsty, but he kept trying. After awhile, he became tired and at last he gave up. He said as he wandered away, "I am sure they are very sour grapes and I don't like sour grapes at all."

---

likes him, recognizes the King loves his subjects, and poisons the lettuce cut for royal consumption. To appreciate Clover's motivation for poisoning the lettuce, students must take the information about Clover's stated goal (poisoning the lettuce) and the King's response to the poisoned lettuce, then make an inference about the relationship between those events. By making the connection between those events, actions, goals, and intentions of the characters, students will appreciate why Clover, the rabbit, is so clever, and why the King thought he had solved two problems at once. This text is textually implicit because the reader has to use the information in the story to make inferences about the character's actions and goals.

An example of a scripturally implicit text, the fable "The Fox and the Grapes," is given in Figure 23.3. In "The Fox and the Grapes," the relationship between the fox's goal of getting the grapes and its final observation that the grapes were sour is not made explicit. To understand the fox's reasons for calling the grapes sour, the reader must identify with the fox's frustrated and unsuccessful efforts in not achieving an important goal. The conclusion that the fox called the grapes sour in order to feel better about not reaching them is drawn exclusively from the reader's own experiences, not from the story.

We recommend beginning story-grammar instruction with stories that are textually explicit (i.e., require little or no background knowledge), short in length, and structurally simple. There should be few characters, and the conflicts, actions, goals, and resolutions should be rather straightforward. As students progress, longer, more complex stories can be gradually introduced. However, the teacher should avoid introducing too much that is new too quickly. For example, it would be inappropriate to introduce scripturally implicit stories that involve multiple characters with many goals, subgoals, plots, and actions after a student has read only textually implicit stories with few characters and a simple storyline.

Teaching Procedures

The following teaching procedures are based on the assumption that students can decode the words in the stories and are capable of answering basic literal-comprehension questions. To introduce story-grammar instruction, the teacher relies on a facilitative questioning strategy that consists of four basic story-grammar questions: (1) Who is the story about? (2) What is she/he trying to do? (3) What happens when she/he tries to do it? and (4) What happens in the end? These core questions will be used to direct the students' attention to the critical parts of each story. The questions are aligned with the important components of story grammar, such as identifying the characters in the story; identifying their goals, the actions and obstacles related to achieving these goals; a resolution, and the final circumstances surrounding the character's goal-related actions; and the story ending. The core questions can also be eventually used as a framework for teaching students to summarize the story in either oral or written form.

Table 23.1 contains a format for introducing story grammar. In this format, students read the story, the teacher stops students at the appropriate

Table 23.1 Format for Introducing Story-Reading Comprehension

Teacher	Students
The teacher writes on the board:	
Who is the story about?	
What is the main character trying to do?	
What happens when the main character tries to do it?	
What happens in the end?	
1. The teacher introduces the story-grammar questions: "When we read this story, we are going to ask four questions." The teacher reads and points to each question on the board.	
a. "What's the first question?" Teacher calls on a student.	"Who is the story about?"
b. "What's the next question we're going to ask about the story?"	"What is the main character trying to do?"
c. "What's the next question?"	"What happens when the main character tries to do it?"
d. "What's the last question?"	"What happens in the end?"
2. The teacher calls on individual students to read the title.	
a. "During the reading of the story, I will stop you to ask one of the questions. The answers to the questions can be found in the story. Let's start by reading the title of the story." Teacher calls on a student to read the story title.	"The Mouse and the Hawk."
b. "Yes, the title tells us that story will be about a mouse and a hawk. So when we read the story, what main characters will we read about?" Teacher calls on a student.	"A mouse and a hawk."
3. Teacher calls on individual students to read the story. Teacher stops students at different points in the story and asks questions.	
a. After reading through the second paragraph, the teacher stops the reader and calls on individual students to answer the following questions: "What is the hawk trying to do?" "What is the mouse trying to do?"	"Kill all the chickens." "Help the townspeople."
b. After reading the next two paragraphs, the teacher stops the readers and asks: "What is the mouse trying to do?"	"Kill the hawk by getting the hawk to fly down on the sharp stick."
c. After reading the last paragraph, the final two questions are asked: "What happens when the hawk tries to get the mouse?" "What happens in the end?"	"It flew onto the sharp stick and was killed." "The mouse is a hero and the people thank the mouse."
4. The teacher summarizes the story using the four questions. "First, who is the story about?" "What are the hawk and mouse trying to do?" "What happens when they try to do these things?" "What happens in the end?"	"The mouse and the hawk." "The hawk is trying to kill chickens and the mouse is trying to help the townspeople get rid of the hawk." "The mouse gets rid of the hawk and chickens are saved." "The mouse is a hero."

points in the story, then asks each story-grammar question. The students then answer the questions. The specific wording used in the format is for such textually explicit texts as "The Mouse and Hawk." The teacher begins the format by telling students the four core questions that they will find answers to when reading the story. The students read the story orally, one student reading several sentences at a time. During the story reading, the teacher asks each story-grammar question at the appropriate place in the story. In addition, the teacher sometimes stops and conducts a cumulative review of the questions previously answered. In the final step of the format, the teacher summarizes by asking the four questions again. Following students' oral answers to the four questions, the teacher requires students to answer written comprehension questions.

In general, the strategy communicates to students that answers to comprehension questions can be retrieved reliably from the story itself. With sufficient practice and guidance, students will eventually learn when to rely on the story to answer questions and when to rely on their own background knowledge and experiences to answer questions.

Corrections

The teacher must demonstrate the relationship between answering the four questions and finding those answers in the story. Sometimes, students' answers will be incomplete or partially correct. For example, when identifying who the story is about, the student may identify a secondary character instead of the main character. In this case, the teacher should respond as follows: "Yes, that tells about one character in the story, but tell me the character the story is mostly about."

In general, the correction procedure should be tailored to the kind of response the student provides. If the response is partially correct, the teacher should acknowledge the specific parts that are correct. When appropriate, the teacher should require the student to locate the correct answer in the story. If an inference is required, the teacher might summarize the relevant information. For example, in the fable "Clover and the King," the student might know that

Clover poisoned the lettuce, but not understand the King's motive for dumping the lettuce next to where the rabbits lived. The teacher should summarize the actions of both "Clover and the King" and discuss with the student the motives of the characters.

Advanced Story-Reading Comprehension Strategy
Overview

Story reading in the upper-grade levels requires more inferential thinking. Unlike stories in the primary-grade levels that are fairly simple, upper-grade short stories are fairly complex. As a result, the comprehension strategy for identifying and understanding story-grammar components needs to be more thorough than the strategy described previously for beginning story reading.

In intermediate grades, stories become more scripturally implicit, and students need to have more background knowledge to comprehend the stories. Similarly, stories are more likely to contain words critical to the meaning of sentences but now known by the student. Before presenting stories to the student, the teacher should preteach any critical information or vocabulary words students need to know.

This section will present teaching procedures for introducing short-story comprehension based on the research by Gurney (1987) and Dimino (1988). The procedures will provide a basic understanding of how to teach intermediate- and secondary-level students to identify and interpret the wide range of characters, actions, events, and situations that take place in short stories.

Story Selection

The short stories that students are required to read in intermediate grades, middle school, and high school are typically found in literature textbooks, basal readers, and student magazines. These stories may range from well-known classics, such as Jack London's "To Build a Fire," to contemporary selections concerned with the problems faced by today's adolescents. Many of these stories have been modified or edited by the publisher. We do not recommend any stories be further rewritten or modified. The preteaching of words difficult to decode or unknown to students should be done prior to short-story reading. By requiring students to read the original stories instead of modified versions, they acquire the comprehension and decoding skills necessary to meet the demands placed upon them in regular reading and English classes.

Although short stories are quite varied in their structure, story grammar, and storyline, the comprehension strategy we propose builds on the four core story-grammar questions taught for comprehending simple stories. We expand these four questions to categories as more complex stories are introduced. These categories, based on Dimino's (1988) analysis, are described as follows.

Category 1: Character Information

The teacher expands the first question, "Who is the story about?" by asking questions about the character. The teacher tries to have students anticipate what a character might do based on the information given. Questions can be asked about the following characteristics:

a. Actions: What the characters do.

b. Dialogue: What the characters say to themselves and each other.

c. Thoughts: What the characters are thinking.

d. Physical Attributes: How the characters look.

Category 2: Conflict or Problem

The second question, "What are the characters trying to do?" is expanded to asking questions about the conflict or problem that exists. The types of conflicts or problems the teacher asks questions about are:

a. Disagreements: A problem arises between two characters. For example, parents disagree with a son over using the car.

b. Tough Decisions: A character is faced with two difficult choices. For example, a character

must choose between keeping quiet or revealing a friend's crime.

c. Struggle for Survival: A character tries to overcome the forces of nature. For example, a character tries to survive in the wilderness during the extreme cold.

Category 3: Attempts/Resolution/Twist

The third question, "What happens when the characters try to do it?" expands to questions about how the characters attempt to solve the conflict or problem. The teacher asks questions about the following:

a. Attempts: What the character does to resolve the conflict or solve the problem.

b. Resolution: The final outcome or attempt that solves or fails to solve the problem.

c. Twist: An unexpected complication that occurs at the end of the story and usually differs from the resolution of the problem.

Category 4: Reactions and Theme

The final question, "What happens in the end?" is expanded in a different way. Instead of focusing on what actually happens at the end of a story, the teacher requires students to focus on the meaning of the author's message. Questions are asked about the following:

a. Reactions: What is the character's response to the events in the story?

b. Theme: What is the underlying meaning of the story? What is the author of the story trying to tell the reader? What is the moral of the story?

Teaching Procedures

The teacher strategy utilizes two unique procedures: (1) a story notesheet designed to help students summarize and clarify the story-grammar components during short-story reading (the outline notesheet appears in Table 23.2), and (2) a think-aloud procedure in which the teacher summarizes and points out how to anticipate story-grammar questions to be asked.

Table 23.2 Notesheet for Short-Story Comprehension Strategy

Student Notesheet

Name _____   Date _____

Story _____

1. Name the problems or conflict._____
_____
_____
_____

2. Identify the main characters and tell about them._____
_____
_____
_____
_____

3. Tell how the characters try to solve the problem._____
_____
_____
_____
_____

4. Tell how the problem is or is not solved._____
_____
_____
_____

5. Is there an added twist or complication at the end of the story?_____
_____
_____
_____

6. What is the theme of the story? What is the author trying to say?_____
_____
_____
_____

Unlike the strategy for simple stories requiring students to ask whom the story is about first, the strategy for comprehending complex stories requires students to identify the problem or conflict first.

The format for teaching short story reading comprehension appears in Table 23.3. Because short stories vary in content and complexity, this format is unlike other formats in the book. Instead of providing detailed teacher wording for each step of the strategy, we provide descriptions of how each of the four categories of story-grammar components can be presented. This format is developed around the short story "To Build a Fire" by Jack London. A summary of this short story follows:

The story begins on an "exceedingly cold and gray" day. The main character is a newcomer to the Yukon Territory and this is his first winter in the land. The man, as London notes, was "without imagination," "quick and alert in the things of life, but only in the things, and not the significances." It is fifty degrees below zero and the man is bound for an old claim where he is to meet "the boys." The man decided to leave the main Yukon trail and is accompanied by a "big native husky" who knew it was not time to be traveling. The man was making 4 miles an hour as he made his way up Henderson Creek. Unexpectedly, the man broke through the ice and wet himself "halfway to the knees." The man built a fire. He felt safe and thought the fire was a success. However, the man had built the fire under a big spruce tree. The fire had warmed the snow until a load of it had fallen on the fire. The man made several attempts to build another fire, but the attempts failed. Soon the newcomer to the Yukon fell asleep in the snow as the day drew to a close and eventually died.

The teacher begins the lesson by giving each student a notesheet. During story reading, students are stopped at designated points and asked the appropriate story-grammar question. The teacher records the information on a transparency of the notesheet while students record it on their individual notesheets. Students are allowed to copy from the transparency but are encouraged to record the information in their own words. Students are advised that after a few stories, they will be responsible for determining and recording the components without the benefit of the transparency or class discussion.

During the first days of story reading, the teacher models asking questions and giving answers. After several lessons, the teacher calls on students to answer questions. For example, after the problem is stated in the story, the teacher asks, "Do we have a problem?"

After weeks of practice, independent exercise is given. In this independent-practice phase,

---

Table 23.3 Format for Introducing Short-Story Reading Comprehension

1. **You're going to learn a strategy that will help you understand short stories. When you read short stories, you're going to be reading about characters, their problems, and how they solve their problems. We'll read a short story and apply the strategy to the story.**

2. **I'll call on different students to read different parts of the story. Read clearly and loudly so that everyone can hear you. If I don't call on another student, continue reading. If you're not reading, be certain to follow along in case I call on you.**

3. (The teacher begins instruction by calling on students to read the title of the short story. Once the title is read, the teacher asks students to make predictions about the story to be read by asking) **"So what do you think the story is going to be about?"**

4. *Identifying the main problem/conflict.*
   (Students begin reading the story and stop at points predetermined by the teacher. At these designated points, the teacher simply asks students to stop. Utilizing a think-aloud strategy, the teacher states) **"I see a problem" or "It looks as if we have a problem."**
   (The teacher states the problem/conflict and writes it on Part 1 of the notesheet that is projected on the transparency for students to see.)
   (When stories contain both major and minor problems, the teacher identifies the problems. For example, during the reading of "To Build a Fire," the teacher states) **"I see a problem. The man is a newcomer and this is his first winter traveling in the Yukon. This may not be a major problem, but I will record it on Part I of the notesheet. As we read on, we will be able to see if this is the major problem."**
   (Students are told to watch carefully as the teacher writes on the notesheet. The teacher should choose the main problem by identifying the one which encompasses most of the action or is the most difficult to solve. Once this problem is identified, the teacher circles it on the notesheet and explains the reasons for its selection.)

5. *Identifying the main character.*
   (Once the main problem is identified, the teacher points out to students that the problem revolves around the main character. The teacher models the thinking-aloud process by restating the problem, then specifying whose problem it is.) **"Now that I found the problem, we can choose the main character by asking ourselves who the problem revolves around. In "To Build a Fire," the problem is a struggle for survival, which revolves around a man who is a newcomer to the winters in the Yukon territory. The man is on a journey through the woods with his dog and his goal is to join some other men at a camp miles away."** (The teacher writes the main character on Part 2 of the notesheet.)

(continued)

Table 23.3 continued

---

6. *Identifying attempts, resolution, and twist.*
   "Now that I have found the problem and main character, we can identify the attempts. The attempts are what the main character does to try to solve the problem." (Students are told to follow along as a group until they are stopped at a designated point. At the point, the teacher models the process by identifying attempts. For example, in "To Build a Fire," the teacher states the following) **"It looks as if the main character tried to solve the problem here. His problem is that he is alone and making his way to a camp that is miles away. It is the middle of winter and it's fifty degrees below zero. He tried to solve his problem by building a fire."** (The students observe as the teacher records the attempt on Part 3 of the notesheet placed on the transparency.)
   "The fire kept him warm for a while, but it melted the snow on a tree. The snow fell and put out the fire. The man couldn't get warm again and died of the cold." (The teacher records the events on Parts 4 and 5 of the notesheet.)

7. *Summary and retell.*
   Students are told that information recorded on Parts 1 (problem), 2 (main character), 3 (attempts), 4 (resolution), and 5 (twist) of the notesheet are used to retell the story. The teacher models retelling the story while pointing to the pertinent information on the notesheet. An example of a retell for Jack London's "To Build a Fire" follows:
   "This is a story about a man and his dog (main characters) **who make a journey alone in the middle of winter when the temperature is fifty degrees below zero** (problem). **The man tried to avoid the springs** (attempt) **along the Yukon river, but fell through the ice** (problem) **and was forced to build a fire** (resolution). **He built the fire under a big spruce. The snow on the spruce melted and put out the fire** (twist). **The man ran to keep warm** (attempt) **but fell and eventually died."**

8. *Identifying the theme.*
   "Now we can talk about the theme of this story. The theme is what the author of the story is trying to tell you. It is the advice the author is giving to the reader."

   a. (Teacher calls on students and asks) **"What is the author trying to tell us?"** (The teacher accepts reasonable answers, then reviews the theme.)
   "The author might be telling us we must be sensitive to the environment. The man was a newcomer to the cold winters in the Yukon and he tended to ignore the significance of things, such as the significance of temperature when it was fifty degrees below zero."

   b. (The teacher calls on several students to retell the story.)

---

identification and discussion of the story-grammar components does not take place until students have recorded the information on their notesheets. Students' responses on the notesheets are monitored, and time is allotted for students to correct their incorrect answers after each story-grammar component is discussed. Since answers are no longer being recorded on the transparency, the teacher must monitor students' written responses carefully. Students can work cooperatively to review their answers.

Correction Procedures

Although the complexity of short stories and the lengthy application of the strategy could prompt a variety of errors, three different types of errors are likely to occur. Each type of error is addressed separately.

Errors Involving Textually Explicit Information

These errors occur when students incorrectly answer questions that require recalling information stated explicitly in the story (e.g., What was the first thing the main character did to solve the problem?). To correct these errors, students should be directed to the portion of the text that contains the answer, then asked to read the passage to find the answer.

Errors Involving Textually Implicit Information

These errors are likely to be more frequent than errors involving textually explicit information. These errors occur when students incorrectly respond to questions that require them to make inferences and judgments about the characters, events, or situations (e.g., What is the main character like? What is the author's message in the story?). To answer these questions correctly, students must assimilate the information given in the story and render a judgment or opinion. To correct these errors, the teacher should first direct the student to the appropriate information on the notesheet or in the story. Once the correct information is found, the teacher should ask questions to assist the student in making a correct inference. For example, if a student responds incorrectly to the following question "Do you think the character will do well in this environment?" The teacher corrects by modeling the following answer: "When the author says that the man was without imagination and was not alert to significances of life, he is using this information to tell the reader that the man was not in tune with his new environment." This correction procedure needs to demonstrate to students the relationship between information in the story and the process of making judgments or inferences about that information.

Errors Involving Theme Identification

Theme identification is likely to be the most difficult aspect of the instructional strategy. Students may have difficulty assimilating the events in the story and formulating a general statement that captures the underlying message. The teacher can model how to state a theme by reviewing themes from previous stories to illustrate how events in a story can be used to develop a theme.

 Application Exercises

Clover and the King

Clover was a very clever rabbit who, along with other rabbits, loved lettuce. They lived outside the King's castle, and soon they had all the lettuce from nearby gardens except for the King's own garden.

    The King loved his garden and grew the best lettuce in all the land. He did not want the rabbits to get any of his lettuce, so his garden was well guarded. The rabbits didn't like the King either and just wanted his lettuce.

    One day Clover got an idea. A rabbit could not sneak into the King's garden, but a rabbit could sneak into the King's kitchen. Clover sneaked into the King's kitchen every morning for several days. Each day the King's men brought in some lettuce for dinner, and each day Clover poisoned the lettuce. Soon, everyone in the King's palace was sick.

    The King was very sad when he learned that his lettuce was making everyone sick. He ordered his soldiers to dig up the lettuce from his garden. Then he ordered the lettuce dumped outside the castle, near where the rabbits lived.

    The King was very pleased with himself. He would solve two problems at once.

1. Assume the role of an elementary student. Fill out the notesheet (Table 23.2) for the story above.
2. Assume the role of the teacher. Rewrite the format for introducing short story reading comprehension (Table 23.3) so that it could be used with the story above. Indicate where you would ask questions during story reading, what the questions would be, and what are acceptable student responses.
3. Predict two serious mistakes students might make. Describe how you would correct each mistake.

Direct Instruction
in Content-Area Reading

The major emphasis in the intermediate grades should move from learning to read to reading to learn. Intermediate children begin extensive reading in expository materials, such as content-area textbooks and reference books designed to convey factual information or to explain what is difficult to understand. These materials differ significantly from the narrative or story material generally found in basal readers. New organizational structures are used, the vocabulary is often more difficult to decode and understand, unique typographic features as well as graphics are introduced, and the density of concepts is higher. Not only are the characteristics of expository materials more difficult for the naive reader to cope with, the demands placed on the reader also increase. The reader is expected to extract, integrate, and retain significant main ideas and details presented in the material and to learn many specialized vocabulary terms, expectations seldom demanded in narrative reading. Due to the unique characteristics of expository materials and the demands placed on the reader, explicit instruction in reading and understanding expository materials must be provided for the intermediate student beginning with classroom content-area textbooks.

This section focuses on content-area reading instruction, beginning with an analysis of the differences between expository and narrative materials.[1] Next, procedures for teaching content-area reading lessons are outlined, including the following steps: (1) teacher preparation for instruction, (2) prereading activities, (3) reading activities, and (4) postreading activities.

Characteristics of Expository Materials

Before discussing teaching procedures for content-area textbooks, it is helpful to examine the unique characteristics of expository materials and some of the problems these characteristics might pose to naive readers. To illustrate these characteristics, examine Figure 24.1, a selection from a sixth-grade science book.

Vocabulary

One of the major differences between narrative and expository materials is the vocabulary used. The

---

1. This chapter was written by Anita Archer and Mary Gleason.

Figure 24.1   Selection From a Content-Area Textbook

Chapter 4

How Rocks Are Formed

Picture Analysis

This rock is made up of different layers. Look closely at the thick layers. Do these layers appear to be about the same size? How does the color of the thin layers differ from the color of the thick ones? Notice the shapes of the two kinds of layers. Are they the same or different?

The rock has been exposed to the weather. What effect do you think heavy rains and strong winds might have had on the rock? What effect do you think they will have in the future?

Preview and Share

Look at the pictures in this chapter. Choose one picture that you want to know more about. Write two questions about it. After you have finished reading the chapter, share your questions with a classmate. Try to answer the questions together.

Science Vocabulary

seismograph	physical property	lava
core	weathering	volcano
mantle	sediment	igneous rock
crust	sedimentary rock	metamorphic rock
rock	pressure	rock cycle
geologist	geyser	
mineral	magma	

Figure 24.1 *(Continued)*

Section 1

THE EARTH'S LAYERS

This is Bryce Canyon in southwest Utah. It was named for Ebenezar Bryce, a pioneer who settled in Utah in 1875. Wind and rain have carved the rocks into these unusual shapes. The rock in this canyon is colored in over sixty shades of red, pink, and beige. Because of the placement of the rock layers, scientists are able to determine the history of their formation. Over one billion years of history are recorded in the layers. When you finish this section, you should be able to:

Figure 24.1 *(Continued)*

■ **A.** Identify the layers of the earth.
■ **B.** Explain how *rocks* and *minerals* are related.
■ **C.** Explain how *rocks* are classified.

Bryce Canyon is 300 meters (1,000 feet) deep. That depth is only a scratch in the surface of the earth. Yet we know what the inside of the earth is like. How do we know? Earthquakes tell us. When there is a strong earthquake, vibrations, or waves, are sent through the earth. The waves are recorded on a **seismograph** (size-muh-graf). The *seismograph* measures the strength of the earthquake waves. It also notes how often the waves occur.

Seismograph: An instrument that detects and records earthquake waves.

Two kinds of earthquake waves travel through the earth. One kind travels through liquids and solid materials. A second kind travels only through solid material. The center of the earth is called the **core**. Scientists have been able to identify earthquake waves that pass through liquid and solid materials in the *core*. Thus, scientists believe that the core is partly liquid. They further believe that the inner core is made of the solid metals iron and nickel.

Core: The hot, partly liquid center of the earth.

Around the core is a thick hot layer called the **mantle**. The earth's *mantle* is a little like plastic. It is not liquid, but it does flow. The kind of earthquake wave that moves only through solids moves through the mantle. So it is thought to be a solid layer.

Mantle: The hot, rocky layer that surrounds the core of the earth.

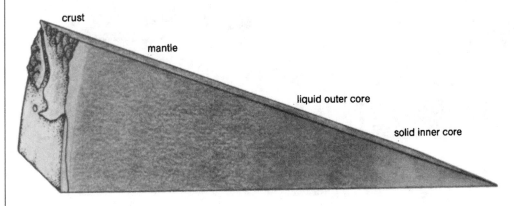

crust

mantle

liquid outer core

solid inner core

Figure 24.1 *(Continued)*

Crust: The thin, rocky outer layer of the earth.

Rock: The material of which the earth's crust is built.

Geologist: A scientist who studies rocks and other features of the earth.

Mineral: A solid material that occurs naturally in the earth's crust.

Physical property: A characteristic, such as color, of a material.

The **crust** of the earth is the part we know most about. The very top part of the *crust* is the surface of the earth, where we live. The crust is only 5 to 70 kilometers (3 to 43 miles) deep. The basic material that makes up the earth's crust is **rock**. *Rock* is what mountains are made of. Stones and pebbles are broken pieces of rock. Sand and soil are very small pieces of broken rock.

Scientists who study rocks and other features of the earth are called **geologists** (jee-**ahl**-uh-jists). *Geologists* have found that all rocks have things in common. All rocks are made of **minerals**. A *mineral* is a solid material that is found in the earth's crust.

The **physical properties** of a mineral are the same no matter where it is found. The *physical properties* of a material make it different from other materials. Color, hardness, and luster are some properties of minerals. About 10 to 15 minerals are commonly found in rocks. The picture on the left shows a rock called granite. To the right of the granite rock are the three minerals of which it is made: quartz (**kworts**), feldspar (**feld**-spahr), and mica (**my**-kuh). Granite may also have a little of some other minerals in it.

granite   quartz   feldspar   mica

Rocks can be classified, or grouped, by their physical properties, such as color. Or they can be classified by their minerals. One way geologists classify rocks is

Figure 24.1   *(Continued)*

according to the way in which the rocks were formed.

Rocks are formed in three different ways. Some rocks are formed from pieces of other rocks and from plant and animal remains. The second kind of rock is formed from hot, melted rock deep in the earth's crust. The third kind is formed from heat and pressure on the other two kinds of rocks.

Excerpts from *Holt Science,* Grade 6, copyright © 1989 by Holt, Rinehart and Winston, Inc., reprinted by permission of the publisher.

vocabulary of content-area materials is often more difficult to decode and pronounce than that found in narrative material. For example, in the selection in Figure 24.1, the student must decode the words *seismograph, identify, geologists, properties,* and *classify*. The density of multisyllabic words and words containing unfamiliar morphemes increases the decoding difficulty of expository materials.

Pronunciation is made more difficult by lack of familiarity with the words and their absence from the student's listening or speaking vocabulary. Though students may use appropriate decoding strategies, they may make slight errors in pronunciation because of their inability to correct the pronunciation against their known vocabulary.

The challenges posed by expository vocabulary go beyond decoding. Expository materials are more likely to include vocabulary terms difficult to understand or unfamiliar to the student. It is unlikely that sixth-grade students have had an opportunity to use such terms as *geologist, seismograph,* or *minerals* in their own speech or have had much prior exposure to their meanings. Expository materials not only present a large number of new vocabulary terms, but also include technical terms (e.g., *meters*), words used in unusual ways (e.g., "the earth's *mantle*"), symbols and abbreviations to convey concepts or to replace vocabulary terms (e.g., 1290° F, 700° C), and figures of speech.

Not only is the vocabulary difficult to decode and unfamiliar to the reader, but the terms are often presented in rapid succession. For example, in one paragraph the terms *geologists* and *minerals* are presented using definitions or contextual cues but with little elaboration. Students, particularly students new to the content area or naive readers in expository materials, will need careful preparation in order to handle the vocabulary and concept load found in content area selections.

Content

In addition to the vocabulary terms, the general content of expository materials is often beyond the student's experiences. While narrative stories generally focus on situations, events, or concepts that the student has dealt with or been exposed to, expository materials include content that is new and unique to the student. Within the illustrated passage, the reader is introduced to the use of the seismograph, the layers of the earth, the characteristics of each layer, the role of geologists, the term *mineral,* and the use of physical properties in classifying rocks. The content includes many unfamiliar concepts as well as a much higher density of ideas than found in narrative materials.

Style and Organization

Expository material is usually written in a terse, straightforward style with explanation minimized, a pattern seldom found in narrative materials. The organization of ideas presented in narrative and ex-pository materials often differs. In narrative or story selections, there is generally a gradual build-ing of sequential events or related ideas, climaxing near the end of the selection and tapering to the se-lection's conclusion. The reader is literally carried by the author from event to event, from situation to situation, from idea to idea. Unlike narrative mate-rials that provide a continuous, uninterrupted stream of information, expository materials usually segment the selection into a number of topics de-lineated by headings and subheadings. Like a huge puzzle, each paragraph provides an explicit or in-ferred main idea with supportive details which, when combined with other paragraphs, define a sin-gle topic. These topical segments, in turn, are com-bined with other segments to form a body of knowledge. For example, the selection in Figure 24.1 begins with a title that presents the chapter's theme. Each of the subsequent major headings in-troduces a different topic concerning the formation of rocks: The Earth's Layers, Sedimentary Rocks, Igneous Rocks, and Metamorphic Rocks. To de-velop the topic, a series of paragraphs, each con-taining a main idea and supportive details, follows each heading.

Other characteristics of organizational design also contribute to the complexity of expository materials. For example, cause-and-effect relation-ships and comparisons are prevalent in expository materials, particularly in science and social stud-ies textbooks. These relationships occur less often in narrative materials. Inverted time sequences are also found in expository materials but seldom in story material. Within narrative materials, the dis-course is smooth and seldom disturbed until the selection's conclusion. However, expository read-ing is interrupted by subheadings and headings; referrals to glossaries and pronunciation keys; and references to graphic aids. These complex organi-zational patterns and disruptions in the discourse can pose problems for the naive reader who has not been systematically introduced to this type of organizational design.

Special Features

Narrative stories have few special features outside of the title and occasional illustrations. The student, however, must cope with and attend to many special features in content area material. Graphics and illus-trations that accompany narrative stories are included to enhance enjoyment and interest and to enrich the story. Graphics and illustrations found in expository materials, however, contribute directly to the infor-mation presented either by supplementing or expand-ing on concepts found in the discourse. In narrative materials, the student need not examine illustrations with any intensity. However, in expository materials, the student must scrutinize graphics and illustrations with special attention given to the title, explanatory notes, and labels. Each new type of graphic aid must be carefully introduced so that the student can locate information, make comparisons, formulate infer-ences, and draw conclusions based on the information presented. In the selection of rocks, a diagram is pre-sented illustrating the various layers of rock found in the earth. Although the written discourse discusses the various layers of rock (e.g., the crust, mantle, and core), their interrelationships are not clear until the student has examined the labeled graphic.

Content-Area Lessons

Content-area lessons should be designed to promote *mastery of the salient information* presented in the selection and *acquisition of critical-reading study skills* that can be applied to other expository materi-als and, at the same time, *foster independence in the learners.* This is a difficult but important balance to reach. Often teachers give total responsibility to stu-dents for reading the selection and answering ques-tions on the content. Although independence is maximized in this case, the lack of preparation for reading and guidance given during reading may re-sult in lowered comprehension and inadequate use of reading-study skills. Yet teachers may provide ex-tensive prereading activities and extensive direction to students across all selections throughout the year.

This introduction to critical-reading study skills would not foster student responsibility for learning or independent use of previously taught reading study skills. For the majority of elementary students and the majority of selections found in content-area textbooks, a compromise between the extremes should be reached. Prereading activities and guidance during reading should be limited to critical passage variables and should be gradually faded as the students become more sophisticated in their reading.

Content-area lessons should include the following steps: (1) teacher preparation for instruction, (2) prereading activities, (3) reading activities, and (4) postreading activities. Prior to instruction, the teacher should determine critical content that students should master, design a chapter examination, and divide the chapter into teachable units. During the prereading activities, instruction is presented on significant variables within the material (e.g., unknown vocabulary concepts, difficult-to-decode words, unique graphics, the structure of the passage) that can contribute to passage comprehension. Prereading activities may also include a survey of the passage's content. These activities are followed by reading of the passage under teacher direction (guided reading or reciprocal reading), in cooperation with a peer (partner reading), or independent reading using a specified learning strategy. Following reading of the selection, students engage in postreading activities (e.g., answering chapter questions, writing a summary of the selection) designed to summarize and synthesize the salient chapter information.

Teacher Preparation for Instruction

Selecting Critical Content

Before teachers can select appropriate prereading, reading, or postreading activities, you must first decide exactly what you would like your students to gain from studying the chapter in the content-area textbook. What ideas, vocabulary, concepts, generalizations, events, and related details would you like them to retain? What concepts are necessary for future study in the content area? To make these determinations, careful reading of the chapter is necessary.

Many teachers find it helpful to take notes on the chapter and to consult the objectives provided in the student or teacher's edition of the textbook. Table 24.1 is a content analysis for the introductory expository material on rock formation. Here, the teacher has listed the vocabulary concepts and general understandings to be stressed for each segment of the chapter. As the teacher prepares prereading, postreading, and reading activities, as well as test items, the teacher can refer to his or her content analysis. Whether a teacher's content analysis takes this form or another form, it is always important to have an instructional map to guide the teacher's work with students.

Designing or Adapting a Chapter Test

When students have completed study on a chapter, it is useful to give a chapter test for a number of reasons. First, an examination over critical content benefits *students.* It encourages students to study and rehearse the salient information that has been stressed in lessons and within the chapter. If the test is well-designed, it can also reinforce what is important in the body of knowledge and, thus, should be retained. Finally, when feedback is given on the test, students have another opportunity to review the critical content. Of course, examinations also serve the *teacher.* Certainly, tests allow teachers to measure the information obtained by their students and to hold them accountable for studying. However, teachers also need feedback on the quality of their instruction. Were the prereading, reading, and postreading activities adequate? Did students focus on the most important information? Without this feedback, instruction cannot be enhanced in the future. Finally, a test on the critical content allows teachers to determine which concepts need reteaching.

While most teachers formulate a chapter test after the chapter has been taught, it is more beneficial to develop it before instruction. If this is done, it will reinforce their instructional focus on critical concepts and ideas. The test that teachers develop or adapt should directly measure the concepts, ideas, and general understandings that they have

Table 24.1 Determination of Critical Content

Chapter 4: How Rocks Are Formed

Section 4.1: The Earth's Layers

Vocabulary: seismograph, core, mantle, crust, rock, geologist, minerals, physical properties
General Understandings:
  The student will be able to

  1. identify the layers of the earth;

  2. describe each layer;

  3. explain how minerals and rocks are related;

  4. tell how rocks are classified.

Section 4.2: Sedimentary Rocks

Vocabulary: weathering, sediment, sedimentary rock, pressure
General Understandings:
  The student will be able to

  1. describe what makes up sediment;

  2. explain how sedimentary rocks are formed;

  3. describe how different sedimentary rocks (shale, sandstone, limestone, gypsum) are formed.

Section 4.3: Igneous Rocks

Vocabulary: geyser, lava, volcano, magma, igneous rock
General Understandings:
  The student will be able to

  1. describe the difference between magma and lava;

  2. describe two ways that igneous rocks are formed and give examples of rocks formed in each manner;

  3. explain how the rate of cooling affects igneous rocks.

Section 4.4: Metamorphic Rocks

Vocabulary: metamorphic rock, rock cycle
General Understandings:
  The student will be able to

  1. describe how metamorphic rocks are formed;

  2. tell what quartz, slate, and marble are made from;

  3. trace the steps in the rock cycle.

---

deemed important and worth retaining. If the test measures irrelevant details, students will come to believe that details should be the focus of their self-study. Whether teachers utilize a chapter test provided in the program or design their own, a teacher's first concern is the importance of the information measured. Next, teachers must be certain that the types of items are appropriate to measure the specific concept or general understanding. For example, if teachers want students to be able to identify the layers of the earth, a labeling task requiring this behavior would be the most appropriate. Examples of objectives and parallel test items are found in Figure 24.2.

Figure 24.2 Development of Appropriate Test Items

For each objective or combination of objectives, select a type of test item that matches the outcome you wish. Use a limited number of types of items, particularly in the early grades.

Examples

Objective: Can identify the layers of the earth.
Type of test item chosen: Labeling
Directions: Label each part of the earth.

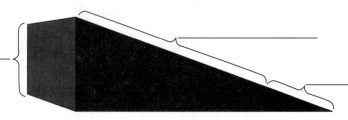

Objective: Describe each layer of the earth.
Type of test item chosen: Multiple choice
Directions: Circle the letter for the best answer.

1. The core of the earth is
   a. at the center of the earth   **c.** very hot
   b. partly liquid   **d.** all of the above.

2. The mantle of the earth is
   a. a hot liquid   **c.** a thick, cool layer of rock
   b. a thick, hot, solid layer   **d.** none of the above.

3. The crust of the earth is
   a. a thin, hot liquid   **c.** the thin, rocky, outer layer of the earth
   b. the thick outer layer of the earth   **d.** all of the above.

Objective: Can define the following vocabulary terms: core, mantle, crust, mineral, sedimentary rock, lava, magma, igneous rock, metamorphic rock.
Type of test item chosen: Matching
Directions: Write the number for the correction definition on the line.

_____ core
_____ mantle
_____ crust
_____ mineral
_____ sedimentary rock
_____ lava
_____ magma
_____ igneous rock
_____ metamorphic rock

1. Rock formed from particles of rock.
2. Hot, melted rock as it comes out of the earth.
3. The thin, rocky, outer layer of the earth.
4. The hot, partly liquid center of the earth.
5. Hot, melted rock under the earth's surface.
6. A solid material that occurs in the earth's crust.
7. The hot, rocky layer that surrounds the core.
8. Rock formed from melted material that has cooled and hardened.
9. Rock formed from sedimentary and igneous rock that has been changed by heat and pressure.

Dividing the Chapter Into Teachable Units

Finally, in preparation for teaching a content-area chapter, divide the chapter into smaller, teachable segments that represent a body of connected discourse on a topic in an amount that can be introduced in one lesson. While many elementary textbook chapters are already broken into teachable segments indicated by lesson numbers and concluding questions, other textbooks have reading segments that are much too long for the naive student. The prereading, reading, and postreading activities will be structured around these lesson-length chapter segments.

Prereading Activities

When critical information that students will be held accountable for has been determined and translated into chapter objectives and test items, the other steps in the content area lesson can be initiated. The first step, preparing students for selection reading, is designed to preteach or alert students to significant variables within the material (e.g., new vocabulary, difficult-to-decode words, organizational patterns, new graphics) that will facilitate comprehension and extraction of the desired information.

The amount of preparation needed for a given selection depends on the complexity of the material, the experience of the students with the given textbook, the amount of prior knowledge that students have on the topic, and the reading skills of the students. Certainly, the fourth grade student reading the first selection in her new social studies book will need substantially more preparation than the more advanced student.

Teaching Difficult-to-Decode Words

Given the increased difficulty of words found in content-area textbooks, the teacher needs to ensure that students can decode and pronounce the words. When selecting words for decoding instruction, focus on words that are difficult "stopper" words, central to the understanding of the passage, and whose pronunciations are not cued within the dis-

course. When presenting the words, the teacher should not restrict the presentation to whole-word methodology, though this will be necessary when teaching irregular words. Instead, the teacher should capitalize on the phonic and structural decoding skills that have been introduced to students using the formats presented throughout this book. Many of the multisyllabic words in content-area textbooks include known prefixes or suffixes. The teacher can ask students to pronounce these known parts and then the entire word. For example, in presenting *mantle,* the teacher can have students pronounce *le,* then the entire word. In other cases, the teacher can indicate parts of the word, have each part read, and have the entire word pronounced. Generally, the pronunciation of words can be introduced at the same time as important word meanings, since the difficult-to-decode words are often the unfamiliar vocabulary. The important thing is that the accurate pronunciation of the words is not assumed, but taught directly. Decoding, while not sufficient for passage comprehension, is necessary.

Vocabulary Instruction

One of the most critical prereading activities is vocabulary instruction. The number of word meanings and concepts that students know directly relates to their ability to comprehend text. Thus, the teacher should introduce the essential vocabulary within a passage to enhance comprehension. Students do not automatically acquire new concepts, suggesting that direct instruction is essential.

Words for vocabulary instruction should be limited to a small number of words that are crucial for passage understanding and beyond the student's experiential background. Children should not be overwhelmed with a large number of difficult-to-understand words in a single presentation. Critical words should be carefully introduced, practiced, and reviewed in subsequent lessons.

There are many methods that the teacher can use to teach and provide practice in vocabulary concepts. However, our discussion will be limited to three procedures: (1) direct instruction procedures, (2) concept maps, and (3) feature analysis procedures.

Direct Instruction Procedures In this book, we have discussed a number of strategies for vocabulary instruction that apply equally well to content-area instruction: (1) teaching through examples, (2) teaching through synonyms, (3) teaching through definitions, (4) locating the meaning in the dictionary or glossary, or (5) using context clues. Though all of these strategies can be used in content-area materials, emphasis should be placed on developing contextual analysis. Since authors of elementary textbooks realize that many of the words will not be in the student's experiential background, explicit and inferred context clues are generally given. Contextual analysis is a student's major tool for vocabulary expansion. Because contextual analysis can be used by the reader when no instructor is present, proficiency in its use leads to independent vocabulary growth. Many children (and adults) have developed the habit of reading right past unfamiliar words. Direct instruction on contextual analysis will alert children to using these clues and encourage them to hunt for the word's meaning within the discourse.

During the vocabulary lesson, students can be asked to determine a word's meaning using context clues found in the passage, the glossary, or a dictionary. When this is not possible, the teacher can directly present a definition or a synonym for the unfamiliar word. However, reading the definition, even verbally repeating the word and its definition, may not improve comprehension of the selection (Beck, McKeown, & Kucan, 2002). In all cases, explicit instruction should follow the introduction of the word and its meaning to ensure that students have adequate practice in using the word. A format similar to those presented earlier in this book can be used. First, the teacher should introduce the word and ask students to locate the definition in the glossary or within the chapter (context analysis). If the word is not adequately defined in the context or included in the glossary, the teacher can directly present a definition or synonym for the word. After the definition has been presented, the teacher should

check students' understanding of the definition by having it repeated or by asking questions about the definition. Next, the teacher should present a number of examples of the word's use to ensure the definition is clear. After this, the teacher should test students' understanding by presenting examples and nonexamples. Finally, the teacher can ask students to generate examples or to use the word in verbal sentences. These teaching procedures are illustrated in Table 24.2.

Another effective method for teaching specific vocabulary concepts through examples is the use of *concept diagrams.* This method also involves presenting an unknown word, its definition, examples, and nonexamples (Bulgren, Schumaker, & Deshler, 1988). In preparing for this instruction, the teacher selects a vocabulary concept from the text material. Next, the teacher constructs a concept diagram that includes the word's definition; characteristics of the concept that are always present, sometimes present, or never present; and examples and nonexamples of the concept. A concept diagram for *natural resources* is found in Table 24.3.

When presenting the concept, the teacher places a blank Concept Diagram on the board or overhead transparency. The teacher then presents and fills in the diagram following a specially designed routine including the following steps: (1) presenting the word and its definition; (2) discussing the "always," "sometimes," and "never" characteristics; (3) discussing one of the examples and one of the nonexamples in relationship to the characteristics; (4) checking other examples and nonexamples to determine if they match the characteristics. Throughout the presentation of the concept diagram, students are actively involved in the discussion.

Concept Maps In expository text, unlike narrative text, the difficult or unfamiliar concepts are generally semantically related. For example, in the text material on the formation of rocks, the highly related terms core, mantle, and crust are presented. It would be useful to teach these terms stressing their interrelationships. Concept maps, also referred to as

Table 24.2 Format for Teaching Vocabulary Using a Synonym or Definition

Teacher	Students
1. Teacher states the new word. Students locate the word's definition in the passage (contextual analysis) or in the glossary. If the definition is not clear in either place, the teacher states the definition.	
a. This word is *export.*	
What *word?*	"export"
b. Find *export* in your glossary.	
c. Read the definition.	"Something that is sent out of the country to be sold in another."
2. Teacher tests understanding of the definition by asking questions and by having the definition repeated.	
a. Where is an export sent?	"to another country"
b. Why is an export sent out of the country?	"to be sold"
3. Teacher presents examples or uses the word in sentences to ensure clarity of the definition.	
a. For example, Japan sends cars to the United States to be sold. Cars are an important Japanese export.	
b. The United States sells wheat to the Soviet Union. That wheat is an important U.S. export.	
4. Teacher presents examples and nonexamples in random order. Students identify examples and nonexamples and tell why it is an example or a nonexample.	
a. Tell me if this is an *export.* Australia sells wool to other countries. Is wool an export of Australia?	"yes"
Why is it an export?	"Because it is sent out of Australia and sold."
b. The United States buys lots of wool from Australia. Is the wool an *export* of the United States?	"no"
Correction: If students make an error, lead them to the correct response.	
Listen again. The United States buys lots of wool from Australia. Does the United States send wool to other countries to sell?	"no"
So is wool an export from the United States?	"no"
c. South Korea sells lots of radios and stereos to Canada. Are radios and stereos an export of South Korea?	"yes"
Why are they exports?	"Because South Korea sells them to Canada."
d. South Korea buys some of the lumber it needs from Canada. Is the lumber a South Korean export?	"no"
Why isn't the lumber a South Korean export?	"Because South Korea doesn't sell the lumber, it buys it."
e. The United States raises lots of cattle and sells the beef in many countries. Is the beef a U.S. export?	"yes"
Why?	"Because the U.S. sells the beef to other countries."
Remember—an export is something that a country sells to another country.	

Table 24.2 continued

Teacher	Students
5. (Optional) Students generate additional examples.	
a. Think carefully. What are some U.S. exports?	(Students suggest U.S. exports.)
b. Recently we studied about China. What do you think some of China's exports might be?	(Students suggest Chinese exports.)
(NOTE: Similar instruction is repeated for other words and definitions. In this lesson, the teacher also taught the following vocabulary terms: import, necessity, and luxury.)	
6. Teacher reviews the new words and their definitions. If related words have been taught, she highlights their relationships.	
a. Is an *export* something that we buy or sell?	"sell"
b. Is an *import* something that we buy or sell?	"buy"
c. If Australia sells wool to the United States, is wool an Australian export or import?	"export"
Is wool a U.S. export or import?	"import"
d. What is a necessity?	"Something you need."
e. What is a luxury?	"Something you want but don't need."
f. Tell me if this is a necessity or a luxury:	
television	"luxury"
food	"necessity"
warm clothing	"necessity"
a fancy sweater	"luxury"

graphic organizers (DiCecco & Gleason, 2002; Griffin, Duncan Malone, & Kame'enui, 1995; Griffin, Simmons, & Kame'enui, 1991; Simmons, Griffin, & Kame'enui, 1988), and visual-spatial displays (Darch, Carnine, & Kame'enui, 1986) allow the teacher to preteach concepts stressing their interrelationships. This not only facilitates initial attainment of the concepts, but subsequent retention and retrieval of information.

A concept map visually represents a body of knowledge including the critical concepts, vocabulary, ideas, events, generalizations, and/or facts using a diagram or other type of visual display. As a result, students gain a holistic view of the body of knowledge before the chapter is read. Not only do students learn critical content before passage reading, they gain an understanding of the chapter's structure. As the name implies, the concept map can serve as a guide to the chapter's content and structure.

The structure of the concept map is dictated by the different types of structure found in expository materials. In many cases, the text material represents a *hierarchy* in which the relationships between major concepts, subordinate concepts, and related details are stressed. The concept map presented in Figure 24.3 illustrates a hierarchical body of knowledge. In this case, the chapter presented the organization of the federal government, the branches of the government, the functions of each branch, and their components. As seen in Figure 24.3, a hierarchy was used to present the major concepts, the subordinate concepts, and the related details.

In some cases, the body of knowledge is best illustrated with a *diagram* that shows the relationship of the *parts* to the *whole*. In Figure 24.4, the concept map illustrates the four layers of the atmosphere by using a diagram. This allows the teacher to preteach the four major chapter concepts as well as related ideas (e.g., the density of gas molecules changes in each

Table 24.3 Example of a Concept Diagram

Concept Name:	Natural Resources
Definitions:	Something that is provided by nature and is valuable to people.

Characteristics Present in the Concept:

Always	Sometimes	Never
provided by nature valuable to people	replaces itself in our lifetime doesn't replace itself or replaces itself very slowly	made by people

Examples	Non-examples
trees	a desk made from wood
water	ice cubes
corn plants	corn flakes

Based on research by J. Bulgren, J. Schumaker, and D. Deshler, "Effectiveness of a concept teaching routine in enhancing the performance of LD students in scondary-level mainstream classes." Presented in *Learning Disability Quarterly, 11*(1988): 3–17.

atmosphere layer, the temperature changes across atmosphere layers). In Figure 24.5, a diagram is used to illustrate the respiratory system. Once again, a diagram is the most appropriate representation since the relationship of the parts (e.g., mouth, larynx, lungs) to the whole (respiratory system) is being stressed.

Many chapters or sections of chapters compare and contrast times (e.g., before and after the Industrial Revolution), objects (e.g., the different types of rocks), people (the past and current cultures of Southwest Native Americans), or concepts (e.g., democracy and communism). In these cases, a chart can be constructed to *compare* and *contrast* information presented in the chapter. This type of structure can be seen in the concept map prepared for a science chapter on land biomes (Table 24.4). Using this chart, students can compare the climates, common plants, and animals in the *biomes.*

In social studies, the structure of the discourse often reflects a sequence of events over time. The most appropriate concept map in this case is a *timeline.* The concept map found in Table 24.5 is a timeline listing the major events in the American Revolution. Before reading each section of the chapter, the teacher went through the sequence of events involved in each major event (see sequences listed under Stamp Act and Boston Massacre). As a result of this preview, students brought a lot of prior knowledge to the passage reading. They could focus on the critical information and fit the new-chapter information into their existing scheme concerning each event.

Other expository materials present *processes* (e.g., how cotton cloth is manufactured) or *cycles* (e.g., the food cycle; the rock cycle). Once again, the structure of the concept map should reflect the structure of the body of knowledge. For example, one science chapter introduced the process involved in the formation of coal, petroleum, and natural gas. A concept map was developed to preteach the basic steps in the process using arrows to show the relationships

Figure 24.3   Example of a Concept Map: Hierarchy

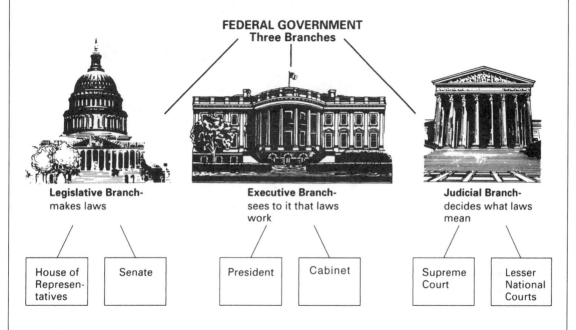

A New Constitution (1787)

1. What kind of government?

Democracy—a government that is run by the people who live in it

Republic—a nation or state in which citizens elect representatives to manage the government.

2. How can we be sure that no part of the government is too powerful?

ANSWER: Divide the powers of the Federal government.

FEDERAL GOVERNMENT
Three Branches

Legislative Branch- makes laws

Executive Branch- sees to it that laws work

Judicial Branch- decides what laws mean

| House of Represen- tatives | Senate | | President | Cabinet | | Supreme Court | Lesser National Courts |

ANSWER: Each branch of government needs help of another branch to do its job.

Legislative Branch makes laws **but President** must sign.

President commands army **but Legislative Branch** decides to spend money for army.

(Note: All words printed in boldface type are provided by the teacher on the worksheet. All words printed in lightface type would be added by students during the lesson.)

between each step (see Figure 24.6). To construct a concept map, the teacher uses the following steps:

1. **Determines the critical content (vocabu- lary, concepts, ideas, generalizations, events, details, facts, etc.) that you wish to preteach to students.**

2. **Organizes the concepts in a visual representation that reflects the structure of the content: hierarchy, diagram, compare- contrast, timeline, or process/cycle.** In some cases, a combination of these structures might be used. For example, in constructing a concept map on a science chapter on protists,

Figure 24.4 Example Concept Map: Diagram

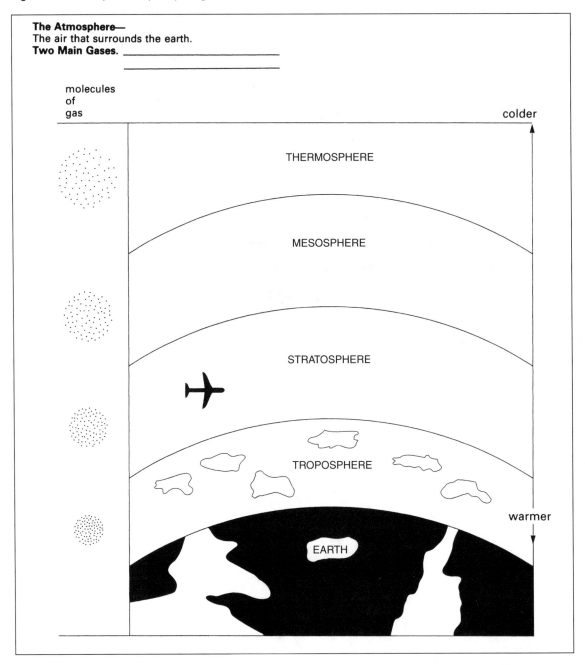

The Atmosphere—
The air that surrounds the earth.
Two Main Gases. _____
_____

molecules
of
gas

colder

THERMOSPHERE

MESOSPHERE

STRATOSPHERE

TROPOSPHERE

warmer

EARTH

Figure 24.5 Example of a Concept Map: Diagram

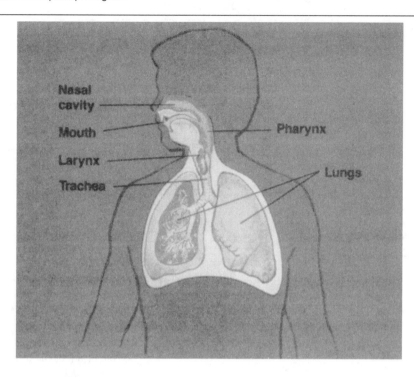

Respiratory System
pharynx—connects nasal cavity and trachea.
trachea—tube that leads to the lungs.
larynx—contains the vocal cords.
lungs—organ where the gas exchange between air and blood takes place.

From ACCENT ON SCIENCE by Robert B. Sund and others, p. 178. Copyright 1985 by Merrill Publishing. Reprinted by permission.

the teacher began with a *hierarchy* showing the relationship of organisms to kingdoms and to the three groups of kingdoms. Next, the teacher used a *compare-contrast* chart to present the various types of protists and their characteristics (see Table 24.6).

3. **Designs a completed concept map.** The teacher should write in the vocabulary, concepts, definitions, details, events, facts, etc. that he or she wishes to preteach. (See Figure 24.7 for an example of a completed conceptual map.) It is helpful to add minimal graphics to the concept map (e.g., an outline of the White House next to the executive

branch; a sketch of a tree next to the word tree). These graphics will increase interest in the concept map and will also help students remember information when a blank concept map is presented.

4. **Creates a partially completed concept map.** (See Figure 24.8.) A partially completed conceptual map includes the major terms and the actual diagram. During the instructional lesson, the partially completed conceptual map will be distributed to students. They will add information such as definitions, examples, and events. Since they will be writing on the concept map, active

Table 24.4 Example of a Concept Map: Compare/Contrast

Biomes A large ecosystem that has similar populations and climate.

	Land Biomes		
	Climate	*Common Plants & Protists*	*Common Animals*
Tundra	very cold, little rain	mosses, grasses, shrubs, lichens	reindeer, foxes, wolves, owls, hawks, eagles, falcons, flies, lemmings
Taiga			
Grassland			
Tropical Rain Forest			
Temperate Forest			
Desert			

participation, subsequent attention, and learning will be increased.

5. **Creates a blank concept map.** The teacher should delete all words, leaving only the diagram or structure of the concept map and any added graphics. The blank conceptual map will be used in a number of ways. First, during initial instruction, it will be used to review and firm up concepts that have been presented. Second, the blank map can be used as a postreading activity in which students or a group of students can recreate the concept map by adding missing information. Third, the blank map can be used in review exercises in which students determine missing information.

The teaching procedures for introducing concept maps will vary considerably depending on the structure of the map. However, the following procedures can generally be used. (See Table 24.7 for an example script that parallels the concept map on natural resources.)

1. **Teachers should distribute partially completed concept maps to students.** During the lesson, the students will fill in additional information.

2. **Teachers should place a transparency of the completed map on an overhead projector.** Teachers should also place a piece of paper under the transparency so that they will expose only those portions they wish students to attend to.

3. **Teachers should introduce the information on the concept map, proceeding in a logical order, stressing the relationships between the vocabulary concepts, events, details, facts, etc.** When introducing vocabulary concepts, teachers should use the direct-instruction procedures discussed earlier. They should introduce the vocabulary concept and its meaning. Teachers should check students on the definition by having students repeat the definition or asking questions about the definition. They should have students record the definition on their concept map. Next, teachers check understanding by presenting examples and nonexamples and by asking students to generate examples. When presenting other aspects of the concept map (e.g., facts, details, events), the teachers present the fact, have students repeat the fact or ask questions about

Table 24.5   Example of Concept Map: Timeline

The Struggle for Independence					
					American Revolution 1775–1783
Stamp Act	*Boston Massacre*	*Boston Tea Party and Concord*	*Battles at Lexington*	*Declaration of Independence*	*Peace With Britain*
1765	*1770*	*1773*	*1775*	*1776*	*1783*
- Parliament passed Stamp Act. ↓ - Colonists had to buy stamp taxes. ↓ - Colonists angry. ↓ - Colonists sent message to Britian. ↓ - Act couldn't be enforced. ↓ - Britain did away with Stamp Act.	- Parliament put a tax on tea and said colonists could only buy tea from Britain. ↓ - Many stopped drinking tea. Some smuggled in tea. ↓ - British soldiers searched for tea. ↓ - Colonists upset. ↓ - Small fight broke out and 5 colonists killed.				

it, then have students record the fact on their concept map. Active participation is critical if teachers wish students to attend during the lesson. Teachers should continually ask students questions and have them record information on their concept maps.

4. **At natural junctures, teachers review and firm up concepts they have introduced.** This can be done by placing the blank map on the overhead and asking students questions concerning the content.

5. **At the end of the lesson, teachers review the critical content again using the blank concept map.**

A concept map may display information from an entire chapter or only a section of a chapter. If it represents information from the entire chapter (as does the concept map on natural resources), teachers introduce the map in sections corresponding to parallel reading assignments. As students proceed through the chapter, the other portions of the concept map can be introduced.

As this section has shown, concept maps are a powerful tool for preteaching and reviewing bodies of knowledge found in science, social studies, and health textbooks. They not only show students the relationship of the concepts and the structure of the chapter, but visually represent the information for easier acquisition, retention, and retrieval. Concept maps are also very useful when teaching

Figure 24.6   Example of a Concept Map: Process

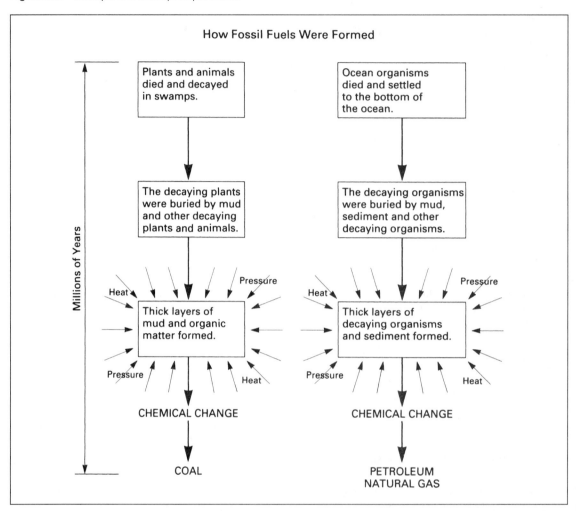

students with very low reading skills. While they may not be able to read the content-area textbook, there is no reason why they cannot learn the important ideas. In addition, early experience with teacher-prepared concept maps will prepare students for designing and using their own concept maps in secondary schools.

Feature-Analysis Procedures Another procedure for presenting related concepts found in a content area chapter is feature analysis (Pittelman, Heimlich, Berglund, & French, 1991). This procedure can be used when the concepts fall in one category (e.g., types of governments, different rock formations, the nine planets). When using this procedure, the teacher organizes the concepts and the features of those concepts in a matrix. For example, a feature analysis on types of government leadership might stress whether the leader's position is inherited, maintained by force, elected by the people or elected by legislators (see Table 24.8). A feature analysis concerning planets might examine whether the planet has life, is hotter or colder than the Earth, is small or large in comparison to the Earth, has

Table 24.6 Concept Map: Multiple Structures

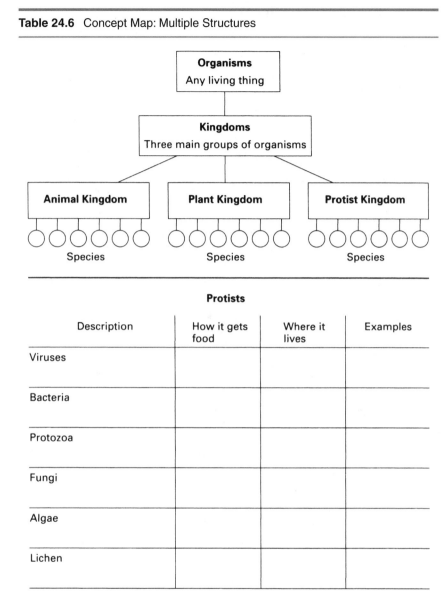

satellites, and has physical characteristics similar or different from those of Earth (see Table 24.9).

When presenting the feature-analysis matrix, the teacher assists students in determining if the concept possesses each of the features. A (+) is recorded if the feature is present and a (−) if the feature is not present. If the students have little prior knowledge of the concepts, the teacher can directly present each of the concepts and their features. The entire feature matrix can be completed prior to reading, or students can complete some aspects of the matrix during or after reading. Once the matrix is completed, the teacher can assist students in noting similarities and differences between the concepts. For example, the teacher might ask questions concerning the planet-feature analysis (see page 287).

Figure 24.7 Completed Concept Map on Natural Resources

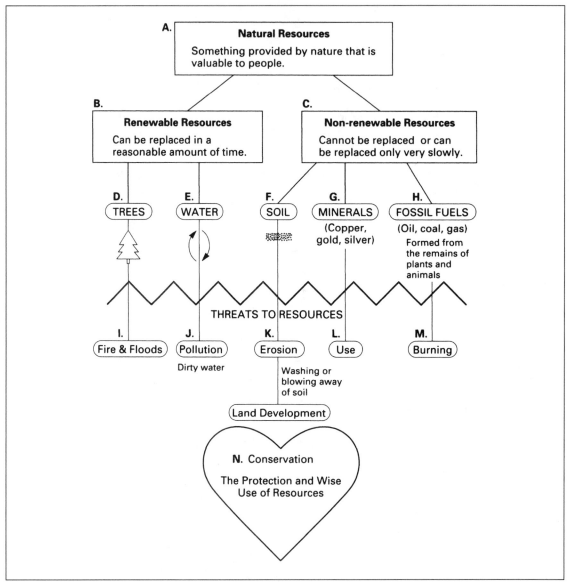

Note: During instruction, the teacher displays this map on an overhead projector.

Figure 24.8 Partially Completed Concept Map on Natural Resources

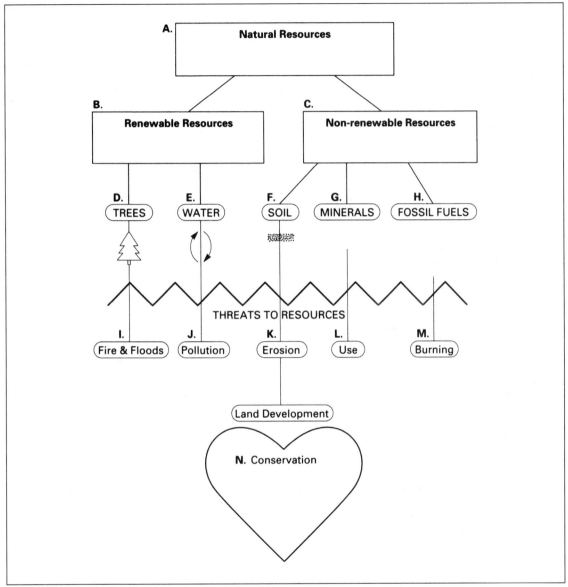

Note: The partially completed concept map would be distributed to students during the lesson. They would add information to the map throughout the lesson.

Table 24.7 Example Lesson for Teaching a Concept Map

First Day

Directions: Hand out partially completed concept map (Figure 24.8). Place completed map on overhead (see Figure 24.7).

T: You are going to be reading a chapter on natural resources. Before you read the chapter, let's learn some of the important concepts.

(Point to Box A on the map.) A natural resource is something provided by nature that is valuable to people. What is a natural resource?

S: Something that is provided by nature that is valuable to people.

T: Yes. For example, trees are a natural resource. They are provided by nature and are valuable to people.

Soil is another example of a natural resource. It is provided by nature and is valuable to people. A chair is not a natural resource. Though the chair contains wood and metal, both of which are natural resources, the chair is made by a person. Tell me if this is a natural resource. Is water a natural resource?

S: Yes.

T: Why? (Call on an individual student.)

S: Because it is provided by nature and is valuable to people.

T: Is gold a natural resource?

S: Yes.

T: Why? (Call on an individual student.)

S: Because it is provided by nature and is valuable to people.

T: Is this gold ring a natural resource?

S: No.

T: Why is this ring not a natural resource? (Call on an individual.)

S: Because it was made by a person.

T: You are correct. The ring is made from a natural resource, gold, but the ring itself is not a natural resource.

In Box A, write the definition for natural resource. (Monitor students as they fill in the box.)

There are two kinds of natural resources. (Point to Box B.) The first kind of natural resource is called a renewable resource. What kind of natural resource?

S: Renewable resource.

T: Renewable resources can be replaced in a reasonable amount of time. How quickly can renewable resources be replaced?

S: In a reasonable amount of time.

T: Yes, these are resources that can be replaced in a reasonable amount of time. For example, they might replace themselves in a month, a year, or one hundred years.

Write the definition for renewable resources in Box B. (Monitor students.)

Find D. (Pause.) What word is written next to D?

S: Trees.

T: Yes, trees are examples of renewable resources. The trees produce seeds or cones. From some of these seeds and cones, new trees grow. This may take a few years, or in some cases, a hundred years. Why are the trees in the forest called renewable resources? (Call on an individual.)

S: Because they replace themselves in a reasonable amount of time.

T: Why are trees important natural resources?

S: (Accept reasonable answers.)

T: Find E. (Pause.) What word is written next to E?

S: Water.

T: Water is another example of a renewable resource. Water replaces itself in a reasonable amount of time. Look at the arrows. Water on the earth evaporates and goes up into the air. Later, clouds are formed and the water returns as rain or snow. Why is water called a renewable resource?

(Call on an individual.)

S: Because water replaces itself in a reasonable amount of time.

T: Why is water an important natural resource?

S: (Accept reasonable answers.)

Table 24.7 continued

     (Place blank concept map on the overhead.)

T: Let's review what we have learned to this point. Turn your maps over. (Point to Box A.) What is the topic of this concept map?

S: Natural resources.

T: Who provides natural resources?

S: Nature.

T: To whom are natural resources valuable?

S: People.

T: Get ready to give me an example of a natural resource.

S: (Give examples.)

T: Great! (Point to Box B.) What is one kind of natural resource?

S: Renewable resources.

T: Can renewable resources be replaced?

S: Yes.

T: How quickly can they be replaced?

S: In a reasonable amount of time.

T: (Point to D.) What is one example of a renewable resource? (Call on an individual student.)

S.   Trees.

T: Why are trees a renewable resource? (Call on an individual.)

S: Because they replace themselves in a reasonable amount of time. (Accept appropriate explanation.)

T: (Point to E.) What is another example of a renewable resource?

S: Water.

T: Why is water called a renewable resource? (Call on an individual.)

S: Because it replaces itself in a reasonable amount of time. (Accept appropriate explanations.)

     (Place the completed map on the overhead.)

T: Find Box C. (Pause.) Now let's study the other type of natural resource, nonrenewable resource. Listen. Nonrenewable resources CANNOT be replaced or can be replaced only very slowly. Read the definition with me. Nonrenewable resources cannot be replaced or can be replaced only very slowly.

S: Nonrenewal resources cannot be replaced or can be replaced only very slowly.

T: When we use some natural resources, we simply use them up. They are not replaced. Other natural resources do replace themselves, but it might take thousands of years. Thus, they are not replaced in our lifetime or in the next generation's lifetime.

T: On your map, write the definition for nonrenewable resources. (Monitor as students write in the definition.)

T: Find F. (Pause.) Read the word written next to F.

S: Soil.

T: Yes, soil is an example of a nonrenewable resource. When soil is blown away, washed away, or carried away, it does replace itself, but it takes thousands of years. Why is soil called a nonrenewable resource?

S: Because it replaces itself very slowly.

T: Why is soil an important natural resource?

S: (Accept reasonable answers.)

T: Find G. (Pause.) Read the word.

S: Minerals.

T: Yes, minerals are another example of a nonrenewable resource. Some examples are copper, gold, and silver. What are some examples of minerals? (Call on individual students.)

S: Copper, gold, or silver.

T: On you map, write *copper, gold,* and *silver* below the word *minerals.* (Monitor.)

T: When we take minerals from rocks or ores to make things, the minerals do not replace themselves. Why are minerals called nonrenewable resources?

S: Because they cannot be replaced.

T: Why are minerals important natural resources?

Table 24.7 continued

S: (Accept reasonable answers.)
T: Find H. (Pause.) Read the words next to H.
S: Fossil fuels.
T: Yes, fossil fuels are also nonrenewable resources. Some examples of fossil fuels are oil, coal, and gas. What are some examples of fossil fuels? (Call on individual students.)
S: (Oil, coal, and gas.)
T: Under the words *fossil fuels,* write *oil, coal,* and *gas.* (Monitor.)
T: Fossil fuels were formed from the remains of plants and animals that were buried under the ground millions of years ago. What were fossil fuels formed from? (Call on an individual.)
S: The remains of plants and animals.
T: Yes, dead animals and plants were buried deep in the ground. Over millions of years, oil, coal, and gas formed from these remains.
     To help you remember how fossil fuels were formed, write "formed from the remains of plants and animals" on your map. (Monitor.)
T: When we burn oil, coal, or gas for energy, they do not replace themselves for millions of years.
     Why are fossil fuels called nonrenewable resources?
S: Because they can be replaced only very slowly. (Accept appropriate explanation.)
T: Why are fossil fuels important natural resources? (Call on an individual.)
S: (Accept reasonable answers.)
T: Now, take some time and study your map. (Monitor.)
     Before we end class today, let's review what we have learned.
       (Place blank concept map on the overhead.)
T: Turn your map over and look here. (Point to Box A.) What are we studying today?
S: Natural resources.
T: What is a natural resource?
S: Something that is provided by nature that is valuable to people.
T: Who uses natural resources?
S: People.
T: (Point to Box B.) What is the first type of natural resource?
S: Renewable resources.
T: Can renewable resources replace themselves?
S: Yes.
T: (Point to D.) What is one example of a renewable resource?
S: Trees.
T: (Point to E.) What is another example of a renewable resource?
S: Water.
T: Excellent. (Box C.) What is the second type of natural resource?
S: Nonrenewable resources.
T: What is a nonrenewable resource? (Call on an individual.)
S: One that cannot be replaced or can be replaced very slowly.
T: (Box F.) What is the first example of a nonrenewable resource?
S: Soil.
T: Can soil be replaced quickly?
S: No.
T: (Box G.) What is the next example of a nonrenewable resource?
S: Minerals
T: What are some examples of minerals? (Call on an individual.)
S: Copper, gold, silver.
T: Can minerals be replaced quickly?

Table 24.7 continued

S: No.
T: What is the last type of nonrenewable resource?
S: Fossil fuels.
T: What are some examples of fossil fuels? (Call on an individual.)
S: Oil, coal, gas.
T: What are fossil fuels formed from? (Call on an individual.)
S: The remains of plants and animals buried in the ground millions of years ago.
T: Can fossil fuels be replaced quickly?
S: No.
T: You have done an excellent job. Tomorrow we are going to talk about some of the things that are hurting our natural resources. Please place your map in your notebook.

Table 24.8 Example of Feature Analysis

	Inherited	Governs by Force	Elected	Elected by People	Elected by Legislators
Monarch (King, Queen)	+	−	−	−	−
Dictator	−	+	−	−	−
President	−	−	+	+	−
Prime Minister	−	−	+	+	+

Table 24.9 Example of Feature Analysis

		Life	Hotter than Earth	Colder than Earth	Big in Relationship to Earth	Small in Relationship to Earth	Satellites	Physical Characteristics Similar to Earth
INNER:	Mercury	−	+	−	−	+	−	+
	Venus	−	+	−	−	−	−	+
	Earth	+	−	−	−	−	+	+
	Mars	−	−	−	−	+	+	+
OUTER:	Jupiter	−	−	+	+	−	+	−
	Saturn	−	−	+	+	−	+	−
	Uranus	−	−	+	+	−	+	−
	Neptune	−	−	+	+	−	+	−
	Pluto	−	−	+	−	+	+	+

Which planets have satellites? Which planets are hotter than Earth? Which planets are colder than Earth? Which planets have a temperature similar to Earth? How does Mars differ from Earth? How is Venus similiar to Earth?

Assistance With Graphics

In addition to assistance with vocabulary meanings and decoding, students will often need preparation to adequately read and interpret visual aids found in the chapter. Since content-area materials generally provide students with their first exposure to charts, tables, graphs, diagrams, maps, and interpretive illustrations and photographs, direct instruction must be provided. The goals of this preparation are to increase the student's ability to read and interpret the information presented as well as to increase awareness of the importance of these features to expository writing.

At the beginning of the school year, the teacher should determine the types of visual aids to be included in the content-area textbook. Generally a few types of visual aids will be repeated throughout a textbook. For example, a social studies textbook might include maps, line graphs, circle graphs, timelines, and tables. Next, the teacher should provide instruction on reading and interpreting each major type of visual aid, preferably before the content-area instruction begins. For example, if maps occur throughout a social studies book, the teacher might teach the following map-reading skills: determining the topic of the map from the map's title, determining directions, locating various places, understanding symbolic language presented in the map, reading the legend of the map, identifying geographic characteristics presented in the map, and reading the map's scale. In the same manner, the teacher can teach students how to read each type of graph (e.g., line graph, pictograph, bar graph) found in the book, stressing the following skills: (1) determining the topic of the graphic material using the title and caption; (2) understanding the organization of the graph; (3) locating information in the graph; (4) making comparisons using the nonnumerical information in the graph (e.g., height of the bars, height of the lines); (5) making comparisons using the numerical information in the graph; and (6) making inferences based on the information. (See Table 24.10 for example teaching script.)

If these skills are taught early in the year, the teacher can focus on interpreting information, forming conclusions, making comparisons, and/or using the information for problem solving when graphics for a specific chapter are introduced. The teacher can ask structured questions about the graph

found in the chapter. The following questions were asked about a bar graph on automobile production from 1900 to 1929: What type of graph is this? What is the title of the graph? What will this graph be about? What do the numbers at the bottom of the graph refer to? What do the numbers on the left side of the graph refer to? In which time period were the most cars produced? In which time period were the fewest number of cars produced? Approximately how many cars were produced between 1910 and 1919? Approximately how many cars were produced between 1920 and 1929? How many more cars were produced in the years 1920 to 1929 than 1910 to 1919? Do you think that car production would be higher today? Why?

In addition to instruction on reading and interpreting graphic aids, students must be taught *when* to refer to graphic material and how to move from discourse to the graphic aid and back. Authors use different techniques to direct the reader's attention to graphic material: explicit directions to refer to graphic material (e.g., "see diagram," "the scale shown in the margin"), general discussion of the graphic material within the discourse, and symbols that appear in the text to indicate to what graphic material a statement refers.

Naive readers could be taught to read the discourse until the author refers to a graphic aid, place their finger at that place in the discourse, refer to the graphic material, examine the material carefully reading all captions, and then resume reading. The critical concept to convey to students is that in content area material, they should never skip over graphs, maps, diagrams, charts, pictures, and other illustrations. They must examine them carefully.

Previewing the Selection

Another prereading activity for expository reading involves previewing information-laden sections of the chapter, such as the chapter title, introduction, headings, subheadings, summaries, and end-of-chapter questions. Through this preview, the reader gains an idea of the content material covered in the chapter and the organization

Table 24.10 Format for Introducing Different Types of Graphs

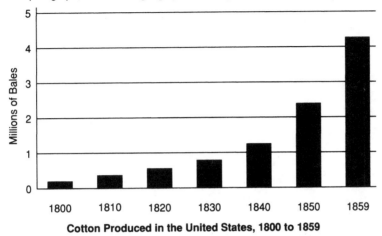

(Adjust the instruction to the specific type of graph: line graph, bar graph, circle graph, pictograph, or table using a graph found in your content area textbook.)

Cotton Produced in the United States, 1800 to 1859

Teacher	Students
1. Introduce the name of the graph (e.g., line graph, bar graph, circle graph, pictograph, table) and the type of information conveyed in the graph.	
a. Look at the graph on page 221. This graph is called a bar graph. What do we call this type of graph?	"A bar graph"
b. A bar graph lets us compare things by comparing the height of the bars.	
2. Introduce the importance of reading the title of the graph and determining the type of information presented.	
a. We read the title of the graph to find out what the graph is about. Read the title of the graph.	"Cotton Produced in the United States, 1800 to 1859."
b. What will the information in the graph be about?	"Cotton production"
3. Introduce the organization of the graph.	
a. This bar graph lets us compare the millions of bales of cotton produced from 1800 to 1859. Look at the numbers across the bottom of the graph. These numbers tell the different years that are compared. Above each of these numbers is a bar.	
b. Put your finger on the highest bar. The highest bar tells you the amount that was produced in 1859. Find the shortest bar. The shortest bar tells you the amount of cotton produced in 1800.	(Students touch the different bars.)
4. Guide students in making comparisons, using the visual display, not the numerical information.	
a. Look at the first two bars. Was more cotton produced in 1800 or 1810? Was more cotton produced in 1850 or 1859?	"1810" "1859"
b. Did cotton production go up or down from 1800 to 1859? When was cotton production greatest?	"Up" "1859"

Table 24.10 continued

Teacher	Student
5. Guide students in making comparisons using the numerical information.	
a. Now, look at the numbers on the left side of the bar graph. We can figure out the millions of bales of cotton by looking at these numbers.	
b. Find the highest bar. Now, look over at the numbers on the left side. A little more than 4 million bales of cotton were produced in 1859.	
c. Find the bar for 1850. Now, look at the numbers on the left side. Approximately, how many millions of bales of cotton were produced in 1850?	"2 million"
Find the bar labeled 1840. Approximately, how many millions of bales were produced in 1840?	"1 million"
6. Guide students in making inferences based on the information reported in the graph.	
a. In the 1800s, did the production of cotton go up or down?	"Up"
b. Slaves were used in all aspects of cotton production. In which of these years would the plantation owners need the most slaves?	"1859"
Do you think the end of slavery would have threatened the plantation owners? Why?	"Yes"

of that information, thus developing a framework for reading the selection.

Previewing the chapter should be teacher guided when the content or organizational structure is complex, the textbook is new to the reader, the readers are less skilled in expository reading, or the information presented in the chapter is beyond students' prior knowledge. Archer and Gleason (2002) developed a teacher-guided survey procedure called *Warm-up*. When using this strategy, the teacher guides students in examining different parts of the chapter and formulating predictions as to the major points to be learned from the chapter. This teaching procedure is outlined in Figure 24.9.

As children become more familiar with the text organization and general content of the book, the teacher may simply review the sections to be previewed to gain a global understanding of the content. Students can then be given a structured activity, such as the worksheet found in Table 24.11 to complete by themselves or with a partner. When all students have previewed the chapter, the teacher and the students can discuss the structure of the chapter and the information that is to be gained by reading the chapter.

Reading Activities

Once students have been properly prepared for reading the passage, the teacher must select a format for the actual passage reading. The type of reading activity depends on the students' reading and comprehension skills and their experience with expository reading. For example, if the students were third-grade students reading the initial chapters of a science textbook, the teacher might choose a teacher-directed procedure to maximize the amount of guidance given to students. As students progress, the teacher might involve the students in a dialogue procedure (reciprocal teaching) in which the students participate as "teachers," asking other students questions about the content-area material. The teacher might also maximize student participation by having students read with a partner, retelling the critical in-

Figure 24.9   Format for Previewing a Chapter: Warm-Up

Warm-Up

Before you read a chapter in your science, social studies, or health book, **warm up.** Get an idea of the chapter's content by previewing these parts.

Beginning	• Title
	• Introduction
Middle	• Headings
	• Subheadings
End	• Summary
	• Questions

Example Lesson

(This format can be adapted to any chapter in an expository chapter. Distribute copies of the warm-up strategy to students before the previewing activity.)

1. Today we will learn how to warm up before reading a chapter in a book. People often warm up before doing an activity. If you go to a baseball game, you see players throwing the ball back and forth and swinging the bat. Before a football game, you see players exercising to warm up their muscles before they start playing the game.

2. Before you read a chapter in a textbook, you need to warm up your mind, just as you warm up your body before an athletic event. When you warm up for reading, you find out what the chapter is about. Read the steps in **Warm-up.**—
What parts of the chapter should we preview before we read the whole chapter?

3. Take out your ____ book.—Turn to page ____.—Let's use **Warm-up** to preview this chapter. Look at the **beginning** of the chapter. Read the title of the chapter.—What will this chapter be about?—(Write the title on the chalkboard.)

4. (If the chapter has an introduction, do this step.) Next we read the introduction to learn more about the chapter. Follow along as I read the introduction. (Read it.) What will this chapter be about?

5. Look at the **middle** of the chapter. Find the first heading.—What is the heading?—So, what will this section of the chapter be about? —(Write the heading on the chalkboard. Continue until all headings and subheadings have been read and written on the chalkboard.)

6. Look at the **end** of the chapter. (If the chapter has a summary, do this step.) Next, we read the summary. Follow along as I read the summary. (Read it.) Tell me some important ideas in this chapter.—As we read the chapter, we would want to learn more about these ideas.

7. Find the questions at the end of the chapter.—Why is it important to read the questions before we read the whole chapter?—Let's read the questions. (Call on individual students to read each question.)

8. Now, think about all of the things that we have read. Tell what this chapter is going to be about.—What are some of the things that you will learn by reading this chapter?

From SKILLS FOR SCHOOL SUCCESS by A. Archer and M. Gleason. Copyright 2002 by Curriculum Associates. Reprinted by permission.

formation to their partner. Finally, as students' experience with expository materials increase, the teacher could give the students an independent reading/learning strategy that can be used for an expository reading.

While the options for reading activities are great, four procedures will be stressed in this section: (1) guided reading, (2) reciprocal teaching, (3) partner reading, and (4) learning strategies. All four reading activities will be modeled using an expository

Table 24.11 Student Worksheet for Previewing Chapter

Directions: As you warm up with your partner, fill in the blanks.

Step 1: Look at the beginning of the chapter. Read the title of the chapter and the introduction.
  What is the title of this chapter? _____
  Does this chapter have an introduction? _____
  Based on the title and the introduction, what is this chapter about?
  _____

Step 2: Look at the middle of the chapter. Read the headings and subheadings.
  List the headings and subheadings you found in this chapter.
  _____
  _____
  _____
  _____

Step 3: Look at the end of the chapter. Read the chapter summary.
  Does this chapter have a summary? _____
  Based on the summary, what are two things that you will learn in this chapter?
  _____
  _____

Step 4: Read the questions at the end of the chapter.
  Does this chapter have questions at the end?
  _____
  Based on the questions, what are two things that you will learn in this chapter?
  _____
  _____

Step 5: Tell yourself. "This chapter will talk about. . . ."
  Finish this sentence. This chapter will talk about
  _____
  _____

passage about fish. Read the passage in Figure 24.10 before continuing with this section.

Guided Reading

When working with young students, such as those having difficulty with comprehension or new to a content-area textbook, the teacher can use a teacher-directed strategy, *guided reading,* similar to the reading formats presented earlier in the book for narrative reading. In this procedure, the teacher presents a guided-reading question or directive (e.g., "Read to find out . . . ") concerning a paragraph or series of paragraphs in the content-area material. This question is meant to direct students' attention to the critical content in the segment of discourse. Next, the students read the segment silently, or with

very poor readers, silently and then orally. After the segment has been read, the teacher asks students questions concerning the main idea of the segment and any critical facts or details that the teacher wishes the students to retain.

To optimize this procedure, the teacher should structure the questions to model the type of self-questioning students should engage in when reading independently. For example, the teacher might begin by asking students the topic of the segment. Next, the teacher might ask students to summarize the information reported about the topic, asking them to stress the most important information. Next, the teacher could ask questions to help students clarify any confusing aspects of the passage. Finally, the teacher could ask students to predict what would be reported in the remaining discourse.

As you will see when you examine the remaining reading activities, this type of questioning would prepare students for participation in *reciprocal teaching,* for the verbal retell in the *partner reading,* and for the rehearsal steps in *learning strategies.* An example of guided reading is found in Table 24.12.

Reciprocal Teaching

In reciprocal teaching (Palincsar & Brown, 1986), the reading activity proceeds in much the same manner as in guided reading; however, the burden of asking questions on the content is shared by the teacher and the students. The students are directly taught four strategies: questioning, summarizing, clarifying, and predicting. Once these strategies have been taught, students, as well as the teacher, ask questions on the content. In this manner, they engage in a dialogue concerning the chapter content. The four strategies are explained below:

- **Question generating:** Using this strategy, the students identify important information within the content, formulate questions concerning this content, and address the questions to peers. Since students are involved in posing as well as answering the questions, they are more involved than if only responding to teacher-generated questions.

Figure 24.10 Expository Text Material

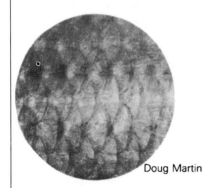

Fish

Fish are the simplest group of vertebrates. They are also the largest group of vertebrates. All fish have similar characteristics. They all have skeletons. Most of the fish you have seen have skeletons made of bone. A few have skeletons made of cartilage (KART ul ihj).

Cartilage is a firm, flexible substance that forms parts of some skeletons. Sharks and rays have cartilage instead of bone. Your body has both bone and cartilage. Feel the tip of your nose. Wiggle it. Compare the tip of your nose to the upper part of your nose. How does the cartilage feel? Where else on your head can you feel cartilage?

Fish also have scales. **Scales** are thin, smooth pieces of a bonelike material that cover the entire body of the fish. Each scale overlaps another scale. The tough, hard scales help protect fish. How are the scales like a coat of armor?

Doug Martin

From ACCENT ON SCIENCE by Robert B. Sund and others, pp. 7–8. Copyright 1995 by Merrill Publishing. Reprinted by permission.

(continued)

Figure 24.10 *(Continued)*

Central Ohio School of Diving (Joey Jacques)

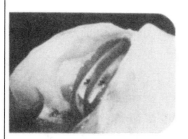

Russ Lappa

Fish live in water. **Gills** are organs through which fish get oxygen from the water. You can see the gills on the side of the fish's head through the openings or slits. As water enters the mouth, it passes over the gills. Oxygen in the water moves into the gills. Carbon dioxide from the body is given off through the gills. The water then passes out of the body through the slits. Find the slits visible on the fish in the pictures. The gills are beneath the slits.

Fish are cold-blooded animals. **Cold-blooded animals** have a body temperature the same as their environment. For example, fish living in warm water have a warm body temperature. Fish living in cold water have a cold body temperature.

Most fish have fins which are bony limbs covered with thin skin. Fish use fins and body movements to move through the water. Count the fins on the fish. How many does it have? Where are the fins located?

Table 24.12 Format for Teacher-Directed, Guided Reading

Teacher	Students
1. Students read the heading or subheading. The teacher asks them to tell what the section will talk about.	
a. Read the heading.	"fish"
b. What will this section of the chapter talk about?	"fish"
2. The teacher directs students to read a segment of the selection, generally a paragraph or a series of paragraphs on the same topic. The segment may be read silently, or the teacher can have the segment read silently and then orally when working with students having decoding difficulties. Before the segment is read, the teacher presents a guided-reading question or direction.	
a. Read the first paragraph to find out what is the same about all fish.	(Students read the paragraph
b. Look up when you have finished reading.	silently.)
3. The teacher asks structured questions about the segment's content. The questions should help students to identify the topic of the paragraph and summarize the critical information. In addition, questions could help students clarify confusing elements of the segment and to predict what might be discussed in subsequent segments.	
a. Tell me in a word or phrase what this whole paragraph talked about.	"fish"
b. Yes, it talked about fish. Tell some of the important things that it said about fish.	"That fish are the largest group of vertebrates."
c. From our past reading, what are vertebrates?	"Animals with backbones."
d. What other important thing did this paragraph tell us about fish?	"That all fish have skeletons."
e. Excellent. Yes, this paragraph talked about fish. It said that fish are the largest group of vertebrates and that all fish have skeletons.	
f. What are most fish skeletons made from?	"bone"
g. What are some fish skeletons made from?	"cartilage"
h. Did the paragraph tell us what cartilage is?	"No."
i. What do you think we will learn about in the next paragraph?	"cartilage"
j. You all know something about fish. Tell me some of the things that we might learn about fish.	"Fish have scales. About the fins on fish. About how fish swim."
4. Repeat this procedure for the remaining paragraphs or segments in the passage.	
5. When the selection has been read, ask students questions over the entire selection that will assist them in summarizing the information and give them practice in rehearsing the critical information.	
a. Let's review what we learned in this selection. Fish are the largest group of vertebrates. What do all fish have?	"skeletons"
b. What two materials can the skeletons be made of?	"bone and cartilage"
c. What is cartilage?	"Flexible stuff like the tip of your nose."
d. What covers the body of fish?	"scales"
e. How do the scales help fish?	"They protect the body of fish."
f. What organs help fish get oxygen from the water?	"gills"
g. Are fish warm- or cold-blooded animals?	"cold-blooded"

Table 24.12 continued

Teacher	Students
h. What are cold-blooded animals?	"Animals that have the same temperature as their environment."
i. So if a fish lives in cold water, what would be the temperature of the fish?	"cold"
j. Fish don't have arms or legs, but they do have limbs. What are those limbs called?	"fins"
k. How do fins help fish?	"They help them move through the water."
6. If time permits, have students retell the content of the selection to a partner. When the partner is done, have their partner add any information that was deleted. This will give your students practice in summarizing the information. This skill can be used in reciprocal teaching, partner reading, and in the independent-learning strategies using verbal rehearsal.	
a. Partner #1, tell your partner what you learned about fish.	(Student retells content to partner.)
b. Partner #2, tell your partner any information that they left out.	(Student tells additional information to his/her partner.)

- **Summarizing:** Here the students are to summarize the information in the segment that has been read, reporting the most important information. As reading proceeds, the students are asked to summarize content across paragraphs and sections of the passage.

- **Clarifying:** Using the clarifying strategy, the students identify elements of the segment that they have read that are unclear (e.g., vocabulary that is unknown) so that they can respond appropriately to facilitate comprehension (ask for help or reread the material).

- **Predicting:** Using this strategy, the students predict what the author will discuss in subsequent paragraphs or sections of the discourse. To do this, students use their prior knowledge of the topic and the information that has already been presented in the discourse.

As Palincsar and Brown (1986) discuss, each of these strategies must be taught before they are used in reciprocal dialogue. Once each of the strategies

has been introduced and students have demonstrated some competency with each, the teacher models the use of the strategies within the context of reading an expository passage. Initially, the teacher leads the dialogue, modeling how the strategies can be used during reading. As instruction proceeds, more responsibility for initiating questions and maintaining the dialogue is transferred to the students. Over time, students take more responsibility for the dialogue, but the teacher continues to guide them in using the strategies. Using the passage on fish, the dialogue (shown in Table 24.13) might result when the teacher and students engage in reciprocal teaching.

Partner Reading

Another way to actively engage students in the reading process is to utilize partner reading. The teacher assigns each student a partner based on their reading levels. Generally, the lowest readers are assigned to middle-performing readers, middle students to low-, middle-, or high-readers; and the highest students to middle- or high-students. The

Table 24.13   Example Dialogue Resulting From the Use of Reciprocal Teaching

(Following silent reading of paragraph #1.)	
Teacher:	Who will be our teacher?
Student 1:	My question is, how are fish all the same?
Student 2:	They all have skeletons.
Student 1:	What are the skeletons made out of?
Student 3:	They are made out of bone.
Student 4:	They are also made out of cartilage.
Student 1:	For my summary now: This paragraph was about fish. All fish have skeletons. Some of the skeletons are made out of bone. Other fish skeletons are made out of cartilage.
Teacher:	Are there any things that need to be clarified?
Student 1:	I think we need to clarify cartilage.
Teacher:	Is cartilage defined in the paragraph?
Student 1:	No.
Teacher:	What do you predict the authors will talk about in the next paragraph?
Student 5:	Cartilage.
Student 1:	Yes, I predict the authors will tell us what cartilage is.
Teacher:	Can you predict any other things that the authors might tell us about fish?
Student 6:	They might tell us about how fish move.
Student 7:	Maybe they will tell us about parts of fish, like the fins.
Student 8:	I bet they will tell us about different kinds of fish.
Teacher:	Those are excellent predictions. Let's read the next paragraph and see if any of your predictions are true.

students must sit next to each other with one or two books between them. The teacher then selects a passage reading procedure. The students can alternate reading after each paragraph, after completing a page, or after a period of time (usually 5 minutes). The students must also be taught how to correct their partner's decoding errors (Fuchs, Fuchs, Mathes, & Simmons, 1996). Teach students an "Ask then Tell" correction procedure. When an error is detected, the partner asks, "Can you figure out this word?" If the word is not correct, the partner tells the word ("That word is _____."). The student then rereads the sentence.

While partner reading will increase the amount of reading practice students receive, full benefit is only gained when comprehension strategies are added. An excellent partner strategy is called *paragraph shrinking* (Fuchs, Fuchs, Mathes, & Simmons, 1996). Using this strategy, one partner (reader) reads a paragraph to his/her partner (coach). After the reader is done, the coach asks the reader to name who or what the paragraph is about. Next, the reader is directed to tell the most impor-

tant thing about the who or what. Finally, the coach instructs the reader to say the main idea of the paragraph in 10 words or less, thus the title of the strategy, paragraph shrinking.

Use of Independent-Learning Strategies

The teacher's ultimate goal in content-area reading, as in all areas of instruction, is to develop independent students who can analyze a task, devise a plan for attacking that task, carry out the plan, and evaluate their own performance. One way to accomplish this goal is to teach students task-specific *learning strategies*. While learning strategies are defined in many ways throughout the literature, we are referring to systematic, student-directed procedures for responding to a specific type of task (e.g., reading expository materials). Learning strategies generally involve a series of steps that the student performs. These steps are meant to enhance students' cognition and attention to critical variables (e.g., important concepts in the expository material) and to increase metacognition, thinking about one's own thinking, through self-monitoring, self-evaluation, and self-correction.

Many learning strategies for reading expository materials have been developed and studied with elementary and secondary students (Deshler, Schumaker, Harris, & Graham, 1999; Gleason, Archer, & Colvin, 2002; Schumaker, Denton, & Deshler, 1984). However, there are some similarities between these strategies. First, all of the strategies attempt to make students more actively involved in the reading process. Instead of passively reading and rereading the chapter, students are asked to formulate questions, take notes on the content, or verbally paraphrase the critical information. Second, all strategies attempt to direct the student's attention to the most important concepts, ideas, and details. Finally, the learning strategies for content area reading engage the student in some type of information rehearsal and practice involving either reciting or writing down critical information. We will explore two types of expository learning strategies: those that involve verbal rehearsal and those that involve written rehearsal.

Verbal Rehearsal Strategies Since Robinson's development of SQ3R (Survey, Question, Read, Recite, Review) in 1941, many similar strategies involving verbal rehearsal or recitation have been developed for use with elementary and secondary students (Archer & Gleason, 2002; Gleason, Archer, & Colvin, 2002; Deshler, Schumaker, Harris, & Graham, 1999). One of these strategies, active reading, is particularly appropriate for elementary students and low-performing secondary students because of its simplicity. The steps in active reading are outlined in Figure 24.11.

Using active reading, the student reads a single paragraph, covers the paragraph, recites the important information, then checks his/her statement of the critical information by examining the paragraph again. This process continues for the entire selection. The student is actively involved in the reading process through a number of overt behaviors: reading the material, placing his/her hand over the material, and verbally reciting the content. Cognition

Figure 24.11 Active Reading Procedure

Active Reading

R = Read

Read a paragraph.
Think about the topic.
Think about the important details.

C = Cover

Cover the material with your hand.

R = Recite

Tell yourself what you have read.
Say the topic.
Say the important details.
Say it in your own words.

C = Check

Lift your hand and check.
If you forget something important, begin again.

From SKILLS FOR SCHOOL SUCCESS by A. Archer and M. Gleason. Copyright 2002 by Curriculum Associates. Reprinted by permission.

(thinking about the information) is enhanced through verbal rehearsal; metacognition (thinking about your thinking) is activated in the check step, where students evaluate their recitation.

As Archer and Gleason (2002) outline in their instructional materials, it is important to teach students verbally to retell content before the *active reading* strategy is introduced. First, they teach students to identify the topics for paragraphs. Once students can say a word or phrase topic for a paragraph, then they are taught to identify critical details in the paragraph and to retell the topic and details in their own words. When students can retell paragraph content, the entire strategy is modeled; guided practice is provided until proficiency is reached, then students practice the strategy independently.

Written Rehearsal Strategies Another way actively to involve students in the reading of expository material is to have them take notes on the critical content. When students take notes, they have to attend closely to the author's message and evaluate what information is important and should be recorded. They emerge from notetaking with a short summary of the content that can be used in subsequent study, writing a paragraph summary of the content, answering chapter questions, or writing a report.

When selecting a notetaking style to teach students, it is important that the form does not take attention from the content. Often teachers introduce formal outlining in which the relationship of ideas in the passage are shown through indentation, numbers (Roman and Arabic), and letters (upper- and lower-case). While outlining might help students organize their *own* ideas in preparation for a speech or writing a paper, it is not an appropriate form when taking notes on written material since many students will be concerned about the appropriate designation (e.g., Should this be a Roman numeral I, a capital A, or a lower-case a?) rather than the author's information. Instead, a simple form of notetaking in which the subordination of ideas is illustrated through systematic indentation of topics and supporting details should be taught. This system is far less complex than parallel systems using number and

letter designations, allowing the student to focus on the relationships between ideas rather than the formality of the outlining system.

One simple system of notetaking developed by Archer and Gleason (2002) is particularly appropriate for elementary students and lower-performing students because the notes follow the structure of the text material and again use the paragraph as the unit of analysis. In this system, students record the heading or subheading in the center of the paper followed by the corresponding page number. Next, students take notes on each paragraph in the section. First, they record a topic for the paragraph. Then, they indent and record the important details in the paragraph. When the notes have been completed and checked for clarity, students go back and record questions in the left-hand margin for each of the paragraphs. Later, when studying their notes, students are taught to cover their notes, ask themselves the question, recite the answer, then check their verbal answer with their notes (see example notes in Table 24.14).

As with all complex skills, careful instruction on notetaking should be given. First, students will need training in identifying paragraph topics and

---

Table 24.14 Example of Indentation Notes

These notes follow the structure of the text material. Notes are taken on each paragraph with a topic and the important details recorded.

Fish

Fish Group
  —simplest group of vertebrates
  —largest group
  —have skeletons
    —bone
    —cartilage

Cartilage
  —firm, flexible
  —some fish skeletons
  —sharks and rays

Scales
  —thin, smooth, bonelike material
  —cover fish
    —scales overlap
    —protect fish

Gills
  —organs that get oxygen from water
    —water comes into mouth
    —oxygen goes into gills
    —water goes out through slits

Cold-blooded
  —temperature same as environment
  —warm water = warm body

Fins
  —limb covered with skin
  —use to move through water

critical details. Next, the notetaking procedure should be modeled. The teacher should read a paragraph, determine the topic of the paragraph and record it on the board or overhead, then indent and record critical details. As the teacher models, the teacher should "think out loud," telling students why the topic and details were chosen. The teacher should stress that the notes should be brief and written in their own words. Students can then be asked to copy the teacher's example notes to reinforce the organization of ideas through indentation.

After modeling notetaking, teachers should lead their students in taking notes. Teachers should have the students read a paragraph and determine a paragraph topic. They should ask students to suggest possible topics and select one topic. The teacher then writes the topic on the board or overhead transparency and has students record it on their papers. Next, students suggest important passage details

and provide feedback on their selections. The students should indent and record the important details under the topic. Again, teachers stress brevity and paraphrasing rather than copying as they record their details. This type of guided practice should be provided for many days until students show proficiency in this skill. At this point, independent practice should be provided and students should be expected to take notes on information-laden portions of their chapters. These same instructional procedures can be used to teach *mapping,* an alternative notetaking system that illustrates the subordination of ideas through a visual display (see Figure 24.12 for an example of mapping).

Notetaking will only benefit students if they are required to take notes and actually study the notes. While collecting and grading students' notes is not necessary, completion and noncompletion of required notes should be recorded in the gradebook

Figure 24.12   Example of Mapping

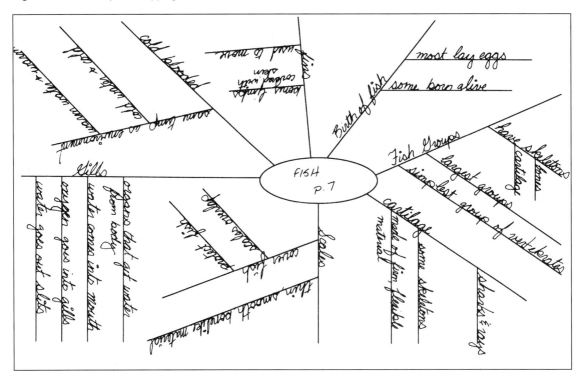

to increase accountability. Students should also be taught how to study their notes. They can use a verbal-rehearsal strategy (e.g., read, cover, recite, check) or a self-questioning strategy (e.g., Read your question. Answer the question. Check your answer with your notes.). Class activities can also be structured for use of the notes. The teacher can ask questions on the content and have students locate the answers in their notes. Similarly, students can ask questions and have their peers locate the answers in their notes. Both of these procedures provide students practice in using their notes and feedback on the adequacy of those notes.

Postreading Activities

The goal of postreading activities is to integrate, synthesize, and consolidate the information that has been read in the selection. Of many postreading activities (e.g., filling in a blank concept map, discussing content using class notes, developing a visual representation of the information), two postreading activities have particular merit: (1) answering written questions and (2) writing a summary of the content. In both cases, the students have an opportunity to study and practice the important information once again and to formulate a written product that can be used in subsequent study.

Written Questions

After reading a passage, students can be assigned written questions on the passage content. To make this activity valuable to students, the teacher should write or select questions that match the following criteria. The questions should (1) stress major concepts presented in the material, not insignificant facts, (2) include both literal- and inferential-comprehension responses, (3) go beyond yes and no responses, and (4) be well worded to promote ease of interpretation. Since one of the purposes of the questions is to ascertain passage understanding, the majority of questions should be "passage dependent," that is, the answers should be based on passage in-

formation rather than solely on experiential background. The answers should also involve significant concepts and relationships. Often teachers and authors write questions that focus on insignificant facts rather than main ideas. As a result, students become detail seekers who cannot separate the important from the unimportant. Teachers can change this pattern through the prudent selection of questions. Teachers should ask themselves, "What do I *really* want the students to remember from this selection?"

Many students lack a strategy for answering chapter questions. For example, they may not read the questions carefully or have a procedure for locating the answer within the chapter. In addition, many students write incomplete sentence answers that do not incorporate wording from the question. To alleviate these problems, students should be taught a specific learning strategy for answering written questions. Using the strategy developed by Archer and Gleason (2002), students are taught to read the question carefully and to change the question into part of the answer and write it down. This step has many benefits. First, it gives the students a way to get the task started. Second, the resulting answer will be a complete sentence and will reflect the question's wording. Finally, changing the question into part of the answer encourages the student to contemplate the question before referring to the chapter. This reduces the possibility of an answer that appears to have no relationship to the question. Next, students locate the section of the chapter that talks about the topic by examining the headings and subheadings. Finally, students locate and complete the answer (see Table 24.15).

As with other learning strategies, the teacher should present the steps in the strategy, model the strategy, guide students in practicing the strategy, and provide independent practice. If this strategy is carefully taught and practiced, the accuracy and quality of students' answers will increase significantly. Once this strategy has been taught, most teachers no longer require that students copy the question since the question wording is incorporated into the answer.

Table 24.15   Strategy for Answering Chapter Questions

Answering Chapter Questions

Use this strategy when you need to answer questions in your science, social studies, or health book.
Remember, words from the question can be used in your answer.

Step 1: Read the question carefully.
Step 2: Change the question into part of the answer and write it down.
Step 3: Locate the section of the chapter that talks about the topic. Use the headings and subheadings to help you find the
section of the chapter that talks about the topic.
Step 4: Read the section of the chapter until you find the answer.
Step 5: Complete the answer.

From SKILLS FOR SCHOOL SUCCESS by A. Archer and M. Gleason. Copyright 2002 by Curriculum Associates. Reprinted by permission.

Written Summaries

Writing a summary on a passage is an excellent postreading activity for a number of reasons. First, summarizing can better help the students understand the organization of the text material. Second, it provides students with practice in determining main ideas and critical concepts in the selection. Third, it provides students needed practice in expressive writing. Finally, the effort to identify critical content during the summarizing process can help students remember those ideas (Gajria & Salvia, 1992).

Despite its many benefits, summarizing is a difficult skill that even high-school students may not be able to do proficiently. Summarizing places great demands on the student. The student must decide what information should be included in the summary, what information should be deleted, and how the information should be organized and reworded. Young and low-performing students are likely to have difficulty deciding what to include and how to condense the information into a concise summary.

Sheinker and Sheinker (1989) have developed a powerful learning strategy to guide students in summarizing content-area material. Their strategy involves the following steps: (1) skim a passage; (2) list key points; (3) combine related points into single statements; (4) cross out least important points; (5) reread list; (6) combine and cross out to condense points; (7) number remaining points in logical order; and (8) write points into paragraph in numbered order (Sheinker & Sheinker, 1989, p. 135). The steps in this process are illustrated in Figures 24.13, 24.14, and 24.15. This step-by-step strategy will benefit all students in learning this important, but difficult skill.

In the instructional procedures outlined by Sheinker and Sheinker, the teacher introduces the purpose of summarizing, situations in which summarizing would be helpful, and a model summary. In a series of carefully structured lessons, the teacher introduces the steps in the strategy, a rationale for each step, and provides drill on the strategy steps. Next, the students write a written summary on a selection following the prescribed steps. Then, all class members brainstorm through the steps, creating a group summary. Students compare their written summary to that generated by the group. This type of instruction is repeated until the students can write summaries both accurately and fluently.

Review Procedures

Feedback on written assignments should be provided through answer keys, while class or small-group corrections should be provided through either written or verbal teacher feedback. Students should be required to complete incorrect or incomplete responses using their textbook. Performance   on   written   exercises   should   be

Figure 24.13   Initial Steps in Writing a Summary

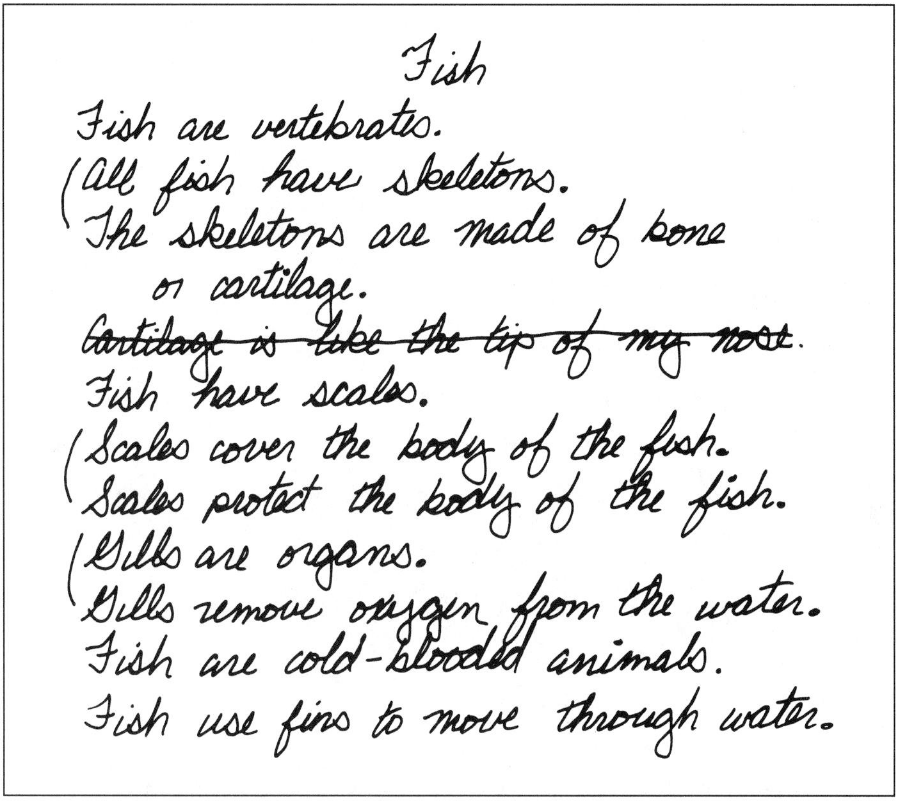

> Fish
>
> Fish are vertebrates.
> (All fish have skeletons.
> The skeletons are made of bone
>   or cartilage.
> ~~Cartilage is like the tip of my nose~~.
> Fish have scales.
> (Scales cover the body of the fish.
> (Scales protect the body of the fish.
> (Gills are organs.
> (Gills remove oxygen from the water.
> Fish are cold-~~blooded~~ animals.
> Fish use fins to move through water.

Following the strategy developed by Sheinker and Sheinker (1989), students skim the chapter and list key points. Next, they combine related points that could be written as single statements. Then, they eliminate the least important points by crossing them out. The first four steps in the strategy are illustrated in this example.

recorded on some type of chart, grade sheet, or assignment sheet. All students should be performing at about a 90% accuracy level. If students are not performing at this level, teachers should increase the preparatory activities and the amount of practice. Typically, lower-performing students function at a low-accuracy level because the assignments presented are too difficult and/or the students do not receive adequate preparation. When students constantly encounter failure, they are likely to develop faulty study habits (random answering just to finish an assignment) and negative attitudes.

Whole-class or small-group discussion designed to firm up difficult concepts can follow individual corrections. The teacher may pose additional literal and inferential questions on the content, elicit verbal answers, and engage the children in discussion. Questions recorded during the chapter preview can be used. To clarify concepts, the teacher may visually summarize information using a table, chart, graph, timeline, or flow chart.

In addition to firming up difficult concepts immediately after completing passage reading and written assignments, critical concepts and

Figure 24.14 Additional Steps in Writing a Summary

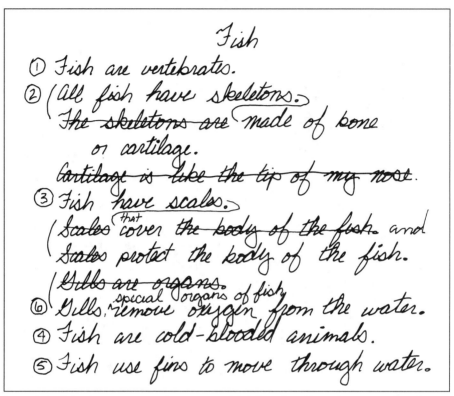

In completing their written summary, students next reread their list and combine and cross out additional points to further condense their list. Next, they renumber the points in a logical order. These steps are illustrated in this example.

relationships should be reviewed in subsequent lessons through teacher-posed verbal questions, written items on later written assignments, or on daily quizzes. End-of-chapter or unit tests can also be used to ensure review of critical concepts. Only through cumulative review will students learn that information presented in the content area textbook is important and should be retained beyond completion of daily assignments.

Summary

Reading in content-area textbooks presents new challenges to intermediate students because of the divergence of expository material from more fa-

miliar narrative or story material. Students need explicit instruction on the use of content-area textbooks that not only promotes mastery of information presented in the text but also assists students in the acquisition of critical-reading study skills that can be used independently. Preparing for content-area lessons begins with the teacher's determination of the information in the selection that should be mastered by the students. This information is translated into a chapter examination and into written assignments that will be completed during or after reading of the selection. The assignments may consist of written questions, directions for completing a written summary, or a visual representation of the infor-

Figure 24.15 Paragraph Summary of Key Points

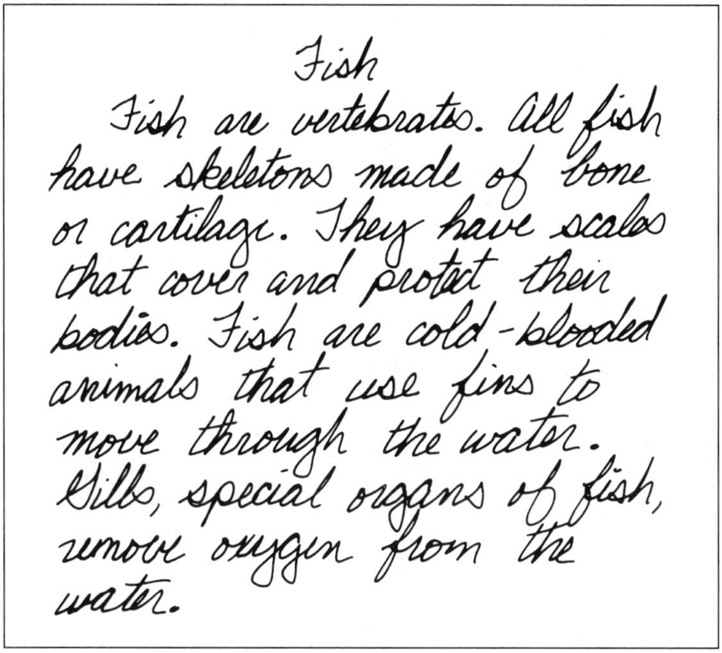

> *Fish*
>
> *Fish are vertebrates. All fish have skeletons made of bone or cartilage. They have scales that cover and protect their bodies. Fish are cold-blooded animals that use fins to move through the water. Gills, special organs of fish, remove oxygen from the water.*

Finally, the student composes a paragraph summary by writing the listed points into a paragraph in the numbered order.

mation, such as a chart, graph, timeline, outline, or concept diagram. The chapter should also be divided into teachable units.

When the critical information has been determined and the written assignment either designed by the teacher or selected from the materials accompanying the content area textbook, the teacher can prepare students for reading of the selection. Preparatory activities may include preteaching vocabulary (decoding and meanings), introducing critical graphics, previewing the selection, instructing on the structure of the passage, and preteaching of concepts through concept diagrams or maps and feature analysis procedures. The amount and type of preparation for passage reading should be adjusted to accomodate the individual differences among students with more preparation given to low-performing students. As the students become more competent content-area readers, the amount of preparation should be gradually faded, leading to independent reading of the selections.

Following preparation for passage reading, students should read the selection through guided, reciprocal, partner, or independent silent reading and use of learning strategies, then complete written exercises on the material. Students should be taught how to take notes, answer questions, and write summaries. When the written assignments are complete, corrections, either group or individual, should be given followed by students correcting any incorrect or inadequate answers. Additional follow-up activities to extend or review critical concepts should also be included.

Application Exercises

Select a chapter in a science, social studies, or health textbook. Complete the following exercises.

Teacher Preparation for Instruction

1. Read the chapter carefully. Determine the critical concepts, vocabulary, general understandings, facts, etc. that you want students to gain from reading the chapter. Write a content analysis similar to that found in Table 24.1.
2. Write or adapt a test for the chapter. Be certain that your test focuses on critical content and uses appropriate items to measure the content.
3. Divide the chapter into teachable segments. Be certain that each segment represents connected discourse on a specific topic and can be taught in one class session.

Prereading Activities

Complete the remaining activities for one segment of the chapter.
1. Reread the segment of the chapter and list words that would be difficult to decode. For each of the words, tell how you would introduce the pronunciation of the word (e.g., as a whole word; by precorrecting affixes; by indicating parts of the word).
2. Select one critical vocabulary concept from the segment. Write an instructional script similar to that found in Table 24.2 for teaching the vocabulary concept.
3. Select another vocabulary concept from the segment. Design a concept diagram (see Table 24.3) that could be used in teaching the concept.
4. Design a concept map that could be used visually to present the critical content within the segment or within the entire chapter. Be certain that the structure of your concept map matches the structure of the discourse (e.g., hierarchy, diagram, compare-contrast, timeline, or process/cycle).
5. For each paragraph or series of related paragraphs in your text selection, write questions that could be used in the guided-reading procedure. See Step 3 of Table 24.12 for example questions.
6. Write example notes for your text selection using the indented notetaking and the mapping styles.

Postreading Activities

1. Write a set of questions that students can complete after passage reading. Be certain that your questions focus on the critical concepts delineated in your content analysis.
2. Create a series of examples that can be used in teaching summary writing. List the key points from your selection. Next, combine related points into single statements and cross out the least important points. Then, condense points further by combining and deleting statements. Number the remaining points in a logical order. Finally, write a summary of the selection.

PART 5

School and Classroom Implementation
Primary and Intermediate Grades

Using Commercial Reading Materials

Late Primary and Intermediate Grades

The reading-to-learn stage follows the learning-to-read stage. As stated earlier, most students complete the learning-to-read stage in approximately 2 years. When they complete this stage and enter the reading-to-learn stage, they can read text with accuracy, moderate fluency (90 words per minute), and basic comprehension. They know all letter-sound correspondences for individual letters and most common letter combinations and can readily apply that knowledge to read words.

During the reading-to-learn stage, only four of the five reading components identified by the National Reading Panel—phonics, fluency, vocabulary, and text comprehension—are continued. The fifth component—phonemic-awareness instruction—is no longer included in reading instruction.

Phonics instruction gradually decreases during this stage as children learn less common letter combinations, prefixes and suffixes, and how to apply this knowledge to read longer multisyllabic words.

Fluency instruction continues until children can read orally at a rate of about 135 words a minute with good expression.

Vocabulary instruction continues throughout the grades. Teachers directly teach the meaning of words that are to be included in text passages and

teach other words that are of general importance. In addition, the teacher implements procedures to encourage students to do a great deal of independent reading.

Comprehension instruction becomes the focus of instruction. It includes the teaching of increasingly complex skills and strategies. Inferential and deductive reasoning strategies become increasingly important.

Writing instruction continues to be integrated into the overall program as children learn the expressive language skills to describe, explain, and convince through written responses.

Constructing a Comprehensive Reading Program

Below are important factors to consider when developing a reading program for the reading-to-learn stage.

Alignment of Instruction

The teaching of all components should be aligned. For example, the passages students read should include words containing phonic elements taught in word-attack exercises. Vocabulary instruction and comprehension-strategy teaching and text-passage exercises should be coordinated. In the past, components of basal programs were rarely aligned, resulting in situations in which workbooks included story comprehension exercises that were not related to the content or skills taught in earlier parts of the lesson.

In-Depth Treatment of Important Content

The coverage of important skills and knowledge should be sufficient to enable students to become proficient. Unfortunately, basal publishers, in their attempt to produce a product that meets the content standards from all states, often provide just surface treatment of important topics in their reading programs. In other words, depth is sacrificed for breadth. For example, commonly an important topic such as main idea appears sporadically throughout a program and receives little more attention than a less-important topic such as placing accent marks. Important topics should receive in-depth treatment. The program should be organized so that there is adequate practice for children to master content. When a new important topic, such as main idea, is presented, instruction in that topic should continue over a series of continuous lessons, and then be reviewed regularly.

Teaching of Prerequisite Background Knowledge and Vocabulary

If children are to be successful in tasks calling for higher-order comprehension skills, teachers must ensure that the children have learned the vocabulary and the background knowledge that is prerequisite for the higher-order tasks. Programs, particularly those for use with at-risk children, need to include the teaching of critical background knowledge and vocabulary that will appear in upcoming text.

Use of Explicit and Clear Strategies With Mediated Scaffolding

Strategies should be designed to enable students to accomplish higher-order tasks. For example, in

teaching students to use deductive reasoning (answering questions based on a given relationship) the teacher should model the strategy of using the stated relationship to answer questions. Then, the instruction should be scaffolded with the teacher guiding the student through application of the strategy a sufficient number of times to develop mastery of the process.

Inclusion of Monitoring and Feedback Procedures

Lessons should be organized so that students receive feedback on their work within a reasonable time. As content becomes more sophisticated, feedback from the teacher does not have to be as immediate as when students are learning beginning reading skills; however, even at a later stage, the feedback should be provided soon enough to prevent any student from being confused or developing misconceptions.

Readability

Readability is a term used to describe the relative ease or difficulty of a passage.[1] The level of difficulty is usually expressed in terms of a grade equivalent. The readability level of the passages in a level of a program should consistently be at the level designated by the publisher. This point is critical. If a great number of selections are at a much higher

---

1. Numerous formulas have been developed to determine readability. While each formula is somewhat unique, some or all of the following factors are taken into consideration in most formulas:
- The average length of words. Passages with longer words are considered more difficult than passages with shorter words.
- The relative frequency of words. Passages with more-common words are easier than passages with less-common words.
- The length of sentences. The longer the average sentence, the more difficult the passage.
- The relative complexity of the sentences. The more clauses used and the greater the use of passive voice, the more difficult the passage.

level than the designated grade level, the program may put at-risk children at their frustration level.

Using and Modifying Materials

The upper-grade levels of basal programs have traditionally not been constructed with the same care as displayed in lower-grade programs. This is in part because of the great number of topics that publishers feel compelled to include in their programs to make them meet various state content requirements.

Teachers, particularly those working with at-risk students, must be prepared to make significant modifications when using basal programs. The remainder of this chapter will focus on how to use their basal programs to best meet the needs of students.

A notable exception to programs that need significant modifications is the *Reading Mastery Series* developed by Siegfried Engelmann. The *Reading Mastery* programs meet all the criteria described earlier in this chapter. We strongly recommend that persons working with at-risk students inspect this program to see a model of how a program can be constructed to meet the needs of their students.

Screening and Placement Assessment at Beginning of the School Year

In the well-organized school, teachers will meet at the end of the school year to make instructional groupings for the next school year. In such schools, teachers will have reliable information on where to begin instruction. Since not all schools provide this valuable information, a teacher must be prepared to determine children's instructional level at the beginning of the year.

This section describes assessment procedures a classroom teacher in the late primary and intermediate grades can use to determine children's instructional level at the beginning of the school year. The procedure described is designed to provide maximum information in a relatively short period of time. (In a day or two a teacher with one parent volunteer could administer assessments that would

provide a basis for initial grouping and placing.) A teacher with 20 to 30 students simply does not have time for time-consuming testing. After a week or two of instruction, the teacher should assess the performance of students to see which students might function better in another group and if groups are placed at appropriate instructional levels. This point is very important: Many students after a week or two of instruction will perform significantly better than they did when the school year started. Reviewing grouping and placement after one to two weeks of instruction is critical.

Teachers using commercial programs must be prepared to obtain or create their own screening and placement assessments because the commercial programs often do not provide these important assessments. A number of commercially produced materials can be utilized. One resource for obtaining information on some of the more widely used reading assessments is a report on a study of assessments conducted for the U.S. Department of Education Reading First program. The report appears on the University of Oregon's Institute for Development of Educational Achievement website: *http://idea.uoregon.edu/*.

We describe three informal assessment instruments for beginning of year screening: a word-attack skills assessment, an informal reading inventory, and a written comprehension test.

Word-Attack Skills Assessment

The word-attack skills test (see Table 25.1) is designed to serve (1) as a quick screening test to determine at what level a student is reading, and (2) as a preliminary indicator of what phonic and structural elements a student does and does not know.

Note that we use the word "indicator" because no one test is definitive. Correctly identifying a word with a phonic element does not necessarily mean that the student could identify the same phonic elements in other words. For example, the student may read the word *hawk* correctly but not be able to generalize to another *aw* word such as *claw*.

The assessment is an individually administered oral test in which students read words in a list. The

Table 25.1   Word-Attack Skills Test

__ 1.	(th)	bath	__ 21a.		happier	__ 41.	(ness)	darkness
__ 2.	(er)	matter	__ 21b.	(y)	funniest	__ 42.	(tion)	invention
__ 3.	(ing)	handing	__ 21c.		cried	__ 43.	(ist)	artist
__ 4.	(sh)	shop	__ 22.	(ay)	pray	__ 44.	(ible)	sensible
__ 5a.		handed	__ 23.	(ou)	proud	__ 45.	(age)	package
__ 5b.	(ed)	licked	__ 24.	(ir)	thirst	__ 46.	(sion)	mission
__ 5c.		hopped	__ 25.	(ur)	curb	__ 47.	(ence)	sentence
__ 6.	(wh)	when	__ 26a.		taped	__ 48.	(ish)	selfish
__ 7.	(qu)	quiz	__ 26b.	(VCe)	hoping	__ 49.	(ation)	vacation
__ 8.	(ol)	fold	__ 26c.		timer	__ 50.	(pre)	preschool
__ 9.	(y)	sunny	__ 27.	(kn)	knock	__ 51.	(ex)	expect
__ 10.	(est)	biggest	__ 28.	(oi)	boil	__ 52.	(over)	overtime
__ 11.	(oa)	loan	__ 29.	(oy)	enjoy	__ 53.	(ion)	million
__ 12.	(ar)	cart	__ 30.	(ph)	graph	__ 54.	(ship)	friendship
__ 13a.		fine	__ 31.	(wr)	wrap	__ 55.	(com)	compare
__ 13b.	(VCe)	hope	__ 32.	(au)	haunt	__ 56.	(ure)	adventure
__ 13c.		cane	__ 33.	(aw)	hawk	__ 57.	(ive)	detective
__ 14.	(ea)	neat	__ 34.	(con)	confuse	__ 58.	(ac)	accuse
__ 15.	(oo)	toot	__ 35.	(ment)	payment	__ 59.	(ous)	joyous
__ 16.	(le)	candle	__ 36.	(teen)	sixteen	__ 60.	(inter)	interfere
__ 17.	(ee)	meet	__ 37.	(ful)	handful	__ 61.	(for)	forward
__ 18.	(ai)	pain	__ 38.	(dis)	distant	__ 62.	(ize)	realize
__ 19.	(ch)	lunch	__ 39.	(able)	enjoyable			
__ 20.	(or)	port	__ 40.	(less)	useless			

words are ordered according to the sequences we recommended for introducing phonic and structural skills. Each word is designed to test a specific phonic or structural skill. The element tested is written in parentheses in front of the word.

The teacher would make a list of the words in regular sized print. This student page would not include the elements in the parentheses in Table 25.1.

Administering the Test

The teacher gives the student a copy of the test, and asks the student to read the words beginning with number 1. The teacher records the student's performance on a copy of the test. The teacher and student should be situated so that the student cannot see the teacher recording on the record sheet.

If a student correctly identifies a word, the teacher writes a plus sign (+) on the line in front of the word. If a student misidentifies a word, the teacher writes the student's response in the space. If the student does not respond to a word within 3 sec-

onds, the teacher can tell the student the word and count it as an incorrect response by writing N.R. for "No Response." The teacher has the student read until the student misses four consecutive words. Class results can be summarized on the group-record form (see Table 25.2).

Informal Reading Inventory

An informal reading inventory (IRI) is a criterion-referenced test constructed by selecting representative passages from the reading series being used in the classroom. One purpose of administering an IRI is to determine the appropriate lesson in the reading series at which to begin instruction. This lesson is usually referred to as the student's *instructional level.*

Constructing the IRI

The IRI is constructed by selecting excerpts from various lessons in the student readers. During the first-, second-, and third-grade levels of most basals, the

Table 25.2 Group-Record Form

Element	Student											
1. th												
2. er												
3. ing												
4. sh												
5. ed												
6. wh												
7. qu												
8. ol												
9. y												
10. est												
11. oa												
12. ar												
13. VCe												
14. ea												
15. oo												
16. le												
17. ee												
18. ai												
19. ch												
20. or												
21. Yderiv.												
22. ay												
23. ou												
24. ir												
25. ur												
26. VCederiv.												
27. kn												
28. oi												
29. oy												
30. ph												
31. wr												
32. au												
33. aw												
34. con												
35. ment												
36. teen												
37. ful												
38. dis												
39. able												
40. less												
41. ness												
42. tion												
43. ist												
44. ible												
45. age												
46. sion												
47. ence												
48. ish												
49. ation												
50. pre												
51. ex												
52. over												
53. ion												
54. ship												
55. com												
56. ure												
57. ive												
58. ac												
59. ous												
60. inter												
61. for												
62. ize												

312

stories become progressively more difficult as the program progresses from beginning to end. The teacher selects a 200-word passage from each 30th lesson.

Starting at fourth grade, the structure of reading books changes. In most programs, the difficulty level of stories does not increase as you progress through the book. A story early in the fourth-grade book may be more difficult than a story appearing later in the fourth-grade book. Since the structure of the fourth-grade and higher-level books differs from first-through third-grade-level books, the way a teacher selects passages for the IRI is different. Beginning at fourth grade, the teacher need select only one passage representative of the stories in the reader for each grade level. We recommend selecting a 200-word passage that does not contain any unusual proper nouns (e.g., difficult-to-decode names or phrases).

The teacher should make a photocopy of each excerpt and prepare one student booklet with the excerpts ordered from lowest to highest grades. For the teacher's use, a separate booklet containing all of the excerpts should be created for each student.

Administering the Informal Reading Inventory

The student should be seated at a desk facing away from the rest of the class. The teacher should be seated to the side of the student so that the student cannot see the teacher recording errors.

Where to Begin

The teacher can use the student's performance on the diagnostic word-attack skills test as a guide at what passage excerpt to begin. (See Table 25.3 for a schedule telling at what level to begin testing.)

1. The teacher explains the purpose of and procedure for the test: "I want to find out at what lesson to start your reading instruction. I am going to ask you to read from different stories. When I say start, begin reading aloud here (indicate). Read across the page. Try to read each word. If you come to a word you don't know, I'll tell it to you. Be sure to do your best reading. Are there any questions?" (The teacher points to where student begins.) "Start now."

2. The teacher should use a stopwatch to time the student on each excerpt. The teacher starts the watch when the student begins to read, and stops it after 1 minute.

3. If a student hesitates more than 3 seconds on a word, the teacher should tell the student the word.

4. If a student misses a word, the teacher says nothing (no correction) unless the student tries to figure out the missed word and hesitates for 3 seconds. After 3 seconds, the teacher says the word.

Table 25.3 Schedule to Determine Beginning Point for IRI

Words Correct on Diagnostic Word-Attack Skills Test	Where to Begin IRI Testing
0–10 words	Beginning first-grade level. Also, administer the beginning-level diagnostic test (see Table 12.2).
11–20 words	Late-first-grade level.
21–30 words	Mid-second-grade level.
31–40 words	Late-second-grade level.
41–50 words	Early-third-grade level.
51–60 words	Late-third-grade level.
61–65 words	Early-fourth-grade level.
66 or more words	Fourth-grade level or higher. Test students on material for their grade level.

5. If a student is reading a passage very laboriously and is making many errors, the student does not have to read the entire passage. The teacher can stop the student and present an earlier passage.

Recording

As the student reads, the teacher records any errors the student makes on the teacher's copy of the excerpt. The following are suggestions for recording errors:

- Student misidentifies a word: The teacher writes the word the student said over the word.

- Student is unable to decode a word within 3 seconds: The teacher writes "N.R." over the word.

- Student omits a word: The teacher writes a little "o" above the omitted word.

- Student inserts a word: The teacher writes a ∧ (caret) where the insertion occurred.

- Student misidentifies, but immediately self-corrects: The teacher writes "S.C." over the word.

The teacher summarizes the student's performance after the student has completed the excerpt. The teacher records the total number of errors the student made. (Self-corrections need not be considered errors, unless students make an excessive number of self-corrects) The teacher also records the number of words read correctly. These numbers can be written on the photocopied excerpt.

What to Do

If a student reads below a 95% accuracy rate, or is reading at a rate lower than the desired rate for the grade level of the passage (see page 193 in Chapter 18), the teacher has the student read the next lower-level passage. The teacher continues testing lower-level passages until the student reads the passage with 95% (or higher) accuracy and with the desired rate.

If a student reads a passage at a 95% (or higher) accuracy rate and above the reading rate for that level, the teacher tests the next higher-level passage. The teacher continues testing higher-level excerpts until the student goes over the error limit or does not meet the fluency criteria.

Written Comprehension Assessment

The third screening assessment we recommend administering is a written comprehension assessment. To prepare this assessment, the teacher would select several written comprehension exercises from material at the student's instructional level (as determined by the student's performance on the IRI). The purpose of this assessment is to provide the teacher additional information in deciding how to group a borderline student and to indicate any students who may have severe comprehension deficits.

The comprehension exercises selected for the assessment should be ones requiring little explanation from the teacher. What the students are expected to do should be obvious. If possible, the teacher should try to select some items that test main idea, inference, sequencing, as well as literal comprehension. A test might include a mix of multiple-choice items and items that require extended written answers so that a teacher can also receive information on the students' writing.

Grouping and Placement

During the reading-to-learn stage, instruction can be provided in larger groups than during the learning-to-read stage. As much as possible, instructional groups should include children at the same instructional level. We recommend no more than two groups per classroom in the intermediate grades. Children performing strongly at grade level can be taught through whole-class instruction beginning the third year of instruction.

In schools where classrooms are formed by other criteria than students' academic level, teachers may find that they have a large range of skill levels in their classroom. In such cases, we recommend that a 150-minute language arts period be established where children switch classrooms for instruction. Teachers working with the higher-performing children would have the most children for reading instruction. Teachers working with the lower-performing children would have the fewest students in their class during reading instruction.

As group size gets larger, teachers should be prepared to provide daily extra instruction in a small-group setting for children who are struggling with any particular skill. The small-group session might last just 10 to 15 minutes while the rest of the class works independently.

Time for Instruction

The number of minutes allocated for reading instruction should be based on how much instruction will be necessary to enable children to reach grade level standards. Each year as children move up in the grades, the amount they have to learn to cover a year's content grows. For example, there is much more new content to be learned in fifth grade than in second grade. Teachers working with children who come from social and home environments that provide little instruction outside of school need to take the responsibility for ensuring that students receive sufficient instruction during the school day to learn all needed information to be at grade level by the end of the school year. For teachers working with large numbers of at-risk students, we recommend at least 150 minutes daily be devoted to reading/language arts instruction with most of this time devoted to direct teaching.

The amount of instructional time for children reading significantly below level should be adequate for children to make significantly more than a year's progress during a school year. In some cases, a daily afternoon reading period, and a daily after-school period may be needed in addition to the 150 minutes a day, which is usually scheduled in the morning.

Adapting Instructional Materials to Meet Needs of At-Risk Students

Teachers working with at-risk students will need to significantly modify most commercially produced materials. As mentioned earlier, most basal-reading programs are designed in a manner that can be described as "too little of too much." This creates problems for many students, particularly at-risk students, because they receive neither enough practice to develop mastery nor enough review to facilitate retention. A second major problem found in basal workbooks is that too much is introduced at one time. The fast introduction can result in student and teacher frustration. A third problem is the lack of guidance provided for the teacher regarding how to teach particular skills.

Teachers can modify commercial programs by incorporating direct instruction principles and procedures. The extent of the modifications needed will depend on (1) how explicitly and systematically the skill and strategies are taught, and (2) the needs of the particular students with whom the teacher is working. Teachers working with higher-performing students may find a particular program to be adequate, while teachers working with more instructionally naïve students will find the program problematic. Teachers must be prepared to make needed modifications if students struggle.

The major steps in making modifications are: (1) determining what to teach on a daily basis, (2) providing more explicit teaching of strategies, (3) providing guided practice to help students apply the strategies, and (4) providing extra practice to enable students to develop mastery and retain information.

Below are specific suggestions for each component of reading instruction.

Phonics Instruction

The teacher examines upcoming lessons to determine if phonic and structural element are clearly taught and if there is sufficient practice. Likewise, the teacher examines irregular words that will appear in upcoming stories to determine if there is sufficient preteaching of words students will not be likely to decode.

If a teacher is using a program that does not provide systematic instruction and practice in word-attack skills, the teacher needs to construct supplementary exercises to teach the skills. The teacher can use the student performance data from the word-attack skills assessment to plan instruction. The teacher refers to the group-record form (see Table 25.2) as a guide to setting up a sequence for introducing phonics skills. The teacher begins the supplementary program with the first phonic or structural element that one or more students missed on the diagnostic test of word-attack skills. (A zero or NR in a column indicates a missed word on the test.) Before spending significant time teaching a new skill, the teacher might retest the students who missed the word containing that tested skill. The retest is to certify that the student does not know the skill. The teacher retests by selecting several words containing that element and having the student read those words.

Appendix A includes a list of words the teacher can use in selecting words for teaching the various elements. When preparing word-list exercises, the teacher should include adequate discrimination practice, presenting not only the new element, but also reviewing the previously introduced elements. The formats for presenting these skills appear in Chapters 15 and 16, in which we discuss phonics and structural analysis.

The teacher focuses on a new element for several days. When the students are able to read words with these new skills, the teacher looks at the chart and determines the next phonic element a student did not know and teaches that element.

Oral Passage Reading and Fluency Instruction

Oral passage reading and fluency-development exercises should be incorporated into daily lessons until students can read fourth-grade materials at a rate of about 135 words per minute with 97% accuracy. The procedures in Chapter 18 can be incorporated into daily lessons. Children would do repeated readings to develop fluency. Teachers would model and students would practice reading with expression.

Vocabulary and Background Knowledge

At-risk children often have difficulty with comprehension exercises because programs do not adequately preteach critical vocabulary and background knowledge. Teachers should examine passages at least several days prior to having students read them. The teacher notes the words that students are not likely to know the meaning of. The teacher compares these words with the words the program presents in vocabulary exercises. If the program does not provide for teaching of the important unknown words, the teacher supplements the vocabulary teaching in the program using the procedures specified in Chapter 20. The teacher would do the same procedure with critical background information, determining what knowledge students will need in upcoming comprehension exercises and creating and implementing exercises to teach this knowledge if the program does not.

Comprehension

Commercial programs vary significantly in the degree that they provide the teacher with specific in-depth guidance on how to teach comprehension. Teachers can use the procedures similar to those described in Chapters 21, 22, and 23 to provide for explicit teaching of strategies. Teachers should examine the teacher's guide days before they are to teach a specific skill and determine the adequacy of teaching the suggested procedures.

Feedback and Corrections

In the upper grades, a larger percentage of student responses are written. A system through which children receive timely feedback on their written work needs to be part of the daily lesson. Such a system should have the following components:

1. Student work should be marked daily. With older students, the teacher can provide the answers orally and have children mark their own papers. The children should use colored marking pencils when marking their papers. The teacher circulates around the room in order to ensure that children are honestly and accurately marking their papers. The teacher randomly checks about one-fifth of the group individually to communicate to children that checking accurately is important.

2. Students should redo any items missed. Note: If students are unable to figure out an answer, they circle the item or write a question mark.

3. The teacher (or a helper) inspects the items the student redid to see if they are correct.

4. The teacher helps students on items they are unable to answer correctly, reteaching the content. Without this last step, children will keep on having problems with the same content. Teachers should look for items missed by a number of children and reteach that content to the entire group.

Record Keeping and Motivation

The students' performance on daily independent reading work should be recorded, as a percentage correct or with some other numerical or letter grade. Recording student performance serves two purposes. First, it provides teachers with specific information on which to determine how well a student is progressing and helps identify children who are struggling. Second, the data on student daily performance can serve to establish a motivation system.

Teachers, particularly those working with at-risk children, will find that some students' performance can be significantly affected by the presence of a system that provides the student with recognition or reward for good performance. With higher-performing, intrinsically motivated students, the recognition can be minimal. Sending a "good-work" letter home for meeting a specified criterion (e.g., 90% or better) for specified periods (e.g., 10

lessons) will usually be sufficient. With less motivated students, a more powerful reinforcement system may be needed. In addition to letters home for good work, rewards such as stickers and points towards earning free time can be powerful motivators.

Progress-Monitoring Assessments

Each few weeks during the school year, the teacher should administer an assessment to determine if children have in fact learned what was taught over the recent lessons. During the first three to four years of reading instruction, we recommend administering oral-reading fluency and accuracy assessments to determine if students are developing sufficient fluency. The teacher selects a passage from the previous lessons and has the students read for 1 minute. In order to be sure that the students are generalizing to other reading materials, the teacher might also test the students on materials from commercially available oral-reading fluency assessment packages several times a year. Comprehension skills and strategies that were recently introduced should also be tested regularly.

Diagnosing

If students are not functioning at about a 85% to 90% accuracy level on their comprehension assignments, teachers need to determine what is causing students difficulty. There are five main reasons why students may be struggling:

1. Motivation

2. Word attack or fluency problems

3. Recall problems

4. Lack of background knowledge or critical vocabulary

5. Lack of appropriate strategy

Teachers should be quite cautious in assuming that errors are caused by lack of motivation. Sometimes students seem like they are not trying when, in fact, they do not know what to do or lack prerequisite skills. In order to determine if motivation is contributing to poor performance, the teacher can put in place some special big rewards for good performance on assignments for several days. If a student who has done poorly on similar assignments does well when a big reward is offered, lack of motivation may be a reason for poor performance. A procedure to increase the student's motivation can be instituted if it appears that motivation is a problem. If students do not respond to increased motivation, the teacher investigates to determine specific problems causing students to struggle.

Oral-reading fluency and word-attack skills should be checked for students performing poorly on comprehension. If a student makes many errors, the teacher would administer the word-attack skills test (page 311) and if necessary provide teaching on phonic elements and also implement motivation procedures to encourage accurate reading. If the student reads slowly or without expression, the teacher would provide extra work on fluency (see Chapter 18).

If the students can read orally with few errors and at a rate which does not interfere with comprehension, the teacher investigates to determine if recall is a problem. Some children do not attend to what they are reading. These children do not remember simple details of the story. The teacher can determine if recall is a problem by examining the students work over a period of days and noting if the child misses simple factual questions. For children with this problem, teachers should ask questions more frequently during passage reading exercises, gradually expanding the number of sentences students read before questions are asked.

If students fail to answer simple recall questions accurately, the teacher checks to determine if students are missing questions because of lack of knowledge of critical vocabulary or background knowledge. The teacher does this by again examining missed items.

Students who need more work on vocabulary, background knowledge, or strategy application can be worked with in a small group. In this small-group session, the teacher more explicitly presents critical vocabulary, background knowledge, and/or strategies to prepare students for upcoming class exercises. The teacher should preteach skills and information to enable the student to be successful on upcoming class work.

✤ Application Exercises

1. Examine how comprehension is taught in a series of five consecutive lessons in a commercial program at second-grade level or above. Indicate what specific skills are presented in the five lessons. Describe how the following components are incorporated into the lessons: in-depth treatment of content, teaching of prerequisite background knowledge and vocabulary, use of explicit and clear strategies with mediated scaffolding, inclusion of monitoring and feedback procedures, and readability.

2. Examine a 20-lesson sequence at the beginning of a second-grade basal program. Indicate the letter-sound relationships that are taught in those lessons. Describe the sequence, the rate of introduction, the teaching procedure, and the amount of practice provided. Indicate what modifications need to be made.

3. At the beginning of the school year, a teacher wants to determine the instructional level of the students in her class. The teacher administers the word-attack skills assessment (Table 25.1) then administers an informal reading inventory.

   Student A: The student reads 15 words correctly on the word-attack assessment. At which level should the passage be for the first excerpt the child reads? In 1 minute the child reads 58 words. What should the teacher do next?

   Student B: The student reads 32 words correctly on the word-attack assessment. At which level should the passage be for the first excerpt the child reads? In 1 minute the child reads 96 words. What should the teacher do next?

Corrective Readers

The results of the 1998 National Assessment of Educational Progress (NAEP) identified 38% of fourth-graders and 26% of eighth-graders as reading at a "below-basic" level. This below-basic level signifies that a student exhibits little or no mastery of the knowledge or skills necessary to perform work at that particular grade level. These statistics indicate that scores of children in elementary schools, middle schools, and high schools need intensive, carefully thought-out interventions if they are to have a chance to develop the literacy needed to be economically viable in our society.

The statistics on this high failure rate do not directly tell the emotional toll being taken on these children. When children are not able to do grade-level work, the school experience is likely to be damaging to them emotionally. Throughout the school day, they will find themselves unable to successfully complete assigned tasks. Children who have fallen behind in reading will usually also have fallen behind in a number of academic areas because of their reading problems.

Teachers and administrators in the late elementary grades, middle school, and high school need to be ready to meet the needs of children who enter their classrooms performing significantly below grade level. Meeting the needs of these students will take a coordinated use of school resources. While individual teachers have a responsibility to meet the needs of all their students, the faculty and administration at a school need to work as a team if students who are behind are to be able to make the needed accelerated progress in all areas of literacy.

Guidelines for Establishing a Comprehensive Program for Children Who Are Behind

Intervene Early

Administer screening assessments at the beginning of the school year to identify children who are performing below grade level. During the school year, administer diagnostic assessments to children who are having difficulty with grade-level work to determine specific skill areas that need to be addressed.

Examine the data from these assessments to identify children who are behind and begin intervention programs immediately for these children.

Provide Extra Instructional Time

Schedule sufficient instructional time to enable students to make more than a year's progress each year in all areas in which they are behind. For children who are behind, we recommend a morning language arts period of 150 minutes, and if at all possible a 30- to 60-minute afternoon period. In addition, after-school and summer instruction should be scheduled for children who need even more extra instruction to reach grade level.

Utilize Small-Group Instruction

Provide instruction in small-group settings for older children who are still in the *learning-to-read stage*, or who are highly inattentive. Make grouping flexible, meaning children can be moved to higher- or lower-performing groups when the student's performance indicates a need for a change. In order to facilitate this flexibility, school schedules need to be coordinated. Meeting the academic needs of students must be a first priority in establishing school schedules.

Use Effective Instructional Materials

Use instructional materials that have proven most effective with students comparable to those being served in the school. The American Federation of Teachers website *(aft.org)* has displayed reports prepared on programs that have data to validate their effectiveness.

Create a Comprehensive Aligned Program

The intervention program should include instruction in all the major areas of reading instruction: phonics; comprehension; fluency; vocabulary; and for children still reading at the beginning level, phonemic awareness as well as relevant language arts topics such as spelling and writing. The instruction should be carefully aligned.

Administer Progress-Monitoring Assessments Frequently

Administer progress-monitoring assessments at least every second week to ensure that students are progressing adequately and learning what is being taught. These assessments can begin with a short test that samples important skills taught to date. Children who do poorly on the screening should receive more in-depth assessment to determine which specific skills have not been mastered. Children having problems on previously taught skills should receive extra instruction on that content. Include oral-reading fluency assessments since oral-reading fluency is a strong predictor of future academic success.

Group for Maximum Efficiency

Arrange instructional groups so that all children are at the same instructional level. Teachers can be most efficient in accelerating the performance of a group of children when all the children in the instructional group are at the same instructional level. Sometimes schools will send all children in a particular grade who are behind to a resource room or special reading teacher for instruction. This arrangement is not efficient because there is likely to be great disparity among the children's instructional level. We recommend arranging the scheduling and grouping of students so that children at the same level receive instruction together. If children are sent to a resource room, the school schedule should be arranged so that children at the same instructional level from several classes go to the resource room at the same time.

Include a Motivational Component

Struggling readers are often unmotivated and understandably so. Think what it would be like to be in a failure situation day after day. No matter how hard you tried, you didn't succeed. Think what that failure would do to your self-image and of how you might react. Then think of the struggling reader who has failed day after day for years, and it is understandable why such a student may not be intrinsically motivated, and it is reasonable to assume that special consideration must be given to motivation.

Foremost in establishing motivation is providing a program in which the student can succeed. Without daily success, it is difficult to change a student's attitude.

In establishing a motivation system, set daily goals that are reachable for the student. With reasonable effort, the student can reach the goal. Initially, teachers can implement a point system or contract that states the student will receive a certain grade, privilege, or prize each week or two. The point system or contract must be carefully designed so that earning the grade or privilege is neither too difficult nor too easy. The grade or privilege must be a functional reward, which means the student will work for it.

Ensure Well-Trained Teaching Personnel

In the past, students who were struggling were often sent to volunteers or other untrained personnel who, with little guidance, were asked to help the students. Volunteers and paraprofessionals can perform very useful functions such as listening to the students read and presenting structured small group and one-on-one tutoring programs from highly prescriptive reading programs. However, careful guidance and direction are required along with careful ongoing monitoring of student performance. Professional development should be provided for the paraprofessionals and volunteers prior to them using a program. The initial training should be followed up by observations and coaching while they work with students. Students with very severe deficits should generally not be assigned to volunteers.

Constructing a Program for Children Reading Below Grade Level

The reading program should include all the components of reading instruction: phonemic awareness, phonics, fluency, vocabulary, and comprehension, with spelling and writing instruction aligned with the reading instruction. (Phonemic awareness would be taught only to children who are at the beginning reading stage.) The materials used in the program need to have all the elements of what make a reading program effective (see pages 120 and 308). Four additional factors should be considered in constructing a program for older students who are behind:

- First, the program must prioritize the essential decoding and comprehension skills.

- Second, the program should be designed to interest older children. Older students often reject pictures and story themes designed for first- or second-graders.

- Third, the materials must be designed so that students may be placed at their specific instructional level. A sixth-grade student reading at second-grade level needs to be taught different content than a sixth-grade child reading at fourth-grade level.

- Fourth, the program should be designed to counter common faulty strategies that children reading below grade level are likely to have developed.

Students who cannot read acceptably at their respective grade levels can be classified in one of the following four categories: nonreaders, confused decoders, moderately developed decoders, and adequate decoders with comprehension difficulty. Correctly classifying students in one of these categories is extremely important because the different categories call for different instruction.

Programs for Nonreaders

Nonreaders are children who are virtually unable to decode. They may be able to identify 50 to 100 words by sight; however, they have no generalizable strategy for decoding words.

These older struggling students should be placed in a program specifically designed to teach beginning-level reading skills to the older nonreader. The program would teach the same skills as in a research-based beginning reading program; phonemic awareness, letter-sound correspondence, sounding out regular words, introduction of common irregular words and passage reading. Phonemic awareness skills, particularly blending and segmenting, would be integrated with the introduction of letter-sound correspondences and word attack. A good deal of practice would be provided with decodable text. The main difference between instruction for the nonreading older student and the beginning student would involve the packaging of the materials and story content. The materials should not look babyish; similarly, story themes should not be too childish.

Concurrently, with the teaching of decoding skills, the overall program should include a component that orally teaches vocabulary and comprehension skills. A more in-depth overview of this language instruction appears at the end of this section.

Confused Decoders

Confused decoders are students who know nearly all individual letter-sound correspondences and can blend sounds to create words. These students, however, do not understand the relationship between the arrangement of letters in a word and the pronunciation of the word. They will say "hat" for *hate* and "ran" instead of *rain.* Confused decoders will demonstrate an overreliance on context usage. They will make errors caused by looking at a letter or two, then saying a word that makes sense in that context (e.g., saying "The boy is happy" for a sentence that reads, "The boy is hungry."). They will

omit or add words in sentences. They will not attend to endings of words, calling *hopping* "hopped" or *played* "plays." They will seem to vacillate in their approach, reading a word correctly in one sentence and incorrectly in the next sentence.

A program for confused decoders need *not* include sounding out, but should concentrate on teaching phonic and structural units such as letter combinations, common affixes, the VCe rule, and how to apply this phonic and structural knowledge to reading words in isolation and in passages. The program also should include passage-reading exercises designed to encourage students to read accurately. These exercises would include specially written stories that are unpredictably written. The style of the writing is not repetitive or predictable regarding what word comes next. Figure 26.1 includes a story designed for the confused reader from a widely used program. Note how a reader must carefully examine the words to read the text. Fluency instruction should be incorporated into the program once students have developed high levels of accuracy

As with the program for nonreaders, concurrently with the teaching of decoding skills, the overall program should include a component that initially teaches comprehension skills. In addition, spelling and writing instruction needs to be aligned with the decoding instruction.

Moderately Developed Decoders

Moderately developed decoders will have mastered most of the phonics skills taught in the learning-to-read stage. They know letter-sound relationships for individual sounds and many letter combinations, are able to read words with a VCe pattern and can read most two-syllable words formed by adding common suffixes to base words. These children, however, have difficulty with longer multisyllabic words and words containing less common letter combinations. Their difficulty with longer words slows down their fluency. When they try to read quickly, they tend to make a number of errors.

A program for these students should include teaching of phonic elements the students do not

Figure 26.1

1	cold st<u>or</u>e <u>that</u> r<u>ea</u>d <u>b</u>ack s<u>oo</u>n j<u>o</u>b b<u>ea</u>ns h<u>e</u>lped h<u>a</u>m bett<u>er</u> thi<u>ng</u>s mu<u>ch</u>	3	<u>Gretta</u> <u>Chee</u> let's day pay played stay someone saying door bigger said I've cook other some don't can't folks didn't another their became one
2	name like came note bone home		

4

CHEE, THE DOG

Gretta got a little dog. She named the dog Chee. Chee got bigger and bigger each day.

On a very cold day, Gretta said, "Chee, I must go to the store. You stay home. I will be back."

Chee said, "Store, lots, of, for, no."

Then Gretta said, "Did I hear that dog say things?"

Chee said, "Say things can I do."

Gretta said, "Dogs don't say things. So I must not hear things well."

But Chee did say things. Gretta left the dog at home. When Gretta came back, Chee was sitting near the door. [1]

Gretta said, "That dog is bigger than she was."

Then the dog said, "Read, read for me of left."

Gretta said, "Is that dog saying that she can read?" Gretta got a pad and made a note for the dog. The note said, "Dear Chee, if you can read this note I will hand you a bag of bones."

Gretta said, "Let's see if you can read."

Chee said, "Dear Chee, if you can read this note, I will ham you a bag for beans." [1]

Gretta said, "She can read, but she can't read well. Ho, ho."

Chee became very mad. She said, "For note don't read ho ho."

Gretta said, "Chee gets mad when I say ho, ho."

Chee said, "Yes, no go ho ho."

Then Gretta felt sad. She said, "I didn't mean to make you mad. I don't like you to be sad. I will help you say things well."

Then Chee said, "Yes, well, of say for things."

So every day, Gretta helped Chee say things. She helped Chee read, too. [1]

Chee got better and better at saying things. And she got better at reading. And she got bigger and bigger. When she was one year old, she was bigger than Gretta.

On a hot day Gretta left Chee at home, but when she got back, Chee met her at the door. "Did you have fun at your job?" Chee asked.

"Yes, I did," Gretta said.

"I don't have much fun at home," Chee said. "I think I will get a job. I don't like to stay at home."

"Dogs can't have jobs," Gretta said.

Chee said, "You have a job. So I will get a job, too." [1]

From Siegfried Engelmann, et al., *Corrective Reading Program: Decoding Strategies, Students' Book B-1,* pp. 26–27. Copyright © 1988 by Science Research Associates. Reprinted by permission.

know. In addition, the program should teach prefixes and suffixes and how to read multisyllabic words and include a good deal of work on increasing student accuracy and fluency in reading passages.

Adequate Decoders With Poor Comprehension

Some students will be able to decode grade-level text with acceptable fluency and accuracy but will have difficulty with comprehension. Quite often these children will not have needed vocabulary and background knowledge and will require systematic and explicit teaching in these areas as well as the teaching of overt comprehension strategies.

Commercial Materials for the Child Who Is Reading Below Grade Level

While numerous commercial materials are designed and available for use with the older child who reads poorly, the challenge is finding materials that can be combined to construct a comprehensive program that teaches all components in an aligned manner. Many commercial materials just deal with one component of reading instruction. For example, a commercial program may teach word-attack skills, but not have decodable text to provide practice on using this knowledge in reading text.

Recently, as the accountability movement has brought to the forefront the reality that there are many older children performing below grade level, publishers have begun to develop more comprehensive programs that are aligned with the scientific research. Two programs developed by persons who have been connected with the University of Oregon have proved particularly effective.

The REACH system incorporates a number of Direct Instruction programs developed by Siegfried Engelmann. The REACH system is a comprehensive program that integrates decoding, comprehension, spelling, vocabulary development, and writing into an integrated multilevel curriculum for older children who are behind. Included in the system are *The Corrective Reading Decoding and*

Comprehension Series, Spelling Through Morphographs and several levels of *Reasoning and Writing*. The REACH system is published by SRA. It includes a sequence that can be used over several years and includes screening and placement assessments as well as progress-monitoring assessments.

Sopris West Educational Services, a publishing company that is committed to publishing programs with a strong research base, publishes a program called REWARDS developed by Anita Archer, Mary Gleason, and Vicky Vachon. REWARDS is designed for the moderately developed decoder. REWARDS teaches students to decode multisyllabic words and includes stories aligned with word-attack exercises to provide practice on utilizing the word-attack strategies. The program also integrates work on fluency.

A number of other programs are available. For information on various programs, examine the National Institute for Literacy website at *www.nifl.gov.*

Language and Comprehension Instruction

Language and comprehension instruction for children performing below grade level needs to be very carefully planned and will require the use of systematically constructed materials. Sophisticated comprehension skills can be taught orally to poor readers while the children are learning beginning level decoding skills. For example, in the comprehension component of the *Corrective Reading Series* developed by Engelmann (1999), the following skill areas are taught orally: analogies and/or logic, classification, deductions, definitions, descriptions, inductions, opposites, statement inference, and true-false.

A mix of text-based comprehension and oral comprehension can be taught as children master beginning decoding. The materials students are to read must be at the students' instructional level if students are to be successful.

Engelmann's comprehension component in the *Corrective Reading Series* provides an excellent illustration of how oral and carefully controlled text comprehension can be aligned with decoding instruction for the poor reader. The teaching is very explicit and systematic. It prioritizes content that students need for future success. Following instructions and analytical skills are stressed. There is a carefully designed sequence in which content taught in early lessons lays the foundation for what comes in later lessons.

Students With Limited English Proficiency

The question of how to best meet the instructional needs of children with limited English proficiency (LEP) is a serious concern. Children who enter school without English proficiency and come from a home in which English is not the primary language are at-risk. The level of risk appears to be in relation to their literacy level in their native language.

The level of literacy in a student's native language impacts their literacy development in English. Teachers must assess and take advantage of the knowledge that students bring to school and use it as a building block during reading instruction. Teachers should assess the students' knowledge in their native language if at all possible before beginning instruction.

When providing instruction to LEP children, it is important to keep in mind that these students are doing twice the cognitive work of native speakers during reading instruction because as well as learning the content being taught, the child is attending to the sounds, meanings, and structures of a new language. The double demands of learning content and a second language should not be underestimated.

Careful coordination needs to occur between the teaching of oral-language skills in English and the teaching of reading. Teachers want to ensure that children understand words they will be reading in English. Reading instruction should be explicit and systematic and include all critical elements identified by the National Reading Panel.

Gersten and Baker (2000) found that LEP instructional interventions with the largest effects in reading were heavily rooted in principles verified by the instructional research literature. Some of these principles included the effective use of time, the provision of frequent, clear feedback to students, and adjusting instruction to the students. These strategies are helpful to all students, but especially to LEP students and struggling readers.

Tutoring Programs

Some tutoring programs have been utilized to improve the performance of children who are behind in reading. Volunteers, other students, and paraprofessionals have been used as tutors. Care must be taken in establishing such programs. Below are guidelines that can be used in establishing a tutoring program:

Guideline 1. Provide tutors working with poor readers with an explicit and systematic reading program that is research-based and highly prescriptive, providing specific guidance to the tutor as well as providing books that the student can read.

Guideline 2. Help tutors figure out where to begin tutoring. A placement test should be included with directions that clearly indicate where to begin instruction.

Guideline 3. Provide systematic training for the tutor. During the training, tutors should see models of what actual tutoring sessions look like and practice presenting lessons so that they are prepared for common difficult situations likely to be encountered. Provide coaching to the tutor during which the tutor is observed working with the student and feedback is provided to the tutor. Training for tutors who work with non-readers needs to be more comprehensive. The tutor needs to know how to say sounds correctly, blend sounds to produce a word, and how to respond when students misidentify a sound or word. Tutors who have difficulty with sounds or blending should not work with children who are nonreaders.

Guideline 4. Schedule enough tutoring time so that there can be significant learning. Tutoring would ideally be scheduled for about 30 minutes every day, but no less than three times a week.

Guideline 5. A supervisor should monitor the progress of students. Measuring student progress and using those findings to adjust tutoring is an important ingredient in improving results.

Below are several tutoring programs that have been successful when well implemented:

- *Project PALS: Peer Assisted Learning System* was developed for children in grades 3 through 12 and adult learners. The curriculum used is the *SRA Corrective Reading* program. The program stemmed from a project in which higher-performing high school students provided tutoring to their peers who were struggling in reading. For information on Project PALS contact Dr. Nancy Marchand-Martella, Department of Counseling, Educational and Development Psychology, Eastern Washington University, 135 Martin Hall, Cheney, WA 99004; tel. 509-359-2821.

- *Reading One-to-One* is designed for grades 1 through 8. The program includes phonemic awareness, explicit instruction on letter-sound correspondence, sight-word practice, decodable text for beginning readers, literature for more advanced readers, comprehension exercises, and writing activities. Students are given initial and regular skill assessments for placement and advancement. For information, contact Reading One-to-One, the University of Texas in Dallas Reading One-to-One Mail Station GR 26, P.O. Box 830688, Richardson, TX 75083-0688; tel. 972-883-2023.

- *Reading For All Learners Program* (RALP) is for students reading at kindergarten through fifth-grade level. The curriculum includes phonemic awareness, explicit phonics, fluency building, explicit instruction on letter-sound correspondence, sight-word practice, and comprehension skills. Tutors receive training on how to use decodable little books with tutoring prompts in small print at the bottom of every page. A fluency building program is provided for upper elementary grades. Typical classroom materials include little books (140 decodable books move from K.0-4.0), a training video, and web and telephone assistance. Assessment and student monitoring black line masters are supplied at no charge. For more information on the program see the web site *www.usu.edu/teach/read*.

✎ Application Exercises

1. Explain the difference between a confused decoder and a moderately developed decoder and the differences in the programs appropriate for each student.
2. Explain how instruction for the third-grade nonreader would differ from instruction for the first-grade nonreader. Also explain how instruction for the older and younger nonreader would be similar.
3. Examine a commercial program designed for children at their grade or higher who are reading significantly below their grade level. Describe the assessment procedure for placing children at their instructional level and indicate any modifications that appear to be necessary. Examine five consecutive lessons in the program. Indicate the objectives of the five lessons. Describe how the following design elements are implemented: clarity of teacher presentation, example selection, practice and review, and sequence for introducing skills. Describe modifications that you would make in these lessons.

Research on Fluency, Word Recognition and Decoding Skills, and Comprehension

Late Primary and Intermediate Grades

This chapter includes an overview and description of some important research findings relevant to reading instruction after the beginning stage. Our review is not meant to be exhaustive. Such a review would necessitate more space than is available. The creation of the Internet and the realization of the importance of relying on research to guide education reform has resulted in access to quality research being much more available now than it was when the first edition of this text was written. In 2001, the No Child Left Behind Act of 2001 (P.L. 107–110) authorized The Partnership for Reading, a national reading research dissemination project. The Partnership for Reading's mission is to make scientifically-based reading research more accessible to educators, parents, policy makers, and other interested individuals. As of the writing of this edition, The Partnership for Reading web site (*http://www.nifl.gov/ partnershipforreading/*) offers a database containing abstracts of approximately 460 research studies related to the teaching of reading in grades K to 3. These studies have met high standards of research.

An overriding theme that emerges from comprehension research of the last several decades is this: Comprehension of text is dependent upon understanding the meanings of spoken words (vocabulary knowledge), accurate and fluent reading of words in text (word recognition and fluency skills), and decoding skills that enable the reader to pronounce new words as they are encountered in increasingly difficult text (phonic and structural analysis). As Vachon explained in the 1997 edition of this textbook:

> . . . . the dependence of reading comprehension on fluent word recognition cannot be ignored. Comprehension of subtle language concepts and relationships are not dependent on word recognition skills until the reader tries to comprehend those concepts and relationships as they are communicated in print. Indeed, word recognition skills lead to improved reading comprehension ability rather than the reverse (Daneman, 1991; Juel, 1991; Stanovich, 1991). According to Stanovich (1991), if fluent word recognition does not produce a clearly identified

word in working memory, "comprehension processes do not have the raw materials to operate efficiently and understanding of text will be impaired." (p. 443) Fluency is a combination of accuracy and reading rate. Word recognition fluency, while not the goal of reading instruction, is necessary for good comprehension. (p. 337)

In this overview, we present research that documents the relationships among fluency, word recognition, and comprehension before presenting a brief summary of research that is focused more exclusively on comprehension.

In the sections devoted exclusively to comprehension, we include discussions of how text organization and text structure affect students' comprehension of expository and narrative text. Particular attention is paid to how those text variables affect diverse students' comprehension and how explicit instruction in text organization facilitates their comprehension.

We conclude this chapter with summaries of research on the relationship between metacognition and reading comprehension. This includes studies which document the effectiveness of direct teaching of strategies such as summarizing, identifying main ideas, using visual imagery, and mapping narrative or expository text.

Fluency

The National Reading Panel (2000) selected reading fluency as one the five major areas of reading instruction. One of reasons the NRP gave for selecting fluency for review and analysis was the concern that children are not achieving fluency in reading. In the late 1990's the National Assessment of Educational Progress conducted a large study of the status of fluency achievement in American education (Pinnell et al., 1995). That study examined the reading fluency of a nationally representative sample of fourth-graders and found 44% of students to be disfluent even with grade-level stories that the students had read under supportive testing conditions. And furthermore, that study found a close relationship between fluency and reading comprehension.

Positive correlations between fluency and comprehension have also been reported by other researchers. Fuchs, Fuchs, and Maxwell (1998) reported that a measure of oral reading rate for text correlated .91 with reading comprehension scores from a widely used standardized measure in a sample of middle-school and junior-high-school students with reading disabilities. Jenkins, Fuchs, Fuchs, and Hosp (2001) reported that measures of oral reading rate were more highly correlated with reading comprehension scores than were measures of silent reading rate in a sample of children whose reading skills varied widely. All of these studies indicate that students who are low in fluency have difficulty getting the meaning of what they read.

Over the past three decades, our understanding of what is involved in reading fluency has been altered and enlarged. One finds, for example, in the 1974 LaBarge and Samuels's article on automatic information processing in reading, an emphasis on word recognition. More recent conceptualizations of fluency, however, have extended beyond word recognition and may embrace comprehension processes as well (Thurlow & van den Broek, 1997). In its early conception, it was recognized that fluency requires high-speed word recognition that frees a reader's cognitive resources so that the meaning of a text can be the focus of attention. However, it is now clear that fluency may also include the ability to group words appropriately into meaningful grammatical units for interpretation (Schreiber, 1980, 1987).

Repeated and Guided Repeated Oral Reading

The National Reading Panel (2000) analysis of studies measuring effects of guided oral repeated readings demonstrated positive effects on reading accuracy and reading fluency. The repeated reading technique was found to be the only method for which there is consistent, positive support of effectiveness in increasing reading fluency. Analysis indicated that repeated reading procedures have a clear impact on the reading ability of nonimpaired readers through at least grade 4, as well as on students with various kinds of reading problems through high school. Although repeated reading of connected text is the most commonly used application of the repeated reading technique, several kinds of fluency-oriented practice have been found to produce gains in reading fluency. Tan and Nicholson (1997) and Levy, Abello, and Lysynchuk (1997) showed that practice reading single words generalized to increases in fluency for text containing those words.

Silent Independent Reading

Fluent readers are likely to read more. Taylor and her colleagues (Taylor et al., 1999a) found that high-achieving primary classes allotted more time for independent reading. For example, in a longitudinal study of 54 children, Juel (1988) estimated that first-grade children with good word-recognition skills were exposed to about twice as many words in basal texts as children with poor word-recognition skills. Biemiller (1977–1978) also reported similar differences in print exposure among readers with different levels of reading ability. The correlation between how much children read and their proficiency in reading led educators to rely on increasing silent reading time as a primary strategy to increase fluency.

The NRP (2000) found no evidence of a causal relationship between silent reading and increased fluency. For example, the NRP examined 14 studies that measured the impact of sustained silent reading (SSR), and similar approaches including USSR (uninterrupted sustained silent reading), DEAR (drop everything and read), and SQUIRT (super quiet reading time). In most cases, these procedures require the provision of approximately 20 minutes per day in which students are allowed to read material silently on their own with no monitoring. In most cases, the students select their own material, and there is no discussion or written assignment tied to this reading. Teachers and other adults in the school setting are to read during this time as well.

Only three studies (Burley, 1980; Davis, 1988; Langford & Allen, 1983) reported any clear reading gains from encouraging students to read independently, and in the third of these studies the gains were so small as to be of questionable educational value. Most of the studies, including the best designed and largest ones (Collins, 1980; Holt & O'Tuel, 1989; Summers & McClelland, 1982), reported no appreciable benefit to reading from such procedures. Holt and O'Tuel (1989) found improvement in vocabulary scores, but these did not translate into better reading comprehension. The most direct test of the effect of silent reading on learning was provided by Carver and Liebert (1995), and they found no clear benefit resulting from 60 hours of additional reading.

The National Reading Panel concluded its report on fluency by indicating that there are still many important questions regarding the development of fluency that need to be answered. One is to explore more carefully how procedures to encourage students to read more could be made to work more effectively in increasing achievement.

Word Recognition and Comprehension[1]

Automatic word recognition, which is dependent on phonic knowledge, allows the reader to attend to meaning; likewise, slow, belabored decoding overloads short-term memory and impedes comprehension (Moats, 1998). Cognitive scientists have shown conclusively that fluent accurate decoding is a hallmark of skilled reading (Adams, Treiman, & Pressley, 1997; Fletcher & Lyon, 1998; Stanovich & Siegel, 1994). Ability to sound out new words accounts for about 80% of the variance in first-grade reading comprehension and continues to be a major factor (Foorman et al., 1997). As whole words, morphemes, and print patterns become increasingly familiar, knowledge of these

---

1. This section is an annotated excerpt from a technical report written by David Chard, Boston University, and Deborah C. Simmons and Edward J. Kame'enui of the University of Oregon entitled, *Understanding the Primary Role of Word Recognition in the Reading Process: Synthesis of Research on Beginning Reading.* The annotated excerpt was prepared by Vicky Vachon, University of Oregon.

larger units of print allows students to read efficiently and spend less attention on sounding out letter by letter (Share, 1995).

Converging evidence suggests that the extent to which reading comprehension is dependent on word recognition varies with the level of reading development. Specifically, normal achievers' comprehension at approximately the end of first grade appears to be strongly affected by word recognition. Sawyer (1992) argued that comprehension's early dependence on word recognition may indicate that facility with the orthographic code (i.e., the printed symbols that represent the letters of the alphabet) is the "principal barrier" to comprehension in the first grade. This barrier posed by orthography is probably a function of the early readers' focus on graphic cues, letter-phoneme or sound correspondences, and smooth-sound blending to encode words that may or may not be a part of their limited vocabularies (Ehri, 1991).

In contrast, once readers achieve a degree of familiarity with the code (generally, sometime after first grade), comprehension seems to have a large direct effect on their word recognition (Sawyer, 1992). For example, readers who have learned the correspondence between letters and sounds may begin to associate certain letter patterns and whole words with their meanings. As their decoding ability becomes more fluent and letter patterns and words become more familiar, skilled readers get better and better at changing clauses or whole sentences into their language equivalents and holding them in their original form in memory (Adams, 1990). That is, they are able to change the coded (written) words into their corresponding language. Even after skilled readers access a word's meaning, they continue to recode the word from its written to its phonological form. Reportedly, this action helps the reader maintain the word's meaning in short-term memory and facilitates reading comprehension (Baddeley, cited in Adams, 1990). Thus, it seems that good word decoders comprehend more; and as expected, stronger comprehension enhances a reader's ability to decode and hold clauses or whole sentences in working memory.

Not surprisingly, less-skilled readers' comprehension continues to be highly dependent on word-recognition skills (Stanovich, 1991). In part, this is because of the relation between the translation of written words into their spoken (phonological) representations, word recognition, and the subsequent storage of the meaning of sentences or clauses in short-term memory. The amount of assistance readers receive from their ability to translate written words to phonological representations varies directly with the speed with which items to be remembered are encoded (Adams, 1990). Poor and young readers who are not yet facile at processing letters and sounding out words fail to recode words in meaningful groups and, therefore, are less likely to maintain the meaning of a clause or sentence in short-term memory (Adams, 1990). In effect, readers who are less able to generate high-quality phonological representations as a part of word recognition are at a disadvantage and at-risk for memory loss (Daneman, 1991). Thus, poor word recognition appears to limit (1) storage of and access to word meanings and (2) ability to access or remember sequences of words.

Once again, our emphasis on reading comprehension's dependence on word recognition is not intended to minimize the significance of reading comprehension. Any comprehensive review of the reading process must address differences of readers' ability to comprehend and understand the message in the print as well as their ability to recognize words from print.

Across the years, decoding deficits among low-performing readers have been well documented. Too often, this has led to wholesale acceptance of any and all instructional programs with a code emphasis. However, cautions against wholesale acceptance of all types of phonics instruction were offered by Beck in 1985. An extensive evaluation of phonics programs led her to conclude that many phonics programs:

- provide the "wrong kind of phonics instruction" that perpetuates word-attack difficulties.

- attempt to teach phonic elements that are too abstract and therefore too difficult.

- teach phonics skills that do not contribute to reading.

- fail to teach an explicit sound-blending technique.

More recently, the NRP (2000) issued a similar caveat against the wholesale adoption of all phonics programs. It is important to remember that not all phonics programs are equally effective.

Vocabulary Acquisition[2]

The enduring effects of the vocabulary limitations of students with diverse learning needs is becoming increasingly apparent. Nothing less than learning itself depends on language. Learning, as a language-based activity, fundamentally and profoundly depends on vocabulary knowledge. With inadequate vocabulary knowledge, learners are asked to develop novel combinations of known concepts with insufficient tools.

Becker (1977) was among the first to highlight the importance of vocabulary development by linking vocabulary size to the academic achievement of disadvantaged students (Baumann & Kame'enui, 1991). He asserted that vocabulary deficiencies were the primary cause of academic failure of disadvantaged students in grades 3 through 12. Almost a decade later, Stanovich (1986) proposed a model of school failure that emphasized the interrelated development of phonological awareness, reading acquisition, and vocabulary growth. A flurry of vocabulary research has been conducted since Becker's observations about the relation between vocabulary knowledge and academic achievement.

Multiple Methods of Enhancing Individual Word Knowledge

Vocabulary research indicates that many different instructional methods have yielded positive results

---

2. This section is an annotated excerpt from a technical report written by Scott Baker, Deborah C. Simmons, and Edward J. Kame'enui of the University of Oregon entitled, *Vocabulary Acquisition: Synthesis of Research*. The annotated excerpt was prepared by Vicky Vachon, University of Oregon.

in increasing vocabulary knowledge. The majority of vocabulary intervention research has examined the effectiveness of increasing students' knowledge of individual, specific words. Many methods to increase vocabulary knowledge have resulted in more words learned than otherwise occurred during normal incidental learning opportunities. However, Beck and McKeown (1991) concluded that a single-best method of vocabulary instruction has not been identified. Recent studies, combined with the information of many secondary sources, provide a clearer picture of the strengths and weaknesses of efforts to increase understanding of individual words.

In considering vocabulary growth, we need to distinguish between *intentional* and *incidental* learning. The majority of word meanings are learned through incidental word learning opportunities (Baumann & Kame'enui, 1991; National Reading Panel, 2000). That is, through normal everyday experiences with oral and written language, students learn most of the approximately seven words they acquire each day. In some cases, however, students learn word meanings intentionally. For example, the classroom teacher may request that students be able to generate original sentences for 10 new vocabulary words per week. Such intentional word-learning opportunities can be either teacher- or student-directed. Intentional vocabulary learning interventions are labor-intensive, however, because they require that direct efforts be expended on word-learning activities. Techniques that utilize high amounts of teacher time are particularly labor-intensive.

Recent Studies on Teaching Specific Words

Baumann and Kame'enui (1991) noted that techniques that involve limited superficial work with words have come under increasingly strong criticism. Recent studies have examined the benefit of using alternative vocabulary-learning techniques, such as semantic mapping/features analysis and keyword and computer-assisted methods, when compared with more traditional techniques.

Semantic Mapping/Features Analysis

Bos and Anders (1990) compared the effects of three knowledge-based interactive vocabulary instructional techniques with a traditional definition approach to vocabulary instruction. Subjects were 61 junior-high students with LD who were learning from science textbooks. The interactive techniques included sematic mapping, semantic-feature analysis, and semantic/syntactic feature analysis. Bos and Anders (1990) found that on the reading test overall (vocabulary and comprehension items), and specifically on the reading-comprehension items, students in the three interactive interventions scored higher than students engaged in definition learning.

Sinatra, Berg, and Dunn (1985) found that the use of two types of semantic maps, one with class, property, and example connections, and one modeled after typical story-grammar elements, resulted in improved reading comprehension scores for three students with learning disabilities on 11 of 15 comparisons.

Fawcett and Nicolson (1991) taught five students with reading disabilities and rich vocabularies and eight students with reading disabilities and poor vocabularies, 24 vocabulary words and 24 matched untrained words. Conditions included (1) an enriched-training condition (i.e., generating sentences and contexts, cross-linking words, and identifying affective reactions, stressing semantic links with related concepts) or (2) a traditional training condition (i.e., worksheets, crosswords, word bingo, and missing letters in order to link words with definitions).

Students were tested on word knowledge using a multiple-choice format and lexical decision speed and accuracy (i.e., deciding if an item was a word or nonword as quickly as possible). All students scored higher on word knowledge at posttest than pretest. Neither the enriched training nor greater amount of training (10 minutes per word vs. 3.3 minutes per word) led to significantly better word knowledge. This finding indicates that if the goal of vocabulary instruction is word knowledge at a rudi-

mentary level (i.e., associative level), then modest amounts of instruction may suffice (Baumann & Kame'enui, 1991). Some evidence in this study suggests that amount of training but not type of training may have influenced another level of word understanding, speed of lexical access. Thus, students trained on words for 10 minutes were able to recognize items as words or nonwords faster than students trained for 3.3 minutes.

Computer-Assisted Methods

Three features, in particular, seem to make computer-assisted interventions attractive. First, such interventions require less direct teacher time than teacher-led instruction. Second, they have the potential to individualize instruction and facilitate the alignment of instructional techniques and vocabulary goals. Third, they have the potential to systematically imbed important instructional design features within the intervention framework, including systematic review, instructional scaffolding, and integration across academic areas.

The National Reading Panel (2000) reported a small but clear trend in recent years showing technology making inroads in literacy and literacy instruction. In addition to the four studies listed in the database of the National Reading Panel, two additional studies have examined the effectiveness of computer-assisted interventions for increasing knowledge of individual words.

Johnson, Gersten, and Carnine (1987) used two computer-assisted instructional vocabulary programs to teach the meaning of 50 words to 25 high-school students with LD. The differences between the groups were (1) the size of the teaching sets (10 or 25 words) and (2) the procedures for cumulative review. The major finding was that significantly more students in the small teaching set reached mastery within 11 sessions than students in the large teaching set group. Students in the small teaching set with cumulative review seemed to learn the material more efficiently.

A second study on computer-assisted instruction by Reinking and Rickman (1990) investigated the effects of providing students immediate access to definitions of difficult words in a passage on a computer screen. That is, students either selected to view the definitions of words at their discretion, or the definitions of the target words were automatically presented. In two non-computer-assisted conditions, students could look words up at their discretion in a dictionary or a glossary. Results showed that students in the two computer-assisted groups scored significantly higher on the multiple-choice vocabulary test and the passage comprehension test than the students in the dictionary or glossary groups. The means between the groups on the multiple-choice vocabulary test, however, indicated that the effects were not particularly strong and may have been attenuated by a ceiling effect.

In summary, vocabulary interventions typically include procedures to enhance student understanding of individual words. In general, innovative vocabulary interventions are superior to traditional instructional procedures that focus on transmitting a single definition of a target word. These more effective procedures include semantic/syntactic features analysis, the keyword method, and computer-assisted methods.

Reading Achievement and Vocabulary Acquisition

Another area of convergence in research on vocabulary development is that students need to develop strong beginning reading skills to be able to engage successfully in the volume of reading necessary for them to learn large numbers of word meanings through reading-connected text (Anderson & Nagy, 1991). The only realistic chance students with poor vocabularies have to catch up to their peers with rich vocabularies requires that they engage in extraordinary amounts of independent reading. Furthermore, research findings are increasingly clear that opportunities for developing adequate reading skills are limited. In fact, the status quo in beginning reading instruction may be entirely insufficient to meet the reading and vocabulary needs of

many diverse learners (Adams, 1990; Liberman & Liberman, 1990). For example, according to Juel's (1988) longitudinal study, there was an 88% chance that a poor reader at the end of first grade would remain a poor reader at the end of fourth grade. Stanovich (1986) explained how the development of strong reading skills facilitated vocabulary growth, which in turn facilitated the further increases in reading. This reciprocal, causal relation between reading and vocabulary seems to continue unabated throughout vocabulary development.

The amount of independent reading that diverse learners need to engage in to reduce the vocabulary gap that separates them from normal achieving peers is extensive. Researchers generally agree that students do learn word meanings in the course of reading connected text, but the process appears to be very time-consuming (Baumann & Kame'enui, 1991; Beck & McKeown, 1991). That is, students have to engage in considerable amounts of reading to be exposed to unknown words a sufficient number of times for them to be learned.

Beck and McKeown (1991) asserted that "research spanning several decades has failed to uncover strong evidence that word meanings are acquired only from context" (p. 799). Their conclusion was that some learning from context does occur, but that the effect is not very powerful. A number of other studies have examined the effects of learning words through normal reading activities (incidental learning). For example, Jenkins, Stein, and Wysocki (cited in Beck & McKeown, 1991) studied the effects of learning words in context with fifth-grade students. The contexts were created so that a word's meaning was either strongly implied or a synonym was provided. Jenkins and coworkers found that students learned the meaning of words that had been encountered 6 or 10 times, unless exposure to meaning occurred prior to passage reading, in which case two encounters were sufficient to produce positive effects. Nagy, Herman, and Anderson (cited in Beck & McKeown, 1991) calculated that the probability of learning a word from a single contextual encounter was between .05 and .11, depending on the learning criterion used.

Even though independent reading may not be an efficient way to learn word meanings, the procedure does not have to be efficient to be effective and, thus, to ultimately result in powerful overall effects (Anderson & Nagy, 1991). Given that students in the primary and middle grades read anywhere from 100,000 to over 10,000,000 words of connected text per year (Nagy & Anderson, 1984), it is unnecessary for students to be efficient in deriving the meaning of words from text for the procedure to result in considerable vocabulary learning. In addition, the connection between reading comprehension and vocabulary knowledge is strong and unequivocal (Baumann & Kame'enui, 1991; Paul & O'Rourke, 1988; Stanovich, 1986), although the precise nature of the causal relation between the two constructs is still under investigation.

Arguing that reading instruction should be an integral component of a comprehensive vocabulary building program we return to Becker's (1977) observation that vocabulary knowledge was the primary factor limiting the reading and academic success beyond grade 3 of students from impoverished backgrounds. We can use a similar rationale to argue that if the spiraling negative effects of reading problems are to be avoided, comprehensive vocabulary development programs should be implemented with students *prior* to grade 3.

Text Organization and Reading Comprehension[3]

In this review of the research on the relation between the organization of text and reading comprehension, three general findings are presented:

- Well-presented physical text facilitates reading comprehension.

- Text structure and student awareness of text structure are highly related to reading comprehension.

- Explicit instruction in the physical presentation of text and/or text structure facilitates reading comprehension.

Well-Presented Physical Text Facilitates Reading Comprehension

Well-presented physical text enables readers to identify the relevant information in text, including main ideas and relations between ideas, skills that are central to comprehension (Seidenberg, 1989). The components of well-presented physical text are the visual cues that highlight or emphasize main ideas and relations between ideas. Visual cues include location of main-idea sentences, author's direct statements of importance, signal words, headings and subheadings, and spacing that divides sentences into "chunks" or meaningful thought units.

Dimensions of Well-Presented Text

The dimensions of well-presented text include those that clearly indicate the main idea, the relations between important information, and the thought units within a sentence.

Clarity and Location of Main-Idea Statements
The ability to identify main ideas is central to comprehension. Seidenberg (1989) cited empirical support showing that the ability to comprehend main ideas differentiates good and poor readers and is directly related to general comprehension ability.

Clear and coherent presentation includes (1) ordering topics systematically, (2) stating a good topic organization in the opening paragraph, (3) placing the topic sentence of a paragraph at the beginning of a paragraph rather than embedding or inferring it, and (4) arranging supporting details in

---

3. This section is an annotated excerpt from a technical report written by Shirley Dickson, Deborah C. Simmons, and Edward J. Kame'enui of the University of Oregon entitled, *Text Organization and Its Relation to Reading Comprehension: Synthesis of Research.* The annotated excerpt was prepared by Vicky Vachon, University of Oregon.

recognizable patterns that exemplify superordi-nate/subordinate relations (Seidenberg, 1989).

Cues to the Relations Between Important Ideas

Another skill that is important for comprehension is the ability to form relations between important information in text. Despite the importance of inter-relations between important ideas, Armbruster and colleagues (cited in Seidenberg, 1989) found many poorly written, incoherent textbooks that failed to use precise language or make clear the relations between concepts, ideas, and sentences. Both normally achieving students and diverse learners have demonstrated difficulty identifying relations between important ideas.

Student Awareness of the Physical Presentation of Text

Student awareness of the physical presentation of text facilitated their ability to identify main ideas and interrelations between important information. Students better identified main ideas and their supporting details if they were aware that main ideas and their supporting details occurred in recognizable patterns that exemplified superordinate and subordinate relations (Seidenberg, 1989). Additionally, student recognition and use of visual textual cues (e.g., headings, signal words, location of main ideas) contributed to their ability to identify the important ideas in text and their interrelations (Seidenberg, 1989).

Strategic Use of Well-Presented Text

To identify the main idea, most readers use simple strategies and prior knowledge matched to the organizational structures of passages (Seidenberg, 1989). Students who were taught the strategy of using headings, subheadings, and paragraph topics to summarize texts recalled text information better than students answering questions or studying the text for a longer period of time (Pearson & Fielding, 1991).

Relations Between Well-Presented Text and Diverse Learners

Students with LD have demonstrated difficulty following main ideas, recognizing main topics and their interrelations, and recognizing that main topics are supported by superordinate and subordinate ideas or examples (Seidenberg, 1989). Seidenberg proposed that when students with LD have comprehension difficulties, teachers need to consider whether the students are able to identify the important information in a reading passage. Therefore, they may need explicit training to increase sensitivity to important text information. Winograd (cited in Seidenberg, 1989) found that poor readers often chose important information based on what was of high personal interest to them and made decisions about what to include in their summaries on a sentence-by-sentence basis, rather than using textual cues to identify important information. Additionally, poor readers demonstrated difficulty integrating separate idea units into larger units (Seidenberg, 1989), and organizing their reading input in a meaningful way (Casteel, 1990).

Text Structure and Reading Comprehension

In general, "text structure" refers to the organizational features of text that serve as a frame or pattern (Englert & Thomas, 1987) to guide and help readers identify important information (Seidenberg, 1989) and logical connections between ideas (Englert & Thomas, 1987; Seidenberg, 1989). Text structure appears to play an important role in reading comprehension. Moreover, there is strong empirical evidence that readers' awareness of text structure is highly related to reading comprehension.

Types of Text Structure

Narrative Text Structure   The most familiar and most studied (Graesser, Golding, & Long, 1991) text structure is narrative text or stories. The oldest and most studied theory of narrative structure is story grammar, which refers to an "abstract linguistic" representation of the ideas, events, and personal motivations that comprise the flow of a story (Pearson & Fielding, 1991, p. 821). Pearson and Fielding (1991) cited five references that support the validity of story grammar as a model of comprehension by providing evidence that adults' and children's story retellings matched the sequential order of story-grammar components and that the frequency of recalled information correlated with the hierarchical position of the information in the story-grammar framework. Despite controversies that center over whether story grammar or other representations of knowledge can explain predictions (i.e., knowledge about planning, social action, motives), Graesser and coworkers (1991) concluded that story grammar unites dozens of empirical trends into one theory of story construction.

Expository Text Structure   In contrast to narrative text which primarily entertains, expository text primarily communicates information (Weaver & Kintsch, 1991). Seidenberg (1989) posited that the ability to comprehend and formulate expository prose is essential for achievement in school. Research evidence suggests that well-structured expository text facilitates comprehension of main ideas or topics, rather than facts. Narrative and expository texts have been found to have differential effects upon readers, with narrative appearing easier to comprehend and monitor than expository text (Zabrucky & Ratner, 1992).

Although well-organized text structure appears important to reading comprehension, the reader's awareness of text structures adds an important dimension. In their review of text-processing and expository-text structure research, Seidenberg (1989), Weaver and Kintsch (1991), and Pearson and Fielding (1991) discussed the importance of the reader's awareness (Seidenberg, 1989), familiarity (Weaver & Kintsch, 1991), or knowledge (Pearson & Fielding, 1991) of text structure. Weaver and Kintsch (1991) reported that learners "familiar" with text structure, who read

well-structured, clearly cued text, performed better on measures of global comprehension (e.g., main topics) than students who did not demonstrate familiarity with text structure.

Research evidence suggests that students vary in their awareness for different text structures. Strong research supports that students have a greater awareness of narrative- than expository-text structures (Graesser, Golding, & Long, 1991), and that students remember and comprehend narrative-text structure easier than they do expository-text structure (Zabrucky & Ratner, 1992). In a study comparing the differences between students with LD and normally achieving students in processing narrative text, Montague and coworkers (1990) concluded that most school-aged children have acquired knowledge of a story schema (awareness of narrative prose) and use that knowledge during story comprehension and production tasks.

Awareness of expository-text structure varies. In a study of expository-text structure, Englert and Thomas (1987) examined student awareness of four types of expository-text structures: description, enumeration, sequence, and comparison/contrast texts. The results indicated that (a) sequence text structure was significantly easier than enumeration and description-text structures, and (b) enumeration and sequence-text structures were significantly easier than compare/contrast text structure. Englert and Thomas (1987) also concluded that awareness of text structure may be developmental, in that the older students (including students with LD) exhibited significantly more awareness of expository-text structure than the younger students.

Seidenberg (1989) reported that a number of studies (e.g., Hiebert, Englert, & Brennan; Kintsch & Yarbrough; McGee, cited in Seidenberg, 1989) have provided evidence that effective readers use strategies linked to text-structure awareness to effectively identify and recall main ideas and supporting information and to summarize (Winograd, cited in Seidenberg, 1989). In contrast, students with LD, although they may have acquired a repertoire of strategies for processing information, do not spontaneously apply them when engaged in activities that require goal-directed or planning activity (Montague et al., 1990).

Relations Between Text Structures and Diverse Learners

Many comprehension difficulties of diverse learners have been attributed to their deficits in text-structure awareness (Englert & Thomas, 1987). Zabrucky and Ratner (1992) found that poor readers did not differ in the number of times they monitored their comprehension by looking back at sentences for narrative and expository texts. Because narrative is easier to comprehend than expository text, Zabrucky and Ratner (1992) concluded that poor readers did not regulate their understanding when reading difficult text. In addition, there was no difference in poor readers' and good readers' detection of inconsistencies during reading. However, poor readers were less able than good readers to comment accurately on passage consistency after reading. Poor readers were no different from good readers in reading problematic or inconsistent text. However, poor readers demonstrated significantly less recall than good readers (Zabrucky & Ratner, 1992).

One hypothesis for why students with LD appear to recall less narrative text than normally achieving students (Montague, Maddux, & Dereshiwsky, 1990) is that they have an incomplete "schema" or awareness of narrative prose. In a primary study of narrative-text structure and students with LD, Montague and coworkers (1990) concluded that the incomplete development of a story grammar by students with LD, as demonstrated in their significantly shorter story recalls, may be because of these students' lack of expertise in interpreting or expressing the affective information about the characters in the story (e.g., human intentions, social interactions, problem solving). Students with LD may also be deficient in their discrimination of various levels of meaning in stories, and less aware of subtle differences in the importance of story propositions compared to students without learning disabilities. Additionally, students with LD had difficulty recalling fine details, using

connective words that signal temporal and causal relations, and identifying text-based inferences in stories.

Englert and Thomas (1987) concluded that the deficit in text-structure awareness in students with LD affected their ability to use the interrelationships in text to predict forthcoming relevant details based on the text structure, to extract essential from nonessential information, and to be sensitive to their own comprehension failures. This study also indicated that similarly to normally achieving students, students with learning disabilities and low-achievers appeared to acquire text structure knowledge developmentally (Englert & Thomas, 1987).

Another area affected by poor readers' lack of sensitivity to text structure is summarization. Seidenberg (1989) reported that eighth-grade poor readers did not appear to use text-structure awareness to summarize text. Although they appeared aware of the need to include important ideas in a summary, they had difficulty identifying important ideas in a reading passage and constructing an internal topic structure representation of the text information. Rather than use the strategic skills required to produce an adequate summary or the meaning of the whole text, they made sentence-by-sentence decisions determined by the position of information and by what was important to them (Winograd, cited in Seidenberg, 1989).

Explicit Instruction in Text Organization Facilitates Comprehension

Research in both the physical presentation of text and text structures support the benefits of explicit instruction in these areas. Instruction in text structures has strong empirical support for benefiting reading comprehension.

Relations Between Instruction in Text Organization and Diverse Learners

Diverse learners have benefited from explicit, task-specific instruction on how to recognize and use the physical structure (e.g., topic sentences, headings, signal words) (Seidenberg, 1989), as well as narrative- (Gurney et al., 1990; Newby, Caldwell, & Recht, 1989) and expository-text structures (Seidenberg, 1989). Instruction in narrative-text structure appeared to provide students with a framework for recalling the important ideas in stories but not the details. Therefore, students with LD may require instructional focus on the goals, motives, thoughts, and feelings of characters in stories (Montague, Maddux, & Dereshiwsky, 1991).

Diverse learners may benefit from instruction in strategies, and when and how to apply them (Seidenberg, 1989). In particular, instruction in strategies for identifying main ideas may be useful for these learners. For students with dyslexia, studies have examined whether to teach using their strengths or remediating their weaknesses (Newby, Caldwell, & Recht, 1989). Newby and colleagues (1989) examined teaching story grammar to five 8- to 10-year-old students using instruction based on their strengths. Two students were identified as having difficulties with the sequential phonetic processes of written text (i.e., dysphonetic or auditory-linguistic dyslexia). Three students were identified as having difficulties processing words as wholes (i.e., dyseidetic or visual-spatial dyslexia). Instruction resulted in recall of a greater percentage of important ideas than in baseline. One of the two dysphonetic students and all of the three dyseidetic students showed clear increases. While this study pointed to the effectiveness of intervention by subtype, more research is required to draw clear conclusions. Newby and colleagues (1989) suggested that the study did not provide enough information to indicate if instruction based on the strengths of dyslexic subtypes was effective, or if training in story grammar in general was just as effective.

In summary, well-presented and structured text results in better comprehension of main ideas and relations between ideas than poorly presented or structured text. Students who are aware of or have had instruction in the physical presentation of text or text structure demonstrate more global comprehension than students who lack awareness or have not had instruction. Although students who are

aware of text structure recall more than students who are not aware of text structure, there is often no difference between these students for local (i.e., details) comprehension.

Metacognition and Reading Comprehension[4]

Research and practice in reading comprehension currently reflect substantial interest in metacognition (Wong, 1992). One emphasis in reading curricula reform is to develop thoughtful readers who plan selectively, monitor comprehension while reading, and reflect on process and content after reading (Paris, Wasik, & Turner, 1991). This current emphasis on thinking about reading reflects the endorsement of many researchers and practitioners that metacognition is an important dimension that enables readers to coordinate and regulate "deliberate efforts at efficient reading and effective studying" (Wong & Wong, 1986, p. 102) and thereby enhance reading comprehension. For diverse learners, there is empirical evidence to support the proposition that metacognition is *one* explanatory factor of reading comprehension difficulties (e.g., Meltzer, 1993; Paris, Wasik, & Turner, 1991). However, the lack of metacognition as an explanation of reading-comprehension difficulties is relatively new (Torgesen, 1985) and in a formative stage of development.

In general, metacognition includes knowledge and self-regulation of one's own learning processes (e.g., Billingsley & Wildman, 1990). Some definitions include motivation as a third component (e.g., Borkowski, 1992; Johnston & Winograd, 1985; Swanson, 1989). There is a general consensus that metacognition derives from an information-processing paradigm, and research of this paradigm provides strong evidence that increased processing speed of basic processes frees capacity for higher-

---

4. This section is an annotated excerpt from a technical report written by Vicky Collins, Shirley Dickson, Deborah C. Simmons, and Edward J. Kame'enui of the University of Oregon entitled, *Metacognition and Its Relation to Reading Comprehension: Synthesis of Research* (1996). The annotated excerpt was prepared by Vicky Vachon.

order organizational and coordinating processes (Torgesen, 1985). Instruction within the information-processing paradigm emphasized teaching cognitive and metacognitive processes in an academic context such as reading comprehension (Wong, 1992). Furthermore, research supports the benefit of such instruction for students with reading comprehension difficulties (e.g., Chan, Cole, & Barfett, 1987; Malone & Mastropieri, 1992; Paris, Wasik, & Turner, 1991; Schunk & Rice, 1992).

Metacognitive Knowledge and Reading Comprehension

The knowledge component of reading metacognition is multifaceted and refers to one's knowledge or awareness of (1) self as a learner; (2) task demands; (3) the relation between reading comprehension and critical-reading variables such as text, prior knowledge, and reading strategies; (4) how, why, and when to perform reading skills or strategies; and (5) resources such as time needed to perform cognitive reading tasks (Billingsley & Wildman, 1990; Palincsar, David, Winn, & Stevens, 1991).

Each of these studies with adequate experimental control (Chan, Cole, & Barfett, 1987; Schunk & Rice, 1992) provided reliable evidence that comprehension differences between groups were due to metacognitive knowledge. For example, in the Chan and colleagues study (1987), normally achieving students and diverse learners were taught to use a cross-referencing technique to identify inconsistent sentences embedded within text. Chan and cohorts randomly assigned 32 average readers and 32 students with learning disabilities, matched on reading level, to specific and general reading groups. Each group received two demonstrations on how to use the cross-referencing strategy. A moderate positive correlation between measures was reported, indicating that student performance on the comprehension monitoring and comprehension measures were related. For example, students who correctly identified wrong passages also tended to correctly identify inconsistent sentences and answer comprehension questions correctly. An instructional method by learner-group

interaction also was reported. Average readers performed better on all measures than students with learning disabilities when instruction was general. Conversely, students with learning disabilities outperformed regular-education students on all measures when instruction was specific (i.e., included an explanation as to why the sentences were inconsistent). These data indicated that diverse learners benefited more from specific instruction than from general instruction.

Schunk and Rice (1992) conducted two studies to investigate whether strategy instruction on main ideas would be more effective for remedial readers if knowledge about strategy usefulness was included. The finding main-ideas strategy had five steps that required students to (1) read the passage questions, (2) read the passage to determine what it mostly was about, (3) think about what the details have in common, (4) think about what would make a good title, and (5) reread critical parts of the passage if they did not know the question answers. Information on strategy usefulness differed between studies. In the first study, Schunk and Rice (1992) gave students feedback on the value of the main-ideas strategy when they answered questions and implemented strategy steps correctly.

Using pretest as a covariate, the authors reported significant differences between groups on the post- and maintenance-comprehension measures. Students in the strategy-value feedback group answered significantly more post- and maintenance-comprehension questions than students in the strategy- and comprehension-only groups who performed comparably. Although strategy-only students performed significantly higher on the post- than precomprehension measure, their progress was not significantly greater than that of the comprehension-only students. Overall, these findings indicated that strategy instruction was beneficial for remedial readers only when strategy-value feedback was provided. Alternatively, perhaps students in the strategy-value feedback group performed better on the comprehension tasks because they were reminded of the relation between strategy use and reading comprehension more frequently than students in the strategy-only group.

In the second study, Schunk and Rice (1992) taught students to modify the main-ideas strategy so that it could be used for locating details. Specifically, students were told that if they changed a step in the main-ideas strategy, they could use the strategy to locate details. Instead of thinking about what details have in common, students were told to look for key words.

Using pretest as a covariate, the authors reported significant differences between groups on the post- and maintenance-comprehension measures. Students in the strategy-modification group answered significantly more post- and maintenance-comprehension questions than students in the strategy- and comprehension-only groups who performed comparably. These data indicated that strategy instruction was beneficial for remedial readers only when strategy-modification instruction was provided. This finding is consistent with those reported in the first Schunk and Rice study (1992) and adds credence to arguments for inclusion of strategy-usefulness information to strategy instruction targeting remedial readers.

Further evidence of metacognitive knowledge facilitating reading comprehension is preliminary, as it was drawn from existing studies that either did not demonstrate experimentally that comprehension differences between groups were due to metacognitive knowledge (Billingsley & Wildman, 1990; Harris & Pressley, 1991; Paris, Wasik, & Turner, 1991; Rottman & Cross, 1990; Wong & Wong, 1986) and/or lacked sufficient detail for evaluating the validity of the findings (Billingsley & Wildman, 1990; Harris & Pressley, 1991; Paris, Wasik, & Turner, 1991; Weisberg, 1988).

Rottman and Cross (1990) taught fourth-grade students with learning disabilities and attention-deficit disorder five Informed Strategies for Learning (ISL), including (1) evaluating the reading task, (2) defining the main idea, (3) summarizing story elements, (4) making inferences, and (5) using prior knowledge. Posttest performances were significantly greater than pretest performances on all but the summarizing story elements measures. Students' overall comprehension and performance on main ideas, using inferences, prior knowledge, and

awareness measures were affected positively by the ISL interventions, however, it is difficult to attribute the results to the ISL modules because a control group was not provided.

In Phase 1 of a quasi-experimental study, Wong and Wong (1986) investigated whether diverse learners and normally achieving students differed in their knowledge of (1) the relation between text variables and reading comprehension, and (2) resources needed to study passages of varying difficulty. Vocabulary difficulty and text organization were the text variables. Time was the resource. Participants were 17 above-average readers, 14 average readers, and 14 readers with learning disabilities. Responses to the metacognitive knowledge tasks were evaluated using a 3 2 2 (Readers 2 Task) research design. A main effect for readers was reported. Above-average readers scored significantly higher than average and LD readers on the selection and explanation tasks. Above-average readers were significantly more likely than average and learning-disabled readers to (1) select the student who increased study time on difficult vocabulary and unorganized passages as the one who would remember more passage information and (2) explain the relation between the text variables, passage comprehensibility, and study time.

Metacognitive knowledge and reading comprehension were related significantly in a number of studies reported in secondary sources (Billingsley & Wildman, 1990; Harris & Pressley, 1991; Paris, Wasik, & Turner, 1991; Weisberg, 1988). Metacognitive knowledge typically was defined as knowledge of the relation between reading variables and reading comprehension. For example, students were told that story mapping (Idol; Idol & Croll, cited in Billingsley & Wildman, 1990) and questioning strategies (Schunk & Rice, cited in Weisberg, 1988; Wong & Jones, cited in Billingsley & Wildman, 1990) increase comprehension.

Diverse learners were the target population in three studies (Idol & Croll; Schunk & Rice; Weisberg & Balajthy, Study 2, cited in Weisberg, 1988), and participants along with normally achieving learners in three studies (Idol; Taylor, cited in Paris, Wasik, & Turner, 1991; Wong & Jones). Diverse learners were defined as (1) learning-disabled, (2) low-achieving, (3) remedial readers, (4) disabled readers, and (5) less-capable summarizers. Learner differences were reported in two of the three studies involving normally achieving and diverse learners (Taylor; Wong & Jones). Taylor (cited in Paris, Wasik, & Turner, 1991) reported that skilled summarizers used text structure to help them identify main ideas, but less-skilled summarizers did not. Wong and Jones (cited in Billingsley & Wildman, 1990; Swanson, 1989) reported that diverse learners performed better than normally achieving learners on a comprehension monitoring task. Moreover, the comprehension performance of normally achieving learners declined after using the self-questioning strategy (i.e., generating and determining answers to questions about passage main ideas). This finding indicated that the self-questioning strategy, while beneficial for diverse learners, was detrimental for normally achieving students.

In summary, it appears that diverse learners benefited from strategy instruction that contained metacognitive features. However, because the contribution of metacognitive knowledge to strategy instruction generally was not investigated in the aforementioned studies, we cannot conclude that comprehension gains were solely attributable to metacognitive knowledge. In terms of learner differences, normally achieving students demonstrated more metacognitive knowledge than diverse learners, but did not benefit more from metacognitive knowledge instruction.

Self-Regulation Facilitates Reading Comprehension

The self-regulation component of reading metacognition is multifaceted and refers to

1. Coordinating metacognitive knowledge (Billingsley & Wildman, 1990), such as combining knowledge of task demands and resources needed to perform reading skills.

2. Planning (Billingsley & Wildman, 1990), such as selecting or scheduling comprehension strategies for a particular type of text, or predicting outcomes.

3. Monitoring reading behaviors (Paris, Wasik, & Turner, 1991), including evaluating understanding of text (Baker & Brown, cited in Chan, Cole, & Barfett, 1987), checking one's comprehension (Billingsley & Wildman, 1990), and evaluating outcomes against an efficacy criterion (Brown, 1987).

4. Identifying causes of one's comprehension failures while reading (Baker & Brown, cited in Chan, Cole, & Barfett, 1987) including incongruity with prior knowledge, text difficulties (e.g., internal consistency, incomplete information, syntactical errors, unorganized content), and failure to attend to reading.

5. Remediating reading failures (Billingsley & Wildman, 1990; Chan, Cole, & Barfett, 1987), such as revising or rescheduling reading strategies (Brown, 1987), and employing "fix-it" strategies (Weisberg, 1988).

The relation between self-regulation and reading comprehension was investigated in five studies—two primary studies (Malone & Mastropieri, 1992; Wong & Wong, 1986) and three studies reported in secondary sources (Cornoldi, 1990; Paris, Wasik, & Turner, 1991; Weisberg, 1988). In most of the studies, self-regulation involved monitoring reading tasks and, to a lesser extent, planning, remediating reading failures, and adjusting study time for difficult passages. Comprehension was measured via story questions, summaries, and number of inferences and main ideas identified. All of the studies provided partial evidence that self-regulation facilitates reading comprehension, while the evidence indicating a causal relation between self-regulation and reading comprehension is preliminary.

Self-Regulation Differences Among Students With Varying Reading Abilities

The relation between self-regulation and reading comprehension among students with varying reading skills has been investigated. Taylor (cited in Paris, Wasik, & Turner, 1991) reported that skilled summarizers planned and monitored the accuracy of their summaries but less-skilled summarizers did not. Bergamo and Cornoldi (cited in Cornoldi, 1990) investigated whether good and poor comprehenders differed in their monitoring, study time, and recall of plausible and implausible passages. All participants rated implausible passages as less comprehensible than plausible passages, although poor comprehenders were less accurate in their monitoring. However, good and poor comprehenders differed in the amount of time they allocated to studying each passage type. Good comprehenders studied implausible passages longer than plausible passages, while poor comprehenders spent approximately the same amount of time studying each passage type. Moreover, good comprehenders recalled more critical passage points than poor comprehenders. These data indicated that poor comprehenders did not use their knowledge of passage comprehensibility to direct their study behavior, and perhaps, as a result, were less successful at remembering main ideas.

Wong and Wong (1986) investigated whether above-average and average readers and readers with identified learning disabilities differed in their study time and comprehension of passages that varied in difficulty. Specifically, they were told to study (1) organized and disorganized passages for recall and (2) hard and easy vocabulary passages for a reading test. The amount of time participants studied each passage was recorded. Comprehension was measured via number of idea units recalled for the organized and disorganized passages, and number of comprehension questions answered correctly for the hard and easy vocabulary passages.

Only the above-average readers studied the disorganized passage significantly longer than the organized passage. This finding indicated that above-average readers applied their knowledge of (1) the relation between text organization and reading comprehension and (2) resources needed to study passages of varying difficulty. Only readers with learning disabilities studied hard vocabulary passages significantly longer than easy vocabulary passages. This finding may indicate that students

with learning disabilities had knowledge of the relation between vocabulary difficulty and reading comprehension and the resources needed to study passages of varying difficulty, but they could not demonstrate or explain such knowledge. Alternatively, perhaps these students may have increased their study time of the hard vocabulary passage because the words were harder to decode or because the hard passage was 69 words longer than the easy vocabulary passage.

In summary, the reviewed studies reported a statistically significant effect of self-regulation on students' reading comprehension. Overall, diverse learners benefited from strategy instruction that contained a self-monitoring component. Moreover, self-monitoring enhanced the efficacy of strategy instruction. In terms of learner differences, normally achieving students demonstrated more self-regulation skills than diverse learners. Additional research on the relation between reading comprehension and strategy instruction containing metacognitive knowledge and self-regulation features is needed.

Metacognitive Instruction Facilitates Reading Comprehension

In this section, the focus is on metacognitive instruction that enhanced reading comprehension rather than instruction that enhanced metacognition. Evidence of instructional applications is preliminary partly because metacognition is a fairly new area of research and partly because most of the analyzed studies contained small numbers of participants, thereby limiting generalizations.

Cognitive Strategies

The most common cognitive strategies in the metacognitive interventions were procedures to *summarize* (Billingsley & Wildman, 1990; Malone & Mastropieri, 1992; Rottman & Cross, 1990; Weisberg, 1988), *identify main ideas* (Billingsley & Wildman, 1990; Schunk & Rice,

Study 2, 1992; Weisberg, 1988), *promote visual imagery* (Chan, Cole, & Morris, 1990; Harris & Pressley, 1991; Weisberg, 1988), and map *expository or story-grammar elements* (Billingsley & Wildman, 1990).

Metacognitive Components

Interventions included various combinations of metacognitive knowledge, self-regulation, and/or motivation. Some studies contained one component; others included several. The *usefulness of a strategy,* a metacognitive knowledge component, was investigated in a number of studies (Borkowski, Carr, Rellinger, & Pressley, cited in Paris, Wasik, & Turner 1991; Duffy et al., cited in Paris, Wasik, & Turner 1991; Hansen & Pearson, cited in Paris, Wasik, & Turner 1991; Palincsar & Brown, cited in Billingsley & Wildman, 1990; Pressley, cited in Harris & Pressley, 1991; Rottman & Cross, 1990; Schunk & Rice, Study 1, 1992; Wong & Jones, cited in Billingsley & Wildman, 1990). Three of these studies taught the usefulness of a strategy as a means to increase motivation; however, it is important to note that each operationalized metacognitive knowledge differently.

While usefulness of a strategy was the most common metacognitive knowledge component in reviewed studies, *knowledge of task demands* was the second most common as found in studies by Chan, Cole, and Barfett (1987), Rottman and Cross (1990), and Schunk and Rice (1992).

The most common self-regulation component was *self-monitoring,* which included (1) reading comprehension or strategy use (Dewitz et al., cited in Paris, Wasik, & Turner, 1991; Malone & Mastropieri, 1992; Markman & Gorin, cited in Paris, Wasik, & Turner, 1991; Palincsar & Brown, cited in Billingsley & Wildman, 1990; Paris & Myers, cited in Paris, Wasik, & Turner, 1991; Schunk & Rice, 1991), (2) reading comprehension using a self-questioning procedure (Billingsley & Wildman, cited in Billingsley & Wildman, 1990; Carnine & Kinder, cited in Billingsley & Wildman, 1990; Chan & Cole, cited in Weisberg, 1988; Clark et al.,

cited in Weisberg, 1988; Singer & Dolan, cited in Billingsley & Wildman, 1990; Wong & Jones, cited in Billingsley & Wildman, 1990), or (3) inconsistent information while reading passages (Baker, cited in Paris, Wasik, & Turner, 1991; Billingsley & Wildman, cited in Billingsley & Wildman, 1990; Chan, Cole, & Barfett, 1987).

Explicit Instruction

Explicit instruction occurred in the majority of the interventions designed to increase metacognition directly or to induce metacognition indirectly (e.g., Chan, Cole, & Barfett, 1987; Chan, Cole, & Morris, 1990; Hansen & Pearson, cited in Weisberg, 1988; Harris, cited in Harris & Pressley, 1991; Markman & Gorin, cited in Paris, Wasik, & Turner, 1991; Paris & Myers, cited in Paris, Wasik, & Turner, 1991; Pressley, cited in Harris & Pressley, 1991; Simmonds, 1990; Wong & Jones, cited in Billingsley & Wildman, 1990). However, explicit instruction was used differently, depending on whether metacognition was directly taught or induced. Direct interventions taught metacognitive components (e.g., the usefulness of a strategy, task demands) explicitly, whereas indirect interventions explicitly taught cognitive strategies (e.g., summarize, predict) with the assumption the strategies would, in turn, enhance metacognition.

Modeling

Modeling is another instructional feature that occurred in the majority of interventions (e.g., Billingsley & Wildman, 1990; Borkowski, 1992; Chan, Cole, & Barfett, 1987; Idol & Croll, cited in Billingsley & Wildman, 1990; Palincsar & Brown, cited in Billingsley & Wildman, 1990; Schunk & Rice, Study 1 & 2, 1992; Simmonds, 1990). One issue concerning modeling is whether it alone is sufficient to benefit reading comprehension or whether modeling must be accompanied by explicit instruction. The evidence is mixed and may depend upon the reading context, tasks, and students' ability.

Interaction

A common assumption of metacognitive instruction is that interaction induces the social construction of metacognition (e.g., Palincsar, cited in Billingsley & Wildman, 1990). For example, dialogue that includes the teacher (1) asking students how to do a task and (2) providing feedback to students' responses facilitates understanding of the purpose of a task and execution of a strategy (Meichenbaum, cited in Harris & Pressley, 1991). Additionally, discussions between students provide opportunities for metacognitive exchanges and modeling (Palincsar, David, Winn, & Stevens, 1991). In reviewed studies, interactions occurred between (1) teacher and students (e.g., Hansen & Pearson, cited in Weisberg, 1988; Harris & Pressley, 1991) and (2) target students and peers (e.g., Palincsar & Brown, cited in Billingsley & Wildman, 1990; Paris et al., cited in Paris, Wasik, & Turner, 1991). Through discussions, cooperative activities, and peer conferences, students interacted to (1) determine goals for instruction; (2) implement, evaluate, and modify strategy acquisition and use; (3) discuss how a strategy could be applied in situations other than the reading lessons (e.g., Palincsar & Brown, cited in Billingsley & Wildman, 1990); and (4) make the strategies concrete and sensible (Cross & Lipson, cited in Paris, Wasik, & Turner, 1991). Borkowski (1992) suggested that students rather than teachers play a major role in dialogue.

Increased Student Control

Billingsley and Wildman (1990) called increasing student control an important dimension of comprehension instruction. In many of the reviewed studies (e.g., Idol & Croll, cited in Billingsley & Wildman, 1990; Idol-Maestas, cited in Billingsley & Wildman, 1990; Palincsar & Brown, cited in Paris, Wasik, & Turner, 1991), instruction occurred along a continuum of teacher versus student control. For example, instruction included three phases: (1) teacher control usually by mod-

eling, (2) a bridge to gradually transfer control to students, and (3) independent student application.

Guided Practice

Chan, Cole, and Morris (1990) concluded that students require adequate time and practice to increase metacognition. Guided practice provides students repeated opportunities to practice the procedures of a strategy or metacognition under the supervision of a teacher. During the guided practice phase of the interventions examined, teachers (1) praised, prompted, or provided additional modeling, as appropriate (Idol & Croll, cited in Billingsley & Wildman, 1990; Palincsar & Brown, cited in Billingsley & Wildman, 1990; Paris et al., cited in Paris et al., 1991; Pressley, cited in Harris & Pressley, 1991); (2) faded the prompts and increased the criterion level as students improved (Harris & Pressley, 1991); (3) referred to the appropriate strategy step (Schunk & Rice, 1992); (4) asked students to verbalize a strategy step (Schunk & Rice, 1992); or (5) provided practice using texts of different lengths (Pressley, cited in Harris & Pressley, 1991) and expository materials rather than brief skill exercises (Paris et al., cited in Paris, Wasik, & Turner, 1991). Billingsley and Wildman (1990) suggested that teachers vary materials appropriate to students' reading levels and background knowledge so that students can concentrate on comprehension, thereby minimizing the effect of decoding problems.

Systematic Feedback

Cross and Lipson (cited in Paris, Wasik, & Turner, 1991) concluded that diverse learners require considerable practice with feedback to increase metacognition. In addition, feedback should be specific, carefully planned, and timed (Billingsley & Wildman, 1990). Several interventions contained feedback for strategy use during comprehension activities (e.g., Harris, cited in Harris & Pressley, 1991; Idol & Croll, cited in Billingsley & Wildman, 1990; Malone & Mastropieri, 1992; Palincsar & Brown, cited in Billingsley & Wildman, 1990; Paris et al., cited in Paris, Wasik, & Turner, 1991; Simmonds, 1990). Feedback specifically linked success in answering questions to strategy use (i.e., strategy-value feedback) (Schunk & Rice, 1992) and included reexplanations and reinstruction as needed (Harris, cited in Harris & Pressley, 1991). In addition to teachers, peers provided feedback that included encouragement and corrections (Palincsar & Brown, cited in Paris, Wasik, & Turner, 1991).

Another common feature was the timing and distribution of feedback. Across interventions, teachers provided feedback at different intervals, including continuously (Palincsar & Brown, cited in Billingsley & Wildman, 1990; Simmonds, 1990), three to four times each to individual students during a 35-minute instructional period (Schunk & Rice, 1992), weekly for performance on comprehension tests (Palincsar & Brown, cited in Billingsley & Wildman, 1990), and at the end of strategy instruction to reinforce the usefulness of a strategy (Wong & Jones, cited in Billingsley & Wildman, 1990).

Summary

The reviewed studies provided evidence that metacognitive instruction enhanced the reading comprehension of diverse learners. However, there was mixed support for the same benefit for normally achieving students. Metacognitive interventions consisted of multiple and varied metacognitive components and instructional features. The most frequent metacognitive components were knowledge of the usefulness of a strategy, knowledge of task demands, and self-monitoring. Generally, metacognitive instruction occurred in the context of narrative and expository passages written for the intervention and concurrently with cognitive strategy instruction. The most common cognitive strategies were summarizing, identifying main ideas, using visual imagery, and mapping narrative or expository text. Instruction was explicit and incorporated modeling, interaction, increased student control, guided practice, and systematic feedback.

Because metacognitive instruction consists of multiple components, it is unclear how to translate research to practice. Future research is required to determine the most effective and efficient balance between cognitive strategies, metacognitive components, and instructional techniques. The balance may vary, depending on student ability and prior knowledge, text type, task demands, and cognitive strategies.

Word Lists*

Contents

---

* Parentheses in Appendix A indicate a minimally different word that can be used in discrimination exercises.

CVC Words Beginning With a Continuous Sound (Chapter 8)

a	*i*	*o*	*u*	*e*
fad				fed
fan	fin		fun	
fat	fit			
lad	lid			led
lag		log		leg
lap	lip			
	lit	lot		let
mad	mid		mud	
		mom	mum	
man				men
map		mop		
mat	mit			met
		nod		Ned
Nat	nit	not	nut	net
nap	nip			
	rid	rod		red
rag	rig		rug	
ram	rim		rum	
ran		Ron	run	
rap	rip			
rat		rot	rut	
sad	Sid	sod		
Sam			sum	
	sin		sun	
sat	sit			set
sap	sip			

CVC Words Beginning With a Stop Sound (Chapter 8)

a	i	o	u	e
bag	big		bug	beg
bad	bid		bud	bed
bam			bum	
bat	bit		but	bet
cap		cop	cup	
cab			cub	
can		con		
cat			cut	
dad	did		dud	
Dan		Don		den
	dig	dog	dug	
	dip			
gas			Gus	
gag				
			gun	
had	hid			
ham	him		hum	
has	his			
hat	hit	hot	hut	
	hip	hop		
		hog	hug	
				hen
jab		job		
jam	Jim			jet
	jig	jog	jug	
	kin			Ken
	kid			
pan	pin			pen
pat	pit	pot		pet
	pig			peg
		pop	pup	pep
tab			tub	
tag			tug	
tan	tin			ten
tap	tip	top		
	Tim	Tom		

CVCC Words Ending With a Consonant Blend
or Double Consonants (Chapter 8)

a		*i*		*u*		*e*		*o*
act	(at)	fill		bump	(bum)	bend	(Ben)	golf
and	(add)	film		bunt	(bun)	bent	(Ben)	honk
ant	(an)	fist	(fit)	bust	(but)	best	(Bess)	lock
band	(bad)	hint	(hit)	dump		belt	(bell)	pond
bank		ink		dust		bent	(Ben)	pomp
camp	(cap)	lick		gulp		dent	(den)	rock
can't	(can)	lift		gust	(gut)	end	(Ed)	romp
cast	(cat)	limp	(lip)	hunt	(hut)	felt	(fell)	sock
damp	(dam)	milk		hung	(hug)	held	(help)	soft
fact	(fat)	mint	(mit)	jump		left	(let)	
fast	(fat)	mist	(miss)	junk		kept		
gasp	(gas)	sick		luck		melt	(mell)	
hand	(had)	tilt	(till)	lump		mend	(men)	
lamp	(lap)	wind	(win)	must		neck		
land	(lad)			punk		nest	(net)	
last				runt	(run)	pest	(pet)	
mask				rust	(Russ)	self	(sell)	
mast	(mass)			suck		send		
pant	(pan)			sung		sent		
past	(pass)					test		
raft	(rat)					tent	(ten)	
sack						weld	(well)	
sand	(sad)					went	(wet)	
sank								

CCVC Words Beginning With a Consonant Blend (Chapter 8)

bl—bled (bed), blot

br—brag (bag), brat (bat), bred (bed), brig (big), brim

cl—clad, clam, clan (can), clap, clip, clot, club (cub)

cr—crab (cab), cram, crib, crop (cop)

dr—drag, drip (dip), drop, drug (dug), drum

fl—flag, flap, flat (fat), fled (fed), flip, flop

fr—frog (fog), from

gl—glad, glum (gum)

gr—grab, gram, grim, grin, grip

pl—plan (pan), plop (pop), plot (pot), plug, plum, plus

pr—prop (pop)

sc—scan, scat (sat), scab

sk—skid, skim, skin, skip, skit

sl—slam (Sam), slap (sap), slat, sled, slim, slip (sip), slob (sob), slot, slug, slum (sum)

sm—smog, smug

sn—snag, snap (sap), snip, snub, snug

sp—span, spat (sat), sped, spin, spit, (sit), spot, spun (sun)

st—stab, stem, step, stop, stun (sun)

sw—swam (Sam), swim

tr—trap (tap), trim (Tim), trip (tip), trot (tot)

tw—twig, twin (tin)

CCVCC, CCCVC, and CCCVCC Words (Chapter 8)

bl—blast, blimp, blunt (bunt), blond, blend (bend), blink, bliss, black (back), block, bluff

br—bring, brunt, brand (band), brass (bass)

cl—clamp (camp), clasp, cling, clump, clung, clink, class, cliff

cr—cramp, crust, craft, crisp

dr—drink, drank, drift, draft, dress, drill

fl—fling, flung, flunk

fr—frost, frank, frisk, frill (fill)

gl—gland, glint, glass (gas)

gr—gramp, grand, grump, grant, grasp, grunt, grass (gas), grill

pl—plant (pant), plump (pump), plank

pr—print, prank, press

sc—scalp

sk—skunk, skill

sl—slang, slant, slump, slept, sling

sm—smack (sack), smell (sell)

sn—snack (sack), sniff

sp—spend (send), spent (sent), spank (sank), spunk (sunk), spell (sell), spill

st—stand (sand), stamp, stump, sting (sing), stink (sink), stomp, still, stiff, stack (sack), stuck (suck)

sw—swift, swang (sang), swung (sung), swing (sing), swell (sell)

tr—tramp, trunk, trust, trend, trick (tick)

tw—twang, twist

spl—split (spit), splint, splat

str—strip, strap, strung, strand, struck

scr—scrap, scram, script

VCe Pattern Words in Which the Vowel Is Long (Chapter 15)

1. Words Beginning With a Single Consonant (CVCe)

a		*i*		*o*		*u*		*e*	
vane	(van)	time	(Tim)	hope	(hop)	cute	(cut)	Pete	(pet)
fade	(fad)	like	(lick)	note	(not)	use	(us)	eve	
made	(mad)	site	(sit)	robe	(rob)	mule			
bake	(back)	Mike	(Mick)	home		cure			
cane	(can)	mile	(mill)	joke		pure	(purr)		
tape	(tap)	ripe	(rip)	hole		fume			
mate	(mat)	file	(fill)	nose		mute			
hate	(hat)	tile	(till)	rope					
sake	(sack)	pile	(pill)	mope	(mop)				
Jane	(Jan)	ride	(rid)	pope	(pop)				
pane	(pan)	mite	(mit)	bone					
same	(Sam)	fine	(fin)	cone	(con)				

a		i		o		u	e
cape	(cap)	wine	(win)	dope			
wave		pike	(pick)	hose			
tame	(tam)	bite	(bit)	note			
take	(tack)	kite	(kit)	yoke			
save		dime	(dim)	poke			
make	(Mack)	hide	(hid)	pole			
gaze		pine	(pin)	rose			
		tide		rode	(rod)		
		side	(Sid)				
		hire					
		fire					
		wire					
		dine					
		dire					
		line					
		like					
		dive					
		five					
		lime					
		bike					
		nine					
		size					

2. Words Beginning With a Consonant Blend (CCVCe)

a		i		o	u
skate		slide	(slid)	spoke	brute
state		snipe	(snip)	broke	
trade		gripe	(grip)	close	
stale	(stall)	prime	(prim)	drove	
scale		spine	(spin)	globe	
snake	(snack)	spite	(spit)	froze	
slave		bride		scope	

a		*i*		*o*	
slate	(slat)	crime		smoke	
scare		pride		stone	
plate		prize		stove	
plane	(plan)	smile		slope	(slop)
grape		stripe	(strip)		
grade					
frame					

3. Multisyllabic Words With a VCe Syllable

a	*i*	*o*	*u*	*e*
careless	perspire	hopeless	excuse	complete
escape	dislike	explode	confuse	stampede
inhale	likely	backbone	reuse	
take-off	umpire	pinhole	costume	
handmade	entire			
grateful	lifetime			
pancake	ninety			
timeless				

Letter Combinations (Chapter 15)

ai aid, aim, bail, bait, claim, fail, fair, laid, maid, mail, main, pail, paid, pain, paint, plain, rain, tail, stair, trait, afraid, complain, remain, explain, tailor, daily, ailment, maintain, obtain, aimed, failing, mailing, painter, raining, aid (add), aim (am), bait (bat), fair (far), maid (mad)

al fall, call, tall, ball, small, wall, mall, salt, false, bald, waltz, also, always, almost, salty, all right, walnut, hallway, walrus, alter

ar arm, bark, barn, card, cart, farm, far, star, hard, harm, mark, park, part, art, car, dark, mars, smart, start, yard, starve, shark, artist, darling, barber, target, party, carpet, partner, harvest, barking, starring, parked, smarter, started, bark (back), hard (hand), art (at), car (care), star (stare), bar (bare)

au fault, vault, sauce, cause, taught, haunt, laundry, author, autumn, August, daughter, applaud, because, auto

aw bawl, brawn, claw, dawn, hawk, jaw, law, lawn, paw, pawn, raw, saw, straw, crawl, shawl, yawn, awful, drawing, lawful, sawmill, lawyer, seesaw, outlaw, strawberry, awkward, awning

ay day, gay, may, ray, say, clay, gray, play, pray, spray, tray, payment, today, played, saying, player, playing, prayed, praying, away, Sunday

<u>ch</u>	chap, chat, chip, chop, cheek, chug, charm, chimp, chain, cheap, chest, chill, chair, champ, catch, match, patch, pitch, switch, ditch, much, march, starch, crunch, arch, pinch, teach, touch, rich, hunch, chip (ship), chop (shop), chap (clap), ditch (dish), catch (cash), catcher, pitcher, pitching, chopped, teacher, touched, rancher, chuckle, chilly, marching
<u>ea</u>	bead, bean, beast, dean, deal, fear, hear, heal, heat, Jean, lead, meal, least, mean, meat, neat, read, sea, seal, seat, speak, steam, east, eat, freak, leave, please, sneak, wheat, treat, bean (Ben), beat (bet), beast (best), meat (met), speak (speck), reason, season, peanut, teacher, eastern, dealing, speaker, sneaker, treated, eating, leaving, hearing, healed, heated, steaming
<u>ee</u>	bee, creep, see, deer, flee, free, green, keep, wheel, three, jeep, creek, fleet, bleed (bled), beet (bet), peep (pep), weed (wed), beetle, between, canteen, fifteen, sixteen, indeed, needle, freedom, coffee, bleeding, creeped, wheeled, peeping
<u>ue</u>	cue, due, sue, rescue, argue, tissue, value, statue
<u>ew</u>	new, few, flew, chew, slew, stew, drew, grew, curfew, nephew
<u>ey</u>	hockey, money, donkey, turkey, whiskey, valley, alley, monkey, honey
<u>igh</u>	fight, light, right, tight, might, high, sigh
<u>ir</u>	bird, birth, dirt, first, shirt, sir, skirt, stir, third, whirl, bird (bid), first (fist), shirt (short), stir (star), dirty, birthday, stirring, whirled, thirsty, thirty
<u>kn</u>	knock, know, knee, knife, knight, knit, knob, knot, known
<u>oa</u>	boast, coat, cloak, float, road, roast, oak, soap, throat, toast, boat (boot), coal (cool), load (loud), oar (our), oatmeal, toaster, unload, approach, railroad, seacoast, soapy, charcoal, coaster
<u>oi</u>	boil, join, noise, point, spoil, soil, moist, oil, voice, coil (cool), foil (fool), coin (con), boiler, appoint, adjoin, disappoint, poison, avoid, joined, noisy, boiling
<u>ol</u>	bold, bolt, cold, colt, roll, fold, gold, hold, hole, scold, sold, told, toll, volt, control, enroll, folder, golden, holder, holster, roller, swollen, unfold, roller, folding, holding
<u>oo</u>	boot, cool, food, fool, hoop, mood, moon, moose, room, soon, tool, pool, stoop, smooth, tooth, too, spoon, shoot (shot), stoop (stop), soon (son), hoop (hop), cartoon, bedroom, noodle, poodle, shampoo, igloo, bamboo, fooling, moody, shooting, raccoon, teaspoon, harpoon
<u>or</u>	born, lord, porch, torn, stork, shore, fort, sport, torch, storm, north, corn (con), for (far), pork (park), port (part), short (shot), normal, order, organ, ordeal, border, conform, escort, forty, hornet, perform, inform, popcorn, story, morning
<u>ou</u>	cloud, clout, loud, pout, pouch, scout, blouse, count, ground, found, out, round, sound, about, aloud, amount, around, counter, thousand, trousers, outside, cloudy, counting, grounder, bout (boot), mouse (moose), noun (noon), mouth (moth), our (or)
<u>ow</u>	blow, crow, glow, grow, know, low, owe, row, slow, show, throw, shown, thrown, grown, elbow, fellow, below, follow, hollow, pillow, shadow, yellow, window
<u>oy</u>	boy, toy, joy, Troy, annoy, employ, enjoy, cowboy, oyster, royal
<u>ph</u>	phone, graph, photo, phrase, photograph, physics, typhoon, alphabet, elephant, dolphin, orphan, pamphlet, trophy, nephew, paragraph
<u>sh</u>	shed, shin, shut, shun, dish, wish, rush, lash, flash, fresh, crash, brush, trash, shine, chime, shame, shape, share, ship (slip), shot (slot), shop (stop), shell (sell), shack (sack), cash (cast), fish (fist)

th   that, them, this, with, tenth, eleventh, twelfth, thirteenth, fourteenth, fifteenth, sixteenth, seventeenth, eighteenth, then (ten), than (tan)

ur   church, curb, cur, hurt, purr, spurt, surf, turn, burst, curse, curve, purse, nurse, purple, turkey, Thursday, disturb, further, return, turtle, injure, burn (born), fur (far), curl (Carl)

wh   when, whip, which, what, white, while

wr   wrap, wreck, wrench, wring, wrist, write, wrong, wrapper, wreckage, wrestle, wrinkle, writer, wrongful

Suffixes (Chapter 16)

a   panda, comma, Anna, soda, drama, china, zebra, mamma, papa

able   likeable, teachable, touchable, expendable, drinkable, enable, unable, portable, reasonable, returnable

age   luggage, package, village, image, voyage, storage, passage, hostage, cottage, manage, language, wreckage, usage

al   sandal, formal, postal, local, vocal, final, journal, metal, total, legal, criminal

ance   clearance, entrance, performance, distance, instance, annoyance

ed   hugged, killed, missed, ripped, tipped, bumped, helped, jumped, picked, rocked, clapped, dripped, dropped, flipped, grabbed, grinned, gripped, pressed, smelled, spelled, tricked, flipped, dotted, patted, petted, dusted, handed, landed, tested, lasted, hunted, ended, blasted, planted, slanted, trusted, twisted

ence   absence, sentence, audience, patience, silence, influence, evidence, confidence

er   batter, bigger, butter, fatter, hotter, letter, madder, sadder, bumper, faster, helper, hunter, blacker, dresser, slipper, speller, sticker, swinger, swimmer

es   glasses, misses, passes, messes, foxes, mixes, taxes, boxes, wishes, dishes, fishes, mashes

est   biggest, fattest, hottest, maddest, saddest, dampest, fastest, blackest, flattest, stiffest

ful   handful, careful, useful, helpful, cheerful, mouthful, watchful, faithful, fearful

ible   horrible, sensible, possible, flexible, admissible, responsible, permissible, convertible, terrible, invisible

ic   traffic, picnic, arctic, antic, frantic, plastic, magic, tragic, comic, panic, basic, music, critic

ing   batting, betting, cutting, digging, filling, getting, killing, letting, petting, bending, dusting, ending, helping, jumping, picking, testing, clapping, dripping, grabbing, grinning, planning, smelling, spending, swimming

ion   fashion, champion, region, union, companion, opinion, religion, million, billion

ish   snobbish, selfish, sluggish, publish, foolish, furnish, establish, accomplish, astonish, punish, finish, radish

ive   active, captive, attentive, expensive, impressive, attractive, constructive, corrective, defective, destructive, positive

le   battle, cattle, juggle, middle, paddle, riddle, saddle, wiggle, apple, bottle, giggle, little, puddle, handle, ankle, bundle, candle, jungle, uncle, grumble, twinkle, trample

ment   agreement, argument, basement, attachment, development, employment, movement, payment, appointment, shipment

<u>less</u>	endless, groundless, matchless, toothless, speechless, sleepless, helpless, careless, restless, lifeless, nameless, useless
<u>ness</u>	madness, badness, freshness, dullness, witness, dryness, likeness
<u>tion</u>	action, mention, fraction, question, invention, inspection, section, suction, portion, construction, celebration, circulation, congratulation, combination, decoration, education, formation
<u>ture</u>	feature, creature, fracture, lecture, picture, puncture, structure, culture, venture, capture, torture, mixture, adventure, furniture, nature, future
<u>ward</u>	northward, inward, forward, backward, coward, skyward, onward, awkward
<u>y</u>	funny, muddy, penny, bunny, happy, jelly, silly, rocky, jumpy, handy, lucky, rusty, sandy, windy, candy, empty, fifty, sixty, smelly, snappy, sticky, clumsy, drafty, grumpy, plenty, sloppy, twenty

Prefixes (Chapter 16)

<u>a</u>	about, alive, alarm, around, along, amount, among, apart, asleep, atop
<u>ab</u>	absent, absentee, absorb, absurd
<u>ad</u>	address, adjust, admire, admit, adverb, advertise
<u>ap</u>	appear, appeal, appendix, applaud, appoint, approach
<u>at</u>	attack, attempt, attend, attic, attach
<u>be</u>	because, become, before, begin, behave, behind, behold, belong, beneath, besides, between, beware
<u>com</u>	combine, command, commit, compete, complain, complex, compute
<u>con</u>	concrete, conduct, confess, confine, confirm, conflict, conform, confuse, connect, conserve, consist, control, consult, convict, contract
<u>de</u>	decay, declare, decoy, defeat, define, defrost, delay, delight, demand, depart, depend, describe, design, desire, destruct, detail, devote
<u>dis</u>	disappear, disappoint, discount, disconnect, discuss, dismiss, dismount, display, displease, disagree, disbelieve, discharge, dishonest, discolor, distance
<u>ex</u>	explain, expect, expense, expert, explode, expand, expire, export, explosive, extoll, exclaim, excuse, exact, exam, except, exit, examine, example
<u>for</u>	forbid, forever, forget, forgive, forward
<u>fore</u>	forbid, forearm, forecast, forgive, forehead, forest, forget, forty, foremost, foreman, foreclosure, forefront
<u>im</u>	imperfect, impact, impeach, impress
<u>in</u>	inclose, income, index, infect, inflate, inform, inspect, intend
<u>mis</u>	miscount, misdeal, misfit, misjudge, mislead, misplace, mistake, mistreat, misspell, misprint, mistrust, mismatch
<u>non</u>	nonsense, nonstop, nonprofit, nonconform, nonsupport

<u>over</u>	overall, overboard, overcast, overcome, overdue, overhead, overload, overlook, overrun, oversight, overtake, overtime, overturn, overstep, overshoes, overshadow
<u>per</u>	percent, perfect, perfume, perhaps, permanent, persist, person, perplex, perspire, perturb
<u>post</u>	postage, postcard, postman, postpone, postmark, postal
<u>pre</u>	predict, pretend, preheat, prepay, prepare, precook, preside, precede
<u>pro</u>	profile, protest, propose, produce, protest, provoke
<u>re</u>	return, rebake, recall, recount, refill, reflex, reform, refresh, refuse, regain, regard, relay, release, remark, repair, repay, report, replay, reprint, respect, retreat, reverse
<u>sub</u>	subdue, subject, submerge, submit, subnormal, subside, subsist, subtract, suburb, subway
<u>super</u>	superman, supervise, supertanker, supersonic, supermarket, supersede, supernatural
<u>trans</u>	transfer, transform, transit, translate, transmit, transparent, transplant, transport
<u>un</u>	unable, unarm, uncage, unchain, unclean, unhappy, uneven, unlock, unreal, untie, unfair, unseen, unsafe, unlucky, unsure
<u>under</u>	undercharge, underdog, undergo, underline, understand, underground, undertake, understood, underworld, underwear
<u>up</u>	uphill, upkeep, uplift, upright, upsidedown, uptown, upward, uphold, upon, uproar, upstream

CVCe Derivative Words (Chapter 16)

(Not all the words in parentheses are minimally different.)

1. Words With *s* Endings

a		*i*		*o*		*e-u*	
canes	(cans)	bites	(bits)	cones	(cons)	Petes	(pets)
cares	(cars)	files	(fills)	globes	(globs)	cubes	(cubs)
hates	(hats)	fines	(fins)	hopes	(hops)	uses	
mates	(mats)	miles	(mills)	mopes	(mops)		
planes	(plans)	shines	(shins)	robes	(robs)		
shakes	(shacks)	times					
stares	(stars)	wines	(wins)				

2. Words With *er* Endings

a		*i*		*o*		*e-u*	
later	(latter)	filer	(filler)	closer	(hotter)	cuter	(cutter)
shaver	(slammer)	diner	(dinner)	smoker	(robber)	ruder	(rudder)
crater	(batter)	finer	(winner)	homer	(logger)	user	

	a		*i*		*o*		*e-u*
braver	(hammer)	riper	(hitter)				
saver	(madder)	timer	(ripper)				
biter	(bigger)						

3. Words With *ed* Endings

	a		*i*		*o*		*e-u*
hated	(tapped)	filed	(filled)	hoped	(hopped)	used
named	(jammed)	smiled	(ripped)	closed	(robbed)	
waved	(fanned)	timed	(kidded)	smoked	(nodded)	
skated	(rammed)	piled	(fitted)	stoned	(rotted)	
blamed	(batted)	glided	(fibbed)	roped	(logged)	
faded	(matted)					

4. Words With *ing* Endings

	a		*i*		*o*		*e-u*
naming	(batting)	filing	(filling)	hoping	(hopping)	using
skating	(tapping)	riding	(hitting)	roping	(robbing)	
waving	(slamming)	timing	(ripping)	closing	(logging)	
hating	(napping)	piling	(kidding)	smoking	(stopping)	
shading	(snapping)	biting	(winning)	roving	(mopping)	

5. Words With *y* Endings

	a		*i*		*o*		*e-u*
gravy	(Tammy)	spicy	(Timmy)	bony	(Tommy)	cuty	(nutty)
shady	(batty)	shiny		smoky	(Dotty)	tummy	
wavy	(fanny)	tiny		stony	(foggy)		
shaky	(Sammy)	wiry					

6. Words With *est* Endings

a	*i*	*u*
bravest	ripest	cutest
latest	wisest	rudest
safest	widest	surest
tamest		

Y-Derivative Words (Chapter 16)

	ier	*iest*	*ied*	*ies*
army				armies
buddy				buddies
bumpy	bumpier	bumpiest		
clumsy	clumsier	clumsiest		
foggy	foggier	foggiest		
funny	funnier	funniest		
greedy	greedier	greediest		
greasy	greasier	greasiest		
grumpy	grumpier	grumpiest		
handy	handier	handiest		
happy	happier	happiest		
holy	holier	holiest		
hungry	hungrier	hungriest		
kitty				kitties
lucky	luckier	luckiest		
muddy	muddier	muddiest		
party				parties
penny				pennies
rusty	rustier	rustiest		
silly	sillier	silliest		
skinny	skinnier	skinniest		
smelly	smellier	smelliest		
ugly	uglier	ugliest		
windy	windier	windiest		
baby			babied	babies
berry				berries
body				bodies
bury			buried	buries
busy	busier	busiest	busied	
carry	carrier		carried	carries
copy	copier		copied	copies
country				countries

	ier	iest	ied	ies
hurry			hurried	hurries
lady				ladies
marry			married	marries
sorry	sorrier	sorriest		
study			studied	studies
worry			worried	worries

Two-Syllable Words With a Single Consonant in the Middle (Chapter 17)

a	e	i	o	u
paper	legal	Bible	frozen	music
satin	fever	visit	holy	bugle
travel	pedal	china	local	punish
cable	meter	prison	profit	human
label	clever	final	moment	super
planet	zebra	limit	copy	pupil
table	seven	finish	motor	humid
chapel	metal	minus	topic	study
rapid	defend	silent	robin	rumor
magic	second	tiger	poker	
crazy	seven	pilot	soda	
favor	devil	spinach	total	
vacant	petal	spider	solid	
taxi	evil	river	robot	
crater		tiny	modern	
panic			proper	
maple			pony	
			comic	
			motel	
			motor	
			promise	
			model	
			robin	
			total	

List of 400 Common Words

a	baby	birthday	car	dog	fat
about	back	black	carry	done	father
after	bag	blue	cat	don't	feet
again	ball	boat	catch	door	few
airplane	balloon	book	children	down	fight
all	bark	both	city	draw	find
almost	barn	box	clean	dress	fire
along	bear	boy	coat	drink	first
also	because	bring	cold	drop	fish
always	bed	brought	colds	duck	five
am	be	brown	come	each	fly
an	bee	build	could	eat	food
and	been	bus	cow	eight	for
animals	before	but	cry	end	found
another	began	buy	cut	enough	four
anything	behind	by	daddy	even	fox
are	below	cage	dark	ever	friend
around	best	cake	day	every	from
as	better	call	did	fall	full
ask	between	called	didn't	family	fun
at	big	came	different	far	funny
ate	bike	can	do	farm	game
away	bird	can't	does	fast	gave

get	hill	left	name	pet	school
girl	him	leg	need	pick	see
give	his	let	never	pig	seen
go	hold	letter	new	picnic	set
goat	home	life	next	picture	seven
goes	hop	light	night	place	shall
going	horse	like	no	play	she
gone	hot	line	not	please	shoe
good	house	little	nothing	pocket	should
good-bye	how	live	now	pony	show
got	hurry	long	number	pretty	side
grass	hurt	look	of	prize	sing
great	I	looked	off	pull	sister
green	ice	lost	often	put	sit
grow	if	made	oh	rabbit	six
guess	I'll	make	old	race	sleep
had	I'm	man	on	rain	so
hair	in	many	once	ran	soon
half	into	may	one	read	some
hand	is	maybe	only	ready	something
happy	it	me	open	red	sound
hard	its	men	or	ride	small
has	it's	met	other	right	start
hat	jump	might	our	road	stay
have	just	miss	out	rocket	step
he	keep	money	over	room	still
head	kind	more	own	round	stop
hear	kitten	morning	paint	run	stopped
heard	knew	most	pan	said	store
hello	know	mother	part	same	story
help	land	much	party	sang	street
hen	large	must	peanut	sat	such
her	last	my	penny	saw	sun
here	laugh	myself	people	say	sure

surprise	they	too	upon	well	with
table	thing	took	us	went	won't
take	things	town	use	were	word
talk	think	toy	used	what	words
tell	this	train	very	when	work
ten	those	tree	wagon	where	world
than	thought	truck	walk	which	would
thank	three	try	want	while	write
that	through	turtle	warm	white	year
the	time	TV	was	who	yellow
their	to	two	wash	why	you
them	today	under	water	will	your
then	together	until	way	window	yes
there	told	up	we	wish	zoo
these	tomorrow				

Outline of Lessons for Beginning Phonics Program

Formats listed in this outline can be found on the following pages:

Lesson One
letter intro.—a
telescoping—sad, if, at
letter intro.—a

Lesson Two
letter intro.—m
letter disc.—m, a
telescoping—it, mad, am
letter intro.—a
letter disc.—m, a

Lesson Three
letter disc.—m, a
segmenting—am, it
letter disc.—m, a
segmenting—Sam, at

Lesson Four
letter intro.—t
letter disc.—t, a, m
segmenting—at, it, Sam
letter intro.—t
letter disc.—t, a, m
segmenting—am, sit

Lesson Five
letter intro.—t
letter disc.—m, a, t
segmenting—am, sad, sit
letter disc.—m, a, t
segmenting—mad, if

Lesson Six
letter intro.—s
letter disc.—m, a, s, t
segmenting—am, sit, Sid
letter intro.—s
letter disc.—m, a, t, s
segmenting—Sam, it

Lesson Seven
letter intro.—s
letter disc.—m, a, s, t
sounding out—am
letter disc.—m, a, s, t
segmenting—at, sit, if
sounding out—am

Lesson Eight
letter intro.—i

letter disc.—m, a, s, t, i
sounding out—am, at
segmenting—sat, it, am
letter intro.—i
letter disc.—m, a, s, t, i
sounding out—am, at

Lesson Nine
letter intro.—i
letter disc.—m, a, s, t, i
sounding out—sat, am
segmenting—if, fat, miss, fig
letter disc.—m, a, s, t, i
sounding out—mat, Sam

Lesson Ten
letter intro.—i
letter disc.—m, a, s, t, f, i
sounding out—am, sat
segmenting—mad, Sid, fit, rat
letter intro.—f
letter disc.—m, a, s, t, f, i
sounding out—at, sat

Lesson Eleven
letter intro.—f
letter disc.—m, a, s, t, f, i
sounding out—Sam, sit
segmenting—rag, fit, sad, add
letter disc.—m, a, s, t, f, i
sounding out—am, it, sat

Lesson Twelve
letter intro.—d
letter disc.—m, a, s, d, f, i
sounding out—mat, sit, sat
letter intro.—d
letter disc.—a, d, i
segmenting—lot, rag, luck

Lesson Thirteen
letter intro.—d
letter disc.—m, a, s, d, f, i
segmenting—not, nut, in, on
letter disc.—a, d, i
sounding out—if, fit, am, fat, Sam
passage reading—am
(sounding out)

Lesson Fourteen
letter disc.—a, m, s, t, i, f, d
segmenting—lot, rat, sick, rip
letter disc.—t, d, i
irregular—is
sounding out—Sid, mad, fat, sad, sit, if
passage reading—Sam
(sounding out)

Lesson Fifteen
letter intro.—r
letter disc.—m, a, s, i, t, r, d
irregular—is
sounding out—mad, sat, it, if, at, sad
letter disc.—r, a, i
segmenting—on, in, ran, rag
passage reading—am, Sam
(sounding out)

Lesson Sixteen
letter intro.—r
letter disc.—m, a, i, t, f, d, s, r
irregular word—is
sounding out—sad, sat, am, fit, mit, mad
letter disc.—r, i, s
segmenting—sick, sock, lot, on, in
passage reading—Sam is sad.
(sounding out)

Lesson Seventeen
letter intro.—o
letter disc.—o, a, i, r, d, f, s, t
segmenting—lock, fig, cat, rag
sounding out—at, it, am, fit, mad, Sam
sight reading—at, it, am
passage reading—it, is, Sam.
(sounding out)

Lesson Eighteen
letter intro.—o
letter disc.—o, a, i, r, d, f, s, t
segmenting—top, got, dad, Tag
sounding out—ram, rid, fit, am, rat, Sam, sit
sight reading—it, at, Sam, sit
passage reading—Sam is sad. Sid is mad.
(sounding out)

Lesson Nineteen
letter intro.—g
letter disc.—o, a, i, r, d, f, t, g
segmenting—rug, cut, cat, did, hot
sounding out—Sam, it, am, sat, rim, fit, mad
sight reading—Sam, it, am, sat
passage reading—Sid is mad at Sam.
(sounding out)

Lesson Twenty
letter intro.—g
letter disc.—o, a, i, r, d, f, t, g
segmenting—dad, got, can, dig, him
sounding out—mom, rod, rat, sit, at, Sid, fit, ram
sight reading—sit, am, at, sad
passage reading—Sam is fat. Mom is fit.
(sounding out)

APPENDIX D

Basic Vocabulary for Beginning Readers and Suggestions for Assessing Student Knowledge

1. **Colors** blue, red, black, orange, green, yellow, pink, brown, white, gray, gold, purple, olive

   Testing Suggestion Use crayons to make marks of each color. Point to each mark and ask, "What color?"

2. **Prepositions** (Synonyms are in parentheses.) in, on, under (below), over (above), next to (beside), between (in the middle of), in front of (ahead), in back of (behind)

   Testing Suggestion Use a pencil and two cups. Place the pencil in various positions and ask, "Where is the pencil?"

3. **Common Objects and Locations**
   Classroom:
   > board, window, reading corner, teacher's desk, bookcase, bulletin board, light switch, doorway, chalk, clothing area, globe, map, stapler, clip, folder, calendar, lunch card holder

   Foods:
   > *fruits:* apricot, apple, cherry, pear, plum, grape, orange, grapefruit, pineapple, blueberry, strawberry
   > *vegetables:* beet, broccoli, cabbage, carrot, celery, onion, pepper, radish, squash
   > *meats:* chicken, ham, liver, steak, turkey
   > *dairy products:* cottage cheese, yogurt, Swiss cheese, American cheese
   > *miscellaneous:* mustard, catsup, salt, pepper, sugar, honey, puddings, bread, cereal

   Locations:
   > park, zoo, restaurant, grocery store, drug store, shoe store, department store, school, garage, church, library, post office, hotel, hospital, forest

   Testing Suggestion Obtain pictures or real objects. Ask, "What is this?"

4. **Pronouns**
   subject—he, she, they, it, you, we
   object—him, her, them, you
   possessive—his, her, their, your, its

Testing Suggestion Get several pictures that are identical except for gender of people (e.g., a picture of girl running and a picture of boy running). Point to appropriate picture and ask questions such as: "Touch *her* hair. Touch *his* hair. Touch the picture that shows *he* is running. Touch *them.*"

5. **Parts of Objects**
   match—stick, head
   pencil—eraser, point, shaft
   hammer—handle, head, claw
   purse—bag, clasp, handle
   wagon—wheels, handle, body
   shoe—sole, heel, laces, top, tongue
   egg—yolk, white, shell
   jacket—hood, zipper, front, back, sleeve
   clock—case, hands, face
   cabinet—handle, doors, shelves
   refrigerator—door, handle, body, freezer door, shelves
   tree—roots, branches, trunk, leaves
   chair—seat, back, legs, rungs
   door—doorknob, key hole, hinges, lock, rod
   cup—bowl, handle
   pot—body, lid, handle
   table—top, legs
   umbrella—frame, handle, covering
   fish—body, tail, fins
   nail—head, shaft, point
   flower—roots, stem, leaves, petal
   glasses—frame, earpieces, lenses
   shirt—collar, pocket, sleeves, cuffs, buttons
   window—frame, lock, handle, panes
   coat—sleeves, collar, buttons, button holes, front, back
   pants—zipper, legs, cuffs, pockets
   broom—handle, bristles
   toothbrush—handle, bristles
   glove—thumb, fingers, cuff, palm
   car—wheels, fenders, windows, doors, bumpers, hood, windshield, headlights, seats, seat belts, steering
      wheel
   rake—handle, prongs
   fork—handle, prongs
   knife—blade, point, handle
   dashboard—speedometer, glove compartment, radio, clock, gas gauge
   shovel—handle, scoop
   jar—lid, mouth, neck, body, label
   belt—strap, buckle, prong, loop, holes
   lamp—shade, stand, cord, switch, bulb
   garbage can—handles, lid, body
   spoon—handle, bowl

staircase—railing, post, stairs

person

face: hair, eyebrow, eyelash, forehead, nostrils, chin

upper body: waist, shoulder, upper arm, lower arm, index finger, ribs, backbone, hips, wrist, elbow, palm, knuckles

lower body: ankle, knee, arch, hips, thigh

Testing Suggestion Obtain pictures or actual objects. Ask, "What part is this?"

6. Characteristics (adjectives)

long—short	few—many	dark—light
big—little	same—different	deep—shallow
hot—cold	old—new	raw—cooked
full—empty	skinny—fat	stale—fresh
wet—dry	clean—dirty	ripe—spoiled
straight—crooked	fast—slow	early—late
rough—smooth	young—old	happy—sad
wide—narrow	tiny—huge	sick—well
quiet—noisy	mild—stormy	easy—difficult
safe—dangerous	ugly—beautiful	careful—careless
sharp—dull	open—closed	tight—loose
whole—part	shiny—dull	
wild—tame	cool—warm	

Testing Suggestion Obtain pictures of objects or actual objects that contain a characteristic. Ask either, "Is this _____?" or "Which one is _____?"

7. Occupations

baker	forest ranger	plasterer
barber	garbage collector	playground supervisor
brick layer	grocer	plumber
bus driver	hair dresser	police officer
carpenter	jeweler	priest
cashier	librarian	printer
clerk	lifeguard	rabbi
cook	logger	roofer
custodian	maid or butler	secretary
dentist	mail carrier	shoe-repair person
dishwasher	mechanic	stewardess or steward
doctor	milkman	taxi driver
dressmaker	minister	teacher
druggist	nurse	telephone-repair person
electrician	painter	truck driver
elevator operator	paper carrier	TV-repair person
farmer	photographer	veterinarian
firefighter	pilot	waiter or waitress
fisherman		

Testing Suggestion Obtain pictures. Ask, "What do we call this person?"

8. **Quantity Words** all, some, none, most, a few, a lot

   Testing Suggestion Put five pencils on a table. Ask, "Give me _____ (all, some, none, most, a few, a lot) of the pencils."

9. **Materials** cardboard, cloth, fur, glass, leather, metal, plastic, rubber, wood, brick

   Testing Suggestion Obtain a piece of material or a picture, Ask, "What is this made of?"

10. **Figures** circle, square, rectangle, oval, triangle

    Testing Suggestion Draw each figure. Ask, "What is this?"

11. **Patterns** plaid, striped, plain, spotted, flowered, checkered

    Testing Suggestion Fill in squares with different patterns. Ask, "What pattern is this?"

REFERENCES

Adams, G. L., & Engelmann, S. (1996). *Research on Direct Instruction: 25 years beyond DISTAR.* Adams and Engelmann Educational Achievement Systems.

Adams, M., Treiman, R., & Pressley, M. (1997). Reading, writing, and literacy. In I. E. Siegel & K. A. Renninger (Eds.), *A handbook of child psychology,* 5th ed., Vol. 4 (pp. 275–355). New York: Wiley.

Adams, M. J. (1990). *Beginning to read: Thinking and learning about print.* Cambridge, MA: MIT Press.

Adams, M. J. (1991). Beginning to read: A critique by literacy professionals. *The Reading Teacher, 44*(6), 371–372.

Adams, M. J., & Bruck, M. (1995). Resolving the "Great Debate." *American Educator, 19*(2), 7–20.

Allington, R. L., et al. (1993). *Celebrate reading.* Glenview, IL: Scott Foresman.

Ambruster, B., & Osborn, J. (Partnership for Reading) (2001). *Put reading first: The research building blocks for teaching children to read.* Washington, DC: National Institute for Literacy, National Institute of Child Health and Human Development, and U.S. Department of Education.

American Institutes of Research (1999). *Educators' guide to schoolwide reform.* Washington, DC.

Anderson, R. C., & Freebody, P. (1983). Reading comprehension and the assessment and acquisition of word knowledge. In B. Hutson (Ed.), *Advances in reading/language research: A research annual* (pp. 231–256). Greenwich, CT: JAI Press.

Anderson, R. C., & Nagy, W. E. (1991). Word meanings. In R. Barr, M. L. Kamil, P. B. Mosenthal, & P. D. Pearson (Eds.), *Handbook of reading research* (pp. 690–724). New York: Longman.

Archer, A., & Gleason, M. (2002). *Skills for school success* (Book 4). North Billerica, MA: Curriculum Associates.

Armbruster, B. B., Echots, C. H., & Brown, A. L. (1983). *The role of metacognition in reading to learn: A developmental perspective* (Reading Education Report No. 40). Champaign-Urbana, IL: University of Illinois, Center for the Study of Reading.

Baker, J. M., & Zigmond, N. (1995). The meaning and practice of inclusion for students with learning disabilities: Themes and implications from the five cases. *The Journal of Special Education, 29*(2), 163–180.

Baker, S. K., Simmons, D. C., & Kame'enui, E. J. (1995). *Vocabulary acquisition: Synthesis of the research* (Technical Report No. 13). Eugene, Oregon: University of Oregon, National Center to Improve the Tools of Educators.

Baker, S., Kame'enui, E. J., Simmons, D. C., & Stahl, S. (1994). Beginning reading: Educational tools for diverse learners. *School Psychology Review, 23*(3), 372–391.

Ball, E. W., & Blachman, B. A. (1991). Does phoneme awareness training in kindergarten make a difference in early word recognition and developmental spelling? *Reading Research Quarterly, 24*(1), 49–66.

Barr, R., Kamil, M. L., Mosenthal, P., & Pearson, P. D. (Eds.) (1991). *Handbook of reading research* (Vol. 2). White Plains, NY: Longman.

Baumann, J. F., & Kame'enui, E. J. (1991). Research on vocabulary instruction: Ode to Voltaire. In J. Flood, D. Lapp, & J. R. Squire (Eds.), *Handbook of research on teaching the English language arts* (pp. 604–632). New York: MacMillan.

Beck, I., & McKeown, M. (1991). Conditions of vocabulary acquisition. In R. Barr, M. Kamil, P. Mosenthal, & P. D. Pearson (Eds.), *Handbook of reading research* (Vol. 2, pp. 789–814). New York: Longman.

Beck, I. L. (1985). Five problems with children's comprehension in the primary grades. In J. Osborn, P. Wilson, & R. Anderson (Eds.), *Reading education: Foundation for a literate America* (pp. 239–254). Lexington, MA: D.C. Heath.

Beck, I. L., McKeown, M. G., & Kucan, L. (2002). *Bringing words to life: Robust Vocabulary Instruction.* New York: The Guilford Press.

Beck, I. L., McKeown, M. G., & Omanson, R. C. (1987). The effects and uses of diverse vocabulary instructional techniques. In M. G. McKeown & M. E. Curtis (Eds.), *The nature of vocabulary acquisition* (pp. 147–163). Hillsdale, NJ: Erlbaum.

Beck, I. L., Perfetti, C. A., & McKeown, R. C. (1982). Effects of long-term vocabulary instruction on lexical access and reading comprehension. *Journal of Educational Psychology, 74,* 506–521.

Beck, I. L., McKeown, M. G., & Kucan, L. (2002). *Bringing words: Robust vocabulary instruction.* New York: Guilford Press.

Becker, W. C. (1973). Applications of behavior principles in typical classrooms. In *Behavior modification in education. The seventy-second yearbook of the National Society for the Study of Education.* Chicago: NSSE.

Becker, W. C. (1977). Teaching reading and language to the disadvantaged—What we have learned from field research. *Harvard Educational Review, 47,* 518–543.

Becker, W. C., & Carnine, D. W. (1980). Direct instruction as a direct approach to educational intervention with disadvantaged and low performers. In B. Lakey & A. Kazdin (Eds.), *Advantages in Clinical Child Psychology* (Vol. 3). New York: Plenum Press.

Bereiter, C., & Kurland, M. (1981–1982). A constructive look at Follow Through results. *Interchange, 12,* 1–22.

Berkeley, M. (2002). The importance and difficulty of disciplined adherence to the educational reform model. *Journal of Education for Students Placed at Risk, 7*(2), 221–239.

Biemiller, A. (1977–1978). Relationships between oral reading rates for letters, words, and simple text in the development of reading achievement. *Reading Research Quarterly, 13,* 223–253.

Billmeyer, R., & Barton, M. L. (1998). *Teaching reading in the content areas: If not me, than who?* Aurora: Mid-Continent Regional Educational Laboratory.

Billingsley, B. S., & Wildman, T. M. (1990). Facilitating reading comprehension in learning disabled students: Metacognitive goals and instructional strategies. *Remedial and Special Education, 11*(2), 18–31.

Blachman, B., Tangel, D., Ball, E., Black, R., & McGraw, D. (1999). Developing phonological awareness and word recognition skills: A two-year intervention with low-income, inner-city children. *Reading and Writing: An Interdisciplinary Journal, 11,* 273–293.

Borkowski, J. G. (1992). Metacognitive theory: A framework for teaching literacy, writing, and math skills. *Journal of Learning Disabilities, 25*(4), 253–257.

Borman, G. D., Hewes, G. M., Overman, L. T., & Brown, S. (2002). *Comprehensive school reform and student achievement: A Meta-analysis.* Baltimore, MD: Center for Research on the Education of Students Placed At Risk (CRESPAR) at Johns Hopkins University.

Bos, C. S., & Anders, P. L. (1990). Effects of interactive vocabulary instruction on the vocabulary learning and reading comprehension of junior-high learning disabled students. *Learning Disability Quarterly, 13*(1), 31–42.

Bower, B. (1992). Reading the code, reading the whole: Researchers wrangle over the nature and teaching of reading. *Science News, 141*(9), 138–141.

Brophy, J. E., & Good, T. L. (1986). Teacher behavior and student achievement. In M. Wittrock (Ed.), *Third handbook of research on teaching* (pp. 328–375). New York: Macmillan.

Brown, A. (1987). Metacognition, executive control, self-regulation, and other more mysterious mechanisms. In F. E. Weinert & R. H. Kluwe (Eds.), *Metacognition, motivation, and understanding* (pp. 65–116). Hillsdale, NJ: L. Erlbaum.

Bulgren, J. A., Schumaker, J. B., & Deshler, D. D. (1988). Effectiveness of a concept teaching routine in enhancing the performance of LD students in secondary-level mainstream classes. *Learning Disability Quarterly, 11,* 3–17.

Burley, J. E. (1980). Short-term, high-intensity reading practice methods for Upward Bound students: An appraisal. *Negro Educational Review, 31*(3–4), 156–161.

Burmeister, L. E. (1968). Usefulness of phonic general-izations. *Reading Teacher, 21,* 349–356.

Byrne, B., & Fielding-Barnsley, R. (1989). Phonemic awareness and letter knowledge in the child's acquisition of the alphabetic principle. *Journal of Educational Psychology, 81,* 313–321.

Byrne, B., & Fielding-Barnsley, R. (1990). Acquiring the alphabetic principle: A case for teaching recognition of phoneme identity. *Journal of Educational Psychology, 82,* 805–812.

California Department of Education (1995). *Every child a reader: The report of the California reading task force* (Bureau of Publications, California Dept. of Education). Sacramento, CA.

Carlson, C. D., & Francis, D. J. (2002). Increasing the reading achievement of at-risk children through direct instruction: Evaluation of the rodeo institute for teacher excellence (RITE). *Journal of Education for Students Placed at Risk, 7*(2), 141–166.

Carnine, D. W. (1976a). *Conditions under which children learn the relevant attribute of negative instances rather than the essential characteristics of positive instances.* Unpublished manuscript, Follow Through Project, University of Oregon.

Carnine, D. W. (1976b). *Establishing a discriminative sequence by distributing attributes of compound stimuli between instances and non-instances.* In W. C. Becker & S. E. Englemann (Eds.), Technical Report 1976-1 Appendix B. Eugene, OR: University of Oregon, Follow Through Project.

Carnine, D. W. (1976c). Effects of two teacher presentation rates on off-task behavior, answering correctly, and participation. *Journal of Applied Behavioral Analysis, 9*(2), 199–206.

Carnine, D. W. (1976d). Similar sound separation and cumulative introduction in learning letter-sound correspondence. *Journal of Educational Research, 69,* 368–372.

Carnine, D. W. (1980a). Three procedures for presenting minimally different positive and negative instances. *Journal of Educational Psychology, 72,* 452–456.

Carnine, D. W. (1980b). Two letter discrimination sequences: High-confusion alternatives first versus low-confusion alternatives first. *Journal of Reading Behavior, 12,* 41–47.

Carnine, D. W. (1980c). Phonic versus whole-word correction procedures following phonic instruction. *Education and Treatment of Children, 3,* 323–330.

Carnine, D. W. (1980d). Relationships between stimulus variation and the formation of misconceptions. *Journal of Educational Research, 74,* 106–110.

Carnine, D. W. (1981a). Reducing training problems associated with visually and auditorily similar correspondences. *Journal of Learning Disabilities, 14,* 276–279.

Carnine, D. W. (1981b). High and low implementation of direct instruction teaching techniques. *Education and Treatment of Children, 4,* 42–51.

Carnine, D. W. (2000). *Why education experts resist effective practices and what it would take to make education more like medicine.* Thomas B. Fordham Foundation report of April 2000.

Carnine, D. W., Crawford, D. B., Harniss, M. K., Hollenbeck, K. L., & Miller, S. K. (in press). Effective strategies for teaching social studies to diverse learners. In E. J. Kame'enui & D. W. Carnine (Eds.), *Effective teaching strategies that accommodate diverse learners.* Columbus, OH: Merrill.

Carnine, D. W., Dixon, R. C., & Silbert, J. (1998). Design considerations for mathematics. In E. J. Kame'enui & D. W. Carnine (Eds.), *Effective teaching strategies that accommodate diverse learners.* Columbus, OH: Merrill.

Carnine, D. W., & Kame'enui, E. J. (1992). *Higher order thinking: Designing curriculum for mainstreamed students.* Austin, TX: Pro-Ed.

Carnine, D. W., & Silbert, J. (1979). *Direct instruction reading.* Columbus, OH: Charles E. Merrill Publishing Company.

Carver, R. P., & Liebert, R. E. (1995). The effect of reading library books in different levels of difficulty on gain in reading ability. *Reading Research Quarterly, 30,* 26–48.

Casteel, C. A. (1990). Effects of chunked text material on reading comprehension of high and low ability readers. *Reading Improvement, 27,* 269–275.

Castle, J. M., Riach, J., & Nicholson, T. (1994). Getting off to a better start in reading and spelling: The effects of phonemic awareness instruction within a whole language program. *Journal of Educational Psychology, 86,* 350–359.

Chall, J. (1992, May). *Whole language and direct instruction models: Implications for teaching reading in the schools.* Paper presented at the meeting of the International Reading Association, Orlando, FL.

Chall, J. (1967). *Learning to read: The great debate.* New York: McGraw-Hill.

Chall, J. S. (1983). *Learning to read: The great debate* (updated edition). New York: McGraw-Hill.

Chan, L. K. S., Cole, P. G., & Barfett, S. (1987). Comprehension monitoring: Detection and identification of text inconsistencies by LD and normal students. *Learning Disability Quarterly, 10*(2), 114–124.

Chan, L. K. S., Cole, P. G., & Morris, J. N. (1990). Effects of instruction in the use of a visual-imagery strategy on the reading-comprehension competence of disabled and average readers. *Learning Disability Quarterly, 13*(1), 2–11.

Chaney, J. H. (1991). Beginning to read: A critique by literacy professionals. *The Reading Teacher, 44*(6), 374–375.

Chard, D. J., Simmons, D. C., & Kame'enui, E. J. (1995). *Understanding the primary role of word recognition in the reading process: Synthesis of research on beginning reading* (Technical Report No. 15). Eugene: University of Oregon, National Center to Improve the Tools of Educators.

Collins, C. (1980). Sustained silent reading periods: Effects on teachers' behaviors and students' achievement. *Elementary School Journal, 81,* 108–114.

Collins, V. L., Dickson, S. V., Simmons, D. C., & Kame'enui, E. J. (1996). *Metacognition and its relation to reading comprehension: A synthesis of the research* (Technical Report No. 23). Eugene, Oregon: University of Oregon, National Center to Improve the Tools of Educators.

Colvin, G., & Lazar M., (1997). The effective classroom—Managing for success. Longmont, CO: Sopris West.

Comprehension: Synthesis of Research (1996). The annotated excerpt was prepared by Vicky Vachon.

Cornoldi, C. (1990). Metacognitive control processes and memory deficits in poor comprehenders. *Learning Disability Quarterly, 13*(4), 245–255.

Cornwall, A. (1992). The relationship of phonological awareness, rapid naming and verbal memory to severe reading and spelling disability. *Journal of Learning Disabilities, 25*(8), 532–538.

Cronbach, L. J., & Snow, R. E. (1977). *Aptitudes and instructional methods: A handbook for research on interaction.* New York: Irvington.

Cunningham, A. E. (1990). Explicit versus implicit instruction in phonemic awareness. *Journal of Experimental Child Psychology, 50,* 429–444.

Daneman, M. (1991). Individual differences in reading skills. In R. Barr, M. L. Kamil, P. B. Mosenthal, &

P. D. Pearson (Eds.), *Handbook of reading research* (Vol. 2, pp. 512–538). New York: Longman.

Darch, C., Carnine, D., & Kame'enui, E. (1986). The role of visual displays and social structure in content-area instruction. *Journal of Reading Behavior, 18,* 275–295.

Davis, Z. T. (1988). A comparison of the effectiveness of sustained silent reading and directed reading activity on students' reading achievement. *The High School Journal, 72*(1), 46–48.

Deshler, D. D., Schumaker, J., Harris, K. R., & Graham, S. (1999). *Teaching every adolescent everyday.* Cambridge, MA: Brookline Books.

DiCecco, V. M., & Gleason, M. M. (2002). Using graphic organizers to attain relational knowledge from expository text. *Journal of Learning Disabilities, 35*(4), 306–320.

Dickson, S., Kame'enui, E. J., & Simmons, D. C. (1995). Instruction in expository text structure: A focus on compare/contrast. *Learning Disabilities Forum, 20*(2), 8–15.

Dickson, S., Simmons, D., & Kame'enui, E. (1995). *Text organization: Curricular and instructional implications for diverse learners* (Technical Report No. 18). Eugene, Oregon: University of Oregon, National Center to Improve the Tools of Educators.

Dimino, J. (1988). *The effects of a story grammar comprehension strategy on low-performing students' ability to comprehend short stories.* Unpublished doctoral dissertation, University of Oregon.

Dixon, R. C., Isaacson, S., & Stein, M. L. (1998). Effective approaches to writing instruction: Common threads. In E. J. Kameenui & D. W. Carnine (Eds.), *Effective teaching strategies that accommodate diverse learners.* Columbus, OH: Merrill.

Dykstra, R. (1968). Summary of the second-grade phase of the Cooperative Research Program in primary reading instruction. *Reading Research Quarterly, 4,* 49–71.

Ehri, L. C. (1991). Development of the ability to read words. In R. Barr, M. L. Kamil, P. B. Mosenthal, & P. D. Pearson (Eds.), *Handbook of reading research* (Vol. 2, pp. 383–417). New York: Longman.

Elliott, S. N., & Shapiro, E. S. (1990). Intervention technqiues and programs for academic performance problems. In T. B. Gutkin & C. R. Reynolds (Eds.), *The handbook of school psychology* (pp. 635–660). New York: John Wiley & Sons.

Ellis, A. K., & Fouts, J. T. (1997). *Research on educational interventions.* Larchmont, NY: Eye on Education.

Engelmann, S., & Bruner, E. (1974). *DISTAR reading I.* Chicago, IL: Science Research Associates.

Engelmann, S., & Bruner, E. (1988). *Reading mastery I.* Columbus, OH: Science Research Associates.

Engelmann, S., & Carnine, D. (1976). A structural program's effect on the attitudes and achievement of average and above average second graders. In W. C. Becker and S. Englemann (Eds.), *Technical Report 76-1. Appendix B: Formative Research.* Eugene, OR: University of Oregon.

Engelmann, S., & Carnine, D. (1991). *Theory of instruction: Principles and applications* (rev. ed.). Eugene, OR: ADI Press.

Engelmann, S., & Davis, K. L. (2001). *Reasoning and writing—Level A: A direct instruction program.* Columbus, OH: Science Research Associates.

Engelmann, S., & Osborn J. (1999). *Language for learning.* Columbus, OH: Science Research Associates.

Engelmann, S., & Osborn J. (2002). *Language for thinking.* Columbus, OH: Science Research Associates.

Engelmann, S., Osborn, J., Osborn, S., & Zoref, L. (1988). *Reading mastery V.* Columbus, OH: Science Research Associates.

Engelmann, S., Osborn, J., Osborn, S., & Zoref, L. (1988). *Reading mastery VI.* Columbus, OH: Science Research Associates.

Engelmann, S., Osborn, S., & Hanner, S. (2001). *Corrective reading program: Comprehension skills.* Columbus, OH: Science Research Associates.

Fawcett, A. J., & Nicolson, R. I. (1991). Vocabulary training for children with dyslexia. *Journal of Learning Disabilities, 24*(6), 379–383.

Fletcher, J. & Lyon, R. (1998). Reading: A research-based approach. In W. Evers (Ed.), *What's gone wrong in America's classrooms* (pp. 49–90). Stanford, CA: Hoover Institution Press.

Foorman, B. R. (1995). Research on "The Great Debate," Code-oriented versus whole-language approaches to reading instruction. *School Psychology Review, 24*(3), 376–392.

Foorman, B. R., Francis, D., Fletcher, J., Schatschneider, C., & Mehta, P. (1998). The role of instruction in learning to read: Preventing reading failure in at-risk children. *Journal of Educational Psychology, 90,* 37–55.

Foorman, B. R., Stuebing, K. K., & Shaywitz, B. A. (1998). Intelligent testing and the discrepancy model for children with learning disabilities. *Learning Disabilities: Research and Practice, 13,* 186–200.

Forness, S. R., Kavale, K. A., Blum, I. M., & Lloyd, J. W. (1997). Mega-analysis of meta-analyses. *Teaching Exceptional Children, 29*(6), 4–9.

Fuchs, D., Fuchs, L. S., Mathes, P. G., & Simmons. D. C. (1996). *Peer-Assisted Learning Strategies in reading: A manual.* (Available from Douglas Fuchs. Box 328 Peabody. Vanderbilt University. Nashville, TN 37203)

Fuchs, L. S., Fuchs, D., & Maxwell, L. (1998). The validity of informal measures of reading comprehension *Remedial and Special Education, 9,* 20–28.

Gajria, M., & Salvia, J. (1992). *The effects of summarization instruction on text comprehension of students with learning disabilities.* Exceptional Children, 58(6), 508–516.

Garner, R. (1987). *Metacognition and reading comprehension.* Norwood, NJ: Ablex.

Gersten, R., & Baker, S. (2000). What we know about effective instructional practices for English-language learners. *Exceptional Children, 66,* 454–470.

Gleason, M. M., Archer, A. L., & Colvin, G. (2002). Interventions for improving study skills. In Mark R. Shinn, Hill M. Walker, & Gary Stoner (Eds.), *Interventions for academic and behavior problems II: Preventive and remedial approaches* (pp. 651–680). Bethesda, MD: NASP Publications.

Goodman, K. (1967, May). Reading: A psycholinguistic guessing game. *Journal of the Reading Specialist,* 126–135.

Goodman, K. (1969). Analysis of oral reading miscues: Applied psycholinguistics. *Reading Research Quarterly, 5,* 9–30.

Goodman, K. (1986). *What's whole in whole language.* Portsmouth, NH: Heinemann.

Goodman, K. (1994). Deconstructing the rhetoric of Moorman, Blanton, and McLaughlin: A response. *Reading Research Quarterly, 29*(4), 340–346.

Gough, P. B., Ehri, L. C., & Treiman, R. (1992). *Reading acquisition.* Hillsdale, NJ: Lawrence Erlbaum Associates, Inc.

Graesser, A., Golding, J. M., & Long, D. L. (1991). Narrative representation and comprehension. In R. Barr, M. L. Kamil, P. Mosenthal, & P. D. Pearson (Eds.), *Handbook of reading research* (Vol. 2, pp. 171–204). White Plains, NY: Longman.

Graves, M. F. (1986). Vocabulary learning and instruction. *Review of Research in Education, 13,* 49–90.

Graves, M. F., Juel, C., & Graves, B. B. (1998). *Teaching reading in the 21st century.* Des Moines, IA: Allyn and Bacon.

Griffin, C. C., Simmons, D. C., & Kame'enui, E. J. (1991). Investigating the effectiveness of graphic organizer instruction on the comprehension and recall of science content by students with learning disabilities. *The Journal of Reading, Writing, and Learning Disabilities International, 7*(4), 355–376.

Griffin, C., Duncan Malone, L., & Kame'enui, E. J. (1995). Effects of graphic organizer instruction on fifth-grade students. *Journal of Educational Research, 89*(2), 98–107.

Grossen, B. J., Carnine, D. W., Romance, N. R., & Vitale, M. R. (2002). Teaching science to accommodate diverse learners. In E. J. Kame'enui & D. W. Carnine (Eds.), *Effective teaching strategies that accommodate diverse learners.* Columbus, OH: Merrill.

Gurney, D. E. (1987, January–February). Teaching mildly handicapped high-school students to understand short stories using a story-grammar-comprehension strategy. *Dissertation Abstracts International, 47*(08), 3047A.

Gurney, D., Gersten, R., Dimino, J., & Carnine, D. (1990). Story grammar: Effective literature instruction for high school students with learning disabilities. *Journal of Learning Disabilities, 23,* 335–342, 348.

Guthrie, J. T. (1977). Follow Through: A compensatory education experiment. *The Reading Teacher, 31*(2), 240–244.

Hanna, P. R., Hanna, J. S., Hodges, R. E., & Rudlof, E. H. (1966). *Phonemegrapheme correspondences as cues to spelling improvement.* Washington, DC: U.S. Government Printing Office.

Harris, K. R., & Pressley, M. (1991). The nature of cognitive strategy instruction: Interactive strategy construction. *Exceptional Children, 57*(5), 392–404.

Hasbrouck, J. E., & Tindal, G. (1992, Spring). Curriculum-based oral reading fluency norms for students in grades 2–5. *Teaching Exceptional Children, 24*(3), 41–44.

Haskell, D. W., Foorman, B. R., & Swank, P. R. (1992). Effects of three orthographic/phonological units on first-grade reading. *Remedial and Special Education, 13,* 40–49.

Hempenstall, K. (1999). Miscue analysis: A critique. *Effective School Practices, 17*(3), 85–93.

Holt, S. B., & O'Tuel, F. S. (1989). The effect of sustained silent reading and writing on achievement and attitudes of seventh and eighth grade students reading two years below grade level. *Reading Improvement, 26,* 290–297.

Hurford, D. P., Darrow, L. J., Edwards, T. L., Howerton, C. J., Mote, C. R., Schauf, J. D., & Coffey, P. (1993). An examination of phonemic processing abilities in children during their first-grade year. *Journal of Learning Disabilities, 26*(3), 167–177.

Irvin, J. L. (1998). *Reading and the middle school student: Strategies to enhance literacy* (2nd ed.). Boston: Allyn and Bacon.

Irvin, J. L. (2001, May). *Strategies to improve reading in the content areas.* Presentation sponsored by Staff Development Resources, Portland, OR.

Jenkins, J. R., & Dixon, R. (1983). Vocabulary learning. *Contemporary Educational Psychology, 8,* 237–260.

Jenkins, J. R., Fuchs, L. S., Fuchs, D., & Hosp, M. K. (2001). Oral reading fluency as an indicator of reading competence: A theoretical, empirical, and historical analysis. *Scientific Studies of Reading, 5*(3), 239–256. Copyright © 2001, Lawrence Erlbaum Associates, Inc.

Jitendra, A., & Kame'enui, E. J. (1994). A review of concept learning models: Implications for special education practitioners. *Intervention in School and Clinic, 30*(2), 91–98.

Jitendra, A., & Kame'enui, E. J. (1988). A design of instruction analysis of concept teaching in five basal language programs: Violations from the bottom up. *The Journal of Special Education, 22,* 199–219.

Johnson, G., Gersten, R., & Carnine, D. (1987). Effects of instructional design variables on vocabulary acquisition of LD students: A study of computer-assisted instruction. *Journal of Learning Disabilities, 20,* 206–213.

Juel, C. (1988). Learning to read and write: A longitudinal study of fifty-four children from first through fourth grade. *Journal of Educational Psychology, 80*(4), 437–447.

Juel, C. (1991). Beginning reading. In R. Barr, M. L. Kamil, P. B. Mosenthal, & P. D. Pearson (Eds.), *Handbook of reading research* (Vol. 2, pp. 759–788). New York: Longman.

Kame'enui, E. J. (1993). Diverse learners and the tyranny of time: Don't fix blame; fix the leaky roof. *The Reading Teacher, 46*(5), 376–383.

Kame'enui, E. J. (1995). Response to Deegan: Keep the curtain inside the tub. *The Reading Teacher, 48*(8), 700–703.

Kame'enui, E. J. (1996). Shakespeare and beginning reading: "The readiness is all." *Teaching Exceptional Children, 28*(2), 77–81.

Kame'enui, E. J., & Carnine, D. W. (1998). *Effective teaching strategies that accommodate diverse learners.* Columbus, OH: Merrill.

Kame'enui, E. J., Simmons, D. C., Baker, S., Chard, D., Dickson, S., Gunn, B., Smith, S., Sprick, M., & Lin, S.-J. (1997). Effective strategies for teaching beginning reading. In E. J. Kame'enui & D. W. Carnine (Eds.), *Effective teaching strategies that accommodate diverse learners.* Columbus, OH: Merrill.

Kame'enui, E. J., & Simmons, D. C. (1990). *Designing instructional strategies: The prevention of academic learning problems.* Columbus, OH: Merrill.

Kavale, K. A., & Forness, S. R. (1987). Substance over error: Assessing the efficacy of modality testing and teaching. *Exceptional Children, 54,* 228–239.

LaBarge, D., & Samuels, S. J. (1974). Toward a theory of automatic information processing in reading. *Cognitive Psychology, 6,* 293–322.

Langford, J. C., & Allen, E. G. (1983). Effects of U.S.S.R on students' attitudes and achievement. *Reading Horizons, 23*(3), 194–200.

Lenchner, O., Gerber, M. M., & Routh, D. K. (1990). Phonological awareness tasks as predictors of decoding ability: Beyond segmentation. *Journal of Learning Disabilities, 23*(4), 240–247.

Levy, B. A., Abello, B., & Lusynchuk, I. (1997). Transfer from word training to reading in context: Gains in reading fluency and comprehension. *Learning Disability Quarterly, 20,* 173–188.

Liberman, I. Y., & Shankweiler, D. (1985). Phonology and the problems of learning to read and write. *Remedial and Special Education, 6*(6), 8–17.

Liberman, I. Y., Shankweiler, D., & Liberman, A. M. (1991). The alphabetic principle and learning to read. In D. Shankweiler and I. Y. Liberman (Eds.), *Phonology and reading disability: Solving the reading puzzle* (pp. 1–33). Ann Arbor: University of Michigan Press.

Liberman, I. Y., & Liberman, A. M. (1990). Whole language vs. code emphasis: Underlying assumptions and their implications for reading instruction. *Annals of Dyslexia, 40,* 51–76.

Lie, A. (1991). Effects of a training program for stimulating skills in word analysis in first-grade children. *Reading Research Quarterly, 26*(3), 234–250.

Lloyd, J. W. (1984). How shall we individualize instruction or should we? *Remedial and Special Education, 5,* 7–15.

Lovett, M. W., Borden, S. L., DeLuca, T., Lacerenza, L., Benson, N. J., & Brackstone, D. (1994). Treating the core deficits of developmental dyslexia: Evidence of transfer of learning after phonologically- and strategy-based reading training programs. *Developmental Psychology, 30*(6), 805–822.

Lovett, M. W., Warren-Chaplin, P. M., Ransby, M. J., & Borden, S. L. (1990). Training the word recognition skills of reading disabled children: Treatment and transfer effects. *Journal of Educational Psychology, 82,* 769–780.

Lundberg, I., Frost, J., & Petersen, O.-P. (1988). Effects of an extensive program for stimulating phonological awareness in preschool children. *Reading Research Quarterly, 23*(3), 263–284.

Lyon, G. R. (1995). Research initiatives in learning disabilities: Contributions from scientists supported by the National Institute of Child Health and Human Development. *Journal of Child Neurology, 10,* 120–126.

Lyon, G. R. (1996). Toward a definition of dyslexia. *Annals of Dyslexia, 45,* 3–27.

Malone, L. D., & Mastropieri, M. A. (1992). Reading comprehension instruction: Summarization and self-monitoring training for students with learning disabilities. *Exceptional Children, 58*(3), 270–279.

Mann, V. (1993). Phoneme awareness and future reading ability. *Journal of Learning Disabilities, 26*(4), 259–269.

Mann, V. A., & Brady, S. (1988). Reading disability: The role of language deficiencies. *Journal of Consulting and Clinical Psychology, 56*(6), 811–816.

Mastropieri, M. A., Scruggs, T. E., & Fulk, B. J. (1990). Teaching abstract vocabulary with the keyword method: Effects on recall and comprehension. *Journal of Learning Disabilities, 23*(2), 92–107.

Mather, N. (1992). Whole language reading instruction for students with learning disabilities: Caught in the cross fire. *Learning Disabilities Research and Practice, 7,* 87–95.

Mathes, P. G., Allor, J. H., Torgeson, J. K., & Allen, S. H. (2001). *Teacher directed PALS (Path to Achieving Literacy Success).* Longmont, CO: Sopris West Educational Services.

Meltzer, L. J. (1993). Strategy use in students with learning disabilities: The challenge of assessment. In L. J. Meltzer (Ed.), *Strategy assessment and instruction for students with learning disabilities* (pp. 93–136). Austin, TX: Pro-Ed.

Mezynski, K. (1983). Issues concerning the acquisition of knowledge: Effects of vocabulary training on reading comprehension. *Review of Educational Research, 53,* 253–279.

Moats, L. C. (2000). Whole language lives on: The illusion of "balanced" reading instruction. Thomas B. Fordham Foundation report of October, 2000.

Moats, L. C. (Spring/Summer 1998). Teaching decoding. *American Educator,* 42–49, 95–96.

Montague, M., Maddux, C. D., & Dereshiwsky, M. I. (1990). Story grammar and comprehension and production of narrative prose by students with learning disabilities. *Journal of Learning Disabilities, 23,* 190–197.

Murphy, J., Weil, M., & McGreal, T. L. (1986). The basic practice model of instruction. *The Elementary School Journal, 87,* 83–95.

Nagy, W. E., Herman, I. A., & Anderson, R. C. (1985). Learning words from context. *Reading Research Quarterly, 29*(2), 233–253.

Nagy, W. E. (1988). *Teaching vocabulary to improve reading comprehension.* Newark, DE: International Reading Association.

Nagy, W. E., & Anderson, R. C. (1984). How many words are there in printed school English? *Reading Research Quarterly, 19,* 304–330.

Nagy, W. E., Anderson, R., & Herman, P. (1987). Learning word meanings from context during normal reading. *American Educational Research Journal, 24,* 237–270.

Nagy, W. E., Herman, P., & Anderson, R. C. (1985). Learning words from context. *Reading Research Quarterly, 20,* 233–253.

National Institute of Child Health and Human Development (2000). Report of the National Reading Panel. Teaching children to read: An evidence-based assessment of the scientific research literature on reading and its implications for reading instruction: Reports of the subgroups (NIH Publication No. 00-4754). Washington, DC: U.S. Government Printing Office.

National Reading Panel (NRP) (2000). Teaching children to read: An evidence-based assessment of the scientific research literature on reading and its implications for reading instruction. Washington, DC: National Institute of Child Health and Human Development.

Newby, R. F., Caldwell, J., & Recht, D. R. (1989). Improving reading comprehension of children with dysphonetic and dyseidetic dyslexia using story grammar. *Journal of Learning Disabilities, 22,* 373–380.

O'Connor, R. E., Jenkins, J. R., Leicester, N., & Slocum, T. A. (1993). Teaching phonological awareness to young children with learning disabilities. *Exceptional Children, 59,* 532–546.

O'Connor, R., Jenkins, J., & Slocum, T. (1995). Transfer among phonological tasks in kindergarten: Essential instructional content. *Journal of Educational Psychology, 87,* 202–217.

Palinscar, A., & Brown, A. (1984). Reciprocal teaching of comprehension-fostering and comprehension-monitoring activities. *Cognition and Instruction, 1,* 117–175.

Palincsar, A., & Brown, A. (1986). Interactive teaching to promote independent learning from text. *The Reading Teacher, 39,* 771–777.

Palincsar, A. S., David, Y. M., Winn, J. A., & Stevens, D. D. (1991). Examining the context of strategy instruction. *Remedial and Special Education, 12*(3), 43–53.

Paris, S. G., & Jacobs, J. E. (1984). The benefits of informed instruction for children's reading awareness and comprehension skills. *Child Development, 55,* 2083–2093.

Paris, S., Wasik, B., & Van der Westhuizen, G. (1988). *Meta cognition: A review of research on metacognition and reading.* Paper presented at the National Reading Conference, St. Petersburg, FL.

Paris, S. C., Wasik, B. A., & Turner, J. C. (1991). The development of strategic readers. In R. Barr, M. L. Kamil, P. B. Mosenthal, & P. D. Pearson (Eds.), *Handbook of reading research* (Vol. 2, pp. 609–640). New York: Longman.

Pearson, P. D., & Fielding, L. (1991). Comprehension instruction. In R. Barr, M. L. Kamil, P. Mosenthal, & P. D. Pearson (Eds.), *Handbook of reading research* (Vol. 2, pp. 815–860). White Plains, NY: Longman.

Pflaum, S., Walberg, H. J., Karigianes, M. L., & Rasher, S. P. (1980). Reading instruction: A quantitative analysis. *Educational Researcher, 9*(7), 12–18.

Pinnell, G. S., Pikulski, J. J., Wixson, K. K., Campbell, J. R., Gough, P. B., & Beatty, A. S. (1995). *Listening to children read aloud.* Washington, DC: Office of Educational Research and Improvement, U.S. Department of Education.

Pittelman, S. D., Heimlich, J. E., Berglund, R. L., & French, M. P. (1991). *Semantic feature analysis: Classroom applications.* Newark, Delaware: International Reading Association.

Pressley, M. (2000). What should comprehension instruction be the instruction of? In M. Kamil, P. Mosenthal, P. D. Pearson, & R. Barr (Eds.), *Handbook of reading research, volume III* (pp. 545–562).

Rack, J. P., Snowling, M. J., & Olson, R. K. (1992). The nonword reading deficit in developmental dyslexia: A review. *Reading Research Quarterly, 27*(1), 29–52.

RAND Reading Study Group (2002). *Reading for understanding: Toward an R&D program in reading comprehension.* A report prepared for the Office of Education Research and Improvement (OERI).

Reinking, D., & Rickman, S. S. (1990). The effects of computer-mediated texts on the vocabulary learning and comprehension of intermediate-grade readers. *Journal of Reading Behavior, 22*(4), 395–411.

Rosenshine, B. (1979). Content, time, and direct instruction. In J. Peterson & H. Walberg (Eds.), *Research on teaching: Concepts, findings and implications.* Berkeley, CA: McCutchan.

Rosenshine, B. V. (1986). Synthesis of research on explicit teaching. *Educational Leadership, 43,* 60–69.

Rosenshine, B., & Stevens, R. (1986). Teaching functions. In M. C. Wittrock (Ed.), *Handbook of research on teaching* (3rd ed.) (pp. 376–391). New York: Macmillan.

Rottman, T. R., & Cross, D. R. (1990). Using informed strategies for learning to enhance the reading and thinking skills of children with learning disabilities. *Journal of Learning Disabilities, 23*(5), 270–278.

Sawyer, D. (1992). Language abilities, reading acquisition, and developmental dyslexia: A discussion of hypothetical and observed relationships. *Journal of Learning Disabilities, 25,* 82–95.

Schreiber, P. A. (1980). On the acquisition of reading fluency. *Journal of Reading Behavior, 12,* 177–186.

Schreiber, P. A. (1987). Prosody and structure in children's syntactic processing. In R. Horowitz & S. J. Samuels (Eds.), *Comprehending oral and written language.* New York: Academic Press.

Schug, M. C., Tarver, S. G., & Western, R. D. (2001). *Direct instruction and the teaching of early reading: Wisconsin's teacher-led insurgency.* Thiensville, WI: Wisconsin Policy Research Institute, Inc.

Schumaker, J. B., Denton, P. H., & Deshler, D. D. (1984). *The paraphrasing strategy.* Lawrence, KS: The University of Kansas.

Schunk, D. H., & Rice, J. M. (1992). Influence of reading-comprehension strategy information on children's achievement outcomes. *Learning Disability Quarterly, 15*(1), 51–64.

Seidenberg, P. L. (1989). Relating text-processing research to reading and writing instruction for learning disabled students. *Learning Disabilities Focus, 5*(1), 4–12.

Share, D. (1995). Phonological recording and self-teaching: Sine qua non of reading acquisition. *Cognition, 55,* 151–218.

Sheinker, J., & Sheinker, A. (1989). *Metacognitive approach to study strategies.* Rockville, MD: Aspen.

Simmonds, E. P. M. (1990). The effectiveness of two methods for teaching a constraint-seeking questioning strategy to students with learning disabilities. *Journal of Learning Disabilities, 23*(4), 229–233.

Simmons, D. C., & Kameenui, E. J. (1996). A focus on curriculum design: When children fail. *Focus on Exceptional Children, 28*(7), 1–16.

Simmons, D. C., & Kame'enui, E. J. (2003). *Early reading intervention program.* Chicago: Scott Foresman/Pearson.

Simmons D. C., Kame'enui, E. J., & Darch, C. (1988). Learning disabled children's metacognition of selected textual features. *Learning Disabilities Quarterly, 11,* 380–395.

Simmons, D. C., Kame'enui, E. J., Dickson, S., Chard, D., Gunn, B., & Baker, S. (1994). Integrating narrative reading comprehension and writing instruction for all learners. In C. K. Kinzer & D. J. Leu (Eds.), *Multidimensional aspects of literacy research, theory, and practice. Forty-third Yearbook of the National Reading Conference* (pp. 572–582). Chicago, IL: National Reading Conference.

Sinatra, R. C., Berg, D., & Dunn, R. (1985). Semantic mapping improves reading comprehension of learning disabled students. *Teaching Exceptional Children, 17*(4), 310–314.

Sindelar, P. T., Monda, L., & O'Shea, L. (1990). Effects of repeated readings on instructional- and mastery-level readers. *Journal of Educational Research, 83,* 220–226.

Smith, R. W. L. (1966). *Dictionary of English word-roots.* Totowa, NJ: Littlefield, Adams & Co.

Smith, S. B., Simmons, D. C., & Kame'enui, E. J. (1995). *Synthesis of research on phonological awareness: Principles and implications for reading acquisition* (Tech. Rep. No. 21). Eugene, OR: University of Oregon, National Center to Improve the Tools of Educators.

Snider, V. E. (1992). Learning styles and learning to read: A critique. *Remedial and Special Education, 113,* 6–18.

Snow, C. E., Burns, S., & Griffin P. (1998). *Preventing reading difficulties in young children.* Washington, DC: National Academy Press.

Snowling, M. J. (1991). Developmental reading disorders. *Journal of Child Psychology Psychiatry, 32*(1), 49–77.

Spector, J. E. (1995). Phonemic awareness training: Application of principles of direct instruction. *Reading and Writing Quarterly, 11,* 37–51.

Sprick, R. (1991). *The solution book: A guide to classroom discipline.* Chicago: Science Research Associates.

Stahl, S. A., & Fairbanks, M. M. (1986). The effects of vocabulary instruction: A model-based meta-analysis. *Review of Educational Research, 56,* 72–110.

Stahl, S. A., & Kuhn, M. R. (1995). Does whole language or instruction matched to learning styles help children learn to read? *School Psychology Review, 24,* 393–404.

Stahl, S. A., & Shiel, T. G. (1999). Teaching meaning vocabulary: Productive approaches for poor readers. *Read all about it! Readings to inform the profession.* Sacramento: California State Board of Education, pp. 291–321.

Stallman, A. C., Commeyras, M., Kerr, B., Reimer, K., Jimenez, R., Hartman, D. K., Pearson, P. D. (1990). Are "new" words really new? *Reading Research and Instruction, 29*(2), 12–29.

Stanovich, K. E. (1985). Explaining the variance in reading ability in terms of psychological processes: What have we learned? *Annals of Dyslexia, 35,* 67–96.

Stanovich, K. E. (1988). Explaining the differences between the dyslexic and the garden-variety poor reader: The phonological-core variable-difference model. *Journal of Learning Disabilities, 21,* 590–612.

Stanovich, K. E. (1991). Word recognition: Changing perspectives. In R. Barr, M. L. Kamil, P. B. Mosenthal, & P. D. Pearson (Eds.), *Handbook of reading research* (Vol. 2, pp. 418–452). New York: Longman.

Stanovich, K. E. (1993). It's practical to be rational. *Journal of Learning Disabilities, 26*(8), 524–532.

Stanovich, K. E. (1994). Romance and reality. *The Reading Teacher, 47,* 280–291.

Stanovich, K. E. (1986). Matthew effects in reading: Some consequences of individual differences in the acquisition of literacy. *Reading Research Quarterly, 21*(4), 360–406.

Stanovich, K., & Siegel, L. S. (1994). The phenotypic performance profile of reading-disabled children: A regression-based test of the phonological-core variable-difference model. *Journal of Educational Psychology, 86,* 24–53.

Sulzby, E. & Teale, W. (1991). Emergent literacy. In R. Barr, M. L. Kamil, P. B. Mosenthal, & P. D. Pearson (Eds.), *Handbook of reading research* (Vol. 2, pp. 727–757). New York: Longman.

Summers, E. G., & McClelland, J. V. (1982). A field-based evaluation of sustained silent reading (SSR) in intermediate grades. *Alberta Journal of Educational Research, 28,* 100–112.

Swanborn, M. S. L., & de Glopper, K. (1999). Incidental word learning while reading: A meta-analysis. *Review of Educational Research, 69*(3), 261–285.

Swanson, H. L. (1989). Strategy instruction: Overview of principles and procedures for effective use. *Learning Disability Quarterly, 12*(1), 3–14.

Talbott, E., Lloyd, J. W., & Tankersley, M. (1994). Effects of reading comprehension interventions for students with learning disabilities. *Learning Disability Quarterly, 17,* 223–232.

Tan, A., & Nicholson, T. (1997). Flashcards revisited: Training poor readers to read words faster improves their comprehension of text. *Journal of Educational Psychology, 89,* 276–288.

Tarver, S. G. (1996). Should method of teaching beginning reading be matched to the student's learning style? *Effective School Practices, 15*(4), 37–38.

Tarver, S. G., in collaboration with the DLD/DR Research Alerts Committee (1999). Focusing on direct instruction. *Current Practice Alerts, 2.* Joint publication of the Council for Exceptional Children's Division for Learning Disabilities and Division for Research.

Tarver, S. G. (2000). Direct Instruction: Teaching for generalization, application, and integration of knowledge. *Learning Disabilities: A Multidisciplinary Journal, 10*(4), 201–207.

Taylor, B. M., Pearson, P. D., Clark, K. F., & Walpole, S. (1999). *Beating the odds in teaching all children to read* (CIERA Rep. No. 2-006). Ann Arbor, MI: Center for the Improvement of Early Reading Achievement, University of Michigan.

Thurlow, R., & van den Broek, P. (1997). Automaticity and inference generation. *Reading and Writing Quarterly, 13*(2), 165–184.

Torgesen, J. K. (1985). Memory processes in reading disabled children. *Journal of Learning Disabilities, 18*(6), 350–357.

Torgesen, J. K., Wagner, R. K., Simmons, K., & Laughon, P. (1990). Identifying phonological coding problems in disabled readers: Naming, counting, or span measures. *Learning Disability Quarterly, 13,* 236–243.

Torgesen, J., Wagner, R. K., Rashotte, C., Rose, E., Lindamood, P., Conway, T. I., & Garvan, C. (1999). Preventing reading failure in young children with phonological processing disabilities: Group and individual responses to instruction. *Journal of Educational Psychology, 91*(4), 579–593.

Traub, J. (1999). *Better by design? A consumer's guide to school reform.* The Thomas B. Fordham Foundation. Available online at http://www.edexcellence.net/library/bbd/better_by_design.html.

Vellutino, F. R. (1991). Introduction to three studies on reading acquisition: Convergent findings on theoretical foundations of code-oriented versus whole-language approaches to reading instruction. *Journal of Educational Psychology, 83,* 437–443.

Vellutino, F. R., & Scanlon, D. M. (1987a). Linguistic coding and reading ability. In S. Rosenberg (Ed.), *Advances in applied psycholinguistics* (Vol. 2, pp. 1–69). New York: Cambridge University Press.

Vellutino, F. R., & Scanlon, D. M. (1987b). Phonological coding, phonological awareness, and reading ability: Evidence from a longitudinal and experimental study. *Merrill-Palmer Quarterly, 33,* 321–363.

Wagner, R. K. (1988). Causal relations between the development of phonological processing abilities and the acquisition of reading skills: A meta-analysis. *Merrill-Palmer Quarterly, 34*(2), 261–279.

Wagner, R., & Torgesen, J. (1987). The nature of phonological processing and its causal role in the acquisition of reading skills. *Psychological Bulletin, 101,* 192–212.

Weaver, C. A., III, & Kintsch, W. (1991). Expository text. In R. Barr, M. L. Kamil, P. Mosenthal, & P. D. Pearson (Eds.), *Handbook of reading research* (Vol. 2, pp. 230–244). White Plains, NY: Longman.

Weinstein, G., & Cooke, N. L. (1992). The effects of two repeated reading interventions on generalization of fluency. *Learning Disability Quarterly, 15,* 21–28.

Weisberg, P., & Savard, C. F. (1993). Teaching preschoolers to read: Don't stop between the sounds when segmenting words. *Education and Treatment of Children, 16,* 1–18.

Weisberg, P., Andracchio, B. J., & Savard, C. F. (1989). Oral blending in young children: Effects of sound pauses, initial sound, and word familiarity. *Journal of Educational Research, 82,* 139–145.

Weisberg, R. (1988). 1980s: A change in focus of reading comprehension research: A review of reading/learning disabilities research based on an interactive model of reading. *Learning Disability Quarterly, 11*(2), 149–159.

White, W. A. T. (1988). Meta-analysis of the effects of direct instruction in special education. *Education and Treatment of Children, 11,* 364–374.

Williams, P., & Carnine, D. (1981). Relationships between range of examples and attention in concept attainment. *Journal of Educational Research, 74,* 144–148.

Wong, B. Y. L. (1992). On cognitive process-based instruction: An introduction. *Journal of Learning Disabilities, 25*(3), 150–152, 172.

Wong, B. Y. L., & Wong, R. (1986). Study behavior as a function of metacognitive knowledge about critical task variables: An investigation of above average, average, and learning disabled readers. *Learning Disabilities Research, 1,* 101–111.

Wren, S. (2002). *Ten myths of reading instruction.* Austin, TX: Southwest Educational Development Laboratory Letter.

Yatvin, J. (1991). *Developing a whole language program for a whole school.* Richmond, VA: Virginia State Reading Association.

Zabrucky, K., & Ratner, H. H. (1992). Effects of passage type on comprehension monitoring and recall in good and poor readers. *Journal of Reading Behavior, 24,* 373–391.

Zigmond, N., & Baker, J. M. (1995). Concluding comments: Current and future practices in inclusive schooling. *Journal of Special Education, 29*(2), 245–250.

Zimmer, J. W. (1978). *s* Paper presented at the annual meeting of the American Educational Research Association, Toronto.

Page numbers in *italic type* refer to figures. Tables are indicated by *t* following the page number.